Windows 2000 Professional In Record Time

Peter Dyson
Pat Coleman

0-7821-2450-X

$29.99

Here's the quickest and easiest way for consultants, power users, and IS personnel to get up to speed with Windows 2000. This step-by-step guide to installing, configuring, and using the workstation version of Windows 2000 gives readers all of the essential skills and practical knowledge that they need. Get clear, concise instructions for using the most practical features of Windows 2000. Designed for people who don't want to spend a lot of time reading a computer book, this straightforward guide offers simple, task-oriented instructions. You find the information you're looking for, accomplish the task at hand, and move on. When you have a Windows 2000 Professional question, this book is the best alternative to "the person in the next cube."

Mastering Windows 2000 Professional

Mark Minasi
Todd Phillips

0-7821-2448-8

$39.99

Mark Minasi, the world's #1 Windows NT authority, brings his technical expertise and ability to make complex topics understandable and enjoyable to Microsoft's new generation of operating systems— Windows 2000. The first section of this book covers all of the essential features and built-in applications of Windows 2000 Professional (Workstation). The second part of the book provides in-depth coverage of all of the advanced topics that most other books merely skim over— subjects such as enterprise networking, scheduling, remote communication, optimization, system-control techniques, and professional troubleshooting advice. For beginners and advanced users alike, this all-in-one volume of essential information is probably the only book on Windows 2000 Professional that you'll ever need.

Mastering Windows 2000 Server, 2nd Edition

Mark Minasi
Christa Anderson
Brian M. Smith
Doug Toombs

0-7821-2774-6

$49.99

Mark Minasi, the world's #1 Windows NT authority, updates his #1 bestselling book for Windows 2000. Every system administrator needs this book! This high-level, irreverent yet readable explanation of Windows 2000 Server provides the best discussion of the architecture, features, and new utilities of the new OS in print. You'll learn from the expert: the differences between NT and 2000; the advantages (and potential pitfalls) of the the new OS; scores of undocumented secrets, tips, tricks, and workarounds; practical, hands-on advice for installing and using Windows 2000 in an enterprise environment; and hundreds of useful and essential nuggets of information that will save you hundreds or thousands of dollars in calls to Microsoft's help desk.

WINDOWS 2000
COMPLETE

SYBEX®

SAN FRANCISCO ▸ PARIS ▸ DÜSSELDORF ▸ SOEST ▸ LONDON

Associate Publisher: Roger Stewart

Contracts and Licensing Manager: Kristine O'Callaghan

Acquisitions and Develpmental Editor: Ellen L. Dendy

Developmental and Compilation Editor: Pat Coleman

Edition Editor: Anamary Ehlen

Production Editor: Elizabeth Campbell

Editors: Maureen Adams, Brianne Hope Agatep, Susan Berge, Bonnie Bills, Tracy Brown, Ellen L. Dendy, Anamary Ehlen, Judy Flynn, Jeff Gammon, Linda Good, Suzanne Goraj, Elizabeth Hurley, Rebecca Rider, Julie Sakaue, Ben Tomkins, and Elizabeth Welch

Technical Editors: Don Fuller, Mark Kovac, Don Meyers, Michelle Poole, Rima Regas, Dallas Releford, John Savill, and Ariel Silverstone

Book Designer: Maureen Forys, Happenstance Type-O-Rama

Electronic Publishing Specialist: Kris Warrenburg

Graphic Illustrators: Tony Jonick, Todd Rinker, and Jerry Williams

Proofreaders: Dennis Fitzgerald, Edith Kaneshiro, Laurie O'Connell, Camera Obscura, and Nancy Riddiough

Indexer: Nancy Guenther

Cover Designer: Design Site

Cover Illustrator/Photographer: Allen Wallace/Photonica

Library of Congress Card Number: 00-103812

ISBN: 0-7821-2721-5

Manufactured in the United States of America

10 9 8 7

ACKNOWLEDGMENTS

This book incorporates the work of many people, inside and outside Sybex.

Gary Masters, Special Projects Editor, hammered out the original idea of an inexpensive compilation of our top-notch Windows 2000 books. Acquisitions and Developmental Editor Ellen Dendy got the project up and running and hired the indispensable editor, Pat Coleman. Pat defined the book's overall structure and contents, and updated, compiled, and adapted all the material for publication in this book.

A large team of editors, developmental editors, and technical editors helped to put together the various books from which *Windows 2000 Complete* was compiled: Anamary Ehlen, Elizabeth Campbell, Maureen Adams, Tracy Brown, Jeff Gammon, Suzanne Goraj, Elizabeth Hurley, Ellen Dendy, Judy Flynn, Julie Sakaue, Brianne Hope Agatep, Rebecca Rider, Ben Tomkins, Susan Berge, Bonnie Bills, Elizabeth Welch, and Linda Good. Technical editors were Don Fuller, Michelle Poole, John Savill, Rima Regas, Mark Kovac, Don Meyers, Dallas Releford, and Ariel Silverstone.

A special thanks to the *Windows 2000 Complete* production team of illustrators Tony Jonick, Todd Rinker, and Jerry Williams; production editors Leslie Higbee, Teresa Trego, Jennifer Durning, and Shannon Murphy; and electronic publishing specialists Kris Warrenburg, Cyndy Johnson, Rhonda Ries, Robin Kibby, Nila Nichols, Grey Magauran, Franz Baumhackl and Bill Gibson, and book designer Maureen Forys.

Finally, our most important thanks go to the contributors who agreed to have their work excerpted into *Windows 2000 Complete*: Pat Coleman, Peter Dyson, Peter D. Hipson, Mark Minasi, Christa Anderson, Brian M. Smith, Doug Toombs, Robert R. King, Todd Phillips, and Jutta VanStean. Without their efforts, this book would not exist.

CONTENTS AT A GLANCE

Introduction   xxxi

Part I   Introducing Windows 2000   1

Chapter 1   Evaluating Windows 2000 Professional   3
Adapted from *Windows 2000 Professional: In Record Time*

Chapter 2   Installing and Upgrading to
Windows 2000 Professional   17
Adapted from *Windows 2000 Professional: In Record Time*

Chapter 3   Exploring the Desktop   35
Adapted from *Windows 2000 Professional: In Record Time*

Chapter 4   Managing Files and Folders   59
Adapted from *Windows 2000 Professional: In Record Time*

Chapter 5   Customizing Your Desktop   83
Adapted from *Windows 2000 Professional: In Record Time*

Chapter 6   Setting Object Properties   107
Adapted from *Windows 2000 Professional: In Record Time*

Chapter 7   Installing and Running Your Applications   121
Adapted from *Windows 2000 Professional: In Record Time*

Chapter 8   Printers and Printing   141
Adapted from *Windows 2000 Professional: In Record Time*

Chapter 9   Sharing Information between Applications   165
Adapted from *Windows 2000 Professional: In Record Time*

Chapter 10   Using the Windows 2000 Professional
Applications   189
Adapted from *Windows 2000 Professional: In Record Time*

Part II   Understanding Active Directory   **229**

Chapter 11   Windows 2000 with ADS   231
Adapted from *Mastering Active Directory, Second Edition*

Chapter 12   Alphabet Soup: ADS, TCP/IP, DNS   259
Adapted from *Mastering Active Directory, Second Edition*

Chapter 13   Building the Active Directory Tree   295
Adapted from *Mastering Active Directory, Second Edition*

Chapter 14   Installing ADS   329
Adapted from *Mastering Active Directory, Second Edition*

Part III   Connecting to the World   **339**

Chapter 15   Introduction to Communications and
Using Phone Dialer   341
Adapted from *Mastering Windows 2000 Professional*

Chapter 16   Using Outlook Express for E-mail and News   371
Adapted from *Windows 2000 Professional: In Record Time*

Chapter 17   Accessing the Internet   401
Adapted from *Mastering Windows 2000 Professional* and from
Windows 2000 Professional: In Record Time

Part IV   Understanding the Registry   **439**

Chapter 18   What Is a Registry and Why?   441
Adapted from *Mastering Windows 2000 Registry*

Chapter 19   Readme.1st: Preventing Disaster!   455
Adapted from *Mastering Windows 2000 Registry*

Chapter 20   Anatomy of the Registry:
The Blood, Gore, and Guts   491
Adapted from *Mastering Windows 2000 Registry*

Chapter 21   Registry Tools and Tips:
Getting the Work Done   521
Adapted from *Mastering Windows 2000 Registry*

Chapter 22   Common Hives and Keys   575

Adapted from *Mastering Windows 2000 Registry*

Part V   Installing and Using Windows 2000 Server   587

Chapter 23   Installing Windows 2000 Server   589

Adapted from *Mastering Windows 2000 Server, Second Edition*

Chapter 24   The Windows 2000 Server User Interface
and MMC   673

Adapted from *Mastering Windows 2000 Server, Second Edition*

Chapter 25   Creating and Managing User Accounts   727

Adapted from *Mastering Windows 2000 Server, Second Edition*

Part VI   Windows 2000 Instant Reference   823

Windows 2000 Instant Reference   825

Adapted from *Windows 2000 Instant Reference*

Index   *950*

CONTENTS

Introduction   *xxxi*

Part I ▶ Introducing Windows 2000   1

Chapter 1 □ **Evaluating Windows 2000 Professional**   **3**

Understanding the Windows 2000 Family   4
   Windows 2000 Professional   4
   Windows 2000 Server   5
   Windows 2000 Advanced Server   8
   Windows 2000 Data Center   9
Comparing Windows 2000 Professional with Other
  Windows Operating Systems   9
   Windows 2000 Professional versus Windows 3.1   9
   Windows 2000 Professional versus Windows 95/98 11
   Windows 2000 Professional versus Windows NT Workstation 4   12
Networking and Windows 2000 Professional   14
What's Next?   15

Chapter 2 □ **Installing and Upgrading to**
        Windows 2000 Professional   **17**

Windows 2000 Professional Hardware Requirements   19
Checking Your Hardware Compatibility   19
Collecting Network Information   20
Making a Backup   20
Should You Upgrade or Make a New Installation?   21
Running Setup   22
   Performing a New Installation   22
   Upgrading to Windows 2000 Professional   24
Choosing a File System   25
   NTFS   25
   FAT and FAT32   26
   A Quick Look at Disk Partitions   26
Setting Up a Dual-Boot Configuration   28
Installing the Add-On Components   31
Creating a New User Account   32
What's Next?   33

Chapter 3 □ Exploring the Desktop   **35**

Logging On   36
Using the Start Menu   37
    Clicking Start   38
    Right-Clicking Start   46
Working with the Taskbar   48
    The Quick Launch Toolbar   48
    The Rest of the Taskbar   49
    Hiding and Displaying the Taskbar   49
Using the Icons on the Desktop   50
    My Documents   50
    My Computer   52
    My Network Places   53
    Recycle Bin   53
    Internet Explorer   54
    Connect to the Internet   54
Creating Shortcuts   55
What's Next?   57

Chapter 4 □ Managing Files and Folders   **59**

Using Explorer   60
Opening Files and Folders   62
Creating a Folder   62
Creating a File   64
Sharing Files and Folders   66
Copying and Moving Files and Folders   68
Renaming Files and Folders   69
Deleting Files and Folders   70
Finding Files and Folders   70
Keeping Files Current with Synchronization Manager   73
Understanding and Using Folder Options   74
Handling Floppy Disks   79
    Formatting a Floppy Disk   79
    Copying a Floppy Disk   80
What's Next?   81

Chapter 5 ▫ Customizing Your Desktop   83

Opening Control Panel   84
Setting Up the Active Desktop   85
Making Windows 2000 Professional More Accessible   86
    Specifying Accessibility Options   87
    Using the Accessibility Accessories   88
Customizing the Keyboard   92
Adjusting Your Mouse   93
Changing the Display   95
    Customizing the Desktop Background   96
    Choosing a Screen Saver   97
    Adjusting the Power Settings   97
    Changing the Appearance of Windows Elements   98
    Enabling Web Content on Your Desktop   99
    Changing Desktop Icons and Effects   99
    Modifying the Display of Colors and Resolution   100
Establishing Your Regional Settings   102
Adjusting the Date and Time   103
Personalizing the Start Menu   103
What's Next?   105

Chapter 6 ▫ Setting Object Properties   107

Right-Clicking in Windows 2000 Professional   108
Using Properties Dialog Boxes   110
Changing File Properties   111
Compressing and Encrypting Files with NTFS   113
Changing Folder Properties   115
My Computer Properties Settings   117
What's Next?   119

Chapter 7 ▫ Installing and Running Your Applications   121

Running Programs from the Start Menu   122
Running Programs from Explorer   123
Running Programs from Search   124
Running Programs from a Document   125
Starting Programs Automatically When You Start
  Windows 2000 Professional   126
Running Programs Minimized   127

Using the Run Command   128
Working from the Command Prompt   129
Adding and Removing Programs   130
    Adding New Programs   131
    Changing or Removing Programs   132
    Adding and Removing Windows Components   133
Looking at the Registry   133
Scheduling Tasks   135
    Adding a New Scheduled Task   137
    Modifying an Existing Scheduled Task   137
    Using the Advanced Menu   138
What's Next?   139

Chapter 8 □ Printers and Printing   141

Adding Printers   142
    Installing a Local Printer   143
    Installing a Network Printer   145
Printing Documents   147
    Printing from the Desktop   148
    Printing from an Application   149
    Printing to a File   151
Managing the Printing Process   152
Customizing the Printer's Properties   154
    The General Tab   155
    The Sharing Tab   155
    The Ports Tab   156
    The Advanced Tab   157
    The Services Tab   158
    The Device Settings Tab   159
    The Security Tab   160
    The Color Management Tab   160
Understanding Fonts   161
What's Next?   163

Chapter 9 □ Sharing Information between Applications   165

Using the Clipboard   166
    Copying, Cutting, and Pasting in Windows Applications   167
    Capturing Screens with the Clipboard   170
Working with the ClipBook Viewer   171

Starting the ClipBook Viewer 172
Pasting an Item into the ClipBook 172
Copying an Item from the ClipBook 173
Sharing ClipBook Pages 173
Clearing the Clipboard 174
Understanding OLE 174
Embedding Objects 175
Linking Objects 177
Communicating and Sharing with NetMeeting 178
Starting NetMeeting 179
Making a Call 181
Using the Chat Application 182
Using Directory Servers 183
Hosting a Meeting 184
Using Video 184
Sharing Applications 185
Transferring Files 186
What's Next? 187

Chapter 10 □ Using the Windows 2000 Professional Applications   189

Listening to Sounds, Watching Movies, and Recording 190
Playing Audio CDs 190
Adjusting the Volume 193
Recording Sounds 194
Using Windows Media Player 195
Playing Games 198
Solitaire 199
FreeCell 199
Minesweeper 200
Pinball 201
Keeping Track of Your Contacts 201
Opening Address Book 202
Adding a New Contact 203
Adding a New Group 203
Locating People 204
Printing Your Address Book 204
Creating a Map 205
Doing Math 206

Using the Standard Calculator   208
Using the Scientific Calculator   208
Creating Text Documents   210
Using Notepad   210
Creating a Document in Notepad   211
Opening and Saving a File in Notepad   213
Using WordPad   213
Creating a Document with WordPad   216
Sending a WordPad Document As an E-Mail Attachment   216
Drawing with Paint   217
Displaying and Editing Digital Images   220
Using Your Computer As a Fax Machine   225
Sending a Fax   226
Receiving a Fax   227
What's Next?   228

Part II ▶ Understanding Active Directory   229

Chapter 11 ▫ Windows 2000 with ADS   231

How Networks Develop   232
The General Goals of ADS   234
Enterprise Management   236
An Industry Standard   236
Vendor Acceptance   237
User Acceptance   238
Single Namespace   245
Namespace   247
Active Directory Names   249
Active Directory in the Windows 2000 Server Architecture   250
The Security Subsystem   252
The Directory Service Module   254
The Internal Architecture of the Active Directory Module   256
What's Next?   257

Chapter 12 ▫ Alphabet Soup: ADS, TCP/IP, DNS   259

TCP/IP Basics   260
The History of TCP/IP   260
Common TCP/IP Protocols and Tools   261

TCP/IP Addressing   263
IP Subnetting   264
Dynamic Host Configuration Protocol (DHCP)   267
Installing DHCP Service   269
How Does DHCP Work?   271
Domain Name System (DNS)   284
So What Exactly Is a DNS Domain?   285
Planning DNS Naming   286
Integrating DNS with Active Directory   288
Installing and Configuring DNS on an
    ADS Domain Controller   289
What's Next?   293

Chapter 13 ▫ Building the Active Directory Tree   295

What Is a Domain?   296
DNS Domains and NT Domains   297
Partitioning the Database   299
Trusts between Domains   301
Administrative Boundaries   304
Organizational Units   305
When to Use a New Domain   307
Designing the OU Model   308
What Makes a Good OU Model?   309
Other Aspects of Planning an OU Model   319
Trees and Forests   321
Special Types of ADS Servers   323
Single Master Functions   325
What's Next?   327

Chapter 14 ▫ Installing ADS   329

Before You Begin   331
Testing DNS   331
Mixed Mode or Native Mode?   332
The ADS Installation Wizard   333
Finishing Your Installation   334
What Does the Wizard Create?   336
Verifying Your Installation   337
What's Next?   338

Part III ▸ Connecting to the World   339

Chapter 15 □ Introduction to Communications and Using Phone Dialer   341

Discovering What's New in Windows 2000 Communications   343
Using the Windows Telephony Interface   343
Installing a Modem   345
Changing Modem Properties   348
    General Properties   349
    Diagnostics   351
    Advanced Settings   352
    Dialing Rules   356
Using Phone Dialer   363
    Starting Phone Dialer   363
    Adding Directories   365
    Programming the Speed Dial List   365
Placing a Call   368
What's Next?   369

Chapter 16 □ Using Outlook Express for E-mail and News   371

Using Outlook Express as Your Mailreader   372
    A Quick Tour   373
    Retrieving Your Mail   375
    Reading and Processing Messages   376
    Creating and Sending Messages   381
    Creating E-mail Messages with HTML   383
    Adding a Signature to Messages   387
    Attaching Files to Messages   388
    Applying Message Rules   389
    Adding and Managing Identities   391
Using Outlook Express as Your Newsreader   393
    Setting Up a Newsgroups Account   394
    Connecting to Newsgroups   395
    Finding a Newsgroup of Interest   396
    Subscribing to a Newsgroup   396
    Reading a Newsgroup   396
    Posting to a Newsgroup   397
Customizing Outlook Express   397
What's Next?   399

Chapter 17 □ Accessing the Internet 401

Understanding the Types of Internet Connections 402
    Using Internet Addresses 405
    Connecting As a Remote Terminal 406
Connecting via Modem 407
    Obtaining the Information You Need from Your ISP 408
    Configuring the Dial-Up Connection 409
    Creating a New Connection to the Internet 410
    Setting Up Your Connection to the Internet Manually 411
    Dialing In to Your Service Provider 412
    Troubleshooting Your Modem Connection 414
Web Cruising with Internet Explorer 415
Setting Internet Explorer Options 418
    Configuring the General Tab 419
    Looking at the Security Tab 420
    Using the Content Tab 422
    Setting Up the Connections Tab 424
    Looking at the Programs Tab 425
    Configuring the Advanced Tab 425
Using Built-In Internet Utilities 426
    Address Resolution Display and Control (ARP) 427
    File Transfer Protocol (FTP) 427
    Finger 429
    Ping 430
    Protocol Statistics (Netstat) 431
    Remote File Copy (RCP) 431
    Remote Program Execution (REXEC) 432
    Remote Shell/Script (RSH) 432
    Remote Terminal (Telnet) 432
    ROUTE 433
    Trace Route (tracert) 433
    Trivial File Transfer Protocol (TFTP) 434
Obtaining Other Internet Applications 434
What's Next? 438

Part IV ▸ Understanding the Registry   439

Chapter 18 □ What Is a Registry and Why?   441

The Organization of the Registry   443
   Hives and Their Aliases   444
   Data Values   445
How Windows 2000 Uses the Registry   447
A Note about Terminology   450
Hints and Kinks from the Experts   452
What's Next?   453

Chapter 19 □ Readme.1st: Preventing Disaster!   455

What's the Deal with the Registry, Anyway?   457
   Where Exactly Is the Registry?   458
Are Two Copies Better Than One?   462
Backup Techniques   464
   Back Up to Tape or to Other Media   464
   Backing Up Using copy or xcopy   465
   What's on My ERD?   470
   Using RegEdit to Back Up the Registry   470
Restoring the Registry   473
   Restoring from Tape   473
   Restoring from Other Media Supported by Backup   474
   Recovering a Copied Registry   475
   ERD Strikes Again: Using Setup to Recover   476
   Loading a .reg File   479
The Recovery Console   480
   Installing the Recovery Console   480
   What's in the Recovery Console?   482
   Using the Recovery Console   483
   Starting the Recovery Console from the Installation CD-ROM   484
   Recovery Console Commands and Options   485
Other Backup and Restore Programs   488
Hints and Kinks from the Experts   488
What's Next?   489

Chapter 20 □ Anatomy of the Registry: The Blood, Gore, and Guts   491

Of Hives and Bees—A Registry Overview   493
   The Registry Hives   493
   Hives, Keys, and Values   494
   Registry Key Data Types   497
HKEY_LOCAL_MACHINE: The Machine's Configuration   501
   HKEY_LOCAL_MACHINE\Hardware:
      The Installed Hardware Key   501
   HKEY_LOCAL_MACHINE\SAM: The Security Access Manager   505
   HKEY_LOCAL_MACHINE\Security:
      The Windows 2000 Security Manager   505
   HKEY_LOCAL_MACHINE\Software:
      The Installed Software Information Manager   506
   HKEY_LOCAL_MACHINE\System:
      The System Information Manager   508
HKEY_USERS: Settings for Users   510
HKEY_CURRENT_CONFIG: The Current Configuration Settings   515
NTUSER: The New User Profile   516
Hints and Kinks from the Experts   518
What's Next?   519

Chapter 21 □ Registry Tools and Tips: Getting the Work Done   521

RegEdit   523
   Using RegEdit   523
   Using RegEdit from the Command Line   534
   Tips for RegEdit Users   535
   Installing Microsoft Remote Registry on
      Windows 95 andWindows 98/98 SE   535
RegEdt32   536
   Using RegEdt32   537
   Tips for RegEdt32 Users   558
Backup's Emergency Repair Disk Features   558
   Creating an Emergency Repair Disk   559
The Reg.exe Registry Editor   560
   The ADD Function   561
   The BACKUP Function   562

The COPY Function 563
The DELETE Function 565
The LOAD Function 566
The QUERY Function 566
The RESTORE Function 567
The SAVE Function 568
The UNLOAD Function 569
The UPDATE Function 570
Hints and Kinks from the Experts 571
What's Next? 573

Chapter 22 □ Common Hives and Keys 575
What's Next? 585

Part V ► Installing and Using Windows 2000 Server 587

Chapter 23 □ Installing Windows 2000 Server 589
Planning and Preparation 590
System Requirements 591
Preparing the Hardware 594
Preparing the BIOS 594
Partitioning 595
File Systems 596
Server Name 598
Network Connection and Options 599
Setting Up and Installing 604
Preinstallation: Phase 1 604
Text-Based Setup: Phase 2 608
Graphical-Based Setup: Phase 3 612
Post-Installation Procedures 618
Performing Unattended Installs 620
Command-Line Automation 621
Answer Files 625
The Setup Manager Wizard 629
Using SYSDIFF 639
Creating the SYSDIFF Package 639
Applying the Difference File 640

Troubleshooting an Installation   641
　　The Recovery Console   642
Installing Windows 2000 on Workstations with
　Remote Installation Services   645
　　RIS Overview   647
　　RIS Limitations   648
　　Steps to Making RIS Work   649
　　Getting Ready for RIS   650
　　Authorizing RIS in Active Directory   652
　　Installing RIS   653
　　Running RISetup   654
　　Enabling RIS for Clients   657
　　Installing Windows 2000 Professional on a
　　　Workstation from the RIS Server   658
　　Creating a System Image with RIPRep   663
　　Reconfiguring the Prototype   664
　　Delivering a RIPRep Image to a Target PC   665
　　Enabling Users to Start RIS Transfers   666
　　Creating the Installers Group   667
　　Restricting RIS Image Choices   669
　Putting It All Together   669
　What's Next?   671

**Chapter 24 ▫ The Windows 2000 Server
　　　　　　　User Interface and MMC   673**

　Where Are They Now?   674
　　Where'd They Put the Network Applet?   675
　　What Happened to User Manager and
　　　User Manager for Domains?   681
　　No More Server Manager?   683
　　Domain Management Functions   685
　　Where Is the Disk Administrator?   687
　　What Happened to the Device Management Tools
　　　in Control Panel?   688
　　Where Is the Services Applet?   690
　　What Is This Network And Dial-Up Connections Tool?   693
　　Where Did They Put NT Diagnostics?   693
　Fixing the Windows 2000 GUI   694
　A Microsoft Management Console Primer   696

What Is This MMC Thing?   696
Why Is MMC Good and Not Evil?   697
MMC Terms to Know   697
The Computer Management Console   700
Other MMC Tools   703
Creating Microsoft Management Consoles   705
Building a Simple Microsoft Saved Console   705
Designing Tools with Taskpad Views   709
Packaging the Tool for Users   723
Distributing the Tool   724
Editing a Custom Console Tool   724
What's Next?   725

Chapter 25 □ Creating and Managing User Accounts   727

Use Computer Management for Local Accounts   728
Use Active Directory Users And Computers for Domain Accounts   731
Where Do User and Group Accounts Live?   732
Security Identifiers   732
Quick Tour of User and Group-Related Functions in
  Active Directory Users And Computers   733
Prebuilt Accounts: Administrator and Guest   735
Creating a New User Account   737
User Account Properties   739
Managing Accounts   750
Understanding Groups   752
Creating Groups   752
Group Types: Security Groups versus Distribution Groups   755
Group Scope: Locals, Globals, and Universals   757
Working with Security Groups   761
User Rights   770
How Do Organizational Units Fit in Here?   775
Working with Group Policies   776
Group Policy Concepts   778
Local Policies and Group Policy Objects   783
Creating Group Policies   785
Filtering Group Policy   791
Delegating Group Policy Administration   794
User and Computer Configuration Settings   796
Managing Group Policies   815
What's Next?   822

Part VI ▶ Windows 2000 Instant Reference   823

Windows 2000 Instant Reference   825

Accessibility   826
Accessibility Options   826
Accessibility Wizard   826
Accessories   826
Active Desktop   827
Active Directory   827
Active Directory Domains And Trusts   828
   Domain Properties   828
   The Active Directory Users And Computers
    MMC Console Snap-In Window   829
Active Directory Sites And Services   829
Add/Remove Hardware   830
Add/Remove Programs   830
Address Book   831
Administrative Tools   831
Backup   831
Browse   832
Calculator   832
Capturing Images   832
CD Player   832
Change Password   833
Character Map   833
   Copying Characters   833
   Advanced View   833
Checking Drives for Errors   834
Clipboard   834
ClipBook Viewer   834
Close   835
COM+ (Component Services)   835
Command Prompt   835
Communications   835
Configure Your Server   836
Component Services   837
   Enabling Security   838

Adding a Network Computer   838
Installing COM+ Applications   838
Compressing Drives, Folders, and Files   839
Computer Management   839
Connect To The Internet   840
Control Panel   840
Copy Files and Folders   841
    Copy Files or Folders Using the Edit Menu   841
    Copy Files or Folders Using the Shortcut Menu   841
    Copy Files or Folders Using Drag-and-Drop   841
Create New Folder   841
Create Shared Folder Wizard   842
Create Shortcut   842
    Using the File Menu in Windows Explorer   842
    Using Shortcut Menus   842
    Using Drag-and-Copy   843
Ctrl+Alt+Delete   843
Data Sources (ODBC)   843
Date/Time   844
Deleting Files and Folders   844
Desktop   844
Device Manager   845
DHCP   845
    DHCP MMC Console Snap-In Window   846
    Enabling DHCP on a Windows 2000 Client   846
DirectX Diagnostic Tool   846
Disk Cleanup   846
    Using Disk Cleanup   847
Disk Defragmenter   847
    Disk Defragmenter MMC Console   847
    Analyzing a Volume   848
    Defragmenting a Volume   848
    Viewing Reports   849
Disk Management   849
    Basic Disks   849
    Dynamic Disks   851
    Upgrading a Basic Disk to a Dynamic Disk   851
Disk Quotas   852
    Quota Tab   852

Quota Entries 852
Quota Entries Window 852
Creating a New Quota Entry 853
Disk Space 853
Display 854
Distributed File System 854
Dfs Types 854
Creating a Domain-Based Distributed File System 854
DNS 855
DNS Domain Name Space 856
Zones 857
Zone Transfers 857
DNS MMC Console Snap-in 857
DNS Client Configuration 858
Documents 858
Drag-and-Drop 858
Dr. Watson 859
Entertainment 859
Event Viewer 859
Event Viewer Logs 859
Event Information 861
Viewing Logs on a Remote Computer 861
Explorer 861
Fax 862
File Signature Verification Utility 862
Folders 863
Folder Options 863
Fonts 863
Format 864
FTP 864
Game Controllers 865
Games 865
Group Policy 865
Group Policy Types 866
Group Policy Inheritance 867
Group Policy Objects and Templates 867
Working with GPOs 867
Help 870
HyperTerminal 870

Creating a New HyperTerminal Connection 870
Opening an Existing Connection 871
Imaging 871
Indexing Drives, Folders, and Files 871
Indexing Service 872
Internet Connection Wizard 872
Internet Explorer 873
Internet Explorer Window 874
Internet Options 874
Internet Services Manager 874
Internet Information Services MMC Console Snap-in Window 875
Action Menu 875
IPCONFIG 875
Keyboard 876
Licensing 876
Local Security Policy 876
Configuring Security Policies 876
Local Users And Groups 878
Lock Computer 878
Logical Drives 878
Log Off 879
Log On 879
Magnifier 880
Make Available Offline 880
Offline Files Folder 881
Map Network Drive 881
Mapping a Network Drive 881
Disconnecting a Mapped Network Drive 882
Maximize and Minimize 882
Microsoft Management Console (MMC) 883
MMC Window 883
MMC Consoles 884
Creating a New MMC Console 887
Microsoft Script Debugger 888
Mouse 889
Move Files and Folders 889
Using the Edit Menu 889
Using the Shortcut Menu 889
Using Drag-and-Drop 890

My Computer 890
My Documents 891
My Network Places 891
    Navigating My Network Places 891
    Add Network Place 892
My Pictures 892
Narrator 892
Net 893
NetMeeting 893
Network and Dial-Up Connections 894
    Network And Dial-Up Connections Folder 894
    Advanced Menu 903
Notepad 905
NTFS 905
On-Screen Keyboard 905
Outlook Express 906
Paint 906
Performance 906
    System Monitor 906
    Performance Logs And Alerts 908
Permissions 910
    Explicit and Inherited Permissions 911
Personalized Menus 911
Phone and Modem Options 911
Phone Dialer 911
Ping 912
Power Options 912
Printers 912
Private Character Editor 913
Recycle Bin 913
Regional Options 913
Registry 914
Removable Storage 914
Restore 915
Routing And Remote Access 915
    Routing And Remote Access MMC Console Snap-in Window 915
Run 916
Run As 916
Safe Mode 917

Scanners and Cameras   917
Scheduled Tasks   918
    Add Scheduled Task   918
    Scheduled Tasks Folder   919
Search   919
Send Fax Wizard   919
Send To   920
Server Extensions Administrator   920
Services   920
    Working with Services   920
Settings   921
Shared Folders   922
Sharing   922
    Sharing a Folder or Disk   922
Shut Down   923
Sound Recorder   923
Sounds and Multimedia   924
Start   924
Start Menu   924
System   925
    General   925
    Network Identification   925
    Hardware   927
    User Profiles   929
    Advanced   930
Synchronize   931
System Information   932
System Tools   932
Taskbar   933
Taskbar & Start Menu   933
    General Tab   933
    Advanced Tab   934
Task Manager   935
    Task Manager Window   935
    Task Manager Menus   935
    Task Manager Tabs   936
    Status Bar   937
Telephony   937
Telnet Client   938

Telnet Server Administration   938
Update Wizard Uninstall   939
User Profiles   939
   Local User Profiles   939
   Roaming User Profiles   940
   Mandatory User Profiles   940
   User Profiles Tab   941
Users And Passwords   941
   Users Tab   942
   Advanced Tab   942
   Adding a User   943
Utility Manager   944
Volume Control   945
Web Sharing   945
What's This   945
Windows Components   946
Windows Media Player   946
Windows Report Tool   947
   Creating and Submitting a Report   947
Windows Update   947
WMI Control   948
WMI Control Properties   948
WordPad   949

Index   950

INTRODUCTION

This 1000-page compilation of information from six of Sybex's books provides comprehensive coverage of Microsoft's latest enterprise operating system, Windows 2000. This book was created with these goals in mind: to offer at an affordable price a thorough guide covering the most important features and gotchas of both Windows 2000 Professional and Server; and to acquaint you with some of our best authors—their writing styles and teaching skills, and the level of expertise they bring to their books—so you can easily find a match for your interests as you delve deeper into this complex operating system. *Windows 2000 Complete* is designed to provide all the essential information you'll need for a solid understanding of the operating system, as well as provide hands-on step-by-step instructions, real-world examples, and troubleshooting tips. At the same time, *Windows 2000 Complete* invites you to explore the even greater depths and wider coverage of material in the original books.

If you've read any Windows NT books, you know that there are many possible approaches to the task of showing how to use Microsoft's high-end operating system effectively. The books from which *Windows 2000 Complete* was compiled represent a range of the approaches to teaching that Sybex and its authors have developed—from the "jump right in" step-by-step style of the In Record Time series to the exhaustively thorough Mastering style. These books also address readers at different levels of computer experience. As you read through various chapters of *Windows 2000 Complete*, you'll see which approach works best for you. You'll also see what these books have in common: a commitment to clarity, accuracy, and practicality.

You'll find in these pages ample evidence of the high quality of Sybex's authors. Unlike publishers who produce "books by committee," Sybex authors are encouraged to write in individual voices that reflect their own experience with the evolution of the computing technology and the Windows operating system. Nearly every book represented here is the work of a single writer or a pair of close collaborators; when Mark Minasi, for example, says, "This, I find, is one of the most convenient ways to do an install...," you know you are getting the benefit of *his* direct experience. Likewise, all the chapters are based on their authors' firsthand testing of prerelease software and subsequent expertise with the final product.

In adapting the various source materials for inclusion in *Windows 2000 Complete*, the compiler preserved these individual voices and perspectives. Chapters were edited only to minimize duplication, and update or add cross-references so that you can easily follow a topic across chapters. A few sections were also edited for length so that other important content could be included.

Who Can Benefit from This Book?

Windows 2000 Complete is designed to meet the needs of a wide range of Windows 2000 users. The books from which this book is compiled are each targeted to a specific audience:

- ▶ *Windows 2000 Professional: In Record Time* is primarily aimed at users who are upgrading from a previous version of Windows and users who are coming to the Windows world from another operating system.

- ▶ *Mastering Active Directory* is primarily aimed at the experienced network administrator who wants to take a look at Active Directory Services, Microsoft's new network directories technology.

- ▶ *Mastering Windows 2000 Professional* is a soup-to-nuts, beginner-to-expert, end-user-to-administrator guide to using and supporting Windows 2000 Professional.

- ▶ *Mastering Windows 2000 Registry* is for general users who are responsible for their own computers, system administrators who are responsible for an organization's computers, and help desk staff.

- ▶ *Mastering Windows 2000 Server* is the premier resource for anyone configuring, administering, and tuning Windows 2000 Server in a large enterprise.

- ▶ *Windows 2000 Instant Reference* has A–Z coverage of every feature and command, and is a perfect reference for every Windows 2000 user.

So, if it seems as if this book contains something for everybody, we've achieved what we started out to do. Whether you're a SOHO (small-office/home-office) user, working with a stand-alone computer or a simple peer-to-peer network with no administrators or technical staff to rely on, or working within a larger network, you'll find information you can use in this book.

We also think this book is a great resource if you are currently evaluating Windows 2000 and considering whether this is the best operating system for either your corporate network or your home office. Rather than wading through mounds of documentation or tomes devoted to all the complicated ins and outs of system architecture, you can get to the heart of the matter quickly.

Although you certainly could read this book from beginning to end, you may not need to read every chapter. The Contents and the Index will help you find specific topics, as will the information in the next section.

How This Book Is Organized

Windows 2000 Complete has 6 parts, consisting of 25 chapters and an Instant Reference.

Part I: Introducing Windows 2000   The 10 chapters in this part of the book are designed to take you step by step through installing and using Windows 2000 Professional. Peter Dyson and Pat Coleman thought about how they and others work with computers and then tailored the topics in this section accordingly, covering such things as how to manage files and folders, how to customize the Desktop, how to set up local and network printers, and how to share files, folders, and applications.

Part II: Understanding Active Directory   The purpose of the chapters in this part of the book is to introduce you to Active Directory. Robert R. King starts by discussing how Active Directory Service (ADS) fits into the overall Windows 2000 philosophy, continues by explaining the communications protocols—in particular how ADS depends on TCP/IP (Transmission Control Protocol/Internet Protocol)—and concludes with a discussion of ADS design theories and information about how to install ADS.

Part III: Connecting to the World   Windows 2000 includes an extensive set of communications tools that let you exchange electronic mail, browse the Internet, and control telephone calls. In the chapters in this part of the book, Mark Minasi and Todd Phillips walk you through the steps to install a modem, use Phone Dialer, send and receive e-mail with Outlook Express, connect to the Internet, and use Internet Explorer as well as other Internet applications.

Part IV: Understanding the Registry   The Registry is the heart and soul of Windows 2000. It contains all the configuration information about hardware, preferences, security, and users. In this part of the book Peter D. Hipson introduces the Registry and tells you about its development history. He then jumps right into how to avoid getting into trouble when you fiddle with the Registry and follows with a chapter that analyzes the Registry contents in depth. In addition, he takes a close look at the Registry tools that are included with Windows 2000.

Part V: Installing and Using Windows 2000 Server   As you may have heard, the Windows 2000 platform actually consists of four products that can work either together or separately: Windows 2000 Professional, Windows 2000 Server, Windows 2000 Advanced Server, and Windows 2000 Data Center. Each product serves a specific purpose and is appropriate for use in particular situations. Windows 2000 Server can be deployed on anything from a small home network to a network of several hundred users.

In this part of the book, Mark Minasi, Christa Anderson, Brian M. Smith, and Doug Toombs provide instructions for installing Windows 2000 Server, explain the user interface and how to use Microsoft Management Console, and guide you through the steps for creating and managing user accounts.

Part VI: Windows 2000 Instant Reference   If you have a specific question about Windows 2000, you might just want to look here first. This part of the book is a distillation of Jutta VanStean's *Windows 2000 Instant Reference,* which is more than 600 pages that cover every Windows 2000 concept, component, and command. For *Windows 2000 Complete,* we omitted the illustrations and the cross-references, but we have kept every single entry and maintained the alphabetic, glossary format. This reference provides information at your fingertips for all levels of users.

A Few Typographical Conventions

When an operation requires a series of choices from menus or dialog boxes, the ➢ symbol is used to guide you through the instructions, like this: "Choose Programs ➢ Accessories ➢ System Tools ➢ System Information." The items the ➢ symbol separates may be menu names, toolbar icons, check boxes, or other elements of the Windows interface or an application—any place you can make a selection.

`This typeface` identifies Internet URLs and HTML code, and **boldface type** is used whenever you need to type something into a text box.

You'll find these types of special notes throughout the book:

TIP

You'll see a lot of these—quicker and smarter ways to accomplish a task, which the authors have based on many, many months spent testing and using your system's hardware and software.

NOTE

You'll see these Notes, too. They usually represent alternate ways to accomplish a task or some additional information that needs to be highlighted.

WARNING

In a very few places you'll see a Warning like this one. There are few because it's not easy to do irrevocable things in Windows 2000 or Windows applications unless you work hard at it. But when you see a Warning, do pay attention to it.

YOU'LL ALSO SEE "SIDEBAR" BOXES LIKE THIS

These boxed sections provide added explanation of special topics that are noted briefly in the surrounding discussion, but that you may want to explore separately. Each sidebar has a heading that announces the topic so you can quickly decide whether it's something you need to know about.

So Where Can I Get These Great Books?

All the Sybex books used to compile *Windows 2000 Complete* are available at book and computer stores worldwide. If you can't find a book
you're looking for (or can't easily get to a bookstore), don't worry. All
Sybex books are available for purchase online at the Sybex Web site, at

    http://www.sybex.com

or through online booksellers, such as Fatbrain (previously known as
Computer Literacy), at

    http://www.fatbrain.com

and Amazon.com, at

    http://www.amazon.com

For More Information...

See the Sybex Web site, www.sybex.com, to learn more about all the
books that went into *Windows 2000 Complete*. On the site's Catalog
page, you'll find links to any book you're interested in.

We hope you enjoy this book and find it useful. Happy computing!

PART i

INTRODUCING WINDOWS 2000

Chapter 1

EVALUATING WINDOWS 2000 PROFESSIONAL

Whether or not you adhere to a purist interpretation of when one century ends and another begins, you have to admit that the approach and celebration of the year 2000 engendered a mind-boggling array of turn-of-the-century transitions—everything from revisiting the prognostications of Nostradamus to making sure your VCR would still work on January 1, 2000. And the computer world took the opportunity to introduce what many describe as major innovations.

Adapted from *Windows 2000 Professional: In Record Time*, by Peter Dyson and Pat Coleman

ISBN 0-7821-2450-X   467 pages $29.99

The Windows 2000 operating system is the latest iteration of what in 1981 appeared as a white A : \ prompt on a black screen. We've now come to expect and assume that our computers and the software they run will become faster and faster, more and more reliable, and easier and easier to use, and, for the most part, we have not been disappointed. Windows 2000 lives up to these expectations.

In this portion of the book, we'll take you through the steps to get started and to use one variation of Windows 2000: Windows 2000 Professional. Before we do that, though, we'll show you how this family of operating systems is structured, how Windows 2000 relates to previous versions of Windows, and how to use Windows 2000 Professional to work more effectively.

UNDERSTANDING THE WINDOWS 2000 FAMILY

The Windows 2000 platform actually consists of four products that can work either together or separately:

- ▶ Windows 2000 Professional
- ▶ Windows 2000 Server
- ▶ Windows 2000 Advanced Server
- ▶ Windows 2000 Data Center

Each product serves a specific purpose and is appropriate for use in particular situations.

Windows 2000 Professional

Windows 2000 Professional is the successor to Windows NT Workstation 4 and looks much like Windows 98. You can run Windows 2000 Professional on a stand-alone machine, on a small network, or on a large corporate network. Its features include a new, simplified Desktop, Internet Explorer 5, tight security options, Plug-and-Play support for hardware, and easy-to-use configuration Wizards. Figure 1.1 shows the Desktop in Windows 2000 Professional.

FIGURE 1.1: The Desktop in Windows 2000 Professional

To exploit many features of Windows 2000 Server, which we'll discuss next, Windows 2000 Professional needs to be installed on users' workstations.

NOTE

In networking, a *workstation* is any personal computer (other than the file server) that is attached to a network. A *server* is any computer that makes access to files, printing, communications, and other services available to users of a network.

Windows 2000 Server

The term *server* can apply to hardware or software. The server machine (hardware) usually has a more advanced processor, more memory, a larger cache, and more disk space than a personal computer used as a workstation. Windows 2000 Server is software that runs on the network server machine.

Windows 2000 Server is the successor to Windows NT Server 4 and was designed to be easier to use, install, and maintain, but it will generally require newer, more powerful computers than Server 4. You can deploy Windows 2000 Server on anything from a small home network to a network of several hundred users.

Table 1.1 compares the hardware requirements for Windows 2000 Server, Windows 2000 Professional, and a few other popular operating systems in use today. Figure 1.2 shows the Desktop for Windows 2000 Server.

TABLE 1.1: Hardware Requirements for Some Current Operating Systems

OPERATING SYSTEM	PROCESSOR	RAM (IN MB)	HARD DISK SPACE
Windows 98 Second Edition	Required: P166 MMX Recommended: PII-300	Required: 24	Required: 260MB using FAT16; 210MB using FAT32
Windows NT Workstation 4	Required: P166	Required: 16 Recommended: 32	Required: 110MB
Windows 2000 Professional	Required: P166 Recommended: PII-300	Required: 32 Recommended: 64	Required: 2GB, with 650MB of free space
Windows NT Server 4	Required: 486DX Recommended: P166	Required: 16 Recommended: 32	124MB
Windows 2000 Server	Required: P166 Recommended: PII-300	Required: 64 Recommended: 128	Required: 400MB Recommended: 1GB
Novell NetWare 5	Required: P166	Required: 64 Recommended: 256	Required: 500MB Recommended: 1GB
Red Hat Linux 6.1	Required: Intel 386 Recommended: Intel 486	Required: 4 Recommended: 16	Required: 200MB Recommended: 500MB

FIGURE 1.2:   The Desktop in Windows 2000 Server

The new features in Windows 2000 Server include the following:

- ► Upgraded user account and system management
- ► Active Directory
- ► Internet and intranet support
- ► Operating stability
- ► Processing power
- ► Internal security
- ► Kerberos authentication
- ► Support for a maximum of four processors

HARDWARE AND WINDOWS 2000

Throughout the development cycle of Windows 2000, Microsoft received the support of all the major hardware vendors, including IBM, Compaq, Dell, Data General, Gateway, Hewlett-Packard, and Toshiba. Dell even offered to preinstall beta releases on systems for corporate customers. Thus, hardware compatibility issues should take a back seat when either you or your organization consider upgrading to Windows 2000 and acquiring new hardware.

In addition, Windows 2000 Professional includes drivers for more than 2,500 different printers. It's highly likely that you'll find yours there when you want to install a new printer.

For the last word on hardware compatibility, go to www.microsoft.com/hwtest/hcl, where you'll find information on a variety of equipment vendors, computer systems, and specific peripherals by name and type.

NOTE

For more information about Windows 2000 Server, see Part V of this book, "Installing and Using Windows 2000 Server."

Windows 2000 Advanced Server

Windows 2000 Advanced Server is for enterprises that use large database applications and online transaction processing (for example, airline reservation systems, banks, and oil companies).

Advanced Server extends the features of Windows 2000 Server to include the following:

- ► Support for a maximum of eight processors
- ► A 64GB memory address space for applications
- ► High-availability clustering (that is, two servers can join in a failsafe configuration that minimizes downtime)

Windows 2000 Data Center

Windows 2000 Data Center is server software that provides maximum processing power for large-scale enterprise Internet and intranet operations. It supports a maximum of 32 processors.

COMPARING WINDOWS 2000 PROFESSIONAL WITH OTHER WINDOWS OPERATING SYSTEMS

You can upgrade to Windows 2000 Professional from the following operating systems:

- ▸ Windows 3.1
- ▸ OS/2
- ▸ Windows 95
- ▸ Windows 98
- ▸ Windows NT 3.51 Workstation
- ▸ Windows NT Workstation 4

As you will see in the next chapter, how you install Windows 2000 Professional depends on which of these systems is currently installed.

Let's take a look at how Windows 2000 Professional compares with some of the operating systems you might be using now.

Windows 2000 Professional versus Windows 3.1

If your workstation or your network is running Windows 3.1 (and we know for a fact that some companies still are) and you are upgrading to Windows 2000 Professional, you are about to take a giant leap forward. Figure 1.3 shows the screen you see when you first open Windows 3.1. Compare this with the Windows 2000 Professional Desktop shown in Figure 1.1, earlier in this chapter. Quite a difference, huh?

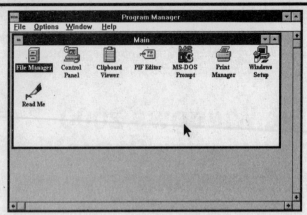

FIGURE 1.3:   The Windows 3.1 interface

Here are just a few of the features that are different from Windows 3.1 in Windows 2000 Professional:

Filenames   You are probably painfully aware that in Windows 3.1 filenames can consist of only eight letters plus a three-letter extension. In Windows 2000 Professional, filenames can contain a maximum of 215 characters, including spaces.

Multitasking   As you probably know, multitasking means doing more than one thing at a time (for example, continuing to edit one document while printing another). Theoretically, Windows 3.1 can multitask, but if you're in the habit of trying to do what we just described, you know it doesn't really work. Fortunately, Windows 2000 Professional has true multitasking; you can even download files from the Internet while calculating a large spreadsheet.

Shortcuts   In Windows 3.1, you can accomplish a lot by left-clicking, but you have to click, and click, and click. In Windows 2000 Professional, you can right-click almost anything to display a shortcut menu from which you can immediately select a command.

Program Manager   Windows 2000 Professional replaces Program Manager with a truly graphical Desktop and the Start menu.

File Manager   In Windows 2000 Professional, you use Windows Explorer to manage your files, and directories have been replaced with folders, many of which also have an Explorer-like appearance.

The Internet and E-Mail   Windows 2000 Professional includes Outlook Express, an Internet mail and news reader, as well as the Internet Explorer Web browser. No longer do you have to install separate applications for these services.

Windows 2000 Professional versus Windows 95/98

As we mentioned earlier, the Windows 2000 Professional interface has the look and feel of Windows 98, as Windows NT Workstation 4 has the look and feel of Windows 95. Obviously, the differences between Windows 2000 Professional and Windows 95/98 are not in the same league as the differences between Windows 2000 Professional and Windows 3.1, but there are some distinct differences and improvements worth mentioning. Here are just a few:

Security   In Windows 95/98, you can password protect your system and files, but you don't have to. And, anyway, all a user has to do to bypass the Password dialog box is to press Escape. This doesn't work in Windows 2000 Professional; you have to know the password and have rights and privileges to start the system or access any files or programs.

The File System   The file system is the set of principles by which files are stored on your hard drive. Windows 95 uses the FAT16 (file allocation table) file system, which stores files in a database in the boot sector of your hard drive (the place that contains the files crucial to starting up your computer). Consequently, if the boot sector becomes damaged, you can lose data. Windows 98 initially also uses the FAT16 file system, but you can convert to the FAT32 file system, which has compression techniques that let you save considerable hard-disk space. With Windows 2000 Professional, you can elect to use either FAT or NTFS (New Technology File System). A number of advantages are associated with using NTFS, including automatic backup of the Master File Table and security controls for files, folders, and programs. For much more information about NTFS, see Chapter 2.

Right-Clicking   Although you can gain quick access to commands and tasks by right-clicking in Windows 95/98, you can right-click almost anywhere in Windows 2000 Professional to make something happen.

Part I

Streamlined Desktop   One of the first things you'll notice about Windows 2000 Professional is the uncluttered, lean Desktop. Quite an improvement over all the stuff that gets displayed in Windows 95/98 (and an even greater improvement if you have an OEM—Original Equipment Manufacturer—version of either operating system).

Personalized Start Menu   By default, the Start menu in Windows 2000 Professional always displays the programs you most frequently use and hides those you don't use.

Searching   The Find command has been replaced with the Search command and is accessible from any open folder window.

Active Desktop   In Windows 2000 Professional, you can specify that your Desktop behave like a Web page. Point to select; click to open. This feature is also available in Windows 98, but not in Windows 95.

Folder Links   Most folder have links to related folders that you can quickly access. For example, from the Printers folder, you can link to Microsoft Support.

Windows 2000 Professional versus Windows NT Workstation 4

Windows 2000 Professional has been described as combining the setup and hardware awareness of Windows 98 with the stability of Windows NT Workstation 4. It has also been described as not just putting a new spin on the interface but as breaking new ground. If you've used NT Workstation 4, you may at first feel as if the new ground is a little shaky; lots of items have been relocated, and some of their names have changed. We'll point these changes out, where appropriate. So, to begin with, let's take a brief look here at some differences between Windows 2000 Professional and Windows NT Workstation 4:

Plug and Play   The Hardware Abstraction Layer (HAL) has been removed, and Windows 2000 Professional is fully Plug and Play. The Plug-and-Play agents check to see what hardware is installed and what configuration is needed, and they communicate that information to the operating system.

Start Menu   The Start menu is now customizable, displaying the items you use most often. If you don't see a familiar item, click the More button at the bottom of a menu. You can also quickly alphabetize Start menu items and rename them.

Folder Bars   The Open and Save As dialog boxes now include an Outlook-like folder bar that you can use to specify a folder quickly.

The Find Command   This command has been renamed Search and is available in any open folder window. You can also extend your search to the Internet.

Network Neighborhood   This has been renamed My Network Places, and, from this folder, you can create Desktop shortcuts to network shares.

Folder Links   Many folders contain links that you can click to quickly open other folders. For example, the My Network Places folder contains links to My Documents and My Computer.

Toolbars   Most folders include a toolbar that is similar to the toolbar in Internet Explorer and contains Back and Forward buttons as well as a History button.

My Pictures Folder   This new folder is the default repository for image files, just as My Documents is for text files.

Folder Views   You can now click the View menu to specify how you want to view the contents of a folder—with large icons or small icons, as a list, or with detailed information.

Favorites Tab   The Help program now contains a Favorites tab in which you can store and quickly access Help topics that you frequently look up.

Windows Update   Choose Start ➢ Windows Update to connect to an area on Microsoft's Web site, where you can download updates, patches, fixes, device drivers, and add-ons.

Disk Defragmenter   With Windows NT 4, you had to purchase a third-party defragmenter tool; it comes with Windows 2000 Professional.

Power Management   Power-conserving schemes are available for both desktop and notebook computers.

Other new features in Windows 2000 Professional include Computer Management, Advanced Configuration and Power Interface

(ACPI) power management, Windows Installer, Safe Mode boot option, interactive troubleshooters, and support for the following:

- ▶ FAT32 volumes
- ▶ Universal Serial Bus
- ▶ Firewire/IEEE 1394 bus
- ▶ DVD (digital video disc)
- ▶ IrDA (Infrared Data Association)
- ▶ Infrared connections
- ▶ Multiple monitors

APPLICATIONS AND WINDOWS 2000 PROFESSIONAL

When a new operating system is released, one big question always concerns which applications can run on it. For the latest information about which applications are ready right now, go to www.microsoft.com/windows/professional/deploy/compatible. You can, however, do your own compatibility testing if you want. Here are the steps:

1. Install and open the application.

2. Verify that the following functions work:

   - ▶ Printing
   - ▶ Saving files
   - ▶ Customizing menus
   - ▶ Exporting data
   - ▶ Cutting and pasting through the Clipboard

3. Run routine tasks to verify that their stability has not been affected.

NETWORKING AND WINDOWS 2000 PROFESSIONAL

While we were writing *Windows 2000 Professional: In Record Time*, we were running Windows 2000 Professional on a couple of small networks.

We mention this for two reasons. First, you can also run Windows 2000 Professional on a stand-alone system, if you want; all the features are enabled except for those related to networking. Second, because we were working on a network, the figures and graphics in Part I of this book reflect that. Nevertheless, everything in this book should work, with very minor differences, whether you are running in stand-alone or network mode.

If you work for a corporation, your computer is probably part of a network, and, furthermore, unless you are the IT (information technology) manager, you probably have or had no part in the decision about what operating system or systems to run. However, if you have a small business or a busy home office, you may decide that a network makes sense for you. A network provides many advantages if you're working with a group of people or simply have multiple computers:

- ▶ You can share a printer or printers.

- ▶ You can easily share files with others.

- ▶ You can back up to another computer if you don't have the space or budget for a zip drive or some other external device.

- ▶ You can share an Internet connection.

- ▶ And, with Windows 2000 Professional, you can secure your systems and your data.

NOTE

In *Windows 2000 Professional: In Record Time*, you'll find two chapters devoted to networks. Chapter 16 tells you step by step how to set up a small network, and Chapter 17 has information on connecting to a corporate network.

WHAT'S NEXT?

In the next chapter, we'll look at how to install and upgrade to Windows 2000 Professional. We'll also go through the steps of running Setup, choosing a file system, and creating user accounts. In Chapter 23, Mark Minasi et al. will show you how to install Windows 2000 Server.

Chapter 2

INSTALLING AND UPGRADING TO WINDOWS 2000 PROFESSIONAL

If you are on a corporate network that has upgraded to Windows 2000 Professional, you probably don't need the step-by-step instructions in this chapter. You will benefit, however, from the information this chapter contains about operating systems and file systems; we recommend that you check out the sections concerning those topics.

Adapted from *Windows 2000 Professional: In Record Time*, by Peter Dyson and Pat Coleman
ISBN 0-7821-2450-X   467 pages $29.99

If you are a current Windows user and are about to install or upgrade to Windows 2000 Professional, this chapter is required reading. Installing or upgrading Windows 2000 Professional is very different from installing or upgrading to previous versions of Windows. Although installing Windows 2000 Professional will probably take you half the time of earlier Windows installations, you need to make some informed decisions during the process. Before you dive into Setup, you need to give some thought to how you currently use your system and how you plan to use it in the future. Some of these decisions can be changed once the installation is complete, but others cannot, and you need to make the right choice the first time. We could have hidden this information away in an appendix at the back of the book, but, because some of the issues involved are so fundamental to how you will use Windows 2000 Professional, we decided to put them right at the front of this book.

Before proceeding with your installation, your to-do list needs to include the following:

- ▶ Make sure your hardware meets the minimum requirements for Windows 2000 Professional.

- ▶ Collect network, workgroup, and domain information from your system administrator if you will be part of a network.

- ▶ Back up your current files before upgrading, in case you need to restore your current operating system.

- ▶ Turn off or uninstall your virus-protection software. Popular antivirus programs such as McAfee AntiVirus version 3 for Windows NT and IBM's AntiVirus are not compatible with Windows 2000 Professional.

- ▶ Decide between upgrading your current operating system and making a completely new installation of Windows 2000 Professional.

- ▶ Choose the file system you want to use.

- ▶ Read the Read1st.txt file on the Windows 2000 Professional CD. This file contains late-breaking information that may affect your installation.

In the sections that follow, we'll go through each of these issues and explain the choices you need to make. Then we'll go through running the Setup program. Finally, we'll create new accounts for each of the people who will use Windows 2000 Professional.

WINDOWS 2000 PROFESSIONAL HARDWARE REQUIREMENTS

Before you install Windows 2000 Professional, make sure your computer meets these minimum hardware requirements:

- A 166-megahertz (MHz) Pentium microprocessor. This is an absolute minimum requirement; we suggest a 300MHz Pentium II for a desktop PC and a 233MHz processor in a notebook computer. (This is definitely a case where more is better.)

- At least 32 megabytes (MB) of RAM; 64MB is recommended, and 4 gigabytes (GB) is the maximum. (Again, as with the processor, as far as memory is concerned, more is better.)

- At least a 2GB hard disk with a minimum of 650MB of free space.

- A VGA or higher-resolution monitor.

- Keyboard.

- Mouse or compatible pointing device.

- CD-ROM drive.

- High-density 3.5-inch floppy disk, unless your CD-ROM drive is bootable and supports starting the Setup program from a CD.

For a network installation, you will also need a compatible network adapter card, a connection to the network, and access to the network share that contains the Setup files.

CHECKING YOUR HARDWARE COMPATIBILITY

The Windows 2000 Professional Setup program automatically checks your hardware and software and tells you of possible problems. To avoid any conflicts, check that your hardware is on the Hardware Compatibility List (HCL) before you start. You can view the Hardware Compatibility List by opening the Hcl.txt file in the Support folder on the Windows 2000 Professional CD. You will find every category of hardware in this list—everything from audio devices to Universal Serial Bus (USB) hubs, stopping at desktop systems,

Part I

Small Computer System Interface (SCSI) controllers, and hard disk drives along the way.

TIP
If you have Internet access, you can view the latest HCL on the Microsoft Web site at http://www.microsoft.com/hwtest/hcl.

If your hardware isn't listed in the HCL file, the Setup program may not work as expected, and your installation may not be successful. Contact the hardware manufacturer and ask if there's a Windows 2000 driver for the component; remember, you don't need any special drivers for your Plug-and-Play devices.

COLLECTING NETWORK INFORMATION

If your computer is going to connect to a network, you need the following information:

- ▶ The name of your computer
- ▶ The name of the workgroup or domain you belong to
- ▶ A TCP/IP address, if your network doesn't have a Dynamic Host Configuration Protocol (DHCP) server

You also need to decide if your computer will be joining a domain or a workgroup. If you don't know which option to choose or if your computer won't be connected to a network, you should select the workgroup option; you can always join a domain later. Your network administrator can provide you with all this information.

MAKING A BACKUP

Upgrading your system to a new operating system or to a new version of an operating system has been described as a quick way to trash all your software. Such a description is supposed to be a joke, but it's not funny when it happens to you. If you're upgrading from a previous version of Windows, you should back up your current files to a disk, to a tape drive, or to another computer on your network. This is mainly a precaution in case something goes wrong during the installation or you decide to return to your previous operating system at some point in the future. If you are upgrading from Windows 95, 98, or 98 Second Edition, use the Backup program; if you are upgrading from Windows NT, use the Windows Backup program.

WARNING

Windows 2000 Professional Backup does not support the restoration of backup files saved to disk using Windows 98.

SHOULD YOU UPGRADE OR MAKE A NEW INSTALLATION?

You can install Windows 2000 Professional as an upgrade to your existing operating system, or you can install it alongside your current operating system and then use one or the other as you see fit. Let's take a look at the differences.

During an upgrade, Setup replaces your existing Windows files but preserves all your current settings and applications. You can upgrade to Windows 2000 Professional from the following operating systems:

- ▶ Windows 95
- ▶ Windows 98
- ▶ Windows 98 Second Edition
- ▶ Windows NT 3.51 Workstation
- ▶ Windows NT Workstation 4

During a new installation, Setup installs Windows 2000 Professional in a new folder. For more details, see "Performing a New Installation" later in this section.

TIP

If you're currently using a non-supported operating system, such as Microsoft Windows 3.1 or IBM OS/2, you must perform a new installation. Once the installation is complete, you will have to reinstall all your applications and reset your settings.

You can also use a dual-boot configuration to run both Windows 2000 Professional and another compatible operating system, such as Windows 98, on your computer. In this case, you should install Windows 2000 Professional on a different hard-disk partition than the one used by your current operating system. We'll look at how to make a dual-boot installation in more detail later in this chapter.

RUNNING SETUP

Whether you make a new installation or perform an upgrade, it's the Setup program that does all the work. Most of the time, Setup is completely automatic, but, from time to time, it pauses to ask you a question or ask you to confirm certain choices, such as time-zone information and other regional settings. Just follow the instructions on the screen.

Setup then copies all the appropriate files to your hard disk, checks your hardware, and configures your installation. Because Windows 2000 Professional supports Plug and Play, all device-driver selection and loading is completely automatic. Setup also restarts your computer several times during the installation. The whole process takes about an hour or so to complete. The method you use to start Setup depends on several things, including whether you are making a new installation or performing an upgrade. We'll look at all these options in the next few sections.

Performing a New Installation

If your current operating system is not supported, if you want to install Windows 2000 Professional in a dual-boot configuration, or if your computer has a blank hard disk, you need to start your computer using either:

- ▶ The Setup boot floppy disks.

- ▶ The Windows 2000 Professional CD—if your CD-ROM drive is bootable. Certain CD-ROM drives can boot from the CD and automatically launch Setup.

WARNING
The Setup start-up or boot disks are not the same as the Windows Emergency Repair Disk.

To start a new installation using the Setup boot floppy disks, follow these steps:

1. With your computer turned off, insert the Windows 2000 Setup boot Disk 1 into your floppy disk drive.

2. Start your computer. The Setup program starts automatically.

3. Follow the instructions on the screen.

MAKING SETUP START-UP FLOPPY DISKS

If you don't have copies of the Setup start-up or boot disks, you can create them yourself. These floppies are used to start Setup if you can't start Setup from your hard drive or from your CD. Here are the steps:

1. Insert a blank, formatted disk into the floppy disk drive and the Windows 2000 Professional CD into your CD-ROM drive. (You will need four blank, 1.44MB, formatted, 3.5-inch disks, labeled "Setup Disk 1," "Setup Disk 2," and so on.)

2. Click Start, and then click Run.

3. At the prompt, type the following command, replacing the letter *d* with the letter of your CD-ROM drive and replacing *a* with the letter of your floppy drive:

   `d:\bootdisk\makeboot.bat a:`

4. Follow the instructions that appear on the screen.

To start a new installation from the CD, follow these steps:

1. Start your computer by running your current operating system, and then insert the Windows 2000 Professional CD into your CD-ROM drive.

2. If Windows automatically detects the CD, click Install Windows 2000. The Setup program then starts.

   If Windows doesn't automatically detect the CD, start Setup from the Run command. In Windows 95, Windows 98, or Windows NT 4, click Start, and then click Run. In Windows NT 3.51 or Windows 3.1, in Program Manager, click File, and then click Run. At the prompt, type the following command, replacing the letter *d* with the letter of your CD-ROM drive:

`d:\i386\winnt32.exe`

If you're using Windows 3.1, type the following command at the prompt, replacing the letter *d* with the letter of your CD-ROM drive:

`d:\i386\winnt.exe`

3. Press the Enter key, and follow the instructions on the screen.

Upgrading to Windows 2000 Professional

Upgrading to Windows 2000 Professional is a straightforward process. The Setup program automatically detects your hardware and installs the appropriate drivers, or, if it finds hardware incompatible with Windows 2000 Professional, it creates a report on devices that cannot be upgraded.

TIP

You must uncompress any DriveSpace or DoubleSpace volumes before upgrading to Windows 2000 Professional.

To upgrade to Windows 2000 Professional from Windows 95, Windows 98, or Windows NT Workstation 4, follow these steps:

1. Start your computer by running your current operating system, and then insert the Windows 2000 Professional CD into your CD-ROM drive.

2. If Windows automatically detects the CD and asks if you want to upgrade to Windows 2000 Professional, click Yes. Otherwise, click Start, and then click Run. At the prompt, type the following command, replacing the letter *d* with the letter of your CD-ROM drive:

`d:\i386\winnt32.exe`

3. Press the Enter key.

4. Follow the instructions on the screen.

Part i

WARNING

If you are upgrading from Windows 95 or Windows 98, you may see some of your applications listed in the Upgrade Report window. These are applications known to have serious problems with the upgrade to Windows 2000 Professional. To prevent problems once the upgrade is complete, you should follow the recommendations given in the Upgrade Report window. See Chapter 7 for more information on running your applications under Windows 2000 Professional.

To upgrade to Windows 2000 Professional from Windows NT Workstation 3.51, follow these steps:

1. Start your computer by running your current operating system, and then insert the Windows 2000 Professional CD into your CD-ROM drive.

2. In Program Manager, click File, and then click Run. At the prompt, type the following command, replacing the letter *d* with the letter of your CD-ROM drive:

   `d:\i386\winnt32.exe`

3. Press the Enter key.

4. Follow the instructions on the screen.

CHOOSING A FILE SYSTEM

Before you install Windows 2000 Professional, you must decide which file system you want to use. The file system consists of the complete set of organizational elements that allow the operating system to communicate with your hard disk. Windows 2000 Professional supports the NT file system (NTFS) as well as the file allocation table file systems FAT or FAT32. You can only use one file system at a time, so let's take a look at the different options.

NTFS

NTFS is the file system recommended for use with Windows 2000 Professional. NTFS is a high-performance file system that provides the following advantages over the FAT and FAT32 file systems:

▶ Increased file security controls.

- ▶ Better disk compression.

- ▶ File encryption.

- ▶ Support for large hard disks of up to 2 terabytes (TB), and, as drive size increases, performance does not degrade as it does with FAT.

- ▶ Better protection from viruses. Most viruses are written to attack FAT and FAT32 file systems and don't know what to do when they encounter NTFS.

- ▶ Long filenames.

NTFS creates backup records of the Master File Table (MFT)—the NTFS version of the FAT file allocation table—so, if the boot sector of your hard disk is damaged by accident, the information can be replaced from one of the backup records. This means you are much less likely to lose data due to disk problems.

MS-DOS, Windows 3.x, Windows 95, and Windows 98 do not understand NTFS, so if you're using a dual-boot configuration with Windows 2000 Professional and one of these operating systems, you won't be able to read the files in the NTFS partition from the other operating system on your computer.

FAT and FAT32

FAT32 is an enhanced version of the FAT file system and is used on drives from 512MB to 2TB in size. FAT and FAT32 offer backward compatibility with operating systems other than Windows 2000 Professional. If you are setting up a dual-boot configuration and it is important that you be able to access from MS-DOS, Windows 3.x, Windows 95, or Windows 98 the files you create with Windows 2000 Professional, you should consider using FAT or FAT32.

Use FAT if the hard disk partition you want to use with Windows 2000 Professional is smaller than 2GB, and choose FAT32 if the partition is 2GB or larger. In fact, if you choose FAT in the Setup program and the partition is larger than 2GB, Setup automatically formats the partition as FAT32.

A Quick Look at Disk Partitions

Disk partitioning is a way of dividing your hard disk so that each section functions as a separate unit. You can create a partition for several reasons, including to back up data, to organize different kinds of information, or to dual boot another operating system. When you create partitions on a disk, you are dividing the disk into areas that can be formatted by different file systems. A hard disk can contain as many as four partitions. Remember to back up any files in a partition that you plan to reformat, because reformatting the partition destroys any data that it contains.

TIP

The Setup program can make changes to your partitions as you install Windows 2000 Professional, but if you prefer to make the changes yourself before you start the installation, use a program such as PartitionMagic from PowerQuest Corporation. PartitionMagic is very powerful but is very easy to use, and you can see exactly what is happening on the screen in front of you. Call 800-379-2566 or point your Web browser to www.powerquest.com for more information.

Depending on your existing hard disk configuration, you have several partitioning options when installing Windows 2000 Professional:

- ▶ If your hard disk is unpartitioned, you can create and size the Windows 2000 Professional partition.

- ▶ If the existing partition is large enough, you can install Windows 2000 Professional in that partition. Installing to an existing partition overwrites any data on that partition.

- ▶ If the existing partition is too small but you have enough unpartitioned space, you can create a new Windows 2000 Professional partition in that space.

- ▶ If the hard disk has an existing partition, you can delete it to create more unpartitioned disk space for the Windows 2000 Professional partition. Deleting an existing partition also erases any data on that partition.

If you're setting up a dual-boot configuration, you must always install Windows 2000 Professional in its own partition. Installing Windows 2000 in the same partition as another operating system will cause Setup to overwrite files required by the original operating system.

TIP

Although Windows 2000 Professional requires a minimum of 500MB of free hard-disk space for installation, using a larger partition gives you the flexibility to add future updates, operating system tools, applications, and other files.

Setting Up a Dual-Boot Configuration

By using a dual-boot configuration on your computer, you can choose between operating systems or even between versions of the same operating system from a menu every time you start your computer. Windows 2000 Professional supports dual-boot configurations with the following operating systems:

- ▶ Windows NT 3.51
- ▶ Windows NT 4
- ▶ Windows 95
- ▶ Windows 98
- ▶ Windows 98 Second Edition
- ▶ Windows 3.x
- ▶ Windows for Workgroups 3.11
- ▶ MS-DOS
- ▶ OS/2

To establish a dual-boot configuration, you must install each operating system into a separate partition. During Setup, you can use the Advanced Setup option to select a folder on an unused partition.

TIP

You can also set up a multiboot configuration and load more than two operating systems onto one computer.

If you are planning a dual-boot configuration, here are some things to think about before you start:

- ▶ Each operating system must be installed on a separate drive or disk partition.
- ▶ Before you start to install the second or subsequent operating system, take the time to create an Emergency Repair Disk if you are using Windows NT Workstation or a Start Up disk if you are using Windows 95 or 98. You might need it later.

▶ Consider using the FAT32 file system for dual-boot configurations. Although using NTFS in a dual boot is certainly supported and offers considerable benefits over FAT32, such a configuration introduces additional operational complexity.

▶ To set up a dual-boot configuration between MS-DOS or Windows 95 and Windows 2000 Professional, you should install Windows 2000 last; otherwise, important files needed to start Windows 2000 Professional could be overwritten. If you want to dual boot between Windows 98 and Windows 2000 Professional, you can install the operating systems in any order.

▶ In a dual boot of Windows 2000 Professional with Windows 95 or MS-DOS, the primary hard-disk partition must be formatted as FAT; for a dual boot with Windows 95, OS/2, or Windows 98, the primary partition must be formatted as FAT or FAT32.

▶ If you're upgrading an NT Workstation dual-boot computer, you can't gain access to NTFS partitions from any operating system other than Windows NT 4 with Service Pack 4 (SP4). Also, if you modify existing files or create new files on the NTFS partition, you can't use those files with any other operating system, including Windows NT 4 with SP4. What this means is that a dual boot with Windows 2000 Professional and any other version of Windows NT is not recommended if the computer uses only NTFS partitions. This is because Windows 2000 Professional supports a new version of NTFS called NTFS 5, which is not compatible with earlier versions of the NT family of operating systems.

▶ If you install Windows 2000 Professional on a computer that dual boots between IBM's OS/2 and MS-DOS, Windows 2000 Professional Setup configures your system so you dual boot between Windows 2000 Professional and the operating system (either MS-DOS or OS/2) that you used immediately before running Setup. This is due to the way that the OS/2 boot manager works.

▶ Don't install Windows 2000 Professional on a compressed drive unless the drive was compressed with the NTFS file system compression utility. You don't have to uncompress DriveSpace or DoubleSpace volumes if you plan to dual boot with Windows 95 or Windows 98, but those compressed volumes won't be available to you while you're running Windows 2000 Professional.

Part I

▶ If the dual-boot computer is part of a Windows NT or Windows 2000 Professional domain, each installation of either Windows NT Workstation or Windows 2000 Professional must have a different computer name.

▶ If you're using NTFS and dual booting with Windows NT, you must upgrade to Windows NT 4 with SP4 or later before continuing with the Windows 2000 Professional installation.

Once you have decided whether these issues are likely to be important in your installation, you can proceed with a new Windows 2000 Professional installation on your system.

CHOOSING BETWEEN NTFS AND FAT32 ON A DUAL-BOOT SYSTEM

If you want to install a Windows 2000 Professional dual-boot system with an existing Windows 98 installation, consider your choice of file system carefully. Windows 98 uses FAT32, and Windows 2000 Professional supports FAT, FAT32, and NTFS. To install Windows 2000 dual boot, you must have two separate hard-disk partitions available—one for Windows 98 and one for Windows 2000 Professional.

The Windows 98 partition will be formatted with FAT32, so that much is given and can't be changed, but with Windows 2000 Professional, you can choose the file system to use. If you install FAT32 on the Windows 2000 Professional partition, you will be able to read files from both partitions using both operating systems. In a typical system, you will have Windows 98 on drive C, Windows 2000 Professional on drive D, and your CD-ROM drive will become drive E. But you get none of the performance or security benefits of NTFS.

If you install NTFS on the Windows 2000 Professional partition, things change quite a bit. When you boot Windows 2000 Professional, you will be able to read the FAT32 files from drive C and the NTFS files from drive D. Your CD-ROM drive stays as drive E. But when you boot Windows 98, the NTFS partition that was drive D disappears along with all the files it contains. You can read the files from the FAT32 partition, and this time your CD-ROM drive becomes drive D. The files on drive D have not been deleted, and they are still there on the disk; it's just that Windows 98 can't see them.

CONTINUED ➡

So it all comes down to how you will use your system. If it is important that you be able to read all files on all disks from both operating systems, install FAT32 on the Windows 2000 Professional partition. If this is not an important operational consideration, install NTFS on the Windows 2000 Professional partition, and take advantage of the better security and increased performance.

INSTALLING THE ADD-ON COMPONENTS

The Windows 2000 Professional CD contains several system elements not included as part of the standard installation. To look at or install these programs, insert the Windows 2000 Professional CD into the CD disk drive, and then click Install Add-On Components to start the Windows Components Wizard. Using the Wizard, you can install:

- Internet Information Services (IIS) Web server and associated files. If you upgrade to Windows 2000 Professional from a previous version of Windows NT Workstation, IIS is installed automatically if Personal Web Server was previously installed on NT.

- Management and Monitoring Tools, including Simple Network Management Protocol (SNMP).

- Message Queuing Services.

- Indexing Service.

- Script Debugger for working with client and server scripts written in VBScript or JScript.

- Networking Services, including RIP (Routing Information Protocol) Listener, and additional TCP/IP (Transmission Control Protocol/Internet Protocol) services such as Quote of the Day.

- Other Network File and Print Services, including Print Services for Unix.

Follow the instructions on the screen to install one or more of these optional elements. See Chapter 7 for more details on adding and removing Windows 2000 Professional optional components.

TIP

You will also find demo versions of non-Microsoft, third-party software in the Valuadd directory on the Windows 2000 Professional CD.

CREATING A NEW USER ACCOUNT

The password you gave Setup during the installation process gives you access to the Administrator account, but once the installation is complete, you should create user accounts for all the people you expect to use the Windows 2000 Professional system. A user account identifies a username and password, group membership, and which network resources can be accessed, as well as personal files and folders.

Windows 2000 Professional has two kinds of user accounts: domain user accounts and local user accounts. With a domain user account, you log on to the domain to access network resources. This kind of account is often used with client/server networks. With a local user account, you log on to a specific computer to access resources available only on that computer. This kind of account is suitable for use on a peer-to-peer network.

To create a new user account, follow these steps:

1. Choose Start ➤ Settings ➤ Control Panel to open Control Panel.

2. Click Users And Passwords to open the Users And Passwords dialog box, which is shown in Figure 2.1.

3. Make sure the Users Must Enter A User Name And Password To Use This Computer check box is checked.

4. Click Add to open the Add New User Wizard. Enter a name for the new user, and click Next.

5. Enter and confirm a password for this user. Click Next.

6. Select the level of access for this user. Choose Standard User, and click Finish.

7. Click Apply and then OK to close the Users And Passwords applet.

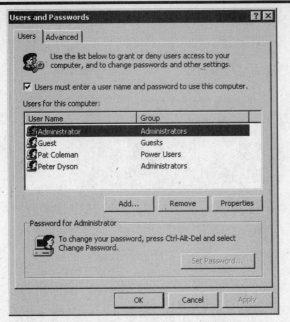

FIGURE 2.1: The Users And Passwords dialog box

Repeat these steps to create an account for each of the people who will be using the system, including one for yourself. Then log off from the Administrator account, and log back on using your new user account:

1. Choose Start ➤ Shut Down, and then select Log Off from the drop-down list. Click OK.

2. Enter your Standard User name and password into the Log On To Windows dialog box.

When you have finished your work, you should choose Start ➤ Shut Down to log off the computer so that other users can log on.

WHAT'S NEXT?

Now that you have Windows 2000 Professional up and running, it's time to take a look at the Desktop, the screen you see when you first start Windows 2000. As we mentioned earlier, the Windows 2000 Desktop is cleaner and slicker than the Desktop in earlier versions of Windows, and certain items have new names or have been relocated. In the next chapter, we'll explore this new Desktop and show you how to use the items on it.

Chapter 3

EXPLORING THE DESKTOP

I f you have been a Windows NT user, the Windows 2000 Professional Desktop will look familiar. However, you will no doubt soon discover that some items have moved to new locations, that there are some new items, and that some items have new names. If you have been a user of Windows 95 or Windows 98 and are upgrading to Windows 2000 Professional, the Desktop will also look familiar. You'll notice right away, however, that it is much less cluttered than the version of Windows you've been using and that you need to right-click to open such essentials as Windows Explorer.

Adapted from *Windows 2000 Professional: In Record Time*, by Peter Dyson and Pat Coleman

ISBN 0-7821-2450-X   467 pages $29.99

In Windows 2000 Professional, you can view the Desktop using the classic Windows interface or the Active Desktop. In the Active Desktop view, your Desktop looks and works like a Web page. You single-click an item rather than double-clicking to open it. By default, the Windows 2000 Professional Desktop displays in classic view, but files and folders display in Web view. This is a hybrid view and is the setup we used as we wrote this book. You can continue to use this view, or you can change it so that everything is either in the classic view or in Web page view. You can also create some other combination. You do all this using the Folder Options applet in Control Panel, and we'll look at this in detail in the next chapter.

In this chapter, we'll look at all the parts and pieces of the Desktop in its default classic view.

LOGGING ON

Although logging on is a simple process and we discussed it at the end of Chapter 2, we're giving it a reprise here—just in case you skipped Chapter 2. You need at least two things to log on: your username and your password. If you are connected to a corporate local area network (LAN), you may also need the name of a domain if you're supposed to log on to a domain other than the default. If this is the case, your network administrator will let you know.

Enter your username and password in the dialog box requesting that information, and click OK. That's really all there is to it, unless you make a typo or you're asked to supply a new password. On corporate networks, most administrators set the system so that user passwords expire every 30 days, and they set password history so that you can't repeat a password until you've used 12 or 13 other passwords. If you think you might not remember the new password, write it down and put it in a safe place—this doesn't mean on a sticky note attached to your computer. Passwords are a vital part of network security, and most organizations have rules about them. Be sure you understand them and implement the policy properly.

TIP

The most common way to mistype your password is to have the Caps Lock key on when it shouldn't be. We have been collectively logging on to networks more years than we want to count, and we still make this mistake. Check the Caps Lock key immediately if your password is not accepted.

USING THE START MENU

If you place your mouse cursor over the Start button, you'll see a ToolTip that says "Click here to begin," and so that's how we'll get started exploring the Desktop. If you don't see the Start button (and the Taskbar, which we'll discuss next), move your mouse cursor to the bottom of the screen. Figure 3.1 shows the Desktop before you click the Start button. Your Desktop will look different from the one shown here. For starters, you probably don't have a FullShot99 icon (FullShot99 is the program we used to create the art for this chapter), and you may have other icons for programs that you or your network administrator has installed.

FIGURE 3.1: The Windows 2000 Professional Desktop

Clicking Start

Clicking Start opens the menu shown in Figure 3.2. Let's briefly look at each of these items, starting at the top.

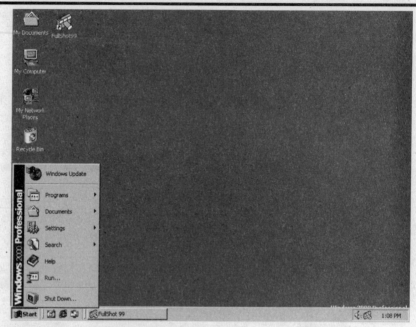

FIGURE 3.2:   The items on the Start menu

Windows Update

When you select Windows Update, you'll be connected to the Microsoft Windows Update site (if you are currently connected to the Internet) and see a page similar to that shown in Figure 3.3. Here you can get up-to-date information and news about Windows products, support, and help. If you scroll down the page, you'll find a link that takes you to a page specific to Windows 2000 Professional that contains information about new features and troubleshooting tips.

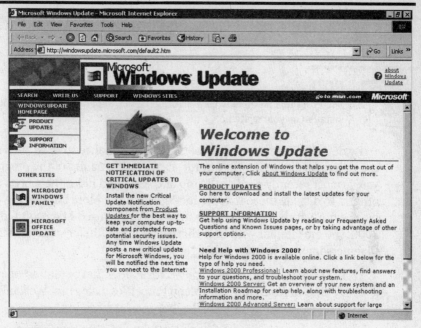

FIGURE 3.3: The Microsoft Windows Update page

Programs

Clicking Programs opens a submenu that contains at least the following items:

Accessories   Contains yet another submenu of programs (see Chapter 10).

Startup   Contains the names of any programs that you want to start every time you start Windows. To place an item on this menu, drag its icon to the Start button, then to the Programs button, and then drop it on Startup.

Internet Explorer   Opens the Microsoft Internet Explorer Web browser. For all the details, see Chapter 17.

Outlook Express   Opens Outlook Express, the mail and
news program included with Windows 2000 Professional. See
Chapter 16 for the details.

NOTE
The Programs menu may contain other items, depending on what you have
installed on your system.

By default, Windows 2000 Professional personalizes menus such as
the Programs menu. In other words, it places the names of the programs
you've most recently used at the top of the list and hides the names of
others. To display those that are hidden, click the More button (the double chevron) at the bottom of the menu. If you've used Microsoft Office
2000, you are familiar with how this works. If you prefer static rather
than personalized menus, follow these steps:

1. Choose Start ➢ Settings ➢ Taskbar & Start Menu to open
    the Taskbar And Start Menu Properties dialog box. We'll take
    a closer look at this dialog box in a later section.

2. On the General tab, click the Use Personalized Menus check
    box to clear it.

3. Click OK.

Documents

Clicking Documents displays a menu that lists the last 15 documents
you've opened as well as your My Documents folder. Clicking My Documents opens that folder in Windows Explorer, and clicking any of the
other documents opens those documents. For the most part, this is a
quick and easy way to open both a document and the program in which
you created it. Some documents, however, do not open in the program in
which you created them. For example, an image file will open in Imaging
Preview. To change the program in which the document will open, follow
these steps:

1. Right-click the document name in the list, choose Open
    With, and then choose Choose Program to open the
    Open With dialog box.

2. Select a program from the list, and click OK. If you don't see the program you want, click Other, select a program, and click Open. Windows 2000 Professional adds the program to the list. Select it, and click OK.

If you want all like files to open in the same program, click the Always Use This Program To Open These Files check box in the Open With dialog box.

RIGHT-CLICKING IN WINDOWS 2000 PROFESSIONAL

In Windows 2000 Professional, right-clicking almost anywhere produces something helpful. In most cases, right-clicking opens a shortcut menu that contains some fairly standard commands such as Send To, Cut, Copy, Delete, Properties, and so on, as well as some items that are specific to what you right-clicked. In some cases, right-clicking opens a What's This? box that you can click to get help on the item.

If you're ever in doubt, just try it. You can't hurt anything; worst case, you'll get nothing.

We'll talk a lot more about the virtues of right-clicking in Chapter 6.

To clear the items in the Documents list, follow these steps:

1. Choose Start ➢ Settings ➢ Taskbar & Start Menu to open the Taskbar And Start Menu Properties dialog box.

2. Click the Advanced tab.

3. Click Clear, and then click OK.

NOTE

Clearing the items in the Documents list does not delete them from your system. It just empties the list and makes room for other, more recent items.

Settings

When you click Settings, you see a menu that contains the following items:

- ▶ Control Panel
- ▶ Network And Dial-Up Connections
- ▶ Printers
- ▶ Taskbar & Start Menu

You will return to these items often as you begin to set up and manage your Windows 2000 Professional system. Let's take a brief look at what you'll find when you select one of these items.

Click Control Panel to open the screen shown in Figure 3.4. These items are often referred to as applets—small programs that you use to take care of a specific task such as adding or removing a program from your system, changing the settings in your display, setting up your connections to the Internet, and so on.

Click Network And Dial-Up Connections to open the Network Connection Wizard and create a connection to another computer or a network, to see the status of a local area connection, and to connect to the Internet.

Click Printers to open the Printers dialog box, which you use to add a printer, manage your print queue, check the status of jobs you've sent to the printer, and so on.

Click Taskbar & Start Menu to open the Taskbar And Start Menu Properties dialog box (see Figure 3.5), which we mentioned earlier. You use the options in this dialog box to customize your Desktop. We'll look at this dialog box in more detail in Chapter 5.

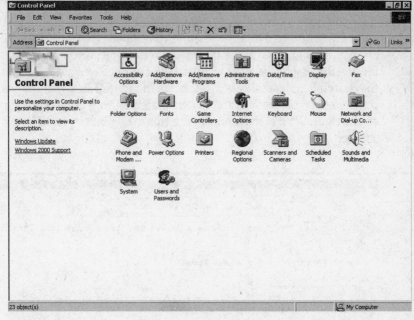

FIGURE 3.4:   Use the options in Control Panel to take charge of your system.

FIGURE 3.5:   The Taskbar And Start Menu Properties dialog box

Search

Have you been looking for the Find command? Well, it's not there; Find
has metamorphosed into Search, and you can use it to locate files, folders, people, and sites on the Internet. For example, if you want to find a
file or a folder, choose Start ➢ Search ➢ For Files Or Folders. You'll see
the Search Results dialog box, as shown in Figure 3.6. When the search is
completed, you'll see files and folders matching your criteria in the pane
on the right. We'll discuss how to use this dialog box in detail in the next
chapter.

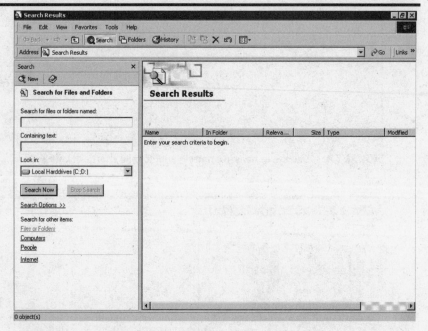

FIGURE 3.6:   Use the Search Results dialog box to find files and folders on your
local drive or on a network.

Clicking On The Internet opens the Search bar in Internet Explorer.
Clicking For People opens the Find People dialog box, which you can use
to locate people in your Address Book or on Internet search services (if
you are connected to the Internet).

Help

Click Help to open the Windows 2000 Professional Help system. You'll
see the screen shown in Figure 3.7. If you've used Help in Windows

applications and in previous versions of Windows, you'll be glad to hear that Windows 2000 Professional Help is really easy to use, and it's fast. Click a tab, click a topic, and then view the information in the right pane.

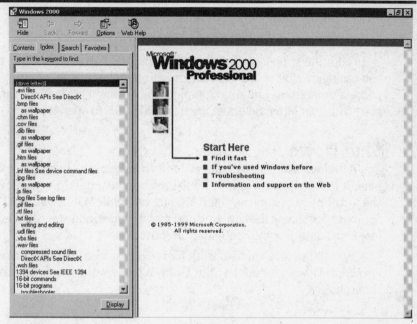

FIGURE 3.7: The Windows 2000 Professional Help system

If you're a seasoned user of either Windows 95/98 or NT, be sure to check out the If You've Used Windows Before topic under Start Here. As we mentioned at the beginning of this chapter, many components have new names and are in new locations. For example, click the first topic in the right pane, Active Desktop. In Windows 98, Active Desktop was on the Settings menu; in Windows 2000 Professional, it's part of Folder Options in Control Panel.

You'll also notice an additional tab, Favorites, which we find particularly useful. With a topic open in the right pane, click the Favorites tab, and then click Add. Now, whenever you want to return to that topic, simply select it from your Favorites list instead of searching for it again.

Run

As you'll find out when you get to Chapter 7, you can run applications from several places in Windows 2000 Professional, including the Run dialog box, which opens when you click Run.

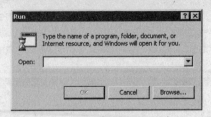

In addition to opening a program by typing its name in the Open box, you can open a folder, a document, or an Internet site. Start entering the name of something, and AutoComplete will display a list of items that start with that letter. Select an item, and click OK to open it.

Shut Down

You'll find out soon enough, if you don't already know, that it's to your benefit to shut down Windows 2000 Professional properly. If you don't, the next time you start up, you'll have to wait while Windows 2000 Professional does some file checking and maintenance, and you could even lose some data or some configuration settings.

When you're through with work for the day or ready to head for bed, click Shut Down to open the Shut Down Windows dialog box. You have three choices:

- ▶ Log Off
- ▶ Shut Down
- ▶ Restart

Choose Log Off to end your current session and leave the computer running. Choose Restart to restart the system (for example, when you are working on a dual-boot system and you want to start the other operating system). Windows 2000 Professional will shut down and then restart automatically. Choose Shut Down when you are ready to power down the computer. Windows 2000 Professional will let you know when it's safe to turn off your computer.

Right-Clicking Start

Remember our earlier declaration about how important right-clicking is in Windows 2000 Professional? It starts with the Start button. Right-click the Start button to open a menu that has the following items.

- ▶ Open
- ▶ Explore

► Search

► Open All Users

► Explore All Users

Open

Click Open to open the Start Menu dialog box, which contains the Programs folder and links to My Documents, My Network Places, and My Computer. We'll discuss these links in the next section.

Explore

Been wondering where Windows Explorer was? Click Explore to open it. As you can see in Figure 3.8, it opens with the Start Menu folder highlighted and its contents in the right pane. When you select another file or folder, its name appears in the title bar. For example, if you select My Computer, the title bar displays My Computer, and the folder contents are displayed in the right pane.

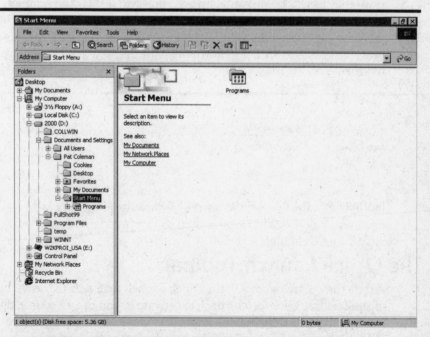

FIGURE 3.8:   Right-click Start and choose Explore to open Windows Explorer.

Search

Click Search to open the Search Results dialog box that we discussed earlier.

Open All Users

Click Open All Users to open the Start Menu folder, which shows the Start Menu items (files, folders, and programs) available to any user who logs on to this computer.

Explore All Users

Click Explore All Users to open the Start Menu folder in Windows Explorer, which will show you the Start Menu items available to any user who logs on to this computer.

WORKING WITH THE TASKBAR

By default, the Taskbar contains the Quick Launch toolbar, the Volume icon, and the clock. You can, however, choose to display the Address, Links, and Desktop toolbars, and you can create and add a new toolbar. We'll look at those options in Chapter 5. In this section, we'll quickly go over the defaults, which are shown in Figure 3.9, and describe how you use them.

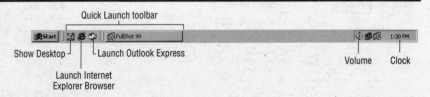

FIGURE 3.9:   The Taskbar in Windows 2000 Professional

The Quick Launch Toolbar

As you can see in Figure 3.9, the Quick Launch toolbar is at the left end of the Taskbar. Click an icon once to activate it. You can, of course, open Internet Explorer and Outlook Express in many other ways, but if you are at the Desktop, using the Quick Launch toolbar is quickest.

Show Desktop   If you have multiple windows open and you need to access something on your Desktop, click Show Desktop to minimize all the open windows. For this to work, you need to be able to see the Taskbar. We'll discuss hiding and displaying the Taskbar later in this section.

Launch Internet Explorer Browser   Click to open Internet Explorer.

Launch Outlook Express   Click to open Outlook Express.

The Rest of the Taskbar

At the right end of the Taskbar are the Volume icon and the clock. Click the Volume icon once to display the volume control slider bar and the Mute check box. If you have speakers and a sound card, you can use this control to quickly adjust the volume. If you want to fine-tune the sound, double-click the Volume icon to open the Volume Control dialog box, as shown in Figure 3.10.

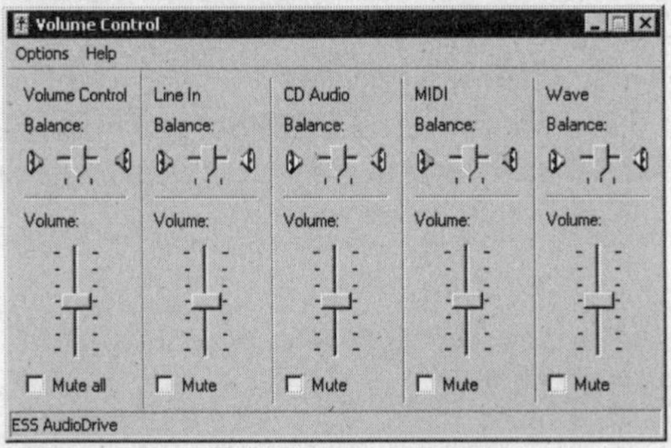

FIGURE 3.10:   Use the slider bars in this dialog box to adjust volume and balance and to mute the sound.

To display the current date, place your mouse cursor over the time at the far right end of the Taskbar. To change the date or time, double-click the time to open the Date/Time Properties dialog box.

Hiding and Displaying the Taskbar

As we mentioned earlier, you need to see the Taskbar if you want to use it when you are working with an application or otherwise not at the Desktop.

If you set up the Taskbar properties correctly, you can hide the Taskbar when you don't need it and display it when you do. Follow these steps so that the Taskbar will only display when you point to the bottom of the screen (regardless of where you are in Windows 2000 Professional):

1. Right-click the Taskbar, and choose Properties to open the Taskbar And Start Menu Properties dialog box.

2. On the General tab, select both the Always On Top and the Auto Hide check boxes.

3. Click OK.

USING THE ICONS ON THE DESKTOP

The icons you see on your Desktop are actually shortcuts to programs and tools on your computer. We'll take a look at using and creating shortcuts in the last section in this chapter, but an important thing to remember about shortcuts is that they are just that—a quick way to open their target (what they point to). They are a representation of the program or tool, not the real McCoy. If you delete a shortcut, you are removing only the representation, not the program or tool itself.

In this section, we'll explore the icons that appear on the Windows 2000 Professional Desktop when you first install the system.

TIP
You can rearrange the icons on your Desktop if you want. Simply click an icon, and then drag it to a new location.

My Documents

Clicking the My Documents icon opens the My Documents folder, which contains a My Pictures folder by default and any other files or folders you've created and stored in the My Documents folder. As you can see in Figure 3.11, folders are displayed in Web view. Simply double-click a folder to display its contents. When you click a folder on the right, information about it is displayed on the left, such as its type, size, date, and attributes. (Attributes are explained in Chapter 6.) Click the Back or Forward button to move from file view to folder view.

The My Documents folder also contains links to My Network Places and My Computer. Click one of these links to open that folder. To delete the My Documents icon from your Desktop, right-click it and choose Delete. Remember, this doesn't delete the My Documents folder but only its representation on your Desktop.

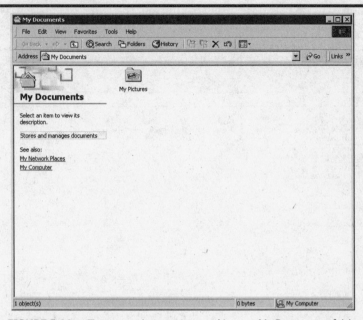

FIGURE 3.11:   To open a document stored in your My Documents folder, click the My Documents icon on the Desktop.

RIGHT-CLICKING A DESKTOP ICON

In Windows 2000 Professional, there's no way to get away from the right-click, nor would you want to. Right-clicking any Desktop icon opens a shortcut menu that contains a few common items such as Open, Explore, Search, Rename, and Properties, as well as items specific to the icon. Right-clicking a Desktop icon is often the most efficient and the fastest way to get information you need or to perform a task.

Take the time to right-click each of these icons and check out the options on its shortcut menu.

My Computer

Clicking the My Computer icon opens a window onto your local computer, as shown in Figure 3.12. This is, in a sense, an overview of what you see in Windows Explorer. Click any icon to view its contents. And, just as you did in the My Documents folder, click the Back or Forward button to move between the big picture and the folder or file view. The pane on the left displays usage statistics about the disk you are viewing.

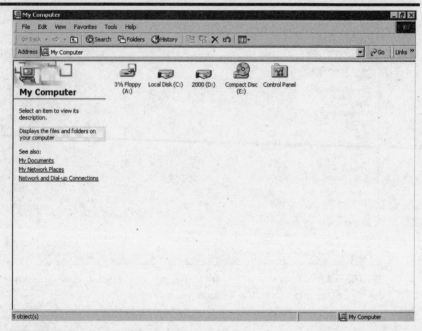

FIGURE 3.12:   The My Computer folder contains big-picture information about the configuration of your system.

TIP

When you want information about your system or any system component, right-click My Computer, and choose Properties to open the System Properties dialog box.

My Network Places

Clicking My Network Places opens a view of your local area network. You use the options in the My Network Places folder (see Figure 3.13) to set up and use the network.

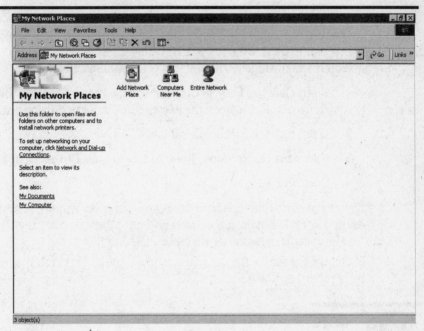

FIGURE 3.13: My Network Places gives you a view of your local area network.

NOTE

In previous versions of Windows, My Network Places was called Network Neighborhood.

Recycle Bin

You probably already know that by default the Recycle Bin is where files and folders go when you delete them from your hard drive. They are not really removed until you empty the Recycle Bin, so up until that point, you can retrieve them. To retrieve a file from the Recycle Bin, follow these steps:

1. Double-click the Recycle Bin to open the Recycle Bin folder.

2. Right-click a file or folder, and choose Restore from the shortcut menu.

To empty the Recycle Bin, right-click it and choose Empty Recycle Bin.

If you want to bypass the Recycle Bin altogether and remove files immediately when you delete them, follow these steps:

1. Right-click the Recycle Bin, and choose Properties from the shortcut menu to open the Recycle Bin Properties dialog box.

2. If necessary, click the Global tab.

3. Check the Do Not Move Files To The Recycle Bin check box.

4. Click OK.

If you have more than one hard drive, you can specify that you want to bypass the Recycle Bin on some drives and not others by selecting the tab for the specific drive rather than the Global tab.

To change the size of the Recycle Bin, move the slider bar in the Recycle Bin Properties dialog box.

NOTE
The Recycle Bin is the only icon on the default Desktop that you cannot rename. Neither can you delete it.

Internet Explorer

Double-click the Internet Explorer icon to open Microsoft Internet Explorer. As you know, you can do the same thing by single-clicking the Internet Explorer icon on the Quick Launch toolbar. See Chapter 17 for information about Internet Explorer.

Connect to the Internet

Click Connect To The Internet to start the Internet Connection Wizard and sign up for a new Internet account, transfer an existing account, or set up an Internet connection through your local area network.

CREATING SHORTCUTS

As we've been looking at the icons on the default Desktop, you've been using shortcuts, and we also mentioned earlier how to move shortcuts around on the Desktop. Because shortcuts are so handy, let's briefly look at how to create them.

When you install an application, the installation process itself will often place a shortcut to it on the Desktop. If it doesn't, you can create one. Follow these steps:

1. Choose Start ➢ Programs.

2. Click the name of the application in the menu, and drag it to the Desktop.

That's all there is to it if you can see the item for which you want to create a shortcut. If you can't see it, follow these steps:

1. Right-click the Desktop, and choose New ➢ Shortcut to open the Create Shortcut dialog box:

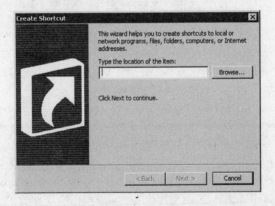

2. Enter the name of the file or folder, or click Browse to locate it.

3. Click Next to open the Select A Title For The Program dialog box.

4. Accept the name that Windows 2000 Professional suggests, or type a new name in the text box.

5. Click Finish.

The shortcut will appear on your Desktop.

To Rename a shortcut, right-click it, choose Rename from the shortcut menu, type the new name, and then click outside the name box on the Desktop.

You can also change the icon of some shortcuts. Follow these steps:

1. Right-click the icon, and choose Properties from the shortcut menu to open the Properties dialog box for that icon.

2. Click the Change Icon button to open the Change Icon dialog box:

3. Select an icon, and click OK.

WINDOWS LOGO KEY SHORTCUTS

If you bought your computer recently, you have a Windows logo key on the keyboard. You can use it in combination with other keys to display essential dialog boxes quickly.

▶ Press Windows+R to open the Run dialog box.

▶ Press Windows+M to minimize all open windows to the Taskbar.

▶ Press Windows+D to minimize or restore all open windows.

▶ Press Windows+F to open the Search Results dialog box.

▶ Press Windows+Ctrl+F to open the Search Results–Computers dialog box.

CONTINUED ➡

▶ Press Windows+E to open the My Computer folder.

▶ Press Windows+U to open the Utility Manager dialog box.

▶ Press Windows+F1 to open Windows 2000 Help.

WHAT'S NEXT?

Using the Desktop is essential to making the most out of Windows 2000 Professional, but an equally essential skill is managing your files and folders, which is the topic of the next chapter. Unless you impose some organization on the contents of your computer system, you could, at the worst, lose information, and at best spend a lot of time searching for what you need. Chapter 4 shows you how to use Windows Explorer and explains file management techniques such as saving, creating, sharing, copying, moving, renaming, and so on.

Chapter 4
MANAGING FILES AND FOLDERS

Although we both work from our home offices now, we spent several years in the corporate world, and our guess is that many of you work in a company or an organization outside your home. Traveling from office to office or even cubicle to cubicle can be a trip into myriad personal styles. Some people decorate their workspace with family photos, mementos, and other objects d'art, while others give no clue that they have a life after work. Some offices are obsessively neat, and others look as if a Texas tornado has just ripped through. We once had a manager whose desk was piled so high with file folders, papers, musical scores, and other documents that we had to walk around it to see him, and he was well over six feet tall.

Adapted from *Windows 2000 Professional: In Record Time*, by Peter Dyson and Pat Coleman

ISBN 0-7821-2450-X   467 pages $29.99

We tend to think that how you organize your physical office probably influences how you organize your computer. Some people use photos of their pets or pithy personal aphorisms as screen savers, and others prefer a blank screen. Regardless of your personal style, however, you'll quickly run into trouble if you don't impose some sense of organization on the files and folders on your system. You need to recognize the names you give them, you need to know where or how to find them, and you need to be able to manipulate them in whatever ways your work requires.

In this chapter, we'll look at what you need to know about files and folders in Windows 2000 Professional, and we'll start with the essential tool, Explorer.

NOTE

Everything in this skill applies equally, whether you're using FAT16, FAT32, or NTFS.

USING EXPLORER

Whether you're coming to Windows 2000 Professional via Windows NT or Windows 95/98, you'll find that Explorer has a new look. As you can see in Figure 4.1, the menu bar, toolbar, and Address bar are borrowed from Internet Explorer. And, as we mentioned in Chapter 3, folders are in Web view by default. In addition, the title bar displays the name of the selected folder rather than the words "Exploring – *folder name*." We think this new version of Explorer is also easier to use than previous versions.

From the Desktop, you can start Explorer in several ways:

- ▸ Right-click Start, and select Explore.

- ▸ Choose Start ➢ Programs ➢ Accessories ➢ Windows Explorer.

- ▸ Right-click My Documents, My Computer, My Network Places, or Recycle Bin, and choose Explore.

The view in which Explorer opens depends on which commands you used. For example, if you open it from the Start menu, the Start Menu folder is selected, the title bar displays Start Menu, and the contents of the Start Menu folder are displayed in the right pane.

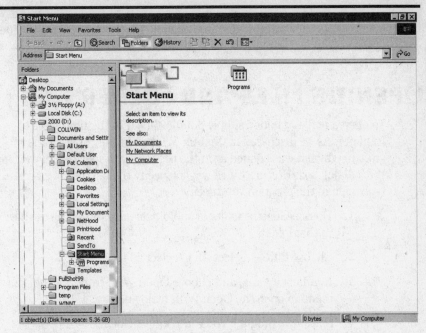

FIGURE 4.1:   The Windows 2000 Professional Explorer has a new look.

You'll also encounter Explorer-like windows in several other places in Windows 2000 Professional (for example, the Search Results window, My Computer, and My Documents). Regardless of where you find an Explorer-like window, you can use the following techniques to display files and folders:

▶ In the Folders pane, select a folder to display its content in the right pane.

▶ In the Folders pane, click the plus (+) sign to display a list of what it contains.

▶ In the right pane, double-click a folder to display subfolders or files.

To flip between folder view and subfolder view or between file view and folder view, click the Back and Forward buttons.

If you can't see all the items in the hierarchical Folders pane, drag the horizontal scroll bar to the right or drag the vertical scroll bar up or down.

In this section, we have rather quickly covered Explorer basics. As we discuss the other tasks related to managing files, we'll look at the other ways you can use Explorer to navigate and organize your system.

OPENING FILES AND FOLDERS

To open any file or folder, simply double-click it in the right pane of Explorer. As we discussed in Chapter 3, it will usually open in the program in which it was created or in the program you specified in the Open With dialog box. Here's a quick way to specify that all files of a certain type open in the program you specify:

1. Double-click the folder or subfolders until you see all the files in that folder.

2. Choose Edit ➢ Select All to select all the folders.

3. Right-click a file, and choose Open With from the shortcut menu to open the Open With dialog box.

4. Select the program you want, and click OK.

NOTE
For more detail about the Open With dialog box, see Chapter 3.

To open a file on another computer on your network, follow these steps:

1. Open My Network Places, and then click the icon for that computer.

2. Keep clicking folders until you find the file you want.

CREATING A FOLDER

You can create a folder either from the Desktop or from Explorer. To create a folder from the Desktop, follow these steps:

1. Right-click an empty space on the Desktop, and choose New ➢ Folder from the shortcut menu.

2. Type a name for the folder, and then click outside it.

This new folder will be stored in the Desktop subfolder in your user-name folder on your hard drive.

To create a folder inside another folder in Explorer, follow these steps:

1. Select the folder.

2. Choose File ➤ New ➤ Folder.

3. Type a name for the folder, and click outside it.

If you're trying to set up a common-sense system for organizing files and folders, it's probably a good idea to create folders in Explorer so that you can see the relationships. You can, however, easily move a folder that you create on the Desktop, as you'll see shortly.

NOTE

If you're working on a corporate network, your network administrator may have specified naming conventions as well as where you are to create and store your files and folders.

NAMING FILES AND FOLDERS

Unless you are coming to Windows 2000 Professional straight from Windows 3.x or MS-DOS, you already know that you are no longer limited to the 8.3 filenaming convention. Filenames can contain a maximum of 215 characters and can contain spaces, commas, semi-colons, equal signs (=), and square brackets ([ ]). Filenames can be in uppercase and lowercase letters.

But don't get carried away. In Explorer, 215 characters is the equiv-alent of a rather longish paragraph, and you'll be hard-pressed to display it easily on the screen.

Be sure, though, to give files and folders names that you will eas-ily recognize several months hence when, for instance, you're try-ing to clean up your hard drive or when you need to send someone the monthly sales report for April of last year.

CREATING A FILE

You can create a file in three ways:

- ▶ From the Desktop
- ▶ From Explorer
- ▶ From within an application

To create a file from the Desktop, follow these steps:

1. Right-click an empty space on the Desktop, and choose New.
2. From the submenu, select the type of file you want to create.
3. Type a name for the file, and then click outside on the Desktop. This file is stored in the Desktop folder in your username folder.

To create a file from within Explorer, follow these steps:

1. Open the folder that will contain the new file (whether it's on your local hard drive or the network).
2. Right-click in a blank space in the right pane of Explorer.
3. Choose New, and then, from the submenu, select a file type.
4. Type a name for the file, and then click outside it in a blank space.

You'll probably most often create a new file from within an application. For purposes of example, here are the steps for creating a new file in Notepad:

1. Choose Start ➢ Programs ➢ Accessories ➢ Notepad to open Notepad.

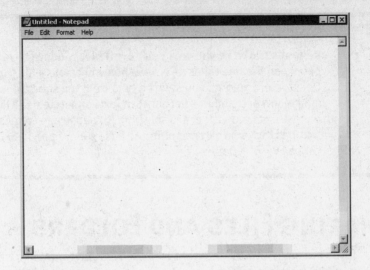

2. Choose File ➤ Save As to open the Save As dialog box.

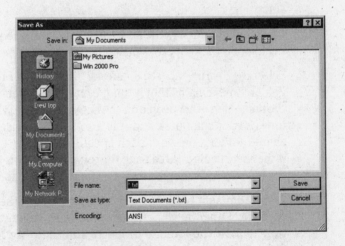

3. Select a folder in which you want to save the document.

4. Enter a name in the File Name box.

5. Click Save.

UNDERSTANDING FILE TYPES

Regardless of how you create or save a file, Windows gives it an extension that identifies its type. When you create a file from the Desktop or Explorer, you select a type from the shortcut menu's submenu. For example, selecting Rich Text Format creates a file that has the `.rtf` extension, and selecting Bitmap Image creates a file that has the `.bmp` extension. To see a file's extension in Explorer, choose View ➤ Details.

SHARING FILES AND FOLDERS

If you are on a network and want to share your files or folders with another computer, follow these steps:

1. Open My Computer, and browse to the object you want to share.

2. Right-click to display the shortcut menu, and choose Sharing to open the Properties dialog box for the selected object.

3. Select the Sharing tab (see Figure 4.2), and choose Share This Folder. Enter a name that is unique on this computer. This is the name that other people on the network will see when they browse your computer, and it is also the name used in the shared folder's network path specification. For example, if the share name is Notes and the computer name is Ferret, the path specification becomes \\Ferret\Notes.

4. In the Comment box, enter a short description of the folder's contents. Other network users can see this comment when they look at the folder's properties in their My Network Places folder.

5. In the User Limit section of this dialog box, you can restrict the number of users who can access this folder simultaneously. On small networks, this is usually left at the default setting of Maximum Allowed.

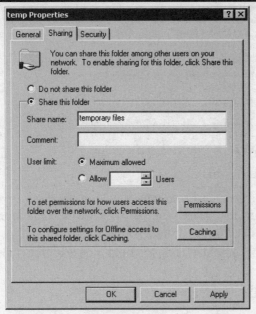

FIGURE 4.2:   The folder Properties dialog box open at the Sharing tab

6. Click the Permissions button to open the Permissions dialog box for the object you selected. You use this dialog box to look at or change the default permissions associated with this folder.

7. The default permission associated with a new shared resource is Full Control To Everyone, which means that anyone on the network can do whatever they like with this resource. If the shared folder is on an NTFS volume, individual files can have their own access restrictions.

8. Click OK or Apply, and the drive or folder will become available to the other users on your network.

COPYING AND MOVING FILES AND FOLDERS

You can copy or move a file or a folder in four ways:

- ▶ By dragging and dropping with the right mouse button
- ▶ By dragging and dropping with the left mouse button
- ▶ By copying and pasting or cutting and pasting
- ▶ By using the Send To command

Which method you use depends on your personal preference and, to some extent, on the circumstances. When you can see both the source and the destination, dragging and dropping is easiest.

To copy or move a file or folder using the right mouse button, follow these steps:

1. Locate the file or folder in Explorer.

2. Right-click it, and then drag it to its destination.

3. Release the mouse button, and then choose Copy Here or Move Here.

If you change your mind en route, press Escape.

To copy a file when the source and destination are on different drives, left-click the file, and drag it to its new location. If you use the left mouse button to drag and drop and the source and destination are on the same hard drive, the file is moved rather than copied. To move a file when the source and destination are on different drives, click the file with the left mouse button, and hold down Shift while you drag the file.

To copy or move a file using the Cut, Copy, and Paste commands, follow these steps:

1. Right-click the source file, and choose Cut or Copy from the shortcut menu.

2. Right-click the destination folder, and choose Paste from the shortcut menu.

Another way to copy a file to a new location, such as a floppy disk or another hard disk, is to right-click the file and choose the Send To command on the shortcut menu. If the shortcut menu doesn't include a destination you want to use regularly, you can add it. Follow these steps:

1. In Explorer, locate your username folder, and then locate the Send To folder within it.

TIP

If you don't see the Send To folder, choose Tools ≻ Folder Options to open the Folder Options folder, and click the View tab. In Advanced Settings, scroll down, click the Show Hidden Files And Folders option, and then click OK. We'll look at the Folder Options dialog box in detail later in this chapter.

2. Select the Send To folder, and then choose File ≻ New ≻ Shortcut to open the Create Shortcut dialog box:

3. Enter the name of the shortcut you want to add, or click Browse to find it.

4. Click Next.

5. Type a new name for the shortcut if you want, and then click Finish.

RENAMING FILES AND FOLDERS

You can easily rename a file or a folder in two ways:

► Left-click twice (wait about a second between clicks) the name of the file or folder, and enter a new name in the highlighted box.

▸ Right-click the name of a folder, choose Rename from the short-cut menu, and then type a new name.

If you change your mind about the new name, you can click Undo, or you can re-rename the file or folder.

DELETING FILES AND FOLDERS

You can delete a file or a folder in three ways:

▸ In Explorer, right-click the name of the file or folder, and then choose Delete from the shortcut menu.

▸ In Explorer, left-click the name of the file or folder, and then press Delete or click the Delete button on the toolbar.

▸ If the Recycle Bin is visible on the Desktop, click the name of the file or folder, and drag it to the Recycle Bin.

TIP

To bypass the Recycle Bin and permanently delete the file or folder from your hard drive, hold down Shift when choosing or pressing Delete.

To restore a file you've sent to the Recycle Bin, follow these steps:

1. Double-click the Recycle Bin to open the Recycle Bin dialog box.

2. Right-click the file, and choose Restore from the shortcut menu.

The file is restored to its original location.

WARNING

You cannot use the Undo command to retrieve a file that you delete from the Recycle Bin.

FINDING FILES AND FOLDERS

As we mentioned in Chapter 3, the Find command that you used in previous versions of Windows is now called Search, and the Search Results dialog box is similar to the Internet Explorer window. If you can't remember where you stored a file or what you named it, you can try to locate it in a couple of ways. You can scroll endlessly through Explorer, or you can right-click a drive and choose Search from the shortcut menu. In the Search Results dialog box, shown in Figure 4.3, you can search for the filename, and you can search for a file containing the contents you specify.

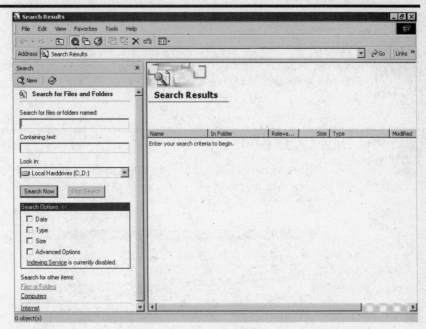

FIGURE 4.3: Use the Search Results dialog box to find files and folders.

In the Search For Files Or Folders Named box, enter your search term, and then click Search Now. All files matching the criteria you entered are displayed in the right pane. If you want to search on file contents, enter your text in the Containing Text box.

TIP

You can also use the wildcard characters * and ? when you're searching. The asterisk represents one or more characters, and the question mark represents a single character. For example, *.doc will find all files that have the .doc extension; chap? will find *chaps* and *chap1* but not *chapter*.

Sometimes you may not remember the filename or part of the filename, but you do remember when you created or last edited the file. To search for a file by date, click Search Options, click the Date check box, and enter your criteria. You can also use Search Options to locate a file by its type or size.

In the Search Options submenu, click the Advanced Options check box to specify subfolders to search or to specify that the search is case sensitive.

NOTE

You can also search for files and folders from the Desktop by choosing Start ➢ Search ➢ For Files And Folders.

INDEXING SERVICE

In the Search Results dialog box, you will also see a link to Indexing Service. When you click it, you'll see the Indexing Service Settings dialog box:

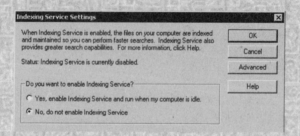

Indexing Service, which is not enabled by default, is a program that reads through files and extracts the text and properties and places them in an index. Searching the index is much faster and can be more powerful than searching all the files themselves.

If you are on a corporate network, see your network administrator for information about enabling or using Indexing Service. For in-depth information about how Indexing Service works, click the Advanced button in the Indexing Service Settings dialog box, and then, in the Indexing Service dialog box, choose Action ➢ Help.

KEEPING FILES CURRENT WITH SYNCHRONIZATION MANAGER

Whether you are working with files on a local area network or on the Internet, you can choose to work with them offline. To enable offline viewing, in My Computer or My Network Places, right-click the file, and select Make Available Offline from the shortcut menu.

To synchronize this file with the one on your network or on the Internet, right-click the file, and choose Synchronize from the shortcut menu. You can also specify that offline files are synchronized when you log on or off your computer at a scheduled time. To set this up, select the file, and then follow these steps:

1. In Explorer, choose Tools ➤ Synchronize to open the Items To Synchronize dialog box:

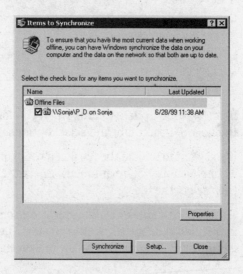

2. Click the check box for the file you want to synchronize, and then click Setup to open the Synchronization Settings dialog box:

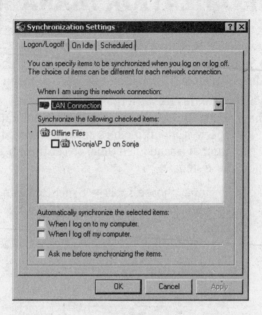

3. If you want to update the file when you log on or off, select the Logon/Logoff tab, and select options.

4. If you want to update the file when your computer is idle (for example, while you're at lunch), select the On Idle tab, and then select the file.

5. To establish another synchronization schedule, select the Scheduled tab, and click Add to start the Scheduled Synchronization Wizard. Follow the on-screen instructions.

UNDERSTANDING AND USING FOLDER OPTIONS

We mentioned in Chapter 3 that, by default, the Windows 2000 Professional user interface is a hybrid—that is, the Desktop uses the classic Windows interface, and folders display in Web view. In Chapter 5, we'll look at how to customize your Desktop, and in this section we'll look at how to set the display for files and folders, using the Folder Options dialog box.

To open the Folder Options dialog box, choose Start ➤ Settings ➤ Control Panel, and then click the Folder Options icon. You'll see the dialog box shown in Figure 4.4, which opens at the General tab.

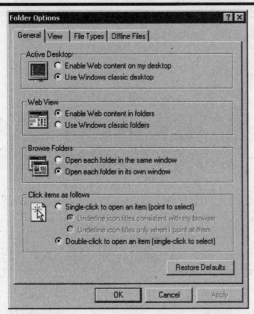

FIGURE 4.4: Use the Folder Options dialog box to specify how files and folders are displayed.

As you can see, in the Web View section, Enable Web Content In Folders is selected. Figure 4.5 shows Control Panel in Web view. Figure 4.6 shows Control Panel as it is displayed when you choose Use Windows Classic Folders. Regardless of which view you choose, Control Panel works the same, as is the case with My Computer, My Network Places, Explorer, and so on. Which view you use is simply a matter of personal preference and, perhaps, the size of your monitor.

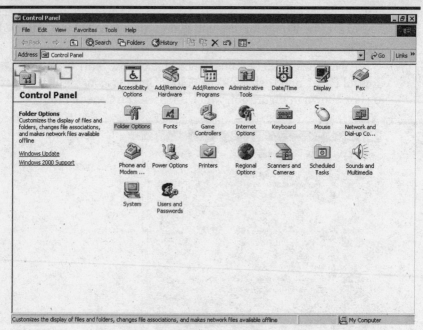

FIGURE 4.5:   Control Panel in Web view

In the Browse Folders section, you can choose to open each folder in the same window or in its own window. Click each of these options to see how this setting affects the display (notice that the icon in this section changes).

In the next section, you can specify whether you want to single-click, as you do on the Web, or double-click to open items.

Select the View tab, as shown in Figure 4.7, to specify how and which folders are displayed. Earlier in this chapter, we used this tab to tell Windows 2000 Professional to display hidden files in Explorer. In the Advanced Settings section, use the scroll bar to check out the other options. If you have already made some changes and want to display all folders as they were when you installed Windows 2000 Professional, click Reset All Folders. If you have made changes to the Advanced Settings and want to restore this area as it was when you installed Windows 2000 Professional, click Restore Defaults.

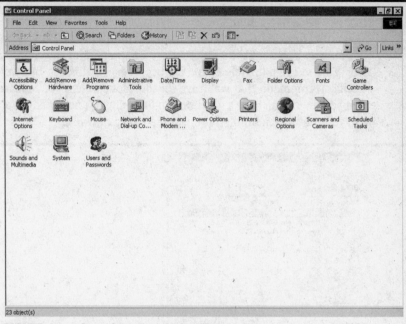

FIGURE 4.6:   Control Panel in classic Windows view

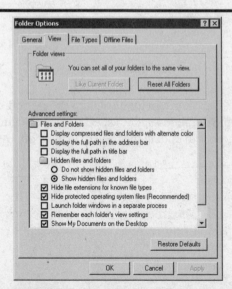

FIGURE 4.7:   Specify which files to display and how in the Advanced Settings section of the View tab.

Select the File Types tab to display the screen shown in Figure 4.8. Here you see a list of filename extensions, their associated file types, and applications that are registered with Windows 2000 Professional. (For information about the Registry, see Chapter 7 and the chapters in Part IV.) You can add, delete, and change items on this list, but we strongly recommend that you leave this list alone unless you really know what you are doing, have a good reason for doing it, and/or have spoken with your network administrator if you are on a network.

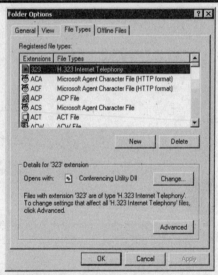

FIGURE 4.8:   The File Types tab in the Folder Options dialog box

Select the Offline Files tab, as shown in Figure 4.9, to enable or disable the use of offline files and reminders and to specify some synchronization options such as whether to update files before logging off.

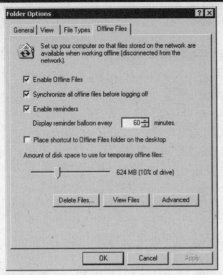

FIGURE 4.9: You can enable and disable offline viewing in the Offline Files tab of the Folder Options dialog box.

HANDLING FLOPPY DISKS

Whether you work on a stand-alone system, you're connected to a local area network, or you live and breathe via the Internet, you probably also use sneakernet from time to time. On a sneakernet, you copy files to a floppy and schlepp the disk over to a coworker. Some of you may think this is tantamount to programming with a pen and quill, but since it's still a fact of life, let's complete this chapter by looking at how you format and copy a floppy.

Formatting a Floppy Disk

Unless you buy formatted disks, you must format a disk before you can store information on it. Formatting a disk that already contains files deletes those files. Follow these steps to format a floppy:

1. Insert a disk in your floppy drive.

2. In Explorer, scroll up in the Folder pane until you see the icon for the floppy, and then right-click it.

3. Choose Format from the shortcut menu to open the Format *drive letter* dialog box:

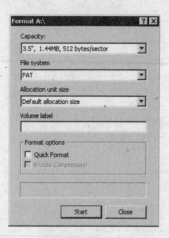

4. Ensure that the correct options are selected, and then click Start. A bar at the bottom of the dialog box will indicate the progress of the format.

5. When Windows 2000 Professional says Format Complete, click OK, and close the Format dialog box.

Copying a Floppy Disk

To copy a floppy disk, follow these steps:

1. In Explorer, scroll up in the Folder pane until you can see the icon for the floppy drive, and right-click it.

2. In the shortcut menu, choose Copy Disk to open the Copy Disk dialog box:

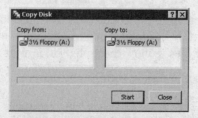

3. When prompted, place the disk you want to copy in the floppy drive, and click OK.

NOTE

If you have more than one floppy drive, you can specify the From and To disks. We know, if you're on a network, you may be lucky to have one floppy drive, much less two. For security purposes, network computers often have no floppy drive.

4. When Windows 2000 Professional has finished reading the source disk, it will ask you to insert the destination disk. Do so, and click OK.

5. When the copy is completed, click Close.

WHAT'S NEXT?

Once you are comfortable with file management techniques and with the skills for using the items on the Desktop, you'll probably find that you'd like to change the way some features work. In Chapter 5, we'll show you how to customize your Desktop, make Windows 2000 Professional more accessible, adjust your mouse, change the display, customize the keyboard, and more.

Chapter 5

CUSTOMIZING YOUR DESKTOP

We've already mentioned a few times in the first four chapters of this book that you can customize your Desktop, and we've taken a couple of quick looks at the instrument you use to do this: Control Panel. The items in Control Panel are variously referred to as applets, folders, icons, tools, and so on. Clicking one of them usually opens a dialog box or another folder in which you can choose options that specify how that particular item will work. For example, if you are left-handed, you can configure your mouse so that the buttons are reversed, and if you move from Bellingham, Washington, to Athens, Greece, you can change the time zone.

Adapted from *Windows 2000 Professional: In Record Time,* by Peter Dyson and Pat Coleman

ISBN 0-7821-2450-X   467 pages $29.99

The changes you make using Control Panel are stored in the Registry, the central database that contains all the configuration settings used on your system. Every time you change an option in an applet, that change is reflected in the Registry. It stays in effect until you change it again and is reloaded every time you start Windows 2000 Professional. In Chapter 7, you'll learn a bit more about the Registry, and in Part IV of this book, you'll learn a great deal more about the Registry. What we want to stress here, however, is that you don't need to use the Registry to customize your system. In fact, you shouldn't; always use Control Panel instead.

If you've been using other versions of Windows, you probably already know basically how you want to set up your system. If something isn't where you expect it to be, check the index of this book or take a look at the If You've Used Windows Before topic in Help. If you're new to Windows or to NT technology, on which Windows 2000 Professional is based, you probably want to become familiar with the default interface before you start changing it.

In addition, if you're on a corporate network, you may need permission to adjust certain items, and you'll find that you need to be logged on as Administrator to tinker with others. Your organization may even have published policies about this. In any event, check with your network administrator.

Now, with all that said, let's open Control Panel, look quickly at how you change the Active Desktop settings, and then check out some other important ways you can set up your system to work the way you want.

OPENING CONTROL PANEL

Choose Start ➤ Settings ➤ Control Panel to open Control Panel, as shown in Figure 5.1. As we mentioned in earlier chapters, Control Panel opens in Web view by default. To open any item, simply click it. To create a shortcut on the Desktop for a Control Panel item, right-click the item and choose Create Shortcut. For more information on creating shortcuts, look back at Chapter 3.

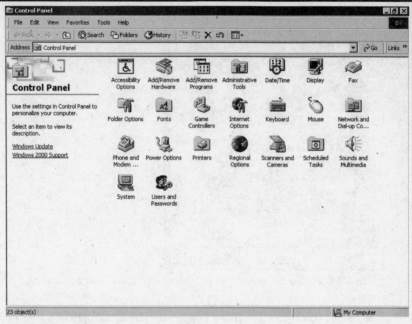

FIGURE 5.1: Control Panel in Web view

SETTING UP THE ACTIVE DESKTOP

As we've mentioned, the default user interface for Windows 2000 Professional is somewhat of a hybrid. It employs the classic Desktop but uses Web view for folders. To change this arrangement, open the Folder Options dialog box, as shown in Figure 5.2. In Chapter 4, we discussed the portions of the General tab that concern folders; here we'll simply look at the options for the Desktop.

Folder Options

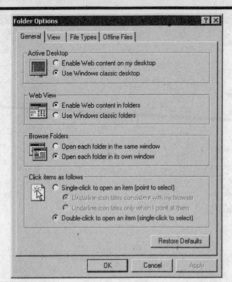

FIGURE 5.2: The General tab of the Folder Options dialog box

To use the Web view instead of the classic Desktop, click Enable Web Content On My Desktop in the Active Desktop section. If you want to open files and folders with a single click instead of a double click, click those options in the Click Items As Follows section. When you're done, click OK.

MAKING WINDOWS 2000 PROFESSIONAL MORE ACCESSIBLE

In the last several years, we have seen many marvelous advances in accessibility technology. Speech recognition systems, alternative keyboards, and adaptive devices for people with spinal cord injuries are but a few of the developments that enable people with physical challenges to improve the quality of their lives by using the computer. Enhancing the accessibility options was key in the development of Windows 2000 Professional. Nevertheless, the current tools provide only a minimal level of functionality for users with special needs.

Most physically impaired users will need special programs and devices. For a list of these and some very helpful information, check

out Microsoft's Accessibility Web site at www.microsoft.com/
enable/ ?RLD=185.

You set up some of the accessibility options in Windows 2000 Professional through the Accessibility Options dialog box; others you can access by choosing Start ➤ Programs ➤ Accessories ➤ Accessibility. In this section, we'll look first at the Accessibility Options dialog box and then look at the features available through the Accessibility accessory, including the Accessibility Wizard.

NOTE

You need Administrator privileges in order to customize some of these features.

Specifying Accessibility Options

Accessibility
Options

To open the Accessibility Options dialog box, click its icon in Control Panel. In this dialog box, you can set keyboard, sound, display, mouse, and administrative options. Figure 5.3 shows the Accessibility Options dialog box open at the Keyboard tab:

▶ Click Use StickyKeys if you have trouble pressing two keys simultaneously, such as Ctrl+Alt.

▶ Click Use FilterKeys if you want brief or repeated keystrokes to be ignored.

▶ Click Use ToggleKeys if you want to hear a high-pitched sound when you press Caps Lock, Scroll Lock, or Num Lock and to hear a low-pitched sound when you turn off these keys.

Here are the features available in the other tabs:

Sound   Click Use SoundSentry if you want a visual cue when your system generates a sound. Click Use ShowSounds if you want to display captions for speech and sounds.

Display   Click Use High Contrast and then Settings to specify that Windows 2000 Professional use black-and-white or a custom color scheme instead of the standard color scheme. You might consider enabling this feature if you are color-blind.

Mouse   Click Use MouseKeys to control the mouse pointer with the keys on the numeric keypad.

General   Use this tab to set a time after which accessibility features are turned off, to tell Windows 2000 Professional that you want a message or sound when turning a feature on or off, to enable an alternative mouse or keyboard device, and to select administrative options.

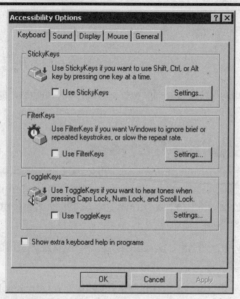

FIGURE 5.3: To set keyboard options, you can use this tab, the Keyboard applet, and the Accessibility Wizard.

Using the Accessibility Accessories

The Accessibility accessories include the Narrator, the Accessibility Wizard, the Magnifier, the On-Screen Keyboard, and the Utility Manager. Let's start with the Narrator, which is new in Windows 2000 Professional.

Running Narrator

To start the Narrator (whose name is Sam, by the way), choose Start ➤ Programs ➤ Accessories ➤ Accessibility ➤ Narrator. You'll see the Narrator dialog box, as shown in Figure 5.4. Click the check boxes that apply to what you want the Narrator to do, and then click the Minimize button.

Now when you open a dialog box, point to an item, or type something, the Narrator will read it to you. To specify the speed at which Sam reads, his volume, or pitch, click the Voice button to open the Voice Settings dialog box. To turn off the Narrator, click the Exit button in the Narrator dialog box.

NOTE

You'll need a sound board, speakers, and text-to-speech program capability to get the benefit of the spoken word.

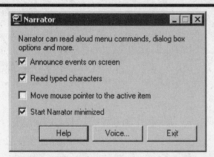

FIGURE 5.4: The Narrator can read items that are displayed on the screen.

Using the Accessibility Wizard

To start the Accessibility Wizard, choose Start ➢ Programs ➢ Accessories ➢ Accessibility ➢ Accessibility Wizard. At the opening screen, click Next. Now follow the on-screen instructions to customize such features as text size, display size, options for vision, hearing, and mobility, and the size and color of the mouse cursor. Figure 5.5 shows the screen on which you can configure your mouse to work with either your left hand or your right hand. When you've set all the options you want, click Finish.

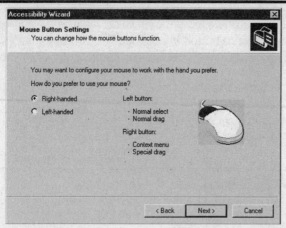

FIGURE 5.5: Use the Accessibility Wizard to configure the mouse for left-hand or right-hand use.

You can also use the Accessibility Wizard to set up Magnifier, and that's what we'll look at next.

Using Magnifier

Magnifier is a utility that displays a magnified portion of your screen in a separate window. To set up Magnifier, follow these steps:

1. Open the Accessibility Wizard, and on the second screen, select Use Microsoft Magnifier, select Large Title And Menus, and click Next.

2. Set the options you want in the Magnifier dialog box, which is shown in Figure 5.6. You can set Magnifier to follow the mouse, the keyboard focus, or text editing.

To return to regular view, click the Close button.

NOTE

When Magnifier is running, you must make selections in the magnified portion of the screen.

To start Magnifier, choose Start ➢ Programs ➢ Accessories ➢ Accessibility ➢ Magnifier.

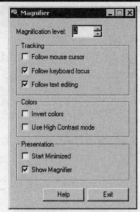

FIGURE 5.6: The Magnifier dialog box

Using the On-Screen Keyboard

If you aren't a good typist or if you have a physical disability that makes typing difficult, you can display the keyboard on the screen and use the mouse to type. To see how this works, follow these steps:

1. Choose Start ➤ Programs ➤ Accessories ➤ Notepad to open Notepad.

2. Maximize Notepad.

3. Choose Start ➤ Programs ➤ Accessories ➤ Accessibility ➤ On-Screen Keyboard. Now your screen looks like the one in Figure 5.7.

4. Click the keys with your mouse to enter text in Notepad. You can alternate between "typing" on the keyboard and choosing commands from the menu in Notepad.

5. When you're finished, click Close to close both Notepad and the keyboard.

TIP

If you can't see the portion of the screen you want to use, click the title bar of the keyboard and move it.

FIGURE 5.7: Use the mouse to type on your on-screen keyboard.

Using Utility Manager

You use Utility Manager to start and stop Narrator and Magnifier and to specify that either program starts when Windows 2000 Professional starts or when you start Utility Manager. To open Utility Manager, choose Start ➢ Programs ➢ Accessories ➢ Accessibility ➢ Utility Manager.

CUSTOMIZING THE KEYBOARD

Keyboard

When you install Windows 2000 Professional, the installation routine recognizes the keyboard installed on your computer system and identifies the keyboard on the Hardware tab in the Keyboard Properties dialog box. Therefore, you normally don't have to fiddle with the keyboard settings. You can, however, use the Keyboard applet to adjust the repeat rate and the cursor blink rate if you want to, and if you need to use more than one language, you can specify the keyboard layout for other languages.

When you select Keyboard in Control Panel, you'll see the dialog box shown in Figure 5.8. The Speed tab contains the following options:

Repeat Delay   Determines the time that passes before a character repeats after you press the key.

Repeat Rate   Determines the speed at which a character repeats when you press and hold down a key.

Cursor Blink Rate   Determines the blinking speed of the cursor.

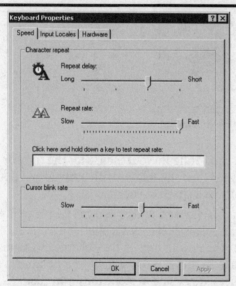

FIGURE 5.8: Use the Keyboard applet to adjust keyboard settings.

Use the settings on the Input Locales tab to set up the keyboard for multiple languages and to specify how the Caps Lock key is turned off (you can either press Caps Lock again or press Shift).

ADJUSTING YOUR MOUSE

Mouse

We mentioned earlier that you can make some mouse adjustments using the Accessibility Wizard. You can make others in the Mouse Properties dialog box, which is displayed when you select the Mouse icon in Control Panel. Figure 5.9 shows the Mouse Properties dialog box open at the Buttons tab.

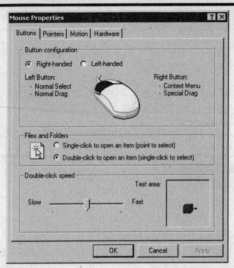

FIGURE 5.9: Use this dialog box to configure your mouse.

In the Buttons tab, you can configure your mouse for the right or left hand, specify whether to open files and folders with a single or a double click, and adjust the double-click speed of your mouse.

In the Pointers tab, you can choose a design scheme for the pointers on your system, and you can even select specific alternate icons for certain pointers. For fun, click the down arrow in the Scheme box to display a list of design schemes. Select Dinosaur to see how your pointers would appear. (None of your choices are etched in stone until you click OK, and then, of course, you can always change them back.) To display a collection of alternate icons, click the Browse button to open the Browse dialog box, as shown in Figure 5.10. If you look closely, you'll see that you can even choose a banana for a pointer!

In the Motion tab, you can adjust the speed of your pointer and specify that the pointer always moves automatically to the default button in a dialog box. The Hardware tab identifies your mouse as it was recognized during installation.

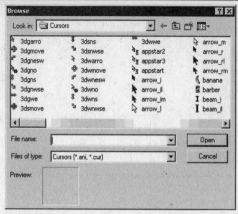

FIGURE 5.10: Move the slider bar to see all your choices.

CHANGING THE DISPLAY

Display

If you're the type of person who likes to make a personal statement with your computer system, you can access a bag of tricks by opening the Display applet. Among other things, you can use the Display Properties dialog box to configure a spiffy background for your Desktop, compose a message to be used as a marquee screen saver, play around with the Windows 2000 Professional color scheme, and change the resolution at which your monitor displays.

To open this dialog box, you can double-click Display in Control Panel, or you can right-click the Desktop and choose Properties. You'll see the screen shown in Figure 5.11.

TIP

If you want to change some settings on only one tab in the Display Properties dialog box, click OK after you make your modifications. If you want to change settings in more than one tab, select the options in the tab, and click Apply. When you've finished making changes in all the tabs you need, click OK.

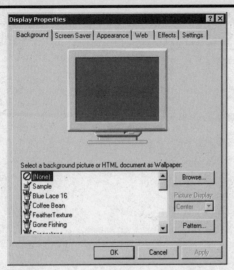

FIGURE 5.11: Use the tabs in this dialog box to customize colors, the background, screen savers, and other Desktop elements.

Customizing the Desktop Background

You have a lot of options when it comes to setting the background, or wallpaper, for your Desktop:

▶ You can choose None, as we have done in the screens in this book.

▶ You can select one of the backgrounds in the list box in the Background tab.

▶ You can browse your local computer, your local area network, or the Web to find a background.

When you choose one of the backgrounds in the list box, a preview is displayed on the monitor in this tab. You can choose to center the background, tile it, or stretch it. If you choose Center, you can click Pattern to select a pattern to fill any leftover space. Some wallpaper can only be displayed if Active Desktop is enabled. When this is the case, you'll be asked if you want to do this.

TIP

To use a graphic you find on the Web as wallpaper, right-click it, and choose Set As Wallpaper.

Choosing a Screen Saver

Use the Screen Saver tab, as shown in Figure 5.12, to select a screen saver, set a password for it if you want, and specify the idle time before the screen saver starts. If you select a screen saver that can be modified in some way, you can click the Settings button to set it up.

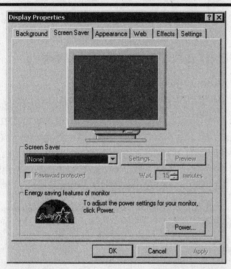

FIGURE 5.12: Specify and configure a screen saver on this tab.

Adjusting the Power Settings

You can also manage the power settings for your computer in the Screen Saver tab. To do so, click Power to open the Power Options Properties dialog box, which has the following tabs:

Power Schemes   Select a scheme that corresponds to your situation, and then specify when or whether to turn off your monitor and hard disks.

Advanced   Click the Always Show Icon On The Taskbar check box if you want to display a power icon in the status area of the Taskbar. You can then click the icon to change your power settings.

Hibernate   Hibernation turns off your monitor and hard drive, saves data to your hard drive, and then turns off your computer. Hibernation is not enabled by default. Click the Enable Hibernate Support check box if you want this option.

APM   To conserve power, you can enable Advanced Power Management by clicking the check box on this tab.

UPS   If you have an uninterruptible power supply, you can configure it using the settings on this tab.

Changing the Appearance of Windows Elements

In this book, we have used the Windows Standard color scheme for elements such as title bars, dialog boxes, menus, and so on, but you can get pretty wild and crazy in this area if you're so inclined. To take a look at the options, select the Appearance tab, which is shown in Figure 5.13, and click the down arrow in the Scheme box. You can use the other options in this tab to color particular items and to change the display font.

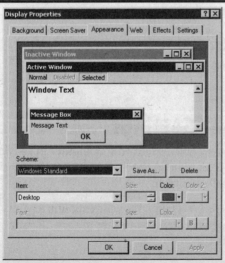

FIGURE 5.13: Changing the color of Windows elements

Enabling Web Content on Your Desktop

Earlier in this chapter, we mentioned how you can enable the Active Desktop in the Folders Options folder and in the Screen Saver tab in the Desktop Properties dialog box. You can also do so by using the Web tab and clicking the Show Web Content On My Active Desktop check box, which is shown in Figure 5.14. To add new items, live Web content, or pictures, click New to open the New Active Desktop Item dialog box. Click Visit Gallery to go to a Microsoft Web site that contains new items you can use on the Desktop. To add a picture or an HTML document, type its URL in the Location box or click Browse to find it.

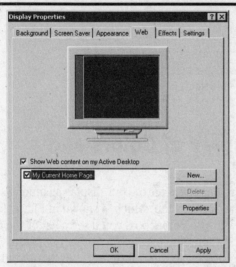

FIGURE 5.14: In this tab, you can enable Web content on the Desktop.

Changing Desktop Icons and Effects

If you're bored with or just plain don't like the default icons on your Desktop, you can change them in the Effects tab of the Display Properties dialog box (see Figure 5.15). In the Desktop Icons section, select an icon, and click Change Icon to see the possible alternatives. To modify the visual effects, click a check box in the Visual Effects section.

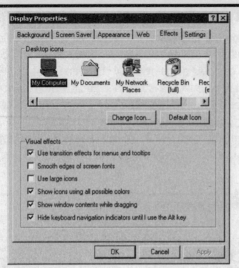

FIGURE 5.15: Modify icons and effects in this tab.

Modifying the Display of Colors and Resolution

Perhaps nothing changes the appearance of your display as much as changing the options in the Settings tab, which is shown in Figure 5.16. If you click the down arrow in the Colors box, you'll see a list of the color settings available on your system. The maximum number of colors that you can display are determined by your monitor and your display adapter. The screenshots in this book were captured with 256 colors because file size was important. A High Color setting displays more than 65,000 colors, and a True Color setting displays more than 16 million colors.

In the Screen Area of this tab, you can change resolution. Resolution is the number of pixels (dots) on the screen and the number of colors that can be displayed at the same time. As strange as it may seem, the higher the resolution, the smaller elements appear on the screen. For example, a resolution of 640 × 480 pixels will display larger icons on the Desktop than a resolution of 800 × 600. But at a lower resolution, you probably won't be able to see all the elements of a Web page, for example. Here are some common settings and the monitors on which they are best used:

640 × 480   A standard Video Graphics Adapter (VGA) display. On a 15-inch monitor, this is quite readable for most people.

800 × 680   A typical super VGA display. On a 15-inch monitor, this is quite small, but it's quite readable on a 17-inch monitor.

1024 × 768   The upper limits of super VGA. If you have good eyesight, it's readable on a 17-inch monitor.

1280 × 1024   For large monitors. Not really readable on a 17-inch monitor.

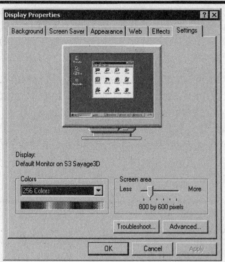

FIGURE 5.16: The Settings tab in the Display Properties dialog box

To change the font size display, click the Advanced button to open the Properties dialog box for your monitor. In the top half of the General tab, select a font size.

When you change the display settings, you often need to restart your computer; if you don't, some programs may not operate properly. By default, however, Windows 2000 Professional is set up so that the new settings apply without restarting. If you want to change this, select one of the options in the Compatibility section of the Properties dialog box.

The other tabs in the Properties dialog box contain information about your display adapter and your monitor, troubleshooting tips for working with your graphics hardware, and options for setting color profiles.

NOTE

In previous versions of Windows, the General tab on the Properties dialog box for your monitor contained an option you could select to place a settings icon on the Taskbar. If you changed resolutions frequently, this was a big time saver. Unfortunately, this option is not available in Windows 2000 Professional.

ESTABLISHING YOUR REGIONAL SETTINGS

Regional Options

By default, Windows 2000 Professional installs so that it is set up for U.S. English, the decimal numbering system, the U.S. measurement system, the U.S. currency system, a time format of h:mm:ss tt (*tt* is A.M. or P.M.), and the standard form of writing dates in the United States (10/30/00; October 30, 2000). To change any of these, open the Regional Options applet, as shown in Figure 5.17. First, select the locale on the General tab, and then modify the settings accordingly in the other tabs.

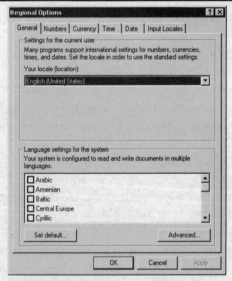

FIGURE 5.17: Modify the system for date and time, currency, numbers, and so on in the Regional Options dialog box.

ADJUSTING THE DATE AND TIME

Date/Time

You adjust the format for the date and time in the Regional Options dialog box, as you have just seen, but you actually change the date and time in the Date/Time Properties dialog box, as shown in Figure 5.18. You can open this dialog box by clicking the Date/Time icon in Control Panel or by right-clicking the time in the Taskbar and choosing Adjust Date/Time from the shortcut menu.

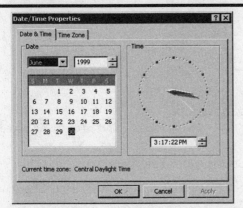

FIGURE 5.18: Change the date or time in this dialog box.

NOTE

You must be logged on as Administrator to change the date and time, which are very important settings on a local area network.

PERSONALIZING THE START MENU

To add, remove, and re-sort items on the Start menu, you use the Taskbar And Start Menu Properties dialog box. To open it, right-click the Taskbar, and choose Properties from the shortcut menu. Select the Advanced tab, as shown in Figure 5.19, to display your options.

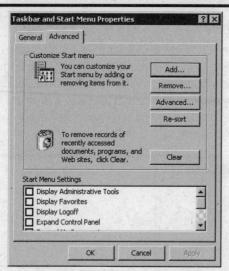

FIGURE 5.19: Customize the Start menu by using the options on the Advanced tab.

To add an item to the Start menu, follow these steps:

1. On the Advanced tab, click Add to open the Create Shortcut dialog box.

2. Enter the location of the item, or click Browse to find it, and then click Next.

3. Select Start Menu, and then click Next.

4. Type a name for the item, and then click Finish.

To remove an item from the Start menu, click the Remove button to open the Remove Shortcuts/Folders dialog box, select the item, and click Remove. To rearrange items on the Programs menu so that they are in default order, click Re-sort.

To add an item in the Start Menu Settings section of the Advanced tab, click it, and then click OK.

WHAT'S NEXT?

In Windows 2000, an *object* is a modem, a file, a folder, a shortcut to other computers on the network, and so on, and all objects have *properties*, settings that affect how the object looks and works. In Chapter 6, we'll take a look at how you establish or change these settings.

Part i

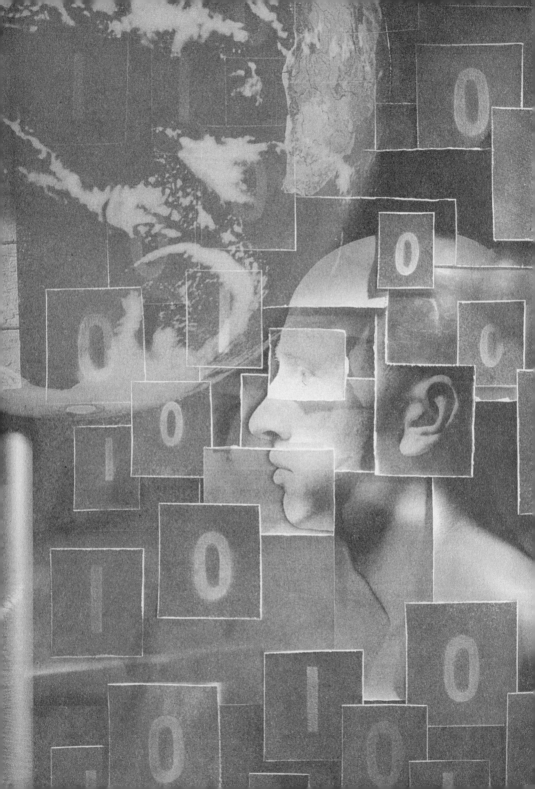

Chapter 6

SETTING OBJECT PROPERTIES

I n Chapters 4 and 5, we looked at how to manage files and folders and how to customize your Desktop. We clicked our way through some of the Control Panel applets, and when working with files, we sometimes right-clicked. In this chapter, we are going to take right-clicking even further and will look at how you can use a right-click to get stuff done faster. We'll start with a quick review of right-clicking, and then we'll take a look at Properties dialog boxes and file properties. We'll examine how to compress and encrypt files and folders in NTFS and then close this chapter with a look at folder properties and the settings you will find associated with My Computer.

Adapted from *Windows 2000 Professional: In Record Time*, by Peter Dyson and Pat Coleman

ISBN 0-7821-2450-X   467 pages $29.99

RIGHT-CLICKING IN WINDOWS 2000 PROFESSIONAL

When you right-click an object in Windows 2000 Professional, a shortcut menu opens containing options that relate to the type of object you are working with. Sometimes the same options are available from the conventional menus, but using a right-click can be faster and more convenient.

NOTE

For all of this discussion, we are assuming that you have not switched the mouse button functions by changing the settings in Control Panel. If you have, you will have to switch this discussion too. And if you don't use a mouse but use some other type of pointing device, such as a trackball, you'll have to find the equivalent right-click button; consult the Help files that come with the pointing device for more information.

You can right-click in many places in the Windows 2000 Professional interface, and you can right-click inside many of today's applications too. For example, Microsoft Word, Excel, and the other Office 2000 applications all support context-sensitive right-clicking, as do many of the Windows 2000 Professional accessory programs and system utilities. When you right-click a spreadsheet cell, the options contained in the shortcut menu will be different from those in the shortcut menu of text or a graphic in Word.

The thing to remember is that right-clicking can do no harm; so if you don't know whether an item will open a shortcut menu, try it and see. If it does, the menu will open; if it doesn't, nothing will happen. Just remember that you can close any Windows 2000 Professional shortcut menu by clicking somewhere else or by pressing the Escape key on the keyboard. Many of these menus will also have some standard entries, such as Cut, Copy, Paste, Open, Print, and Rename.

TIP

Many of today's keyboards have a right-click or menu key located between the Windows key and the right-hand Ctrl key; you can press it to trigger a right-click for the currently highlighted object. If you are a touch typist, using this key will be faster than moving your hand to the mouse, moving the mouse pointer, and clicking the right button.

Here's a quick review of what happens when you right-click certain common objects:

► Right-click the Desktop and you will see the menu we covered in Chapter 5, which is used to customize your Desktop.

► Right-click the Start button to open a menu that contains Open, Explore, and Search options, as well as two entries relating to users.

► Right-click a blank part of the Taskbar to open a menu you can use to manage any windows open on the Desktop, run the Task Manager, or look at the Taskbar properties. We'll be looking at properties in more detail later in this chapter.

► Right-click a program icon on the Taskbar. This opens the application's System menu, just as if you had right-clicked the application window's title bar or clicked the System button. Use the selections it contains to resize the application window or to close the application.

► Right-click a file, and the menu contains lots of options, including opening the file with its associated application program. Depending on the file type, you will also see Open With, which allows you to specify the program you want to use to open this file.

► Right-click a folder, and the menu you see is similar to the one for a file. If you choose Open, you will see the contents of the folder.

► Right-click a printer in the Printers folder to set a printer as the default printer or, if you are on a network, to work offline.

For example, if you right-click the My Computer icon on the Desktop, you'll see this menu:

And if you right-click the Taskbar, this is what you'll see:

Many Windows 2000 Professional objects, such as My Network Places, My Computer, printers, and folders, have the shortcut menu item Explore, which opens the item in an Explorer two-pane format, with the object in the left pane of the window and its contents in the right pane. The contents will vary according to the object and can include other computers on the network, disk drives, files, folders, and even print jobs being processed by your printer.

TIP

Certain items, such as fax modems, hard disks, and printers, have a Sharing selection in their shortcut menus, so you can specify how each item is shared with other users on the network.

Certain applications will add their own entries to a shortcut menu. For example, the file-compression program WinZip adds the menu selection Add To Zip so that you can select files to add to an archive.

USING PROPERTIES DIALOG BOXES

All objects in Windows 2000 Professional—from modems, folders, files, and shortcuts to other computers on the network—have properties, or settings, that affect how the object looks and, oftentimes, how the object operates. These properties are collected together and displayed on one or more tabs in a special dialog box called a Properties dialog box. When you install a new printer or set up your modem, for instance, the Wizard that walks you through the configuration steps collects all the information together and places that information in the appropriate Properties dialog box.

The very last item in many of the shortcut menus that we looked at in the preceding section is Properties, which gives you fast and easy access to these Properties dialog boxes. You can also get to an item's properties through Control Panel, and many dialog boxes have a Properties button that performs the same function. Once a Properties dialog box is open, you can not only display the current settings but can also change them. Some Properties dialog boxes have a single tab with just a few settings, while others may have multiple tabs; it all depends on the complexity of the object you are working with.

TIP

To open an object's Properties dialog box from the keyboard, highlight the object, and press Alt+Enter.

CHANGING FILE PROPERTIES

Right-click a document file and choose Properties to open the file's Properties dialog box, as Figure 6.1 shows. The document file in Figure 6.1 is a Microsoft Office document created by Word, and you'll see that there are several tabs, because Word keeps its property information in several locations; files created by other applications may display a dialog box with just a single tab.

The information shown on the General tab includes the document type and the name of the application associated with this file type, its location and size, as well as the create, last modified, and last accessed dates.

The document shown in Figure 6.1 is on a hard disk formatted with FAT32 and includes these three attribute check boxes:

Read-Only   Set this attribute to prevent anyone from doing anything to this file other than reading it.

Hidden   Check this box to hide the file. It will function as normal, but you won't be able to see it in the Explorer or other programs.

Archive   A check in this box indicates that the document has not been backed up since it was created or last modified.

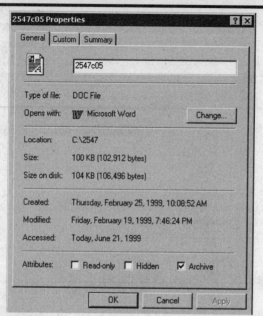

FIGURE 6.1: A Properties dialog box for a Word document file on the FAT32 file system

The Custom tab lets you create your own properties to attach to this file, and the Summary tab details the document title, subject, author, and other details, such as page and character count and the revision number.

The Properties dialog box for the same Word file created on a hard disk formatted with NTFS is shown in Figure 6.2. Now there are four tabs: General, Custom, Summary, and a new one called Security.

The General tab contains the same information as under FAT32, except this time only two attributes, Read-Only and Hidden, are shown.

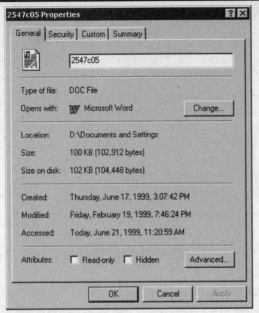

FIGURE 6.2: A Properties dialog box for a Word document file on the NTFS file system

COMPRESSING AND ENCRYPTING FILES WITH NTFS

Using NTFS allows you to take advantage of advanced file-system features not present on a FAT or a FAT32 drive, such as file compression and encryption. Right-click a file on an NTFS disk, choose Properties, and click the Advanced button on the General tab to open the Advanced Attributes dialog box, which is shown in Figure 6.3. The attributes shown here are only available with NTFS. They are not available if you are using FAT32; the Advanced button will not even be present.

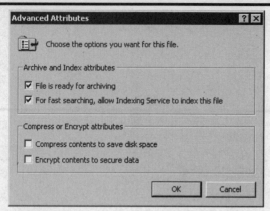

FIGURE 6.3: The Advanced Attributes dialog box

At the top of the Advanced Attributes dialog box, you will see two check boxes:

File Is Ready For Archiving   Specifies whether the file has been changed or modified since it was last backed up.

For Fast Searching, Allow Indexing Service To Index This File   Specifies whether the contents of the file should be indexed to allow for faster searching. Once the contents are indexed, you can search for text within the file as well as for properties, such as the create date or other attributes. We looked at indexing and how to use the Indexing Service in detail in Chapter 4.

At the bottom of the Advanced Attributes dialog box, you will see two more check boxes:

Compress Contents To Save Disk Space   Check this box to compress the file so that it occupies less space on your NTFS hard disk. Files are compressed by about one-third, so a 200MB file shrinks down to 135MB. This is a great way to keep large files that you only need to access occasionally. The next time you use the file, it is automatically uncompressed; you don't have to do anything special. You shouldn't compress certain types of files, however. For example, most multimedia and graphics files are already stored using their own compression scheme, and there is no point in compressing a database file since the added overhead of decompressing the file for each transaction you run could seriously affect performance. If you compress a file, you cannot encrypt it.

Encrypt Contents To Secure Data Check this box to encrypt a file so that others cannot read it; only the user who encrypted the file can open it. If you encrypt a single file, you are asked if you also want to encrypt the folder containing the file. Once the file is encrypted, you can open and change the file just as you would normally; you don't have to decrypt the file before you can use it. Mobile users can encrypt important files so that if their computer is stolen, the thief cannot access those files. If you encrypt a file, you cannot compress it, and you can't encrypt Windows 2000 Professional system files.

The Windows 2000 Professional Encrypting File System (EFS) forms the basis for encrypting files on NTFS hard disks. Before you rush off and encrypt all your files, though, here are some operational points to consider:

- ▸ If you are part of a network, remember that encrypted files cannot be shared, and files opened over the network will be decrypted before they are transmitted.

- ▸ When you move or copy an encrypted file to a non-NTFS disk, the file is decrypted.

- ▸ Any user with Delete permission can delete an encrypted file or folder, so encryption is not protection against accidental deletion.

- ▸ Use Cut and Paste to move a file into an encrypted folder; if you use drag-and-drop, the file will not automatically be encrypted.

- ▸ If you use applications that create temporary files, such as Microsoft Word, encrypt at the folder level so that these temporary files are encrypted automatically. If you encrypt only a single important document, the Word temporary files will not be encrypted. You should also encrypt the Temp folder on your hard disk for this same reason.

CHANGING FOLDER PROPERTIES

Many of the properties we looked at in the last section also apply to folders. Figure 6.4 shows the Properties dialog box for a folder on an NTFS volume.

FIGURE 6.4: A Properties dialog box for an NTFS folder

To change folder properties, right-click the folder, select Properties, choose the General tab, and then click the Advanced button to open the Advanced Attributes dialog box for this folder, where you can compress or encrypt the folder. Again, as with files, these are mutually exclusive choices: you must choose one or the other. When you apply compression or encryption at the folder level, you are asked if you want the change to apply to all subfolders as well.

If you add or copy a file into a compressed folder, the file is compressed automatically by Windows 2000 Professional. If you move a file from another NTFS drive into a compressed folder, the file is compressed automatically. However, if you move a file from a folder on the same NTFS drive into a compressed folder, the file stays in its original state, either compressed or uncompressed.

To display a compressed file or folder in a different color, follow these steps:

1. Choose Start ➢ Settings ➢ Control Panel to open Control Panel.

2. Open the Folder Options applet.

3. Select the View tab.

4. In Advanced Settings, check the Display Compressed Files And Folders With Alternate Color check box.

5. Click OK to close the Folder Options applet.

TIP

You can also encrypt or decrypt a file or folder from the command prompt using the cipher command. Type **cipher** /? at a command prompt for more information. And for more on using the command prompt, see Chapter 7.

MY COMPUTER PROPERTIES SETTINGS

Once the Windows 2000 Professional installation is complete, you will see a number of icons arranged down the left side of the Desktop, depending on the options you or your system administrator chose for your system. One of these icons is My Computer, which gives you access to some of the most important sets of properties in Windows 2000 Professional. Right-click the My Computer icon, and choose Properties to open the System Properties dialog box, which is shown in Figure 6.5. Click the General tab to bring it to the front.

The General tab lists detailed information about your computer, including the processor and the amount of memory installed. When someone asks you a technical question about your system, this is likely the place to find the answer.

The Network Identification tab details the information that identifies your computer to others on the network. Click Network ID to open the Network Identification Wizard, which guides you through making the changes, or click Properties to change the name of your computer or to change your workgroup or domain membership; consult your system administrator before making any changes here.

The Hardware tab gives you access to the Hardware Wizard, which is used to install or remove hardware components from your system, and the Device Manager, which is used to adjust hardware configuration. Hardware Profiles is the place you go to create different hardware configurations. You can create additional profiles to enable or disable certain hardware devices on your system. Once you have two or more hardware profiles, you will be prompted to choose one of them when Windows 2000 Professional starts. You can also create different hardware profiles for different users.

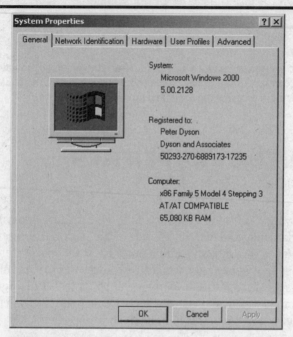

FIGURE 6.5: The System Properties dialog box for My Computer open at the General tab

The User Profiles tab lets you save different Desktop configurations, which can be associated with different users. You can also create a roaming profile that provides your Desktop appearance to every computer on your network, so, no matter where you log on to the network, you will always have your own configuration available.

The Advanced tab, shown in Figure 6.6, contains three sets of options: Performance, Environment Variables, and Startup And Recovery.

The Performance options control how your computer responds to applications versus background system services, allowing you to set the system responsiveness and to look at and change the computer's virtual memory settings. It's best to leave these alone and let Windows 2000 Professional manage virtual memory automatically, unless you really know what you are doing.

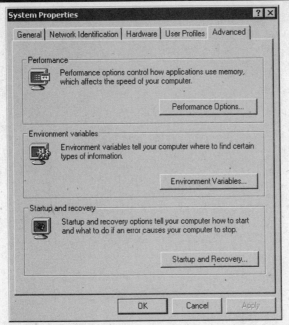

FIGURE 6.6: The System Properties dialog box for My Computer open at the Advanced tab

The Environment Variables options let you tweak system variables, such as the system path—something you might want to change from time to time.

The Startup And Recovery options let you choose a different operating system to load on restart, assuming that you installed Windows 2000 Professional as a dual-boot system. You can also specify what you want Windows 2000 Professional to do when it encounters a serious system error, such as a system halt. For example, you can specify that if the system stops, Windows 2000 Professional will log the event to the system log, send an alert, or reboot automatically.

What's Next?

When any new operating system is released, a big question is, how do you install and run applications on it? We'll answer this question in Chapter 7 and, in addition, we'll discuss a bit about the Registry and show you how to schedule programs to run automatically.

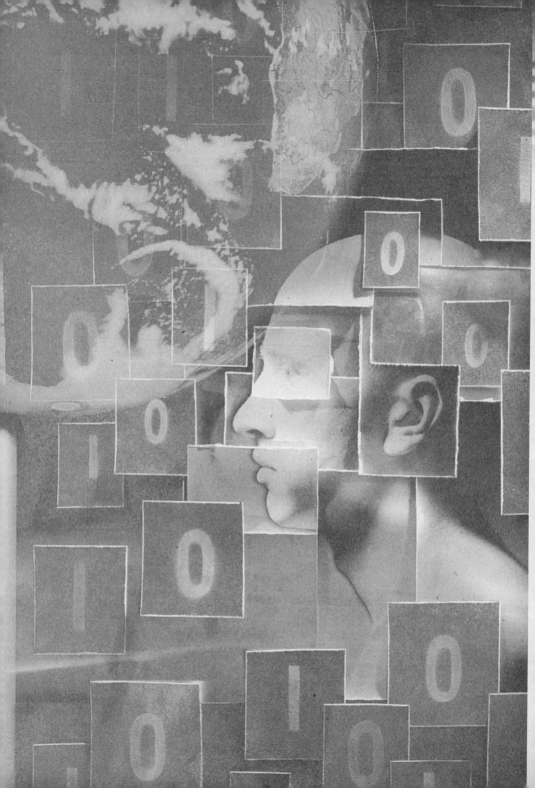

Chapter 7
Installing and Running Your Applications

The reason you installed Windows 2000 Professional in the first place was to have a secure, stable platform upon which to run your applications, right? As you might expect with Windows 2000 Professional, you can start an application in several ways, and you can manage that application in several ways once it is running. In this chapter, we'll look at all the ways you can do these things. We'll also explain how to add and remove applications and Windows 2000 Professional components, and we'll take a quick look at the Registry and explain how it plays a central role in application configuration. Finally, we'll explain how you can make Windows 2000 Professional run your applications at specific times.

Adapted from *Windows 2000 Professional: In Record Time,* by Peter Dyson and Pat Coleman

ISBN 0-7821-2450-X   467 pages $29.99

RUNNING PROGRAMS FROM THE START MENU

As its name suggests, you can use the Start button to begin anything in Windows 2000 Professional. To start an application previously installed on your system for your use, follow these steps:

1. Click the Start button to open the Start menu.

2. Click Programs. Along with some application names, your Programs menu will likely include several folders for different categories of programs, such as Accessories and a folder for startup programs that run automatically when you start Windows 2000 Professional; more on this in a later section in this chapter.

3. Choose the program group that includes the application you want to start.

4. Click the program you want to start from the selections listed in the submenu.

The next thing you see on the screen will be the application starting to run, unless the program has been configured to run minimized, which is something we'll be looking at in a later section. Windows 2000 Professional also provides keyboard alternatives to using the mouse:

▶ To open the Start menu from the keyboard, press Ctrl+Escape, or press the Windows key if your keyboard has one.

▶ To move around inside the menus, use the cursor movement keys (sometimes called the arrow keys) to highlight the entry you are interested in, and then press Enter to launch it.

BUT WILL MY OLD APPLICATIONS RUN ON WINDOWS 2000 PROFESSIONAL?

The answer to that question is that it all depends. Almost all MS-DOS and Windows 3.x applications bypass certain portions of the operating system and manipulate the computer hardware directly, and that is something that violates Windows 2000 Professional system security. So they won't run. Even some Windows 95 programs

CONTINUED ▶

will not run properly under Windows 2000 Professional, and if you run a proprietary in-house application, consult your system administrator for more information on how to proceed.

New applications, particularly those that display the Certified For Windows 2000 logo, certainly will run, and you can be sure that certified applications have passed a stringent battery of tests and are capable of taking advantage of all the operating system services built into Windows 2000 Professional.

If you are concerned about whether your favorite application will run on Windows 2000 Professional or whether it is, as they say, Windows 2000 Professional compliant, check the constantly updated catalog of Windows 2000–ready products at www.microsoft .com/windows2000/ready. You can search through a database by product name, product category, or company name to find the application you are interested in.

RUNNING PROGRAMS FROM EXPLORER

Another way to start an application is to click its name or icon in a folder or in the Explorer window. Alternatively, you can right-click the icon and choose the Open command from the shortcut menu, or you can select the item and press the Enter key. This also applies to the other Explorer-type windows in Windows 2000 Professional such as My Computer and My Documents, and you can open any application you are authorized to use from My Network Places. Figure 7.1 shows the contents of a Microsoft Office folder open in Explorer; click the Microsoft Word icon to start the application running.

TIP
See Chapter 3 for details about how to add your own shortcuts to the Start menu.

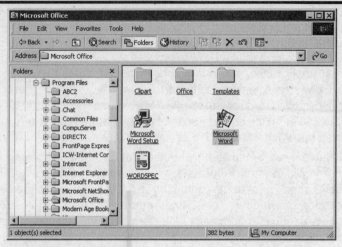

FIGURE 7.1: Click the Microsoft Word icon to run the application

RUNNING PROGRAMS FROM SEARCH

Another window that works like the Explorer is the Search Results window, and you can launch applications from it in a similar way. Search is particularly useful for applications that do not appear in any of the Start button Program submenus but are located somewhere on your hard disk or on the network. Follow these steps:

1. Choose Start ➤ Search ➤ For Files And Folders. Alternatively, right-click the Start button, and choose Search.

2. Enter the name of the file you want to locate in the Search For Files Or Folders Named field. You can use the * wildcard character to search for files with similar names. And if you don't know the name of the file you are looking for, you can locate all the executable files (in other words, all the program files) by entering *.**exe**.

3. Use the drop-down list from the Look In field to select the drive you want to search; you can search any drive attached to your computer, including floppies and CD-ROMs as well as mapped network drives.

4. Click the Search Now button to start the search. You can wait until the search completes, or if you spot the file you are looking for, click Stop Search.

Once the search is complete, the Search Results dialog box lists all the files that match your search criteria. The example in Figure 7.2 shows all the files on drive D with the filename extension of .exe. To run one of the programs listed, highlight it and choose File ➢ Open, or right-click the program and choose Open, or just double-click the program name.

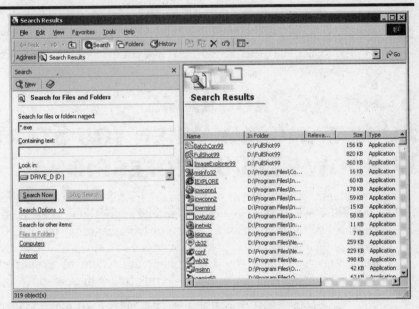

FIGURE 7.2: A list of files displayed in the Search Results window

RUNNING PROGRAMS FROM A DOCUMENT

As you go about your day-to-day work, opening applications and creating documents, Windows 2000 Professional keeps track of your 15 most recently used documents and makes these documents available from the Documents menu on the Start menu. To open one of these documents and open the parent application at the same time, choose Start ➢ Documents, and then choose the name of the document you want to work with. The application starts running and opens the appropriate document on the Desktop.

The Documents submenu can only hold a maximum of 15 documents; as you continue to work, new items replace the least recently used items. If you start a new project and realize that all the documents on your menu are now out of date, follow these steps to clear the entire menu and start over:

1. Choose Start ➢ Settings ➢ Taskbar & Start Menu.

2. In the Taskbar And Start Menu Properties dialog box, click the Advanced tab to bring it to the front.

3. Click the Clear button, and click OK to close the dialog box.

STARTING PROGRAMS AUTOMATICALLY WHEN YOU START WINDOWS 2000 PROFESSIONAL

You can also specify that applications start automatically every time you start Windows 2000 Professional by adding applications to a special folder called the Startup folder. Everyone has at least one program that they use on a regular basis (a word processor or a spreadsheet, perhaps), so you may as well have your most commonly used programs start every time you start up your computer. To do this, follow these steps:

1. Choose Start ➢ Settings ➢ Taskbar & Start Menu to open the Taskbar And Start Menu Properties dialog box.

2. Click the Advanced tab to bring it to the front, and click the Advanced button to open the Start Menu folder.

3. Find the shortcut to the program you want to start automatically when you start Windows 2000 Professional, and drag it to your Startup folder.

The next time you start Windows 2000 Professional, this application will be started automatically. In Figure 7.3, you can see an application called FullShot99 within Peter Dyson's Startup folder.

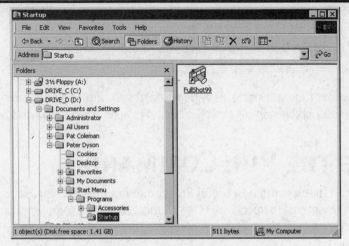

FIGURE 7.3: This Startup folder contains FullShot99.

RUNNING PROGRAMS MINIMIZED

You can also specify that any application you use is run minimized so that it appears as a button on the Taskbar rather than as an open window on the Desktop. By setting the Run Minimized option in an application's Properties dialog box, every time you run the application, it will automatically run minimized.

Automatically running a program minimized can be a very useful way to start a program that you know you will need but that you don't want to run at start-up. And if you have a collection of applications in your Startup folder, you can configure them to run minimized so that they don't take up space on your Desktop.

To specify that any application run minimized, follow these steps:

1. Choose Start ➢ Settings ➢ Taskbar & Start Menu to open the Taskbar And Start Menu Properties dialog box.

2. Click the Advanced tab to bring it to the front, and click the Advanced button to open the Start Menu folder.

3. Find the shortcut to the application you want to start minimized in the Start Menu folder, and select it.

4. Choose File ➤ Properties to open the Properties dialog box for that application, and then click the Shortcut tab.

5. In the Run list box, select Minimized.

6. Click OK to close the dialog box.

The next time you start this application, it will start as a minimized button on the Taskbar; simply click the button to open a full-sized window.

USING THE RUN COMMAND

The Start menu contains a useful Run command that you can use to launch programs, to open folders, to connect to shared computers, and even to open Web sites. The Run command is most useful when:

▶ The program you want to run is not available on your Programs menu or as an icon on the Desktop.

▶ You want to rerun or reopen a recently used program, document, or folder.

▶ The program you want to run requires one or more command-line parameters.

As Figure 7.4 shows, the Open field in the Run dialog box presents as a default the name of the program or document you last opened; to rerun this item, simply click OK. Better still is that the Open field is really a drop-down list; click the arrow to the right to see a list of your most recently used Run commands. Select the one you want from the list, and click OK. You can also connect to the Internet or to a corporate intranet using Run. For example, to reach the Sybex Web site, type www.sybex.com in the Open field, and click OK.

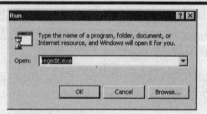

FIGURE 7.4: Use the Run dialog box to launch programs that don't appear in your Programs menu.

WORKING FROM THE COMMAND PROMPT

Windows 2000 Professional also contains a command prompt you can use to start programs and run utility programs. To open a Command Prompt window, choose Start ➤ Programs ➤ Accessories ➤ Command Prompt, or choose the Run command from the Start menu, enter **cmd** in the Open box, and click OK. To close the Command Prompt window, type **exit** and press Enter, or click the Close button. Figure 7.5 shows a Command Prompt window.

```
Command Prompt                                                    _ □ ×
 /D              Same as wide but files are list sorted by column.
 /L              Uses lowercase.
 /N              New long list format where filenames are on the far right.
 /O              List by files in sorted order.
 sortorder       N  By name (alphabetic)       S  By size (smallest first)
                 E  By extension (alphabetic)   D  By date/time (oldest first)
                 G  Group directories first     -  Prefix to reverse order
 /P              Pauses after each screenful of information.
 /Q              Display the owner of the file.
 /S              Displays files in specified directory and all subdirectories.
 /T              Controls which time field displayed or used for sorting
 timefield       C  Creation
                 A  Last Access
                 W  Last Written
 /U              Uses wide list format.
 /X              This displays the short names generated for non-8dot3 file
                 names.  The format is that of /N with the short name inserted
                 before the long name.  If no short name is present, blanks are
                 displayed in its place.
 /4              Displays four-digit years

Switches may be preset in the DIRCMD environment variable.  Override
preset switches by prefixing any switch with - (hyphen)--for example, /-W.

D:\>
```

FIGURE 7.5: A Command Prompt window open on the Desktop

TIP

When using a command prompt, you can get simplified help for utilities and commands by typing the command name followed by /?. For example, to see help information on the directory command, type **dir /?**.

To open another Command Prompt window, type **start** or **start cmd** at the command prompt. If you want to customize the appearance of the Command Prompt window, click the window's Control menu icon to open the shortcut menu, and select Properties. You can change the font, colors, cursor size, and other options used in the window.

ADDING AND REMOVING PROGRAMS

So far in this chapter, we have looked at how you can run application programs from various places in Windows 2000 Professional. In this section, we'll look at how you can add new programs and Windows components as well as how to remove them from your system if you find that they are underused and just taking up space.

In the past, every application provided its own Setup program, so each application had to manage installation and removal. Quite often, applications installed an older version of a file over a newer version, causing an apparently unrelated application to stop working. Some programs provided an installation program but no way to uninstall the package if you decided you didn't want to use it any more. All that has changed with the Windows 2000 Professional Installer service. The Installer service manages all aspects of application installation and removal as well as installation of updates and the separate configuration of components of larger packages such as the Office 2000 suite.

And the best thing about the Installer service is that you don't have to know anything about it at all. The Add/Remove Programs applet in Control Panel helps you to manage programs on your system and guides you through the process of installing new or removing existing programs and optional Windows 2000 Professional system components.

WARNING
You can only install programs written for Windows with the Add/Remove Programs applet.

To start Add/Remove Programs, choose Start ➢ Settings ➢ Control Panel, and then select the Add/Remove Programs applet. The opening screen is shown in Figure 7.6 and includes three options down the left side of the window: Change Or Remove Programs, Add New Programs, and Add/Remove Windows Components. We'll begin with Add New Programs.

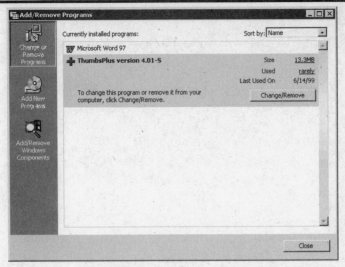

FIGURE 7.6: The Add/Remove Programs applet opening screen

Adding New Programs

Click the Add New Programs button on the left side of the Add/Remove Programs window, and you will see the screen shown in Figure 7.7. If you want to add a new program using floppy disks or a CD, click the CD Or Floppy button. If you want to connect to Microsoft's Windows Update Web site and download new Windows 2000 Professional features, device drivers, and other updates over the Internet, click the Windows Update button. A Wizard then guides you through the remaining installation and configuration steps; just follow the instructions on the screen.

TIP

You can also choose Start ➤ Windows Update to connect to the Windows Update Web site.

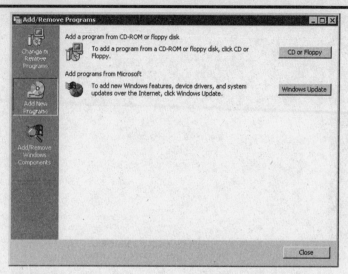

FIGURE 7.7: Adding a new program from CD or floppy disk

If you are connected to a network, any programs you are authorized to install over the network are listed at the bottom of the Add New Programs window. If your system administrator has organized several types of applications into different groups, you can select a different option in Category to find the program you want to install. Select the program or programs you want to install, and click Add. Follow the instructions on the screen.

Changing or Removing Programs

You can also use the Add/Remove Programs applet to change existing installations of large software packages such as Microsoft Office 2000 and to remove programs you no longer use. Click the Change Or Remove Programs button on the left side of the Add/Remove Programs main window to see a list of the applications currently installed on your system displayed to the right. You can sort these programs by name, size, date last used, or frequency of use to get an idea of how useful or important they are to the way you work. To remove or change one of the applications, select it in the main window, click the Change/Remove button, and follow the instructions on the screen.

Using Add/Remove Programs is the only safe way to remove installed applications and to be completely certain that all the appropriate files have been removed and that all the appropriate Registry entries have been changed as required. We look at the Windows 2000 Professional Registry in the next section and discuss why the Registry is so important.

TIP

For even more information on the Registry, see Part IV.

Adding and Removing Windows Components

As you saw in Chapter 2, the Windows 2000 Professional CD contains several optional components that you can install if you need to use them. By using Add/Remove Programs, you can fine-tune your selection of these optional elements, adding or removing them as appropriate.

Be sure that your Windows 2000 Professional CD is in your CD-ROM drive, and then click the Add/Remove Windows Components button to the left of the main window. The Windows Components Wizard opens to guide you through the installation, configuration, or removal of these optional components. See Chapter 2 for more details on these optional components.

LOOKING AT THE REGISTRY

In the last section, we mentioned the Windows 2000 Professional Registry and that it is important to the normal operation of the system. In this section, we'll look at the Registry in a bit more detail. Simply put, the Registry is just a database that contains all the configuration settings used on your system. Everything, from users and accounts to applications and the kinds of documents they create, to Properties settings for your Desktop, to printers, modems, and other hardware, has entries in the Registry.

Registry entries are updated automatically by Windows 2000 Professional operating system services when they receive a request from one of the Control Panel applets, so most of the time you don't need to worry about the Registry. However, we need to get a couple of warnings out of the way before we go too much further in this discussion. So here they are.

WARNING

Be absolutely sure you know what you are doing before you change anything in the Registry. Making a mistake can turn your system into a boat anchor (in other words, render it completely unusable).

WARNING

Any changes you make in the Registry are made immediately, and there is no undo function in the Registry Editor. You only get one chance, and it's got to be right the first time.

With these warnings in mind, it is OK just to *look* at the contents of the Registry, and we use the Registry Editor to do that. To open the Registry Editor, choose Start ➢ Run, and then type **regedit** in the Open box. The Registry Editor presents the information contained in the Registry in a hierarchical structure, as Figure 7.8 shows.

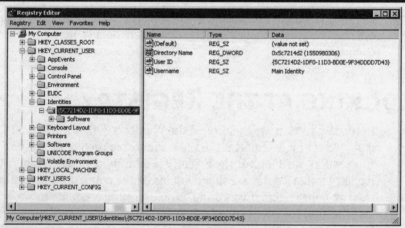

FIGURE 7.8: The Registry Editor presents Registry information in a hierarchical structure.

In the left pane of the Registry Editor, you will see these subtrees:

HKEY_CLASSES_ROOT   Contains information on file-association data and about OLE; see Chapter 9 for more on OLE.

HKEY_CURRENT_USER   Contains information about the user currently logged on to this computer.

HKEY_LOCAL_MACHINE   Stores information about the hardware available on your computer, as well as device drivers, device settings, and hardware profiles.

HKEY_USERS   Stores information about users and their preferences, along with network and Desktop settings.

HKEY_CURRENT_CONFIG   Contains information about the currently active hardware configuration.

Below these subtrees, you will see keys represented as folder icons in the left pane of the Registry Editor window. These keys contain values, and these values are displayed in the right pane. Each value has three parts: a name, a data type, and some sort of associated value. This data can be of several types, including binary, hexadecimal, or text. You navigate your way up and down the Registry Editor's left pane in the same way you navigate folders displayed in Explorer.

To change a value's data, double-click the value; a dialog box opens to receive the new data. To add a value, first select the appropriate key, choose Edit ➢ New, and then choose whether the new data will be in the form of a string value or one of the other data types. Chose Edit ➢ Find to locate specific keys in the Registry database.

In this chapter so far, we have talked about all the ways that you can run your favorite applications, but wouldn't it be neat if you could start running programs while away from your computer? Well, you can if you use the Task Scheduler, which is explained in the next section.

SCHEDULING TASKS

Windows 2000 Professional contains a Task Scheduler, which is a program you can use to run selected applications at specific times—daily, weekly, or even monthly—without any input from you or involvement on your part. The Task Scheduler starts running in the background every time you start Windows 2000 Professional; it just sits there until the time comes to run one of your selected tasks, and then it moves into action.

Certain tasks are well suited to unattended automatic operation, such as making a tape backup or running hard-disk utilities. You can run these programs while you work, but it often makes more sense to run them when your system is turned on but is not too busy, such as at lunch time, when you are attending a regularly scheduled company meeting, or during the night.

You can open the Task Scheduler in several ways:

▶ Double-click the Task Scheduler icon on the Taskbar if the Task Scheduler is already running.

▶ Open the Scheduled Tasks folder in Control Panel.

▶ Choose Start ➢ Programs ➢ Accessories ➢ System Tools ➢ Scheduled Tasks.

The main Task Scheduler window opens as shown in Figure 7.9, listing any currently scheduled tasks along with information about when they will run next and when they were run last.

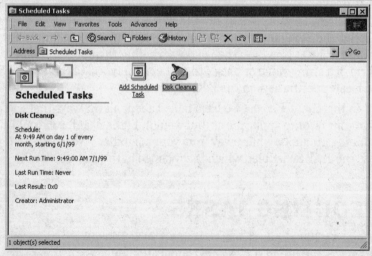

FIGURE 7.9: The Scheduled Tasks main window lists currently scheduled tasks.

Adding a New Scheduled Task

To add a new scheduled task, follow these steps:

1. Open the Scheduled Tasks folder in Control Panel, or double-click the Task Scheduler icon on the Taskbar to open Task Scheduler.

2. Click Add Scheduled Task to open the Scheduled Task Wizard.

3. The Wizard presents a list of programs you can run unattended; click Browse to look for more. Make a selection, and then click Next.

4. Select the frequency at which you want the program to run, and click Next.

5. Select the time and day when you want the program to run, and click Next.

6. Enter a username and password; the program you have chosen will run as though started by that user. Click Next.

7. The Wizard confirms the task name and tells you when the task will run next. Click Finish to add this task to your Windows schedule.

Modifying an Existing Scheduled Task

To modify an existing task, right-click the task, and then choose Properties from the shortcut menu to open a dialog box for that task. The dialog box contains the following tabs:

Task   Changes the name of the program you want to schedule.

Schedule   Changes when the program is run.

Settings   Customizes the task configuration.

Security   Specifies the security for the task.

NOTE

You will not see the Security tab unless you are using the NTFS file system.

To halt a scheduled task that is currently executing, right-click to open the shortcut menu, and then select End Task; to resume the task, right-click, and choose Run. To remove a task, right-click it, and select Delete from the shortcut menu.

Using the Advanced Menu

The Task Scheduler Advanced menu includes the following options:

Stop Using Task Scheduler　Turns the Task Scheduler application off and halts all scheduled tasks. Task Scheduler will not start automatically the next time you start Windows. This menu selection changes into Start Using Task Scheduler so that you can use it to restart operations.

Pause Task Scheduler　Temporarily stops the Task Scheduler. This menu item changes into Continue Task Scheduler so that you can restart operations. Any tasks that were due to run during the time Task Scheduler was paused will not run until their next scheduled time.

Notify Me Of Missed Tasks　Informs you of any scheduled tasks that did not run.

AT Service Account　Specifies the account used for the Task Scheduler. In previous versions of Windows NT software, the Task Scheduler was known as the AT command.

View Log　Opens the Task Scheduler log file in a Notepad window.

WHAT'S NEXT?

No matter how much we would all like to dispense with the mounds of paper that cross our desks daily, we find ourselves still dependent on printers and printed output. In the next chapter, we'll tell you how to install a network printer and a local printer, how to print from Windows and from an application, how to print to a file, how to manage the print queue, how to customize printer properties, and how to work with fonts.

Part I

Chapter 8

PRINTERS AND PRINTING

We have a friend who is bound and determined to have a paperless office. He's on the road a lot and has office space at corporate headquarters and at home. Two things really set off this Type-A guy, however: not being able to get on e-mail and not being able to print. No matter how much we may strive to work electronically, Hewlett Packard and the rest of the printer manufacturers are thriving.

Adapted from *Windows 2000 Professional: In Record Time,* by Peter Dyson and Pat Coleman

ISBN 0-7821-2450-X   467 pages $29.99

Installing and using printers becomes easier and easier with each new generation of equipment, which, by the way, continues to decrease in cost and size and increase in output speed and number of features. In addition, each new version of Windows includes tools that make installing a printer easier and faster. In this chapter, we will go step by step through the process of installing both a network and a local printer, and then we'll discuss how to establish the settings that are most appropriate for how and what you print.

TIP

When you buy or acquire a new printer, put the manual somewhere where you can find it. Each printer or series of printers has idiosyncrasies, such as how you change the cartridge and the type of cartridge to use, and you'll need to follow the manufacturer's advice about these things.

ADDING PRINTERS

If you have a stand-alone system and upgraded to Windows 2000 Professional, you may not have to install your printer; the installation routine should have recognized it, as it did your keyboard, mouse, monitor, and so on. If you did a clean install on a new machine or a new partition on your hard drive, however, you will need to install your printer. If you're on a corporate network, your network administrator has, no doubt, done this for you, and you can skip to the "Printing Documents" section of this chapter.

Obviously, if you've just bought a new printer or are connecting to a different printer, you'll need to install it. Installing involves more than simply plugging in the printer. Installing is a matter of giving Windows 2000 Professional the information it needs so that it knows how to use your printer.

Before we get down to business, though, we need to define a couple of terms. A *local* printer is one that is physically attached to your computer by a cable. A *network* printer is a printer that is attached to another computer on your network; that computer becomes a *print server,* and you access it via the network, just as you access other network resources.

To install either a local printer or a network printer, you use the Printers folder. Let's start by looking at how to install a local printer.

Installing a Local Printer

You can open the Printers folder, which is shown in Figure 8.1, in two ways:

▶ Choose Start ➢ Settings ➢ Control Panel, and then click the Printers icon.

▶ Choose Start ➢ Settings ➢ Printers.

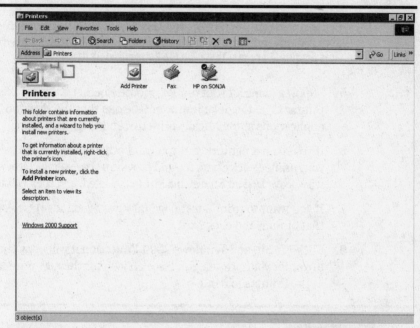

FIGURE 8.1: Use the Printers folder to add, remove, and configure printers.

To add a new printer to your system, first be sure that the printer cable is securely connected to both the printer and to your computer. Also, be sure you've followed any setup instructions that came with the printer. Now, turn on the printer, click Add Printer to open the Add Printer Wizard, which is shown in Figure 8.2, and follow these steps:

1. At the Welcome screen, click Next.

2. Click Local Printer. If you want Windows 2000 Professional to find and install your printer, leave the Automatically Detect And Install My Plug And Play Printer check box checked. Otherwise, click this check box to clear it, and click Next.

3. Select the printer port to use (most likely, LPT1, which is selected by default), and click Next.

4. Select the manufacturer and model of your printer, and click Next.

NOTE

If you don't see your printer listed and you have the CD or floppy disk that came with your printer, click Have Disk. If you don't see your printer listed and no disk came with your printer, check your printer manual to see if your printer emulates (imitates) a printer that is on the list, and select that one.

5. Supply a name for your printer, choose whether you want this printer to be the default printer (the one that Windows and applications automatically print to), and then click Next.

6. If you're on a network and you want others to be able to use your printer, click Share As, and provide a share name. Otherwise, leave Do Not Share This Printer selected, and click Next.

7. If you want to print a test page (always a good idea), select that option, and click Next.

8. Click Finish, and Windows 2000 Professional will copy the driver for your printer. You'll see an icon for the new printer in the Printers folder.

FIGURE 8.2: To install a printer, you use the Add Printer Wizard.

WHAT TO DO IF YOUR TEST PAGE DOESN'T PRINT

Most of the time, installing a printer is a straightforward process, but if your test page didn't print or didn't print correctly, the first thing to do is click No in the dialog box that asks about this. You'll be presented with a list of troubleshooting steps, which you'll also find in the Troubleshooting section of Help.

If you work through these and you still can't print, make sure your printer is on the Hardware Compatibility List, which you'll find at www.microsoft.com.

If your printer is on the list, locate your printer manual, and look for a telephone number for technical support. We know from personal experience that sometimes even the printer driver on the CD or disk that comes with your printer may not be the correct one. (A printer driver, by the way, is a program that controls or regulates the printer.) If the correct driver is not installed, the printer won't work or won't work properly. In the worst case, you may have to acquire the appropriate driver from the manufacturer.

To delete a printer from the Printers folder, right-click it, and choose Delete from the shortcut menu. To rename a printer, right-click it, choose Rename, type a new name in the box, and then click outside the box. To set a different printer as the default, right-click the printer, and choose Set As Default Printer from the shortcut menu. To create a shortcut to this printer on the Desktop, right-click it, and choose Create Shortcut from the shortcut menu.

Installing a Network Printer

Before you can install a network printer, you or someone else must do the following:

1. Physically connect the printer to the network cable or to a computer on the network. (To connect the printer to the network cable, the printer must have a network interface card installed.)

2. Install the printer on a computer on the network.

3. Set the printer up as a shared printer.

4. Get the network up and running.

5. Turn on the printer.

When all that's been taken care of, you're ready to start your installation. Follow these steps:

1. Choose Start ➢ Settings ➢ Printers to open the Printers folder.

2. Click the Add Printer icon to start the Add Printer Wizard.

3. At the Welcome screen, click Next.

4. Select the Network Printer option, and click Next.

5. Enter the name of the network printer you want to use. If you don't know the name, click Next to open a screen that displays the resources available on your network (this may take a few seconds, depending on the speed of your network). When you find the printer, click it, and then click Next.

6. If you want to set this printer as the default, click Yes. (Remember, you can always do this later by right-clicking this printer in the Printers folder and selecting Set As Default Printer.) Click Next to continue.

7. Click Finish to copy the driver and print a test page.

To remove a network printer from the Printers folder, to rename it, to set it as the default printer, or to create a shortcut to it on the Desktop, right-click it, and choose the appropriate command from the shortcut menu.

SHARING A NETWORK PRINTER

Before you can install and use a network printer, that printer must be shared. And, if you have a printer that you want others on the network to be able to use, you must share it. To share a printer, follow these steps:

1. In the Printers folder, right-click the printer, and choose Sharing from the shortcut menu to open the Properties dialog box for that printer.

CONTINUED ➡

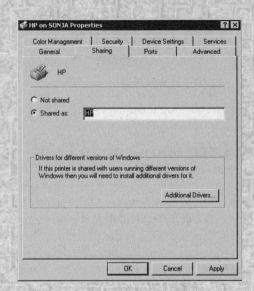

2. Click the Shared As option button.

3. Accept the name that is generated, or enter a new one.

4. Click the General tab if you want to enter a comment about this printer.

5. Click OK.

The icon of this printer in the Printers folder will now have a hand under it to indicate that it is shared.

PRINTING DOCUMENTS

After you add a printer, either local or network, you're ready to print, and you can do so either from the Desktop or from an application. Regardless of where you print from, Windows 2000 Professional is actually handling the process. The print spooler program accepts the document and holds it on disk or in memory until the printer is free, and then the printer prints it.

If you want to print an existing document, the quickest way is to print from the Desktop.

Printing from the Desktop

You can print from the Desktop in a couple of ways:

▶ By using drag-and-drop

▶ By right-clicking the document

Using Drag-and-Drop to Print

To print with drag-and-drop, you need a shortcut to your printer on the Desktop, and you need an open folder that contains the file. In other words, you need to be able to see both the printer icon and the filename or icon. Simply click the file, and drag it onto the printer icon. Windows 2000 Professional opens the file in the program in which the document was created or in the program you've associated with the file by using the Open With command, and then it prints the file. Figure 8.3 shows a file being dragged to the printer on the Desktop.

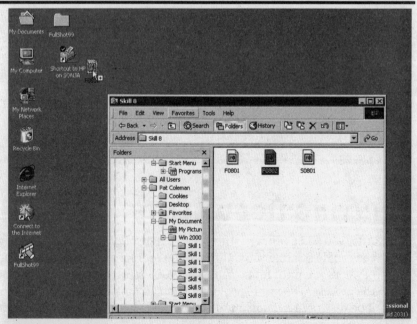

FIGURE 8.3: Printing with drag-and-drop

When you print in this manner, you use the default options in the Print dialog box, which we'll look at in the upcoming "Printing from an Application" section. The entire file is printed, only one copy is printed, the printed output is in portrait orientation (vertical), and the default paper tray is used. You have no opportunity to modify these settings.

Right-Clicking to Print

To print using the right-click method in Windows, open a folder that contains the file you want to print, right-click the file, and select Print from the shortcut menu. In a flash, the program associated with the file opens, and the document prints. Just as when you drag and drop to print, the default settings in the Print dialog box are used.

Printing from an Application

If you want more control over how your document is printed, such as the orientation of the paper, the number of copies, and so on, you'll want to print from the application. You can usually print in a couple of ways in an application:

▸ By clicking the Print button on the toolbar

▸ By choosing File ➤ Print

If you click the Print button, usually the document is immediately spooled to the printer, and you have no opportunity to specify the number of copies, exactly what you want to print, and so on. Choosing File ➤ Print opens the Print dialog box, which is shown in Figure 8.4, in which you can specify the options that control what is printed and how. The specific options you see in the Print dialog box depend on your printer. For example, if your printer can print both in color and in black-and-white, you'll see both those options.

NOTE

The steps are the same whether you are printing on a local printer or a network printer. But remember, the options in the Print dialog box will vary depending on the printer.

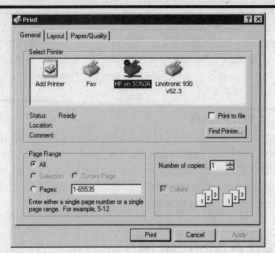

FIGURE 8.4: Specify printing options in the Print dialog box.

To see how this works, let's walk through the steps to print a document from WordPad, one of the applications that comes with Windows 2000 Professional (we'll look at WordPad in more detail in Chapter 10). Follow these steps:

1. Choose Start ≻ Programs ≻ Accessories ≻ WordPad.

2. Open an existing document, or create a new one.

3. Choose File ≻ Save As, and save the document if it is new (it's usually prudent to save before you print).

4. Choose File ≻ Print to open the Print dialog box at the General tab, which you can see in Figure 8.4.

5. In the Select Printer area, click the printer you want to use. If you place the mouse cursor over the printer icon, you'll see a ToolTip that displays its status—whether it's ready to print or if documents are waiting in the print queue. (We'll look at how you manage the print queue later in this chapter.)

6. In the Page Range area, choose whether to print the entire file, only a selection, the current page, or selected pages. To print a selection, you need to select it first and then open the Print dialog box.

Part i

7. In the Number Of Copies box, select the copies to print. When you print more than one copy, they are collated by default. If, for some reason, you don't want them collated, clear the Collate check box.

8. To specify that your document print in landscape mode (horizontally) rather than portrait (vertically), click the Layout tab, which is shown in Figure 8.5.

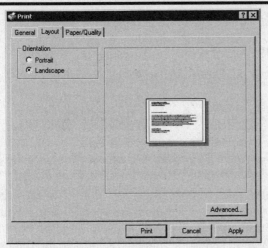

FIGURE 8.5: Click Landscape if you want to print horizontally instead of vertically.

9. To specify the paper source, the kind of paper, the print quality, and the color (if you have a color printer), click the Paper/Quality tab, and select the appropriate options.

10. Click Print.

TIP

To see how your printed document will look before you actually print it, click the Print Preview button or choose File ➢ Print Preview.

Printing to a File

Printing to a file is not necessarily something that most people do every day, but, on occasion, it's a handy thing to know about. When you print to a file, you save on disk the codes and data that are normally sent to the printer. In our work, we sometimes need to supply the publisher with a file that has been saved to disk so that it can be printed on their printer. When you want to do this, you can even install on your hard drive a printer that isn't physically installed on your system or the network, and then print the file to that printer.

To print to a file, follow these steps:

1. Choose File ➤ Print to open the Print dialog box.

2. Select the printer, and then click Print To File.

3. Click Print.

4. Enter a name for the file in the Print To File dialog box, and click OK.

By default, these files are stored in your My Documents folder.

MANAGING THE PRINTING PROCESS

If you've ever meant to print a short paragraph from a file but forgot to click the Selection option and ended up printing an 80-page document instead, you know how important it is to be able to stop the printing process. And if you've ever sent something to the printer and then waited and waited in vain for the document to print, you know you need a way to find out what's going on. To halt printing, to check the status of a document you've sent to the printer, or to clear all documents out of the print queue, you use the printer window that opens when you double-click the printer in the Printers folder. Figure 8.6 shows the printer window for one of the printers on our network.

You'll need to maximize this window and drag the horizontal scroll bar to see all the information it contains:

Document Name   The name of the document and the total number of pages

Status   Whether the document is printing, paused, or being deleted

Owner   The name of the person who sent the document to the printer

Pages   The number of pages currently printed

Size   The size of the document in bytes

Submitted   The time the document was sent to the printer

Port   The printer port being used

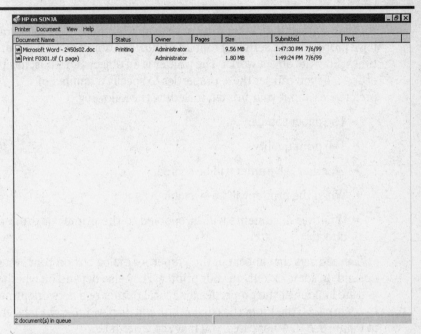

FIGURE 8.6: Status information is displayed in a printer window.

Once you know what's happening or about to happen in the print queue, you can take charge of it:

- ▶ To cancel the printing of a document, right-click the document in the print queue, and choose Cancel from the shortcut menu.

- ▶ To cancel the printing of all documents in the print queue, choose Printer ➢ Cancel All Documents.

- ▶ To temporarily halt the printing of a single document, right-click the document, and choose Pause.

- ▶ To resume the printing of a document you have paused, right-click the document, and choose Resume.

NOTE

When you choose Pause or Cancel, the printing probably won't stop right away. Whatever has already been spooled to the printer's buffer must print before the printing stops.

Customizing the Printer's Properties

As we discussed in Chapter 6, all objects in Windows 2000 Professional have properties (or settings) that affect how the object looks and, oftentimes, how the object works. The printer is an object and, thus, has properties, and you can set those properties to specify a number of preferences about your printer, including the following:

▶ The paper source

▶ The print quality

▶ Whether the printer will be shared

▶ When the printer will be available

▶ Whether documents will be spooled to the printer or printed directly

The settings that appear in the Properties dialog box on your system depend, to some extent, on your printer. They also depend on whether you are looking at the properties for a local printer or a network printer. In some cases, the Properties dialog box will display the eight tabs shown in Figure 8.7. In other cases, you may see fewer tabs.

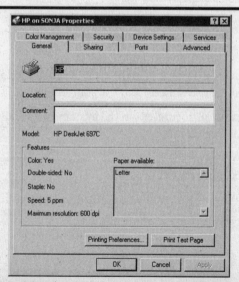

FIGURE 8.7: The printer Properties dialog box

NOTE

You can change the printer settings only if you have the permission to do so.

To open the Properties dialog box for a printer, right-click its icon in the Printers folder, and then click Properties. You will notice that some of the items on the shortcut menu take you directly to a portion of the Properties dialog box. For example, you can click Sharing to display the Sharing tab.

In this section, we'll look at each of the tabs in the printer Properties dialog box and describe some of their typical settings.

NOTE

The settings you specify in the printer Properties dialog box become the default settings for that printer. You can, of course, change them at any time.

The General Tab

On the General tab, which is shown in Figure 8.7, you can change only a couple of fields: Location and Comment. For a network printer, you might use the Location box to describe where the printer is situated (for example, "Third-floor printer room"), and you can use the Comment box to say something pertinent about the printer (for instance, "Legal-size paper only").

To specify layout (portrait or landscape), paper source, print quality, and color, click the Printing Preferences button to open the Printing Preferences dialog box. In this dialog box, click the Advanced button to open the Advanced Options dialog box, which contains a description of a number of printer features and in which you can also change the paper size. Back in the General tab, you can click Print Test Page to do just that.

The Sharing Tab

If you want to share your printer with other users on your network, click the Sharing tab, which is shown in Figure 8.8. As we mentioned earlier in the "Installing a Network Printer" section, click the Shared As option button, and then enter a name for the printer. If you will be sharing this printer with people running versions of Windows other than Windows 2000 Profes-sional, click the Additional Drivers button to open the Additional Drivers dia-log box. You'll see a list of systems. Click a system so that users on that system can automatically download the driver when they connect to your printer.

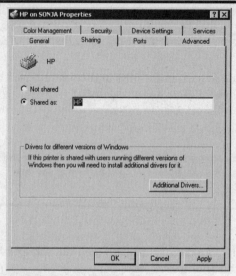

FIGURE 8.8: The Sharing tab

The Ports Tab

You normally don't need to be messing around with the settings in the Ports tab, which is shown in Figure 8.9, and, indeed, if you are on a corporate net-work, you shouldn't (in addition, you probably don't have permission). On this tab, you'll see a list of ports on your computer, and you'll see buttons to add, delete, and configure ports. Adding and deleting a port is relatively easy; retrieving a deleted port is not. Unless you have permission *and* know exactly what you're doing, don't fiddle with the options on this tab.

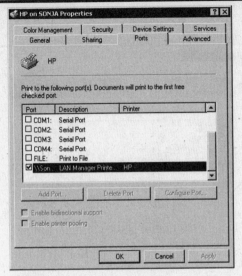

FIGURE 8.9: The Ports tab

The Advanced Tab

You can use the Advanced tab to set a number of options such as the following:

- ▶ When the printer is available for use
- ▶ The priority of the printing document (1 is the lowest; 99 is the highest)
- ▶ The printer driver name
- ▶ Whether documents will be spooled to the printer
- ▶ To check for mismatched documents (a document whose setup doesn't match the printer setup)
- ▶ To store printed documents so that they can be printed from the print queue rather than being spooled again

The Enable Advanced Printing Features check box is enabled by default. This means that certain features such as page order and pages per sheet are available, depending on your printer.

Clicking Printer Defaults displays the dialog box in which you can specify the layout, paper size, and printing quality. This is the same dialog box you see when you click Printing Preferences in the General tab. Figure 8.10 shows the Advanced tab.

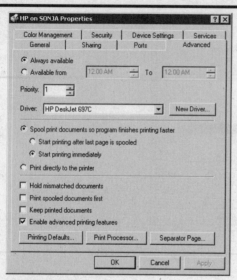

FIGURE 8.10: The Advanced tab

One other handy option on the Advanced tab is the Separator Page button. A separator page identifies the beginning of a document. When several print jobs are being sent to a network printer, a separator page makes it easy for users to locate their particular documents. To specify a separator page, follow these steps:

1. Click Separator Page to open the Separator Page dialog box.

2. In the Separator Page box, enter a filename for the page you want to use, or click Browse to locate one. You'll find some already-existing separator pages in the System 32 folder.

3. Click OK.

The Services Tab

Whether you have the Services tab and its contents depends on your printer. As you can see in Figure 8.11, we can use the options on this page to align or clean the print cartridges on our Hewlett Packard DeskJet.

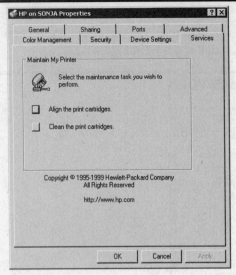

FIGURE 8.11: The Services tab

The Device Settings Tab

If your printer has more than one paper tray, you can use the options on this tab, which is shown in Figure 8.12, to specify which size paper is printed from which tray. You can then select a tray when you print from applications.

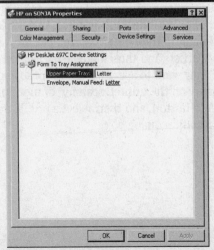

FIGURE 8.12: The Device Settings tab

The Security Tab

If you have the appropriate permissions, you can assign printer permissions on the Security tab, which is shown in Figure 8.13.

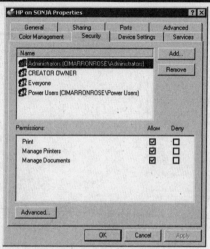

FIGURE 8.13: The Security tab

The Color Management Tab

When you install a new scanner, printer, or monitor, Windows 2000 Professional automatically installs a color profile that is used when colors are scanned, printed, or displayed. For most desktop systems, this profile is sufficient and is selected by default in the Color Management tab, as you can see in Figure 8.14. Graphic artists and those doing complicated color desktop publishing, however, may want to specify a color profile in order to better control the color quality on the printer, scanner, or monitor. To add a color profile, click the Add button, and then select a profile from the list in the Add Profile Association dialog box.

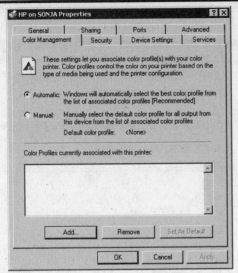

FIGURE 8.14: The Color Management tab

UNDERSTANDING FONTS

Before we complete our discussion of printers and printing, we need to take a quick look at fonts. In Windows 2000 Professional, a font is the name of a typeface, and a font can have size, which is usually described in points, and a style, such as bold or italic. Most fonts are TrueType fonts; that is, their printed output is identical to what you see on the screen.

NOTE

A point is 1/72 inch.

Some fonts are not TrueType fonts, however, and they are identified with this symbol. They are not scalable and, thus, look really bad at larger point sizes.

Fonts identified with this symbol are the new OpenType fonts, which are outline fonts and are an extension of TrueType. You can scale and rotate both TrueType and OpenType fonts.

To see the fonts installed on your system, click the Fonts icon in Control Panel to open the Fonts folder, which is shown in Figure 8.15. To see what an individual font looks like at several sizes, double-click a font. Figure 8.16 shows representative sizes of the Comic Sans MS font and displays some information about this font. To see printed output of a particular font, simply click the Print button, which is shown in Figure 8.16.

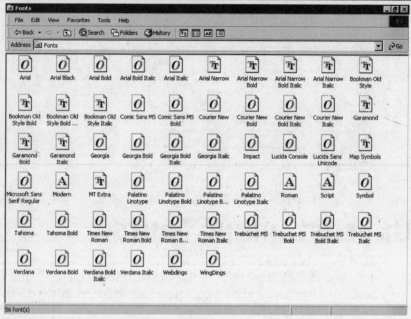

FIGURE 8.15: The Fonts folder

If you are overwhelmed by the number and type of fonts shown in the Fonts folder, choose View ➢ Hide Variations (Bold, Italic, etc.). To see a list of fonts that are similar, follow these steps:

1. In the Fonts folder, choose View ➢ List Fonts By Similarity.

2. In the List Fonts By Similarity To drop-down list, select a font.

You'll see a list of font names, in order from the most similar to the least similar.

FIGURE 8.16: A sample of what's available in the Comic Sans MS font

Although Windows 2000 Professional comes with a great many fonts installed, you may well want to install other fonts for particular purposes. Follow these steps:

1. In the Fonts folder, choose File ➢ Install New Font to open the Add Fonts dialog box.

2. Select the drive and the folder containing the font.

3. Click OK.

By default, fonts are installed into the Fonts folder.

WHAT'S NEXT?

Information has been called the "coin of the age," and the sharing of information has always been key to the development of Windows. In the next chapter, we'll look at how to share information between Windows applications, and we'll also look at how to share information via Net-Meeting, a conferencing application that's included with Windows.

Chapter 9

SHARING INFORMATION BETWEEN APPLICATIONS

U nless you are brand new to the Windows environment, you have probably used the Cut, Copy, and Paste commands, and you may have even embedded and linked objects—all without knowing you were using Object Linking and Embedding (OLE). In this chapter, we'll quickly go over the steps for these tasks and take a look at the underlying structure that makes OLE work.

Adapted from *Windows 2000 Professional: In Record Time*, by Peter Dyson and Pat Coleman

ISBN 0-7821-2450-X   467 pages $29.99

You will probably find that a couple of the topics in this chapter are new to you. In Windows 2000 Professional, the ClipBook Viewer has replaced the Clipboard Viewer, and it includes some features that were not previously available in Clipboard Viewer. (The ClipBook Viewer, however, has been around in previous versions of NT.)

Another topic that you may not be familiar with is NetMeeting, although it has been included with Internet Explorer since version 4. It is now an integrated part of Windows, and you can use it to share and collaborate on applications, video and audio conference, phone a friend via the Internet, transfer files, and finger-chat over the Internet. You'll find in Chapter 15 that you can use Phone Dialer to do some of these things, but, in our opinion, using NetMeeting is much more convenient.

The idea of sharing information has always been central to the development of the Windows family of operating systems, and, of course, it is the heart and soul of the Internet. In this chapter, we'll start with the basics and then have some fun with NetMeeting, which, by the way, has a new interface in Windows 2000 Professional.

USING THE CLIPBOARD

The Clipboard is an area in memory that serves as the temporary storehouse for an item that you cut or copy. When you paste an item, a copy stays on the Clipboard until you cut or copy another item, close Windows 2000 Professional, or intentionally clear the Clipboard. Thus, you can paste the same item multiple times.

How much you can store on the Clipboard depends on the available memory. You don't normally need to be concerned about this unless you are cutting and pasting very large files such as graphics, video, and sound.

NOTE

When you cut an item, you actually remove it from the source document and place it in the destination document. When you copy an item, it remains in the source document, and a duplicate is placed in the destination document.

Windows 2000 Professional includes the ClipBook Viewer, a utility that you can use to save and share items that you place on the Clipboard.

After we look at the various ways you can use the Clipboard in Windows applications, we'll take a look at the ClipBook Viewer.

Copying, Cutting, and Pasting in Windows Applications

You can cut, copy, and paste as follows:

- ▶ Within a document
- ▶ Between documents in the same application
- ▶ Between documents in different applications
- ▶ Between applications in different versions of Windows
- ▶ Between applications running on other computers on a local network
- ▶ Between a site on the Web and an application on your local drive or a network drive

Regardless of the source and destination, the process is the same. Here are the steps:

1. Open the source document, and select what you want to cut or copy.

2. Choose Edit ➢ Cut (or press Ctrl+X) or Edit ➢ Copy (or press Ctrl+C). The item is now stored on the Clipboard.

3. Open the destination document, and place the insertion point where you want the item.

4. Choose Edit ➢ Paste (or press Ctrl+V).

You choose Edit ➢ Paste Special if you want to link or embed an object within a document, and we'll look at that in the "Understanding OLE" section, later in this chapter.

Figure 9.1 shows a selection that's being copied from the Sybex Web site, and Figure 9.2 shows that selection copied into WordPad.

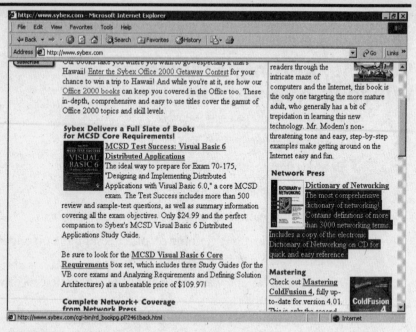

FIGURE 9.1: Copying a selection from a Web page

You can also use drag-and-drop to cut, copy, and paste, and you can right-click a selection to use the shortcut menu for these tasks. To use drag-and-drop, follow these steps:

1. Open both the source document and the destination document so that both are visible on the Desktop.

2. Select what you want to cut or copy, right-click the selection, drag it to the destination document, and release the mouse button.

3. From the shortcut menu that appears, choose Move Here, or choose Copy Here.

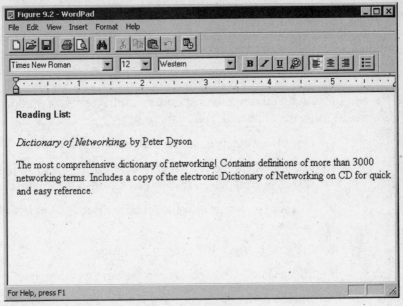

FIGURE 9.2: Pasting the selection into WordPad

To use right-click, follow these steps:

1. Select the source item, and right-click to open the shortcut menu.

2. Choose Cut or Copy.

3. Open the destination document, place the insertion point where you want the item, and right-click.

4. From the shortcut menu, choose Paste.

NOTE

See the section "Working with the ClipBook Viewer," later in this chapter, for information on how to clear the Clipboard.

Capturing Screens with the Clipboard

If you ever create documentation, training materials, or promotional materials about software, you may find it quite handy to capture screens with the Clipboard. If you do a lot of this, you'll want to use a professional program such as Collage or FullShot99, especially if you need to edit the image. You can, however, capture a full screen or a window and save it using the Clipboard. Follow these steps:

1. Open the window or screen that you want to capture.

2. Press Alt+Print Screen to capture the entire screen, or press Ctrl+Alt+Print Screen to capture only the open window.

3. To save the image as a file, choose Start ➤ Programs ➤ Accessories ➤ Paint.

4. In Paint, press Ctrl+V to open the image.

5. Choose File ➤ Save As to open the Save As dialog box.

6. Select a folder in which to save the file, enter a name for the file in the File Name box, and choose the type in which you want to save it from the drop-down Save As Type box. You have the following options:

   ▶ 256 Color Bitmap (*.bmp, *.dib)

   ▶ Monochrome Bitmap (*.bmp, *.dib)

   ▶ 16 Color Bitmap (*.bmp, *.dib)

   ▶ 24-bit Bitmap (*.bmp, *.dib)

7. Click Save.

The file is now saved as a separate document, and you can insert it in your document. For example, to insert the screen capture into a Microsoft Word document, follow these steps:

1. Open the destination document in Word.

2. Choose Insert ➤ Picture ➤ From File to open the Insert Picture dialog box.

3. Select the file, and click Insert.

You can now save the image as part of the destination document. If you do so, the image will reside both in that document and as a separate file in the folder where you originally saved it.

You can also copy the image from the Clipboard directly into a destination document if you want. In that case, the image is not saved as a separate file but as part of the document in which you place it.

Figure 9.3 shows a screen capture inserted in a Word document.

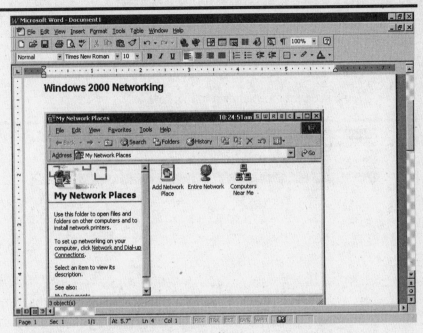

FIGURE 9.3: Even if you don't have a professional program, you can easily capture screens using the Clipboard.

WORKING WITH THE CLIPBOOK VIEWER

As we mentioned in the introduction to this chapter, the Clipboard Viewer in previous versions of Windows has been replaced with the ClipBook Viewer. Using the ClipBook Viewer provides several advantages over the Clipboard Viewer:

▶ You can save what is on the Clipboard as a page and reuse it at a later time. In fact, you can save as many as 127 pages.

▸ You can give a page a descriptive name of as many as 47 characters.

▸ You can share pages with others on your network.

Starting the ClipBook Viewer

To start the ClipBook Viewer, follow these steps:

1. Choose Start ➢ Run to open the Run dialog box.

2. In the Open box, type **clipbrd**, and click OK.

You'll see the screen shown in Figure 9.4.

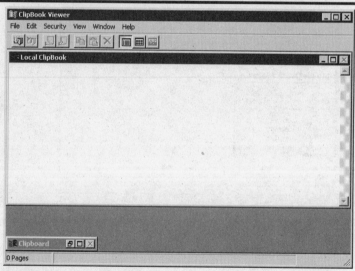

FIGURE 9.4: The ClipBook Viewer

Pasting an Item into the ClipBook

To use the ClipBook, you paste items from the Clipboard into pages. Here are the steps:

1. Cut or copy something to the Clipboard.

2. Open the ClipBook Viewer.

3. Choose Edit ➤ Paste to open the Paste dialog box:

4. In the Page Name box, enter a name for the page, and click OK.

You'll now see the item in Thumbnail view in the Local ClipBook. You can also view it on the Clipboard. To change the view, choose View ➤ Table Of Contents to display an alphabetic list of your pages. To display the contents of a page, choose View ➤ Full Page.

Copying an Item from the ClipBook

To copy an item from the ClipBook into an application, follow these steps:

1. Open ClipBook Viewer.

2. In the Local ClipBook, click the page you want to copy.

3. Choose Edit ➤ Copy.

4. Open the document in the application to which you want to copy the item.

5. Place the insertion point where you want the item.

6. Choose Edit ➤ Paste.

Sharing ClipBook Pages

If you are on a local area network, you can share ClipBook pages with other users who also have ClipBook Viewer installed. Follow these steps:

1. In the Local ClipBook, click the page you want to share.

2. Choose File ➤ Share to open the Share ClipBook Page dialog box.

3. To start the program with which the page was created when a user inserted the page in a document, click the Start Application On Connect check box. To also run the program minimized, also click the Run Minimized check box.

4. If you want to ensure that users can't edit or delete the page, click the Permissions button to open the ClipBook Page Permissions dialog box.

5. After you set the permissions, click OK twice.

Clearing the Clipboard

To clear the contents of the Clipboard, follow these steps:

1. Open the ClipBook Viewer.

2. Click the Clipboard window.

3. Choose Edit ➤ Delete, and then click Yes.

UNDERSTANDING OLE

When you use the Clipboard to insert an item from a document in one application into a document in another application, you are inserting a static element. For example, if you insert an Excel worksheet or a portion of a worksheet into a Word document, the worksheet is not updated in Word when you update it in Excel. In addition, you cannot edit the worksheet in Word.

Most of the time, this is probably what you want. However, in some cases it is really helpful to insert a copy of a document that changes whenever it's edited in the originating application; it can also be useful to be able to edit the source document right inside the destination document. For example, you are working on a report that contains the next quarter's budget, which is in a state of flux. The report is created in Word, and the budget worksheet is being created in Excel. You have a couple of choices here:

► Insert a new copy of the worksheet every time it is updated.

► Insert a link to the worksheet so that changes to it are reflected in the Word document.

Obviously, the most efficient choice is to link to the worksheet. The technology that makes this possible is OLE (Object Linking and Embedding), which has been available in the Windows family of operating systems since Windows 3.1. OLE allows you to create *compound* documents that contain linked or embedded *objects*.

A compound document is simply one that consists of portions created in different applications. For example, our report might contain text created in Word, the budget worksheet created in Excel, and a company logo created in Paint. An object is the portion of the document that you either link or embed, and it can be text, graphics, sound, or video.

To use OLE, all the programs involved must support it. How can you tell if this is the case? If the Paste Special item is not present on the Edit menu, the program does not support linking and embedding. You'll see why this is important in the next section.

Before we get down to the nuts and bolts of linking and embedding, though, we need to define both these terms and explain the differences between them. When you *link* an object to a document, the document contains only a link to the object. To change the object, you edit the original file. Any such changes are reflected in the linked object.

When you *embed* an object in a document, the document contains a copy of the object. Any changes made to the original object are not reflected in the document unless the embedded object is updated. Embedding an object is rather similar to inserting a static element via the Clipboard; the difference is that you can click an embedded object to edit it in the application in which it was created.

Whether you link or embed an object depends on the situation. If it's important for the document to be current at all times, link the object. Otherwise, you can embed the object. Now, let's walk through the steps for doing both and take a look at how you edit an object.

Embedding Objects

To embed an object, follow these steps:

1. Open the application that contains the information you want to embed, and select the information.

2. Choose Edit ➢ Copy.

3. Open the document that will contain the embedded object.

4. Place the insertion point where you want the object, and then choose Edit ➤ Paste Special to open the Paste Special dialog box:

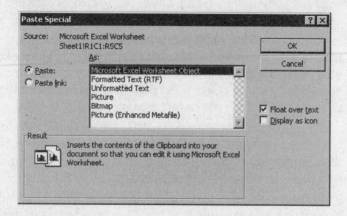

5. Click Paste, and select the format you want to use.

6. Click OK.

To edit an embedded object, follow these steps:

1. Open the document that contains the object.

2. Double-click the object to open it in an editing window that displays the tools and menus of the application in which the object was created.

3. Edit the object, and then click outside it.

Figure 9.5 shows an embedded object ready for editing.

TIP

To view an embedded object in Word, you need to be in Page Layout view.

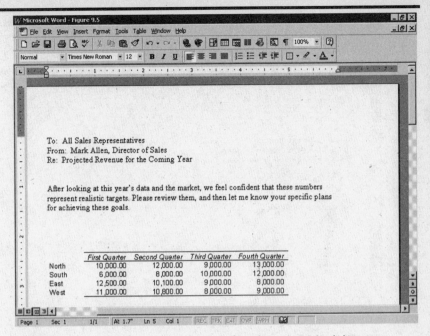

FIGURE 9.5: This Excel worksheet is ready for editing in a Word document.

Linking Objects

To link an object, follow these steps:

1. Open the application that contains the information you want to link, and select the information.

2. Choose Edit ➤ Copy.

3. Open the document that will contain the embedded object.

4. Choose Edit ➤ Paste Special to open the Paste Special dialog box.

5. Click Paste Link, and select a format for the object.

6. If you want to display a copy of the object in the document, click Float Over Text. If you want to display an icon instead, click Display As Icon.

7. Click OK.

Figure 9.6 shows a Word document with an icon that indicates an Excel worksheet is linked to the document.

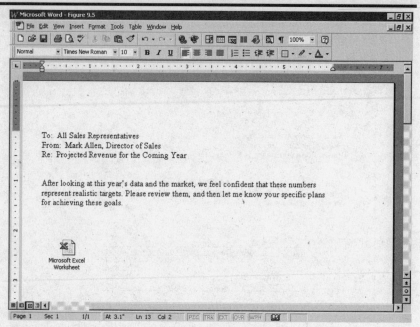

FIGURE 9.6: A Word document with a linked Excel worksheet

To edit a linked object, follow these steps:

1. Open the document that contains the link.

2. Double-click the link (whether it floats on the page or is an icon) to open the originating application and the document that contains the information that was linked, and make your changes.

3. Save the file, and then close the application. Changes are reflected in the linked object.

COMMUNICATING AND SHARING WITH NETMEETING

NetMeeting is an application that you can use to do the following:

► Chat with someone over the Internet, via a telephone or by typing on the screen

► Audio conference

- ▶ Video conference
- ▶ Share applications
- ▶ Collaborate on documents
- ▶ Transfer files
- ▶ Draw on the Whiteboard

Obviously, you need the proper equipment to do some of these, and, as we look at the individual features of NetMeeting, we'll point that out.

Starting NetMeeting

Before you can use NetMeeting for the first time, you need to configure it a bit and give it some information about yourself. You do this with a Wizard that starts up the first time you open NetMeeting (choose Start ➤ Programs ➤ Accessories ➤ Communications ➤ NetMeeting). After you complete the setup, NetMeeting places a shortcut to itself on your Desktop so that you need only to click the shortcut to start the program.

Let's go quickly through the steps you need to take before you can work (and have fun) with NetMeeting. The first screen presents an overview of NetMeeting. Take a look at it, click Next, and then follow these steps:

1. In the boxes provided, enter at least your first name, your last name, and your e-mail address, and then click Next.

2. If you want to log on to a directory server whenever you start NetMeeting, click Log On To A Directory Server When Net-Meeting Starts. If you don't want your name to appear in the directory listing for that server, click Do Not List My Name In The Directory. Click Next.

NOTE

Directory servers are maintained by organizations or companies and provide a list of people who are logged on to the server and have chosen to display their names. If you are connected to the Internet and log on to a directory server, you can click a name in the list to connect to that person. We'll look at exactly how this works in a later section in this chapter and also talk about why you might or might not want to display your name.

3. In the next screen, specify your modem speed or connection mode, and then click Next.

4. If you want quick access to NetMeeting, leave the options selected in this screen so that you display a shortcut to Net-Meeting on your Desktop and an icon on the Quick Launch bar. Click Next to start the Audio Tuning Wizard, and then click Next again.

5. If you have sound equipment (speakers and a sound card), click the Test button to sample the volume, and then change it as necessary.

6. If you have a microphone, speak into it to ensure that the record volume is correct. Click Next.

7. Click Finish.

You're now ready to start using NetMeeting, which is shown in Figure 9.7.

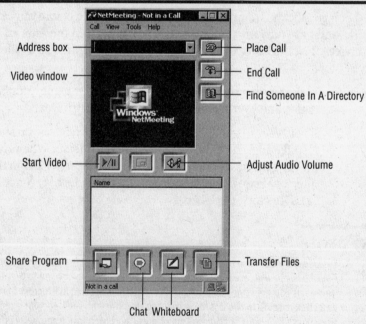

Address box
Video window

Place Call
End Call
Find Someone In A Directory

Start Video

Adjust Audio Volume

Share Program

Transfer Files

Chat Whiteboard

FIGURE 9.7: The opening NetMeeting window

Making a Call

When you make a call in NetMeeting, you can use an e-mail address, an IP address, a network address, or a modem phone number for the person you are calling. The only requirement is that both people must be running NetMeeting.

When you make the connection, you can communicate in several ways, depending on your equipment:

▶ If both people have microphones, sound cards, and speakers, you can talk just as you would over the telephone.

▶ If both people have microphones, sound cards, speakers, video cards, and video cameras, you can talk and be seen on the screen.

▶ If you don't have any of this equipment or just prefer it, you can communicate via the Chat application.

NOTE

You can see video even if you don't have a camera, and you can hear another person who is using a microphone if you have speakers. Video runs in the Video window.

To make a call, follow these steps:

1. Click the Place Call button to open the Place A Call dialog box:

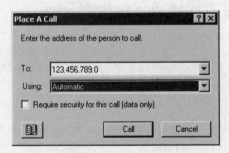

2. In the To box, enter the address (an IP address, an e-mail address, a modem phone number, or the name of the computer).

3. Click Call.

FINDING AN IP ADDRESS

An IP (Internet Protocol) address is a unique number that identifies your computer on the Internet, for example, 209.254.117.155. The first three parts of this number refer to your ISP (Internet Service Provider), and the last three digits refer to your computer. Unless you have a permanent connection to the Internet such as your ISP has, each time you log on you are assigned a different IP address. As we've mentioned, using an IP address is one way to connect through NetMeeting with others who are on the Internet.

To find out what your current IP address is, follow these steps:

1. Choose Start ➤ Run.

2. In the Open box, type **ipconfig** to open the IP Configuration dialog box.

Now you can share your IP address with someone who wants to call you. We've done this via e-mail before, and it works great. If the person you want to call is not running Windows 2000 but Windows 95/98 instead, he or she can type **winipcfg** to find out his or her IP address. Remember, though, every time you disconnect from the Internet or lose your connection, you lose that IP address. You'll get another one when you connect again.

Using the Chat Application

If you've visited chat rooms on the Web, you know how to use chat. What you type appears on the screen for you and others to see. Figure 9.8 shows the Chat window. To open Chat, click the Chat button in the main NetMeeting window.

To use Chat, you need to know only the following:

▶ Click in the Message box, type, and press Enter to send your words of wisdom.

▶ If the session involves more than one person, click the down arrow in the Send To box to specify whether to send your chat lines to an individual or to the whole group.

▶ To save the contents of a Chat session, choose File ➤ Save As.

▶ To end a session, close the Chat window.

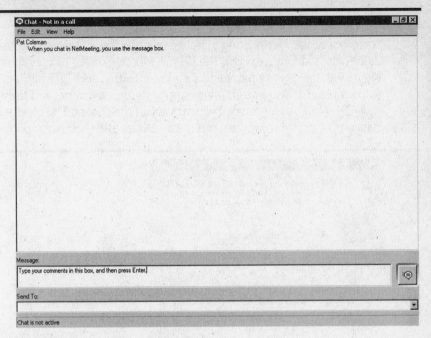

FIGURE 9.8: Chatting in NetMeeting

TIP

To customize the format of the Chat window, such as the fonts used and the display of information, choose View ➢ Options.

Using Directory Servers

As we mentioned earlier, a directory server is a service maintained by an organization or a company, and when you connect to it, you can see the names, e-mail addresses, and so on of all the others who are logged on and have chosen to display their names. You can also see whether they are available for video and audio transmission.

By default, NetMeeting points you to the Microsoft Internet Directory service. To log on to it, choose Call ➢ Directory, which opens the Find Someone dialog box. To communicate with someone on the list, click the name. NetMeeting locates the computer of the person and displays a message that someone is calling. If the other person accepts the call, you are connected and ready to interact.

Hosting a Meeting

You can also use NetMeeting to hold a meeting. To set this up, choose Call ➢ Host Meeting to open the Host A Meeting dialog box, as shown in Figure 9.9. Specify the parameters for the meeting, such as whether only you can place or accept calls, share applications, and so on, and then click OK. Now others can call you or you can call others. The meeting lasts until you end it (or until you or the others lose their connections).

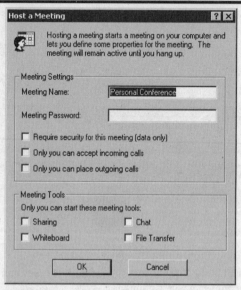

FIGURE 9.9: Setting the guidelines for a meeting

Using Video

When you are receiving or sending video, images are displayed in the video window. To set up video transmissions, choose Tools ➢ Options to open the Options dialog box, and click the Video tab, which is shown in Figure 9.10. You can specify when to send and receive video, the size of the image, its quality (do you want speed or clarity?), and the properties of your camera.

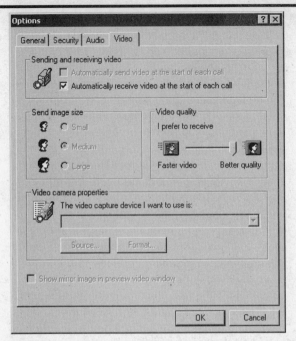

FIGURE 9.10: Setting up video transmission

Sharing Applications

While you are in a call or in a meeting, you can share documents and applications. To do so, open the program you want to share, and then click the Share Program button to open the Sharing dialog box, as shown in Figure 9.11. Specify the program to share and who will control it, and then click Close. Others will now be able to see and interact with you and your application.

NOTE

To share the Whiteboard, click the Whiteboard button.

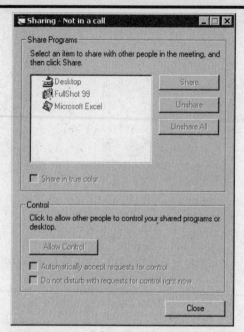

FIGURE 9.11: Getting ready to share an application

Transferring Files

Whenever you are in a call, you can transfer files. Simply click the Transfer Files button to open the File Transfer dialog box, and follow these steps:

1. Click Add File to select the file to send.

2. Click the name of the person to whom you want to send the file.

3. Click Send All.

To receive a file, click Accept. Received files are stored in the Received File folder in the NetMeeting folder, unless you specify otherwise.

What's Next?

Windows 2000 Professional comes with a number of applications that
you access from the Accessories menu. In the next chapter, Pat Coleman
and Peter Dyson will close out this part of the book with an overview of
how to access and use these applications.

Chapter 10

USING THE WINDOWS 2000 PROFESSIONAL APPLICATIONS

To access the applications that are included with Windows 2000 Professional, you choose Start ➢ Programs ➢ Accessories. The Accessories menu includes a number of items that are standard issue with Windows, such as Games and Notepad. If you haven't noticed, however, the Accessories menu now contains Windows Explorer and a few other relocated items.

Adapted from *Windows 2000 Professional: In Record Time*, by Peter Dyson and Pat Coleman

ISBN 0-7821-2450-X   467 pages $29.99

We look at some of these programs in other chapters:

- ▶ Chapter 5 discusses the Accessibility applet.
- ▶ Chapter 9 discusses NetMeeting.
- ▶ Chapter 15 discusses Phone Dialer.

You may find that you frequently use some of the applications on the Accessories menu and never use others. Nevertheless, after working through this chapter, you'll know where to find an applet when you need it, and you'll know how to use it. Let's begin by looking at how you can use your computer as a media player and as a recorder.

LISTENING TO SOUNDS, WATCHING MOVIES, AND RECORDING

Whether you ever do so or not, you probably know that you can play audio CDs from your CD drive, watch movies using the Windows Media Player, and, if you have the proper equipment, make sound recordings.

Playing Audio CDs

Playing an audio CD is probably the easiest thing you'll ever do with your computer: just put the CD in the drive and close it. In a second or two, CD Player will display on your screen. In Windows 2000 Professional, CD Player has a sleek, new look. As you can see in Figure 10.1, it resembles the CD player you might have in your car and even has some of the same buttons and dials.

TIP

If you don't want the CD to play automatically, hold down Shift while you insert the CD.

Volume Control
Mute

Pause   Scan   Next   Mode
Forward Track

Scan   Previous Stop Eject
Back   Track

FIGURE 10.1: You use the Windows 2000 Professional CD Player in much the same way you use any CD player.

Before we get into how you actually use CD Player, we need to explore one new feature. When you put a new CD in the drive, in a second or two, before the music starts, you'll see the following dialog box:

To download information about the artist, title, and tracks, click one of the option buttons. As the music begins to play, CD Player looks at a site on the Internet for this data (if you are connected to the Internet). If it can't find it, you'll see the message "The album was not found on the Internet."

By default, CD Player searches the Tunes.com site. You can, instead, search another site: Music Boulevard. To do so, follow these steps:

1. In CD Player, click Internet.

2. Choose Internet Music Sites ➢ Go To Music Boulevard.

This information is stored in the Album Information database. To display it, click Options, choose Preferences, and click the Playlist tab.

Now let's look at the controls in CD Player. Table 10.1 shows what each one does.

TABLE 10.1: The CD Player Controls

CONTROL	WHAT IT DOES
Pause	Stops the CD. When you click Pause, this control then becomes the Start button.
Stop	Halts the playing of the CD. To start it again, click the Pause button until it becomes the Start button, and then click again.
Eject	Opens the CD-ROM drive.
Scan Back	Moves backward through the current track bit by bit.
Scan Forward	Moves forward through the current track bit by bit.
Previous Track	Plays the previous track.
Next Track	Plays the next track.
Mode	Opens a menu of playing modes, including Standard, Random, Repeat Track, Repeat All, and Preview. Selecting Preview plays a snippet from the beginning of each track.
Volume Control	Adjusts the volume. With the hand that appears, click and drag the little red button to raise or lower the volume.
Mute	Silences the music. This works just like the Mute button on your TV remote control. The CD continues to play, but you can't hear it.

In this section, we haven't covered everything you'd ever want to know about CD Player, but it's enough to get you started. One way to get the hang of it is to experiment. You can also open CD Player, click the Options button, and choose CD Player Help.

TIP
You can also manually open CD Player. To do so, choose Start ➤ Programs ➤ Accessories ➤ Entertainment ➤ CD Player.

Adjusting the Volume

In the last section, you saw how to adjust the volume on CD Player by turning the "knob." You can also adjust the volume of the current sound by left-clicking the Volume icon in the Taskbar. You'll see a slider bar like this:

To adjust the volume of the CD Player as well as other sounds, use the Volume Control dialog box, as shown in Figure 10.2. To open the Volume Control dialog box, right-click the Volume icon, and choose Open Volume Controls from the shortcut menu, or choose Start ➤ Programs ➤ Accessories ➤ Entertainment ➤ Volume Control.

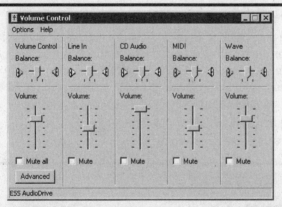

FIGURE 10.2: What you see in the Volume Control dialog box depends on which sound devices are installed on your computer.

The features you see in the Volume Control dialog box depend on the sound devices you have on your computer. For example, if you have a microphone, you'll see a control for it; if you don't have a microphone, you won't. Thus, you may see some or all these devices or more:

▸ Volume Control is the master switch. It controls the volume and balance of all sounds coming out of your computer.

▶ Line In controls volume and balance for an audio tap, an FM tuner, or a similar device.

▶ CD Audio controls the volume and balance for an audio CD you play in your CD-ROM drive.

▶ MIDI, pronounced "middy," is an acronym for Musical Instrument Digital Interface, which is the format in which synthesized sounds are stored on your computer. Use the MIDI control to adjust their volume and balance.

▶ Wave sets the volume and balance for playing .wav files. The sounds that accompany many Windows actions, such as exiting Windows, are .wav files. If you'd rather not hear them, click the Mute button in the Wave control.

To adjust the volume or balance of any control, move its slider. If you want to make even finer adjustments to your audio, click the Advanced button to open the Advanced Controls For Volume Control dialog box.

Recording Sounds

If you have all the necessary equipment, you can make your own voice recordings or record from another sound source. To make voice recordings, you need a microphone and a sound card. To record sounds from another device such as an audio CD or a stereo receiver, you'll need a Line In connector to your sound card.

To open Sound Recorder, which is shown in Figure 10.3, choose Start ➢ Programs ➢ Accessories ➢ Entertainment ➢ Sound Recorder.

FIGURE 10.3: The Sound Recorder dialog box

Use the buttons at the bottom of the Sound Recorder dialog box to control recording and playback:

- ▶ Seek To Start moves to the beginning of a sound file.

- ▶ Seek To End moves to the end of a sound file.

- ▶ Play starts the playback of a recording.

- ▶ Stop ends playing or recording.

- ▶ Record begins the recording process.

To make a voice recording, follow these steps:

1. Open Sound Recorder.

2. Choose File ➢ New.

3. Turn on your microphone.

4. Choose File ➢ Properties to open the Properties For Sound dialog box.

5. In the Choose From drop-down list, select Recording Formats, and click Convert Now to open the Sound Selection dialog box.

6. In the Name drop-down list, select a recording quality—CD, radio, or telephone.

7. Click OK twice.

8. Click the Record button, and speak into the microphone.

9. When you're finished, click Stop.

10. Choose File ➢ Save As to save your recording as a file.

Using Windows Media Player

You use Windows Media Player to play audio, video, and mixed-media files that you find on the Internet or that are stored on your local area network or your own system. When you open one of these files, Media Player starts automatically, behind the scenes. Before we get into the nuts and bolts of how Media Player works, let's take a look at what it does. Follow these steps:

1. Connect to the Internet, and open Internet Explorer.

2. Go to www.hipclips.com.

3. Select a clip.

In a small window on the left, the clip loads and plays. And that's all there is to it.

NOTE

Your Internet viewing and listening experience will be more satisfying if you have at least a 56Kbps connection.

Now let's take a look at Media Player itself. To open Media Player, choose Start ➤ Programs ➤ Accessories ➤ Entertainment ➤ Windows Media Player, or choose Start ➤ Run, type **mplayer2** in the Open box, and press Enter. You'll see the screen shown in Figure 10.4.

TIP

If you know the name of the file you want to play, you can also type it in the Open box (for example, mplayer2 http://webserver/directory/filename).

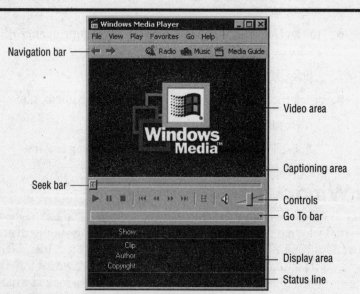

FIGURE 10.4: The Windows Media Player

Depending on the type of media file you are playing, you'll see the following components in the Windows Media Player:

Navigation bar   Click the Forward and Back buttons to open a file you played earlier in the current session; click Web Events to go to WindowsMedia.com, which contains a number of links to media files that you can play and download.

Video area   The video you are viewing displays in this area.

Captioning area   If the file you are playing provides it, this area displays closed-captioning. (Choose View ➤ Captions.)

Seek bar   If the content of the file you are playing makes the Seek bar available, you can drag the slider bar to play a specific section of the clip.

Controls   The controls in Media Player correspond to those on your audio CD player, and you use them in exactly the same way.

Go To bar   Click the down arrow to display a list of markers in the file, if the file provides it. Click a marker to play the section of the file associated with the marker.

Display area   If the file provides it, this area displays the show title, clip title, author, and copyright notice.

Status line   This area displays icons for sound and closed captioning and the following information for the current playing file:

- ▶ Connecting
- ▶ Buffering
- ▶ Playing
- ▶ Paused
- ▶ Reception quality
- ▶ Time elapsed
- ▶ Total time

Most of the time, the files you access with Media Player will be those you find on the Internet. You need to know that these files are in streaming media format, which means that as the file is transmitted to your computer it begins playing before all of it is stored in memory. As the file plays, Media Player stores the rest in memory. If you have a slow connection, the play may be jerky at first.

You'll need the very latest version of Media Player to play some files, and you can download it by choosing Go ➤ Windows Media Player Home Page.

Before we, of necessity, leave this all-too-brief discussion of Media Player, we need to take a look at the types of files you can play with it:

Microsoft Windows Media Formats   These files have the extensions .avi, .asf, .asx, .rmi, and .wav.

Moving Pictures Experts Group (MPEG)   These files have the extensions .mpg, .mpeg, .m1v, .mp2, .mpa, and .mpe.

Musical Instrument Digital Interface (MIDI)   These files have the extensions .mid and .rmi.

Apple QuickTime®, Macintosh® AIFF Resource   These files have the extensions .qt, .aif, .aifc, .aiff, and .mov.

Unix Formats   These files have the extensions .au and .snd.

TIP

For much more information about Media Player, including how to customize it, choose Help in Media Player.

PLAYING GAMES

And now we come to what many consider an essential life skill: playing computer games. A stroll down the games aisle of any software emporium will be enough to convince you, if you aren't already convinced, of the enormous popularity of computer games. In addition, you can download games from many Web sites.

Your easiest access to games, however, is through the Games item on the Accessories menu in Windows 2000 Professional (choose Start ➤ Programs ➤ Accessories ➤ Games). In previous versions, Windows included four games: Hearts, Solitaire, FreeCell, and Minesweeper. In Windows 2000 Professional, Hearts has been replaced with Pinball.

In this section, we're going to take a brief look at each of these games and show you their interfaces. We won't get into step-by-step instructions for a couple of reasons. First, you probably already know how to play most of them, and, second, if you don't, all you need to do is open the game and choose Help. Let's start with the old favorite and one of the world's greatest time-wasters, Solitaire.

Solitaire

Solitaire is the American name given to a number of card games that can be played by one person. The English name for the game is Patience. When you open the game, the first hand is dealt for you, as Figure 10.5 shows. To deal a new game after you complete one, choose Game ➤ Deal. To turn over cards from the deck, click the deck; to move a card or a stack of cards, drag it.

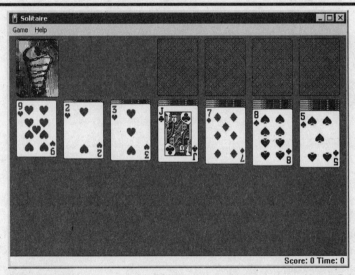

FIGURE 10.5: You can choose from among 12 decks when playing Solitaire.

FreeCell

Unlike Solitaire, it is believed (though not proven) that it is possible to win every game of FreeCell. Like Solitaire, in FreeCell you lay out a tableau of cards and then attempt to arrange them in their respective suits. The object is to move all the cards to the home cells, stacked by suits in order from ace through king. To start a game, choose Game ➤ New Game. Figure 10.6 shows a freshly dealt hand of FreeCell.

Free cells   Home cells

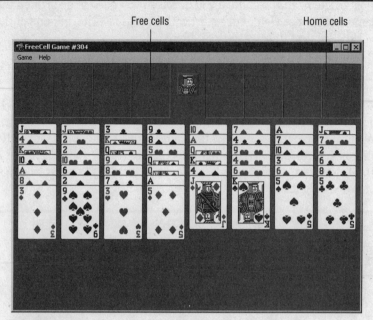

FIGURE 10.6: In theory, you can win every game of FreeCell.

Minesweeper

Minesweeper has to do with deduction and logic. The object is to uncover all the squares in a minefield that don't contain mines and to mark the squares that do contain mines as quickly as possible. (We prefer not to think about any real-world analogy to this game.) Figure 10.7 shows the opening grid of Minesweeper.

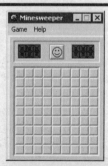

FIGURE 10.7: Click a square to uncover it.

Pinball

Space Cadet 3D Pinball is the electronic version of the pinball machines found in the typical arcade. Unlike the other three Windows games, Pinball is played with the keyboard. The object is to launch the ball and earn lots of points by hitting bumpers, targets, and flags. You begin each game with three balls and at the rank of Cadet. Figure 10.8 shows a game in progress. Even if you aren't a pinball wizard, open and start this game just to hear the great sound effects (unless you're at work, of course).

FIGURE 10.8: A game of Pinball in progress

And that's a very quick trip through the game scene in Windows 2000 Professional. Now, let's get back to business.

KEEPING TRACK OF YOUR CONTACTS

Although Address Book is a great time-saver when you're composing e-mail since it can automatically store the e-mail address of anyone to whom you reply, you can use Address Book to store much more than e-mail addresses. If you want, it can become the central repository of all the information you need to keep about your contacts, including:

▶ Home and business addresses

- ▶ Phone, fax, pager, and mobile numbers
- ▶ Web page addresses
- ▶ Job-related data
- ▶ Personal info such as spouse's name, children's names, anniversaries, and birthdays
- ▶ Conferencing connections
- ▶ Digital IDs

Opening Address Book

You can open Address Book in the following ways:

- ▶ Choose Start ➤ Programs ➤ Accessories ➤ Address Book.
- ▶ In Outlook Express, click Addresses on the toolbar in the main window. (Chapter 16 discusses Outlook Express.)
- ▶ When composing a message in Outlook Express, click the To or Cc icon in the New Message window.

Figure 10.9 shows the Address Book window, empty and waiting to be filled with contact information.

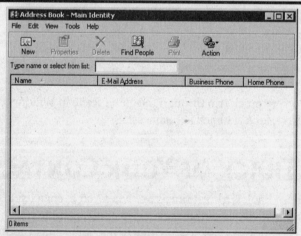

FIGURE 10.9: The main Address Book window

Adding a New Contact

To add information for a new contact, follow these steps:

1. In Address Book, click the New icon, and then choose New Contact to open the Properties dialog box:

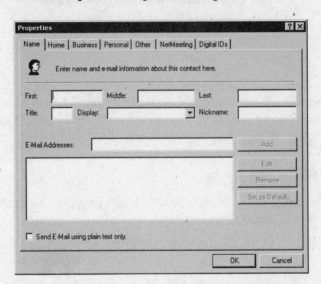

2. Fill in as much or as little information as you want on the tabs, which include Name, Home, Business, Personal, Other, NetMeeting, and Digital IDs.

3. When you're finished, click OK.

Now you'll see your new contact's information in the main window.

Adding a New Group

You can also set up a group, or distribution list, in Address Book, which lets you send the same message or file to a number of people without entering all their e-mail addresses. Follow these steps:

1. Click the New icon, and then choose New Group to open the Properties dialog box.

2. In the Group Name box, type a name for the group.

3. Click Select Members to open the Select Group Members dialog box.

4. Select a name from the Name list, and click the Select button for the names you want to add to the group. (You can use all the usual Windows selecting techniques.)

5. Click OK.

The group name now appears in boldface in the Name list in the main window.

Once you have collected some information in your Address Book, you can sort the list in a number of ways: by name, e-mail address, business phone, home phone, first name, last name, and so on. To do so, choose View ➢ Sort By, and then select a sorting style from the list.

Locating People

You can also use Address Book to locate people in the various directory services. Follow these steps:

1. In the main window, click Find People to open the Find People dialog box.

2. Click the Look In down arrow to display the list of services you can search.

3. Select a service, and then fill in the information you know about this person.

4. Click Find Now.

Printing Your Address Book

If you ever need or want to, you can print your Address Book. Simply click the Print icon to open the Print dialog box. You can print in three formats:

Memo   Prints all the information you have stored for selected contacts

Business Card   Prints the information from Address Book that you would typically find on a business card

Phone List   Prints all phone numbers you have stored for the selected contact

Creating a Map

To display a map for a specific address, connect to the Internet, and follow these steps:

1. In the Address Book main window, right-click a name, and choose Properties from the shortcut menu to open the Properties dialog box for that person.

2. Click either the Home or Business tab, whichever contains the address you want to map.

3. Click View Map.

You'll see something similar to Figure 10.10.

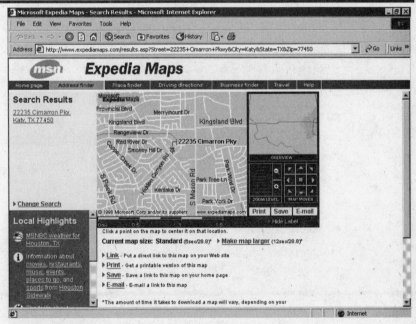

FIGURE 10.10: Creating a map in Address Book

IMPORTING AND EXPORTING AN ADDRESS BOOK

If you have an address book in any of the following, you can import it into the Windows 2000 Professional Address Book:

▶ Eudora Pro or Light Address Book (through version 3)

▶ LDIF – LDAP Data Interchange Format

▶ Microsoft Exchange Personal Address Book

▶ Microsoft Internet Mail for Windows 3.1 Address Book

▶ Netscape Address Book (version 2 or 3)

▶ Netscape Communicator Address Book (version 4)

▶ Text File (Comma Separated Values)

To import an address book, follow these steps:

1. In the Address Book main window, choose File ➢ Import, and then select either Address Book (WAB) or Other Address Book.

2. Select the file.

3. Click Import.

You can also export a Windows 2000 Professional Address Book that you create to any of the following:

▶ Other Windows Address Book files

▶ Microsoft Exchange Personal Address Book

▶ Text File (Comma Separated Values)

To export your Address Book, follow the earlier steps for importing, but choose Export instead.

DOING MATH

Calculator is simply an on-screen version of the handheld variety, and, essentially, you use it in the same way. It's available in two versions: Standard and Scientific. When you open Calculator (choose Start ➢ Programs ➢ Accessories ➢ Calculator), it displays in the version last used. Figure 10.11 shows Calculator open in Standard view. To change the view, choose View, and then select Standard or Scientific. If you want results displayed with comma separators, choose View ➢ Digit Grouping.

FIGURE 10.11: Calculator in Standard view

In Standard and Scientific view, Calculator has the following keys:

*   Represents the multiplication sign (×).

/   Represents the division sign (÷).

Backspace   Erases a single digit.

CE   Clears the last entry. You can also press Delete to do the same thing.

C   Clears the calculation altogether. You can also press Escape to do the same thing.

MC   Clears a number from Calculator's memory.

MR   Recalls a number from Calculator's memory.

MS   Stores a number in Calculator's memory and removes what was already there.

M+   Adds a number to the number in Calculator's memory.

In Standard view, Calculator also has the following keys:

sqrt   Calculates the square root of a number.

%   Lets you add, subtract, divide, and multiply a number by a percentage.

1/x   Is the Inverse key. You use it to divide 1 by a value.

Using the Standard Calculator

To add, subtract, multiply, divide, and perform any other standard arithmetic operations, follow these steps:

TIP

You can select Calculator's buttons with the mouse, with the numbers at the top of the keyboard, or with the numeric keypad. To use the numeric keypad, press Num Lock.

1. Enter the first number in the calculation.

2. Click the operator key.

3. Enter the next number.

4. Click = to get the result.

Using the Scientific Calculator

Figure 10.12 shows Calculator in Scientific view. You use this view to calculate logarithms, to convert values to other number systems, and to perform statistical calculations.

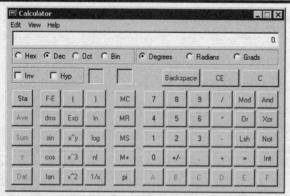

FIGURE 10.12: Calculator in Scientific view

To perform a scientific calculation, follow these steps:

1. Click an option button to select a number system:

   Hex   Hexadecimal

   Dec   Decimal

   Oct   Octal

   Bin   Binary

2. Enter the first number, and then click an operator.

3. Click = to display the result.

To perform a statistical calculation, follow these steps:

1. Click Sta to open the Statistics Box:

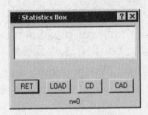

2. Click Dat to enter the data.

3. Continue to enter numbers, clicking Dat after each.

4. Click Sta to once again display the Statistics Box, and click RET to return to Calculator.

5. Click the statistics function you want.

The Statistics Box contains the following buttons:

RET   Closes the Statistics Box

LOAD   Displays the number selected in the Statistics Box in Calculator's display area

CD   Removes the selected number

CAD   Clears the Statistics Box

CREATING TEXT DOCUMENTS

Windows 2000 Professional includes a couple of word-processing programs: Notepad and WordPad. Notepad is a simple text editor, and WordPad is a simple word processor. Which you use depends on the task at hand, but you will, no doubt, use a full-fledged, fully featured word-processing program, such as Microsoft Word, most of the time when you create large, complicated documents.

In this section, we'll take a look at both Notepad and WordPad and discuss how to put each to its best use.

Using Notepad

As we just pointed out, Notepad is a simple text editor, which means that you can use it to view and edit only .txt files. Such files are pure text and contain only basic formatting. Normally, you use Notepad to display the contents of the Clipboard, program files, ReadMe files, and your autoexec.bat and config.sys files.

In previous versions, Notepad could not open any file that was larger than 64KB; if you attempted to do so, you received a message asking if you'd rather open the file in WordPad instead. With Windows 2000 Professional, this has changed. Notepad can now load at least a 7MB file. And this is good news for those who like to create Web pages by handcoding HTML rather than using an HTML editor such as Microsoft FrontPage.

When you use Notepad to create HTML documents, there is no way that you can accidentally save special formatting. Special characters inserted in an HTML document may not appear when the page is opened in a Web browser, and, in addition, they can even produce errors.

When you open a Web page in Internet Explorer and choose View ➤ Source, the HTML document opens in Notepad. Figure 10.13 shows the underlying source for a Web page open as an HTML document in Notepad.

Now, let's take a brief look at how to use Notepad to enter text.

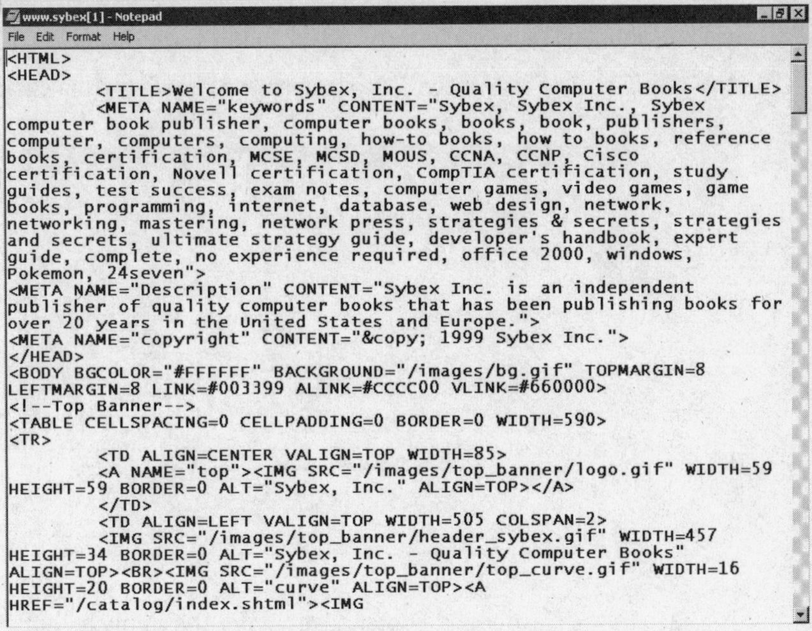


```
<HTML>
<HEAD>
        <TITLE>Welcome to Sybex, Inc. - Quality Computer Books</TITLE>
        <META NAME="keywords" CONTENT="Sybex, Sybex Inc., Sybex
computer book publisher, computer books, books, book, publishers,
computer, computers, computing, how-to books, how to books, reference
books, certification, MCSE, MCSD, MOUS, CCNA, CCNP, Cisco
certification, Novell certification, CompTIA certification, study
guides, test success, exam notes, computer games, video games, game
books, programming, internet, database, web design, network,
networking, mastering, network press, strategies & secrets, strategies
and secrets, ultimate strategy guide, developer's handbook, expert
guide, complete, no experience required, office 2000, windows,
Pokemon, 24seven">
<META NAME="Description" CONTENT="Sybex Inc. is an independent
publisher of quality computer books that has been publishing books for
over 20 years in the United States and Europe.">
<META NAME="copyright" CONTENT="&copy; 1999 Sybex Inc.">
</HEAD>
<BODY BGCOLOR="#FFFFFF" BACKGROUND="/images/bg.gif" TOPMARGIN=8
LEFTMARGIN=8 LINK=#003399 ALINK=#CCCC00 VLINK=#660000>
<!--Top Banner-->
<TABLE CELLSPACING=0 CELLPADDING=0 BORDER=0 WIDTH=590>
<TR>
        <TD ALIGN=CENTER VALIGN=TOP WIDTH=85>
        <A NAME="top"><IMG SRC="/images/top_banner/logo.gif" WIDTH=59
HEIGHT=59 BORDER=0 ALT="Sybex, Inc." ALIGN=TOP></A>
        </TD>
        <TD ALIGN=LEFT VALIGN=TOP WIDTH=505 COLSPAN=2>
        <IMG SRC="/images/top_banner/header_sybex.gif" WIDTH=457
HEIGHT=34 BORDER=0 ALT="Sybex, Inc. - Quality Computer Books"
ALIGN=TOP><BR><IMG SRC="/images/top_banner/top_curve.gif" WIDTH=16
HEIGHT=20 BORDER=0 ALT="curve" ALIGN=TOP><A
HREF="/catalog/index.shtml"><IMG
```

FIGURE 10.13: You can safely view and edit HTML documents in Notepad.

Creating a Document in Notepad

To begin a document in Notepad, simply open Notepad (choose Start ➢ Programs ➢ Accessories ➢ Notepad), and start typing. To start a new paragraph, press Enter. To delete the preceding character, press Backspace. To delete several characters, a sentence, a paragraph, and so on, select the text by dragging the mouse over it, and press Delete.

Also new to this version of Notepad (which is version 5) is the Format menu. After you enter text, select it, choose Format ➢ Font to open the Font dialog box, and choose a font, style (Regular, Italic, Bold, Bold Italic), and size for your text.

If you are creating a document of several pages and want to insert headers and footers on the printed pages, follow these steps:

1.   Choose File ➤ Page Setup to open the Page Setup dialog box:

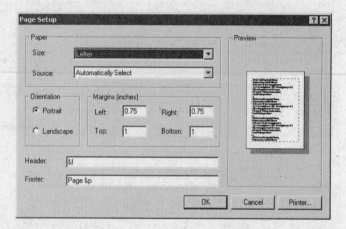

2.   In the Header and Footer boxes, enter the character and letter combination shown in Table 10.2 that corresponds to the information you want.

TABLE 10.2: Entering Header and Footer Information

TO DO THIS	TYPE THIS
Insert the filename	&f
Insert the date	&d
Insert the time	&t
Insert page numbers	&p
Left-align the header or footer	&l
Center the header or footer	&c
Right-align the header or footer	&r

3.   Ensure that the paper size, orientation, and margins are the way you want them, and click OK.

NOTE

For information about printing in Windows 2000 Professional, see Chapter 8.

If you've used previous versions of Notepad, you may have noticed that the menu bar no longer contains the Search menu. Find and Replace commands have been relocated on the Edit menu. The Edit menu now also contains a Go To command. To go to a specific line of text, choose Edit ➢ Go To to open the Goto Line dialog box, enter a line number, and click OK.

Opening and Saving a File in Notepad

To open a file in Notepad, choose File ➢ Open to display the standard Windows Open dialog box, select the file, and click Open.

To save a file you just created in Notepad, choose File ➢ Save As to open the standard Windows Save As dialog box, locate the folder in which you want to store the document, give the file a name, and choose Save.

To save a file you've saved before, choose File ➢ Save.

Using WordPad

To open WordPad, choose Start ➢ Programs ➢ Accessories ➢ WordPad. If you've used other Windows word processors, this screen, which is shown in Figure 10.14, will look familiar. Figure 10.14 contains labels for the buttons on the standard toolbar, and Table 10.3 explains what these buttons do.

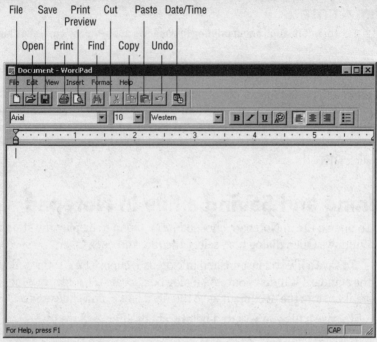

FIGURE 10.14: WordPad includes several of the features you'd find in a full-fledged word-processing program, such as Microsoft Word.

TABLE 10.3: The Toolbar Buttons in WordPad

BUTTON	WHAT IT DOES
New	Opens a new, blank document
Open	Opens an existing document
Save	Saves your document
Print	Prints your document
Print Preview	Displays on-screen what your printed document will look like
Find	Searches for text you specify
Cut	Moves your selection to the Clipboard
Copy	Duplicates your selection on the Clipboard
Paste	Inserts the contents of the Clipboard at the insertion point
Undo	Reverses your last action
Date/Time	Inserts the current date and time

As we pointed out, Notepad provides only minimal, basic formatting. WordPad, on the other hand, provides a great many formatting features, including bullets and the ability to format text in colors. To format, you can use the commands on the Format menu, or you can use the Format bar:

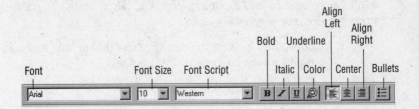

Table 10.4 describes what the Format buttons do. If you don't see the Format bar on your screen, choose View ➤ Format Bar.

TABLE 10.4: The Buttons on the Format Bar

BUTTON	WHAT IT DOES
Font	Displays a drop-down list of fonts you can use for the current text selection.
Font Size	Displays a drop-down list of font point sizes you can use for the current text selection.
Font Script	Displays a drop-down list of eight non-Western alphabets you can use if your keyboard and system are set up to do so.
Bold	Boldfaces the current text selection.
Italic	Italicizes the current text selection.
Underline	Underlines the current text selection.
Color	Displays a list box of colors you can use to color the current text selection.
Align Left	Left-aligns the current text selection.
Center	Centers the current text selection horizontally.
Align Right	Right-aligns the current text selection.
Bullets	Turns the selected paragraphs into a list of bullet points. Click the Bullets tool again to return to regular text formatting.

Creating a Document with WordPad

You create a basic document in WordPad much as you would in Notepad, but you have a great many more options for formatting and for choosing formats in which to save your documents. (Interestingly enough, you can't insert headers and footers in WordPad documents.) To create a document, follow these general steps:

1. Choose File ➤ New to open the New dialog box, and select a type for your document. The choices are:

   ▶ Word 6 Document

   ▶ Rich Text Document

   ▶ Text Document

   ▶ Unicode Text Document

2. Click OK.

3. When WordPad asks if you want to save changes to this document, click Yes to open the Save As dialog box.

4. Select a folder in which to save the document, type the name for the document in the File Name box, and click Save.

5. Enter your text, and format it using the tools on the Format bar.

6. When you're finished, choose File ➤ Save to save the document.

You can now print your document if you need to distribute it that way, or you can send it as an e-mail attachment, as you'll see in the next section.

Sending a WordPad Document As an E-Mail Attachment

You will see in Chapter 16 how to attach a file to an e-mail message. In WordPad, you do the opposite: you create the file and then compose the message. Here are the steps:

1. After you create and save a document, choose File ➤ Send to display the New Message window in Outlook Express. The Attach line includes the document name.

2. Fill in the To and Subject lines, type your message, and click Send. A copy of your message is placed in your Outbox in Outlook Express.

3. If you want to send the message immediately, connect to the Internet, open Outlook Express, and click Send And Receive.

TIP

You can insert any of a number of objects in a WordPad document, including another WordPad document, a Word document, a bitmap image, a video clip, clip art, and a wave sound. To do so, choose Insert ➤ Object, and make a selection in the Insert Object dialog box.

DRAWING WITH PAINT

Paint is an application you can use to develop and edit graphic images: diagrams, logos, scanned photographs, original art, and so on. You can even set one of your creations as Desktop wallpaper. To open Paint, choose Start ➤ Programs ➤ Accessories ➤ Paint. You'll see the screen shown in Figure 10.15.

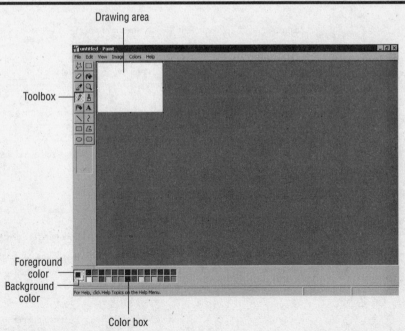

FIGURE 10.15: You can use Paint to create and edit graphic images.

To work with or create an image in Paint, you use the tools in the Toolbox, some of which are the electronic equivalents of the utensils you'd use on paper or canvas. Table 10.5 describes what each tool does.

TABLE 10.5: The Paint Tools

Tool	Name	What It Does
	Free-Form Select	Selects an irregularly shaped area of the image.
	Select	Selects a rectangular-shaped area of the image.
	Eraser/Color Eraser	Removes an area of the image as you move the eraser over it.
	Fill With Color	Fills an area with the color you selected.
	Pick Color	Selects the color of an object you click.
	Magnifier	Enlarges the area you select.
	Pencil	Draws a freehand line one pixel wide.
	Brush	Draws lines of different shapes and widths.
	Airbrush	Draws using an airbrush of the size you select.
	Text	Inserts text into an image.
	Line	Draws a straight line. Hold down Shift to create a really straight line.
	Curve	Draws a curved line.
	Rectangle	Draws a rectangle. Choose Rectangle, and hold down Shift to draw a square.

CONTINUED ➡

TABLE 10.5 CONTINUED: The Paint Tools

TOOL	NAME	WHAT IT DOES
	Polygon	Draws a figure of straight lines connecting at any angle.
	Ellipse	Draws an ellipse. Choose Ellipse and hold down Shift to draw a circle.
	Rounded Rectangle	Draws a rectangle that has curved corners.

To erase your most recent squiggle, choose Edit ➢ Undo, or press Ctrl+Z. To get rid of everything in the Drawing area and start over fresh, choose Edit ➢ Select All, and press Delete.

If you've never worked with Paint before, you'll find that it takes some practice to become comfortable with the drawing tools and to achieve the result you expect. Follow these steps to create a simple image:

1. Choose File ➢ New.

2. Optionally, choose Image ➢ Attributes to open the Attributes dialog box in which you can specify the size and shape of your picture, the unit of measure, color or black-and-white, and so on. Click OK when you're done.

3. Click a drawing tool to select it.

4. Choose a line width, brush shape, or rectangle type from the Toolbox.

5. Click a color in the color box to select a foreground color.

6. Right-click a color in the color box to select a background color.

7. When you're finished, choose File ➢ Save As to save your drawing.

By default, Paint saves your drawing in the number of colors set in the Settings tab of the Display Properties dialog box. To change this, click the down arrow in the Save As Type box, and select another type. You can save a Paint drawing in the following graphic formats:

- ▶ 256 Color Bitmap (*.bmp, *.dib)

- ▶ Monochrome Bitmap (*.bmp, *.dib)

- ▶ 16 Color Bitmap (*.bmp, *.dib)

- ▶ 24-bit Bitmap (*.bmp, *.dib)

DISPLAYING AND EDITING DIGITAL IMAGES

The Imaging application is not new to Windows 2000 Professional, and you may have used it in a previous version of Windows without realizing it. For example, unless you've associated another program with graphic files, clicking a graphic in Windows Explorer opens it in Imaging Preview. But you can use Imaging for much more than quickly displaying a graphic.

If you have a scanner or a digital camera, you can send images you capture with those devices directly to the Imaging application, in which you can resize them, change their colors, annotate them, change their file type, print them, send them as e-mail, and so on. An image can be any photograph, text, or drawing that is digitized.

NOTE

You also use Imaging to view and print received and sent faxes, as you will see in the last section in this chapter.

To open the Imaging application, choose Start ➤ Programs ➤ Accessories ➤ Imaging. Figure 10.16 shows a sample image open in Imaging.

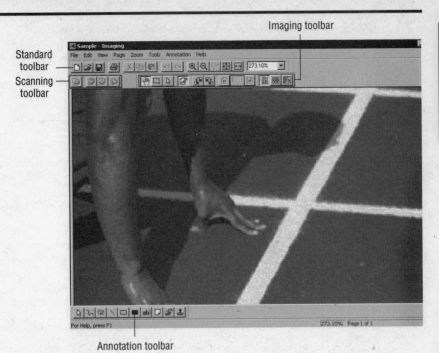

Imaging toolbar

Standard toolbar

Scanning toolbar

Annotation toolbar

FIGURE 10.16: A sample image open in the Imaging application

To capture or manipulate images, you use the tools on the Standard, Imaging, Annotation, and Scanning toolbars. Table 10.6 describes the tools on the Standard toolbar, Table 10.7 describes the tools on the Imaging toolbar, and Table 10.8 describes the tools on the Annotation toolbar. You'll notice that some of the tools on the Annotation toolbar are similar to those in Paint. If you have a scanner, you can use the tools on the Scanning toolbar to scan a new image, insert a scanned page, append a scanned page, and rescan a page.

TABLE 10.6: The Tools on the Standard Toolbar

TOOL	NAME	WHAT IT DOES
	New Blank Document	Creates a new, blank document
	Open	Opens an existing document

CONTINUED ➡

TABLE 10.6 CONTINUED: The Tools on the Standard Toolbar

TOOL	NAME	WHAT IT DOES
	Save	Saves the active document
	Print	Prints the active document
	Cut	Cuts the selection and places it on the Clipboard
	Copy	Copies the selection and places it on the Clipboard
	Paste	Inserts the Clipboard contents in the upper-left corner of the window
	Undo	Reverses the last action
	Redo	Redoes the last action that was undone
	Zoom In	Zooms the image to twice its current size
	Zoom Out	Zooms the image to half its current size
	Zoom To Selection	Zooms in on the current selection
	Best Fit	Displays the image to include the entire page in the window
	Fit To Width	Displays the image to fit the width of the window
273.10%	Zoom	Selects a predefined zoom factor

TABLE 10.7:   The Tools on the Imaging Toolbar

TOOL	NAME	WHAT IT DOES
	Drag	Selects the dragging tool
	Select Image	Selects the Image Selection tool
	Annotation Selection	Selects the Annotation Selection tool
	Annotation Toolbar	Displays or hides the Annotation toolbar
	Rotate Left	Rotates the current page 90 degrees to the left
	Rotate Right	Rotates the current page 90 degrees to the right
	Previous Page	Displays the previous page of the document, if there is one
	Page	Displays the page you specify
	Next Page	Displays the next page of the document, if there is one
	One Page View	Displays the document one page at a time
	Thumbnail View	Displays the pages of the document as thumbnails (little pictures)
	Page And Thumbnails View	Displays the active page and thumbnails

Part i

TABLE 10.8: The Tools on the Annotation Toolbar

Tool	Name	What It Does
	Annotation Selection	Selects the Annotation Selection tool
	Freehand Line	Selects the Freehand Line annotation tool
	Highlighter	Selects the Highlighter annotation tool
	Straight Line	Selects the Straight Line annotation tool
	Hollow Rectangle	Selects the Hollow Rectangle annotation tool
	Filled Rectangle	Selects the Filled Rectangle annotation tool
	Text	Selects the Text annotation tool
	Attach-A-Note	Selects the Attach-A-Note annotation tool
	Text From File	Selects the Text From File annotation tool
	Rubber Stamp	Select the Rubber Stamp annotation tool

Many of the items on the menus in Imaging duplicate tools found on the various toolbars, and the menus also include such standard Windows commands as File ➢ Save As and File ➢ Open. Some menu items are, however, specific to the Imaging application. Table 10.9 lists and explains those.

TABLE 10.9: Menu Items Specific to Imaging

Menu	Command	What It Does
File	New	Opens the New Blank Document dialog box, in which you can choose a file type, color, compression ratio, resolution, and size
	Color Management	Opens the Color Management dialog box, in which you can specify the color profiles in which pictures appear on your monitor or in print
View	Scale To Gray	Displays black-and-white images as grayscale images
Tools	General Options	Opens the General Options dialog box, in which you can specify how you want to view documents
	Scan Options	Opens the Scan Options dialog box, in which you can specify how to compress scanned images in terms of quality and size
	Thumbnail Size	Opens the Thumbnail Size dialog box, in which you can specify the size at which thumbnails display on the screen
Annotation	Make Annotations Permanent	Burns the annotations into the image so that they are no longer treated separately but as part of the image

USING YOUR COMPUTER AS A FAX MACHINE

If you have a fax modem, you can send and receive faxes with the Fax accessory. These days, most modems have fax and data capabilities. If you don't know whether your modem has fax capabilities, choose Start ➤ Settings ➤ Printers to open the Printers folder. If you have an icon for a fax printer, your modem has fax capabilities. Windows 2000 Professional detects this when you install the operating system and installs the fax service and the associated fax printer.

NOTE
You cannot share a fax printer with others on your network.

Sending a Fax

You can fax a document from within any Windows program that contains a Print command. For purposes of example, let's fax a document from WordPad and assume that this is your first time to fax a document in Windows 2000 Professional. Follow these steps:

1. Choose Start ➤ Programs ➤ Accessories ➤ WordPad to open WordPad.

2. Open an existing document, or create a new one.

3. Choose File ➤ Print to open the Print dialog box.

4. Select the Fax icon, and then click the Fax Options tab.

5. Click Print to start the Send Fax Wizard.

6. At the Welcome screen, click Next.

7. Enter the information that will be included in all your cover pages.

8. In the Fax Properties dialog box, click the Status Monitor tab to specify how you want to be notified when you send or receive a fax. Click OK to open the Recipient And Dialing Information screen of the Send Fax Wizard.

9. Fill in the name and fax number, or select these items from your Address Book if they are stored there. Click Next to open the Preparing The Cover Page screen.

10. Add any additional comments or information that you want to include on your cover page, and click Next to specify when to send the fax.

11. Click Finish.

You'll see the Fax Monitor open on your screen, in which you can track the progress of your fax transmission.

Receiving a Fax

Before you can receive a fax, you must set up your fax service to do so. In order to do this, you need to be logged in with Administrator privileges. Follow these steps:

1. Choose Start ➢ Programs ➢ Accessories ➢ Communications ➢ Fax ➢ Fax Service Management to open the Fax Service Management dialog box:

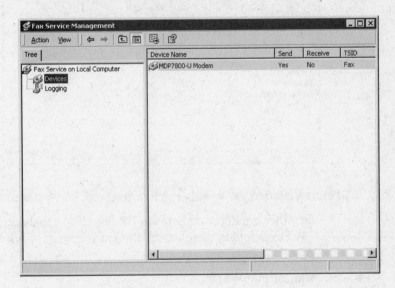

2. In the Tree column, click Devices to display the name of your fax modem.

3. In the Receive column, right-click No, and choose Receive from the shortcut menu so that Yes is displayed in the Receive column.

4. Close the Fax Service Management dialog box.

Now, when you receive a fax, you'll be notified in whatever way you specified in the Monitor tab of the Fax Properties dialog box. Faxes are stored in the My Faxes folder:

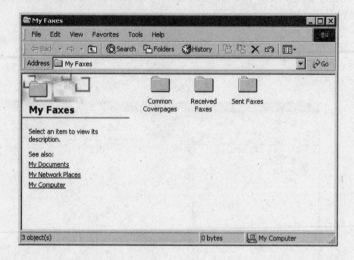

To print a fax that you've either sent or received, follow these steps:

1. In either the Received Faxes or the Sent Faxes folder in the My Faxes folder, double-click the fax you want to print to open it in Imaging.

2. Choose File ➢ Print.

WHAT'S NEXT?

Active Directory is a service in Windows 2000 Server that lets you identify resources, called objects, in the network and make those resources accessible to users via a single logon. In Part II, Robert R. King explains how Active Directory works and walks you through designing and implementing an Active Directory tree.

PART II

UNDERSTANDING ACTIVE DIRECTORY

Chapter 11

WINDOWS 2000 WITH ADS

Windows 2000 Server moves Microsoft networking away from the dated (and limiting) domain-based architecture of earlier releases and toward the true directory service–based architecture necessary in today's complex networks. In Windows 2000, Active Directory is a scalable directory service that lets you identify resources in the network and make those resources accessible to users via a single login.

Adapted from *Mastering Active Directory, Second Edition*, by Robert R. King

ISBN 0-7821-2659   517 pages $39.99

This part of the book introduces Active Directory Service (ADS). I'll begin in this chapter by discussing how ADS fits into the overall Windows 2000 philosophy. In Chapter 12, I'll explain the communication protocols that Windows 2000 can use, and I'll explain how to design a stable ADS structure in Chapter 13. Finally, in Chapter 14, I'll tell you how to install ADS.

NOTE
You'll find information about how you use ADS to manage a Windows 2000 network in Chapter 25.

How Networks Develop

Few networks are installed all at once, especially in medium to small companies. Most networks grow over time—almost like a fungus! First, the accounting department installs a server. They get it configured properly (this *can* take some time) and start bragging about it around the company. The folks in the production department see what the accountants are doing and decide to install their own server, creating their own domain in the process. The sales department staff suddenly wants Internet mail, so they bring in a consultant and have their own server installed, creating yet another domain. Before you know it, the company is NT-based, but there are no connections between the various departments.

The next step in the development of the network is sharing resources between departments. First someone in sales needs access to the quarterly accounting reports. Then someone in production wants to look over the marketing materials in order to stock inventory based on what the company is advertising. Departmental administrators start creating local accounts and trusts between domains to allow for this unplanned resource-sharing. Before you know it, a complete trust domain structure is born!

As you may know, the three big benefits of domains over older, server-based networks are:

- Single logon
- Universal resource access
- Central administration

The "network on the fly" scenario that I just described has the potential to provide all three. The question is, do the benefits outweigh the costs? Managing a larger domain-based network with lots of trusts can be overwhelming! In a complete trust design, the number of trusts is $D \times (D - 1)$, where D is the number of domains involved. This doesn't seem like a lot—until you do the math for a few networks, as shown in Table 11.1.

TABLE 11.1 Trusts in a Complete Trust Network

NUMBER OF DOMAINS	NUMBER OF TRUSTS
2	2
3	6
4	12
5	20
6	30
7	42
8	56
9	72
10	90

As you can see, even a small company with five or six departments (or sites) will generate a relatively large number of trusts. This is compounded by the fact that most small companies either have no staff administrators or have an administrator who doesn't have a lot of experience.

Of course, not a lot of management is involved with trust relationships once they are created—it is the global groups, local groups, global accounts, and local accounts that will turn you in circles. As an example, look at the environment shown in Figure 11.1. Jim works in the Seattle office, but he needs access to resources in Tampa.

In a domain-based system, two solutions are possible:

▶ Connect the two domains by a trust relationship.

▶ Create a local account for Jim in the Tampa domain.

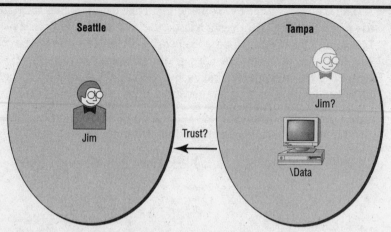

FIGURE 11.1: Jim's dilemma

In either event, the administrators have to decide which is the appropriate method. If they choose to create the trust, they will have to remember that the Tampa domain now trusts the entire Seattle domain. If the administrators decide to create an account for Jim in the Tampa domain, they will have to train Jim in the skills necessary to connect to resources in Tampa. Either way, they will have increased the potential amount of management required on their system.

THE GENERAL GOALS OF ADS

The overall goal of Windows 2000 Server and Active Directory Services can be stated simply:

> To reduce both the user and the administrative overhead associated with computer networks.

As a proposal, it's fairly simple. As an implementation, it becomes much more difficult. This has been the goal of most network operating systems since networking began. The biggest problem is that this "goal" is really made up of two areas:

▶ User access

▶ Network administration

Often these two goals are at odds. Making a network easier for the user ends up creating more administrative overhead. Conversely, giving more responsibility to users usually means less work for the administrators. Placing higher demands on system users is not a realistic expectation. Given the complex nature of today's networks, users cannot be expected to understand many of the necessary technologies.

The result is that the complexity of networks has forced both end-users and administrative personnel to become more network literate. Users are becoming more and more aware of the network, and administrators are being forced to master more and more complex technologies. At some juncture, this spiral will reach a point of diminishing returns. Users will be forced to master technology at the expense of their ability to perform their job functions (in other words, users will spend more time worrying about the network and less time being productive). Network administrators will spend such a large amount of time managing existing systems that no time will be left for improvement or optimization.

Since technological advances do not appear to be slowing (much to the relief of those of us who make our living writing about them) and these advances have the potential to increase the productivity of end-users, something must be done to avoid that point of "diminishing returns." Network directories in general, and Active Directory specifically, attempt to accomplish this by providing a simpler, more intuitive interface to the increasing complexities of a network. ADS attempts to provide two things:

- ▸ A common interface to network resources

- ▸ An intuitive interface to network resources

At first glance, these two goals might appear to be identical. The truth is, however, that we have intuitive interfaces in many of today's technologies. Almost every vendor realizes that easing access and management—through GUIs (graphical user interfaces), online help systems, and the like—is critical to success. The problem is the lack of a "standard" method of presenting information to end-users, administrators, or even other vendors.

ENTERPRISE MANAGEMENT

ADS aims to allow you to manage your entire network (and all its associated resources) in a consistent manner: more specifically, through a series of tools used to access configuration information stored within the ADS database. At first glance, this might not seem like such a revolutionary change to network management. If you stop and think about it, though, a *single* tool to manage *all* network resources—users, printers, servers, routers, switches—is indeed a lofty goal. If successful, accomplishing this goal could change the way that network administrators approach their current responsibilities.

Three prerequisites must be met before this goal can be reached:

▸ Design of an industry-standard method for storing and accessing configuration information

▸ Acceptance of this standard by third-party vendors of hardware and software

▸ Customer buy-in to the products created (and brought to market) by these vendors

An Industry Standard

ADS is the embodiment of the first of these three prerequisites. In ADS, Microsoft provides the framework for an industry-standard method of storing, accessing, and using configuration information for network resources. Through ADS, Microsoft defines how information should be formatted. By embracing industry recommendations and standards, such as X.500 and LDAP (Lightweight Directory Access Protocol), Microsoft makes ADS accessible to any vendor who wants to take advantage of it. More important, by creating a system for easily extending the schema of the ADS database, Microsoft creates an environment that all vendors can use.

I cannot overstress the importance of an open environment. By creating a directory service that is easy to access and utilize, Microsoft brings the first truly "open" directory service to the networking industry. Although there have been other commercially successful directories (Novell's NDS, for example), none has been as easily accessible or extensible as ADS. Developers can use simple tools to extend the capabilities of ADS to meet their needs. This openness is the first step in fulfilling the second of our three prerequisites.

Vendor Acceptance

With an open environment, backed by Microsoft, the stage is set for the completion of the second prerequisite: acceptance of a standard by product vendors. Given the clout that Microsoft wields in the industry, this would seem a foregone conclusion. In reality, ADS must provide some added value (over older, proven technologies) before products will be written to take advantage of ADS.

NOTE

At a recent trade show, it was rumored that Microsoft offered incentives to any vendor that would fly an "ADS-ready" flag on its booth. Although many booths had this logo, most were demonstrating products that did nothing more than trust ADS to perform user authentication. In other words, most of the products were not, in fact, ADS-based; rather, they were ADS-friendly. A large difference!

At first, this added value will probably consist of products that utilize ADS services to authenticate users to control access, use information stored in ADS, or perhaps automatically add data to standard attributes of an object class. For instance, consider the following:

▶ Most so-called ADS products will accept the identity of a user once authenticated through the ADS database. This information can then be used to control access to specific features of the product.

▶ Other products might access the information stored within the directory. A simple example is a company directory (phone book) that gathers its information dynamically from user attributes and provides a user-friendly interface to LDAP queries of that data.

▶ Some products might actually make the jump to placing data in the ADS database. The installation software for a printer, for instance, might automatically fill in the make, model, and serial number attributes of a printer object in the directory.

Although each of these applications would be an improvement over non-ADS-enabled products, none of them is really revolutionary in design. Before ADS can become the industry standard, Microsoft must entice developers to create products in which ADS is an integral component. Such products would depend on ADS for a portion of their functionality. A few examples might include:

▶ Devices that store their configuration in the directory database rather than in a local file. These devices will have to include firmware that can find an ADS server so that this information can be gathered as they initialize.

▶ Software that stores a user's preferences (such as default fonts, colors, or even the location of stored data) in ADS. By moving this information to a central database, a user's preferences will be available to her no matter where she is on the network.

▶ Software that knows where other copies of itself are located. If a server becomes unavailable, a user can be routed to another copy of the software—without any interruption of normal network services.

Given the strength of a directory service, these few suggestions are just the tip of the iceberg. The big question is, what will Microsoft do to justify the costs involved in reengineering products to be ADS-aware? Without this justification, third-party providers will not take a chance on this new technology. Three aspects of ADS will provide this justification:

▶ Microsoft's large market share in both the desktop and networking arenas. Developers are confident that any Microsoft product will be successful—and a large installed base increases their own odds of success.

▶ Microsoft has made programming ADS applications as easy as possible. You can create ADS applications using most of today's prevalent tools, including Microsoft Visual Basic and C++.

▶ Microsoft has made ADS easy to access through the use of industry-standard protocols such as LDAP.

User Acceptance

The last prerequisite to the success of ADS is user acceptance. Two types of users must be considered, and each type will have its own criteria for accepting any product:

▶ End-users

▶ Administrators

End-Users

A common maxim of older networks has always been that "the best networks are those of which the user is unaware." In a nutshell, this credo of network administration implies that end-users should not have to be concerned with the mechanics of networking. Users should see their computer as just another tool—no different from a screwdriver—for doing their jobs.

With Windows 2000 Server and Active Directory Services, this credo might be changed to "the best networks are those that intuitively guide users to the resources they need." As I mentioned earlier, networks (and the resources they provide) have become much more sophisticated over the last few years. Networks provide many more services than they used to, and this increase in service has pushed users into becoming more computer (and network) savvy. Typical office workers are now required to understand both the specific applications they use to manipulate information *and* the networks that connect them. The argument over whether this is a good trend will probably continue for years. The simple truth is that users must have a basic understanding of networks to survive in today's business world.

From an end-user perspective, some of the most basic aspects of ADS might be the best selling points. ADS promises the following benefits to users:

A single logon for *all* network resources.   Many users are faced with multiple logons to access the varied resources on their networks—one for the local area network (LAN), another for the mainframe, and yet another for some legacy system down the hall. With ADS, the user will be authenticated to the Windows 2000 network, and this authentication should be valid across multiple environments.

Dynamic mapping to network resources.   Users are often overwhelmed by the task of remembering the locations and names of resources throughout a large network. Using ADS to represent resources, such as applications, printers, and shared data, makes the process of accessing resources as easy as clicking an icon.

A consistent set of services on the network.   Users are often confused by changes to their environment. By providing a central database to store all of a user's preferences, policies, and other unique configuration information, ADS can re-create a user's environment—no matter where he logs on to the network.

For ADS to become successful, Microsoft must make the information that the directory database holds easily (and readily) available to end-users. Moving to a graphical interface is a first step. The simple fact that

Microsoft owns the most popular end-user operating systems (Windows 95/98/98 SE and Windows NT Workstation) gives ADS a leg up on the competition. Almost every end-user will understand the process of using a Windows-based application.

NOTE

The next step is to design the killer application—in other words, some application that becomes indispensable to the average end-user. I've mentioned some applications for directory services, everything from an employee telephone directory to automatic configuration of network devices. None of these examples, however, is really indispensable to the average end-user. What is needed is a new application that insinuates itself so thoroughly into business that it becomes as commonplace as the calculator and as indispensable as the fax machine. Although I'm sure that this application will be developed, there is no telling at this point what its purpose will be.

Administrative Users

Although ADS can provide numerous services to end-users, its primary function is that of network resource management. As such, ADS will first and foremost have to be sold to network administrators—administrators who have little time or patience for new technologies that promise the world but do not deliver! As a group, network administrators are mostly overworked and underappreciated (until an information emergency, that is) but are fascinated by the possibilities of technology. If ADS fulfills its promise, it should be an easy sell to these individuals. For administrative personnel, ADS can provide the following:

A single point of management for each user.   Administrators will no longer have to create multiple accounts for a user who needs to access multiple environments. The same account information (or at least the same account object within the database) can be used to access many types of systems: NT servers, Novell NetWare servers, mainframe systems, and even Unix boxes.

A single interface for managing products from multiple vendors.   Since ADS can be extended to hold the configuration information for any type of object, a single set of tools should be able to manage any resource that can be represented by an object within the database.

The ability to provide a uniform configuration for a like set of resources.   ADS provides the ability to *copy* objects. From an administrative perspective, this means that like objects (for instance, two routers) should have to be configured only once; the second can be configured by copying the configuration of the first.

The ability to provide a standard set of policies across an entire network.   For resources that are so enabled, administrators can use ADS tools to create policies of use. Such resources will accept the identity of the user (as confirmed by the network) to enable or disable services. A router, for example, might limit access to a particular route (the Internet, perhaps) based on membership in an ADS-defined group.

The ability to selectively delegate administrative responsibility based on an object's location in the tree structure.   In ADS, each container can act as a security boundary. In other words, if you have created a users container, you can delegate the administrative tasks for the objects it contains. This allows you to limit the areas in which a particular user might have administrative powers.

The ability to selectively delegate administrative responsibility based on an object's attributes.   You can, for instance, allow all members of the help desk group to change passwords for all user objects, without allowing them any other administrative privileges.

The ability to distribute printer drivers from a central location.   ADS will store the drivers necessary for a client to use a particular printer. When a user attempts to print, the driver can be automatically installed (or upgraded) on her computer.

NOTE

This ability to distribute printer drivers from a central location is not new—both NT 4 and Novell NetWare also have this capability.

All in all, what administrators need is an environment in which new technologies mesh easily with old technologies and an environment in which management tasks do not consume every waking hour and can be customized to fit the specific needs of the business. In other words, what administrators need is ADS! Active Directory includes many tools that bring it close to achieving these lofty goals.

Extensibility   One of the major features of the Active Directory database is that it can be extended to include *any* information that might be necessary in a particular environment. Suppose, for example, that Company XYZ is in a business that requires employees to travel regularly. In this type of company, each office probably has one person responsible for arranging travel—flights, hotels, auto rentals, perhaps even tickets to activities such as plays or ballgames.

If user Carrie is based in Grand Rapids, Michigan, the local travel personnel probably knows all about Carrie and her travel preferences. They know whether she likes window or aisle seats and whether she prefers nonsmoking or smoking rooms. They are aware of the appropriate type of automobile for her—that is, whether she needs a van to carry equipment or whether a compact car meets her needs. When Carrie needs to travel, she just calls the local person and gives her destination and travel dates, and everything is arranged.

If Carrie is away from home, though, this scenario changes a bit. Either Carrie calls her office to arrange travel (which means faxing itineraries and being on the phone a lot), or she talks to the travel person at the branch nearest her. The problem is that this travel person doesn't know all of Carrie's preferences. He either has to ask Carrie—who is busy working on her project—or call her office and have the material faxed to him (okay—he could probably do this through e-mail). Either way, information that should be readily available, based on the type of company we have described, is not!

In an ADS-based environment, this scenario changes. After analyzing the business needs of the company, the administrators decide that the ADS database should store travel preferences as properties of the user account. Using fairly straightforward tools, they extend that property list of user accounts to include things such as airline of choice, frequent flyer identification, smoking/nonsmoking, special diet needs, and perhaps even hobbies (so that entertainment arrangements can be made or suggested). Now, wherever Carrie travels, her preferences are available to the local staff. If her plans change, they can make arrangements easily. If she's doing a really great job, they can check her entertainment preferences and arrange tickets to a ballgame. In other words, the data that is needed is readily available.

The process of changing or adding to the properties of objects is known as *extending* the schema of the database. Extensibility ensures that ADS can be customized to fit the needs of any size or type of business.

Integration with DHCP (Dynamic Host Configuration Protocol)

Since TCP/IP (Transmission Control Protocol/Internet Protocol) is the protocol of choice for Windows 2000 networks and is mandatory for Active Directory Services, many of the traditional TCP/IP tools have been improved in Windows 2000. One of the most basic, yet critical, tools is DHCP. DHCP is used to dynamically configure the TCP/IP protocol stack on clients—automatically as they boot rather than manually at each computer.

Traditionally, as DHCP clients initialize, they broadcast a packet on the network requesting the services of a DHCP server. This DHCP server responds with an offer that includes all the pertinent TCP/IP configuration parameters. The DHCP server keeps a database of available IP addresses and is responsible for ensuring that no duplicate addresses are given out.

In Windows 2000, DHCP services have been integrated with ADS. First, the DHCP database of IP addresses has been moved into the Active Directory database. This allows central control of all DHCP services; more important, it also negates the necessity to implement DHCP relay agents or configure routers to pass BootP (Bootstrap Protocol) broadcast packets.

Another benefit of integrating DHCP into the Active Directory database is that the IP addressing information is moved to a more accessible forum. You'll see the benefit of this in the next section.

Integration with DNS (Domain Name System)   DNS is used to resolve user-friendly names, such as www.royal-tech.com, into the IP address of a resource. The biggest drawback to the original DNS was its static nature—each entry had to be created manually for each resource or service. This limitation meant that while DNS was great for some resources (e-mail servers, Web servers, and the like), it wasn't all that great as an all-around resource locator. (This was why WINS—Windows Internet Naming Service—was created.) For Windows 2000, Microsoft has integrated a new version of DNS—Dynamic Domain Name System

(DDNS)—into Active Directory. With DDNS, a resource can dynamically register itself in the DNS database. The bottom line here is that the resource records can be created on the fly as each resource initializes. This turns DNS into a dynamically maintained database of active resources—in other words, it replaces the DNS/WINS combination that was used in earlier versions of Microsoft networking.

Global Catalog Server   If I use the Active Directory database to find phone numbers for users around the globe, the traffic generated could outweigh the benefit of the central database. To reduce this network overhead, Windows 2000 includes a component known as the Global Catalog. This service is installed by default on the first domain controller in your forest.

The Global Catalog contains a partial replica of every object defined in every domain in your forest—in other words, a list of everything in your environment, but with only part of the actual data. Only selected properties of each object are stored in the Global Catalog, specifically those properties that are most likely to be searched upon.

Let's take my company phone book as an example. If my company's network spanned the globe, I would probably have created multiple domains. Remember that each domain represents a partition of the overall Active Directory database. As such, if I were to search my local partition (domain database) for the phone number of a fellow employee whose account resides in another domain, the information would not be available (at least not from my local server). Without any additional components, my local server would have to access a domain controller at the remote domain and perform the query on my behalf, ultimately returning the information that I requested. The problem here is that my request has now traveled across the wide area network (WAN) links that connect my network. The amount of traffic generated for a single query would probably not affect the performance of my network, but if we extrapolate that traffic for 1,000 users—well, suddenly we have a problem.

The Global Catalog acts as a reference point for these types of queries. In the scenario I just described, my local server would forward my query to the Global Catalog server. There, we would hope, the requested information would be found. The best part of this entire process is that I have complete control over which properties are stored in the Global Catalog and who can access the information.

I can also designate multiple servers to hold the Global Catalog, thus ensuring that a catalog is available locally to all of my users. (Of course, the more Global Catalog servers I have, the more traffic is generated to keep the replicas up-to-date.)

Policy-Based Administration   Earlier versions of Windows NT had the ability to create policy files to control certain aspects of a user's environment. Although this capability was useful, it was limited in scope—you could create policies only for users, groups, or computers. The level of control was also limited to a select set of parameters, things such as access to the display options on a computer or the ability to disable the Run option on the Start menu. Administrators had more control than was available with earlier operating systems, but the capabilities were too limited.

In Windows 2000, policies have been expanded so that they can apply across a site, a domain, or an organizational unit (OU) as defined in the Active Directory database. The controls available have also been expanded so that administrators can now control just about every aspect of a user's environment.

Policies now include options that allow central administration of items such as operating system updates, installation of applications (either mandatory or user-controlled), user profiles, and the traditional Desktop.

SINGLE NAMESPACE

Within the realm of networks and network applications, you can identify resources in numerous ways. Within a single environment, administrators and users are often forced to understand (and use) multiple methods for naming and finding the resources they need.

One common method of naming servers and share points is to use UNC (Uniform Naming Convention) names. UNC names adhere to the following format:

`\\<server name>\<share point>\<path to resource>`
where

▶ `<server name>` refers to the name of the device that holds the resource.

▶ `<share point>` refers to the name given to the shared data area.

Part II

▶ `<path to resource>` refers to the logical directory structure used to find the requested information.

NOTE

The abbreviation UNC is also interpreted as Universal Naming Convention in many current texts. Since UNC is a Microsoft term and this book is about Microsoft technology, I've decided to go with the original.

Although users have grown accustomed to this format, it is not necessarily either intuitive or convenient. Users must know the entire UNC name to use an object on their network. This is one of the reasons that graphical interfaces are so popular: users can click to an object rather than having to remember its name.

Another confusing environment can be that of messaging systems. Exchange Server, for example, generates multiple names for each recipient created. These names follow the format of various standards and foreign mail systems (thus allowing mail to be routed to and from other environments). A typical recipient will have names matching the following standards:

▶ Distinguished names (or X.500 names)

▶ X.400 names

▶ Lotus cc:Mail names

▶ Microsoft Mail names

For our purposes, we do not need to examine each of the naming standards in detail. Besides, most of this is done behind the scenes, meaning that the mail administrator doesn't necessarily have to understand each naming standard. At times, however, such information is critical to troubleshooting a message delivery problem. The problem with this type of system is that no one can be expected to have detailed knowledge of all of these standards (especially for systems one has never worked with).

With Windows 2000 Server and ADS, each object in the directory has one unique name that can be used to reference it. ADS uses X.500 names to represent each of the objects that it contains. In an X.500 environment, the complete, or *distinguished,* name of any object is a complete path to the top of the tree structure, as shown in Figure 11.2. From an administrative perspective, this means that only one naming format is in use on a network.

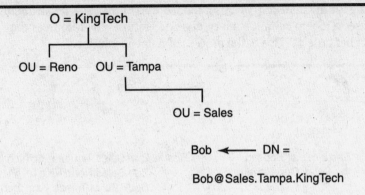

FIGURE 11.2: Distinguished object names

As you can see in Figure 11.2, all objects named within a particular ADS tree have certain similarities. At the very least, every object share's name includes the name of the root object, much as all members of a family might share a common last name. Just as you can refer to my family as "the King family," you can refer to an ADS tree by its topmost object (the root).

Namespace

The root object of a tree defines the beginning of a *namespace*. The concept of a namespace is critical to understanding ADS. A namespace is a structure in which a name (in this case, the name of the root object of the ADS database) is applied to all the objects it contains.

NOTE
In other words, a namespace is any specific context in which a name can be resolved to a resource.

Name Resolution

Name resolution is the process that uses the name of an object to find some information about that object. Probably the most common name resolution process is using the telephone book. With a telephone book, you use a name to find a telephone number or address.

In ADS you can use the name, or even just a portion of the name, of an object to find the value of its attributes, as shown in Figure 11.3. Susan is looking for the mail-stop of a user named Bob in the sales department. She uses a tool to submit a query, and ADS returns the resources that match her criteria. This is the process of name resolution.

Susan

Query: Show me all Bobs in   Result: Bob.Sales.Tampa.KingTech
        the Sales Department   Bob.Sales.Reno.KingTech
                                              BobP.Sales.Tampa.KingTech

FIGURE 11.3: Name resolution

When you create the tree structure for an ADS tree, its contents are organized in a hierarchical (and, ideally, logical) manner. Each department, workgroup, or object class can be given its own container. These containers relate to the original Active Directory namespace, as shown in Figure 11.4.

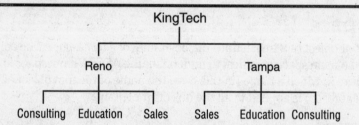

FIGURE 11.4: The ADS hierarchical structure

The King Technologies tree has two regional containers, or organizational units:

- ▸ Tampa.KingTech
- ▸ Reno.KingTech

Each region is divided into three departmental OUs. For the Reno office, these are Consulting.Reno.KingTech, Education.Reno .KingTech, and Sales.Reno.KingTech. In our previous example, if

Susan had known which office Bob worked in, she could have limited her search to the appropriate area of the ADS structure by specifying the `Sales.Reno.KingTech` container. This shows the hierarchical nature of the ADS tree structure. It also demonstrates the concept of namespace: each object in the context `KingTech` can be resolved to a unique name.

Active Directory Names

In an ADS directory, each object has a unique name within the structure. Three types of names are used, depending on the function being performed:

- ▶ Distinguished names
- ▶ Relative names
- ▶ User principal names

NOTE

I know that I said there was a single naming standard; as I discuss each of the three name types, you will find that they are all derived from the same single namespace.

Distinguished Names

The *distinguished name (DN)* of any object identifies the entire path through the ADS structure to that object. Every object within an ADS tree has a DN. For example, Katie King, who works in the Reno sales department of King Technologies, has the following DN:

```
Katie King@Sales.Reno.KingTech.com
```

- ▶ `Katie King` is the actual name given to the object in the ADS database.
- ▶ `Sales` is an OU within the `Reno` container.
- ▶ `Reno` is an OU within the `KingTech` container.
- ▶ `KingTech` is the organization at the top of the structure.
- ▶ `com` represents the container in which the `KingTech` namespace is defined on the Internet.

A distinguished name is the most accurate and complete way to represent any object within the ADS tree. DNs can, however, be cumbersome to use in a productive manner—can you imagine typing Katie's entire DN each time you want to send her an e-mail or manage her object? Luckily, a few shortcut naming standards can reduce the length of names used to access resources.

Relative Names

A *relative name (RN)* is made up of the parts of an object's DN that are attributes of the object itself. Katie's RN is Katie King because this is the only part of her DN that is specific to her object. The rest of her name is made up of RNs of the containers used to make up her DN. Sales, for instance, is the RN of her parent container.

NOTE

The term *parent* is used to describe any object above another in an ADS tree.

User Principal Names

The *user principal name (UPN)* is the name a user uses to log on to the network. Katie *could* use her DN—Katie King@Sales.Reno.KingTech .com—but this could be confusing for her. The UPN is a shortcut made up of her RN and the DNS name of the container in which she resides: Katie King@KingTech.com.

A major goal of ADS is to simplify the process of finding information about resources on a network. By using a standard set of rules to create DNs, RNs, and UPNs for objects, Microsoft begins the process of removing multiple naming formats from large environments. This can help to reduce both user and administrative confusion, easing the process of resolving names to resources.

ACTIVE DIRECTORY IN THE WINDOWS 2000 SERVER ARCHITECTURE

When reading (or writing) a book about Active Directory, one tends to forget that ADS is just one small piece of the overall Windows 2000 Server environment—although a critical small piece! Before we get into the specifics of ADS, we need to see how ADS fits into the overall architecture of Windows 2000 Server.

As you can see in Figure 11.5, the Active Directory subsystem is contained within the security subsystem—more specifically, within the *Local Security Authority (LSA)* subsystem of the security environment. The specific module that contains Active Directory within the LSA is the *Directory Service module*. Understanding how these modules are organized can help when designing your ADS network for optimal efficiency and performance.

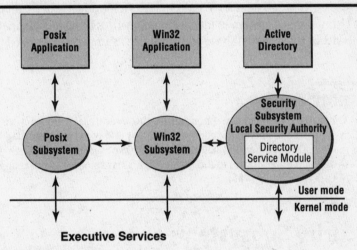

Executive Services

FIGURE 11.5: ADS in the Windows 2000 Server architecture

The modular design of Windows 2000 Server means that each component is a separate and distinct piece that is responsible for a particular function. These components work together to perform operating system tasks. Active Directory is a part of the component called the security subsystem, which runs in *User mode*. User mode is a separate section of memory in which applications are executed. Applications running in user mode do not have direct access to the operating system or hardware; each request for resources must be passed through various components to determine whether the request is valid. One such component is the security subsystem. *Access Control Lists (ACLs)* protect objects in the Active Directory structure. ACLs list who or what has been given permission to access the resource. Any attempt to gain access to an ADS object or attribute is validated against the ACL by Windows 2000 Server access validation functions.

The Windows 2000 Server security infrastructure has four primary functions:

- ▶ To store security policies and account information

- ▶ To implement and enforce security models for all objects

- ▶ To authenticate access requests to ADS objects

- ▶ To store trust information

The security subsystem for Windows NT is a mature, stable component. Using this subsystem to manage ADS ensures that the information stored within the ADS database will be secure against unauthorized access.

NOTE

There have been a few changes to the overall NT architecture with Windows 2000 Server: the addition of Plug-and-Play and power management modules; the addition of Quality of Service (QOS), asynchronous transfer mode (ATM), and other drivers to the I/O manager; and some low-level changes to the operating system kernel.

The Security Subsystem

Active Directory is a subcomponent of the LSA, which is in turn a subcomponent of the security subsystem. The LSA is a protected module that maintains the security of the local computer. It ensures that users have system access permissions. The LSA has four primary functions:

- ▶ To generate tokens that contain user and group information, as well as the security privileges for a particular user

- ▶ To manage the local security policy

- ▶ To provide the interactive processes for user logon

- ▶ To manage auditing

The LSA itself is made up of various components, each of which is responsible for a specific function, as shown in Figure 11.6.

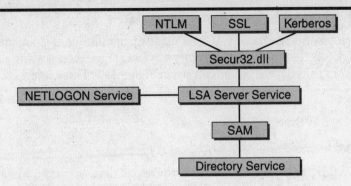

FIGURE 11.6: LSA components

Part II

Netlogon.dll   Maintains the secure connection to a domain controller. It passes the user's credentials to a domain controller and returns the domain security identifiers and user rights for that user. (In Windows 2000 Server, the NETLOGON service uses DNS to locate the domain controller.) If the environment is a mix of NT 4 and Windows 2000 servers, the NETLOGON service also controls the replication process between the PDC (Primary Domain Controller) and BDCs (Backup Domain Controllers).

Msv1_0.dll   The Windows NT LAN Manager (NTLM) authentication protocol.

Schannel.dll   The Secure Sockets Layer (SSL) authentication protocol.

Kerberos.dll   The Kerberos v5 authentication protocol.

Lsasrv.dll   The LSA server service, which enforces security policies.

Samsrv.dll   The Security Accounts Manager (SAM), which enforces stored policies.

Ntdsa.dll   The Directory Service module, which supports LDAP queries and manages partitions of data.

Secur32.dll   The multiple authentication provider, which manages the rest of the components.

The Directory Service Module

The Directory Service module is itself made up of multiple components that work together to provide directory services. These modules are arranged in three layers, as you can see in Figure 11.7. These layers are

- Agents
- Directory System Agent
- Database

These three layers control access to the actual database itself, which is known as the *Extensible Storage Engine (ESE)*.

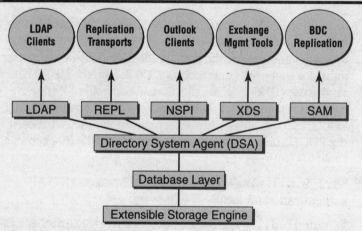

FIGURE 11.7: Directory Service components

Agents Layer

Five interface agents gain access to the directory through internal functions:

- Lightweight Directory Access Protocol (LDAP)
- Intersite and intrasite replication (REPL)
- Name Service Provider Interface (NSPI)
- Exchange Directory Service (XDS)
- Security Accounts Manager (SAM)

Each of these interfaces uses a different method to access the information stored within the database.

Directory System Agent (DSA) Layer

The DSA is responsible for creating a hierarchical treelike namespace from an existing flat namespace. This arrangement allows you to view objects in a more logical manner, rather than as a flat list. The database itself is not really a "tree"—the DSA uses the information found for containers to create the logical structure that you see in the various management tools. The DSA has the following responsibilities:

- ▶ To enforce all Directory Service semantics
- ▶ To process transactions
- ▶ To enforce the common schema
- ▶ To support replication between ADS servers
- ▶ To provide Global Catalog services
- ▶ To propagate security descriptors

Database Layer

The database layer provides the functionality needed to access and search the directory database. All database access is routed through the database layer. It controls the ways in which the data is viewed.

Extensible Storage Engine

The ESE is the actual database used to store the Active Directory database. It is a modified version of the JET database used in Microsoft Exchange versions 4 and 5. The ESE enables you to create a 17-terabyte database that (theoretically) can hold a maximum of 10 million objects.

The JET database engine has been used for Microsoft Exchange Server for some time. The version used by ADS comes with a predefined schema (the definition of object classes and their attributes). ESE reserves storage only for the space actually used. If you create a user object, for example, which *could* have 50 predefined attributes, but you only give values to 4 of them, ESE will use only as much storage space as needed for the 4 attributes. As you add values to other attributes for that user, ESE will dynamically allocate space for the growth in record size. ESE can also store multiple values for a single attribute (such as telephone numbers). It will allocate space as needed for each telephone number added to a user object.

The Internal Architecture of the Active Directory Module

The rootDSA object is inside the DSA in the Directory Service module. It is the top of the logical namespace defined by the ADS database and therefore at the top of the LDAP search tree, as shown in Figure 11.8.

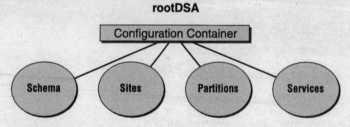

FIGURE 11.8: ADS internal architecture

The rootDSA object contains a configuration container, which in turn holds data about the entire ADS network. The information stored in the configuration container provides the data necessary to replicate the directory database, to specify how this server relates to the overall namespace, and to specify how the database is partitioned. This information is known as the *name context* for the various types of information. The four name contexts described under the configuration container are:

Schema   Contains the definitions of all object classes and their attributes

Sites   Contains information on all sites in the Enterprise network, the domain controllers in those sites, and the replication topology

Partitions   Holds pointers to all the partitions of the directory database

Services   Holds the configuration information for network-wide services such as Remote Access Service, system volumes, and DNS

WHAT'S NEXT?

Microsoft Active Directory Services is intended to tie together all of the diverse aspects of network management within a single database, which can be accessed using a single set of tools. Once implemented, ADS should ease the administrative burdens placed upon network administrators.

Now that we've looked at the goals and the architecture of ADS, we can turn our attention to specific pieces of ADS. In the next chapter, we'll take a closer look at how domains exist in a Windows 2000 Server environment and how ADS implements backward compatibility with older NT systems.

Part ii

Chapter 12

ALPHABET SOUP: ADS, TCP/IP, DNS

Although Microsoft Windows 2000 Server can use many communication protocols, ADS depends on TCP/IP. Before you can install and configure an ADS environment, you must have a strong foundation in TCP/IP and the various TCP/IP tools and techniques. I'll begin by discussing some basic elements of the TCP/IP suite, move to a section on IP subnetting as it relates to Windows 2000 Server and ADS, and then go on to a few of the TCP/IP tools you'll need to understand to implement ADS.

Adapted from *Mastering Active Directory, Second Edition*, by Robert R. King

ISBN 0-7821-2659   517 pages $39.99

TCP/IP Basics

TCP/IP (Transmission Control Protocol/Internet Protocol) is a suite of protocols designed to achieve two specific goals:

- ▶ Allow communication across WAN (wide area network) links
- ▶ Allow communication between diverse environments

Understanding the roots of these protocols leads to an understanding of their importance in today's networks.

The History of TCP/IP

In the late 1960s and early 1970s, the U.S. Department of Defense Advanced Research Projects Agency (DARPA) conducted a series of tests with packet-switching networks. These tests had two goals:

- ▶ To develop a network that would allow research facilities to share information (at the time, DARPA discovered that numerous universities were conducting the exact same research but did not have the ability to share their results)
- ▶ To develop a network that would act as a link between defense sites in the event of a nuclear attack

NOTE

The second of these goals might sound kind of silly in light of today's global political situation, but at the time, the threat of "nuclear holocaust" was a fact of life. Many of today's most important technologies were developed with the Cold War in mind.

These experiments finally came together in what we now call the Internet. The TCP/IP suite, which was developed as part of these experiments, continues to evolve to meet the needs of changing technology.

The Internet Society is responsible for the internetworking technologies and applications used on the Internet and oversees the development of TCP/IP. The Internet Architecture Board (IAB), an advisory group of the Internet Society, is responsible for setting Internet standards. Internet technologies are defined through a series of articles known as RFCs: Requests for Comments.

If a member of the IAB believes that she has a new technology for the Internet or an improvement to an existing technology, she writes a Request for Comments that outlines her idea and submits it to the IAB, which then posts the RFC for discussion. (Hence, the name Request for *Comments*.) If the idea has merit, it might eventually become part of a standard definition. Posting each proposed change on a public forum for discussion fosters an environment of cooperative development. This process also helps to ensure that any change is well thought out and tested before implementation.

Common TCP/IP Protocols and Tools

Over the years, many RFCs have been added to the standard definition of the TCP/IP suite. TCP/IP has developed into a rich, if somewhat complex, set of protocols perfectly suited to the task of managing a complex network. The mature status of most of the technologies is one reason that Microsoft selected TCP/IP as its protocol of choice for Windows NT and 2000 networks. Table 12.1 lists some of the more common TCP/IP protocols and the purpose of each.

TABLE 12.1: TCP/IP Protocols

PROTOCOL	PURPOSE
Simple Network Management Protocol (SNMP)	A protocol designed to be used by network management software. Specifically designed to allow remote management of network devices. This definition has been expanded to include the management of just about any network resource.
Transmission Control Protocol (TCP)	A communication protocol that is connection-oriented and provides guaranteed delivery services.
User Datagram Protocol (UDP)	A communication protocol that uses a connectionless delivery scheme to deliver packets. This is a nonguaranteed delivery protocol.
Internet Control Message Protocol (ICMP)	A protocol used for special communication between hosts, usually protocol management messages (errors and reports).

CONTINUED ➡

Part ii

TABLE 12.1 CONTINUED: TCP/IP Protocols

PROTOCOL	PURPOSE
Internet Protocol (IP)	A protocol that performs addressing and routing functions.
Address Resolution Protocol (ARP)	A protocol used to resolve IP addresses into hardware addresses.
Simple Mail Transfer Protocol (SMTP)	A protocol specifically designed to handle the delivery of electronic mail.
File Transfer Protocol (FTP)	A protocol used to transfer files from one host to another.

NOTE

Although this is not a complete list of the various protocols that make up the TCP/IP suite, it shows some of the more important protocols in use. As we add complexity to our networks, we must add complexity to the protocols that provide network functionality.

Every network administrator should be aware of a standard set of TCP/IP tools. Table 12.2 lists a few of the more common utilities and their functions.

TABLE 12.2: Common TCP/IP Utilities

UTILITY	FUNCTION
File Transfer Protocol	This utility is listed as a protocol in Table 12.1, but it is also considered a critical TCP/IP utility. You can use FTP to test the transfer of files to and from hosts.
Telnet	Provides terminal emulation to a host running Telnet server software.
Packet Internet Groper (Ping)	Used to test TCP/IP configurations and connections.
IPCONFIG	Verifies the TCP/IP configuration on the local host.
NSLOOKUP	A command-line tool used to read records in the DNS (Domain Name System) database.
TRACERT	Used to display the route taken between two hosts.

You will need to be proficient with each of these tools in order to set up and troubleshoot an ADS environment.

TCP/IP Addressing

In a TCP/IP environment, each network host (any device that uses TCP/IP to communicate) needs a unique identifier. This identifier is known as its *IP address*. IP addressing is well beyond the scope of this book, but I will cover the basics just to ensure that we are speaking the same language.

Without getting into too much detail (I'll suggest some additional reading at the end of this chapter), here's an overview. Each IP address is made up of 32 bits. Since computers use a binary system to represent information, each of those bits has one of two values: 0 or 1. The arrangement of those bits must be unique among all computers on any network that a host can communicate with. A typical IP address looks something like this:

    10000011.01101011.00000010.11001000

Notice that the 32 bits are divided into 4 *octets* (an octet is a grouping of 8 bits). Each octet is 1 byte of data. Although this is actually what the computer "sees," it is not how humans think (or at least most of us don't think in binary). Rather than using the binary value, IP addresses are converted into their decimal equivalent. We see IP addresses in a format known as *dotted decimal*. The dotted decimal representation of the address shown above is

    131.107.2.200

An IP address has two parts:

▶ The network address

▶ The host address

The *network address* is used to route information to the correct network segment, and the *host address* identifies a particular device within that segment. This is really no different from the street addresses used by the U.S. Postal Service, as you can see in Figure 12.1.

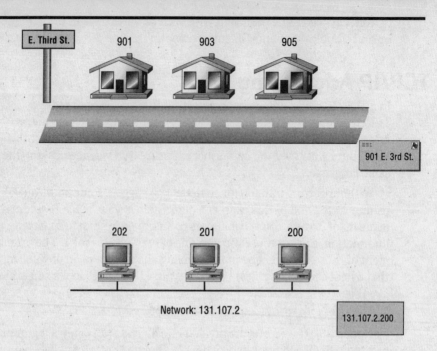

FIGURE 12.1: IP addresses

The address line on a letter contains both the house number and the street name. This allows the post office to sort the mail (using the street name) so that the appropriate carrier receives it and can identify which house it should be delivered to. The same process is used with IP addresses: the network portion allows routers to deliver packets to the correct network, and the host portion identifies which host should receive them.

IP Subnetting

IP addressing is a little more complex than I just described. When a company requests a network address (either from the Internet authorities or from an Internet Service Provider), it is given a range of possible addresses. The three most common classes of addresses are A, B, and C.

NOTE

There are actually more than three classes of IP network addresses, but we will stick with the more common classes here.

The ABCs of IP Addresses

Class A addresses begin with a first octet value in the range 1 through 127. The high-order bit in a class A network is always zero, which leaves 7 bits available to define 127 networks. In other words, the entire Internet can have only 127 class A networks. (Needless to say, no more class A addresses are available.) The first octet is the network portion of the IP address, and the last three octets represent the host portion. Each class A network can support more than 16 million hosts. Now you can see why only a few of these addresses are needed—not many companies have that number of hosts on their networks. Examples of class A networks include General Electric, IBM, Apple, Xerox, and Columbia University. Although address 127 is a class A address, it cannot be used for host addresses because it is reserved for loopback testing.

NOTE

How do you calculate the number of hosts a network can support? On a class A network, only the first octet represents the network. This means that 3 octets—or 24 bits—are used to provide the host portion. In a binary system, you can determine the number of unique combinations by raising 2 to the number of bits available. In this case, 2 raised to the 24th power equals 16,777,214—more than 16 million available combinations. Without going into the binary math involved, two of the possible combinations are illegal, so really there are 16,777,212 hosts available on a class A network.

Class B networks begin with a first octet value in the range 128 through 191. In a class B network, the first two octets represent the network, and the last two represent the node portion of an IP address. This means that only 16,384 class B networks are possible, each of which can support 65,534 hosts. All the class B networks are in use, and no more are available. Examples of class B networks include Microsoft and Exxon.

Finally, class C networks begin with a first octet value in the range 192 through 223. On a class C network, the first three octets represent the network, and the last octet represents the host portion. This means that some 2 million class C networks are possible, but each can support only a maximum of 254 hosts. Class C networks are still available.

Subnetting IP Addresses

The problem with the standard address classes is that they assume no routers between the various hosts on the network. In other words, if you were given a class B network address, it is assumed that you have somewhere in the neighborhood of 65,000 hosts on a single network. In reality, this situation would be intolerable. Even if you could find a topology that would support it, the amount of traffic on such a network would slow performance to a crawl.

To overcome this limitation, you can *subnet* IP network addresses. The process of subnetting can be extremely confusing (especially since this is not something you consider every day), but the theory is fairly straightforward.

When a company is given a network address, it is given the *network portion* of each valid IP address for the network. In other words, if a company is given a class B address of 131.107.0.0, each IP address on its network *must* begin with 131.107. This is the portion of the address used by network devices to route packets to the network.

Another way to look at this is to see the network portion as mandated by some external entity (the Internet, for instance). The local administrator owns the host portion, such as the last two octets in our example. He can do what he likes with them. This means that with a class B license, the local administrator has 16 bits to use as he sees fit. To control traffic, the local administrator might choose to use some of these bits to represent local network addresses. Although this *does* make the process of assigning IP addresses much more complex, it offers a few advantages that cannot be ignored:

- ▸ Since internal routers will direct traffic to the appropriate local network, congestion is reduced. Each network segment will carry only traffic intended for local hosts.

- ▸ Each topology has limitations on the number of hosts that can be physically attached to a single network wire. Subnetting allows the administrator to control how many hosts are on each internal network.

▶ Later you will see that we can define ADS *sites* that are used to control directory database replication. These sites are based on IP subnet addresses.

NOTE

As you can see, TCP/IP addressing can be a complex subject, well beyond the scope of this book. For more information, I suggest you read one of the books recommended at the end of this chapter.

Now that we've taken a look at some of the basic principles of TCP/IP, we can examine a few of the utilities designed to make managing a network easier.

Dynamic Host Configuration Protocol (DHCP)

Each host on a typical routed IP network must have certain parameters set correctly in order to communicate. The three most common parameters are

IP address   Used to uniquely identify the host

Subnet mask   Used to determine which portion of the IP address represents the network address

Default gateway   Used to represent the IP address of the router to which all nonlocal traffic will be directed

Traditionally these parameters were configured manually on each device on the network. From a management perspective, this meant that an administrator had to visit each device to configure its IP parameters. Entering this information manually took a lot of time and was prone to error. Although there is a better way to accomplish this task, you can still opt for manual configuration of a Windows 2000 Server computer if you desire.

TCP/IP addresses in Windows 2000 are configured in much the same way as they were in NT 4. There are, however, a few changes to the interface. To access the configuration window, follow these steps:

1.   Click the My Computer icon on the Desktop to open My Computer, as shown in Figure 12.2.

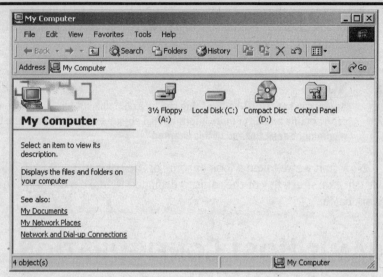

FIGURE 12.2: My Computer options

2. Click the Network And Dial-Up Connections link to open the Network And Dial-Up Connections folder, as shown in Figure 12.3.

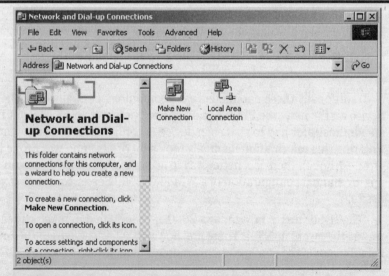

FIGURE 12.3: The Network And Dial-Up Connections folder

3. Right-click the Local Area Connection icon, and choose Properties to open the Properties dialog box for that connection.

4. Highlight the Internet Protocol (TCP/IP) option, and again choose Properties to open the Internet Protocol (TCP/IP) Properties dialog box, as shown in Figure 12.4.

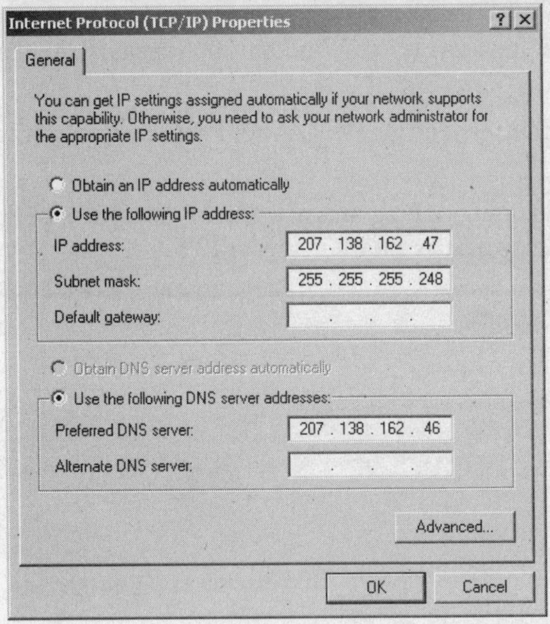

FIGURE 12.4: Internet Protocol (TCP/IP) Properties dialog box

5. Click the Use The Following IP Address option, enter your parameters, and click OK.

Our discussion of how to manually configure the IP parameters on a Windows 2000 Server computer is mostly academic. You will use this method primarily to configure static IP addresses for special-case devices. Microsoft's preferred method for configuring IP hosts is to use Dynamic Host Configuration Protocol (DHCP).

Installing DHCP Service

DHCP uses the BootP protocol to automatically configure TCP/IP clients as they join the network. DHCP services must be installed on a

Windows 2000 server. The basic premise of DHCP services is that clients can be configured automatically as they join the network, rather than manually as the computer is installed. Since configuration occurs each time the client computer attaches to the network, changes to the configuration are dynamically updated on the client.

The DHCP installation process has been modified from the NT 4 process, so let's take a good look at it.

To install DHCP services on your Windows 2000 server, follow these steps:

1. Choose Start ➢ Settings ➢ Control Panel to open Control Panel.

2. Click Add/Remove Programs to open the Add/Remove Programs dialog box, as shown in Figure 12.5.

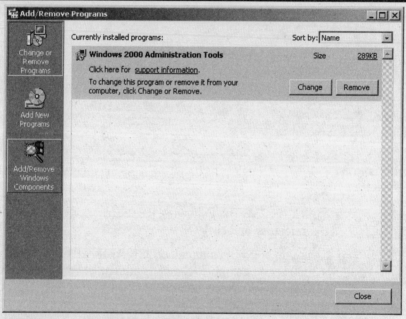

FIGURE 12.5: The Add/Remove Programs dialog box in Windows 2000 Server

3. Click Add/Remove Windows Components to start the Windows Components Wizard, as shown in Figure 12.6.

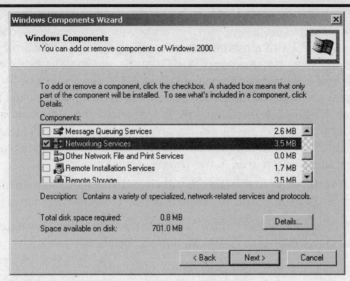

FIGURE 12.6: The Windows Components Wizard

This window displays the components that you can install on your server. The DHCP service is part of the Networking Services selection.

4. Make sure that Networking Services is selected, and click Details.

5. You will notice numerous components for this option; make sure that only the items you want installed at this time are chosen, and then click OK.

6. Click Next, and then click Finish to complete the installation.

Once DHCP services are installed, you will find a new tool in your Administrative Tools group: DHCP.

How Does DHCP Work?

You need to consider two procedures when looking at DHCP services:

▶ Configuring the DHCP server

▶ Configuring clients as they attach to the network

The next couple of sections discuss these processes.

Configuring the DHCP Server

When configured properly, DHCP servers provide an important service to the network. As with most important functions, though, an incorrectly configured (or worse, unplanned) DHCP server can wreak havoc on your orderly world. Remember the major task of DHCP servers: to give IP addresses and other configuration parameters to clients as they join the network. If a DHCP server is incorrectly configured, it could conceivably hand out IP addresses that are either invalid or—worse—already in use on your network. For this reason, each DHCP server must be authorized before it can function in an Active Directory environment.

Each server in an Active Directory environment will function in one of three roles: domain controller, member server, or stand-alone server.

► Domain controllers contain a copy of the Active Directory database and manage accounts for domain members.

► Member servers do not maintain a replica of the Active Directory database, but they have joined a domain and have an associated record in the ADS database.

► Stand-alone servers do not hold a replica of the ADS database and are not members of any domain. Basically, stand-alone servers announce their presence as members of a workgroup.

Only domain controllers and member servers can act as DHCP servers in an ADS environment. By mandating that all DHCP servers be verified as legal, Windows 2000 provides a level of security that was unavailable in earlier operating systems. Not only does this protect against "industrial espionage" (I've always wanted to use that phrase in a book—of course, I had a spy novel in mind), but it also epitomizes one of the biggest advantages of a directory service: central control. The central Information Services (IS) department no longer has to worry about some hotshot in Cleveland installing a DHCP server without understanding IP addressing or subnetting.

Authorizing a DHCP Server

To authorize a server to act as a DHCP server, first install DHCP services as described earlier, and then follow these steps:

1. Choose Start ➢ Programs ➢ Administrative Tools to open the Administrative Tools folder.

2. Click DHCP to open the DHCP management tool as shown in Figure 12.7.

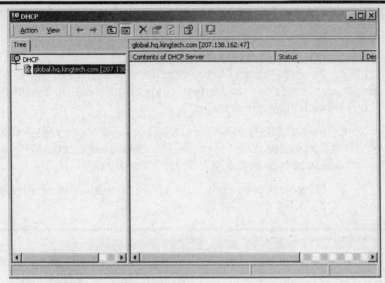

FIGURE 12.7: The DHCP management tool

3. Choose Action ➤ Manage Authorized Servers to open the Authorize DHCP Server dialog box, as shown in Figure 12.8.

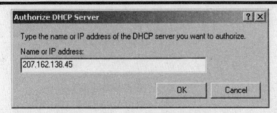

FIGURE 12.8: Authorizing DHCP servers

4. Enter the name or IP address of the server you want to add, and click OK.

Creating a Scope

At the server, you must create a *scope*, which is a database of the parameters that the DHCP server will pass to clients as they initialize. The DHCP server can provide more than just an IP address, a subnet mask, and a default gateway. You might need to configure numerous TCP/IP parameters on any given client, and DHCP can designate all of them!

To create a scope, open the DHCP management tool located in the Administrative Tools group. You can complete most tasks in two ways: manually or with the aid of a *Wizard*. (A Wizard is just a script that walks you through the steps involved in configuring an item.) Personally, I like the Wizards—even though I'm fairly comfortable with most items, Wizards ensure that I don't inadvertently forget something. To use the New Scope Wizard, follow these steps:

1. In the DHCP management tool, highlight the server to which you want to add the scope, and then choose Action ➢ New Scope to start the New Scope Wizard.

2. Click Next to open the Scope Name screen, as shown in Figure 12.9.

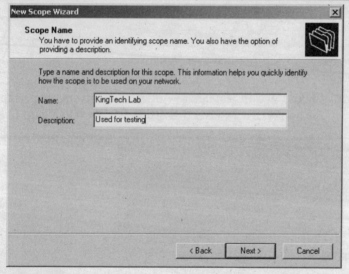

FIGURE 12.9: Entering the new scope name and comments

TIP

The scope name should be something that will remind you of the purpose of the scope, such as "KingTech Test Lab." You can also add an administrative comment, such as "IP addresses not valid on the Internet."

3. Enter a name and description, and then click Next to open the IP Address Range screen, as shown in Figure 12.10.

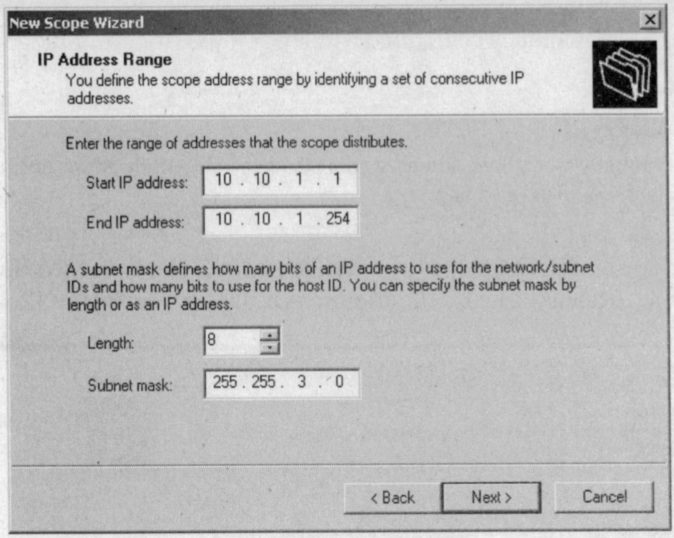

FIGURE 12.10: Defining the range of addresses

4.   Enter the range of addresses that the DHCP server will give
     out when using this scope. (This is where knowledge of the
     IP addressing scheme discussed earlier will come in handy!)
     Then configure the subnet mask, and click Next to open the
     Add Exclusions screen, as shown in Figure 12.11.

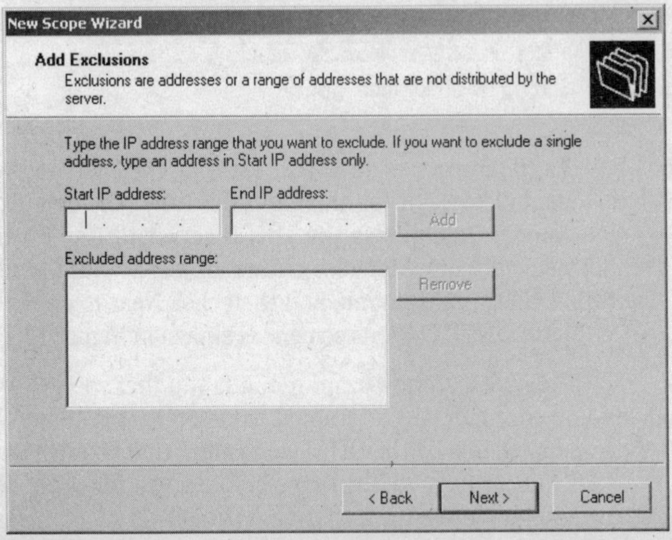

FIGURE 12.11: Excluding IP addresses

5. You might need to exclude addresses if you have devices that are manually configured with an address from your range.

NOTE

Manually configured addresses are also known as static addresses because they should never change.

Enter the addresses you want to exclude, and then click Next to open the Lease Duration screen, as shown in Figure 12.12.

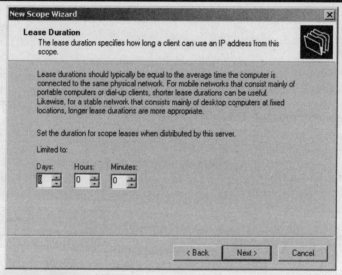

FIGURE 12.12: Setting lease duration

6. When a client receives an IP address from the DHCP server, the client "leases" it for an amount of time (the default is eight days). This allows the DHCP server to free up the address if the computer goes offline for an extended period of time. Specify a duration, and then click Next to open the Configure DHCP Options screen, as shown in Figure 12.13.

7. The last screen of the Wizard reminds you that you will still have to configure any additional parameters that should be passed to clients by the DHCP server and that you will have to activate, or turn on, the scope before it will function. You can configure these options now or do so later.

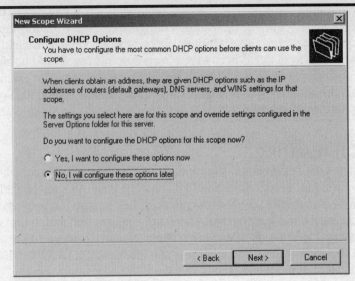

FIGURE 12.13: Additional options

After you create the scope, it is added to your view in the DHCP management tool, as shown in Figure 12.14.

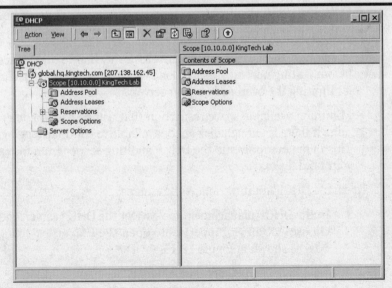

FIGURE 12.14: The KingTech Lab scope

To configure additional parameters, right-click Server Options in the DHCP management tool, and choose Configure Options from the shortcut menu to open the Server Options dialog box. A complete discussion of the options available is beyond our purposes, but you should be aware that no scope is complete without a few additional options. For example, you will probably want to configure the default gateway option (003 Router) for most clients.

DHCP Auditing

Although DHCP is an established and reliable process, in some circumstances you may need to track the DHCP actions taken on a server. Perhaps you suspect that unauthorized computers are being placed on your network, or maybe you want to track who is utilizing your services so that you can "charge back" usage time to other departments or justify an increase in the IS budget. For these and other reasons, the version of DHCP services included with Windows 2000 includes the ability to audit its services.

Once enabled, DHCP logging creates comma-delineated text files that document the actions taken by the DHCP service. Administrators can control the placement, size, and use of DHCP auditing. You can set the following parameters:

▶ Placement of the log files.

▶ Maximum size limit (in megabytes) for all DHCP log files.

▶ How often the DHCP service checks for available disk space before writing new records to a log file. This parameter is useful for limiting the overhead on your server.

▶ Minimum available space restriction that will be used to determine if there is enough disk space available to continue logging. This parameter prevents the DHCP auditing service from filling your hard disks.

To enable DHCP auditing, follow these steps:

1. In the DHCP management tool, select the DHCP server, and choose Action ➤ Properties to open the Properties dialog box, as shown in Figure 12.15.

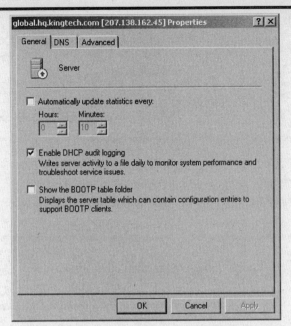

FIGURE 12.15: Enabling DHCP audit logging

> **2.** Make sure that the Enable DHCP Audit Logging check box is checked, and then select the Advanced tab.

On the Advanced tab, you will be able to set the path to the audit files. This allows you to place them on a partition that has enough available disk space.

Once logging is available, you will want to check the audit files regularly. Below is the output from a sample log file:

```
Microsoft DHCP Service Activity Log

ID Date,Time,Description,IP Address,Host Name,MAC Address
00,11/26/99,13:34:12,Started,,,
55,11/26/99,13:34:43,Authorized(servicing),,WORKGROUP,
01,11/26/99,13:51:10,Stopped,,,
```

As you can see, each entry provides an event code that identifies the action taken, the date, the time, and a short description. The trailing commas represent other fields that will be available when appropriate: IP address, Host name, and MAC address. Our sample is a simple example of a DHCP log file. You'll want to become familiar with the numerous event codes. I've listed a few of the more important ones in Table 12.3.

TABLE 12.3: DHCP Log File Event Codes

Event ID	Name	Description
00	Start	The log was started.
01	Stop	The log was stopped.
02	Pause	The log was paused due to low disk space.
10	Lease	A new IP address was leased to a client.
11	Renew	A lease was renewed by a client.
12	Release	A client has released its IP address.
13	Duplicate	An IP address was found in use on the network.
14	Out of addresses	A lease request was denied because the DHCP server had no available addresses.
15	Denied	A lease request was denied.
50	Unreachable domain	The server was unable to find the domain in which it is configured (probably followed by more events).
51	Authorization succeeded	The service was authenticated and started.
52	Upgraded to Windows 2000	The service was recently upgraded to Windows 2000, so unauthorized DHCP server detection was disabled.
53	Cached authorization	The server was unable to contact ADS but used cached information to start.
54	Authorization failed	(Usually followed by more event records to explain the problem.)
55	Authorization (servicing)	Successful authorization occurred.
56	Authorization failure, stopped servicing	The attempt to authenticate failed, so DHCP services were stopped.
59	Network failure	The system is unable to communicate on the network; services stopped.

NOTE

You'll find more event codes in the DHCP help file and in the Windows 2000 Resource Kit.

DHCP and Clustering

In this part of the book, we are concentrating on mastering one very specific topic: Active Directory. Windows 2000 includes many other new technologies, tools, and advances to make your computing environment more efficient, easier to manage, and more reliable. I can touch on only a few of those in this chapter. One noteworthy new technology is *clustering*. Clustering, available only with Windows 2000 Advanced Server and Datacenter Server, allows a group of independent computers, known as *nodes*, to work together as a single unit. Many advantages are associated with a clustering environment, including:

▶ The ability to manage a group of servers as a single entity

▶ Improvement in workload distribution

▶ Fail-over in the event of hardware failure

A basic cluster is made up of two or more computers attached to one or more storage systems. Each node runs software that allows it to monitor the status of the other nodes in the cluster. You can configure the cluster so that in the event of a failure, the affected computer's critical services restart or applications on other computers in the cluster restart. You can also configure the system to spread the workload of an application or service across multiple machines.

NOTE

A complete discussion of clustering technology is beyond the scope of this text. For more information, see *Mastering Windows 2000 Server*, 2nd ed., by Mark Minasi, Christa Anderson, Brian M. Smith, and Doug Toombs (ISBN 0-7821-2774-6, Sybex, 2000).

You can configure the DHCP service to take advantage of a clustered environment. This configuration allows you to ensure that DHCP services are constantly available through cluster fail-over. This type of fault tolerance is critical in today's high-volume, constant-use, mission-critical networks.

To configure DHCP to take advantage of clustering, certain prerequisites must be met. The cluster itself must have a shared disk resource configured and working. You must then create an IP address resource (to act as the IP address of the DHCP service) and a name resource (to represent the DHCP service).

The IP address cluster resource represents the IP address that will be assigned to the DHCP service (as opposed to a specific host). You must configure this "virtual IP address" statically, and it must be valid on your network. The DHCP service will bind to the virtual IP address instead of the address of a physical device.

You must also configure each node in the cluster with its own IP address. You then configure the DHCP named cluster resource with the IP address of the preferred node and the IP addresses of any node that should take over in the event of failure. Since the cluster shares a disk subsystem, the DHCP database is available even though the original DHCP server might be unavailable. In the event of a failure, the clustering software starts the DHCP service on another node, and the service will continue normally.

The DHCP Client Configuration Process

Four packets are involved in configuring a DHCP client:

- ▶ Discover
- ▶ Offer
- ▶ Request
- ▶ Acknowledgment

The process is as follows:

1. As a DHCP client initializes, it sends a *discover packet* out on the wire. This packet is a broadcast, so all computers on the local network will pick it up to determine whether they need to respond.

2. Any DHCP server that receives the broadcast discover packet will respond. Each such server first checks its scope to determine whether it has an IP address available. If so, it marks an address as temporarily in use and sends an *offer packet* to the client. The offer also uses a broadcast packet because the client is not yet configured with an address.

3. The client accepts the first offer that it receives (more than one DHCP server might respond). It broadcasts a *request packet* on the wire. The client uses a broadcast for two reasons:

   - ▶ The client still has no IP address, so broadcasts are mandated.

   - ▶ This informs all other DHCP servers that the client has made a selection.

4. Finally, the DHCP server broadcasts an *acknowledgment packet* and marks the client's IP address as being in use. Any other DHCP server that responded also receives the broadcast and can free up the address that it had temporarily marked as unavailable.

Many types of clients can take advantage of the DHCP service—all of the current Microsoft operating systems (Windows 95/98/98 SE, Windows NT 4, Windows 2000), of course, plus various other local operating systems currently on the market (for example, various flavors of Unix). Each local operating system is configured to act as a DHCP client in a slightly different manner. Most, however, have certain things in common. For example, most will be configured in the same way as other network-related options (text files, some applications, or perhaps as part of the operating system installation). Microsoft products, for example, are configured in the same place as the TCP/IP protocol.

Although DHCP does reduce administrative overhead by centralizing control over IP configurations, a few problems do arise with the traditional implementation. First and foremost, DHCP is a broadcast-based technology. Most administrators tend to avoid broadcast-based technologies for two reasons:

▶ Broadcast packets place unwanted overhead on the network. Every computer that receives a broadcast packet must open it to look inside and determine whether the computer needs to respond. In effect, broadcast packets use processing power on every computer that receives these packets.

▶ More important, most of today's routers are configured to prevent broadcast packets from being forwarded to other networks. This means that broadcast packets are limited to the home network of the originating computer. With DHCP, this means you must have a DHCP server on each segment or you must manage some other solution (either configuring your routers to forward DHCP broadcasts or installing a DHCP proxy).

Microsoft has integrated ADS, DHCP, and DNS to solve these problems, as you'll see later in this chapter.

Part ii

DOMAIN NAME SYSTEM (DNS)

As I discussed earlier, DNS is the directory used by traditional TCP/IP environments (such as the Internet) to resolve user-friendly names into IP addresses. DNS is a group of name servers linked together to create a single namespace.

NOTE

Remember that a namespace is just a system in which all resources share a common trait. In the case of the Internet DNS, the common trait is the Root object.

The namespace defined by the DNS system is logical in nature—in other words, it presents a group of text files as a single entity. The servers that hold these data files are known as *name servers*. Clients that query the name servers for name resolution are known as *resolvers*.

The DNS namespace itself is presented graphically as a hierarchical system, much like the system of folders and subfolders that make up a file system. In DNS, each folder is considered a DNS *domain* (not to be confused with an NT domain). Any domain that contains subdomains is considered the *parent* of those domains, and the subdomains are considered *child domains*. (A domain can be both a child of one domain and the parent of another.) Each domain has one, and only one, parent domain. At the top of the structure is the *root domain*; this is the only domain that has no parent. Planning the structure of domains and subdomains is a large part of planning any DNS installation.

Domains are named by the complete path to the root domain. In Figure 12.16, the complete name of the Royal-Tech domain is `royal-tech.com`.

NOTE

The root domain is not included as part of the complete name. It is assumed that every DNS name ends with the root domain.

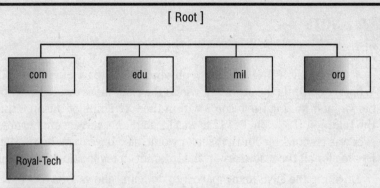

FIGURE 12.16: The royal-tech.com domain

DNS is critical to an ADS environment because ADS uses DNS to resolve host names into IP addresses for internal functions, such as the replication of the directory database. Without a properly functioning DNS system, ADS will not function correctly. In other words, DNS is something that you will have to be familiar with in order to plan your ADS-based network properly.

So What Exactly Is a DNS Domain?

You can look at DNS domains in two ways:

► Physically

► Logically

You will need to understand both views in order to install and configure the DNS service properly on your Windows 2000 server.

Physically, a DNS domain is really a piece, or a partition, of a large distributed database. It exists as a text file stored on a server that is running DNS services. The file that holds the records for a domain is often called the *zone file*. The syntax used in the zone file is arcane—remember, the same people who designed the original Unix interface created this technology. Luckily, Microsoft's implementation of DNS uses a graphical interface to create the records in the zone file.

NOTE
We'll look at the DNS Manager tool a little later in this chapter.

Logically, a DNS domain represents a boundary of responsibility. Whoever controls the server on which the zone file is located is responsible for maintaining the records within the file. Think of this in terms of the Internet. If one big DNS file was located on a server somewhere, whoever was responsible for that server would also have to maintain the DNS records for all the resources on the Internet—a big job, to say the least!

Breaking the DNS namespace into domains allows for a *distributed database*, which allows for delegating responsibility. Even if your company is not connected to the Internet, you can still use these principles to distribute both the overhead and the administrative tasks on your DNS servers.

Planning DNS Naming

When planning your DNS naming structure, you must answer a series of questions:

- ▶ Will this system be connected to the Internet?

- ▶ How heavily will DNS be used?

- ▶ How can the system best be organized to provide an intuitive environment for end-users?

Will This System Be Connected to the Internet?

If your system will be connected to the Internet, certain aspects of the DNS namespace will be mandated for you. You will need to register a domain with the Internet Society and follow certain rules governing your configuration. For information about this process, go to `http://rs .internic.net`.

NOTE
If you are not connecting to the Internet, the same rules apply, but you will have a little more freedom in naming your domain. Just remember that the name must be unique if you are ever going to connect to the Internet.

How Heavily Will DNS Be Used?

If you expect your DNS system to be heavily utilized, you might want to consider setting up multiple DNS servers. DNS can replicate zone files from a master DNS server to secondary servers. Although you can change only the primary copy, the secondary servers can act both as a fault-tolerant copy of the zone file and as another name server to split the workload of resolving names. This consideration is not applicable if you decide to implement DNS as a portion of ADS, a choice I'll discuss in a bit.

How Can the System Best Be Organized to Provide an Intuitive Environment for End-Users?

This is probably the hardest part of designing a DNS system. Creating multiple subdomains can ease the overhead on each DNS server (since each server holds less of the database), but this can be confusing for your users. Microsoft recommends that the DNS structure not be more than three to five layers deep and that you keep names as short as possible. This reduces the users' learning curve considerably. Table 12.4 lists the common steps involved in designing a DNS domain structure, using `Sales.royal-tech.com` as the example.

TABLE 12.4: Planning Your DNS Domain Structure

LEVEL	EXAMPLE	CONSIDERATIONS
Top	.com	This level will usually be mandated by the Internet Society. Certain top-level names are associated with different types of organizations: .com for commercial, .org for nonprofit organizations, .edu for educational facilities, and so on.
Top of local domain	royal-tech	This should be descriptive of your company, such as its name, product, or function. This is the domain name you register on the Internet, and it is often not exactly what you want. (My company's name is King Technologies, but the closest I could get was Royal-Tech.)
Child domains	Sales.royal-tech.com	The entire purpose of creating child domains is to be able to delegate responsibility for administration of the zone file. Usually these names will indicate the department or organization that is responsible for each.

Integrating DNS with Active Directory

When you deploy Microsoft DNS services in an ADS environment, you have two choices:

- ▶ Use traditional, text-based zone files.
- ▶ Integrate the zone information with Active Directory.

Microsoft suggests the latter option! When you integrate DNS with ADS, all zone information is stored in the ADS database: a distributed, replicated, fault-tolerant database, which is then stored on all the ADS servers within your organization.

ADS can store one or more DNS zones. All domain controllers can then receive dynamic DNS information sent from other Windows 2000 computers. Each Active Directory server can also act as a fully functional DNS authority, updating the DNS information stored on all your ADS servers.

NOTE

In other words, once DNS has been integrated with ADS, every ADS server acts as a primary DNS server for all zones. In fact, all zones stored by ADS must be primary—if you need to implement old-fashioned secondary zones (perhaps in a mixed DNS environment), you will have to stick with the old-fashioned text-file-based DNS.

In addition to integration with Active Directory, the Microsoft implementation of DNS provides the following functionality:

SRV resource records   These are a new type of record (defined in RFC 2052) that identifies the location of a service rather than a device.

Dynamic update   Microsoft DNS is more properly called DDNS: *Dynamic* Domain Name System. It can allow hosts to register their names dynamically with the zone, thereby reducing administrative overhead.

Secure dynamic update   Windows 2000 Server security is used to authenticate hosts that attempt to register themselves dynamically within the zone.

Incremental zone transfer   Only changed data is replicated to other ADS servers.

Interoperability with DHCP   A server running DHCP services can register host names on behalf of its clients. This allows non-DDNS clients to register dynamically with the zone.

Active Directory uses DNS to locate domains and domain controllers during the logon process. This is made possible by the inclusion of SRV-type records in the DNS database. Each Windows 2000 domain controller dynamically registers an SRV record in the zone. This record represents the domain NETLOGON service on that server. When a client attempts to log on, it will query its DNS server for the address of a domain controller. The bottom line here is that even if you are not going to use DNS for anything else, you will have to install and configure it for the logon process to work properly. Let me stress this one more time—DNS is critical to an ADS environment!

Installing and Configuring DNS on an ADS Domain Controller

If you are upgrading an existing NT 4 server that has DNS installed and configured, the installation of ADS will automatically upgrade DNS for you. If not, you will have to install DNS as a separate step (part of the Networking Services you installed with DHCP services).

If you have to configure a new DNS server, you will use the DNS Manager tool located in the Administrative Tools group. Here you will see your server listed, as shown in Figure 12.17.

To create a new zone, right-click the name of your server, and choose Create A New Zone from the shortcut menu. The New Zone Wizard will start and walk you through the steps involved. You will first be asked whether you want a traditional DNS system (stored in text files) or want DNS integrated into ADS, as shown in Figure 12.18.

If you are going to create a reverse lookup zone, you will be asked for its network address, as shown in Figure 12.19; otherwise, you will have to provide only the name for the new domain.

Part II

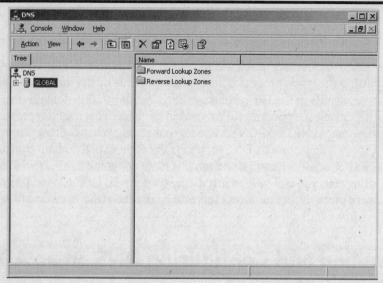

FIGURE 12.17: The DNS Manager

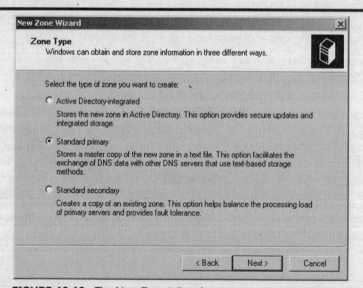

FIGURE 12.18: The New Zone Wizard

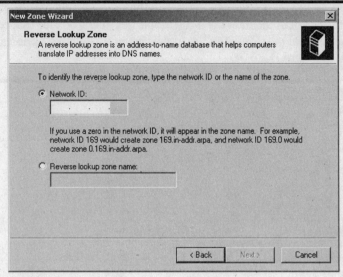

FIGURE 12.19: Configuring a reverse lookup zone

NOTE

For more information about the specifics of DNS (such as reverse lookup zones), I suggest reading *MCSE: TCP/IP for NT Server 4 Study Guide*, 4th ed., by Todd Lammle with Monica Lammle and James Chellis (ISBN 0-7821-2725-8, Sybex, 2000).

DNS and Dynamic Updates

One of the most exciting new features of Windows 2000 DNS is the ability to configure the system to accept dynamic updates from clients. This allows clients to register and dynamically update their DNS records as they boot or as their configuration changes. In older systems, especially those on which computers were frequently moved or reconfigured, keeping the DNS files up-to-date was a full-time job. Windows 2000 clients and servers support dynamic updates as defined in RFC 2136—in other words, through an industry standard method.

In Windows 2000 DNS servers, you can enable or disable dynamic updates on a zone-by-zone basis. By default, all Windows 2000 clients attempt to dynamically register themselves with DNS as they boot or as changes occur. Enabling or disabling dynamic updates is a fairly simple process. In the DNS manager, right-click the zone, and choose Properties from the shortcut menu to open the Properties dialog box for that zone. On the General tab, configure the Allow Dynamic Updates? option as shown in Figure 12.20.

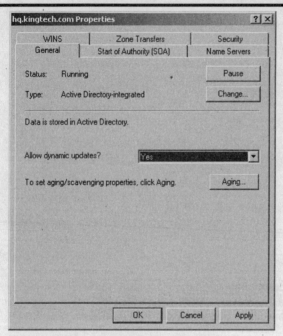

FIGURE 12.20: Allowing dynamic updates

Clients register themselves using their FQDN (fully qualified domain name). The FQDN is the NetBIOS computer name followed by the text placed in the Primary DNS Suffix Of This Computer configuration parameter. This parameter can be found in the Network Identification tab of the System Properties dialog box, as shown in Figure 12.21. (Notice that the computer in the graphic is a domain controller, so this parameter cannot be changed.)

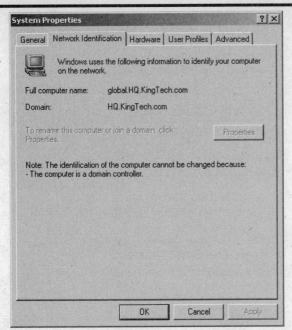

FIGURE 12.21: Fully qualified domain name

WHAT'S NEXT?

A basic level of TCP/IP knowledge is mandatory when configuring ADS. Our discussion has been limited to an overview. For a more detailed explanation of the technologies presented, I recommend the following titles, available from Sybex:

- ▶ *MCSE Exam Notes: TCP/IP for NT Server 4* by Gary Govanus (ISBN 0-7821-2307-4, 1998)

- ▶ *MCSE: TCP/IP for NT Server 4 Study Guide,* 4th ed., by Todd Lammle with Monica Lammle and James Chellis (ISBN 0-7821-2725-8, 2000)

- ▶ *Mastering TCP/IP for NT Server* by Mark Minasi and Todd Lammle (ISBN 0-7821-2123-3, 1997)

In the next chapter, we will take a look at domains in an ADS environment: why they exist, their function in today's networks, and how to manage them.

Chapter 13

BUILDING THE ACTIVE DIRECTORY TREE

I n this chapter, we will look at both the theory and the mechanics of building your ADS tree structure. Of the two topics, the theory is probably more important; the "mechanics" involve just knowing where to click your mouse. (And Microsoft is always changing the interface, anyway!) Knowing the theory allows you to build a stable structure that does not place undue stress on any single point of your network. Creating an ADS tree without knowing the theory is a crapshoot—you *might* produce a design that is stable, but then again, you might not.

Adapted from *Mastering Active Directory, Second Edition*, by Robert R. King

ISBN 0-7821-2659   517 pages $39.99

WHAT IS A DOMAIN?

You might recall the definition of a *domain* from earlier versions of NT: a logical grouping of computers and users managed through a central security accounts database. According to this definition, a domain was:

▶ Logically, an organizational grouping of resources allowing central management of those resources

▶ Physically, a database containing information about those resources

Combining the logical with the physical gave you a management or security boundary: administrators for a domain could manage all resources in that domain by default.

The definition of a domain has not changed in Windows 2000 Server. The only real change is that we now have to work this definition into a bigger picture—that of the entire network. In earlier versions of NT, we tied domains together by establishing trust relationships between them. In Windows 2000 Server, trusts still exist, but they are established by default and function quite differently than they did in NT.

In Windows 2000 Server, domains act as the building blocks for an ADS tree structure. The first domain you create becomes the *root domain*. The root domain acts as the top of the structure and determines the beginning of the ADS namespace. The name of this domain *must* match the top level of your desired namespace. After you create the first domain, each subsequent domain is added to the tree somewhere beneath it. In other words, additional domains are always children (although not necessarily children of the root domain), whereas the root domain has no parent. Figure 13.1 illustrates this concept.

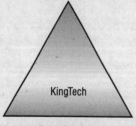

Root Domain

FIGURE 13.1: The root domain

In Figure 13.1, the first domain for the company King Technologies is named KingTech. As the first domain added to the tree, it becomes the root domain. All subsequent domains will follow the naming pattern of <something>.KingTech, as shown in Figure 13.2.

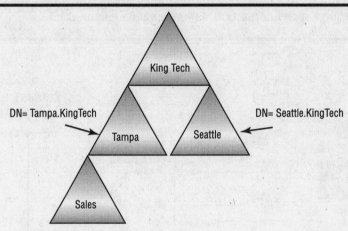

FIGURE 13.2: Subsequent domains

Figure 13.2 demonstrates the principle of *hierarchical naming*. Each subsequent domain adds the names of all domains above it together to create a distinguished name.

DNS Domains and NT Domains

In Chapter 12, I discussed DNS (Domain Name System) domains. A DNS domain represents a piece of the overall DNS namespace. DNS is a service used to find resources: A process submits a host name, and DNS attempts to find a record that matches. If a match is found, DNS returns the appropriate IP address to the requestor. Therefore, we can define a DNS domain as *a bounded portion of a DNS namespace used to find IP host information.*

In this chapter, we will discuss Windows 2000 domains, concentrating on how they relate to Active Directory. For our purposes, we can define an NT domain as *a bounded area of an ADS namespace used to organize network resources.*

Comparing the two definitions, we can make two generalizations:

- ▶ DNS domains are for finding resources.

- ▶ ADS domains are for organizing resources.

I know that I have said that the Active Directory database is used to "find" resources, so let me clarify. Although ADS holds information about resources on the network, it uses DNS to find and resolve distinguished names into IP addresses. In other words, ADS and DNS work together to return connection information to users or to other processes that request such information, as you can see in Figure 13.3.

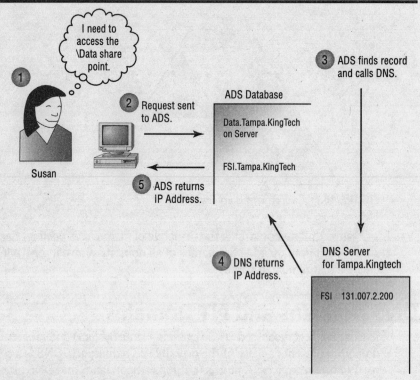

FIGURE 13.3: ADS and DNS work together to provide services.

In Figure 13.3, Susan uses the ADS database to find a share point. Here is what happens:

1. Susan browses the directory and clicks the \Data resource.

2. The client software sends a request to an ADS server.

3. The ADS server searches the directory database for the resource record. In the record, it finds the DNS name of the

server on which the share point is located. ADS queries DNS for the IP address of the appropriate server.

4. DNS searches its database for the record for server FS1 .Tampa.KingTech. Once it finds this record, DNS returns the IP address to ADS.

5. ADS returns the IP address of server FS1.Tampa.KingTech to the client.

At this point, the client software can establish a connection with the server using the appropriate TCP/IP technologies.

NOTE

DNS is a critical piece of the ADS puzzle. Without DNS, ADS cannot resolve user requests into IP addresses of resources. For this reason, you must have a good grounding in DNS before installing and configuring Active Directory.

Partitioning the Database

In large environments, the ADS directory database can become huge. The X.500 recommendations specify a method of breaking the database into smaller pieces, known as *partitions*, and distributing them across multiple servers. The X.500 recommendations also include a methodology for replicating changes to multiple copies of the same partition.

For the Active Directory database, domains act as the boundaries of partitions. In other words, each domain represents a partition of the overall directory database, as shown in Figure 13.4. Breaking the database into smaller pieces places less overhead on each Active Directory server. It also gives the administrator more control over the amount and route of traffic generated by the database replication process. Consider the environment depicted in Figure 13.5. Since only one domain is defined, each ADS server holds records for every resource in the enterprise. If a new printer is installed in Seattle, information about that printer will have to be updated on every ADS server in the entire company. The same holds true for *every* change made to the database. If user Katie in Tampa changes her password, that change will have to be replicated to every ADS server across the entire network. Although this design is functional, it is probably not the best design possible for the network.

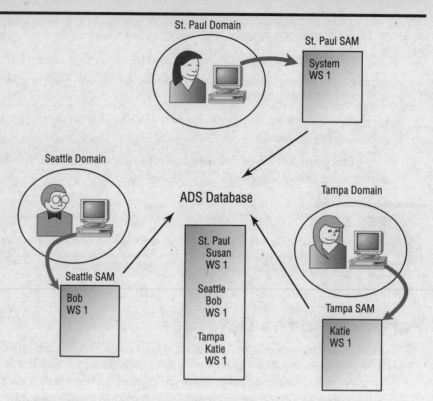

FIGURE 13.4: Each domain is a partition of the ADS database.

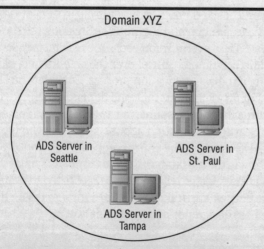

FIGURE 13.5: Company XYZ domain structure

The KingTech Company has come up with a much better design, as you can see in Figure 13.6. In this design, each server contains records only for objects that are in its own geographic area. This design has two benefits:

▶ It limits the amount of traffic generated between the two locations.

▶ It ensures that no server is overburdened by holding records that are of no real value to its purpose.

We'll look at various design strategies in more detail later in this chapter.

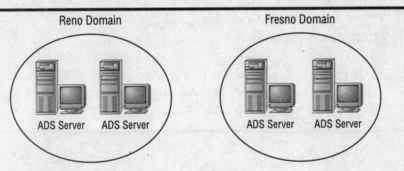

FIGURE 13.6: KingTech domain structure

Trusts between Domains

Domains not only act as partition boundaries for the database; they also act as boundaries for various administrative functions. In NT 4, a trust is a secure connection between two domains. Without some sort of trust, domains will not communicate and cannot share resources. This is also true in Windows 2000 Server—except that trusts are created automatically, and they work a little differently.

Trusts in NT 4 and Earlier

As a quick review, let's take a look at how trusts worked in NT 4. Version 4 used two types of trusts: one-way and two-way. In Figure 13.7, the Tampa domain trusts the Reno domain. In effect, this means that accounts that exist in the Reno domain can be granted permissions to access resources in the Tampa domain. *But not vice versa!* A one-way trust implies that only one of the domains is trusted and that only the trusted domain can access resources in the other.

FIGURE 13.7: One-way trust

In Figure 13.8, a two-way trust has been established between the Tampa and Reno domains. In this configuration, accounts from both domains can be granted permissions in either domain.

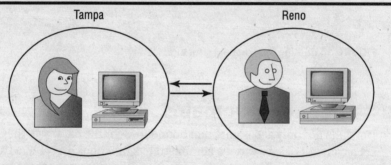

FIGURE 13.8: Two-way trust

In NT 4 and earlier, trusts were non-transitive. This meant that trusts had to be explicitly defined between any two domains. For example, look at Figure 13.9. In this figure:

▶ The Tampa domain trusts the Reno domain.

▶ The Reno domain trusts the St. Paul domain.

▶ The Tampa domain does not trust the St. Paul domain.

NOTE

To put it simply, if A trusts B, and B trusts C, this does not imply that A trusts C.

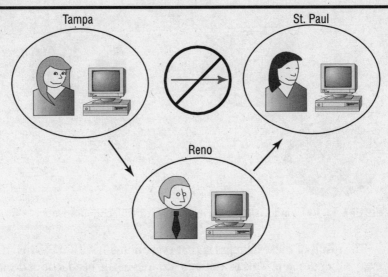

FIGURE 13.9: Non-transitive trusts in NT 4

Trusts in Windows 2000 Server

In Windows 2000 Server, trusts have changed. First, in earlier versions of NT trusts were not defined automatically. You had to set up all trusts manually. In Windows 2000 Server, a two-way trust is established between every domain and its parent domain in the tree, as shown in Figure 13.10.

The second (and probably more significant) change in trust relationships in Windows 2000 Server is that trusts are now transitive. To put it another way, if A trusts B, and B trusts C, then A trusts C. Take another look at Figure 13.10.

NOTE

With transitive trusts, every domain in the tree trusts every other domain by default.

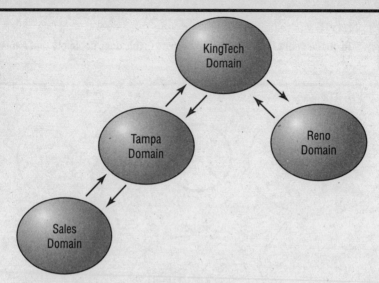

FIGURE 13.10: Windows 2000 Server's default trust configuration

The result of these changes is that every domain within the tree trusts every other domain. This rids administrators of the headache of designing and manually configuring an environment in which users can be given permissions to all resources within the enterprise.

ADMINISTRATIVE BOUNDARIES

Domains act as administrative boundaries: it is easy to give one administrator control over all resources within a domain. In many cases, though, using domains as the boundary for administrative privileges does not offer enough granularity of management. Administrators want the ability to limit an assistant's power to a particular group of users or to a geographic area. For these needs, ADS includes the Organizational Unit (OU) object class.

NOTE

The OU object is a container object used to organize the resources in your directory.

Organizational Units

OUs form logical administrative units that can be used to delegate administrative privileges within a domain. Rather than add another domain to an existing structure, it is often more advantageous to create another OU to organize objects.

Organizational units can contain the following types of objects:

- ▶ Users
- ▶ Computers
- ▶ Groups
- ▶ Printers
- ▶ Applications
- ▶ Security policies
- ▶ File shares
- ▶ Other OUs

NOTE

Remember that the ADS schema is extensible, so the preceding list might change if you change the schema of your tree.

NOTE

There is only one type of object that an OU cannot contain, and that is any object from another domain.

Easier Access, Easier Management

You could define an OU as a container object designed to allow organization of a domain's resources. An OU is used in much the same way as a subdirectory in a file system. An old adage about creating subdirectories in DOS states:

There are only two reasons to create a subdirectory: to ease access or to ease management.

You might, for example, create the DOS structure shown in Figure 13.11. Most of us would find this type of layout comfortable (and familiar). If you take the time to analyze why this structure works so well, you'll find that all subdirectories were created for one of two reasons: management or access.

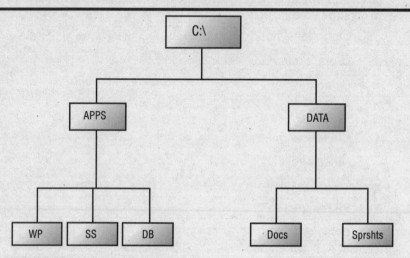

FIGURE 13.11: Typical file structure

APPS   Naming a subdirectory APPS lets a user know exactly where to find applications, making access easier. It also lets an administrator know where to place any applications stored in the file system, making management easier.

DATA   Again, the name helps both access and management. Placing both the APPS and DATA directories directly off the root of the drive makes navigation easier for users. Separating the data from the applications also simplifies setting up backup programs (you can back up everything under DATA rather than all .doc files in \apps\wp and all .xls files in \apps\ss, and so on).

The same reasoning applies to every directory in the file structure shown in Figure 13.11. This philosophy also works when designing the structure of your ADS tree. OUs should reflect the business structure of your company. Do not create containers for political reasons or just for the sake of structure.

TIP

The bottom line is: if you can't justify a container for either management or user convenience, you probably don't need the OU.

Creating Containers

With that said, there are a few good business reasons for creating containers:

- ▶ To delegate administrative control, allowing an individual the ability to add, delete, or modify objects in a limited portion of the tree.

- ▶ To ease management by grouping like objects. You might, for example, create a container to hold users with similar security requirements.

- ▶ To control the visibility of objects.

- ▶ To make administration more straightforward, assigning permissions once to the OU rather than multiple times for each object.

- ▶ To make administration easier by limiting the number of objects in a single container. Even though the limit on the number of objects within a single container is large (well over a million), no one wants to page through a huge list every time they need to manage one object.

- ▶ To control policy application.

- ▶ To be used as a holding container for other OUs. This would be the same as the APPS directory in our DOS example. The APPS directory does not really hold any files; it just acts as an organizer for other directories.

- ▶ To replace NT 4 domains. In earlier versions of NT, delegation of administration was achieved by creating multiple domains.

When to Use a New Domain

A Windows 2000 domain can grow to 1 million objects or until the partition occupies more than 17 terabytes of storage space. This means that most companies will not be forced into a multiple-domain configuration by the limitations of the directory. Multiple domains will be used to facilitate solutions to common network problems. Here are the primary reasons for creating an additional domain (rather than an OU):

- ▶ When management of users or resources needs to be decentralized and administrators do not want to share control of a domain

- ▶ When you want to make delegation easier in cases of diverse environments, such as a network in which different languages are spoken

- ▶ If unique domain-level security policies are mandated

- ▶ When you want to control directory replication traffic (for example, across a WAN link with limited bandwidth)

- ▶ If you will have more than 1 million objects in the database

- ▶ When you are upgrading from an earlier version of NT that was configured as a multidomain environment

- ▶ If you have autonomous divisions that require unique namespaces

- ▶ When you are preparing for future changes to the company

- ▶ If the default trust relationships do not meet your needs

To be truthful, you will usually create new domains to control network traffic. A prime concern in most wide area networks is bandwidth limitations on the wide area links. Controlling the traffic placed on these links is the driving force behind most directory designs. Once this consideration is taken into account, the administrator is left with the task of designing the OU model for each domain.

DESIGNING THE OU MODEL

Organizational units provide structure within a domain. This structure is hierarchical in nature, just like the structure built by adding domains together. Each OU acts as a subdirectory to help administrators organize the various resources described within the directory. This structure must be meaningful to users and administrators alike for it to be of any value to the network. A structure designed without people in mind can be of more harm than good, as demonstrated in Figure 13.12.

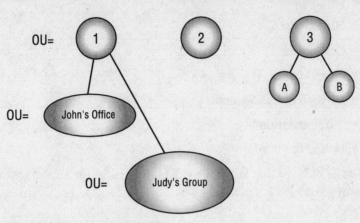

FIGURE 13.12: Bad OU structure

A couple of problems are inherent in this design:

▶ Many of the OU names are not user friendly. A name of 1 might mean something to the administrator who created it, but it will probably mean nothing to the system's users.

▶ Naming containers after people *might* make things easier for a while, but as soon as there is a change in personnel or business structure, all such containers will need to be renamed.

What Makes a Good OU Model?

A model defines categories of OUs and the relationships between them. The model you create for your tree should follow the business practices of your company. More than in any other form of network, a directory-based network demands that administrators understand the business practices and workflow of their company before designing the system.

Creating an OU model can be a difficult task—especially on your first attempt. Since a good design makes your life (and the lives of your users) easier in the long run, you should come up with a good, stable design the first time! With this in mind, some "cookie-cutter" models have been designed to act as guides during the planning stage of your own design.

Microsoft suggests seven basic models for OU structures:

- ▶ Geographic
- ▶ Object-based
- ▶ Cost center
- ▶ Project-based
- ▶ Division or business unit
- ▶ Administration
- ▶ Hybrid or mixed

In the sections that follow, we will take a look at the advantages and disadvantages of each design model.

Geographic Model

A geographic model structures its OUs by geographic location, as shown in Figure 13.13. The KingTech Corporation created a first level of OUs to represent continents and a second level to represent countries. This type of configuration is helpful if each country has its own administrator; you can easily grant administrative privileges to a local user account.

A number of advantages are associated with a geographic model:

- ▶ OUs will be fairly stable: most companies sometimes reorganize internal resources, but the locations of their offices are usually stable.

- ▶ Corporate headquarters can easily dictate domain-wide policies.

- ▶ It is easy to determine where resources are physically located.

- ▶ A geographic naming standard is easy for both users and administrators to understand.

Some disadvantages are also associated with a geographic model:

- ▶ This design does not mirror the business practices of KingTech in any way.

- ▶ The entire structure is one large partition (single domain). This means that *all* changes to all objects must be replicated to all ADS servers worldwide.

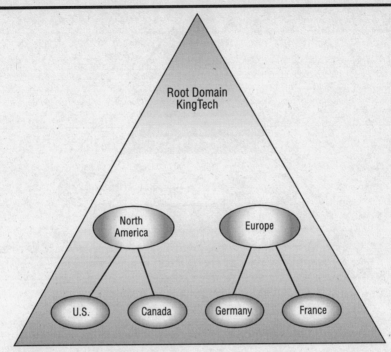

FIGURE 13.13: Geographic model

NOTE

In most cases, the replication traffic on the wide area links will outweigh any of the benefits of using this model.

Object-Based Model

The design of an OU structure can also be based on object types, as illustrated in Figure 13.14. A first-level container is created for each class of object that exists in the tree. Below this first level, a geographic layout might make administration easier.

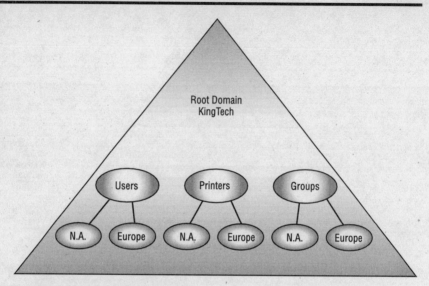

FIGURE 13.14: Object-based model

Here are some advantages of the object-based model:

▶ Resource administration is easier because each OU represents a specific class of object.

▶ Permissions are based on OUs. It's easy to create OU-wide permissions, such as, "All users should be able to use all printers."

▶ Administration can easily be delegated by resource type. For example, you can create a Printer Administrator who has permissions to add, delete, and modify all printers in the enterprise.

▶ A company reorganization should have little effect on the design. The same resources (with the possible exception of users) should exist no matter how the company is organized.

▶ Distinguished names are consistent for all objects in a class.

▶ It resembles the DNS structure, so it may lessen the learning curve for some administrators.

Disadvantages of the object-based model include the following:

▶ It is more difficult to define OU-based policies because all users are in the same containers.

► You have to create this flat structure in each domain.

► Too many top-level OUs can make navigating the Administrative Tools more difficult.

► If the schema is extended to accept new object types, you will have to create new OUs.

I've been working with directory-based networking for quite some time, and I've never liked the object-based design. It offers the administrator little opportunity for customizing the environment to meet a particular business need. I might, for instance, have a printer that should be visible only to a particular group of users. Although this goal is possible with the object-based model, accomplishing it is more work than it might be in other models.

Cost Center Model

A company may decide that the OUs within its ADS tree should reflect its cost centers, as shown in Figure 13.15. You might want to use this model in a company in which budgetary concerns outweigh other considerations. A nonprofit organization, for example, might have separately defined divisions, each of which is responsible for its own management and cost controls.

The cost center model has one main advantage: each division or business group manages its own resources.

This model also has some disadvantages:

► Users might not be grouped together in a way that reflects their resource usage. A color printer, for example, might belong to one department but be used by other departments as needed.

► Delegation of administrative privileges can be confusing.

The cost center design does not really take full advantage of the power of Active Directory. Most companies have departments, and each department might have its own budget—but there is usually some overlap of resources.

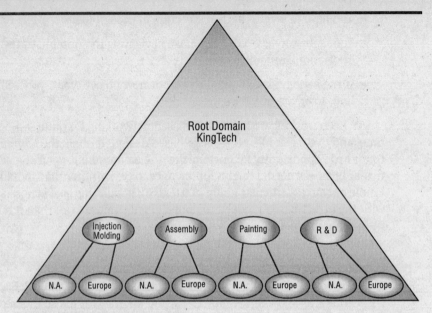

FIGURE 13.15: Cost center model

Project-Based Model

Some companies prefer an OU structure that is based on current project teams. A manufacturing firm, for example, could create an OU for each resource group in a shop floor manufacturing process. The project-based model is shown in Figure 13.16.

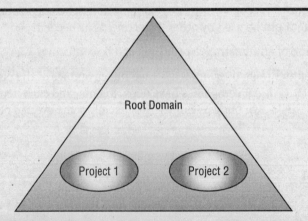

FIGURE 13.16: Project-based model

For certain environments, the project-based model offers some definite advantages:

▶ This model works well in an environment where resources and costs must be tracked.

▶ Because each project group is a separate OU, security between groups is easy to maintain.

Project-based design also has a couple of disadvantages:

▶ Projects often have a finite lifetime, so many OUs will have to be deleted and the resources redistributed.

▶ If projects change frequently, this type of structure will require a lot of maintenance.

I've found that a project-based structure works for smaller companies with a limited product line. As a company grows (along with the number of active projects), the workload of maintaining a project-based design gets out of hand.

Division or Business Unit Model

The OU structure can also reflect a "well-known" business structure if such a structure exists. A typical well-known structure involves the various departments within a law enforcement agency. You can see an example in Figure 13.17. Here are some advantages of the division or business unit model:

▶ This structure is user friendly, because it is based on a structure with which users are already familiar.

▶ For the same reason, it is easy to locate resources.

And here is a disadvantage: Although the structure is based on a "well-known" environment, there is always the chance that the business divisions will change. Any such change would force a redesign of the OU structure.

TIP

This model works well in environments that are defined in a rigid fashion, such as police departments and government offices.

Part ii

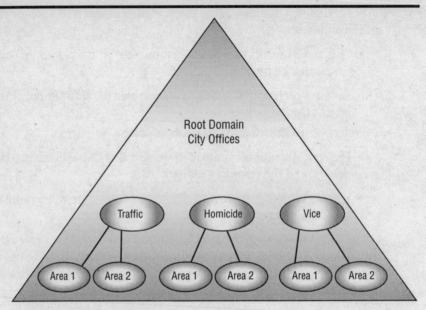

FIGURE 13.17: Division or business unit model

Administration Model

One of the more frequently used models is a structure based on common administrative groupings within a company, as shown in Figure 13.18. This model works well because it is based on the actual business structure of the particular company.

The administration model offers these advantages:

▶ This model is designed from the perspective of the network administrator and makes the administrator's job easier.

▶ Since most companies are departmental—from both a physical and a logical perspective—this model fits most enterprises.

It also has these disadvantages:

▶ Since this model is division oriented, all resources from a single division or department will be grouped under a single OU. This might be confusing for users.

▶ In companies that share many resources between departments, this model might not reflect the business model of the company.

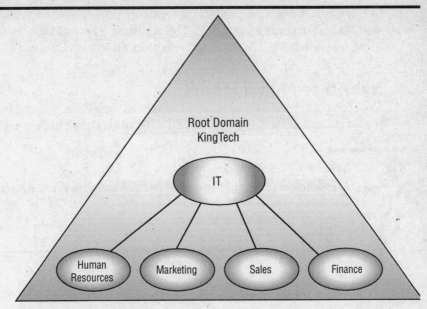

FIGURE 13.18: Administration model

This is one of the more commonly implemented OU models. It works reasonably well for most companies.

NOTE

Probably the biggest advantage of the administration model is that in most companies this design matches the organizational chart. In other words, the design has already been created—all the network administrator has to do is implement it!

The administration model also matches the way many NT 4 networks were created. First one department installs an NT server, creating its own domain and user accounts. Later, another department sees the benefits enjoyed by the first department and in turn installs its own NT server. In the process, this department creates its own domain and SAM (Security Accounts Manager) database. Next, the two departments see the potential benefits of sharing resources and create trusts. The end result is a network already modeled on the administrative groupings within the company.

During the upgrade to Windows 2000 Server, the administrator has the option of redesigning the structure, but since the users are already familiar with the "departmental" concept of multiple domains, it makes sense to keep the structure as it is. This results in less confusion for end-users, less retraining, and less productivity lost due to confusion.

Hybrid or Mixed Model

Most companies settle on a hybrid structure that combines two or more of the "standard" models. A typical hybrid structure is shown in Figure 13.19.

TIP

Remember that a structure is more stable and needs fewer adjustments if it accurately reflects the business structure of your company. The standard models are often too rigid to do this.

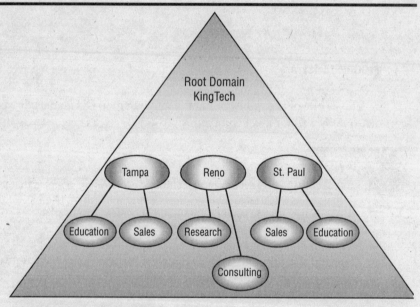

FIGURE 13.19: Hybrid model

The hybrid model has these advantages:

▶ You can customize the structure to closely match the way in which the company conducts business.

▶ Employees are usually comfortable with the design, since it reflects the way they actually work.

This model does have one disadvantage: it requires a greater understanding than the other models do of the company for which it is intended. For this reason, many outside consultants will avoid hybrid models.

Because of its flexibility, the hybrid model is probably the best overall design. It does, however, require more planning before implementation than the other models. Administrators of a hybrid model ADS have to create a set of rules governing when, why, and where new containers will be created. Here are some questions to ask yourself during this process:

▶ Which resources are departmental?

▶ Which resources are regional?

▶ Which resources are dedicated to a specific project?

Once you answer these questions, you can start designing a structure that closely mirrors the way in which your business is structured.

NOTE

The biggest problem with the hybrid model is that most businesses are dynamic. In other words, the way that they do business changes as the market changes. Such changes could result in a design that no longer meets the needs of the organization.

Other Aspects of Planning an OU Model

After you choose the overall structure that you will use for your OU model, you need to consider a few other things before you start implementation. Most of the following topics are administrative concerns. Proper planning of these details will make administering your network easier down the line.

Name Standards

The names you give to OUs are used internally within the domain and can be seen when searching for particular objects. It is important, therefore, that the names you choose are meaningful *both* to your users and to your administrators.

Part II

NOTE

OU names are not part of the DNS namespace. Users do not use DNS services to "find" an OU. This makes sense, since OUs are not physical resources—they are logical structures used to organize the objects in your database.

OUs are identified by a distinguished name—also known as a *canonical name*—that describes their location in the hierarchical structure. Basically, this is the X.500 name for the object in the tree. An OU named `Tampa` that is located in the `KingTech` container would be known as `Tampa .KingTech`. These names are used most often for administrative tasks.

OU Ownership

Each OU in the structure has an object that acts as its owner. The owner of an OU can:

- ▸ Add, delete, and update objects within the container

- ▸ Decide whether permissions should be inherited from the parent container

- ▸ Control permissions to the container

- ▸ Decide whether permissions should be propagated to child containers

NOTE

By default, the user who creates an OU is its owner.

Delegating Administration of OUs

For every OU in a domain there is a set of permissions that grant or deny Read and Write access to the OU. This allows for a delegation of administrative privileges down to the lowest level of your structure. Any permissions assigned at the OU level pertain to all objects within that OU. You might want to delegate various levels of authority to other administrators:

Changing container properties   Administrators can change OU-wide properties, such as OU policies and other attributes.

Creating, deleting, and changing child objects   These objects can be users, groups, printers, and so on.

Updating attributes for a specific class of object   Perhaps your help desk personnel should be allowed to change *only* users' passwords (but not any other attributes of a user account).

Creating new users or groups   You can limit the class of objects that an administrator has the permission to create.

Managing a small subgroup of objects within the tree   You might want an administrator to manage only objects in a particular office.

Trees and Forests

In the discussion so far, I have limited myself to environments with only one ADS tree. In a single-tree environment, each domain is added to the structure as a new partition of a single database to create the tree, as shown in Figure 13.20.

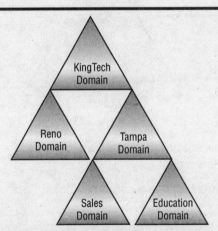

FIGURE 13.20: Single-tree environment

This configuration works well in most environments, but it has one big limitation: all objects within the structure *must* be a part of the same namespace.

NOTE

Remember that a namespace can be defined as a system in which all objects have a similar attribute to their name.

In the case of KingTech, the name of every object will end in `.KingTech` `.com`. Therein lies the problem: what if a company has a reason for some objects to belong to one namespace and other objects to a different namespace? Such a situation might occur when an environment requires a substantial amount of separation between domains that must still share resources. For example, partnerships or joint ventures might require that two distinct businesses share resources. These two companies would each have a unique namespace, so both could not fall under a single root domain.

Two separate ADS trees can establish a relationship, thereby forming an ADS *forest*. A forest is just a collection of trees that share a common schema and Global Catalog server. The trees establish a trust relationship between their root domains, as shown in Figure 13.21.

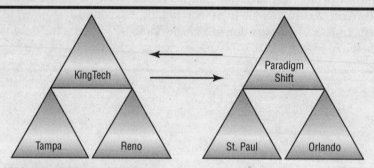

FIGURE 13.21: An ADS forest

Once you've established this relationship, you have formed a forest. A forest allows you to do the following:

- Search across all domains through a common Global Catalog server.

- Maintain existing DNS names (during an acquisition, for instance).

- Control trust relationships with partnering systems. Rather than creating a two-way trust between the trees, you could opt for a one-way trust to limit access to one system.

A forest configuration can also come in handy if you need to establish a relationship with an outside company. Let's say your company makes widgets. Your widgets come in many colors. You have the paint made to your custom specifications—your own version of candy apple red, perhaps. If the company that produces your paint is also working on a Windows 2000 network, you could create a trust between your two trees (thus creating a forest). This would allow your widget-color-scheme designers to be granted access to resources in your vendor's environment or to check on your orders to plan for paint production.

Special Types of ADS Servers

I've discussed various aspects of computers acting as Active Directory servers. I've discussed the Active Directory database, how it is partitioned into domains, and how these replicas stay in sync through a replication process. What I haven't talked about are some of the special function servers that exist in an Active Directory environment.

Global Catalog Servers

I briefly discussed the role of a Global Catalog server in the last chapter; now let's finish the topic. A Global Catalog server is an ADS server that holds a partial replica of the entire tree. This replica holds a limited amount of information about every object within the forest, usually those properties that are necessary for network functionality or those properties that are frequently requested.

The list of properties will be different for each class of object. User objects, for instance, will need to store certain information for network functions—a great example is their Group Membership list. During the logon process, the user's object is checked to retrieve this list. ADS will then confirm the user's membership with each group using information stored in the Global Catalog. Once membership has been confirmed, the Security IDs for each group can be added to the user's security token. The Global Catalog might also contain various properties that might be frequently searched on—telephone numbers, for example. On the other hand, the Global Catalog will probably store less information about Printer objects because fewer of their properties will be needed regularly.

By default, the Global Catalog is created on the first domain controller installed in the ADS forest. The service itself has two major functions. First, it is critical to the logon process. When a user logs on to the network, a security token is created for them. This token includes information about the groups of which they are a member. If a Global Catalog server is not available during the logon process, the user will not be able to log on to the network—instead they will be limited to logging on to the local computer.

NOTE

Members of the Domain Admins group can log on to the network without accessing the Global Catalog. If this were not the case, a malfunctioning Global Catalog server could conceivably prevent an administrator from logging on to fix the problem.

The second function of the Global Catalog is to facilitate searches of the Active Directory database. If you perform a search for, let's say, the phone number property of a user in another domain, your request could be answered by the Global Catalog server rather than by a domain controller from the target domain. To put it more simply, searches can take place on servers that are more local to the user—thereby reducing network traffic and decreasing the time it takes to receive results.

The second function of Global Catalog servers brings us to an important design issue. Although by default only one Global Catalog server is created, the system can support an unlimited number of them. To reap the benefits of the Global Catalog, you must think about how many you would like and place them appropriately. It is best to have a Global Catalog server at each physical location—otherwise, your search will cross your WAN links, thereby eliminating the benefits of the service. This design also prevents the situation in which users are unable to log in to the network because a WAN line has gone down.

On the flip side, though, too many Global Catalog servers can increase network traffic. Remember that the catalog contains an incomplete copy of every object in your forest. Let's say that user Joe changes his phone number; this change would have to be replicated to every Global Catalog server in your environment.

NOTE

This explains why the Global Catalog does not contain every property of every object. The traffic generated to keep complete replicas up-to-date would probably exceed the bandwidth available on most networks.

Windows 2000 creates the first Global Catalog server for you and determines which properties of each object class it will store. In most cases, this default list of stored properties will be sufficient. In some situations, though, you might want to add a property to the list that the Global Catalog stores. You can control the attributes of each object class stored in the partial partition of the Global Catalog by using the Active Directory Sites And Services tools.

Single Master Functions

In short, single-master environments use a single instance of a database to accept and then replicate changes. Multiple-master environments allow changes to any replica of the database. Each replica can update all other replicas with changed data. Most of the changes made to the Active Directory database are handled in a multiple-master manner. The change will occur at any local ADS server, and that server will synchronize those changes with the rest of the ADS servers in the domain (and the Global Catalog server, if necessary).

Certain operations, however, by the nature of what they do, need to be handled in a single-master manner. For these operations, one server is designated as the *operation master*. All updates or changes occur at the operation master, and this server is responsible for synchronizing the changes to all other servers. Because you can move these responsibilities from server to server (as best fits your network), Microsoft refers to them as "flexible single-master operations."

NOTE

Do not let the word "flexible" confuse you—this is mostly a marketing phrase. These operations are truly "single-master." They are "flexible" only in that you can determine which server will perform them.

Some single-master operations are forest-wide tasks. In other words, one server performs the task for your entire ADS forest. Other operations are performed by one server in each domain. In either case, only one server performs the operation, so it is important that you take these tasks into account when planning server functionality (and disaster recovery). By default, the first domain controller installed in your forest or in each domain, as appropriate, is assigned the role of operation master for each function.

Forest-Wide Operations

There are two forest-wide operation master roles:

▶ Schema master

▶ Domain naming master

Once again, let me stress that only one server in the entire forest performs these tasks. You must ensure that this server is reliable and has enough horsepower. You should also place it in a physical location where any outside links are fairly reliable. If these servers or the links to them are unavailable, certain administrative functions will not be accessible.

The *schema master* controls the structure of the ADS database. Any updates or modifications made to the database structure must be made on this server first. It will then replicate these changes to the rest of the ADS servers in your forest. This ensures that all ADS servers are "speaking the same language." There should never be a case in which one server knows about a new object class or property but another server does not.

The *domain naming master* is responsible for adding or removing domains from the forest. It ensures that each domain is given a unique name when added to the forest and that any reference to a removed domain is cleaned up.

Domain-Wide Operations

There are three domain-wide operation master roles:

- ▶ Relative ID master
- ▶ Primary Domain Controller (PDC) emulator
- ▶ Infrastructure master

Once again, only one server in each domain performs each of these tasks. These servers will need to be both powerful enough to handle the extra workload and reliable enough to be available when necessary.

The *relative ID master* controls the creation of security IDs for new objects created in the domain. Each object has a security ID that is made up of a domain identifier (the same for every object in the domain) and a unique relative ID that differentiates the object from any other in the domain. To ensure that these IDs are unique, only one server in each domain generates them.

The *PDC emulator master* can act as a PDC for non–Windows 2000 clients and NT 4 (and earlier) BDCs. This allows for a mixed environment of Windows 2000 and earlier NT version servers on the same network. Even in a completely Windows 2000 ADS environment, though, the PDC emulator performs an important function. When a user changes their password, whichever domain controller accepts the change will first pass the change to the PDC emulator operation master. This server then uses a high-priority function to replicate this change to all the other domain controllers in the domain.

Each domain controller in a domain knows which server is acting as the PDC emulator. If a user tries to log on to the network but provides an incorrect password, the domain controller will first query the PDC emulator to ensure that it has the latest password for the user before denying the request to log on. This prevents a denial of service in the event that a user attempts to use their new password before it has had a chance to be replicated to all the domain controllers in the domain.

The *infrastructure master* is responsible for updating group-to-user references when group members are renamed or relocated. It updates the group object so that it knows the new name or location of its members.

WHAT'S NEXT?

Designing the structure of your Active Directory is an important task that should be completed *before* implementation. As you have seen, proper planning of domains and organizational units can make life easier for both users and administrators. Here are some suggestions for your design:

▶ Use as few domains as possible. Windows 2000 Server greatly increases the capacity of a single domain. You should use multiple domains only when there is a specific need for such a configuration.

▶ Limit the number of OU levels. As with the file system, the deeper things are hidden, the harder they are to find! Because of the way ADS searches for objects, deep structures are less efficient than shallower ones.

▶ Limit the number of child objects for any given OU. Although a Windows 2000 Server domain can now support up to a million objects, no one wants to page through that many objects to find a specific user or printer.

▶ Remember that administrative privileges can be delegated at the OU level. You no longer have to create a new domain in order to limit administrative power.

In Chapter 14, we'll look at how to install ADS.

Part II

Chapter 14

INSTALLING ADS

N ow that we have looked at some of the variables that go
into planning your ADS tree, we can turn our attention
to the mechanics involved. Once you have settled on a
design, the next step is to install ADS.

Adapted from *Mastering Active Directory, Second Edition*,
by Robert R. King

ISBN 0-7821-2659   517 pages $39.99

In earlier, domain-based versions of Windows NT, the accounts database (known as the SAM for Security Accounts Manager) was stored on special servers known as *domain controllers*. There were two types of domain controllers:

▶ One primary domain controller (PDC) for each domain

▶ An unlimited number of backup domain controllers (BDCs)

NOTE

As you will recall, the PDC was responsible for synchronizing changes to the database to all the BDCs.

One of the biggest problems with this older system was the inability to reconfigure servers "on the fly." Although you could promote a BDC to the position of PDC, it was impossible to demote a domain controller or promote a member server (any NT server that was not acting as a domain controller) without reinstalling Windows NT. In other words, once you chose a role for an NT server—domain controller or member server—you were stuck with that role. The only way to change a server's role was to pull out the NT CD-ROM and reinstall the operating system.

One of the biggest "incidental" advances that Microsoft has made to Windows 2000 Server is that you can install or remove ADS without affecting the underlying operating system. If you decide that a certain server should act as an ADS server, only to learn later that the server just doesn't have the necessary horsepower to perform the task, you can remove ADS. If you install a Windows 2000 server without ADS and later decide you need to add the service, all you have to do is run an Administrative Wizard.

ADS has become "just another network component" of the Windows 2000 operating system. This flexibility allows network administrators the opportunity to make mistakes without fear of losing network functionality while *another* reinstallation takes place.

BEFORE YOU BEGIN

Before you can begin the actual installation of the Active Directory service, you must complete certain preliminary tasks. Specifically, DNS *must* be configured and working properly before you begin the installation process. You should verify the following:

- You have decided on and configured DNS names for each of your Active Directory servers.

- DNS is installed and working.

- You have configured DNS for your environment. Specifically, ensure that

    - Lookups work properly.

    - All DNS servers are configured for forward lookups as needed.

    - Your reverse lookup zones are working properly.

- You have configured DNS to allow dynamic updates.

Testing DNS

Testing DNS is beyond the scope of this book, but here are a couple of suggestions:

- Use Ping to confirm communication between *all* Active Directory servers. If you Ping each server by its host name, you will also test DNS at the same time.

- Use NSLOOKUP to test functionality for forward lookup, reverse lookup, and root zones.

NOTE

For more information on these tools, I suggest *Mastering Windows 2000 Server*, 2nd ed., by Mark Minasi, Christa Anderson, Brian M. Smith, and Doug Toombs (ISBN 0-7821-2774-6, Sybex, 2000) or *MCSE: TCP/IP for NT Server 4 Study Guide*, 4th ed., by Todd Lammle, Monica Lammle, and James Chellis (ISBN 0-7821-2725-8, Sybex, 2000).

Mixed Mode or Native Mode?

You must also decide on one other facet of your ADS environment: whether your ADS server should be configured to run in *mixed* or *native* mode.

A mixed-mode ADS server can interact with domain controllers running earlier versions of NT. Basically, the ADS server becomes the primary domain controller (PDC) for the existing domain, and it will update the older servers in a manner similar to that of an NT 4 server. (For this reason, ADS servers are sometimes referred to as domain controllers.) This allows you to update your servers one at a time without having to be concerned about backward compatibility issues. Although this process is certainly not as efficient as moving everything to ADS, it does allow you a gradual upgrade of your environment.

NOTE

Unfortunately, terminology in the Microsoft world is often a little confusing. A Windows 2000 Server acting as an ADS server can emulate the functions of a domain controller from earlier versions of Windows NT. Since it is performing the same functions as an NT domain controller, many documents will refer to it as a domain controller. You should be aware that there is a subtle difference between old and new—and an ADS server just acts like a PDC.

A native-mode ADS server cannot act as part of an older environment. As soon as all of your older servers have been upgraded to Windows 2000 and ADS, you should switch your servers to native mode. "Mixed mode" basically refers to a process running on your Windows 2000 server, using processor power and memory.

NOTE

It is not necessary to use mixed mode if all your servers are running Windows 2000.

THE ADS INSTALLATION WIZARD

To install ADS, you use the Active Directory Installation Wizard (the actual file is named DCPromo.exe and is located in the <windows_root>\system32 directory). The Wizard leads you through the entire process, asking you for information on the first domain controller, domain, site, and so on. You must install ADS on a volume that has been formatted with NTFS 5 or higher.

The Wizard itself is fairly straightforward. It starts with the obligatory Microsoft Welcome screen to identify what you are about to do (just in case you ran the wrong program). On the second screen, you will be asked to select your server type, as shown in Figure 14.1.

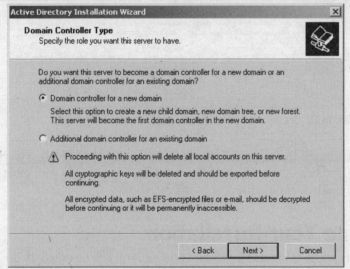

FIGURE 14.1: Specifying the domain controller type

There are two choices on this screen:

Domain controller for a new domain   This server will be the first domain controller. Make this choice if this is the first ADS server for a domain.

Additional domain controller for an existing domain   Use this option if there is already an ADS server within this NT domain. This server will receive a replica of the local domain's partition.

The next screen also has two choices, as shown in Figure 14.2. Here you will have to decide if you would like to create a new domain tree or add this domain to an existing tree.

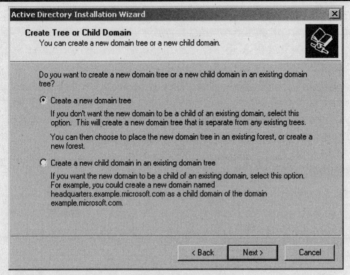

FIGURE 14.2: Create a tree or a child domain.

I discussed the tree and forest issue in the last chapter. Here you will make decisions that will affect the number of domains in your environment and how their namespaces will interact.

Finishing Your Installation

If you choose to create a new child domain, you will be asked for an administrative account and password for an existing domain in the tree, as shown in Figure 14.3.

If you choose to create a new tree, the next screen will ask you for the full DNS name for the new domain, as shown in Figure 14.4. Remember that this name *must* be resolvable through DNS.

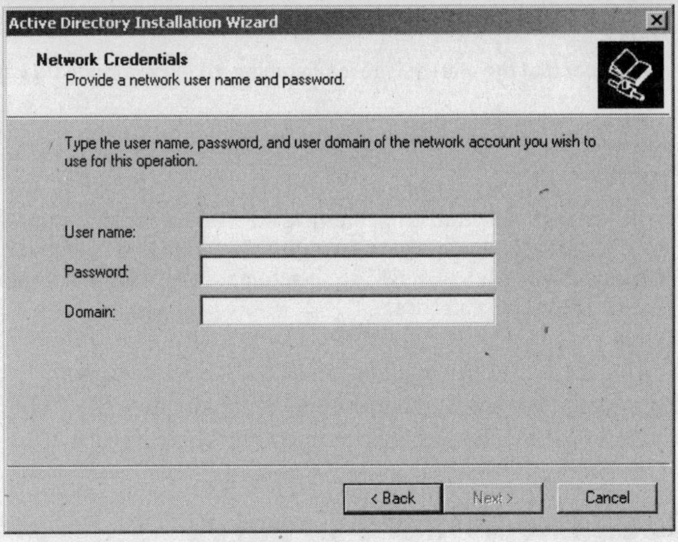

FIGURE 14.3: Network credentials

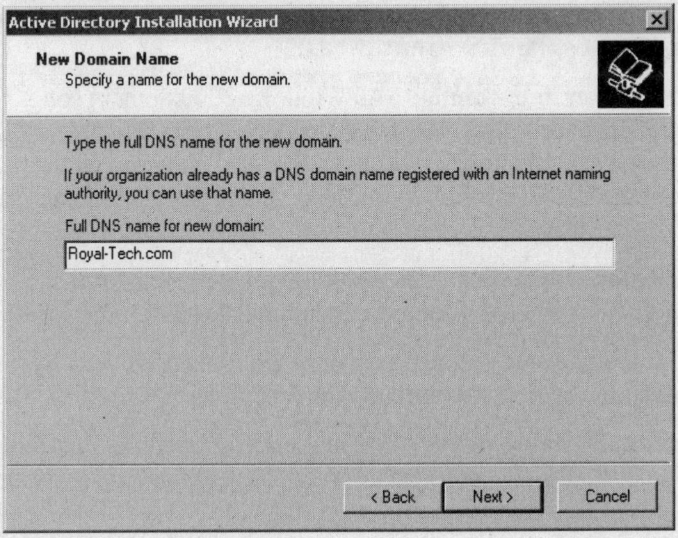

FIGURE 14.4: New domain name

Part ii

NOTE

Remember that the prerequisite for installing ADS is a working DNS system!

NOTE

If the Installation Wizard cannot resolve the name of the server through DNS, it will ask if you would like to have DNS installed and configured on this machine. If you say yes, it will do so automatically, adding the appropriate records to the DNS database.

That's all there is to the installation of ADS. So far, so good! Actually, creating a good design is the hardest part of moving to a directory-based environment—the mechanics are just knowing where to click.

What Does the Wizard Create?

The following items are created during the ADS installation process:

Database   This is the directory database for the new domain. The default location for the database and its associated log files is `<systemroot>\Winnt\Ntds`.

Shared system volume   All Windows 2000 domain controllers have a share point used to store scripts that are part of the group policy objects for both the local domain and the enterprise. The default location for these files is `<system-root>\Sysvol\sysvol`.

Domain controller   The first domain controller for the domain is created during the first installation of ADS.

First site name   A *site* is a logical grouping of servers. By default, the first site contains the first domain controller.

Global Catalog server   The first domain controller in a site becomes the Global Catalog server. The Global Catalog server holds a partial replica of every domain in the forest. This replica holds a subset of the attributes for each object—those attributes most commonly used for searches. The Global Catalog server facilitates forest-wide searches for objects.

Root domain   If you create a new tree (rather than join an existing one), this domain will become the root domain for the new tree.

The installation also creates a series of organizational units:

Built-in   This contains default security groups, such as Account Operators, Administrators, and so on.

Foreign Security Principals   When a trust is made with a domain outside of the tree, this container is used to hold references to objects from the outside environment that have been granted local permissions.

Users   This is the default location for user accounts.

Computers   Likewise, this is the default location for computer accounts.

Domain controllers   I bet I don't even have to tell you. (Just in case, though, this container is the default location for domain controller accounts.)

After your installation is complete, all components are ready to go. The process even creates an OU structure for you. This structure is more than sufficient for many companies. The installation process also creates a log file that lists the results of each step in the process. This log file is located in the \winnt\debug folder.

Verifying Your Installation

Once you have completed the installation of ADS, it is a good idea to confirm that everything went as planned. The only real problem with Wizards is that you click, they do, and you are never sure if they have done what you wanted them to do! The most important process that must be completed during the installation is the addition of the service records, or *SRV records,* to the DNS database.

NOTE

Since ADS uses DNS to find domain controllers, it is imperative that each server have a record in the database.

To confirm that DNS has been updated correctly, you need to do two things.

First, check the local DNS file to ensure that the proper entries have been made. This file is located in the \<*systemroot*>\System32\ Config folder and is named Netlogon.dns. The first record you should see is the server's LDAP service record. The LDAP SRV record should look something like this:

```
_Ldap._tcp.<Active_directory_domain_name> IN SRV 0 0 389
<domain_controller_name>
```

Here's an example:

```
_Ldap._tcp.KingTech.com IN SRV 0 0 389 ADS1.KingTech.com
```

Second, to ensure that the SRV records in the DNS database are working correctly, use the NSLOOKUP tool. The following steps will confirm their functionality:

1. At the command prompt, type **NSLOOKUP**, and press Enter.

2. Type **SET TYPE = SRV**, and press Enter.

3. Type **ldap.tcp.<*Active_directory_domain_name*>**, where <*Active_directory_domain_name*> is the name of your company's Active Directory domain. Press Enter.

If this process returns the server name and IP address, the SRV records are performing correctly.

What's Next?

These days, almost anybody who has a computer is connected to the Internet, and being connected is often the reason a person buys a computer in the first place. Windows 2000 includes all sorts of tools and features that make connecting easy. In Part III, we'll take a look at how to get connected and then at how to send and receive e-mail and access resources on the Internet.

PART III
CONNECTING TO THE WORLD

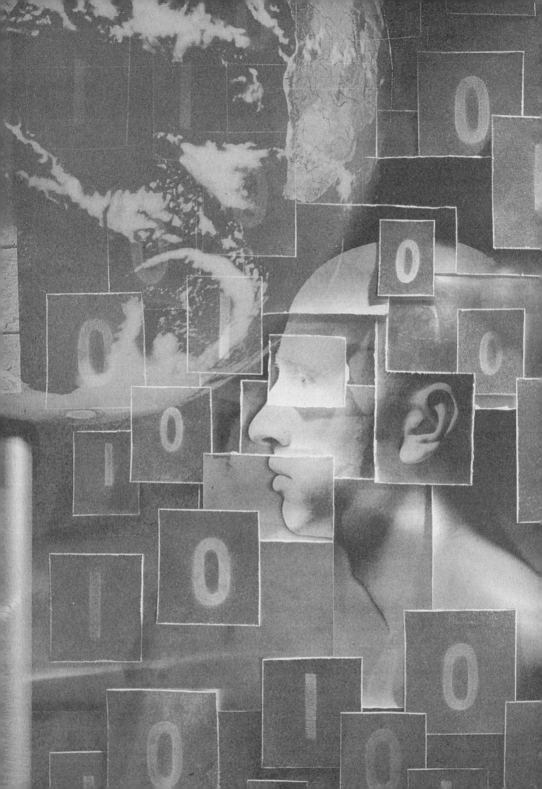

Chapter 15

INTRODUCTION TO COMMUNICATIONS AND USING PHONE DIALER

Will Rogers once explained that the telephone is like a very big dog; when you pulled on its tail in New York, the dog would bark in Los Angeles. Radio, he said, works exactly the same way, but without the dog. In Windows 2000 Professional, communications functions—including data transfer, electronic mail, and control of voice telephone calls—are integrated into the operating system. Maybe Will Rogers would have said that the dog is now using a keyboard and a modem.

Adapted from *Mastering Windows 2000 Professional,* by Mark Minasi and Todd Phillips

ISBN 0-7821-2448-X   1163 pages $39.99

When you first got your computer, you probably planned to use it for word processing, financial record keeping and analysis, and maybe playing some games. You would tap information into the keyboard, the computer would do its thing, and after a while, it would print the result on a piece of paper or display the result on your screen. At that point, your computer was probably a stand-alone device, not connected to any other computers. If you needed to exchange data with somebody else, you could use a floppy disk to move files from one machine to the other (this technique is sometimes called sneakernet).

But when you start connecting them together, stand-alone computers become extremely flexible tools for communication. Relatively early in the development of computer technology, people figured out that it wasn't particularly difficult to transfer information through a wire from one computer to another. As long as the computers on both ends use the same technical standards, you can move messages, programs, text, and data files back and forth. And when you connect a *lot* of computers together through a network, you can communicate with any other computer on the same network, just as you can reach any other telephone connected to the global telecommunications system from the one on your desk.

Under the broad category of communications, your PC can send and receive text, program files, sounds, and images. It can also exchange images of fax pages with a distant fax machine. This data can enter and leave your PC through a modem, a network interface card, or a direct cable connection to another computer.

Communications capability has been part of DOS and Windows since the earliest IBM PCs. Windows 2000 includes an extensive set of communications tools that enable you to exchange electronic mail with other computers, browse the Internet, and use your computer to control telephone calls. This chapter starts with an overview of the communications features of Windows 2000, shows how to configure Windows 2000 to work with your modem, and concludes with a discussion of how to configure and use the Phone Dialer applet. You can find more specific information about communications applications in the remaining chapters of this part. Chapter 16 covers Outlook Express, the Windows 2000 Professional control center for messaging components. Chapter 17 describes how to use Windows 2000 Professional to connect your computer to the rest of the world.

DISCOVERING WHAT'S NEW IN WINDOWS 2000 COMMUNICATIONS

Windows 2000 includes some major improvements over the way earlier versions of Windows and NT handled communications:

- ▶ It's a lot happier about sending and receiving data at high speeds.

- ▶ It can transfer data in the background without interfering with other applications.

- ▶ It doesn't require you to shut down a program that waits for incoming messages or faxes before you try to use the same modem to place an outgoing call.

In addition, Microsoft has replaced the old Terminal program in previous versions of Windows and NT with a completely new set of applications for connecting to distant computers through a modem and for sending, receiving, and managing messages, data files, and faxes. Windows 2000 Professional also has a Telephony Application Program Interface (TAPI) that integrates your PC with a telephone system. You may notice, in Control Panel, the Phone And Modem Options applet. This provides an interface for installing future telephony drivers, once they become more widely available. Two Microsoft-supplied drivers are installed with Windows 2000 Professional—namely, the Unimodem driver and TAPI. Overall, Windows 2000 goes a long way toward turning your stand-alone computer into a tool that can be linked to other computers and other communications devices anywhere in the world.

USING THE WINDOWS TELEPHONY INTERFACE

NT 4 and Windows 95/98 included TAPI—a set of software hooks to applications that control the way your computer interacts with the telephone network. Windows 2000 implements a newer version of TAPI that gives you some additional capabilities. TAPI is an internal part of Windows 2000 Professional rather than a specific application program—it provides a standard way for software developers to access communications ports and devices, such as modems and telephone sets, to control data, fax, and voice calls. Using TAPI, an application can place a call, answer an incoming call, and hang up when the call is complete. TAPI also supports features such as hold, call transfer, voicemail, and conference calls. TAPI-compliant applications work with conventional telephone lines, Private Branch Exchange (PBX), and Centrex systems; these applications also work with specialized services such as cellular and Integrated Services Digital Network (ISDN).

By moving these functions to a common program interface, Windows 2000 Professional prevents conflicting demands for access to your modem and telephone line from multiple application programs. Therefore, you no longer need to shut down a program that's waiting for incoming calls before you use a different program to send a fax.

Unless you're planning to write your own communications applications, you won't ever have to deal directly with TAPI, but you will see its benefits when you use the communications programs included in Windows 2000 Professional—HyperTerminal, Outlook Express, Phone Dialer, and Remote Access—and when you use new NT or Windows 95/98–compatible versions of third-party communications programs such as Pro-Comm and WinFax.

Windows 2000 Professional includes a fairly simple telephony application called Phone Dialer (which we talk about later in this chapter), but this application only begins to show what TAPI can do. NT 4 also included Phone Dialer, but the version in Windows 2000 Professional is a whole new animal. Phone Dialer now delivers on some of the promise that TAPI showed us in NT and Windows 95. This application can not only dial the phone, it can connect to video conference sessions over your local area network (LAN) or place a voice call to an Internet address by modem or network connection.

Eventually, you can expect to see a lot of new Windows telephony products that will move control of your telephone to the Windows 2000 Professional Desktop. For example, you might be able to use the telephone company's caller-ID service to match incoming calls to a database that displays detailed information about the caller before you answer, or you may be able to use an on-screen menu to set up advanced call features such as conference calling and call forwarding, which now require obscure strings of digits from the telephone keypad.

INSTALLING A MODEM

Every time you installed a new communications application in earlier versions of Windows or NT, you had to go through another configuration routine—you had to specify the port connected to your modem, the highest speed the modem could handle, and so forth. Because there was no central modem control, each program required its own setup.

This changed in NT 4 (and Windows 95/98), which uses a *universal modem* driver called *Unimodem*. Unimodem is the software interface between all of your computer's 32-bit Windows-compatible communications applications (including the ones that use TAPI) and your modem or other communications hardware. It includes integrated control for port selection, modem initialization, speed, file transfer protocols, and terminal emulation. Because Unimodem handles the modem configuration, you only have to specify setup parameters once.

If you're using third-party communications applications left over from earlier versions of Windows, they'll usually work with Windows 2000 Professional, but you'll still have to configure them separately. When you replace them with newer, Windows 2000–compatible updates, they'll use the settings already configured in your Control Panel.

WARNING

Some communications packages written for Windows 3.*x* provided their own version of several key system files such as comm.drv or winsock.dll. If you install such a program, it may adversely affect your 32-bit communications software by overwriting the system files on which they depend.

In most cases, you need a modem to use the communications features of Windows 2000 Professional. Your modem might be an internal expansion board, an external modem plugged into a serial port, or a credit-card–sized PCMCIA (Personal Computer Memory Card International Association) modem. You can choose to install a modem during the Network Setup portion of Windows 2000 Professional Setup by telling Setup that your computer will participate on a network through a dial-up connection. To install your modem later, you can use the Phone And Modem Options applet in Control Panel, or you can configure the modem from a communications application such as Phone Dialer or HyperTerminal.

Follow these steps to install a modem from Control Panel:

1. Choose Start ≻ Settings ≻ Control Panel to open Control Panel.

2. If you're using an external modem, turn it on, and make sure it's connected to both the telephone line and a serial port on your computer.

3. Double-click the Phone And Modem Options icon to open the Phone And Modem Options dialog box, which is shown in Figure 15.1.

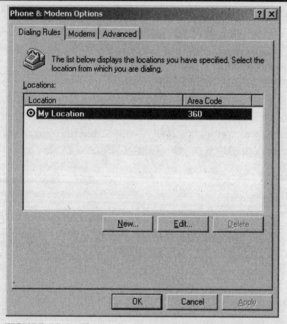

FIGURE 15.1: This is the Phone And Modem Options dialog box. Click the Add button on the Modems tab to install a new modem.

4. Click the Modems tab, and then click the Add button to start the Install New Modem Wizard.

5. Because you turned on the modem in step 2, you can let the Wizard try to identify your modem type. Click the Next button.

6. If you have an external modem, you will see the lights flash on the front panel while the Wizard tests it. When the tests are complete, the Wizard displays the final dialog box, which is shown in Figure 15.2.

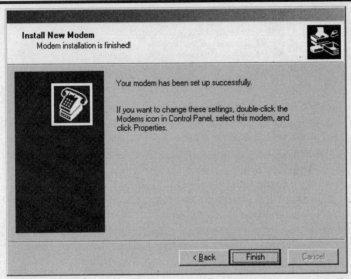

Install New Modem
Modem installation is finished!

Your modem has been set up successfully.

If you want to change these settings, double-click the Modems icon in Control Panel, select this modem, and click Properties.

< Back   Finish   Cancel

FIGURE 15.2: The Install New Modem Wizard tells you that it has finished installing a new modem.

7. If the Wizard is not able to identify your modem, you will be prompted to choose its make and model from a list. If your modem is not listed, look in the modem manual for an equivalent type or select the Generic Modem Drivers item in the Manufacturers list. Windows 2000 Professional supports most modems on the market today, but it also allows for new models that will inevitably be released in the future. If you own a modem that is not listed, contact the vendor for updated drivers, or use the disk that was provided with the modem. In this case, use the Have Disk button to install the driver. Be sure to load the Windows 2000 version of the driver.

8. Click Next, select the COM port (typically COM 3 or 4), and click Next and then Finish to complete the modem installation. If you haven't already entered your location and area

Part III

code, the Location Information dialog box in Figure 15.3 asks for this information.

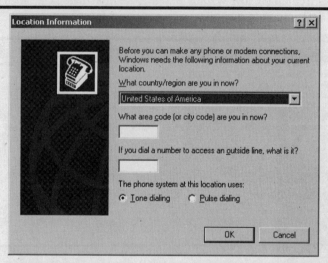

FIGURE 15.3: This is the Location Information dialog box. Choose your location from the drop-down menu, and type your area code.

9. If your modem is connected to a line that uses Touch-Tone dialing, choose Tone. If not, choose Pulse.

CHANGING MODEM PROPERTIES

After you install your modem, all your TAPI-aware communications programs will use the same configuration settings. When you change them in one application, those changes carry across to all the others. In general, you won't want to change the default modem properties, which specify settings such as the loudness of the modem's speaker and the maximum data-transfer speed. If you replace your modem, or if you use different modem types in different locations, you can install an additional modem from Control Panel.

To change the modem properties after installation is complete, open Control Panel, and double-click the Phone And Modem Options icon to open the Phone And Modem Options dialog box. Click the Modems tab, select the modem you want to modify, and then click the Properties button to display the Properties dialog box for that modem. Figure 15.4 displays the Properties dialog box for a U.S. Robotics modem.

NOTE

Other applications that work with modems, such as HyperTerminal, also provide access to the Modem Properties dialog box. The tabs visible in this dialog box depend on whether you are working from Control Panel or from another application.

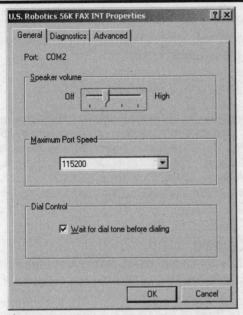

FIGURE 15.4: Use this Properties dialog box to change your modem configuration.

General Properties

The General tab of the Modem Properties dialog box has four settings:

- ► Port
- ► Speaker Volume
- ► Maximum Port Speed
- ► Dial Control

Port

The port that your modem is using is displayed in this area. Unlike NT 4, you can't change the port setting here. Instead, use the Advanced tab to alter the port usage for the modem. (We'll look at the settings on the Advanced tab later in this section.) Internal modems are usually installed on COM ports 3 or 4. External modems are normally installed on COM 2.

Speaker Volume

The Speaker Volume control is a slider bar that you can use to specify the loudness of the speaker inside your modem.

NOTE

Some modems support only one volume level besides Off, and if you happen to be using a generic modem driver, this volume control may be disabled. In this case, you can still control the speaker. In the Modem Properties dialog box, click the Advanced tab, and in the Extra Initialization Commands box, enter **ATM1** (for sound) or **ATM0** (for no sound). For more information on the AT commands for your modem, consult the manual that came with your modem.

Maximum Port Speed

When your modem makes a connection, it will try to use the maximum speed to exchange data with the modem at the other end of the link. As a rule, if you have a 33,600 bits per second (bps) or faster modem, the maximum speed should be three or four times the rated modem speed (for example, set your modem speed to 115,200) to take advantage of the modem's built-in data compression.

Dial Control

This setting is a simple check box that enables or disables the option to Wait For Dial Tone Before Dialing. If your modem doesn't recognize the dial tone used by your current location, or if you need to manually dial your modem connection, you should clear this check box.

Not all modems support this setting. If your modem does not support this, the check box will be grayed out.

Diagnostics

The Diagnostics tab is new to many NT users, but should be familiar to users of Windows 95/98. The Diagnostics tab is extremely useful for troubleshooting communications issues. Clicking the Diagnostics tab displays the dialog box shown in Figure 15.5.

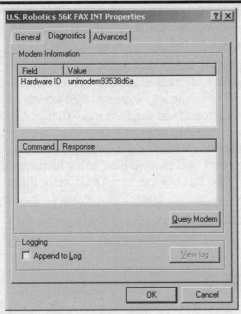

FIGURE 15.5: The Diagnostics tab of the Modem Properties dialog box lets you test your modem configuration and set logging options.

Part iii

Query Modem

This button is important if you plan to use a modem in Windows 2000 Professional. Clicking the Query Modem button sends a series of commands to your modem, testing its response. The first thing this tells you, hopefully, is that you actually *have* a modem and that it is working correctly. The next thing it reveals is which attention commands (AT commands) are supported by your hardware.

The responses to your test, if any, will be displayed in the two text boxes of the Modem Information area of the Diagnostics tab.

Logging

The Logging section is at the bottom of the Modem Properties dialog box. The first setting that you can control here is whether to create a new modem log for each session or to append the new information to the existing file. To add new information to the end of an existing file, check the Append To Log check box.

Clicking the View Log button opens the log file in Notepad. The naming convention of this log file has changed somewhat for Windows 2000 Professional. In Windows 95/98, the log file was named modemlog.txt. But in Windows 2000 Professional, you can have more than one modem attached to your computer, so the name must reflect this. The name used by Windows 2000 Professional is ModemLog_<Your Modem Name> .txt. For example, a Sportster 56K modem has the log filename of ModemLog_Sportster 56k Data Fax.txt. Quite a mouthful!

These log files contain information gathered while the modem was being queried for diagnostics and information gathered while the modem was in normal use.

Advanced Settings

Many of the, pardon the term, *advanced* settings have been moved out of the way and consigned to the Advanced tab (see Figure 15.6). This is partly an effort to shield the average user from the possible complexities of configuring a modem in Windows 2000 Professional and partly because you just won't have to use these settings very often.

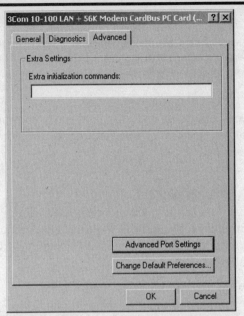

FIGURE 15.6: The Advanced tab of the Modem Properties dialog box

Extra Settings

This Extra Settings section contains the Extra Initialization Commands text box for entering any additional AT commands you want to use while initializing the modem. We've found this area useful when working with several modems under Windows 95/98 or NT, such as the U.S. Robotics Sportster. This modem and several others by various manufacturers don't seem to like the initialization string that Microsoft wrote for them. Symptoms of this may be anything from dropped sessions to failed file transfers. You can use the Extra Settings section to correct this problem. Simply type **&F1** in the Extra Initialization Commands box, and click OK. This command tells the modem to ignore the initialization string it just received and to use its built-in factory settings instead. Perfect!

Part III

WARNING

You should exercise some caution here, though, and consult the documentation for your modem to verify the actions of the command before using it. If the command isn't right for your modem, using it could cause some real damage to your modem.

The Extra Initialization Commands option enables you to control all the functions of your modem, such as the speaker volume or whether it waits for a dial tone before dialing.

Change Default Preferences

Clicking the Change Default Preferences button opens the Default Preferences dialog box for your modem. Using the General and the Advanced tabs, you can alter the configuration for your modem, including port speeds, compression, and advanced port settings.

The General tab contains settings for Call Preferences and Data Connection Preferences. The Call Preferences section has a couple of settings that govern how the call session will be handled. The first is whether the modem should hang up automatically after it has been idle for a set number of minutes. Check the box next to Disconnect A Call If Idle For More Than x Minutes, and enter the number of minutes that you want the modem to sit idle before being disconnected. The default is 30 minutes.

The second option under Call Preferences is to Cancel The Call If Not Connected Within x Seconds. The default is 60 seconds. This option tells your modem to continue trying to connect for up to the number of seconds you specify.

The Data Preferences section contains the following settings that affect the transfer of data across this modem session:

Port Speed   Sets the data transfer rate for the communications port. As a rule, set this to at least twice the rated speed of your modem to allow for modem data compression.

Data Protocol   Controls the error-correction scheme that your modem will use for sessions. The default setting of StandardEC enables your modem to negotiate the highest level of error correction that both modems in a session will support. This is usually the best setting since it allows for some flexibility. The ForcedEC setting causes the modem to use only V.42

error correction. If this fails, the call will be terminated. The Disabled setting turns off error correction entirely. Click the down arrow to display the ForcedEC and Disabled settings.

Compression   Tells the modem to use hardware-based data compression. This usually results in faster communications, except when you are transferring large files that are already compressed. In this case, enabling hardware compression can actually slow down your session because you are trying to compress something that is already compressed.

FlowControl   This setting controls the method used to signal transmission of data. Many programs require some kind of indication that the data sent was received on the other end. Typically, this can be done through hardware or software methods. The hardware method uses a scheme called Ready to Send/Clear to Send (RTS/CTS), which depends on the modem hardware to handle the signaling. The software method is called XON/XOFF, which relies on the operating system to send a signal when the modem is through transmitting. The Disabled option disables flow control altogether. Use this option mostly for troubleshooting.

The Advanced tab has the following settings, some of which you may recognize if you've been using your modem for a while under older operating systems:

Data Bits   Sets the number of bits that will be used for transmitting a single character of text. Typically, most online services and bulletin board systems use eight bits per character, though some systems use seven. If you don't you use the same setting that the modem you are calling is using, you won't be able to communicate correctly.

Parity   Determines whether the session will use parity bits for error checking. If you are using this method of error checking, the modem will append a single bit that indicates whether the number of bits set to the value of one in a character is even or odd. This is a fairly primitive method of checking for errors and has been replaced with much more sophisticated routines. Typically, this option is set to None. This setting must match that of the other modem with which you are communicating.

Stop Bits   Tells the system that a byte of data has been sent. Stop bits are almost always set to a value of one.

Modulation   This setting determines the protocol used to translate the data signals from the digital form used by computers to the sounds that can be transmitted across the phone line. Normally, you would use the Standard modulation protocol, but if you are having problems connecting, try changing to the Non-Standard (Bell, HST) modulation.

Dialing Rules

This is one of the new areas in Windows 2000 Professional. In NT 4, you used the Dialing Properties dialog box to dictate the configuration of your TAPI location. Windows 2000 Professional uses the Dialing Rules tab of the Phone And Modem Options dialog box. You can access this information in a couple of ways: you can use Control Panel, or you can use any TAPI-aware application.

When TAPI was first released (with Windows 95), it was a great boon to people who traveled with their computers. Establishing the communications settings just once and having them apply equally to all communications programs was really nice. But you probably live in a place where the phone companies have been splitting areas into smaller geographic segments and assigning these segments new area codes. If you use an ISP in an area code different from your own but access that ISP as a local call it can be enough to drive you crazy.

Windows 2000 Professional can help end *that* suffering by letting you set up rules for your 10-digit dialing pleasure. The Dialing Rules tab of the Phone And Modem Options dialog box lets you create, modify, or delete TAPI locations. Put simply, a TAPI *location* is a collection of the dialing properties for the place from which you are calling.

To create a new location or to edit a location, follow these steps:

1. Open Control Panel, and double-click the Phone And Modem Options icon to open the Phone And Modem Options dialog box.

2. On the Dialing Rules tab, click the New button to open the New Location dialog box, or click Edit to open the Edit Location dialog box, which is shown in Figure 15.7.

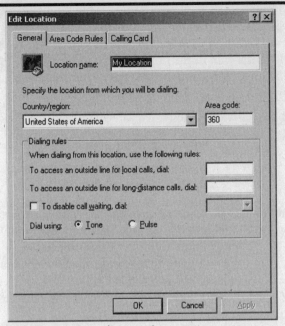

FIGURE 15.7: The Edit Location dialog box gives you access to all of the important settings to control dialing from one place.

NOTE

Both the New Location and the Edit Location dialog boxes contain the same options, and you can also open them from any TAPI-aware communications program in Windows 2000 Professional.

3. Type a name that you will use to identify this location in the Location Name text box.

4. Under Country/Region select the appropriate country. This will determine the correct country code for dialing long distance. In the United States, the country code is 1.

5. In the Area Code text box, type the area code for the location you will be dialing from.

6. In the Dialing Rules section, you need to tell Windows 2000 Professional how to dial from this location. If you dial a special number to access an outside line (such as 9 on a PBX system at work), enter that in the first text box. In the second text box, you can enter the number you use to dial an outside line for long distance, if it's different from the first number.

7. If you have call waiting, you can disable it by checking the To Disable Call Waiting check box and then selecting the correct numeric code.

NOTE

To find out the correct code for disabling Call Waiting in your area, look in the front of your local telephone directory or call your telephone business office.

8. Finally, select the correct radio button for the type of modulation your phone system uses to dial. This will most likely be Tone dialing, but if your phone system uses Pulse dialing you will need to select Pulse in order to dial correctly.

9. Click OK.

If you want to change the area code settings to outsmart the new 10-digit dialing for local calls, you will need to complete a few more steps. On the Area Code Rules tab, you can establish the rules for dialing within your area code and for calling other area codes. Basically, you need to separate long distance from local calling whether it's in your own area code or another. To create a new area code rule, follow these steps:

1. On the Area Code Rules tab of the New Location dialog box or the Edit Location dialog box, click the New button to open the New Area Code Rule dialog box, which is shown in Figure 15.8.

2. Type the area code for which you want to create the rule in the Area Code text box.

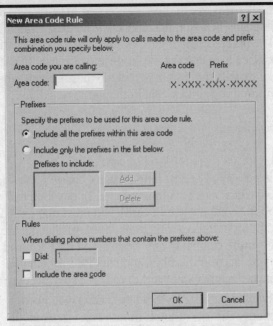

FIGURE 15.8: The New Area Code Rule dialog box enables you to define combinations of area code and prefix that are to be dialed as local calls.

3. In the Prefixes section, click either Include All The Prefixes Within This Area Code to dial all the prefixes as local, or click Include Only The Prefixes In The List Below if you want to customize the list. To add new prefixes to the list, click the Add button to open the Add Prefix dialog box, and type the prefixes in the Prefixes box. Separate multiple prefixes with either a space or a comma.

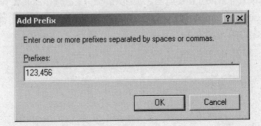

Part iii

4. Finally, check the boxes in the Rules section of the New Area Code Rule dialog box that describe how this rule should be applied. The first box tells Windows 2000 Professional to dial your country code before the area code and number. The second check box tells the system to include the area code when dialing any area code and prefix in the list.

5. Click OK.

Calling Card

Calling cards are a good way to handle long distance charges, especially if you will be expensing costs back to your employer. To pay for a call with a calling card (a telephone company credit card), you must dial a special string of numbers that includes a carrier access code, your account number, and the number you're calling. In some cases, you have to call a service provider, enter your account number, and wait for a second dial tone before you can enter the number you want to call.

To use your calling card automatically when dialing, you need to specify the card to use, along with the account number and Personal ID Number (PIN). To do this, click the Calling Card tab of either the New Location dialog box or the Edit Location dialog box, and in the Card Types list, click the name of the calling card you use. If your card isn't listed, you can create a new definition by clicking the New button. The Calling Card tab is shown in Figure 15.9.

The Card Types list includes the most commonly used telephone credit cards in the United States—those issued by AT&T, MCI, and Sprint, as well as some of the more common international cards such as British Telecom. If you choose a calling card from the list, the program automatically uses the correct calling sequence for that long-distance carrier. But if you need a special calling sequence, click the New button and type the sequences for local, long distance, and international calls in the New Calling Card dialog box.

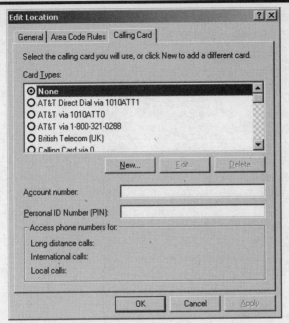

FIGURE 15.9: Use the Calling Card tab in either the New Location dialog box or the Edit Location dialog box to specify your telephone credit-card type and number.

To create a new calling card definition, follow these steps:

1. In Control Panel, open the Phone And Modem Options applet.

2. Click the Dialing Rules tab, and select the TAPI location you want to edit. If you are creating a new location, refer to the steps earlier in this chapter, and then follow the steps here to modify the calling card.

3. Click Edit to open the Edit Location dialog box, and then click the Calling Card tab to display the list of predefined calling cards available.

4. Click the New button to open the New Calling Card dialog box, as shown in Figure 15.10.

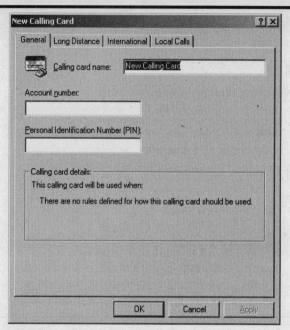

FIGURE 15.10: The New Calling Card dialog box enables you to create your own calling card definitions.

5. On the General tab, fill in a name to describe this card. This name helps you identify this card definition; it is not *your* name. Fill in the account number of your calling card, if it has one, and then fill in the PIN.

6. On the Long Distance tab, enter the phone number you call to place your long distance call with this card.

7. Select the steps you need to perform to place a call. This sets the exact order in which the information needs to be provided so the computer can use the calling card. For instance, if your card requires you to enter your PIN and then the destination number, click the PIN button, and then click the Destination Number button. The steps will be displayed in the Calling Card Dialing Steps text box. You can easily move them up or down by highlighting them and pressing the Move Up or Move Down buttons until the order is correct.

8. Repeat steps 6 and 7 for the International and Local Calls tabs until you have provided the information for every type of call you will be making with this card.

9. Click Apply or OK to save your card definition.

In Windows 95/98 and NT 4, you needed some complicated scripting to create the procedure we just completed. Windows 2000 Professional has made calling cards much easier to deal with by shielding you from the need to understand script variables and formatting.

USING PHONE DIALER

In NT 4, Phone Dialer was a simple application that placed outgoing voice telephone calls through your modem. You could tell Phone Dialer what number you wanted to dial by typing the number, choosing it from a Speed Dial list, or clicking numbers on an on-screen keypad. After you called a number, you could select it from a list of recent calls. After dialing the call, Phone Dialer connected the line to the telephone set plugged into the phone jack on your modem so you could pick up the handset and start talking.

Windows 2000 also has a Phone Dialer application, but it has much more functionality than the one in NT 4. Instead of simply being a handy way to place a voice call using your computer to dial, the new Phone Dialer can perform voice or video conferencing over your local network or the Internet. You can still use a telephone connected to your modem's pass-through jack, or you can use a sound card, microphone, or video camera directly through your computer.

Starting Phone Dialer

To start Phone Dialer, choose Start ➤ Programs ➤ Accessories ➤ Communications ➤ Phone Dialer. If you use Phone Dialer frequently, you can create a shortcut for this application.

When you start the program, the main Phone Dialer screen, shown in Figure 15.11, appears. To place a call, simply click the Dial button on the toolbar, or choose Phone ➤ Dial to open the Dial dialog box, which you can use to enter the phone number. (Be sure that the Phone Call option button in the Dial dialog box is selected.) Phone Dialer will dial telephone numbers literally as you enter them, so be careful to enter all the numbers you want.

Part III

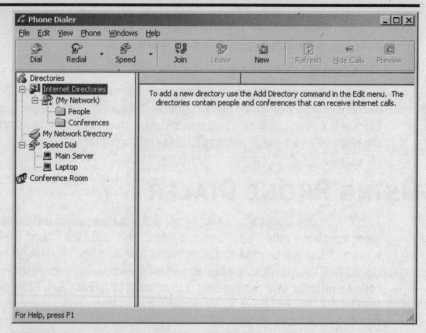

FIGURE 15.11: The main screen of the Phone Dialer application includes an Explorer-like interface for storing call information.

Dialing a number with Phone Dialer is exactly like dialing a number from your telephone. Therefore, you must include all the prefixes required by the phone company for this kind of call, such as a 1 for prepaid long-distance calls or a 0 for operator-assisted calls. On the other hand, if you're using an office telephone that requires 9 or some other access code for an outside line, you can use the Edit Location dialog box or New Location dialog box (discussed earlier in this chapter) to add the code for all calls. Follow these steps:

1. In Phone Dialer, choose Edit ➤ Options to open the Options dialog box.

2. Click the Phone And Modem Options button to open the Phone And Modem Options dialog box.

3. Click the New button to open the New Location dialog box, or click the Edit button to open the Edit Location dialog box.

4. In the Dialing Rules section, enter the necessary access codes, and then click OK.

The new capabilities of this application enable you to use the Internet and your computer to place calls. This conferencing option even works well on your local network. To use this feature, follow these steps:

1. Click the Dial button to open the Dial dialog box.

2. Click the Internet Call option, and then enter the person's name, computer name, or IP address. The number field also acts as a recently called list. You can drop down this list to select a connection that you recently used.

3. Click Place Call.

Whether you use this tool to save money on long distance (by connecting to a friend in another part of the world) or just as a convenient video conferencing tool, Phone Dialer is an application with which you should become familiar.

Adding Directories

Phone Dialer uses directory servers to keep track of people and computers. You can access directories on the Internet or on your local network. The Active Directory on Windows 2000 Server can provide this service for Phone Dialer, as well as many directory servers on the Internet. Phone Dialer uses the Internet Locator Service (ILS) or Lightweight Directory Access Protocol to find people or computers on your local network or the Internet. You need to have at least one directory server added to your configuration to use Phone Dialer this way.

To add a new directory to your Phone Dialer configuration, follow these steps:

1. Right-click either Internet Directories or My Network Directory in the left pane of Phone Dialer's main window, and then choose Add Directory from the shortcut menu to open the Add Directory Server dialog box.

2. Enter the name or IP address of a directory server, and then click Add.

Programming the Speed Dial List

The Speed Dial list in Phone Dialer lets you easily and quickly connect to people, computers, addresses, or phone numbers that you've connected

Part iii

to before. With the Speed Dial list set with the numbers you use the most, connecting can be as easy as double-clicking an entry. The Speed Dial list, contained in the left pane of the main Phone Dialer window, is shown in Figure 15.12.

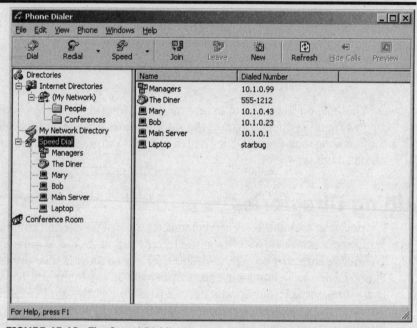

FIGURE 15.12: The Speed Dial list lets you quickly connect to a phone number, network address, or conference.

You can add a new entry to the Speed Dial list in several ways. The easiest is to right-click the Speed Dial icon in the left pane of Phone Dialer's window and select New Speed Dial from the shortcut menu. Select Edit Speed Dial List from the shortcut menu if you want to change an existing entry or perhaps create more than one new entry. You can also add a new Speed Dial entry when placing a call, as shown in Figure 15.13. Simply check the box next to Add Number To Speed Dial List to add the current number to your list.

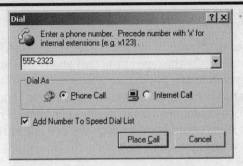

FIGURE 15.13: You can add a new Speed Dial entry when placing a call.

In addition, you can add a new Speed Dial entry by choosing Edit ➤ Add To Speed Dial List. Doing so opens the Speed Dial dialog box. For any method you choose, you will be prompted for a display name for the entry, the number to dial, and the type of number. For example, using our local network, we could create the entry in Figure 15.14 to connect to Ted at his computer in the Accounting department.

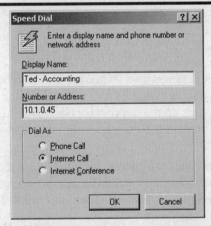

FIGURE 15.14: A sample entry for the Speed Dial list

PLACING A CALL

When you place a call through Phone Dialer, the windows slide out from the side of your screen and display the type of call that you're making, as well as the number or name to which you're trying to connect. For Internet calls (calls placed over a network), a Preview window shows you whether the other party has a camera attached to their computer. The Preview window also has slider controls with which you can adjust the microphone and speaker volumes.

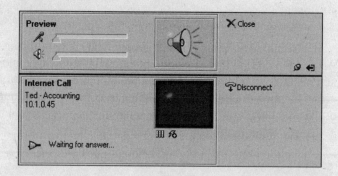

As Phone Dialer places the call, you will hear the dialing tones (or pulses) and the ringing signal or busy signal through the modem's speaker. The Phone Call window lets you know when the call has gone through. To transfer the call to your telephone set (if your telephone is on the same line as your modem), pick up the handset, or click Disconnect to break the connection. If the modem detects a busy signal, you will see a failure message instead.

After you pick up the receiver, your call passes through the modem to your telephone set. At this point, there's no real difference between a Phone Dialer call and one placed directly from the telephone itself. To end the call, simply hang up the telephone.

If you are using Phone Dialer at work through a PBX system, and you are trying to dial an extension number instead of a full phone number, type an **x** at the beginning of the number to tell Phone Dialer to dial the number as an extension. For example, if you want to dial someone at extension 45234, type **x45234** in the Dial dialog box, and set the call type to Phone Call.

As we mentioned earlier, Phone Dialer is a simple tool that does what its name implies. You can, of course, purchase more-sophisticated software (it might even come with your modem) that provides voicemail boxes, fax-on-demand—even call-routing and PBX support.

WHAT'S NEXT?

Now that you have a working knowledge of how to get connected to the outside world using Windows 2000 Professional, we are ready to take a look at Outlook Express. In Chapter 16, Peter Dyson and Pat Coleman discuss the program you use to send and receive e-mail—the most-used feature of the Internet.

Chapter 16

USING OUTLOOK EXPRESS FOR E-MAIL AND NEWS

O f all the features of the Internet, intranets, and local area networks, e-mail is, without question, the most used. Instead of playing phone tag with a colleague at work, you send her e-mail. Millions of extended families stay in touch via e-mail, and an e-mail address has become an expected component of a business card.

Windows 2000
Professional

In Record Time

Teach Yourself Essential Windows 2000 in no time

Adapted from *Windows 2000 Professional: In Record Time*, by Peter Dyson and Pat Coleman

ISBN 0-7821-2450-X   467 pages $29.99

Outlook Express is an Internet standards e-mail reader you can use to access an Internet e-mail account. An Internet e-mail account is not the same thing as an account with an online information service. The difference is that an Internet account provides services such as Point-to-Point protocol, Internet access, and e-mail but does not include services such as chat rooms, access to databases, conferences, and so on. Consequently, you cannot use Outlook Express to access an e-mail account with MS Mail, cc:Mail, CompuServe, America Online, or versions of Microsoft Exchange Server prior to version 5.

TIP

You can use Outlook Express to set up and access a free Hotmail account. To set up a Hotmail account, choose Tools ➤ New Account Signup ➤ Hotmail, and follow the on-screen instructions.

In addition to being an e-mail reader, Outlook Express is also a news reader. In the first part of this chapter, we'll look at e-mail features, and in the second part we'll look at how to access and post to newsgroups.

USING OUTLOOK EXPRESS AS YOUR MAILREADER

The quickest way to start Outlook Express is to click the Launch Outlook Express icon on the Quick Launch toolbar. You can also start it by choosing Start ➤ Programs ➤ Outlook Express or, from within Internet Explorer, by choosing Tools ➤ Mail And News and then selecting an item from the submenu.

NOTE

Before you can use Outlook Express to send and receive e-mail, you need to configure Outlook Express to use your Internet connection. In Outlook Express, choose Tools ➤ Accounts to open the Internet Accounts dialog box, choose Add ➤ Mail to start the Internet Connection Wizard, and follow the on-screen instructions.

A Quick Tour

When you first open Outlook Express, you'll see a screen similar to the one shown in Figure 16.1.

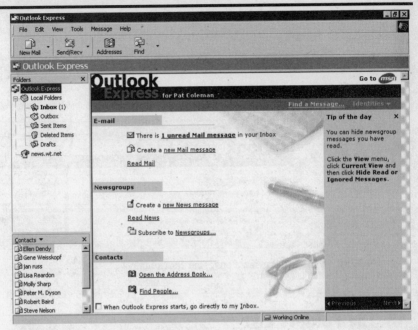

FIGURE 16.1: The opening screen in Outlook Express

To read your mail, click Read Mail, or click Inbox in the Folders list. As you can see in Figure 16.2, initially the Preview Pane is split horizontally; header information is displayed in the upper pane, and the message is displayed in the lower pane.

TIP

To change the arrangement of the Preview Pane, choose View ➤ Layout to open the Window Layout Properties dialog box, and select options to show or hide certain parts.

Part iii

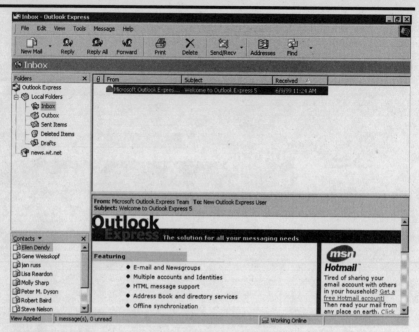

FIGURE 16.2: The Preview Pane, split horizontally

The Folders List

The Folders List is a tool for organizing messages. Initially, it contains the following folders, although you can create additional folders, as you'll see later in this skill:

- ▶ Inbox contains both newly received messages and messages that you have not yet disposed of in some way.

- ▶ Outbox contains messages that are ready to be sent.

- ▶ Sent Items contains copies of messages that you have sent (a handy device if you send lots of e-mail).

- ▶ Deleted Items contains copies of messages that you have deleted.

- ▶ Drafts contains messages that you are working on but which are not yet ready to be sent.

The Contacts Pane

The Contacts pane contains the names of people in your Address Book (for information on Address Book, see Chapter 10). To compose a message to anyone on this list, simply double-click the name.

Retrieving Your Mail

If you are connected to your Internet account, Outlook Express will automatically check the server for new messages and download them when you open Outlook Express. By default, Outlook Express will also check for new mail every 30 minutes, as long as you are connected. To adjust this time interval, follow these steps:

1. Choose Tools ➢ Options to open the Options dialog box:

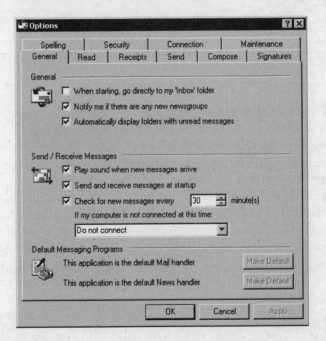

2. Click the up or down arrow to change the Check For New Message Every *x* Minutes option.

3. Click OK.

You can also check for new mail by choosing Tools ➤ Send And Receive ➤ Receive All or by clicking the Send/Recv button on the toolbar in the main window.

Reading and Processing Messages

If you are working in the split Preview Pane view, simply click a message header to display the message in the lower pane. Otherwise, simply double-click a header to view the message.

Printing Messages

For various reasons, it's often handy to have a paper copy of e-mail messages. You can print in a couple of ways:

▶ To print a message without opening it, select its header, and click the Print icon on the toolbar in the main window.

▶ To print an open message, click the Print icon on the toolbar in the message window.

Marking Messages

If you're like us, you don't always handle each message as you receive it or immediately after you read it, and it's easy to forget that you need to take some action or follow up on a message unless it stands out from the others in the header list. One trick that we use is to mark a message as unread even though we have read it (select the header and choose Edit ➤ Mark As Unread). When you mark a message as unread, the header is displayed in boldface. You can also select the header and choose Message ➤ Flag Message to display a red flag to the left of the message header.

In addition, you can mark an individual message as read, and you can mark all messages as read.

Moving Messages

You can easily move a message from one folder to another by dragging and dropping it. For example, if you receive a message that you want to modify and send to someone else, select the message header, and then drag it to the Drafts folder. Open it, revise it, and then send it on its way.

Saving Messages

You can save messages in folders you create in Windows Explorer, and you can save messages in Outlook Express folders. You can also save attachments as files.

Saving Messages in Windows Explorer Folders   To save messages in a folder in Windows Explorer, follow these steps:

1. Open the message or select its header.

2. Choose File ➤ Save As to open the Save Message As dialog box:

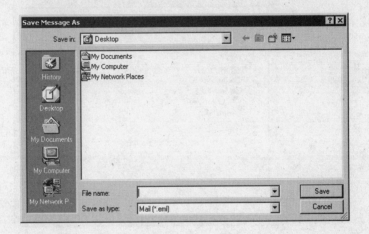

3. Select a folder in which to save the message. Outlook Express places the subject line in the File Name box. You can use this name or type another name.

4. Select a file type, and then click Save.

NOTE

In Windows Explorer, when you click a file that has the .EML extension, it opens in Outlook Express. If you save a message as an HTML file, it opens in Internet Explorer.

Part iii

Saving Messages in Outlook Express Mail Folders   As we've mentioned, you can create your own Outlook Express folders. For example, you might want to create folders for people with whom you regularly correspond, or you might want to create folders for current projects. To create a new folder, follow these steps:

1. Choose File ➤ New ➤ Folder to open the Create Folder dialog box:

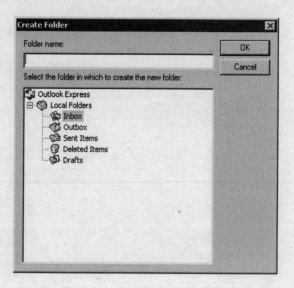

2. In the Folder Name box, type a name for your folder.

3. Select a folder in which to place the new folder, and click OK.

You now have a new folder in your Folders list, and you can drag any message to it. You have, however, an even easier and more efficient way to save messages in Outlook Express folders, and we'll look at that in the "Applying Message Rules" section later in this chapter.

Saving Attachments   An attachment is a file that is appended to an e-mail message. You'll know that a message has an attachment if the header is preceded by the paper clip icon. When you open the message, you'll see the filename of the attachment in the Attach line in the header. To open an attachment, double-click its filename.

To save an attachment, follow these steps:

1. Open the message, and choose File ➢ Save Attachments to open the Save Attachments dialog box:

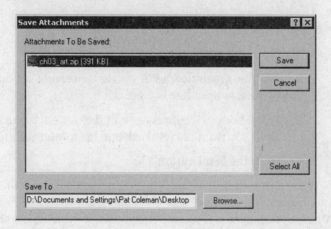

2. Select a folder in which to save the file, and click Save.

We'll discuss how to attach a file to a message later in this chapter in the "Attaching Files to Messages" section.

Replying to Messages

To reply to a message, click the Reply button on the toolbar in the message window. If the message is addressed to multiple recipients and you want to reply to all of them, click the Reply All button.

TIP

This is a quick and easy way to note the person's e-mail address. By default, Outlook Express automatically places the names of the people you reply to in your Address Book. For more on Address Book, see Chapter 10.

By default, Outlook Express includes the text of the original message in your reply. According to Internet tradition, this squanders bandwidth, and it's better not to include the original message unless it's really necessary. When is it necessary?

▶ When you want to be sure that the recipient understands the nature of your reply and the topic to which it is related

Part iii

▶ When your message is part of a series of messages that involve some sort of question-and-answer sequence

▶ When it's important to keep track of who said what when

An alternative is to include only the relevant portions of the original message in your reply. To do so, follow these steps:

1. Open the message, and click the Reply button.

2. The message is now addressed to the original sender, and the original subject line is preceded by Re:.

3. In the body of the message, edit the contents so that the portions you want are retained, and then enter your response.

4. Click the Send button.

If you don't want to include the original message in your reply, you can simply open the message, click the Reply button, choose Edit ➤ Select All, and press Delete. If you're rather sure that you almost always don't want to include the original message, choose Tools ➤ Options, and in the Options dialog box, click the Send tab. Clear the Include Message In Reply check box.

Forwarding Messages

Forwarding an e-mail message is much easier than forwarding a letter through the U.S. mail, and it actually works. To forward a message, follow these steps:

1. Open the message.

2. Click the Forward button on the toolbar in the message window.

3. Enter an address in the To field.

4. Add your own comments if you want.

5. Click Send.

Deleting Messages

To delete a message, you can select its header and click Delete, or you can open it and then click Delete. The message is not yet really deleted, however; Outlook Express has placed it in the Deleted Items folder. By default, the Deleted Items folder is emptied when you close Outlook Express.

If you want to delete items from the Deleted Items folder yourself, follow these steps:

1. Select the Deleted Items folder.

2. Choose Edit ➤ Empty 'Deleted Items' Folder.

3. When Outlook Express asks if you are sure you want to delete these items, click Yes.

Creating and Sending Messages

In this section, we'll walk through the steps to create and send a simple message. You can, however, create messages in HTML (HyperText Markup Language) and include hyperlinks, pictures, colorful formatting, sounds, and so on. We'll look at that in the next section.

To begin a new message, you can click the New Mail button in the main window to open the New Message window, as shown in Figure 16.3. If the intended recipient is in your Address Book, you can double-click that person's name in the Contacts pane to open the New Message window; the To line will display the recipient's name.

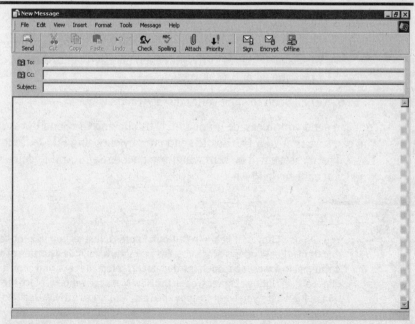

FIGURE 16.3: You create a new message in the New Message window.

If your New Message window includes a Formatting toolbar, the message you compose will be formatted as HTML. For our purposes here, we want only plain text. So, if necessary, choose Format ➤ Plain Text before you begin composing your message. Now, follow these steps:

1. If necessary, enter the address of the primary recipient in the To field. If you are sending a message to multiple primary recipients, separate their addresses with semicolons.

2. Optionally, enter e-mail addresses in the Cc (carbon copy) and Bcc (blind carbon copy) fields. To enter a Bcc recipient, click the Cc icon, enter the name in the Select Recipients dialog box, and click Bcc.

3. Enter a subject line for your message.

NOTE

If you don't enter a subject line, Outlook Express will ask if you're sure you don't want a subject line. Unless you have a good reason not to do so, enter some text in the subject line. Your recipient will see this text in the header information for the message and will then have a clue as to the nature of your message.

4. Enter the text of your message.

5. If appropriate, establish a priority for your message. Choose Message ➤ Set Priority, and then choose High, Normal, or Low. The default is Normal.

6. Click Send to start your message on its way.

You can send your message immediately by clicking the Send button, or you can save it in your Outbox to send later by choosing File ➤ Send Later. The message will be sent when you choose Send And Receive All or when you choose Send All.

TIP

You can use Copy and Paste in Outlook Express, just as you use those commands in other Windows programs. For example, to include a portion of a Word document in a message, open the document, select the text, and copy it to the Clipboard. In Outlook Express, open the New Message window, place the insertion point where you want to copy the text, and press Ctrl+V. Use this same process to copy portions of e-mail messages to other messages or to documents in other applications.

Creating E-mail Messages with HTML

In the previous section, we created a plain text message, but, as we mentioned, you can also compose messages in HTML and include all sorts of neat effects. Before you send a formatted message, be sure that your recipient's e-mail program can display it effectively. When you open the New Message window and choose Format ➤ Rich Text (HTML), the message you compose is essentially a Web page. Newer e-mail programs such as Netscape Messenger and the commercial version of Eudora, Eudora Pro, can read, compose, and send HTML messages, but many others cannot, including America Online and the freeware version of Eudora. An easy way to find out if your recipient's e-mail program can handle HTML is to send a simple plain text message and ask.

That said, let's look at some bells and whistles you can include in Outlook Express e-mail messages. Click the New Mail icon to open the New Message window, and be sure that the Rich Text (HTML) option is selected. You'll see the screen shown in Figure 16.4. Notice the Formatting toolbar, which contains many of the same tools you see and use in your Windows word processor. You'll also see the Font and Font Size drop-down list boxes that are present in your word processor.

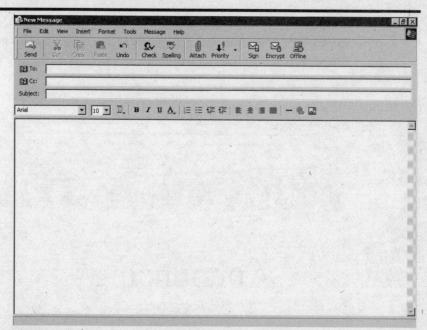

FIGURE 16.4: You can use the Formatting toolbar when creating a message in HTML.

Part iii

As you create your message, just pretend that you're using a word processor, and use the Formatting tools to apply emphasis to your message. All the usual design rules apply, including the following:

- ▶ Don't use a lot of different fonts.

- ▶ Remember, typing in all capital letters in e-mail is tantamount to shouting.

- ▶ Don't place a lot of text in italics. It's hard to read on the screen.

- ▶ Save boldface for what's really important.

To insert a horizontal line that spans the message window, choose Insert ➢ Horizontal Line.

 To apply HTML styles such as Definition Term or Definition, click the Paragraph Style button on the Formatting toolbar.

 USING STATIONERY

In addition to formatting, you have another way to add some class or some comedy to your e-mail messages: stationery. In the New Message window, choose Message ➢ New Using, and then choose a predesigned format from the list in the submenu or click Select Stationery to open the Select Stationery dialog box and select from a larger list. Here's one example of what you'll find:

CONTINUED ➡

To customize stationery, click Create New in the Select Stationery dialog box to start the Stationery Setup Wizard. Follow the on-screen instructions.

Adding Pictures to Messages

You can insert a picture in a message in two ways:

- ► As a piece of art
- ► As a background over which you can type text

To insert a picture as a piece of art that you can size and move, follow these steps:

1. In the New Message window, choose Insert ➤ Picture to open the Picture dialog box.

2. Enter the filename of the picture in the Picture Source text box, or click the Browse button to locate it.

3. Optionally, in the Alternate Text box, enter some text that will display if the recipient's e-mail program cannot display the picture, and specify layout and spacing options if you want. (You can also size and move the picture with the mouse once you place it in the message.)

4. Click OK.

To insert a picture as background, follow these steps:

1. In the New Message window, choose Format ➤ Background ➤ Picture to open the Background Picture dialog box.

2. Enter the filename of the picture, or click Browse to select a predesigned stationery background or locate another file.

3. Click Open, and then click OK to insert the background.

Part III

Adding a Background Color or Sound to Messages

To apply a color to the background of your message, choose Format ➤ Background ➤ Color, and select a color from the drop-down list. Now type something. Can you see it on the screen? If not, you have probably chosen a dark background and your font is also a dark color—most likely black if you haven't changed it from the default.

 To make your text visible, click the Font Color button, and select a lighter color from the drop-down list.

To add a background sound, follow these steps:

1. In the New Message window, choose Format ➤ Background ➤ Sound to open the Background Sound dialog box.

2. Enter the filename of the sound, or click Browse to locate a sound file.

3. Specify the number of times you want the sound to play or whether you want it to play continuously. (In our opinion, a sound that plays continuously while the recipient is reading the message is far more likely to annoy than to entertain.)

4. Click OK.

Including Hyperlinks in Messages

When you insert a hyperlink in a message, the recipient can go directly to the resource simply by clicking the hyperlink. You can insert a hyperlink in three ways:

▶ Simply type it in the message body. Be sure to include the entire URL.

▶ In the New Message window, choose Insert ➤ Hyperlink to open the Hyperlink dialog box, and then enter the URL in the text box.

▶ In Internet Explorer, choose Tools ➤ Mail And News ➤ Send A Link to open the New Message window. The URL of the current page is automatically inserted in the message body.

Adding a Signature to Messages

We know people who never sign their e-mail messages. After all, their name is in the From line in the message header. We also know people who append elaborate signatures, touting their accomplishments or advertising their businesses. We usually just sign our first name at the bottom of messages, but what you do depends on your personal style or whether you're sending business or personal correspondence.

To create a signature that's automatically added to all your outgoing messages, follow these steps:

1. Choose Tools ➤ Options to open the Options dialog box.

2. Click the Signatures tab.

3. Click New.

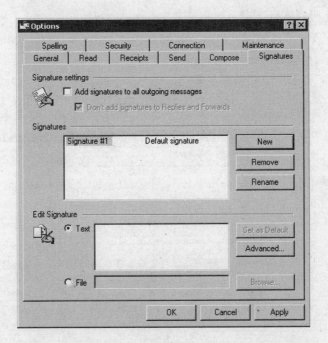

4. To create a text signature, enter the content in the box next to the Text option button.

5. If you want to use a file you've already created as your signature, click the File option button, and enter the filename or click Browse to locate it.

6. If you have multiple e-mail accounts, click the Advanced button to open the Advanced Signature Settings dialog box, and specify which accounts should use this signature.

7. Click the Add Signature To All Outgoing Messages check box, and click OK.

If you don't want the signature automatically appended to all outgoing messages, leave the Add Signature To All Outgoing Message check box unselected. Then, to add this signature to a message, choose Insert ➢ Signature in the New Message window.

Attaching Files to Messages

In Outlook Express, sending a file or multiple files along with your message is painless and simple. Follow these steps:

1. In the New Message window, choose Insert ➢ File Attachment to open the Insert Attachment dialog box:

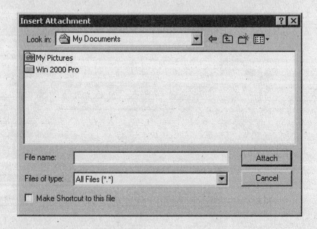

2. Select a file, and click Attach.

Your message now contains the name of the file in the Attach line.

TIP

If the file is large or if you know that the recipient has a slow connection, you'll want to compress it using a program such as WinZIP. For a list of Web pages from which you can download or purchase such a program, in Internet Explorer search on *compression utilities.*

Applying Message Rules

Using the Rules Editor, you can specify where messages go after they are downloaded, block unwanted messages, and, in general, manage incoming messages more efficiently—especially if you deal with a lot of e-mail. In this section, we'll give you a couple of examples that illustrate the possibilities, but, as you will see, there are lots of possibilities, and you'll need to apply the options that make the most sense for your situation.

Let's start by establishing a rule that sends all mail from a particular person to that person's Outlook Express folder. Follow these steps:

1. In the main Outlook Express window, choose Tools ➢ Message Rules ➢ Mail to open the New Mail Rule dialog box:

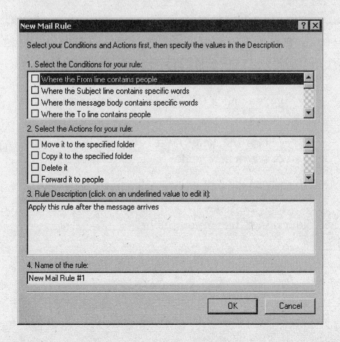

2. In the Select The Conditions For Your Rule section, click the Where The From Line Contains People check box.

3. In the Select The Actions For Your Rule section, click the Move It To The Specified Folder check box.

4. In the Rule Description section, click Contains People to open the Select People dialog box:

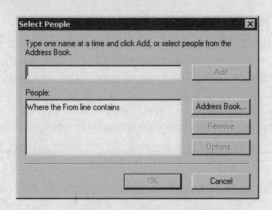

5. Enter a name, or select a name from your Address Book, and click OK.

6. Click Specified to open the Move dialog box.

7. Select the folder where you want this person's messages to go, and click OK. If you need to create a folder, click New Folder.

8. Accept the name of the rule that Outlook Express proposes or type a new name.

9. Click OK.

Now, when messages arrive from that person, you'll find them in his or her folder rather than in your Inbox.

TIP

To delete a rule, select it, and click Remove in the Message Rules dialog box. To modify a rule, select it, and click Modify.

To establish a rule that blocks unwanted messages, follow these steps:

1. In the main Outlook Express window, choose Tools ➤ Message Rules ➤ Blocked Senders List to open the Message Rules dialog box at the Blocked Senders tab.

2. Click Add to open the Add Sender dialog box:

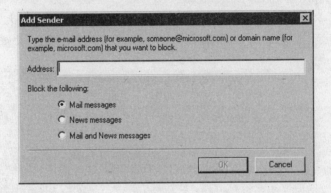

3. Enter the e-mail address that you want to block, specify whether you want to block mail, news, or both from this person, and click OK.

4. Click OK again in the Message Rules dialog box.

Mail from that address will now go immediately to the Deleted Items folder. News from that person will simply not be displayed. (More on news in the last part of this chapter.) To change or delete this rule, open the Message Rules box, select the address, and click Modify or Remove.

Adding and Managing Identities

If several people use the same computer either at home, at the office, or elsewhere and thus also use Outlook Express, you'll probably want to take advantage of the Identities feature, which lets each person view his

Part iii

or her own mail and have individualized settings and contacts. Once you set up Identities, you can switch between them without shutting down the computer or disconnecting from and reconnecting to the Internet.

NOTE

You can also set up Identities in Address Book by choosing Start ➤ Programs ➤ Accessories ➤ Address Book.

When you install Windows 2000 Professional, you are set up in Outlook Express as the Main Identity. To set up other identities in Outlook Express, follow these steps:

1. In the main Outlook Express window, choose File ➤ Identities ➤ Add New Identity to open the New Identity dialog box:

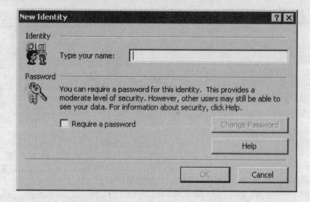

2. Enter the name of the identity you want to establish. If you want to establish identities for the members of your family, for example, you could simply enter a person's first name.

3. If you want to password protect this identify, click the Require a Password check box. Enter the password twice— once in the New Password box and again in the Confirm New Password box. Click OK twice.

4. Outlook Express asks if you want to switch to this new identify now. If you do, click Yes; otherwise, click No.

5. In the Manage Identities dialog box, click New if you want to set up another identity; otherwise, click Close.

The first time you log on as a new identity, you will be asked for some information about your Internet connection. To switch from one identity to another, choose File ➢ Switch Identity to open the Switch Identities dialog box. Select the identity, and click OK. To log off from an identity, choose File ➢ Identities ➢ Logoff *identity*.

To delete an identity, select the identity in the Manage Identities dialog box, and click Remove.

USING OUTLOOK EXPRESS AS YOUR NEWSREADER

A newsgroup is a collection of articles about a particular subject. A newsgroup is similar to e-mail in that you can reply to what someone else has written (the newsgroup term for this is to *post*), and you can send a question or a response either to the whole group or to individuals within the group.

The primary (but not sole) source of newsgroups is Usenet, which is a worldwide-distributed discussion system consisting of newsgroups with names that are classified hierarchically by subject. In a newsgroup name, each component is separated from the next by a period. For example, `rec.crafts.metalworking` is a recreational group devoted to the craft of metalworking. The leftmost portion represents the largest hierarchical category, and the name gets more specific from left to right. Table 16.1 lists the major top-level newsgroup categories and explains the topics each discusses. Currently, there are thousands and thousands of newsgroups on every conceivable topic. For an extensive listing of them, go to `sunsite.unc.edu/usenet-i/hier-s/master.html`.

TABLE 16.1: The Major Newsgroups

NEWSGROUP	WHAT IT DISCUSSES
alt	Newsgroups outside the main structure outlined below
comp	Computer science and related topics, including operating systems, hardware, artificial intelligence, and graphics
misc	Anything that does not fit into one of the other categories
news	Information on Usenet and newsgroups

CONTINUED ➡

Part iii

TABLE 16.1 continued: The Major Newsgroups

NEWSGROUP	WHAT IT DISCUSSES
rec	Recreational activities such as hobbies, the arts, movies, and books
sci	Scientific topics such as math, physics, and biology
soc	Social issues and cultures
talk	Controversial subjects such as gun control, abortion, religion, and politics

You access newsgroups by accessing the server on which they are stored. Not all servers store the same newsgroups. The network administrator or the owner of the site determines what to store. Almost all news servers "expire" articles after a few days or, at most, a few weeks because of the tremendous volume. Although they might be archived at the site, these articles are no longer available to be viewed by users.

WARNING

Newsgroups are uncensored. You can find just about anything at any time anywhere. Nobody has authority over newsgroups as a whole. If you find certain groups, certain articles, or certain people offensive, don't go there, or use the Rules Editor that we talked about earlier to prevent certain articles from even being displayed. But remember, anarchy reigns in newsgroups, and you never know what you might stumble upon in the least likely places.

Setting Up a Newsgroups Account

Before you can read newsgroups, you must set up a newsgroups account. Begin by getting the name of your news server from your ISP, and then follow these steps:

1. In the main Outlook Express window, select the Outlook Express folder, and, in the pane on the right, click Set Up A Newsgroups Account to start the Internet Connection Wizard.

2. Supply the information that the Wizard requests, and click Finish when you are done.

You'll now see a folder in the Folders list for your news server.

Connecting to Newsgroups

The next task is to download the list of newsgroups from your server. When Outlook Express asks if you want to do this, click Yes. This may take a while if you have a slow connection, but notice the incrementing number of newsgroups in the Downloading Newsgroups dialog box. In the process of writing this section, we downloaded a list of more than 25,000 newsgroups.

TIP

Only the names of the newsgroups are downloaded to your computer; their contents remain on the news server. Periodically, you can update this list by clicking Reset List.

When the list has finished downloading, you'll see the Newsgroup Subscriptions dialog box, as shown in Figure 16.5.

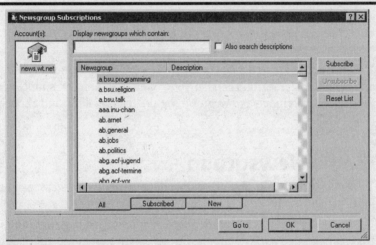

FIGURE 16.5: Use this dialog box to search for and subscribe to newsgroups.

Part iii

Finding a Newsgroup of Interest

You can select a newsgroup to read in two ways:

- ▶ You can scroll through the list (this will take a lot of time).
- ▶ You can search on a term.

Just for the sake of doing it, scroll the list a bit. As you can see, it's in alphabetic order by hierarchical categories. If you don't see anything right away that strikes your fancy, you can perform a search. Enter a term in the Display Newsgroups Which Contain text box, and then don't do anything! In a second, you'll see a list of newsgroups that contain articles about your topic.

Subscribing to a Newsgroup

Subscribing to a newsgroup doesn't involve a fee or any other transaction. Subscribing means simply creating a subfolder for a particular newsgroup in your news folder. Then, instead of selecting it from the Newsgroup Subscriptions dialog box, you can simply click the newsgroup's folder to see the list of articles in it.

Once you've located a newsgroup you want to read, you can select it and click Subscribe and then Go To to open it, or you can simply click Go To. To unsubscribe to a newsgroup, right-click its folder, and choose Unsubscribe.

Reading a Newsgroup

To read an article, simply click its header to display the message in the lower pane.

Outlook Express is a threaded newsreader in that it groups messages that respond to a subject line. If you see a plus sign to the left of a newsgroup header, you can click the plus sign to display a list of related messages. The more up-to-date term for threads is *conversation*. Newsgroup articles are grouped by conversations by default, but you can also organize mail messages by conversations. With your Inbox selected, choose View ➤ Current View ➤ Group Messages by Conversation.

To read the articles from another newsgroup or to search for another newsgroup, double-click your main news folder, and then click Newsgroups to open the Newsgroup Subscriptions dialog box.

Posting to a Newsgroup

Replying to a newsgroup article or sending a message to a newsgroup is known as posting. You post to a newsgroup in much the same way that you compose and send e-mail. To send an original message to a news-group, open the newsgroup and click the New Post button. The New Message window will open with the group's name in the To line.

To reply to an individual article, click the Reply button, and to reply to the entire newsgroup, click the Reply Group button.

CUSTOMIZING OUTLOOK EXPRESS

Throughout this chapter, we've mentioned from time to time ways that you can specify how Outlook Express handles certain features, such as signa-tures. In most cases, you do this through the Options dialog box (shown in Figure 16.6), which you open by choosing Tools ➢ Options. Here's a quick rundown of what to use each tab for in the Options dialog box:

General   Use this tab to specify settings for how Outlook Express starts and for sending and receiving messages.

Read   Use this tab to set options for reading news and mail. For example, you specify a maximum number of news article headers to download at one time.

Receipts   Use this tab if you want to verify that your message has been read by the recipient.

Send   Use this tab to set, among other things, the format (HTML or Plain Text) in which you will send all messages and the format you'll use to reply to messages. You can also specify whether copies of sent messages will be stored and whether you want Outlook Express to put the names and addresses of peo-ple you reply to in your Address Book.

Compose   Use this tab to specify the font and font size for mail messages and news articles that you create and to select stationery fonts for HTML messages.

Signatures   For details about how to use this tab, see the sec-tion "Adding a Signature to Messages."

Security   Use this tab to specify your desired Internet Security zone and to get a digital ID. (For more information on Internet security, see Chapter 19.)

Connection   Use this tab to specify how Outlook Express handles your dial-up connection.

Maintenance   Use this tab to specify what Outlook Express does with deleted items and to clean up downloaded messages, as well as to specify that all server commands are stored for troubleshooting purposes.

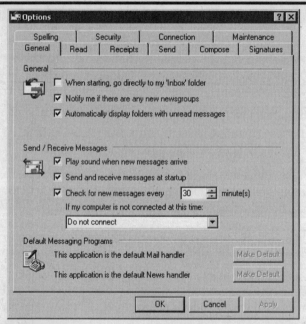

FIGURE 16.6: You use the Options dialog box to customize Outlook Express for the way you work.

WHAT'S NEXT?

E-mail is arguably the most-used feature of the Internet, but to access many Internet resources you need a Web browser. In the next chapter, Mark Minasi and Todd Phillips will take a look at Internet Explorer, the Web browser that's included with Windows 2000, and discuss some built-in Internet utilities.

Part iii

Chapter 17

ACCESSING THE INTERNET

As you're probably well aware, the Internet is the world-wide interconnection of computers and computer networks that permits exchange of messages, data, and files among millions of users. Windows NT Workstation upped the ante in Internet interconnectivity by including not only a Web browser and several of the obligatory Unix-style command-line tools, but also, for the first time, a built-in Web server, an FTP server, and a Gopher server, enabling you to turn your NT Workstation PC into an Internet information server.

Adapted from *Mastering Windows 2000 Professional*, by Mark Minasi and Todd Phillips

ISBN 0-7821-2448-X   1163 pages $39.99

and from *Windows 2000 Professional: In Record Time*, by Peter Dyson and Pat Coleman

ISBN 0-7821-2450-X   467 pages $29.99.

Windows 2000 Professional takes that a little further by including new versions of the Internet Explorer browser, Outlook Express, and of course Internet Information Services (IIS). This time, Microsoft has built in a fully featured Internet server, with nearly all the same components that IIS on Windows 2000 Server boasts.

In this chapter, we discuss the various types of Internet connections and then go through the procedures for connecting your PC to the Internet. We also look at Microsoft's Internet Explorer and various command-line tools and discuss where you can download great Internet software.

UNDERSTANDING THE TYPES OF INTERNET CONNECTIONS

You can connect a PC to the Internet in at least four ways:

- ► The older, more limited way is as a remote terminal on a host computer already connected to the Internet.

- ► The ideal way (because it's fast) is through a Network Interface Card (NIC) to a local area network (LAN) that's connected to the Internet.

- ► The most common way is through a dial-in TCP/IP (Transmission Control Protocol/Internet Protocol) connection to an Internet Service Provider (ISP).

- ► And finally, also quite common is accessing the Internet via an online information service such as America Online or CompuServe.

In the next section, we look at how to configure Windows 2000 Professional to connect via modem to an ISP. If you're fortunate enough to have a LAN connection to the Internet, you won't need a modem, and you probably also won't need to make any changes to your TCP/IP configuration.

NOTE

An ISP is a business or nonprofit organization that supplies dial-in or private-line connections to the Internet.

Right now, let's look at three of these connection options in a little more detail. (We won't be talking about online services in detail because they typically can be accessed just like an ISP. For specific information about their features, consult the documentation for the online service.) To better understand the similarities and differences among these connection methods, it's helpful to know that the Internet uses TCP/IP, a common set of rules, commands, and procedures that enables many kinds of computers to communicate. To send and receive data through the Internet, you must either use TCP/IP software on your computer or move the data through another computer that converts it to and from TCP/IP. All types of connections except a shell account (remote-terminal) use TCP/IP protocols.

Figure 17.1 shows a remote-terminal connection. In this case, your PC uses a conventional communications program, such as HyperTerminal or ProComm, to exchange data with a second computer called a *host*, which is connected to the Internet. As far as the host is concerned, your PC is just like a terminal that does not have its own computer processor. For this reason, communications programs such as HyperTerminal are also called *terminal-emulation* programs. Unless the host is located in the same building, you probably use a modem to connect to the host through a telephone line. You may also see this kind of Internet access called a *shell account* because many host computers employ a user interface called a *shell*.

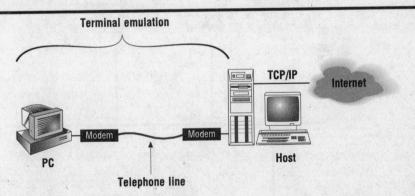

FIGURE 17.1: A remote-terminal connection to the Internet uses TCP/IP programs on a host computer.

Remote-terminal access to the Internet has advantages and disadvantages. Although you still need a modem, remote-terminal access is frequently less expensive than other types of Internet connections because remote terminals usually put very little strain on a host computer. Thus, a host computer can support a large number of simultaneous remote-terminal sessions. And because the TCP/IP gateway and data caches are located on the host, not on your PC, you can use a slower modem and a less powerful computer. Of course, if your PC is powerful enough to be running Windows 2000 Professional, it is certainly more than capable of supporting a "real" TCP/IP connection. (Windows 2000 Professional can even be used as a host computer to connect other users to the Internet, but that's another subject.) A remote-access connection generally uses a command line (such as the DOS or Unix prompt) rather than a graphical interface, limits you to the Internet tools loaded on the host, and takes a lot longer to transfer files from a distant computer because you have to relay the files through a host.

Figure 17.2 shows a connection through a local area network (LAN), and Figure 17.3 shows a direct TCP/IP link through a Serial Line Internet Protocol (SLIP) or Point-to-Point Protocol (PPP) connection. The Internet tools that control such functions as e-mail, news (Usenet), and file transfer all run on your PC. If you're already connected to a LAN, connecting the whole network to the Internet is generally more efficient because a network connection is usually much faster than a modem link.

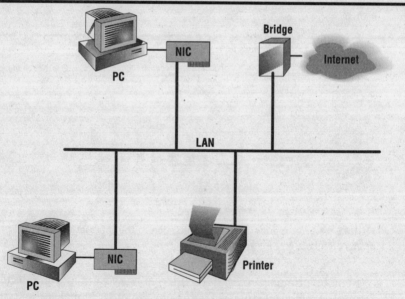

FIGURE 17.2: A LAN connection to the Internet provides access to all the computers on a local area network.

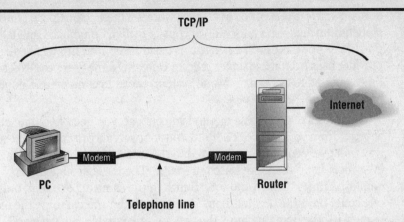

FIGURE 17.3: SLIP and PPP connections to the Internet communicate directly to the Internet using TCP/IP protocols.

The advantages of a direct TCP/IP connection to the Internet are speed and flexibility. Many Windows programs provide graphical displays, drag-and-drop file transfer, and other features that are not available through a remote-terminal connection. On the other hand, TCP/IP connections are usually a bit more expensive than shell accounts, and they require higher-speed modems (*minimally* 14,400bps) or other kinds of (usually costly) data links between your PC and an Internet *point of presence*. A point of presence for the Internet is any point at which you can connect to the network. Your ISP is a point of presence. The fact is, you'll likely only find TCP/IP connections today due to the popularity of the Web and the many features offered by graphical environments such as Windows.

Using Internet Addresses

Every computer on the Internet has a unique identity in the form of a 32-bit (4-byte) number, which for readability's sake is usually shown as a four-part numeric address. Some folks refer to this number as *dot notation* or a *quad address*. For example, a typical address (Microsoft's) looks like this:

    198.105.232.30

In most cases, the address also exists as a name, with a *domain* that shows either the type of business or other institution that uses this address (such as com for commercial, edu for educational, or gov for government), or the country in which it's located. For example, Microsoft's domain address is `microsoft.com`, whereas the Pacific Space Centre, a planetarium and observatory in Vancouver, British Columbia, Canada, uses `pacific-space-centre.bc.ca` as its address. Your Internet access provider uses a database server called a Domain Name Service (DNS; sometimes referred to as Domain Name System) server to convert from domain names to numeric addresses.

Regardless of the access method you choose, you need to obtain an account from your network administrator or service provider. In the same way that every computer connected to the Internet has its own address, every user has a distinctive account name. Therefore, if a business employs Frances Smith and Fred Smith in the same department, only one could have the account name `fsmith`. When you combine the username with the domain name, the two are separated by an *at* sign (@) so you can identify (and send mail to) anybody with an account on any Internet system in the format `name@address.domain`. Here are some typical Internet account names:

```
bluebottle@finchly.uk
yokum@dogpatch.com
snorkel@swampy.mil
```

In addition to your account name, address, and password, your service provider or network administrator may also give you several other pieces of information that you need to set up your Internet account. These may include the dial-in Internet host's telephone number and the numeric addresses of the servers for name conversion, mail, and network news.

NOTE

In the not-too-distant future, we will have a new version of TCP/IP addressing. The new version, referred to as IPv6 or TCP/IP version 6, will boast completely different addressing than our current IPv4. The new addresses will have eight groups of four hexadecimal numbers. Hexadecimal is a base 16 number system in which the possible values range from zero to F. A possible IPv6 address could look like this: `FEDC:BA98:1234:5678:0BCA:9987:0102:1235`.

Connecting As a Remote Terminal

When you use a communications program such as HyperTerminal to dial into a host computer, your PC becomes a terminal on that host. If the host is connected to the Internet, you must use Internet programs resident on the host.

The most common remote-terminal access to the Internet is through a Unix host or a host that recognizes Unix-like Internet commands such as Telnet, FTP (File Transfer Protocol), and so forth.

NOTE

Unix is a widely used computer operating system that is available for many kinds of computers, including desktop systems, mainframes, and everything in between. Unix enables more than one program to run at a time, and multiple users can share a single computer.

As far as Windows 2000 Professional is concerned, your PC is running a modem communications program to move ASCII characters or binary files through a modem when you use a shell account. All the TCP/IP activity is happening at the host. In other words, when you type commands on your PC's keyboard, those commands pass through your computer to the host, which runs the programs that communicate with the Internet.

If you have a remote-terminal connection to the Internet, you don't need to worry about network configuration because the administrator of the host computer has taken care of all that for you. After you know your account name, password, and the host's Internet address (name), you're ready to go.

As mentioned earlier, we assume in this chapter that you will want to connect via LAN or modem to the Internet. Connecting via LAN simply requires that you have your networking hardware installed and connected to the network, and that you have the necessary Windows 2000 Professional software installed to get on the network. To put it simply, once you're on the network, you're also on the Internet!

CONNECTING VIA MODEM

To connect to the Internet by modem, if you haven't already, you need to select an ISP in your area and sign up for a dial-in account. After your account is set up, you need to do the following:

1. Get the connection information (phone number, user ID, password, and TCP/IP settings) from your ISP. They will mail this to you, but you may want to ask for it over the phone to get started sooner.

2. Install Windows 2000 Professional modem support for your modem (and the modem itself, if necessary!).

3. Configure your Dial-Up Networking connection.

That's it—simple, eh? In case you don't think it's so simple, we've broken down each step into the following procedures, and you shouldn't have any trouble if you follow the steps carefully. Remember that you'll only have to do them once (assuming all goes well). After that, connecting each time to the Internet will be a piece of cake. You can even have your modem dial silently and automatically whenever you start up any Internet application (such as your Web browser).

Obtaining the Information You Need from Your ISP

Most ISPs are very good about providing exactly the pieces of information you need. In what we hope is becoming a standard, several of them are giving out handy laminated cards containing all the necessary information, complete with technical support phone numbers.

Here are the items you need to know:

▶ Primary (and secondary, if it exists) DNS server

▶ User ID

▶ Password

▶ Dial-in phone number

▶ E-mail server information for sending and receiving e-mail

If your service provider does not use dynamic address assignment (most do), you also need to obtain your Internet Protocol (IP) address and gateway address from the service provider. Also, you should find out whether this is a SLIP or a PPP account (if they don't mention this, it is likely PPP, but it won't hurt to make sure).

After that's done, the next step is to install your modem—by that we mean the Windows 2000 Professional modem driver software. However, if you haven't done so already, install the modem itself first. See Chapter 15 for information on how to install the modem.

Configuring the Dial-Up Connection

In times past, setting up a connection to the Internet was quite a complex operation, but that is no longer the case. The Internet Connection Wizard walks you through the steps of setting up your Internet connection. All you need is an account with an ISP and your credit card number, and you're all set. You can start the Internet Connection Wizard in several ways:

▸ Click the Connect To The Internet icon on the Desktop. Once you set up your Internet connection, this icon will disappear from the Desktop.

▸ Choose Start ➢ Programs ➢ Accessories ➢ Communications, and then select Internet Connection Wizard.

▸ Choose Start ➢ Settings ➢ Control Panel ➢ Internet Options to open the Internet Properties dialog box, select the Connections tab, and click the Setup button.

▸ In Internet Explorer, choose Tools ➢ Internet Options to open the Internet Options dialog box, select the Connections tab, and click the Setup button.

No matter which method you use, the Welcome screen, shown in Figure 17.4, appears and gives you three choices:

I Want To Sign Up For A New Internet Account. (My Telephone Line Is Connected To My Modem)   Select this option if you do not already have an Internet account. The Wizard takes you through the steps of finding an ISP and starting an account and sets up the dial-up link for you.

I Want To Transfer My Existing Internet Account To This Computer. (My Telephone Line Is Connected To My Modem)   Select this option to set up a connection to your existing Internet account or to revise the settings for your current account.

I Want To Set Up My Internet Connection Manually, Or I Want To Connect Through A Local Area Network (LAN) Select this option to set up your account configuration manually.

Click Tutorial to learn more about the Internet, or click Cancel if you want to close the Internet Connection Wizard without setting up your Internet account.

Part iii

FIGURE 17.4: Starting the Internet Connection Wizard

Creating a New Connection to the Internet

To create a new dial-up connection to the Internet, start the Internet Connection Wizard, and then follow these steps:

1. At the Welcome screen, choose the first option to select an ISP and set up a new Internet account, and then click Next.

2. The Wizard dials out on your modem, connects to the Microsoft Internet Referral Service, and downloads information on ISPs. Not all the ISPs available in your area will be listed here; most of those listed are actually nationwide services.

3. Select one of the ISPs, and click Next. The information shown in the next two dialog boxes depends on which of the ISPs you chose in the last step.

4. Enter your name, address, and phone number in the next dialog box. This information is used for billing purposes only and is only sent to the ISP you selected. Click Next.

5. Choose a billing option from those shown on the screen, and click Next.

6. Choose a method of payment, enter the details of your credit card, and click Next.

7. The Internet Connection Wizard connects to the ISP, selects a user ID and password, and completes the configuration of your Internet connection. Follow the prompts on the screen to complete your setup.

Setting Up Your Connection to the Internet Manually

You don't have to use the ISPs listed by the Microsoft Internet Referral Service. If you want to use an ISP whose name is not listed by the Internet Connection Wizard—perhaps a local ISP known for offering a particularly good service or an ISP recommended by a friend—choose the third option on the Internet Connection Wizard opening screen, and follow these steps:

1. Phone the ISP you have chosen, and ask for a dial-up account that will give you e-mail and Internet access; some ISPs also assign space on their systems so you can create a small Web site of your own. The ISP will send you details of the servers they operate, including the names of the mail and news servers; you will need that information to complete the steps outlined below.

2. Start the Internet Connection Wizard, and in the opening dialog box, select the third option to set up a connection manually.

3. Choose the method you want to use to connect to the Internet. Most people will check the I Connect Through A Phone Line And A Modem option. Click Next.

4. In the next dialog box, enter the phone number to dial to make the connection to your ISP.

5. In the next dialog box, enter your username and password information. These will be provided by your ISP, and remember to enter them in the same case, either uppercase or lowercase, as specified by your ISP. Click Next.

6. Enter the name you want to use for this connection; choose something easy to remember, such as the name of your ISP. Click Next.

7. You'll then be asked if you want to set up an Internet e-mail account; click Yes and then Next to specify whether you want

to use an existing account or create a new one. If you opt to continue using an existing account, you will be asked to confirm your e-mail account settings; if you establish a new account, you will have to enter this information from scratch. Click Next.

8. Finally, click the Finish button to complete the configuration, close the Wizard, and connect to the Internet.

Dialing In to Your Service Provider

After you configure your account using the Internet Connection Wizard, you can dial in using the Network And Dial-Up Connections folder, which you can open in a couple of ways:

▶ Choose Start ➤ Programs ➤ Accessories ➤ Communications ➤ Network And Dial-Up Connections.

▶ Double-click My Computer to open the My Computer folder, and click the Network And Dial-up Connections link.

In either case, you'll see the folder shown in Figure 17.5.

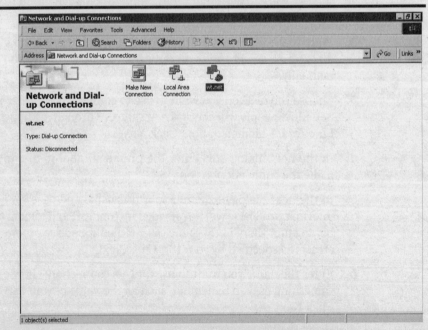

FIGURE 17.5: Opening the Network And Dial-Up Connections folder

Use the following procedure to initiate dial-in:

1. Double-click the icon for the connection you want to dial to open the Connect dialog box:

2. In the User Name and Password text boxes, if necessary, enter your username and password exactly as given by your ISP (these are usually case sensitive). Normally, Windows 2000 Professional picks up your username from the information you provided when you ran the Internet Connection Wizard.

3. Click the Save Password check box. If you don't, you will always have to type the password before connecting to the Internet. If you're concerned about someone else using your Internet connection, leave this unchecked.

4. Click Dial. After dialing, you should hear the modem establish handshaking. If all goes well, you may see a message saying you're successfully connected. Click the Don't Show This Message Next Time check box if you don't want to be bothered with this message in the future.

Congratulations! You are now connected to the Internet. You should be able to run any Winsock-compliant software, such as Web browsers, FTP, Ping, newsreaders, and so on.

If you are having problems connecting and you're sure it's not due to a busy signal at your ISP's number, first go back through the setup procedure

Part iii

outlined above. If you still cannot connect, see the next section, "Troubleshooting Your Modem Connection."

After your computer is connected to the Internet, regardless of the type of connection you're using, your Winsock applications will automatically find your connection. If you close one application and start another, or run more than one application at the same time, the second (and subsequent) applications will use the same Winsock connection to the Internet.

Troubleshooting Your Modem Connection

If you have any problems with connecting or staying connected to your ISP, or you cannot get your Web browser to work after you're connected, the following suggestions may help. If all else fails, don't forget that you can call your ISP tech support. If you call, ask specifically for any Windows 2000 Professional experts on staff.

If your modem connection "rudely" disconnects you:

- ▶ Your connection may be set to disconnect after some number of idle seconds. To avoid disconnects completely, make sure this is set to zero. Right-click your connection in the Network And Dial-Up Connections folder, and choose Properties to open the Properties dialog box. Click the Options tab, and in the Idle Time Before Hanging Up drop-down list box, select Never.

- ▶ Your ISP may have its own idle disconnect time-out. If the disconnect occurs only when you aren't actively surfing the Net or transferring data, and if your disconnect time-out is set to Never, this is most likely what's happening.

- ▶ Your modem speed setting could be too high. In Control Panel, open the Phone And Modem Options applet, click the Modems tab, select your modem, and click Properties to open the Properties dialog box for that modem. In the Maximum Port Speed drop-down list box, select a lower speed.

- ▶ You might need to disable modem hardware flow control in the Properties dialog box for the modem. Click the Advanced tab, click Change Default Preferences, click the down arrow in the Flow Control drop-down list box, and choose None.

▶ Your modem cable may have a bad connection. Replace it, or at least double-check that both ends are securely connected and that no wires are loose and no pins are missing on the connectors.

▶ You may have a faulty telephone cable. Check the plastic connectors at both ends to be sure that all wires appear to make contact with the metal connectors in the plug.

▶ Your modem's initialization string may be incorrect. Check your modem's manual for details on the correct string. In many cases, you can add **&F1** in the Extra Settings box on the Advanced tab of the modem's Properties dialog box, in effect telling your modem to ignore what Windows 2000 Professional just told it and to use its default settings instead. Your modem's manual should have the correct settings to add.

If your connection seems to transfer files abnormally slowly:

▶ You may simply be connected to a busy Web site. Try jumping to a few other locations or return to this site later and try transferring the file again.

▶ You may be transferring compressed data, in which case disabling modem compression *and* software compression can sometimes help significantly. Both of these are actually a hindrance when transferring very compressed data (such as .zip files, compressed image files, and the like). Disconnect, and reconfigure your modem so that it won't use modem and software compression, and then dial again.

WEB CRUISING WITH INTERNET EXPLORER

Probably the first thing you'll want to try after connecting to the Internet is cruising the Web by using your Web browser. Certainly, you can use

Part III

Netscape's Navigator browser, but because Windows 2000 Professional comes with Microsoft's Internet Explorer 5 (MSIE), that's the one we'll assume you're using for this little test cruise.

You can open Internet Explorer in several ways:

▶ Click the Launch Internet Explorer Browser button on the Quick Launch toolbar.

▶ Double-click the Internet Explorer shortcut on the Desktop.

▶ Choose Start ➢ Programs ➢ Internet Explorer.

Figure 17.6 shows the page you'll see when you open Internet Explorer the first time, which is known as your home page. You can specify any page on the Internet as your home page, as you'll see later in this chapter.

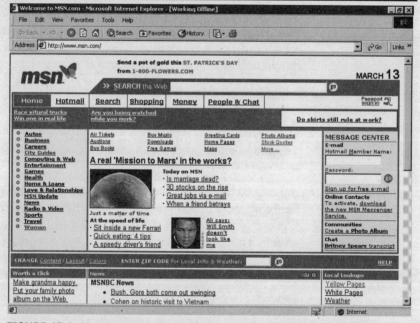

FIGURE 17.6: You can retain the www.msn.com page as your home page or select any other page that suits your fancy.

When Internet Explorer opens, you can type a Uniform Resource Locator (URL), such as `microsoft.com` or `Webcrawler.com`, into the Address bar and press Enter. If you're connected, within seconds the page should begin loading.

As you jump from page to page, all previous pages you've visited are saved in a temporary cache, so returning to them next time is much quicker (unless the cache has been cleared in the meantime). Note that you can jump ahead and back by clicking the Back and Forward buttons on Internet Explorer's toolbar. Pressing the PgUp and PgDn keys scrolls up or down a screen at a time, and the up and down arrows scroll up or down by a much smaller amount. To print whatever page(s) you're looking at, click the Printer button on the toolbar, or choose File ➤ Print to open the Print dialog box.

Then, of course, there's the Favorites button on the toolbar (and the Favorites menu), which you use to "bookmark" those places you want to return to easily later. If you're a typical Web user, you'll likely fill up your Favorites folder with favorite pages; at some point you'll have to create subfolders for sorting the bookmarks into categories to make them manageable. You can place these bookmarks anywhere—on your Desktop, in another folder, or even within an e-mail message (if you're using Outlook Express to send your e-mail, refer to Chapter 16).

Another nice thing you can do in Internet Explorer is right-click any image in a Web page, which displays a shortcut menu that includes options to make this image the current wallpaper or to save the image in a handy format for later wallpapering or viewing. You can also right-click any background wallpaper in the browser and set this as your Desktop wallpaper or save it to a file for later use.

TIPS FOR USING INTERNET EXPLORER

Internet Explorer is so easy to use that you hardly need a how-to book, a manual, or even this chapter. You can start browsing immediately by simply clicking links. Here are some tips, though, that might speed the exploration process:

▶ You can start Internet Explorer from any document in any Windows application that includes a hyperlink if Internet Explorer is your default browser.

▶ To see the underlying HTML for any open Web page, choose View ➤ Source.

▶ To access a resource other than an HTML document, enter the full URL.

CONTINUED ➡

Part iii

▶ Textual links are underlined and are usually in a different color from normal text. To find out if an image or a symbol is a link, place the mouse pointer over it. If it's a link, the pointer becomes a hand with a pointing finger.

▶ Click Home at any time to return to your home page.

▶ To interrupt the loading of a page (perhaps because it is so slow), click Stop.

▶ To send a link to the current page, click the Mail button, and choose Send A Link. In the New Message window, address your message, compose your message, and click Send. If your recipient is connected to the Internet and has a Web browser, he or she merely needs to click the link in the message to open that page.

SETTING INTERNET EXPLORER OPTIONS

In Windows 2000 Professional, you can view or change the configuration options relating to Internet Explorer in two ways:

▶ Choose Start ➢ Settings ➢ Control Panel, and click Internet Options to open the Internet Properties dialog box.

▶ In Internet Explorer, choose Tools ➢ Internet Options to open the Internet Options dialog box.

NOTE

In the first case, the dialog box is titled Internet Properties; in the second case, the dialog box is titled Internet Options. The options are exactly the same in both dialog boxes. In this section, we'll explain these options using the Internet Properties dialog box.

This dialog box has six tabs, and in the next few sections, we'll review the most important configuration choices you can make on each of these tabs. We'll start with the General tab.

Configuring the General Tab

Figure 17.7 shows the Internet Properties dialog box open at the General tab. It contains these groups of settings:

Home Page   Lets you choose which Web page opens each time you connect to the Internet. A home page is the first Web page you see when you start Internet Explorer. Click Use Current to make the current page your home page (if you are online to the Internet), click Use Default to return to the default setting, and click Use Blank to start each Internet session with a blank screen. To use a different Web page as your home page, type the URL in the Address box.

Temporary Internet Files   Lets you manage those Web pages that are stored on your hard disk for fast offline access. If these files are occupying too much hard-disk space, click the Delete Files button to remove them. To control how these files are stored on your hard disk, click Settings to open the Settings dialog box. Click the option that applies to when you want Internet Explorer to check for newer versions of these stored Web pages. You can use the slider to specify how much hard-disk space is given over to these temporary Internet files. Click Move Folder if you want to use a different folder to hold your temporary Internet files; you must remember to restart your computer after making this change so that the new folder is used in place of the default. Click View Files to open an Explorer window listing all the Web and graphics files in the folder, or click View Objects to open an Explorer window listing all the other Web-related files such as ActiveX controls and Java-related files.

History   Contains a list of the links you have visited so that you can return to them quickly and easily using the History button on the Internet Explorer toolbar. You can specify the number of days you want to keep pages in the History folder; if you are running low on hard-disk space, consider reducing this number. To delete all the information currently in the History folder, click the Clear History button.

Colors   Lets you choose which colors are used as background, links, and text on those Web pages for which the original author did not specify colors. By default, the Use Windows Colors option is selected.

TIP

You can always change the Windows colors. In Control Panel, click Display, and then select the Appearance tab.

Fonts   Lets you specify the font style and text size to use on those Web pages for which the original author did not make a specification.

Languages   Lets you choose the character set to use on those Web pages that offer content in more than one language. English is rapidly becoming the most common language in use on the Internet, so you may not use this option often.

Accessibility   Lets you choose how certain information is displayed in Internet Explorer, including font styles, colors, and text size. You can also specify that your own style sheet is used.

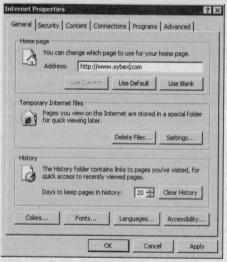

FIGURE 17.7: The General tab in the Internet Properties dialog box

Looking at the Security Tab

The Security tab, which is shown in Figure 17.8, lets you specify the overall security level for each of four zones. Each zone has its own default security restrictions that tell Internet Explorer how to manage dynamic Web page content such as ActiveX controls and Java applets. The zones are:

Internet   Sites you visit that are not in one of the other categories; default security is set to Medium.

Local Intranet   Sites you can access on your corporate intranet; default security is set to Medium-Low.

Trusted Sites   Web sites you have a high degree of confidence will not send you potentially damaging content; default security is set to Low.

Restricted Sites   Sites that you visit but do not trust; default security is set to High.

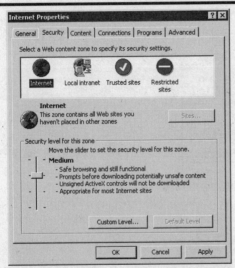

FIGURE 17.8: The Security tab in the Internet Properties dialog box

To change the current security level of a zone, just move the slider to the new security level you want to use:

High   Excludes any content capable of damaging your system. Cookies are disabled, and so some Web sites will not work as you might expect. This is the most secure setting.

Medium   Opens a warning dialog box in Internet Explorer before running ActiveX or Java applets on your system. This is a moderately secure setting that is good for everyday use.

Medium-Low   Same as Medium but without the prompts.

Low   Does not issue any warning but runs the ActiveX or Java applet automatically. This is the least secure setting.

Click the Custom Level button to create your own settings in the Security Settings dialog box, which is shown in Figure 17.9. You can individually configure how you want to manage certain categories, such as ActiveX controls and plug-ins, Java applets, scripting, file and font downloads, and user authentication.

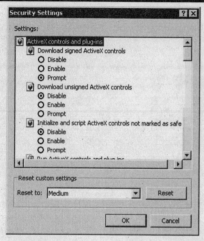

FIGURE 17.9: The Security Settings dialog box

Using the Content Tab

The Content tab, which is shown in Figure 17.10, contains settings you can use to restrict access to sites and specify how you want to manage digital certificates:

Content Advisor   Lets you control access to certain sites on the Internet and is particularly useful if children have access to the computer. Click Settings to establish a password, and then click OK to open the Content Advisor dialog box. Use the tabs in this dialog box to establish the level of content you will allow users to view:

Ratings   Lets you use a set of ratings developed by the Recreational Software Advisory Council (RSAC) for language, nudity, sex, and violence. Select one of these categories, and then adjust the slider to specify the level of content you will allow.

Approved Sites   Lets you create lists of sites that are always viewable or always restricted regardless of how they are rated.

General   Specifies whether people using this computer can view material that has not been rated; users may see some objectionable material if the Web site has not used the RSAC rating system. You can also opt to have the Supervisor enter a password so that users can view Web pages that may contain objectionable material. You can click the Change Password button to change the Supervisor password; remember that you have to know the current Supervisor password before you can change it.

Advanced   Lets you look at or modify the list of organizations providing ratings services.

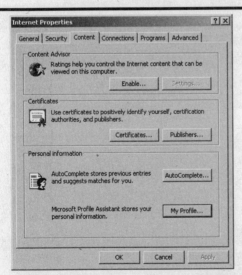

FIGURE 17.10: The Content tab in the Internet Properties dialog box

Certificates   Lets you manage digital certificates used with certain client authentication servers. Click Certificates to view the personal digital certificates installed on this system, or click Publishers to designate a particular software publisher as a trustworthy publisher. This means that Windows 2000 Professional applications can download, install, and use software from these agencies without asking for your permission first.

Personal Information   Lets you look at or change the settings for Windows AutoComplete and your own personal profile. Click AutoComplete to change the way that this feature works within Windows 2000 Professional, or click My Profile to review the information sent to any Web sites that request information about you when you visit their site.

Setting Up the Connections Tab

The Connections tab, which is shown in Figure 17.11, allows you to specify how your system connects to the Internet. Click the Setup button to run the Internet Connection Wizard and set up a connection to an Internet Service Provider. (See the Internet Connection Wizard section earlier in this chapter for complete details.) If you use a modem, click the Settings button to open the Settings dialog box, where you can specify all aspects of the phone connection to your ISP.

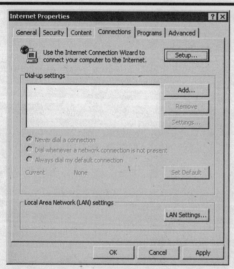

FIGURE 17.11: The Connections tab in the Internet Properties dialog box

Looking at the Programs Tab

The Programs tab, which is shown in Figure 17.12, lets you set your default program choices for HTML editor, e-mail, newsgroup reader, Internet call, calendar, and contact list.

Finally, you can specify that Internet Explorer check to see if it is configured as the default browser on your system each time it starts running.

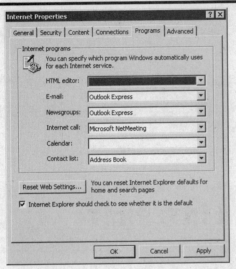

FIGURE 17.12: The Programs tab in the Internet Properties dialog box

Configuring the Advanced Tab

The Advanced tab, which is shown in Figure 17.13, lets you look at or change a number of settings that control much of Internet Explorer's behavior, including accessibility, browsing, multimedia, security, the Java environment, printing and searching, the Internet Explorer toolbar, and how HTTP 1.1 settings are interpreted. Click a check box to turn an option on; clear the check box to turn the option off.

Changes you make here stay in effect until you change them again, until you download an automatic configuration file, or until you click the Restore Defaults button, which returns the settings on the Advanced tab to their original values.

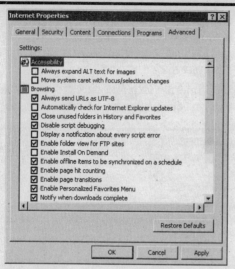

FIGURE 17.13: The Advanced tab in the Internet Options dialog box

USING BUILT-IN INTERNET UTILITIES

Windows 2000 Professional includes several standard Internet utilities. These programs are in most cases functionally identical to the same programs or commands found on pretty much every flavor of Unix. Although most people are not going to use these nearly as often as they will their Web browsers, we describe each in the following sections so you at least know what they are. It is useful to acquaint yourself, for example, with FTP—if you are ever on a Windows 2000 Professional system that for some reason does not have a Web browser, knowing how to use FTP to transfer files enables you to connect to Spry, Netscape, or Microsoft and download a browser.

Following this brief rundown of each of the tools, we will look at other Internet applications you can download via the Internet. Note that with each of the following programs, you can get help by typing the program name at the command prompt followed by -? (hyphen, question mark).

To open any of the following utilities, you type a command at a command prompt. To open a command prompt window, do one of the following:

► Choose Start ➤ Run, and in the Open text box, type the command (the name of the utility).

► Choose Start ➤ Programs ➤ Accessories ➤ Command Prompt.

Address Resolution Display and Control (ARP)

The ARP program is used to display and/or modify entries in the Internet-to-Ethernet (or Token Ring) address translation tables that are used by the Address Resolution Protocol (ARP). Various command-line switches are documented in the -? option. To use ARP, type **arp** at the command prompt.

File Transfer Protocol (FTP)

FTP is the standard TCP/IP file transfer protocol used for moving text and binary files between computers on the Internet. If you have an account on a distant computer on the Internet, you can use FTP to download files from the other computer to your PC and to upload files from your PC to the host. In addition, there are tens of thousands of *anonymous* FTP archives all over the Internet that accept logins from anybody who wants copies of their files.

The Windows 2000 Professional FTP program (and the others mentioned here) can be found in the Winnt\System32 folder, which is included in your search path. Therefore, you don't have to specify the path when you enter an FTP command. To connect to an FTP server, follow these steps:

1. At a command prompt, type the following, and then press Enter:

   FTP *<host name>*

2. Windows 2000 Professional displays the `ftp>` prompt:

3. After FTP connects to the server, the server asks for your username and password. If you're connecting to an anonymous FTP server, type **anonymous** as your username, and type your Internet address as your password. Use the standard *name@address.domain* format.

Most FTP servers use the same system of directories and subdirectories that you may be familiar with from DOS and Windows. To see the contents of the current directory, type **dir** or **ls** at the `ftp>` prompt.

A *d* as the first letter in a listing indicates that the item in that line is a directory. If a hyphen is the first character, the item is a file. The name of the file or directory is at the extreme right.

Use the command **cd *name*** (but type the name of the subdirectory in place of *name*) to move to a subdirectory.

Use the command **cd ..** to move to the next higher level.

When you download a file from an FTP server, you must specify that it is either an ASCII text file or a binary file. As a general rule, binary files that you can read on a PC have a `.dos` file extension (other than `.txt` for a text file or `.ps` for a Postscript print file), but you really can't be certain. ASCII text files may or may not have a file extension.

When you initially connect to an FTP server, you're in ASCII mode. Before you try to transfer a binary file, you have to change modes. To switch to binary mode, use the command **binary**. To switch back to ASCII mode, use the command **ascii**. The host acknowledges your mode-change command.

To download a file from the server, use the command **get** *filename* (typing the name of the file in place of *filename*). If you want to store the file on your PC with a different name, use the command **get** *filename* *newname* (typing the file you want to get in place of *filename* and the name you want to store the file under in place of *newname*). When the file transfer is complete, the host sends you another message, shown below.

```
ftp> get Yellball.gif
200 PORT command successful.
150 Opening BINARY mode data connection for Yellball.gif(582 bytes).
226 Transfer complete.
ftp: 582 bytes received in 0.01Seconds 58.20Kbytes/sec.
ftp>
```

When you are finished with your FTP session, type **disconnect** to break the connection to the server. You can connect to another host by typing the new server's address.

To close the FTP utility, type the command **quit**.

TIP

One handy use for the command-line FTP client is automating file transfers. Because FTP accepts scripts (via the -s:filename switch), you can easily create a script (which is just a text file of FTP commands) to log on to an FTP server, switch to a particular directory, transfer a long listing of files in one or both directions, and then log off. You can even set this to occur at a given time of day, by using the Windows 2000 Professional at command. (For details on using the at command, type **help at** from any command prompt.)

Finger

The finger program can be used to retrieve user-supplied information about a user (or host computer). Unfortunately, many users do not have a finger file for others to retrieve and view (or even know about creating one), and some host computers do not provide finger services, so your mileage will vary. On the other hand, some universities and institutions do use finger services, and on these you can find some useful (or at least interesting) information. To use finger, type **finger** *auser@someplace*.**com**. Enter a valid username or at least a host name, and press Enter, and you may get a listing of information.

Part III

Ping

Ping is a useful diagnostic utility that tests your ability to connect your computer to another device through the Internet by sending an echo request and displaying the number of milliseconds required to receive a reply. Whenever you need to diagnose your Internet connection problems, pinging a known host computer is a good first test.

To set up a Ping test, follow these steps:

1. At a command prompt, type **ping** *destination*. Use the domain name or the IP address of the host you want to test in place of *destination*. If you do not get a response when using the domain name of the destination, try the IP address of the destination instead.

2. Ping sends four sets of Internet Control Message Protocol (ICMP) echo packets to the host you specify and displays the amount of time it took to receive each reply, as shown below.

The important part of the Ping display is the "time</>*nnn*ms" section of the Reply lines. Ping's capability to connect to the distant host tells you that your connection to the Internet is working properly; the number of milliseconds can tell you if you have an efficient connection to this particular host (anything less than about 500ms is usually acceptable).

Protocol Statistics (Netstat)

Use the Netstat command to display a list of currently active Internet connections. At the command prompt, type **netstat**. A list of connections similar to the ones in the following illustration appears:

A Netstat report includes the following information:

Proto   Shows the networking protocol in use for each active connection. For PPP or SLIP connections to the Internet, the Proto column always reads TCP, which specifies a TCP/IP connection.

Local Address   Indicates the identity of your PC on the network.

Foreign Address   Shows the address of each distant computer to which a connection is currently active.

State   Shows the condition of each connection.

Remote File Copy (RCP)

If you've ever wanted to copy a file from one directory or drive to another, on a remote computer, without having the file go through your modem twice (as a normal copy or xcopy would), you understand the purpose of the RCP program. You can also use RCP to copy files from one remote computer to another remote computer without being copied to your computer first. Not all systems permit you to use this command, and if they do, of course you are limited to the directory areas for which you have access rights. Type **-?** for specific usage and option information. To use RCP, open a command prompt, and type **rcp.**

Part iii

Remote Program Execution (REXEC)

The REXEC program is just as powerful as Remote Shell/Script (RSH; discussed in the next section), if not more so, and likewise is quite restricted by most system administrators. It functions just like RSH, except that it starts binary programs on the remote host rather than scripts. Windows 2000 stations *do* permit remote execution of programs, provided the system administrator has enabled this and given you the necessary access rights. To run REXEC, type **rexec** at a command prompt.

Remote Shell/Script (RSH)

Another potentially powerful utility, RSH is used to start a script program on a remote host. Again, some host computers do not support this, and of those that do, your access rights may preclude or severely limit what you can do. To use RSH, type **rsh** at a command prompt.

Remote Terminal (Telnet)

Telnet is one of the utilities you are somewhat more likely to use, particularly in university settings or when data you need to access without using HTML is stored on a remote host (a less and less common scenario, thankfully). When you connect through a Telnet connection, your PC becomes a terminal on the distant system. In most cases, a Telnet login requires an account on the host (remote) machine, but many systems accept logins from anybody who wants to connect. Among the most common public Telnet sites are online library catalogs. Other public Telnet sites let you use certain character-based Internet services that may not be available on your computer.

To set up a Telnet connection, type **Telnet *hostname*** at a command prompt (using the domain name or IP address of the computer to which you want to connect in place of *hostname*). Telnet connects your computer to the host whose name you supplied and displays messages from that host in the Telnet window.

Most Telnet hosts display a series of login prompts as soon as you connect. If you're connecting to a public Telnet host, it will probably tell you how to log in.

NOTE

Telnet is also used to configure most routers. If you are interested in network design and management, you might want to focus some attention on Telnet.

ROUTE

You can use ROUTE to view, add to, or modify a routing table on a Windows 2000 Professional computer with more than one network interface. If you have a *multihomed* computer (one with multiple network cards) and have enabled IP forwarding in the TCP/IP Properties dialog box, you can use the ROUTE command to view and modify the table of information that tells Windows 2000 Professional where to direct TCP/IP data from one interface to another. Using this command on a computer with one network interface will also display basic routing information. To use ROUTE, type **route** at a command prompt.

Trace Route (tracert)

In most cases, when you set up a connection to a distant computer through the Internet, your signal path passes through several routers along the way. Because this is all happening in a fraction of a second, these intermediate routers are usually invisible. But when you're having trouble making a connection, the trace route command can help isolate the source of the problem.

To run a trace route test, type **tracert *target*** at a command prompt. In place of *target*, type the address of the distant system. A trace route report appears in the prompt window.

In many cases, your connection will pass through one or more backbone networks between your connection to the Internet and your ultimate destination. For example, the tracert report in Figure 17.14 shows a route from a PC in Seattle to The WELL, near San Francisco. In this case, the connection passes through backbone networks operated by Sprintlink and AlterNet.

```
C:\WINNT\System32\cmd.exe                                    _ □ X
C:\>tracert well.com
Tracing route to well.com [206.15.64.10]
over a maximum of 30 hops:

  1    47 ms    47 ms    47 ms  gateway.gte2.rbl.bel.nwlink.com [209.20.176.1]
  2    15 ms    31 ms    16 ms  gte1-rbl-bel-cr1.nwlink.com [209.20.128.14]
  3    16 ms    31 ms    31 ms  902.Hssi4-0.GW2.SEA1.ALTER.NET [137.39.136.129]
  4    16 ms    31 ms    31 ms  104.ATM3-0.XR2.SEA1.ALTER.NET [146.188.200.54]
  5    15 ms    32 ms    31 ms  194.ATM3-0.TR2.SEA1.ALTER.NET [146.188.200.118]
  6    32 ms    46 ms    63 ms  110.ATM5-0.TR2.SCL1.ALTER.NET [146.188.137.189]
  7    31 ms    31 ms    47 ms  198.ATM6-0.XR2.SJC1.ALTER.NET [146.188.146.49]
  8    46 ms    47 ms    47 ms  192.ATM3-0-0.SAN-JOSE9-GW.ALTER.NET [146.188.144
.133]
  9    47 ms    47 ms    47 ms  198.32.184.34
 10   141 ms    46 ms    63 ms  sf-cust1-fe0-0.core.hooked.net [206.80.17.13]
 11    47 ms    63 ms    47 ms  well.com [206.15.64.10]

Trace complete.
C:\>
```

FIGURE 17.14: The tracert command produces a list of intermediate routers between your PC and an Internet host.

Tracert steps through the connection route, one step at a time. For each step, it shows the amount of time needed to reach that router, in milliseconds. If an intermediate router or a connection between two intermediate routers fails, tracert will not display any steps beyond that point in the route. If that happens, you can assume that the failed site is the reason that you are unable to connect to your intended destination.

Trivial File Transfer Protocol (TFTP)

This program is similar in usage and functionality to the more well-known FTP utility, but is used to transfer files to or from a remote computer that is running Trivial File Transfer Protocol (TFTP).

FTP uses the TCP protocol, which guarantees safe delivery of the data. TFTP uses User Datagram Protocol (UDP), which does not provide reliable delivery and hence is somewhat faster. Windows 2000 Professional does not provide a TFTP server, but some are available for download on the Internet.

OBTAINING OTHER INTERNET APPLICATIONS

The inclusion of Internet Explorer in Windows 2000 Professional, along with Telnet and the other utilities, gives you a good start on accessing information on the Internet. However, as you browse the Web, you will likely want to use additional client software to interact with other users or to make your use of the Web more appealing and intuitive.

In this section, we'll provide a brief description of some of the types of Internet software you may find helpful and want to locate and download. An easy way to start finding good software is to point your Web browser to any search engine page, and enter search words such as **Internet Windows 2000 software**. Many of these Internet applications are also referred to as Winsock applications. Thus, Winsock is another good search word. Try a search by using the words **Winsock software**, and you'll find plenty of locations filled with listings of good freeware and shareware.

PERFORMING A SIMPLE SEARCH

Regardless of what you're looking for—information about a topic, an e-mail or a mailing address, a business, a Web page, and so on— the way to find it is to use a search service. *Search service* is a relatively new term for what we referred to in the past as a search engine, a program that can search a file, a database, or the Internet for keywords and retrieve documents in which those keywords are found.

Examples of search services that you may have used include Yahoo!, Excite, InfoSeek, AltaVista, and Lycos. To search with one of these services, you go to the site (for example, http:// www.yahoo.com), optionally select a category, enter a keyword or phrase, and click Search (or some similar button). Although these search services are very efficient, you are accessing only one of them at a time.

In Internet Explorer 5, you can use the Search Assistant to search several services simultaneously. Let's do a simple search to see how this works. Follow these steps:

1. In Internet Explorer, click the Search button on the Standard toolbar to open the Search bar.

2. In the Find A Web Page Containing box, type **Internet Windows 2000 software**.

3. Click Search.

Internet Explorer displays a list of links to sites that contain your search phrase. If you want to find Web pages similar to the current page, choose Tools ➢ Show Related Sites. A list of links is displayed in the Search bar.

The need for File Transfer Protocol (FTP) clients has been somewhat mitigated by the ease of downloading files via today's Web browsers. However, sometimes you may wish to download several files at once or to download without opening a Web browser, and for this you still need an FTP client. Many FTP programs are available on the Web. One good freeware version is called Winsock FTP. Winsock FTP is a lot easier to use than the command-prompt version included with Windows 2000 Professional. Figure 17.15 shows the main Winsock FTP window.

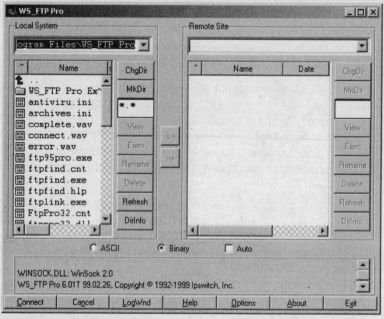

FIGURE 17.15: Winsock FTP is a great improvement over the FTP utility supplied with Windows 2000.

You can obtain Winsock FTP via anonymous FTP from FTP.usma.edu, in the directory /pub/msdos/winsock.files. The file is called ws_FTP .zip. You'll need an unzip program such as PK_UNZIP to uncompress the file after you download it. Winsock FTP includes a list of other FTP archives that contain additional Winsock applications. If you like Winsock FTP, be sure to check out another FTP client, called CuteFTP or CuteFTP32.

Because much of the DOS, Windows, NT, and Windows 2000 software on the Internet is compressed, you'll likely appreciate WinZip, FreeZip, or another such utility that lets you graphically view and extract the contents of compressed files.

Internet Relay Chat (IRC) is quite popular among many Internet users as a way to communicate in real time with other users. By downloading and installing one of the many good IRC client programs, you'll be able to type and read messages "live" with other users. One popular Windows IRC client is WinIRC.

If you literally want to talk across the network, try VocalTec's IPhone (see Figure 17.16) or Camelot's Digiphone. These and several other similar products let you talk with anyone else over a TCP/IP connection and require only the software, almost any sound card, and an inexpensive microphone. The amazing thing about these products (aside from the fact that they actually work) is their relatively low bandwidth; for example, you can be chatting with someone while simultaneously viewing Web pages with Mosaic or Netscape over even a 14.4Kbps Internet connection. The only problem with these programs is their lack of standards, which means you can chat only with other users of the same software. Windows 2000 Professional includes this capability with Phone Dialer, which was discussed in Chapter 15.

FIGURE 17.16: Internet Phone (IPhone) from VocalTec lets you communicate with voice over any TCP/IP connection.

Part iii

Taking the above ideas a step further, videoconferencing applications—such as CU-SeeMe and VidPhone—let you send still or motion video to other users. Besides the software, you need either a camcorder (usually on a tripod) or a small camera designed for videoconferencing that perches on your monitor. In addition, you need a video capture card, typically used to convert video from a VCR or camcorder into a signal you can display on your computer monitor and also used to create movie or graphics files. For less-than-full-motion video, even a 14.4Kbps modem connection can be used to send a few frames a second; on a faster network connection, these video-conferencing applications can meet or exceed movie-quality video.

As you can see, the Internet is a virtual hotbed of new technology. By adopting TCP/IP as your network protocol, you can ensure easy expansion into a wide area network, plus have the freedom to assimilate Internet media technologies to your network, even if you decide not to connect your company's network to the Internet.

NOTE

For a more detailed guide to exploring the Internet, check out *Internet Complete* (Sybex, 1998).

WHAT'S NEXT?

Now that you are connected to the world, we'll turn to an internal matter. In Windows 2000, the Registry is a system database that contains configuration information—information about the system's hardware, software, preferences, security, and users. In Part IV, Peter D. Hipson will explain what the Registry is, how it works, how you can edit it, and how to do so safely.

PART iV
UNDERSTANDING THE
REGISTRY

Chapter 18

What Is a Registry and Why?

Some users of Windows NT know exactly what the Registry is: a system designed to cause users and administrators to lose their hair. I know this is true because I can no longer feel the wind ruffling through my hair. Oh, I feel the wind; I just don't feel the hair.

Adapted from *Mastering Windows 2000 Registry,*
by Peter D. Hipson
ISBN 0-7821-2615-4   725 pages $39.99

The Registry, like Windows, evolved. The Registry was preceded by a pair of flat-text files, called `Win.ini` and `System.ini`. These two files live on even today in Windows 2000, though they are virtually unchanged from Windows NT version 4. The first Registry to appear in Windows was created to solve a number of problems: poor performance (retrieving information from the original flat-text `.ini` files was cumbersome), size limitations (the `.ini` files could be only so large), and maintenance problems (the `.ini` files were organizationally impaired!).

Today, the Windows 2000 `.ini` files contain only a few entries used by legacy 16-bit applications. They are of no importance to us, and we ignore them. It's the Registry that is important, because it contains the heart and soul of Windows 2000. Without the Registry, Windows 2000 would be nothing more than a collection of programs, unable to perform even the basic tasks that we expect from an operating system. Every bit of configuration information that Windows 2000 has is crammed into the Registry. Information about the system's hardware, preferences, security, and users—everything that can be set is set in there.

The Registry has a limit in size too; it's not infinitely large. A message telling you that you are low on Registry quota indicates that the Registry has grown too large for the current size allocation. Unless you change it, the Registry size is set to 25 percent of the paged pool size; for most computers, the paged pool size is approximately equal to the amount of installed RAM, up to a maximum of 192MB. The Registry can be set to 80 percent of the paged pool size (80 percent of 192MB is just under 154MB, though good sense says to round down to 150MB).

Windows 2000 will adjust this size based on the currently installed RAM. Several Registry entries affect Registry size, though most users will find that the defaults are acceptable for their use. To create a very large Registry, ensure that the amount of RAM installed is sufficient, and set the `RegistrySizeLimit` and `PagedPoolSize` entries.

NOTE

Microsoft limits the size of any object that is stored in a Registry data key to 1MB. This limit is basically only meaningful for REG_BINARY objects, because strings and such are unlikely to become this large. If you find that you must store more than 1MB in a Registry object, it will be necessary to store the information in a file and store a pointer to the file in the Registry. Without this limitation, the Registry could easily grow to be the largest file on your system.

THE ORGANIZATION OF THE REGISTRY

The Registry is organized into five major sections. These sections are called *hives*, which are analogous to root directories on your hard drive. Each hive, by definition, has its own storage location (a file) and log file. If necessary, you can restore a given hive without affecting the others.

Inside a hive you find both keys and subkeys (which are analogous to directories and subdirectories on your hard disk). A key may have information, or data, assigned to it (referred to as a *value entry*), making the key analogous to a file on your hard drive as well.

A key or a subkey may have zero, one, or more value entries, a default value, and from zero to many subkeys. Each value entry has a name, a data type, and a value:

▶ The entry's name is stored as a Unicode character string.

▶ The entry's type is stored as an integer index. The type is returned to the querying application, which must then map this type to the type that the application knows.

▶ The entry's value is stored as necessary to allow efficient retrieval of the data when needed.

Both the Windows 2000 operating system and applications store data in the Windows 2000 Registry. This is both good and bad. It is good because the Registry makes an efficient, common storage location. Here's the bad part: as more and more applications and systems store information in the Registry, it grows larger, and larger, and larger.

It is most unusual for the Registry to become smaller—I'm unaware of any application that does a really complete job of cleaning up all its own Registry entries when the application is uninstalled. Many applications leave tons of stuff in the Registry when they are uninstalled, and not many applications clean up unused entries as a routine process. The end result is that the Registry will grow, like Jack's magic beanstalk, over time.

NOTE

From time to time in this book, I will refer to hives, keys, subkeys, and values using the generic term *object*. When I use *object*, assume that the item could be any valid item in the Registry!

Hives and Their Aliases

The Windows 2000 Registry contains a number of hives and their accepted abbreviations:

- ► HKEY_CLASSES_ROOT, a.k.a. HKCR

- ► HKEY_CURRENT_USER, a.k.a. HKCU

- ► HKEY_LOCAL_MACHINE, a.k.a. HKLM

- ► HKEY_USERS, a.k.a. HKU

- ► HKEY_CURRENT_CONFIG, a.k.a. HKCC

NOTE

The HKEY_DYN_DATA hive, which has no abbreviation, disappeared in Windows 2000, though Microsoft had originally intended to include information about Plug and Play in this hive. So where is PnP data saved if the HKEY_DYN_DATA hive is gone? It is integrated with the main Registry rather than in a separate hive.

Each hive begins with HKEY_. HKEY is an abbreviation of "hive key," though the significance of this is not terribly important in understanding the Registry. The H also signifies that the name is a "handle" for a program to interface with the Registry. These handles are defined in the file winreg.h, included with the Windows 2000 SDK (Software Development Kit).

The Registry contains duplication—sort of. For example, you'll notice that everything in HKEY_CURRENT_USER is also contained in the hive HKEY_USERS. But these aren't two different sets of the same information; rather, they're two names for the same set of information. Microsoft needed to make some parts of the Registry appear to be in two places at one time, but it didn't want to copy these sections, because that could have created problems with keeping each section current. Instead, Microsoft created an alias, or another name, for some Registry components. The alias points to the original component and is updated whenever the original is updated. Only Windows can create these aliases. You, as a user, can't create an alias in the Registry no matter how hard you try!

The most common alias is the Registry hive HKEY_CURRENT_USER. It is an alias to either the .DEFAULT user in HKEY_USERS or to the current user in HKEY_USERS. If you take a quick peek at HKEY_USERS, you will see several keys: one is .DEFAULT, and the others are named with long strings of characters. These are SIDs (security identifiers), which Windows 2000 uses to identify users. One of these subkeys for the currently logged-on user consists of just the SID, and the other consists of the SID suffixed with _Classes. For example, on one Windows 2000 server, the administrator has the two subkeys HKEY_USERS\S-1-5-21-1004336348-842925246-1592369235-500 and HKEY_USERS\S-1-5-21-1004336348-842925246-1592369235-500_Classes.

NOTE

The default user, used when no user is logged on, has only one subkey, which is named .DEFAULT.

The Registry also contains other aliases. For example, the Registry key HKEY_ LOCAL_MACHINE\System\CurrentControlSet is an alias to one of the other control sets—ControlSet001, ControlSet002, or sometimes ControlSet003. Again, this is that same magic: only one Registry object is there; it just has two names. Remember, in modifying a specific Registry key or subkey; don't be surprised when another Registry key or subkey seems to magically change also!

Data Values

A value can contain one or, in some instances, more than one data item. The only type of multiple-item value entry that the Registry editor can handle is REG_MULTI_SZ, which may contain zero, one, or more strings.

Data is stored in a number of different formats. Generally, the system uses only a few simple formats, although applications, drivers, and so forth may use more complex types defined for a specific purpose. For example, REG_RESOURCE_LIST is a complex Registry type used primarily by drivers. Though it would be inefficient, all Registry data could be considered REG_BINARY data.

Data types for value entries include:

- REG_BINARY
- REG_COLOR_RGB
- REG_DWORD
- REG_DWORD_BIG_ENDIAN
- REG_DWORD_LITTLE_ENDIAN
- REG_EXPAND_SZ
- REG_FILE_NAME
- REG_FILE_TIME
- REG_FULL_RESOURCE_DESCRIPTOR
- REG_LINK
- REG_MULTI_SZ
- REG_NONE
- REG_QWORD
- REG_QWORD_LITTLE_ENDIAN
- REG_RESOURCE_LIST
- REG_RESOURCE_REQUIREMENTS_LIST
- REG_SZ
- REG_UNKNOWN

NOTE

REG_QWORD is new to Windows 2000 and is a quad-word (64-bit) numeric entry; REG_QWORD_LITTLE_ENDIAN is the same as REG_QWORD.

Applications can access each of these data types. Additionally, some applications store data in formats that only they understand. Actually, a provision in the Registry allows the storing application to assign a specific type to the Registry data. Any application or component that doesn't understand the format simply treats the data as a REG_UNKNOWN type and reads the data as binary.

NOTE

Oops, did I say something special? Yes! Don't forget that applications can and do store data in the Registry.

HOW WINDOWS 2000 USES THE REGISTRY

How does Windows 2000 use the Registry? When is the Registry first opened and used?

The Registry is a tree-based hierarchical system that provides quick access to data stored in almost any format. Actually, the Registry is a rather flexible database, and the information in it comes from a number of sources:

- ▶ From installing Windows 2000

- ▶ From booting Windows 2000

- ▶ From applications, systems, and user interaction

Every component of Windows 2000 uses the Registry, without exception. A set of APIs allows both Windows 2000 and other applications to access Registry information easily and quickly.

Windows 2000 starts to use the Registry at the very beginning stages of system boot-up. The Windows 2000 boot process is based on which file format is installed, though the important parts are identical in either case. The unimportant parts are the loading of the specific drivers to read the NTFS (New Technology File System).

NOTE

Throughout this book, unless I say otherwise, I'm referring to Windows 2000 installed on an Intel *x*86 platform. The boot process on RISC-based systems (such as the Digital Alpha system) is different, though the differences are not terribly significant, considering how the Registry is used.

The Windows 2000 boot process consists of the following steps:

1. The system is powered up, the video is initialized, and the hardware self-tests are performed. The BIOS performs these tests, which are called POSTs (power-on self-tests). Usually, the memory test is the most visible one; its progress is shown on most computer screens.

2. After running POST, the system initializes each adapter. If the adapter has its own built-in BIOS, the adapter's BIOS is called to perform its own initialization. Some adapters, such as Adaptec's SCSI (Small Computer System Interface) adapters, both display messages and allow the user to interact. Some adapters that don't have a BIOS aren't initialized until Windows 2000 loads their drivers much later in the boot-up process.

3. After all the adapters that have a BIOS are initialized, the system boot loader reads in the sector located at the very beginning of the first bootable disk drive and passes commands to this code. This sector is called the *boot sector*, or the MBR (Master Boot Record), and the operating system writes it when the operating system is installed.

4. The code in the MBR then loads the NTLDR (a small program in the root directory of the boot partition of the server's hard disk). (This file has no extension, though it is an executable file.) Once the NTLDR is loaded, the MBR passes control to the code in NTLDR. When NTLDR is initialized, it displays the message "Windows NT Portable Boot Loader." Since our computers are so fast today, we never actually see this message—the screen is almost immediately cleared when NTLDR reinitializes the video system.

5. NTLDR then switches into 32-bit mode (remember, an Intel *x*86 processor always boots into 16-bit real mode). It then loads a special copy of the necessary file system I/O files and reads in the file boot.ini.

6. The file boot.ini has information about each operating system that can be loaded. Remember, Windows 2000 supports multiboot configurations. It is trivial to create a Windows 2000 installation that can boot Windows NT, Windows 2000, and Windows 95 or Windows 98. The boot loader can even

boot two different copies of Windows 2000 with either the same or different version numbers. NTLDR then processes the boot.ini file, displaying boot information to allow the user to select which operating system will be loaded. At this point, let's assume that Windows 2000 will be loaded.

7. When you select Windows 2000 to be loaded, NTLDR loads the file NTDETECT.COM. This program then collects information about the currently installed hardware and saves this information for the Registry. Most of this information is stored in the HKEY_LOCAL_MACHINE hive.

8. Once NTDETECT has detected the hardware, control is passed back to NTLDR, and the boot process continues. At this point, the Registry has been substantially updated with the current hardware configuration, which is stored in HKEY_LOCAL_ MACHINE\Hardware.

9. You will then see the following prompt: "Press spacebar now to invoke Hardware Profile/Last Known Good menu." Pressing the spacebar forces Windows 2000 to use a specific configuration stored in the Registry hive HKEY_LOCAL_ MACHINE.

10. Following the detection of NTDETECT, NTLDR loads and initializes the Windows NT kernel, loads the services, and then starts Windows.

11. When the kernel is loaded, the HAL is also loaded. (The HAL—Hardware Abstraction Layer—is used to manage hardware services.) Next, the Registry system subkey HKEY_LOCAL _MACHINE\System is loaded into memory. Windows 2000 scans the Registry for all drivers with a start value of zero. This includes those drivers that should be loaded and initialized at boot time.

12. You can see the beginning of the next stage, kernel initialization. The screen switches to a blue background, and you will see a message about the Windows 2000 build number and the number of system processors. Again, the system scans the Registry and finds all drivers that must be started at the kernel initialization stage.

13. From this point, Windows 2000 starts various components and systems. Each component and system reads the Registry and performs various tasks and functions. The final stage is to start the program that manages the user logon, WinLogon. WinLogon allows the user to log on and use Windows 2000.

Once Windows 2000 is booted, both the operating system and applications use the Registry. The Registry is dynamic, but usage of the Registry may be dynamic or static. That is, some Registry items are read one time and never reread until the system is restarted. Other items are read every time they are referenced. There is no fixed rule as to what is read each time it is needed and what is not, but to be on the safe side, follow these guidelines:

▶ Application-related data is probably read when the application starts. If you change application-based data, restart the application. In fact, the best path to follow is this: do not change application-based data while the application is running.

▶ User-interface data is sometimes dynamic, sometimes static. With user-interface data, the way to go is to change the data and wait to see the results of the change. If the change doesn't appear, try logging on again.

▶ System data is usually either static or buffered. Many system-related Registry changes won't become effective until the system is restarted. Some system data is rewritten or created at start-up time, precluding changes by users. Many of the items in HKEY_LOCAL_MACHINE may be reset at system boot time, especially those items that are hardware related.

A Note about Terminology

The Registry is made up of hives, keys, subkeys, and value entries. Well, actually, depending on the source, you may be faced with hives and data keys; or keys and items; or just data keys; or who knows what else.

There is some indication that Microsoft wants to drop the original term for a Registry section—the *hive*—and replace this term with the word *key*. In the Windows NT Resource Kit, Microsoft defines the following:

> The Registry is divided into parts called *hives*. A hive is a discrete body of keys, subkeys, and values rooted at the top of the Registry hierarchy. Hives are distinguished from other groups of keys in that they are permanent components of the Registry; they are not created dynamically when the system starts and deleted when it stops. Thus, HKEY_LOCAL_MACHINE\ Hardware, which is built dynamically by the Hardware Recognizer when Windows NT starts, is not a hive.

In the Windows 2000 documentation, Microsoft says a hive is:

> A section of the Registry that appears as a file on your hard disk...

These definitions are absolute and state exactly what is a hive and what is not. However, in the real world, no one follows this exact definition. Many authors call all holders of information *hives* (or *subhives*) and call data objects *keys*. Others never refer to hives at all and instead call all holders *keys* or *subkeys* and refer to data objects as *values*.

Virtually every definition leaves something to be desired. To call the thing that holds data a "value entry" sometimes makes it awkward to refer to the contents. Consider these examples:

The value entry named asdf contains the value 1234.

The value called asdf contains the value 1234.

The following example is much more readable:

The value entry asdf is a REG_DWORD with a value of 1234.

Is there a need to distinguish between what Microsoft calls a "hive" (a top-level, permanent, Registry component) and what Microsoft calls a "key"? When does a hive become a key, and is this important? I can't think of any context in which anything is gained by making this distinction. Referring to the top-level objects as *hives* certainly frees up the term *key* to be used elsewhere, but why not stick to one term?

Table 18.1 compares Registry terminology against the terminology used for the Windows file system—and gives the terminology I'll be using in the chapters in this part of the book.

TABLE 18.1: Registry Terminology Explained

Context	Root Collections	Subcollections	Objects	Data
Disks	Root directories		Files	Data
Older Registry terminology	Hives	Subhives	Data keys	Data
Newer Registry terminology	Hives	Keys/subkeys	Value entry	Data
Registry terminology in this book	Hives	Keys/subkeys*	Value entry	Data

*Just to keep things easy to read, I'll use the term *key* to refer to both keys and subkeys.

HINTS AND KINKS FROM THE EXPERTS

In each chapter in this part of the book, I'll present a few hints and kinks from the experts. These experts are a number of people who have a lot of experience working with the Windows Registry. They have learned from their experiences and the experiences of others.

For example, every expert will tell you the same thing: the minute you start tinkering with the Registry, you will create a mess that is so bad that only a clean reinstall (or restoration from a backup) will fix it. To restore the backup, you would boot from the installation disks and choose Repair, insert the ERD (emergency repair disk), and restore the Registry—not a full backup. (A full backup would only work if you'd selected to back up System State data.)

The first time I had a serious Registry problem, I'd change something, and things would just get worse. Some Registry problems cannot be "hacked," or fixed manually. The only fix for these problems is to either reinstall or restore the system. However, this type of situation is unusual. My experience has been that these problems happen only when hardware (such as the Registry's drive) fails or when an incredibly errant program totally trashes the Registry. Neither of these happens often.

Most users make minor tweaks or fixes in the Registry. Most of the time, things go OK. Sometimes things go awry. Through it all, we toast the Registry, and then it's back to the proverbial drawing board. Such is life.

What's Next?

Now that you know what the Registry is and why it's important, you need to know how to use it, how to back it up, and how to restore it—all topics that I'll deal with in the next chapter.

Chapter 19

Readme.1st: Preventing Disaster!

Preventing disaster is important. No one wants a system failure or to have to reinstall Windows 2000.

Adapted from *Mastering Windows 2000 Registry*, by Peter D. Hipson

ISBN 0-7821-2615-4   725 pages $39.99

You are reading this chapter for your own particular reason. Perhaps, as I am recommending, you are here because you want to do everything possible to prevent a disaster with your Windows 2000 installation. Or maybe you really, really want to recover from an existing disaster. If you are recovering from a problem, you may want to skip to the section later in this chapter titled "Restoring the Registry." For those of you who never do anything wrong, read on.

The Registry has always been the one part of Windows that virtually every user has neither understood nor trusted. Just when things go well, the Registry gets corrupted, and it is time to reinstall everything.

The Windows 2000 operating system is quite robust; however, many things can cause problems. For example, a hard drive failure (even a small soft error on the system drive in the Registry files), a controller failure, or a more complex memory bit that sometimes doesn't set correctly all can cause many problems with Windows 2000 and the Registry.

WARNING

Windows 2000 is robust, but our hardware is not. Most Pentium systems do not have memory parity. Though earlier PC systems used memory parity, this feature disappeared quietly a few years back when memory prices skyrocketed and there was a serious effort to keep computer prices to a minimum. Most of the newest computers now do support memory parity; many of the systems still in use do not, and as a result, routine memory errors won't be detected until it is much too late.

In this chapter, we'll cover a number of potential problem areas:

Backup   You'll learn a number of ways to back up that pesky Registry.

Restoration   What's difficult even under the best of conditions will be made simpler after you've perused these pages.

Recovery techniques   You'll discover ways to recover from a Registry failure and retain as much of the existing installation of Windows 2000 as possible.

Hints and kinks from the experts   This is stuff from the Resource Kit and a few ideas from some experts on how to keep things going well.

WHAT'S THE DEAL WITH THE REGISTRY, ANYWAY?

One of the biggest problems with the Registry is that Windows uses it constantly. The entire process of backing up and restoring the operating system is much more difficult because Windows must have the Registry files open during a restore.

You can solve this problem in several ways: One solution is to use the backup program supplied with Windows 2000. Another is to use an aftermarket backup program. Such a backup program has to contain the code necessary to back up and restore the Registry.

TIP

Oh, joy! The backup program that is included with Windows 2000 allows backing up to media other than tape drives. Now it is possible to back up to other hard drives (a technique that I use), Zip drives, and other storage media.

However, these techniques may not work well under your circumstances. You may already have had a Registry failure, and you may have no Registry backup to rely on for recovery. Backing up and recovering the Registry without a tape backup is excruciatingly difficult using previous versions of the backup program.

Using the ERD (Emergency Repair Disk) is easy, but you cannot simply stick in a diskette, type **restore registry**, and expect it to work. Windows 2000 does not store any Registry information on the ERD (Microsoft recognized that the Registry was becoming too large to store on a typical diskette). The Windows 2000 ERD contains only three files: autoexec.nt, config.nt, and setup.log. The directory %*systemroot*%\repair (the same location in which they are stored in Windows NT 4) holds all the Registry files that are backed up.

In fact, restoring the Registry from the %*systemroot*%\repair directory requires the Windows 2000 installation program. It's not that bad; you don't have to reinstall Windows, but the installation program will restore the Registry from the backup, if necessary.

The menu that you see when you boot up Windows 2000 also allows you to restore parts of the Registry based on copies of the Registry saved from previous sessions.

TIP

Always, always make sure that you back up the Registry whenever you install new software or hardware or remove anything from your computer. If you do not back up the Registry, and you restore a previous copy from an old backup, the system will not work as expected!

Where Exactly *Is* the Registry?

In order to back it up, you need to know where the Registry is located. Sometimes you get to the Registry as if by magic—the standard Registry editors don't tell you where the Registry is; they simply load it automatically. However, many times you need to know where to find the Registry files. They're not too difficult to find; the Registry's files are in the directory *%systemroot%*\System32\config.

ENVIRONMENT VARIABLES

Every Windows 2000 installation automatically has some shortcut variables installed that are accessible to the user and the system. These variables are called environment variables. One environment variable, *%systemroot%*, contains the drive, path, and directory name for the directory in which Windows 2000 was installed.

Using these environment variables makes it easy to write batch files and to otherwise locate components of your current Windows 2000 installation. For example, you might type the following at a command prompt:

    CD %systemroot%

This command then changes to the directory in which Windows 2000 was installed.

Using the environment variables can also be useful when you are writing software that must run on a number of different Windows 2000 installations, especially when these installations are made to different drives or directories.

The *%systemroot%*\System32\config directory includes the following set of files, each of which is a critical component of the Registry.

These files are backed up to the `repair` directory, so that they can be restored as necessary in the event of a Registry failure.

Autoexec.nt   Used to initialize the MS-DOS environment unless a different start-up file is specified in an application's PIF (Program Information File).

Config.nt   Used to initialize the MS-DOS environment unless a different startup file is specified in an application's PIF.

Default   The default Registry file.

SAM   The SAM (Security Accounts Manager) Registry file.

Security   The security Registry file.

Setup.log   The file that contains a record of all files that were installed with Windows 2000. Service packs and other components of Windows 2000 use the information in this file to update the operating system.

Software   The application software Registry file.

System   The system Registry file.

You use two additional files to reconfigure security when repairing the Registry. These are contained only in the `repair` directory, and not in the `%systemroot%\system32\config` directory:

SecDC.inf   The default security settings that have been updated for domain controllers.

SecSetup.inf   The out-of-the-box default security settings.

In a typical Windows 2000 installation, the `%systemroot%\system32\config` directory contains these files:

AppEvent.Evt   The application(s) event log file.

DEF$$$$.DEL   The default Registry recovery file.

Default   The default Registry file.

Default.sav   A backup copy of the information contained in the default Registry file.

DnsEvent.Evt   The DNS (Domain Name Service) server event log.

File Rep.evt   One of two File Replication Service event log files.

Netlogon.dnb   A NetLogon support file.

Netlogon.dns   A NetLogon support file.

NTDS.Evt   The Windows 2000 directory service event log.

NtFrs.Evt   The second of two File Replication Service event log files.

SAM   The Security Accounts Manager Registry file.

SecEvent.evt   The security event log.

Security   The security Registry file.

SOF$$$$$.DEL   The software Registry recovery file.

Software   The application software Registry file.

Software.sav   A backup copy of the information contained in the software Registry file.

SYS$$$$$.DEL   The system Registry recovery file.

SysEvent.evt   The system events log.

System   The system Registry file.

SYSTEM.ALT   A copy of the information contained in the system Registry file.

System.sav   A backup copy of the information contained in the system Registry file.

Userdiff   Migrates preexisting user profiles from previous versions of Windows NT to Windows 2000.

In the Registry, the most important files are those with no extensions—these are the current Registry files. Another important file is SYSTEM.ALT, a duplicate of the System Registry file.

The files in the %*systemroot*%\System32\config directory that have the extensions .log or .sav contain a history that you can view with the Event Viewer program. For example, files with the extension .sav were saved using the Last Known Good booting process. Files with the .log extension are records of changes made to the Registry when Registry auditing is turned on. Though the .log and .sav files are not strictly necessary to have a working Windows 2000 installation, it is best to consider each of these files a member of a complete set.

WARNING

Be careful not to replace one file in the Registry without replacing all the others. It is simply too easy to get one file out of sync with the remaining Registry files, and this would spell disaster.

SIDE TRIP: RESTORING WINDOWS 2000

Restoring a copy of Windows 2000 from a backup can be a difficult process. First, without a working copy of Windows 2000, you can't run the backup and restore programs. This means you have to install a new copy of the operating system to be able to run the restore program. You'd then use this copy of Windows 2000 to restore the original system from the backup. Some users will reformat the drive, reinstall Windows 2000 into the same directory that the original installation was made to, and restore on top of this new installation. There's nothing wrong with doing this, as long as you remember one critical point: If you installed any Windows 2000 service packs on your original installation, these service packs must also be installed on the new installation being used to run the restoration program. If you don't install the service packs, Windows 2000 restores system files from the original installation (with the service pack) on top of the new files (without the service pack); the files will be out of version sync with the existing operating system files and the Registry. This will usually cause the restore to crash without much of a warning as to what happened.

To perform a full restore of Windows 2000 (and everything else on the drive) do the following:

1. Reformat the drive. Remember that you're doing a full restore here, and nothing that was on the drive is considered valuable at this point.

2. Install Windows 2000, using your original distribution CD-ROM.

3. Install the service packs that were installed with the version of Windows that is being restored. Remember that the service

CONTINUED ➡

Part iv

packs are cumulative, so you need only reinstall the last service pack. For example, if Service Pack 3 was installed, it will not be necessary to install Service Packs 1 and 2. You only need to reinstall Service Pack 3.

4. Reinstall your backup/restore program, if necessary, and begin your restoration process.

ARE TWO COPIES BETTER THAN ONE?

Generally, two of anything is better than one. It's easier to ride a bicycle than a unicycle. However, it is even easier to drive a car—you don't even have to keep your balance. Where the Registry is concerned, keeping *at least* two copies of it is a good idea. I'd recommend that you keep at least four:

▶ The copy created by the Windows 2000 backup program, stored in %*systemroot*%\repair. The Windows 2000 Setup program is able to use this copy to restore the Registry.

▶ A backup copy of the Registry files found in %*systemroot*%\repair, saved in a safe and convenient location. Consider a Zip disk or some other type of removable storage media for this copy.

▶ One (or more) backup copies, created using a backup technique on a type of medium that is compatible with the backup and restore program of choice. (I'll discuss backup methods to use in the next section.)

▶ A copy of the Registry files contained in %*systemroot*%\System32\config stored on separate medium, such as a different drive, diskettes, a Zip drive, CD-RW, or some other easily accessible, writeable media. Try to avoid media that require special drivers and such, because these drivers may not work when you need to restore that pesky Registry. This copy can only be made by dual-booting into another copy of Windows 2000 (or Windows 95/98 if the drive is FAT compatible).

NOTE

In Windows NT 4, keep the special copy created by the RDisk utility that is stored in the Windows NT directory %*systemroot*%\repair. This copy of the Registry can only be used by the Windows NT Setup program to repair an existing copy of Windows NT. Also keep the copy created by the RDisk utility that is stored on the Windows NT ERD. Again, this copy of the Registry can only be used by the Windows NT Setup program to repair an existing copy of Windows NT. Windows 2000 doesn't support RDisk. Instead, the Registry backup and ERD-creation functionality is incorporated into the finally-useful-for-everyone Backup program.

Be absolutely sure you keep these copies secure. Lock 'em up, stash 'em away. Oh, and by the way, that lock on your desk drawer is not good enough; use a fireproof safe or a strong box.

DANGER, WILL ROBINSON, DANGER!

Throughout this chapter, I'll talk about backing up the Registry, saving the Registry to diskettes, other drives, and tapes. That's all well and good. However, you must remember that the Registry contains sensitive information, especially if it is for a Windows 2000 server.

The Registry contains information critical to both the operation and security of Windows 2000. Someone can use your backup Registry files in many ways to breach your system's security, perhaps costing you money or (gasp!) your job.

Be absolutely sure you maintain the highest levels of security for any copies of the Registry that you make. If you save the Registry to external media (diskettes, tapes, or Zip drives, for example), make sure these copies are securely locked up. Why? Someone could, with little effort, completely subvert system security and then use the backup copies of the Registry to hide their actions.

I recommend you use a quality fireproof safe or a strong box for storing your Registry backup copies. Me, I use a fireproof, locked strong box inside a federal government–rated Mosler safe—and I don't think I'm being overly protective, either.

BACKUP TECHNIQUES

Windows 2000 supports two different file systems: FAT (File Allocations Table) and NTFS (New Technology File System). The FAT file system is identical to the file system used with both DOS and Windows 95/98. The FAT file system is not secure and presents no resistance to hackers and others who want to access files improperly. The FAT file system comes in three flavors: FAT12, FAT16, and FAT32. Windows 2000 fully supports FAT32 and FAT16. This support allows compatibility with Windows 98's large disk support.

NOTE

Windows NT 4 does not support FAT32 except in a very limited, read-only manner. You cannot install Windows NT 4 onto a FAT32 drive. FAT12 is antiquated and is unlikely to be found on Windows NT systems.

NTFS is unique to Windows 2000. Though it is possible to read an NTFS drive from DOS or Windows 95 using shareware utilities, it is generally not possible to write to an NTFS drive unless you are using Windows 2000. However, System Internals (see their Internet site at http://www .sysinternals.com) has two utilities that allow you to write to an NTFS volume from DOS or Windows 95/98.

Back Up to Tape or to Other Media

The Windows 2000 backup program, Backup (NTBackup.exe), is one of a whole slew of compatible backup programs that allow backing up the system Registry to tape, diskettes, other hard drives, or for that matter, any Windows 2000–supported writeable medium. The process is straightforward and can be done as part of a regular backup cycle or whenever desired. Just check System State in the backup tree to back up using Backup. When it stores the System State, Backup saves the following items:

- ▶ Active Directory—the database of information about objects on the network

- ▶ Boot files—the files used to boot the system

- ▶ COM+ Class Registration database—the COM+ classes' registration

- ▶ Registry—the set of files that constitute the configuration of Windows 2000

- ▶ SysVol—a shared directory that contains the server's public files that will be replicated on all other domain servers on the network

NOTE

In Windows 2000, to create an ERD, you use the Backup program. Choose Tools ➤ Create An Emergency Repair Disk. Backup will prompt for diskettes as needed.

Using Backup is simple if you are familiar with creating and restoring tape backups. However, a few difficulties arise when you use backups of the Registry. First, to keep the Registry backup easily accessible, it is wise to place the Registry backup on its own medium. If the medium is inexpensive, this is viable, but if you are paying an arm and a leg for the medium, this can be costly, because each Registry backup is relatively small as far as backups go.

Second, the Registry backups must be secure, perhaps more secure than standard backups. Everyone's situation is different; just realize that unrestricted access to the Registry allows unrestricted, unaudited access to everything else as well.

Finally, tape backups are sometimes slow. Stick the tape in the drive and the first thing that happens is that the tape gets rewound (to re-tension it). This process alone can take some time—time that is not available when you are working on getting a server up and running. Consider instead backing up the Registry to a local hard drive (a drive other than the system drive, however).

Backing Up Using *copy* or *xcopy*

It is not possible to copy back the current Registry while Windows 2000 is using the Registry. Period. Therefore, to restore the Registry using either copy or xcopy, you must shut down Windows 2000 and start another operating system, such as DOS, Windows 95/98, or a second copy of Windows 2000. Which operating system you use depends on which file system is being used on the computer. If the file system is FAT, start DOS or Windows 95/98. If the file system is NTFS, start a second copy of Windows 2000.

Backing up the Registry with copy or xcopy is easier than using Backup. Run the Backup program, create an ERD, and then simply copy the backup of the Registry found in the %systemroot%\repair directory to another location. Then (this is optional, but can't hurt), xcopy the current Registry files in the %systemroot%\system32\config directory using the /c option, which tells xcopy to ignore errors. (Since the currently opened Registry cannot be copied, these files will generate an error.)

Backing Up If You're Using FAT

If you are using Windows 2000 and the FAT file system, you can simply boot a DOS or Windows 95/98 (if FAT32 is used) diskette that was for-matted with the /sys option. This will give you a DOS command prompt that allows you to read from and write to the hard drive quite easily.

To create a bootable disk, simply use the Windows 95/98 or DOS FORMAT command with the /s system option, and then copy the xcopy command's files (xcopy*.*) to the diskette too. This disk can then be booted in the Windows 2000 computer, allowing unrestricted accesses to all FAT drives that are installed on that computer. When using Zip drives, you may need to add DOS drivers for these drives to your boot diskette.

NOTE

If the system is already configured for dual-booting, you can probably use the second operating system instead of using a boot diskette. It probably won't matter which alternate operating system is installed (DOS, Windows 95/98, or even Windows NT); all will work fine for the purpose of backing up the Registry. You don't need boot diskettes in this situation.

After you boot into a command prompt, it is a simple task to copy the Registry files to a safe location, such as another hard drive, a set of diskettes (the Registry won't fit on a single diskette), a Zip drive, a CD-RW drive, or other supported medium.

NOTE

Some computers can boot from the CD-ROM drive. If this is the case for your computer, it is also possible, if you have a CD-RW drive, to create a bootable CD.

Backing Up If You're Using NTFS

Users with NTFS are presented with a much more difficult problem. The NTFS file system is a secure file system that other operating systems such as DOS or Windows 95/98 cannot easily access. Files on an NTFS drive can only be written by Windows 2000 and not by other operating systems. Sure, there are utilities that allow NTFS to be accessed from Windows 95/98, but the mode of access is read-only; therefore, restoring is not possible

To be able to access the Registry files on an NTFS drive, you need to install a second copy of Windows 2000. Actually, this is not a major problem because everyone should have at least two installations of Windows 2000. Windows 2000 supports multiple boot configurations quite effectively. To create a multiple boot installation of Windows 2000, simply follow these steps:

1. Ensure that you have sufficient space on your hard drive for a second copy of Windows 2000. This second copy requires a minimal amount of disk space since it is only a basic operating system. Figure 100MB to 150MB of hard disk space for this installation, depending on how much additional software and how many features you install.

2. Using the Windows 2000 installation boot diskettes, begin your installation. When prompted for a destination, specify a new directory. If you are farsighted enough and are doing this before disaster has struck, you can install directly from the distribution CD without using the boot diskettes. To do so, run the Windows 2000 Setup program to begin the installation process.

WARNING

Don't install to the same directory in which your current working installation of Windows 2000 is installed. That won't create a second copy of Windows 2000.

3. The Windows 2000 Setup program configures the Boot Manager (creating new entries in the boot menu) so that you can choose which copy of Windows 2000 you want to boot.

Part iv

CUSTOMIZING THE BOOT MENU

Once you install a second copy of Windows 2000, your boot menu will list both copies of the operating system. This can be confusing since the descriptions are almost identical.

The solution is to customize the boot menu. The boot drive's root directory contains a file called boot.ini, which includes the boot options for each installed copy of Windows 2000. Before you can edit boot.ini, you need to remove the system, read-only, and hidden attributes. At a command prompt, type **c:\> attrib c:\boot.ini –r –s –h**. Don't forget to restore these attributes afterward.

The boot.ini file includes a text string that describes the installation:

```
type boot.ini
[boot loader]
timeout=30
default=signature(9e2ebb84)disk(0)rdisk(0)parti-
tion(1)\WINNT
[operating systems]
signature(9e2ebb84)disk(0)rdisk(0)partition(1)\WINNT
="Microsoft Windows 2000 Server" /fastdetect
multi(0)disk(0)rdisk(0)partition(1)\WINNTBU="Windows
NT Server"
multi(0)disk(0)rdisk(0)partition(1)\WINNTBU="Windows
NT Server" /basevideo /sos
```

You can modify anything in the quoted strings. I suggest that you call your backup installation of Windows 2000 just that—"Windows 2000 B/U." For example:

```
multi(0)disk(0)rdisk(0)partition(1)\WINNTBU="Windows
2000 Server Registry B/U"
multi(0)disk(0)rdisk(0)partition(1)\WINNTBU="Windows
2000 Server Registry B/U [VGA mode]" /basevideo /sos
```

Don't forget to use Control Panel's System applet to change the default boot to the version of Windows 2000 that normally is booted by default. After you reinstall Windows 2000, the installation (Setup) program makes the latest installation the default operating system.

To *copy* or to *xcopy*, That Is the Question

Users of FAT file systems can access the Registry with a DOS boot disk, and users of either FAT or NTFS can gain access with a second copy of Windows 2000 as described earlier. Once you establish a method for accessing the Registry, it is a simple task to completely back up the Registry.

Typically, I'll use a command window (a "DOS box" or command prompt), because I use NTFS and have a second copy of Windows 2000 installed. I'll show you how I back up the Registry on my Windows 2000 server.

Using the md (make directory) or mkdir command, I create a new directory called \RegBU on another drive (my system has five hard drives):

```
md d:\RegBu
xcopy g:\winnt\system32\config\*.* D:\RegBu\*.* /s
```

I then use the copy command (or xcopy) to copy the Registry files in g:\winnt\ system32\config directory to the RegBU directory. My main copy of Windows 2000 is installed in the winnt directory..

This example saves a backup to a subdirectory on the D: drive. This is a good solution. If the system (G:) drive becomes unreadable, the backup copy is still accessible. Other alternatives include backing up to a removable (Zip) drive or a network drive on a different computer.

If things are going well, I also use PKZIP to back up the Registry files to a set of diskettes. In my system, the files in my config directory are just over 16MB in size. Am I typical? No. I have only a few users in my user database, so my Registry is smaller than most. PKZIP can compress the files to only two diskettes, which is a reasonable number. Of course, if I used a Zip drive, I could put these files on a single cartridge, but in my case that would be a waste of space.

Once you've copied your Registry files to a safe location, simply remove the boot diskette (if used), and reboot the computer. This will give you a copy of the Registry that you can later restore using an almost identical technique: boot to DOS and restore the files.

TIP

What the heck is a safe location? A safe location is typically another drive, a Zip drive, or perhaps even diskettes. Diskettes present a small problem in that the Registry files are typically going to total 10 to 20MB. Using a utility such as PKZIP, you can write these large files to a number of diskettes while at the same time compressing them, which reduces the number of diskettes to a minimum.

What's on My ERD?

The Windows 2000 ERD contains a number of files in addition to the Registry files:

Autoexec.nt Not part of the Registry, this file is used to initialize the MS-DOS environment.

Config.nt Not part of the Registry, this file is used to initialize the MS-DOS environment.

Setup.log This file contains information about the initial setup of Windows 2000. It is critical when restoring the Registry using the Setup program's repair function.

Using RegEdit to Back Up the Registry

Using the Windows 95/98 Registry Editor, you can make an additional copy of the Registry and restore it by double-clicking a single icon. The Windows 95/98 Registry Editor, RegEdit, is included with Windows 2000.

NOTE

If you are a system administrator and you have Windows 95/98 systems, you can use the following technique for these computers as well. Actually, this technique works better with Windows 95/98 than with Windows 2000, but we'll keep that our carefully guarded secret.

If you follow the steps outlined shortly, you can create a copy of the system Registry that includes everything except the Security and SAM Registry keys. When backing up a Windows 2000 workstation on a network, RegEdit usually uses this technique to save everything needed. You can back up the security database using other methods, though they are awkward and somewhat difficult to manage: it is easier to use the techniques described earlier in this chapter to do a complete Registry backup. Because the `Security` and SAM keys are not backed up, this is not a complete backup technique. Rather, this is a quick and easy way to back up the other major parts of the Registry.

To use RegEdit to back up the Registry, follow these steps:

1. At a command prompt, type the command **regedit**, or choose Start ➢ Run to open the Run dialog box, type **RegEdit** in the Open box, and click the OK button to open the Registry Editor:

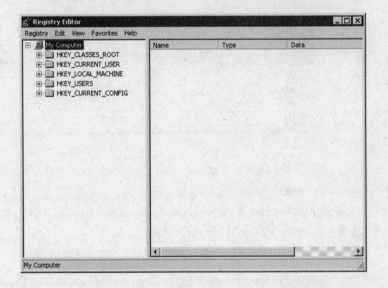

2. Notice that My Computer is highlighted. If My Computer is not highlighted, select it to ensure that the entire Registry, not just part of it, is backed up.

3. Choose Registry ≻ Export Registry File to open the Export Registry File dialog box:

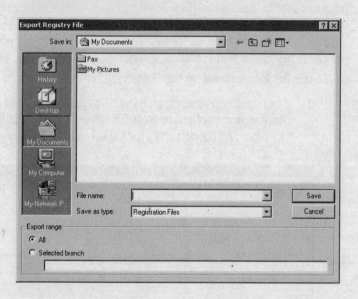

4. In the Save In text box, click the down arrow and select Desktop.

5. In the File Name text box, type a name for the file (for example, Registry), and then click Save.

6. Click the Close button to exit the Registry Editor.

You'll now see a shortcut to the Registry backup on your Desktop.

Unlike earlier versions of RegEdit, the version that is supplied with Windows 2000 writes the Registry file in Unicode format (each character is two-bytes long). Editors and utilities that do not understand Unicode character sets will have difficulty working with this file. To convert a Unicode text file to a one-byte text format, use the `type` command, with the output redirected to a new file. For example:

```
type "file in unicode.reg" >"file in text.txt"
```

If you use the Registry Editor to back up the Registry immediately after installation, you can quickly and easily restore the system to a known state. Simply double-click the Registry shortcut on the Desktop to reload this file as the current Registry.

NOTE

You can place the saved Registry file anywhere you want. In some cases, placing a Registry restore capability on the user's Desktop is tantamount to courting disaster. Some users will click it just to see what will happen. One solution is to hide the file or save it to an offline storage location.

RESTORING THE REGISTRY

To restore the Registry, you must consider how the Registry was saved. You can save a Registry in four ways, each of which differs in just how much of and where the Registry was saved:

▶ You can use a backup program to copy the Registry to a tape or other offline location. The backup program will then restore the Registry backup to its original location.

▶ You can copy the Registry (as described earlier), creating identical copies of the Registry that you can then recopy to the original Registry location. This requires that you use a second operating system (or a second copy of Windows 2000) to restore the files.

▶ The Backup program saves the Registry to the %system-root%\repair directory. You can then use the Windows 2000 Setup program to restore these files.

▶ You can use the Registry Editor to save the Registry in a text file with an extension of .reg. Windows 2000 knows that this is a Registry file (because the .reg file type is a registered extension) and will reload the file automatically into the Registry if you double-click the file in Explorer or on the Desktop. From a command prompt, enter the command **start *filename*.reg**; *filename* is the name of the Registry backup file.

Restoring from Tape

Restoring a tape backup is a simple though time-consuming process. When you use a backup-and-restore program compatible with Windows 2000, be sure that you select the option to restore the local Registry. Whether you restore other files at this time depends on your circumstances. If you suspect that other system files are corrupted, or if you are simply not sure of the state of the system, I would recommend repairing Windows 2000 or restoring the entire operating system and the Registry at the same time. If you know that the Registry is the only damaged component, simply restoring the Registry and not other system files may save some time.

Restoring from Other Media Supported by Backup

Restoring backups saved on other media (such as disks, diskettes, Zip drives, and so on) is a simple and often fast process. Use the Windows 2000 Backup program, and select System State from the list of backed up items to restore.

NOTE

It is not possible to restore only part of the System State data; you must restore it all.

If your backup includes files in addition to the System State, you can restore those files at the same time. The decision to restore these other files depends on your circumstances. If you suspect that other system files are corrupted or if you are simply not sure about the state of the system, I recommend repairing Windows 2000 or restoring the entire operating system and the Registry at the same time. If you know that the Registry is the only damaged component, simply restoring the System State and not other system files may save a certain amount of time.

You cannot restore the System State when Active Directory is running. This limitation requires that you stop the Active Directory services by doing the following:

1. Reboot Windows 2000.

2. Select the advanced start-up option Directory Services Restore Mode.

3. Once the system has completed the boot, restore the System State.

4. Reboot Windows 2000 a second time.

If you're using another backup program, simply follow the instructions provided with the program. The same general cautions about which files to restore (only the System State or the entire operating system) still apply. The main difference between most backup programs is the user interface.

NOTE

When restoring, be especially careful that you do not restore the wrong version of the System State. Generally, you want to make sure that you restore the most current working version of the Registry.

Recovering a Copied Registry

You restore a Registry that has been backed up using copy or xcopy in the opposite manner from which you backed it up. For example, if you have the NTFS file system, you have to restart the system using your backup copy of Windows 2000.

FAT and NTFS

When restoring a Registry on a FAT file system running Windows 2000, you must boot DOS, Windows 95/98, or a second copy of Windows 2000. If you have a dual boot installed (either DOS or Windows 95/98), you can use the dual boot to get to the other operating system.

If you are restoring the Registry on an NTFS system, dual-boot into the copy of Windows 2000 that you installed to back up the Registry.

WARNING

Once you are running the alternate operating system, find your latest working copy of the Registry *before* you copy it over the Registry that you think is corrupted, and back up the current Registry to another location. Take this precaution just in case the current Registry is not the problem (it happens) and the backup copy is not as good as you think it is.

You can follow these steps to restore your Registry from a backup you created:

1. Boot to another operating system: Windows 2000/NT, DOS, or Windows 95/98 for FAT; Windows 2000/NT for NTFS.

2. Save the current Registry to a safe location just in case it is not the problem.

3. Copy your saved Registry (from wherever it was stored) to the Registry location.

4. Boot the original version of Windows 2000, and test to see if the restoration worked. If it didn't, keep reading; more golden tips are coming up soon.

ERD Strikes Again: Using Setup to Recover

If you have no other backup copies of the original Registry, you'll have to fall back on the ERD diskette and the repair directory. This technique is fraught with peril, including the fact that the saved Registry may not have all the necessary information.

Properly restoring the system Registry from the repair directory and the ERD diskette requires running the Windows 2000 Setup program. When it starts, Setup examines the hard drive and looks for already-installed copies of Windows 2000 and their repair directories. Once the examination is complete, Setup will give you four choices:

- ► Help (press F1).

- ► Set up Windows 2000 (press Enter).

- ► Repair a damaged Windows 2000 installation (press R).

- ► Quit, because this was all just a big mistake (press F3).

Now, we know that we are in trouble—the only option is to consider whether it might be possible to recover from the problems without doing a complete reinstallation of Windows 2000.

Let's say that we are going to try to repair. Press **R** to select the repair option. At this stage, the Setup program switches to repair mode and continues. The next screen displays four choices. You can choose any combination or all of them:

Inspect Registry Files   This choice allows the repair program to check and repair the Registry files. This is the option that most of us will select. The repair program will need either an ERD diskette or the files stored in the %*systemroot%*\ repair directory.

Inspect Start-up Environment   The start-up environment is the Boot Manager, which is called by the program contained in the boot sector. Other supporting files—including boot.ini, ntdetect.com, and others—must also be validated. The repair program will repair or replace these files as best as it can, but be prepared for some items to be restored to the state they were in when you installed Windows 2000.

Verify Windows 2000 System Files   Verifying the system files is a process in which the repair program will go through the root directory and all the system directories (such as the Windows and System directories) and verify that each and every file is valid. This process is used when a hard disk error (especially on an NTFS volume) has made one or more system files invalid. Careful! You will loose all service packs installed to this repair process. Reinstall your service packs immediately after choosing this option.

Inspect Boot Sector   You inspect (and repair) the boot sector for several reasons. For example, if you inadvertently install another operating system with boot sector virus infections, this could damage the boot sector, especially with the FAT file system.

All four of these options are selected by default. You can use the selector bar (use the arrow keys) to highlight and deselect any option that you don't want; press Enter to select or clear an option.

After you elect to continue, Setup will check the devices. This is the same check that is done prior to an installation of Windows 2000.

The next stage is to determine where the Registry repair information will be coming from. Remember, you can use either the ERD or the copy stored in the repair directory. If you have multiple installations of Windows 2000, be sure to choose the correct repair directory from which to repair.

TIP

The ERD will tell Setup which copy of Windows 2000 you are attempting to repair. You *cannot* use the ERD from one installation of Windows 2000 to repair another installation of Windows 2000. It just won't work.

If you don't have an ERD (or you don't want to use it), Setup will search your drive for Windows 2000. You may have multiple installations of Windows 2000; this is common, considering how many times I've recommended installing at least two copies. If this is the case, Setup lists each installation that it finds. Select the version of Windows 2000 you want to repair, and press Enter.

WARNING

Careful! Be sure that you repair the correct Windows 2000 installation if you have more than one copy of the OS installed. Nothing is worse than successfully repairing a copy of Windows 2000 that wasn't broken in the first place.

Next, Setup checks the drives. The message indicates that drives are being checked, and the status indicator at the bottom of the screen shows the progress. Actually, Setup checks only the boot (C:) drive, but that's probably all that is needed right now.

The next prompt, which is displayed when you choose to repair the Registry repaired, is to determine which key or keys are to repair:

- ▸ System
- ▸ Software
- ▸ Default
- ▸ ntuser.dat
- ▸ Security
- ▸ SAM

Replacing some hives and not others might result in some problems if items in the Registry have been updated since the Registry was last saved. Typically, it is best to replace all files to avoid any problems with different versions.

Once the Registry is updated, the Setup program prompts you to remove the diskette from its drive and reboot the computer. If all went well, the computer will reboot and run.

Loading a *.reg* File

You can usually load any .reg file created by RegEdit (discussed earlier) by simply double-clicking the Registry shortcut in the Explorer program or on the Desktop.

You can also open the Registry Editor to load the .reg file. Choose Registry ➤ Import Registry File to open the Import Registry File dialog box. Actually, when you double-click a .reg file, Windows 2000 opens the Registry Editor. The main advantage of loading a Registry file from the Registry Editor is that you're able to see the effect of the Registry load.

A .reg file, being a text file, can be *carefully* edited. Did I emphasize *carefully* enough? Realize that you are making a Registry change if you modify the .reg file and then reload it. And make certain that the editor you use understands Unicode. Notepad will work fine; just remember not to use the default .txt file extension that Notepad uses when saving the file.

You will not be able to use this technique if you are unable to boot or run Windows. This is another good reason to have multiple backups of the Registry in different formats.

NOTE

When you are restoring the Registry, several errors are displayed. Some errors will state "System Process - Licensing Violation" and advise the user that the system has detected tampering with the product registration component of the Registry. Click OK when these messages appear and also when another error stating that it was not possible to write to the Registry shows up. This final error is actually an artifact of the licensing violation errors and does not indicate a failure of the entire process.

To make the restored Registry active, restart Windows 2000. (Windows 2000 caches most of the Registry while it is running.) There is no prompt to restart; however, some changes to the Registry will not be reloaded until the system is restarted. Choose Start ➤ Shut Down to open the Shut Down Windows dialog box, select Restart, and then click OK.

NOTE

It is not uncommon for applications to update the Registry using a . reg file during program installation. This is one method used by software developers. Why? Simple: this allows the Registry to be repaired, restoring the application's default values without having to reinstall the entire program.

THE RECOVERY CONSOLE

The Recovery Console is a tool that was added to Windows 2000 to allow recovery from a number of failures. Previously, all we could do was to boot another copy of Windows 2000 and hack our way around, replacing files, even Registry components, in the blind hope that we would somehow fix the problem.

Now, with Windows 2000, we have two new tools: the Recovery Console and the Safe Mode feature.

The Recovery Console is a powerful, simple (no, that's not an oxymoron!) feature that is supplied with Windows 2000. Now, realize that the Recovery Console is not installed by default. You must install the Recovery Console before you can use it. Installing the Recovery Console after the system has failed is quite like locking the barn door after the horse has been stolen—it really won't work that well.

Installing the Recovery Console

To install the Recovery Console, you use the Windows 2000 distribution CD (or share, if installing from a network device). The Recovery Console is installed using the winnt32.exe program. The winnt32.exe program is the same program that is used to install Windows 2000; however, by selecting the correct option, you are able to tell winnt32.exe not to install Windows 2000, but to install the Recovery Console instead.

NOTE

It is not possible to install the Recovery Console at the same time as Windows 2000. You must first install Windows 2000 and then install the Recovery Console. If you have multiple copies of Windows 2000 installed, you need to install the Recovery Console only once—the Recovery Console will work with as many copies of Windows 2000 as are installed.

Follow these steps to install the Recovery Console:

1. Insert the distribution CD, and change into the i386 directory.

2. Run winnt32.exe, using the /cmdcons option. Typically, no other options are needed, though you may want to specify source options, especially if you are installing from a network share rather than a hard drive.

3. The winnt32.exe program displays the dialog box shown in Figure 19.1. This dialog box allows you to cancel the installation if you need to.

NOTE

Multiple installations of the Recovery Console will simply overwrite previous installations; in such cases, no error is generated.

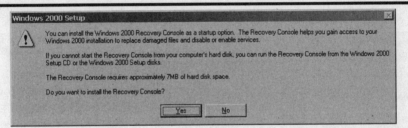

FIGURE 19.1: Setting up the Recovery Console using winnt32 /cmdcons bypasses all other setup options.

4. If there are no errors, the dialog box shown in Figure 19.2 is displayed. The Recovery Console is ready for use at this point.

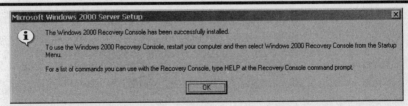

FIGURE 19.2: The Recovery Console has been successfully installed.

Part iv

What's in the Recovery Console?

The Recovery Console consists of a minor modification to the `boot.ini` file and the addition of a *hidden* directory on the boot drive. The added directory's name is `cmdcons`. The change to the `boot.ini` file is simply the addition of a line providing for a new boot option:

```
C:\CMDCONS\BOOTSECT.DAT="Microsoft Windows 2000 Recovery
Console" /cmdcons
```

This option consists of a fully qualified filename (`c:\cmdcons\bootsect.dat`), a text description (`Microsoft Windows 2000 Recovery Console`), and a boot option (`/cmdcons`).

As you probably know, the Windows 2000 Boot Manager can boot virtually any operating system (assuming that the operating system is compatible with the currently installed file system). The Recovery Console does qualify as an operating system, though it is very simple—and limited.

Is the Recovery Console secure? In most situations, it is actually quite secure. The user, at start-up of the Recovery Console, is prompted for two pieces of information:

▶ Which Windows 2000 installation is to be repaired (assuming that there is more than one Windows 2000 installation!).

▶ The Administrator's password for that installation. The Recovery Console then uses the installation's SAM to validate this password to ensure that the user has the necessary permission to use the system.

If the Administrator's password is lost or otherwise compromised, not only might it be impossible to use the Recovery Console, but anyone with access to the compromised password would be able to modify the system with the Recovery Console. This is not really an issue, though. If the Administrator's password is lost, that's life. It will be difficult, if not impossible, to recover the password. If the security of the Administrator's password is compromised, it will be necessary to repair the damage—changing the password is mandatory in this case. In either case, the Recovery Console is no less secure than Windows 2000.

The `cmdcons` directory contains more than 100 files. Most of these files are compressed, and the Recovery Console will uncompress them when they are needed. Here's a list of the uncompressed files in this directory:

```
C:\cmdcons\autochk.exe
C:\cmdcons\autofmt.exe
C:\cmdcons\biosinfo.inf
C:\cmdcons\BOOTSECT.DAT
C:\cmdcons\disk101
C:\cmdcons\disk102
C:\cmdcons\disk103
C:\cmdcons\disk104
C:\cmdcons\kbdus.dll
C:\cmdcons\migrate.inf
C:\cmdcons\ntdetect.com
C:\cmdcons\setupldr.bin
C:\cmdcons\setupreg.hiv
C:\cmdcons\spcmdcon.sys
C:\cmdcons\system32
C:\cmdcons\txtsetup.sif
C:\cmdcons\winnt.sif
C:\cmdcons\system32\ntdll.dll
C:\cmdcons\system32\smss.exe
```

The files disk101, disk102, disk103, and disk104 are disk image identifier files, and they contain nothing but a single space and a carriage return/line feed. The BOOTSECT.DAT file is the bootable boot sector image file. The migrate.inf file contains information used to update the Registry if needed. The setupreg.hiv file is used to update the Registry; however, this file is in a special format that can only be used with certain applications. The cmdcons directory also contains the subdirectory system32. This subdirectory contains two files, ntdll.dll and smss.exe.

Using the Recovery Console

Once the Recovery Console is installed, it will appear in the Start menu as the last item in the list, named Microsoft Windows 2000 Recovery Console.

WARNING

I strongly recommend that you not use the Recovery Console unless it is absolutely necessary! The Recovery Console commands are powerful, and if you use them improperly, you can destroy a Windows 2000 installation.

To use the Recovery Console, follow these steps:

1. Boot the system.

2. When the start-up screen is displayed, select Microsoft Windows 2000 Recovery Console.

3. Select the installation to be repaired if you have multiple Windows 2000 installations.

4. Enter the correct Administrator password for the installation to be repaired.

5. Use any Recovery Console commands (see the next section) needed to do the repair.

When you've repaired the installation, simply enter the **exit** command to restart the computer.

Starting the Recovery Console from the Installation CD-ROM

Follow these steps to start the Recovery Console for computers that either do not have the Recovery Console installed or cannot be booted (perhaps due to errors in the partition table or MBR):

1. Boot the system, using the CD-ROM disk or diskettes as appropriate.

2. When the initial setup text screen is displayed, press **R** to select Repair.

3. At the prompt, press **C** to select Recovery Console.

4. Select the installation to be repaired if you have multiple Windows 2000 installations.

5. Enter the correct Administrator password for the installation to be repaired.

6. Use any Recovery Console commands (see the next section) needed to do the repair.

When you have repaired the installation, enter the **exit** command to restart the computer.

Recovery Console Commands and Options

When the computer is started in the Recovery Console mode, a prompt similar to a command prompt is the only interface available. The Recovery Console's functionality is limited, and there is only support for the following commands:

attrib   Changes file attributes. The read, hidden, and system attributes may be either set or cleared as desired.

batch   Allows execution of a set of Recovery Console commands that have been saved in a text file. You just specify both the filename and the extension for the batch command to work. This command allows specifying an output file as well.

chdir (cd)   Works identically to the command session's cd command, changing the current working directory to the directory specified or, if no directory is specified, displaying the current working directory.

chkdsk   Works similarly to a command session's chkdsk command. Two options are available: /p specifies that the drive is to be checked regardless of whether the dirty flag is set; /r specifies that chkdsk should repair any bad sectors found.

cls   Works identically to the command session's cls command—clears the screen.

copy   Copies a file from a source location to a destination location. The file, if compressed, is uncompressed when copied. No wildcards are permitted with the copy command. This command has no options.

delete (del)   Works much like a command session's delete command. This command deletes the specified file or files. It will only work in the system directories of the installation being repaired, in hard drive root directories, and with local installation source files.

dir   Works similarly to a command session's dir command. This command will display the names of files and subdirectories in the location specified. The dir command has no options, listing file sizes, modification dates, and attributes.

Part IV

disable   Used to disable a service or device driver. The service or device driver to be disabled is marked as SERVICE_DISABLED to prevent it from being started when the system is subsequently restarted.

diskpart   Manages partitions on disk devices. This command is able to add or delete partitions as desired. When adding a partition, a command parameter specifies the size of the partition in megabytes.

enable   Used to enable a service or device driver. The service or device driver to be enabled is marked with the user-specified service type: SERVICE_AUTO_START, SERVICE_DISABLED, SERVICE _DEMAND_START, SERVICE_BOOT-START, or SERVICE_SYSTEM _START.

exit   Ends the Recovery Console session and reboots the computer.

expand   Works similarly to a command session's expand command. This command allows expanding files from a source CAB file. Two options are available: /d displays the contents of the CAB file; /y suppresses any overwrite warnings that may be given.

fixboot   Repairs or replaces the (optional) specified drive's boot sector.

fixmbr   Repairs or replaces the (optional) specified drive's master boot record.

format   Works similarly to a command session's format command. This command allows formatting disks using FAT, FAT32, and NTFS. One option, /q, allows quick formatting without a scan when the drive is known to be good.

help   Lists the available Recovery Console commands.

listsvc   Displays a list of services and drivers that are currently available on the computer.

logon   Run automatically when the Recovery Console is first started, this command is used to log on to an installation of Windows NT 4 or Windows 2000.

map   Used to display a list of all drive mappings. This command's output is very useful for the `fixboot`, `fixmbr`, and `fdisk` commands.

mkdir (md)   Works similarly to the command session's `md` (`mkdir`) command. This command allows creating directories within the system directories of the currently logged-on installation, removable disks, root directories of hard disk partitions, and local installation sources.

more   Works like the command session's `type` command. Displays the file's contents on the screen. There are no parameters for the `more` command.

rename (ren)   Allows the user to rename a file. This command does not support wildcard specifications.

rmdir (rd)   Works similarly to the command session's `rd` (`rmdir`) command. This command allows deleting directories within the system directories of the currently logged-on installation, removable disks, root directories of hard disk partitions, and local installation sources.

set   The Recovery Console supports a limited set of environment variables. These variables affect Recovery Console commands only.

systemroot   Changes to the current installation's `%systemroot%` directory. Functionally equivalent to `cd %systemroot%` in a normal command session.

type   Works like the command session's `type` command. This command displays the file's contents on the screen. There are no parameters for the `type` command.

You can install the Recovery Console permanently so that whenever the system is booted, you can select the Recovery Console. This works well for installations that will still boot to the Start menu (where one selects the installation or operating system to be booted). The Recovery Console is placed in the `cmdcons` directory, located on the boot drive.

NOTE

The `cmdcons` directory is always located on the boot drive, not on the system drive, unless the boot drive is also the system drive.

OTHER BACKUP AND RESTORE PROGRAMS

One excellent source for other Registry backup and restoration programs is the Windows 2000 Resource Kit's REG program, which has backup and restore functionality.

HINTS AND KINKS FROM THE EXPERTS

Here's another installment of good stuff from the Windows gurus.

Why Don't My Changes to the Registry Take Effect?

Always reboot. Reboot after restoring any Registry values. Windows 2000 does not reload many values except at boot time. There's nothing worse than wondering why your "fix" didn't work when Windows 2000 was simply not loading it.

Users Never Have a Current System State Backup!

In most sites, users rarely have a current System State backup when they need one. Give them one with this procedure. Use the scheduler (the AT command or a good one like OpalisRobot) on each workstation to schedule a save of the System State. The batch file to schedule is:

```
net use x: /delete
net use x: \\YourServer\RepairShare$ /persistent:no
if not exist x:\%computername% md x:\%computername%
REM - Use NTBackup to save the system state!
REM - '/l: f' used to create a full backup log.
ntbackup backup systemstate /f "x:\%computername%\System
State" /l:f

net use x: /delete
exit
```

In this batch file, %computername% is a subdirectory of the hidden share on the server (one for each workstation). When you need the System State for that workstation, just reattach the share to the target system.

The scheduler must be run under the system context and allowed to interact with the desktop or under the context of an administrative user. If you use the system account, you can't schedule the copy because the system account has no network access. Use a ROBOT account that is a member of the Administrator group with a non-blank, non-expiring password. Use full path names for all files.

Here is a sample schedule for workstation wsA:

```
AT \\wsA 01:00 /interactive every:M,T,W,Th,F,S,Su
\\YourServer\RepairShare$\Repair.bat
```

You can dress up the Repair.bat with logging, messaging, and so on.

What's the Difference between the Contents of the ERD and the Repair Directory?

The ERD and the repair directory contain the same files. One is as good as the other. You can have as many ERDs as you want, but you can have only one repair directory. In fact, I'd recommend at least three or four ERDs for each Windows 2000 installation you have—more if you can find the diskettes.

WHAT'S NEXT?

If you've just been reading this chapter and haven't backed up the Registry on your system, now would be a good time to do that. In the next chapter, we'll get into the nitty-gritty of the Registry—hives and keys, and if you have a backup, you needn't be concerned about accidentally making an unwanted change as you follow along.

Part iv

Chapter 20

ANATOMY OF THE REGISTRY: THE BLOOD, GORE, AND GUTS

I n Chapter 18, I talked a little about what the Registry is and the terminology used for its various components. In this chapter, I'll get more into the details of what actually is in the Registry. If you're only interested in how to use (or recover) the Registry, but not *what* the Registry is, it's possible to skip this chapter. However, if you're unsure about this, I'd recommend reading it.

Adapted from *Mastering Windows 2000 Registry*, by Peter D. Hipson

ISBN 0-7821-2615-4   725 pages $39.99

Now humor me for just a moment; I think I'm going to back up my Registry. In fact, it is a good time for *you* to do a backup as well, since it is entirely possible that at any time you might have some kind of problem (or disaster) with the Registry and really need that backup copy to restore it. Start Backup, and select the System State in the Backup tab, and back up to a safe location. Then in the Welcome tab, select Emergency Repair Disk.

Next, let some time pass....

Ah, that feels better. I've got a fresh backup copy of my Registry just in case I do something stupid, and so do you—not that we ever do anything stupid, right?

The Registry is subdivided into a number of clearly defined sections, called *hives*:

- ▶ HKEY_CLASSES_ROOT

- ▶ HKEY_CURRENT_USER

- ▶ HKEY_LOCAL_MACHINE

- ▶ HKEY_USERS

- ▶ HKEY_CURRENT_CONFIG

Some hives are less important than others. For example, you can probably recover a damaged Security Accounts Manager key (SAM) easily without serious, permanent problems. You could possibly lose the entire user database, so no users would be able to log on to the server. However, as long as you can log on as Administrator, the worst case is that you have to enter the other user information again. The default SAM Registry will contain at least the initial Administrator user ID and password, which you would have to know.

However, say you lose the system component of the Registry without adequate backup. In that case, it is unlikely that you'll be able to recover without reinstalling Windows 2000, and that would be a painful experience at best.

OF HIVES AND BEES—A REGISTRY OVERVIEW

As I discussed in Chapter 18, the Windows 2000/NT Registry (and the Registry for Windows 95/98) is arranged into logical units called *hives*. Though I can't vouch for its truth, legend has it that some unnamed programmer at Microsoft seemed to see a relationship between the various keys in the Registry and the structure of a beehive. Now me, I just don't see this, so let's consider the two following alternative analogies:

▶ The Registry is arranged just like the folders and files contained on your hard drive. Hives are analogous to root folders, and keys are like subfolders and files. In fact, this relationship is almost 100 percent parallel: Hives are usually shown separated by backslashes (just like folders on the drive) from keys, and keys typically (but not always) have values. Remember, a file can also be empty.

▶ The Registry is arranged as a hierarchical database, nothing more and nothing less. If you are a database person, this view of the Registry might make more sense to you. In truth, the database arrangement is more like the Registry's actual construction.

Specific data is assigned to a key. As I've mentioned, some Registry keys don't have a value set; this is also acceptable.

WARNING

Be careful not to delete keys just because they are empty. Even though they don't have a value, their presence in the Registry may be necessary for the health and well being of Windows 2000. Never, ever, delete a key unless you know that there will be no adverse side effects.

The Registry Hives

The Registry is divided into five hives, and each is named with the prefix HKEY_. Each hive embodies a major section of the Registry that has a specific functionality. Each hive is separate from the other hives and is typically stored as a file in the %*systemroot*%\System32\config folder. Hive storage files have no extension or file type, making them easier to find.

Hives, Keys, and Values

I use a terminology similar to that used when referring to disk drives, folders, subfolders, files, and the contents of files. Often Microsoft confuses the issue somewhat. I try to keep it clear:

Hive   A hive is similar to a root folder on a drive. Inside a hive are keys (like files and subfolders). A hive is the highest level; a hive cannot be a sub-hive inside another hive. An example of a hive in the Registry is HKEY_LOCAL_MACHINE.

Key   A key is similar to a subfolder or a file and is found inside a hive. Inside a key can be other keys (like files) that contain values or other keys (like subfolders) that contain both values and keys. A key has either a hive or a key as a parent above it and *zero* or more keys contained within it. Sometimes Microsoft refers to a key as a sub-hive. An example of a key in the Registry is HKEY_LOCAL_MACHINE\SAM.

Value   A value is similar to a file's data. Each key has one value (though the value may consist of many parts) or no value set at all. There is also something called the *default value* (sometimes called the *unnamed value*), which is an object that may or may not be assigned a value.

HKEY_CLASSES_ROOT

The HKEY_CLASSES_ROOT hive contains information about both OLE (Object Linking and Embedding) and various file associations. The purpose of HKEY_CLASSES_ROOT is to provide for compatibility with the existing Windows 3.*x* Registry.

The information contained in HKEY_CLASSES_ROOT is identical to information found in HKEY_LOCAL_MACHINE\Software.

HKEY_CURRENT_USER

The HKEY_CURRENT_USER hive is used to manage specific information about the user who is currently logged on. This information includes:

▶ The user's Desktop and the appearance and behavior of Windows 2000 to the user.

▶ All connections to network devices, such as printers and shared disk resources.

- ► Desktop program items, application preferences, screen colors, and other personal preferences and security rights. This information is stored for later retrieval by the system when the user logs on.

All other environment settings are retained for future use.

By accessing the roaming user profile, Windows 2000 can make any workstation that the user logs on to appear the same to the user. Domain users need not worry about having to set up or customize each workstation that they will be using.

The information contained in HKEY_CURRENT_USER is updated as users make changes to their environments.

HKEY_LOCAL_MACHINE

The HKEY_LOCAL_MACHINE hive contains information about the computer that is running Windows 2000. This information includes applications, drivers, and hardware. HKEY_LOCAL_MACHINE contains five separate keys:

Hardware   The key used to save information about the computer's hardware. To allow new hardware to be added easily, the Hardware key is always re-created when the system is booted. Changes to this key are not meaningful. Contained within the Hardware key are the following four subkeys:

Description   Contains information about the system, including the CPU (Central Processing Unit), FPU (Floating Point Unit), and the system bus. Under the system bus is information about I/O, storage, and other devices.

DeviceMap   Contains information about devices (keyboards, printer ports, pointers, and so on).

ResourceMap   Contains information about the HAL (Hardware Abstraction Layer). Remember, as we approach the year 2001, HAL is not a talking computer on a spaceship; HAL is the hardware. Also contained are I/O devices, drivers, SCSI (Small Computer System Interface) adapters, system resources, and video resources.

SAM   The Security Accounts Manager (SAM) stores information about users and domains in the SAM key. You cannot access this information using any of the resource editors; use the administrator's User Manager program instead.

Security   Contains information about local security and user rights. A copy of the SAM key is found in the Security key. As with SAM, the Security key is not accessible using the resource editors; use the administrator's tools instead.

Software   Contains information about installed system and user software, including descriptions. There are generally sub-keys for each installed product in which the products store information—including preferences, configurations, MRU (most recently used) file lists, and other application-modifiable items.

System   Contains information about the system start-up, device drivers, services, and the Windows 2000 configuration.

HKEY_USERS

The HKEY_USERS hive contains information about each active user who has a user profile. A minimum of two subkeys are in the HKEY_USERS key: .DEFAULT and information for the currently logged-on user. The purpose of the .DEFAULT key is to provide information for users who log on without a profile. Information for the current user is stored under the user's SID (security identifier).

Personal profiles are contained in the %*systemroot*%\Profiles folder or the %*sysdrive*%\Documents and Settings\Default User folder, unless roaming profiles are used, in which case a copy will be stored there, but the original will reside on a server.

HKEY_CURRENT_CONFIG

The HKEY_CURRENT_CONFIG hive contains information about the system's current configuration. This information is typically derived from HKEY_LOCAL_MACHINE\System and HKEY_LOCAL_ MACHINE\ Software, though HKEY_CURRENT_CONFIG does not contain all the information that is contained in the source keys.

NOTE

As I noted in Chapter 18, the HKEY_DYN_DATA hive no longer exists in Windows 2000. In Windows NT 4, this hive was intended to contain information about the system's PnP (Plug and Play) status. However, since Windows NT 4 does not support PnP, this key is empty.

Registry Key Data Types

Values have different data types:

REG_BINARY   Represents binary values. They may be edited or entered as hexadecimal or binary numbers. Figure 20.1 shows the RegEdt32 Binary Editor dialog box. RegEdit has a similar edit window, though it is not as flexible in how data is entered.

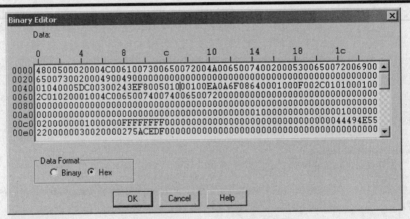

FIGURE 20.1: The Binary Editor dialog box for RegEdt32

REG_SZ   Stores Registry keys that contain strings. Editing is easy; just type the new string. Case is preserved, but the string is initially selected; so be careful not to inadvertently delete it. Strings are of fixed length and are defined when the key is

Part iv

created. Figure 20.2 shows a string being edited in the String Editor dialog box. You can lengthen a string key by adding more characters; the key is reallocated when you lengthen it.

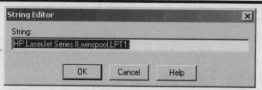

FIGURE 20.2: The String Editor dialog box for RegEdt32

REG_EXPAND_SZ   Stores keys that contain an environment variable that must be expanded. Some keys need to contain values that reference environment variables, much like a batch file—for example, if a string contains the field %*systemroot%*\ System32, and it is necessary for the %*systemroot%* part of the string to be replaced with the value that is assigned to it in the environment. To make this substitution, you must define this string as a REG_EXPAND_ SZ type string. The result of the expansion is then passed to the requestor. %*systemroot%* as a standard environment variable containing the location, drive, and folder where Windows 2000 is installed. To enter a REG _EXPAND_SZ key, you use the String Editor dialog box, as shown in Figure 20.3.

NOTE

Any environment variable, either system-created or created by the user, can be used in a REG_EXPAND_SZ key.

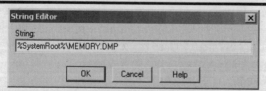

FIGURE 20.3: The String Editor dialog box for RegEdt32

REG_DWORD   A 32-bit value. The value is entered as decimal, hexadecimal, or binary. In the DWORD Editor dialog box, which is shown in Figure 20.4, you can enter only valid numeric data, which prevents sloppy typing.

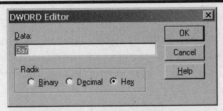

FIGURE 20.4: The DWORD Editor dialog box for RegEdt32

REG_MULTI_SZ   Stores multiple strings in a single Registry key. Normally, a string resource in the Registry can contain only one line. However, the multi-string type allows a string resource in the Registry to hold multiple strings as needed. Figure 20.5 shows multiple strings being edited, with two lines present in this example.

NOTE

The Windows 95/98 Registry editor, RegEdit, does not support the REG_MULTI_SZ type. If you edit a REG_MULTI_SZ item with RegEdit, you may corrupt the data that is contained in it.

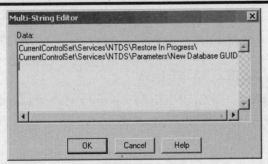

FIGURE 20.5: The Multi-String Editor dialog box for RegEdt32

REG_FULL_RESOURCE_DESCRIPTOR Manages information for hardware resources. No one should edit the items that appear in the Resource Editor fields. Figure 20.6 shows a disk resource object displayed in RegEdt32. However, these objects are never changed manually with the resource editors.

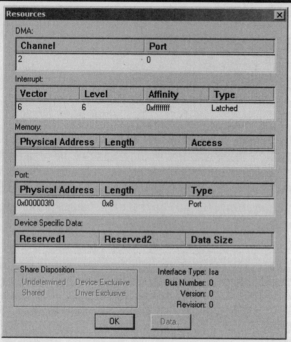

FIGURE 20.6: A disk resource shown in the Resources dialog box for RegEdt32

REG_NONE An identifier used when no data are stored in the key. It doesn't take a rocket scientist to figure out that there is no editor for the REG_NONE type.

REG_UNKNOWN REG_UNKNOWN is used when the key's data type cannot be determined.

HKEY_LOCAL_MACHINE: THE MACHINE'S CONFIGURATION

The HKEY_LOCAL_MACHINE hive contains information about the current hardware configuration of the local computer. The information stored in this hive is updated using a variety of processes, including Control Panel, hardware and software installation programs, administrative tools, and sometimes Windows 2000.

It is important not to make unintended changes to the HKEY_LOCAL_MACHINE hive. A change here could quite possibly render the entire system unstable.

NOTE

All the settings in the HKEY_LOCAL_MACHINE hive are recomputed at boot time. If a change has been made, and the change is causing problems, first try rebooting the system. The Windows 2000 Boot Manager should rebuild the HKEY_LOCAL_MACHINE hive at reboot time, discarding any changes made.

HKEY_LOCAL_MACHINE\Hardware: The Installed Hardware Key

HKEY_LOCAL_MACHINE\Hardware contains information about the hardware configuration of the local machine. Everything hardware related (and I do mean everything) is in this hive.

In Windows 2000, the HKEY_LOCAL_MACHINE\Hardware key is subdivided into three keys:

Description   Contains descriptive information about each device, including a general description and basic configurations.

DeviceMap   Contains information about devices, including the location in the Registry where a device's full configuration is saved.

ResourceMap   Contains translation information about each major component that is installed in the system. Most keys contain a set of value entries named .Raw and .Translated.

Part IV

NOTE

In Windows NT 4, the Hardware key contains another subkey, OWNERMAP, which contains information about removable PCI-type devices. These devices plug into the system's PCI bus, but are generally not permanently installed on the system's motherboard. However, not all PCI-type devices will be listed in OWNERMAP.

DESCRIPTION

Within HKEY_LOCAL_MACHINE\HARDWARE\Description is a wealth of information about the installed hardware. The only subkey, System, describes the CPU and I/O fully. Items in the Description key are always redetected at boot time. The following subkeys are contained in the System subkey:

CentralProcessor   Contains information about the CPU. This includes speed, which is an identifier that contains the CPU's model, family, and Stepping. Also included in this subkey is vendor information; for example, a "real" Intel CPU has the VendorIdentifier string "GenuineIntel".

FloatingPointProcessor   Describes the system's FPU in a set of entries similar to that of the CPU. The fact that the typical CPU has an integral FPU is not considered here; the FPU is listed separately, regardless.

MultiFunctionAdapter   Describes the system's bus (PCI [Peripheral Component Interconnect]), any Plug-and-Play BIOS installed, and other devices, including the controllers for disk drives, keyboards, parallel and serial ports, and the mouse. If a mouse is connected to a serial port, the mouse is listed under the serial port; if a mouse is connected to a PS/2 mouse port, it will be shown connected to a pointer controller as a separate device.

ScsiAdapter   Describes the system's IDE (Integrated Drive Electronics) interfaces, if there are any. Windows 2000 lists these as SCSI interfaces, and they include the controllers for IDE disk drives, IDE CD-ROM drives, and other supported IDE devices.

NOTE

ScsiAdapter lists only the devices attached to the IDE controller. The IDE controller itself is described in HKEY_LOCAL_MACHINE\Hardware\DeviceMap.

Typically, you can use the Description key to determine what hardware is installed (and being used) and how the installed hardware is connected. However, some devices, such as storage devices (non-IDE hard drives, SCSI devices, non-IDE CD-ROM drives, video cards, and network interface cards), are not listed in HKEY_LOCAL_MACHINE\Hardware\ Description. Instead, they are listed in HKEY_LOCAL_MACHINE\ Hardware\DeviceMap. Why? Because these devices are not detected at boot-up stage; instead, they are detected when they are installed.

DeviceMap

The HKEY_LOCAL_MACHINE\Hardware\DeviceMap subkey contains information about devices, arranged in a similar fashion to the HKEY _LOCAL_MACHINE\HARDWARE\Description subkey discussed earlier. In the Devicemap subkey, the following subkeys are found:

KeyboardClass   Contains the address of the subkey that manages information about the keyboard itself.

PARALLEL PORTS   Contains the address of the subkey that manages information about the parallel printer ports.

PointerClass   Contains the address of the subkey that manages information about the system mouse.

Scsi   Contains information about each SCSI interface found on the computer. Windows 2000 pretends that IDE devices, as well as many CD-ROM devices that are connected to special interface cards, are SCSI devices. This is a management issue. Windows 2000 is not converting these devices to SCSI, nor is it using SCSI drivers; rather, Windows 2000 is simply classing all these devices under a common heading of SCSI.

SERIALCOMM   Contains the address of the subkeys that manage information about the available serial ports. In Windows NT 4, if the system mouse is connected to a serial port and not to a PS/2 mouse port, that port is not listed in the **SERIALCOMM** subkey.

Part iv

VIDEO   Contains the address of the subkey that manages the video devices. Two devices are typically defined in VIDEO: the currently used adapter and a backup consisting of the previously installed (usually the generic VGA [Video Graphics Adapter]) adapter's settings to use as a backup in the event of a problem with the video system.

NOTE

In NT 4, DeviceMap includes two additional subkeys. KeyboardPort contains the address of the subkey that manages information about the keyboard interface unit, often called the 8042 after the original chip that served as the keyboard controller in the original PC. PointerPort contains the address of the subkey that manages information about the port to which the system mouse is connected.

ResourceMap

All hardware device drivers use the ResourceMap subkey to map resources that they will use. Each ResourceMap entry contains information about the usage of the following:

- ▶ I/O ports
- ▶ I/O memory addresses
- ▶ Interrupts
- ▶ Direct memory access (DMA) channels
- ▶ Physical memory installed
- ▶ Reserved memory

The ResourceMap subkey is divided into subkeys for each class of device (such as Hardware Abstraction Layer), and under these subkeys lie subkeys for different devices.

Windows 2000 includes a new key in ResourceMap, called PnPManager. This key contains Plug-and-Play information.

HKEY_LOCAL_MACHINE\SAM: The Security Access Manager

HKEY_LOCAL_MACHINE\SAM contains information used by the Windows 2000 security system. It also contains user information (permissions, passwords, and the like). The SAM key is mirrored in HKEY_LOCAL_MACHINE\Security\SAM; making changes to one changes the other.

NOTE

Can't see the SAM or Security key? Use RegEdt32 to select the subkey you cannot see, choose Security ➢ Permissions, and then change the Type of Access from Special Access to Full Control.

In Windows 2000, this information is set using the Microsoft Management Console (MMC), Local Users and Groups branch. If the Windows 2000 system is a domain controller, the SAM is not used (we have the Active Directory services now). To modify the SAM subkeys (both in HKEY_LOCAL_MACHINE\SAM\SAM and HKEY_LOCAL_MACHINE\Security\SAM),use the MMC in Windows 2000 or the User Manager administrative programs in Windows NT. However, attempts to modify information that is in the SAM subkeys typically result in problems. For example, users will be unable to log on, wrong permissions will be assigned, and so on.

WARNING

Don't attempt to modify the SAM or Security key unless you have made a full backup of your Registry, including the SAM and Security keys.

HKEY_LOCAL_MACHINE\Security: The Windows 2000 Security Manager

The key HKEY_LOCAL_MACHINE\Security contains information relevant to the security of the local machine. This information includes:

- ► User rights
- ► Password policy
- ► Membership of local groups

Typically, you set this information using the Administrative User Manager or User Manager for Domains program.

NOTE

Under Windows NT 4, modify the `Security` subkeys using only the User Manager or the User Manager for Domains. With Windows 2000 Active Directory, use only the Active Directory administrative programs (Active Directory Users and Computers). Attempts to modify information in the `Security` key typically result in problems. For example, users are unable to log on, wrong permissions are assigned, and so on.

HKEY_LOCAL_MACHINE\Software: The Installed Software Information Manager

The `HKEY_LOCAL_MACHINE\Software` Registry key is the storage location for all software installed on the computer. The information contained in `HKEY_LOCAL_MACHINE\Software` is available to all users and consists of a number of standard subkeys as well as a few subkeys that may be unique to each computer.

One computer on my network, a Windows 2000 server, has the following subkeys in `HKEY_LOCAL_MACHINE\Software`. These subkeys correspond to items that I have installed on my computer:

Adobe   Contains information about the copy of Adobe's Acrobat program that was recently installed.

Federal Express   Contains information about the FedEx online access and support I have on my computer. My computer produces all my FedEx airbills, making shipments much easier.

INTEL   Contains information about the Intel 3D Scalability Toolkit that I installed at some point. I don't remember when or why, but it's there.

Intuit   Contains information specific to the financial software that is Intuit's specialty.

Qualcomm   Contains information specific to the Eudora e-mail program. The nice thing about Eudora is that there is a free version for private use.

The following are system subkeys probably installed on your computer; however, some of these subkeys, such as ODBC and Clients, may not be present on some minimal installations:

Classes   Contains two types of items: file-type associations and COM (Common Object Model) associations. A typical file-type association entry might have the name DIB, with a string that associates this name with the application Paint Shop Pro. An example of the COM association is the extension .doc that is associated with Microsoft Word and with WordPad, the default viewer for .doc files. Both WordPad and Word can be embedded in other applications. For example, Outlook, Microsoft's upscale e-mail system, can use Word-formatted documents and embed either Word or WordPad to display and edit these documents.

Clients   Contains client-server relationships. For example, Microsoft Outlook is a multipurpose program with e-mail, a calendar, contact lists, news, and other features. Each part of Outlook has a complex series of calling protocols that are defined in the Clients subkey.

Microsoft   Stores a number of items that pertain to Microsoft products or parts of Windows 2000. You may find as few as 20 or as many as 100 entries in the Microsoft subkey.

ODBC   Stores items that pertain to Open Database Connectivity, which allows applications to retrieve data from a number of data sources. Many users install ODBC, either knowingly or as a side effect of installing another product.

Program Groups   Contains one value entry, Converted-ToLinks, which indicates whether the program groups were converted. A value of one (0x1) indicates that the conversion is complete. Even a system installed on a new computer that didn't require conversion will have this value.

Secure   If you say so. The Secure subkey is the location in which any application can store "secure" configuration information. Only an Administrator can modify this subkey, so mere mortal users can't change secure configuration information. Not many, if any, applications use the Secure subkey.

Windows 3.1 Migration Status   Indicates whether the computer was upgraded from Windows 3.x to Windows NT 4/ 2000. Though at one time there were many upgrades, more users today are likely to be doing clean installations—virtually all existing Windows 3.x systems have already been upgraded. This key contains two subkeys: IniFiles and REG.DAT. These values show whether the .ini and Reg.dat files have been migrated successfully to later formats.

NOTE

In NT 4, a Description subkey contains names and version numbers for software installed on the local computer. Though any vendor can use this subkey, the author can see only one entry, which is entered during installation of Windows 2000. Microsoft RPC (Remote Procedure Call) has several entries in this subkey.

HKEY_LOCAL_MACHINE\System: The System Information Manager

The HKEY_LOCAL_MACHINE\System subkey holds start-up information that Windows 2000 uses when booting. This subkey contains all the data that is stored and not recomputed at boot time.

NOTE

A full copy of the HKEY_LOCAL_MACHINE\System information is kept in the file System.alt, found in the %systemroot%\System32\config folder.

The HKEY_LOCAL_MACHINE\System key (a.k.a. the System key) is organized into control sets (such as ControlSet001, ControlSet002, and CurrentControlSet) that contain parameters for devices and services. (The key Clone, present in versions of Windows NT, is not found in Windows 2000.)

The main control sets are:

ControlSet001   The current and the default control set that boot Windows 2000 normally. Mapped to Current-ControlSet at boot time, ControlSet001 is the most critical component in the Registry in the normal boot-up process.

ControlSet002   A backup control set from the Last Known Good boot that boots when the default control set (`Control-Set001`) fails or is unusable for some reason.

ControlSet003   `ControlSet003` (and `ControlSet00n`, where n is greater than 3) is a backup control set from the Last Known Good boot that can be used to boot when the default control set (`ControlSet001`) fails or is unusable for some reason.

CurrentControlSet   The `CurrentControlSet` is the control set from which Windows 2000 has booted. It is usually mapped to `ControlSet001`.

NOTE

The `Clone` control set in NT 4 is the volatile copy of the control set (usually `ControlSet001`) that was used to boot the system. Created by the system kernel during initialization, this key is not accessible from the Registry Editor.

There are three or four other items in the HKEY_LOCAL_MACHINE\ System key:

MountedDevices   Contains items for each locally attached storage device that is available to the system.

DISK   Contains items for each mapped CD-ROM drive. For example, I map my CD-ROM drives to drive letters after S, so I have three entries in this subkey mapping each CD-ROM drive to a different drive letter. The Disk Administrator tool updates this subkey.

Select   Contains four subkeys. It also has information on which control set was booted and which subkey is the Last Known Good set. Also, if there is a "failed" control set, the failed control set's identity is found in the `Select` subkey.

Setup   Contains information used by Setup to configure Windows 2000. This information includes locations of drives and folders, the setup command line, and a flag indicating whether setup is currently in progress.

Part iv

The HKEY_LOCAL_MACHINE\System key is critical to both the boot process and the operation of the system. Microsoft has created a number of tools and processes that help protect the HKEY_LOCAL_MACHINE\System key information. These include the Last Known Good boot process, which allows mapping in a known (or so we hope) copy of the control set, which in turn allows the system to boot if the original control set is too damaged to be booted.

WARNING

Do not, I repeat, *do not* boot using the Last Known Good control set unless it is necessary! Any changes made to the system during the previous session will be lost, gone, forever and ever!

When modifying the control sets, be aware of the process of booting and creating the control sets. Generally, modifying a backup control set won't affect the system.

WHEN IS THE CURRENT CONTROL SET THE LAST KNOWN GOOD CONTROL SET?

At some point in the boot process, the current control set is copied into the Last Known Good control set. In Windows 2000, the process of replacing the Last Known Good control set occurs after the initial logon. This allows the system to catch any problems related to the logon process.

HKEY_USERS: SETTINGS FOR USERS

Current user configurations are saved in HKEY_USERS, which contains three keys. The first key, .DEFAULT, is the default user profile, which is used when no user is currently logged on. Once a user logs on, their profile is loaded and stored as the second and third keys in HKEY_USERS.

The second key, the user profile for the user who is currently logged on, appears as something like this:

S-1-5-21-45749729-16073390-2133884337-500

The second key is for a specific user's profile. The profile is either the user's own profile or is copied from the default user profile (found in %systemdrive%\Documents and Settings\All Users) if the user has not established their own profile.

The third key looks something like this:

S-1-5-21-45749729-16073390-2133884337-500_Classes

This key contains information about the various classes registered for the current user.

These last two long, magical Registry keys need some explanation. The number, as a whole, is called a SID, which contains a lot of information. For example, the ending three- or four-digit number identifies both the user and, for some users, the type of user. Table 20.1 lists a number of general user types that might be assigned. In this part of this book, the most commonly seen value is 500, which is assigned to me, the system administrator account.

TABLE 20.1: Common SID Values

USER GROUP	SID
DOMAINNAME\ADMINISTRATOR	S-1-5-21-*xxxxxxxxx-xxxxxxxxxx-xxxxxxxxxx*-500
DOMAINNAME\GUEST	S-1-5-21-*xxxxxxxxx-xxxxxxxxxx-xxxxxxxxxx*-501
DOMAINNAME\DOMAIN ADMINS	S-1-5-21-*xxxxxxxxx-xxxxxxxxxx-xxxxxxxxxx*-512
DOMAINNAME\DOMAIN USERS	S-1-5-21-*xxxxxxxxx-xxxxxxxxxx-xxxxxxxxxx*-513
DOMAINNAME\DOMAIN GUESTS	S-1-5-21-*xxxxxxxxx-xxxxxxxxxx-xxxxxxxxxx*-514

General users might be assigned SIDs ending in four-digit numbers starting at 1000. My domain has a user called Pixel, whose SID ends in 1003, and another user, Long, whose SID ends in 1006. Get the picture?

There are also a number of built-in and special groups of SIDs, as shown in Tables 20.2 and 20.3.

TABLE 20.2: The Built-in Local Groups

BUILT-IN LOCAL GROUPS	SID
BUILTIN\ADMINISTRATORS	S-1-2-32-*xxxxxxxxx-xxxxxxxxxx-xxxxxxxxxx*-544
BUILTIN\USERS	S-12-32-*xxxxxxxxx-xxxxxxxxxx-xxxxxxxxxx*-545
BUILTIN\GUESTS	S-1-2-32-*xxxxxxxxx-xxxxxxxxxx-xxxxxxxxxx*-546
BUILTIN\POWER USERS	S-1-2-32-*xxxxxxxxx-xxxxxxxxxx-xxxxxxxxxx*-547
BUILTIN\ACCOUNT OPERATORS	S-1-2-32-*xxxxxxxxx-xxxxxxxxxx-xxxxxxxxxx*-548
BUILTIN\SERVER OPERATORS	S-1-2-32-*xxxxxxxxx-xxxxxxxxxx-xxxxxxxxxx*-549
BUILTIN\PRINT OPERATORS	S-1-2-32-*xxxxxxxxx-xxxxxxxxxx-xxxxxxxxxx*-550
BUILTIN\BACKUP OPERATORS	S-1-2-32-*xxxxxxxxx-xxxxxxxxxx-xxxxxxxxxx*-551
BUILTIN\REPLICATOR	S-1-2-32-*xxxxxxxxx-xxxxxxxxxx-xxxxxxxxxx*-552

TABLE 20.3: The Special Groups

SPECIAL GROUPS	SID
\CREATOR OWNER	S-1-1-0x-*xxxxxxxxx-xxxxxxxxxx-xxxxxxxxxx-xxx*
\EVERYONE	S-1-1-0x-*xxxxxxxxx-xxxxxxxxxx-xxxxxxxxxx-xxx*
NT AUTHORITY\NETWORK	S-1-1-2x-*xxxxxxxxx-xxxxxxxxxx-xxxxxxxxxx-xxx*
NT AUTHORITY\INTERACTIVE	S-1-1-4x-*xxxxxxxxx-xxxxxxxxxx-xxxxxxxxxx-xxx*
NT AUTHORITY\SYSTEM	S-1-1-18-*xxxxxxxxx-xxxxxxxxxx-xxxxxxxxxx-xxx*

Naturally, there are many more SID codes and definitions. Tables 20.1 through 20.3 simply show a few of the more commonly used SIDs.

NOTE

Remember to differentiate between the HKEY_USERS hive and the HKEY _CURRENT_USER hive. HKEY_CURRENT_USER contains a pointer that references the current user in HKEY_USERS.

The content of a user's profile, as it is found in the HKEY_USERS hive, is interesting. For example, the following keys are present in a typical user's profile (usually, there is nothing to guarantee that they will all be present or that others might not be added):

AppEvents   Contains information about events (an event is an action such as closing, minimizing, restoring, or maximizing) in a key called `EventLabels`. This information includes a text label for the event, such as the label "Close program" for the event close. These labels are used for a number of purposes, but one that most of us see is in Control Panel's Sounds applet. A second section in `AppEvents` is `Schemes`, which lists labels for each application that uses specific sounds for its own events.

Console   Contains the default command-prompt configuration. You can customize this configuration for each command prompt individually, or you can change the global default, which would be used for all new command prompts that are created.

Control Panel   Contains information saved by many Control Panel applets. Typically, these are default, or standard, values that are saved here, not user settings, which are stored elsewhere.

Environment   Contains the user environment variables for a user. To set user and system environment values, in Control Panel click System to open the System Properties dialog box, click the Advanced tab, and then click the Environment Variables button to open the Environment Variables dialog box.

EUDC   Contains the definitions and other information about End User Defined Characters (EUDC). Users can use the `eudcedit.exe` program to edit/design characters that are specific to their needs.

Identities   Contains the information to link users and software configurations. Most configurations are Microsoft based, such as Outlook Express.

Keyboard Layout   Contains the keyboard configuration. Most users, at least those in the United States, will have few or no substitutions. However, users who are using special keyboards or non–U.S. English keyboards will have some substitutions for special characters found in their languages.

Network   Contains mappings for each network drive connected to the computer. Information about the connections includes the host (server), remote path, and username used for the connection. The Network key is not typically found in the .DEFAULT key because users with no user profile are not automatically connected to a remote drive.

Printers   Contains mappings for each remote (network) printer connected to the computer. Information about the printer connection includes the host (server) and the DLL file used to manage the connection. The Printers key is typically not found in the .DEFAULT key because users with no user profile are not automatically connected to a remote printer.

RemoteAccess   Contains the various remote access configurations. The connections are managed using Control Panel's Network and Dial-up Connections applet.

Software   Contains information about installed software, including components such as Schedule, Notepad, and so on. Also included in Software is Windows 2000 itself, with configuration information specific to the currently logged-on user.

System   Contains information about items such as backup configurations and files that are not to be backed up.

UNICODE Program Groups   Contains information about program groups that use Unicode. More commonly found on computers configured for languages other than English, Unicode is the scheme for displaying characters from both English and non-English alphabets on computers.

Volatile Environment   Contains information about the logon server that will be placed in the environment. One typical item is the logonserver environment variable. All items in Volatile Environment are dynamic; that is, they are created each time a user logs on. Other dynamic environment information might be contained in this key as well.

HKEY_CURRENT_CONFIG: THE CURRENT CONFIGURATION SETTINGS

The Registry hive HKEY_CURRENT_CONFIG is created from two Registry keys, HKEY_LOCAL_ MACHINE\System and HKEY_LOCAL_MACHINE\Software. Because it is created dynamically, there is little value in modifying any of the objects found in the HKEY_CURRENT_ CONFIG hive.

The HKEY_CURRENT_CONFIG hive is composed of two major subkeys:

Software   Contains current configurations for some software components. A typical configuration might have keys under Software for Microsoft Internet Explorer, for example.

System   Contains information about hardware. The most common device found in this key is the video display adapter (found in virtually all configurations) and sometimes information about the default video modes as well. The video mode settings contained here are typical for any video system: resolution, panning, refresh rates (didn't you wonder where refresh rates were saved?), and BitsPerPel (color depth).

Generally, you modify the source settings for a hardware device in HKEY_ LOCAL_MACHINE\System\ControlSet001\Hardware Profiles\Current\System\CurrentControlSet\Services\ <device>\Device0, where <device> is the device being modified. For example, my Matrox Millennium is listed under the device name MGA64.

TIP

For more information about the source for HKEY_CURRENT_CONFIG, take a look at HKEY_LOCAL_MACHINE, described earlier in this chapter.

NTUSER: THE NEW USER PROFILE

The Windows 2000 installation process will create a default user profile and configuration. This information is located in *%systemdrive%*\Documents and Settings\ Default User. Whenever a new user logs on to a workstation or a domain, this default user profile is copied to the user's profile. After that, the user modifies the profile to their own requirements and needs.

For example, the Windows 2000 default language is typically U.S. English. (There are other language editions of Windows 2000; for this example, I'm assuming the U.S. English version.) Whenever a new user logs on, the user will have U.S. English as their language, even if the system administrator has selected a different, non-English locale.

The default user profile is saved in the \Documents and Settings\ Default User [WINNT] folder. WINNT is the folder in which Windows 2000 was installed. In Windows NT 4, the default user information was stored in *%systemroot%*\ Profiles\Default User. User information is always saved in a file named NTUSER.DAT. There is an entire configuration for new users in this folder—check out the Start menu, Desktop, and other folders too. You will find that interesting modifications can be made that enable new users to become proficient quickly without spending too much time customizing their computers.

WARNING

This technique is an advanced use of the Registry Editor, and you must exercise care not to inadvertently modify the wrong Registry or the wrong keys. Back up the Registry *before* doing the following.

First, to make this new user profile accessible to remote users (that is, to all users other than those who log on locally), you must copy the Default User folder to the Netlogon share. This share is typically located in the folder at *%systemroot%*\ sysvol\sysvol\, in a folder that is named for the server. (For Windows NT 4 users, look in *%systemroot%*\ System32\ Repl\Import.) One way to copy these files is to create a new custom profile and copy the new custom profile. In Control Panel, click System to open the System Properties dialog box, and click the User Profiles tab.

If there are BDCs (Backup Domain Controllers), you actually edit the file in the Export folder (same initial path) because this folder is locally replicated to the Import folder and to the other BDC Import folders, although it might be located elsewhere. You can quickly locate the Net-Logon share q by typing the following at a command prompt:

```
net share
```

Follow these steps to modify the default new user profile in your new `Default User` folder (remember to create a new `Default User` folder, saving the current `Default User` folder as a backup):

1. Start RegEdt32 using either a command prompt or the Start menu's Run command. Don't use RegEdit for this process, because RegEdit is unable to load the NTUSER.DAT file.

2. Click the title bar of the HKEY_USERS on Local Machine window to make the window active.

3. Choose Registry ➤ Load Hive from the RegEdt32 menu.

4. Open the hive found in *%systemroot%*\Profiles\ Default User or *%systemdrive%*\ Documents and Settings\Default User. This hive has the filename NTUSER.DAT.

5. RegEdt32 will prompt for a new key name. Use the name **NTUSER**.

6. Change whatever keys in NTUSER need to be modified. The new profile will contain a slew of changeable items, including AppEvents, Console, Control Panel, Environment, Keyboard Layout, Software, and Unicode Program Groups. When adding new keys, do be careful to ensure that all users have at least read access to the new keys. No read access means that the key won't be accessible to the user.

TIP

To set the permissions for a key, select the key, and then choose Security ➤ Permissions from the RegEdt32 menu. Ensure that the group Everyone has at least read access. Resist the urge to give everyone more than read access to this key. Too much power can be a dangerous thing!

7. After modifying NTUSER, choose Registry ➤ Unload Hive from the RegEdt32 menu.

8. Exit RegEdt32.

Once this profile is saved in the NetLogon share location, new users will get this new profile each time they log on.

HINTS AND KINKS FROM THE EXPERTS

Another installment of good stuff from the Windows gurus.

How Can I Tell What Changes Are Made to the Registry?

Using the `regedit.exe` program, you can export portions of the Registry. Follow these steps:

1. Start the Registry Editor (`RegEdit.exe`).

2. Select the key you want to monitor.

3. Choose Registry ➢ Export Registry File to open the Export Registry File dialog box.

4. Enter a filename (if you want to export the whole Registry, select All in the Export Range section), and click OK.

5. Perform the change (install some software or change a system parameter).

6. Perform Steps 1 through 4 again using a different filename.

7. Run the two files through a comparison utility such as `windiff.exe`.

8. If you are using WinDiff, choose File ➢ Compare Files, and you will be prompted to select the two files to compare.

9. Once the files are compared, a summary will be displayed, stating whether there are any differences. To view the changes, double-click the message.

10. Press F8 or choose View ➢ Next Change to view the next change.

You have now found what changed.

(Courtesy of John Savill.)

WHAT'S NEXT?

In the next chapter, we'll look again at RegEdit and RegEdit32 with a view to using them to do some real work. I'll also go into more detail about the features of the ERD and take a look at the Windows 2000 Resource Kit. Of course, you'll also find the usual hints and kinks at the end of the chapter.

Chapter 21

REGISTRY TOOLS AND TIPS: GETTING THE WORK DONE

Windows 2000 includes two Registry editors: RegEdit and RegEdt32. Two—did I say *two* Registry editors? Why do we need two of them? Actually, each Registry editor has advantages and disadvantages. RegEdit was created for Windows 95 and provides a few functions that RegEdt32 doesn't, such as importing and exporting Registry files and good search capabilities.

Adapted from *Mastering Windows 2000 Registry*,
by Peter D. Hipson

ISBN 0-7821-2615-4   725 pages $39.99

RegEdt32 is the "native" Windows 2000 Registry editor. An MDI (multiple document interface) application, RegEdt32 displays each of the main hives in the Registry in its own window. RegEdt32 has powerful administrative tools that RegEdit doesn't support, including read-only mode and security configuration, that allow you to restrict access to some Registry hives, keys, and subkeys.

Both Registry editors are valuable. I use either one depending on my mood and on what I am doing. I find RegEdit easier to use, but RegEdt32 is much more powerful.

The Windows 2000 Resource Kit, which is not included with Windows 2000, also provides a Registry tool, RegistryREG, which you run at a command prompt. Because of its flexibility, you can use REG to manipulate the Registry, replacing earlier versions of a number of other Resource Kit components.

NOTE

There are two resource kits: one is included with the operating system, on the distribution CD, and has only limited contents. The other is both a book and a CD that contains many more utilities and is available from Microsoft Press. Try the URL http://mspress.microsoft.com/reslink for more information.

If you are still using older Resource Kit components in legacy support systems, there is no urgent need to change or migrate to the newer tools in the Windows 2000 Resource Kit. However, I don't recommend that you use the older utilities when updating support facilities; integrate the new tools wherever possible.

Many of the Resource Kit utilities are command-prompt driven. However, being experienced users, we are not afraid of a command prompt, are we?

TIP

Found a program you don't know about? When in doubt, enter a command with either no options or a /? option, and you should see some form of help. Not all commands display significant help, and some do not provide any help at all. However, the Resource Kit utilities won't cause damage if this help convention is used.

In Chapter 19, we looked at how to use RegEdit to back up and restore the Registry. In this chapter, we'll take a look at all three of the Registry editors I've just described, starting with an in-depth exploration of how to use RegEdit. Whether you open RegEdit or RegEdt32, the dialog box that opens has Registry Editor in the title bar.

RegEdit

RegEdit is the Windows 95/98 Registry editor. Microsoft was smart enough to make RegEdit work well with Windows 95/98 and Windows 2000, which means that Windows 2000 users can choose between Registry editors. One of the nicest things about RegEdit is its simplicity. A quick user interface, easy to understand options, and a clean, uncluttered look make RegEdit a favorite for many users.

REGISTRY CHANGES ARE PERMANENT!

All changes that you make with RegEdit are immediate and, for all intents, permanent! Though you can go back and manually undo a change made with RegEdit, everything that you change with RegEdit affects the current Registry. Unlike RegEdt32, RegEdit does not have a read-only mode. There is no safety net, nothing to catch your bloopers, and generally you'll have to clean up your own mess.

In other words, you are editing the real, working, live, honest-to-goodness Registry—not a copy. There is no Save command in RegEdit; you type in a change, and it is saved right then and there.

So, make sure you have a backup of the Registry files before diddling with the Registry.

Using RegEdit

As you may remember from Chapter 19, using RegEdit is as simple as starting it. From a command prompt, type **regedit** and press Enter, or from the Desktop, choose Start ➢ Run to open the Run dialog box, type **RegEdit** in the Open box, and click the OK button.

RegEdit displays the current Registry (see Figure 21.1). By default, RegEdit opens the local Registry. To open a Registry on a remote computer, follow these steps:

1. Choose Registry ➢ Connect Network Registry to open the Connect Network Registry dialog box.

2. In the Computer Name box, enter the name of the computer whose Registry you want to open.

3. Click OK.

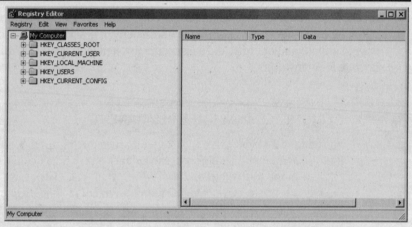

FIGURE 21.1: RegEdit opens the current, local Registry automatically.

MAKING REGEDIT DO WHAT IT USED TO DO!

In Windows 2000, when you open the Registry Editor for the first time, you'll see the display shown in Figure 21.1. When you open the Registry Editor the next time, the last open key from RegEdit's previous session is displayed. Some users like this feature; others do not. Currently, there is no easy way to disable this functionality, though perhaps Microsoft will give us the option to do so at a later time. Until that time, you can use RegEdt32 to try to disable the feature (you cannot use RegEdit to do this). Follow these steps:

1. At a command prompt, type **regedt32** to open the Registry Editor.

CONTINUED ➡

2. Open `HKEY_CURRENT_USER\Software\Microsoft\Windows\CurrentVersion\Applets\Regedit`.

3. Edit the `LastKey` value, and change its contents to an empty string.

4. Select the `RegEdit` key.

5. Choose Security ➤ Permissions to open the Permissions For RegEdit dialog box.

6. Clear the Full Control permission for every user in the list.

7. Click OK.

This procedure prevents RegEdit from saving a value in this key. (It also prevents RegEdit from saving any defaults or favorites.)

One improvement made to RegEdit in Windows 2000 is the addition of a Type column in the pane on the right. Although RegEdit displays the names of all the data types available to Windows 2000, the user is still restricted to editing string, binary, and DWORD data types.

RegEdit has a straightforward set of menus. You use the items on the Registry menu to save and load text-based `.reg` (Registry) files, connect to and disconnect from a network Registry, and print the current branch or the entire Registry.

You use the items on the Edit menu to create a new key or value entry. Because data types in RegEdit are restricted to string, binary, and DWORD, you'll have to use RegEdt32 if you need to create a Registry data type unique to Windows 2000. You can also use the items on the Edit menu to delete an object, rename a key or a subkey, or copy a key name to a new name. At the bottom of the Edit menu are Find and Find Next options.

Use the View menu to hide or display the status bar, to resize the panes, and to refresh the screen.

Also, new to the Windows 2000 version of RegEdit is the Favorites menu. You can place subkeys in a list of favorites and, thus, quickly navigate to a subkey.

Choose Help ➤ Help Topics to open Registry Editor Help.

Part IV

Importing and Exporting Registry Hives and Keys

The ability to export a Registry hive or key (or the entire Registry, if necessary) is a powerful feature of RegEdit. Once a Registry is open, select a hive or a key (or select My Computer to export the entire Registry), and choose Registry ➤ Export Registry File to open the Export Registry File dialog box (see Figure 21.2).

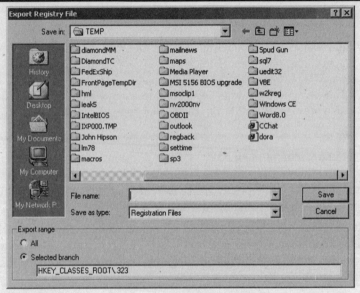

FIGURE 21.2: Exporting the currently selected hive or key is easy!

NOTE

The typical Windows 2000 Registry will contain anywhere from several thousand to hundreds of thousands of lines. The Registry on my server has more than 130,000 lines. At 66 lines per page, the report would run to at least 2,000 pages. At least, you say? Yes, many Registry lines require more than one line to print, so the report would actually run to much more than 2,000 pages.

A hive is exported into a Unicode text-based file, which you can open with almost any text editor (such as Notepad), search, and modify (carefully). This file has no comments; some of the Resource Kit Registry tools do comment exported sections of the Registry. Any changes you make to the exported text file can be incorporated into the Registry by simply importing the modified file.

To import a file that RegEdit previously exported, follow these steps:

1. Choose Registry ➤ Import Registry File to open the Import Registry File dialog box.

2. In the File Name box, enter the name of the Registry file to import.

3. Click Open.

WHAT IS AN EXPORTED REGISTRY FILE?

A Registry file exported by RegEdit starts with the line Windows Registry Editor Version 5.00. The following line is the first hive exported in a hierarchical format:

```
Windows Registry Editor Version 5.00
[HKEY_LOCAL_MACHINE]
[HKEY_LOCAL_MACHINE\Hardware]
[HKEY_LOCAL_MACHINE\HARDWARE\Description]
```

Generally, a full export of a Registry starts with an export of the HKEY_LOCAL_ MACHINE hive, as the above example shows.

The contents of an exported Registry are arranged in the file as a hive and key combination (fully qualified, enclosed in brackets), with the data value name in quotes and the value following the equal sign:

```
[HKEY_LOCAL_MACHINE\HARDWARE\DESCRIPTION\System\
➡ FloatingPointProcessor\0]
"Component Information"=hex:00,00,00,00,00,00,00,00,
➡ 00,00,00,00,01,00,00,00
"Identifier"="x86 Family 5 Model 4 Stepping 3"
"Configuration Data"=hex(9):ff,ff,ff,ff,ff,ff,ff,ff,
➡ 00,00,00,00,00,00,00,00
```

This example shows the three value entries that FloatingPoint-Processor contains.

Why export the Registry? First, none of the search capabilities in any of the Registry editors is optimal. (Well, that's my opinion!) Loading an exported Registry file into an editor allows you to quickly search for strings using the editor's search capability.

Another benefit is that it is easy to export the Registry before installing an application or system extension. After an installation, it is also a good idea to export the Registry. Then, using one of the system comparison tools (such as FC or WinDiff), you can compare the two versions of the Registry and see what the installation has changed. Bingo—a quick way to see what's happening to the Registry on installations.

Connecting to and Disconnecting from Remote Registries

As I mentioned earlier, the local Registry is opened by default when RegEdit starts. You can then open the Registry on a remote computer (see Figure 21.3) and even connect to many remote Registries at one time. When you are connected to a remote Registry, you cannot close, or disconnect from, the local Registry. So you need to be sure that when you make changes, you make them in the correct Registry.

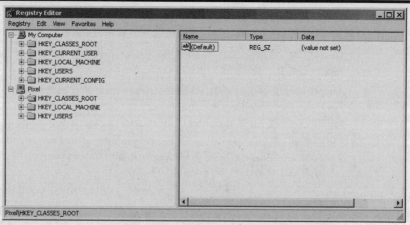

FIGURE 21.3: A remote Registry and the local Registry open in RegEdit

NOTE

The computer with the remote Registry must be on the network, must have remote administration enabled, must share the drive that the Registry is on (for Windows 2000/NT computers only), and must be running the remote Registry service.

Some functionality doesn't span multiple Registries (such as searching), but generally everything that you can do on a local Registry may also be done on a remote Registry.

TIP

When you finish working with a remote Registry, disconnect from it to prevent unexpected modifications of the wrong Registry.

Printing the Registry

As I mentioned earlier, printing an entire Registry is not a great idea—you'd have to make a major investment in paper and printer supplies. But printing sections of a Registry can be useful, for example, when you need a paper copy for a meeting.

To print a hive or a subkey, follow these steps:

1. Select the hive or the subkey, and then choose Registry ➤ Print to open the Print dialog box, as show in Figure 21.4.

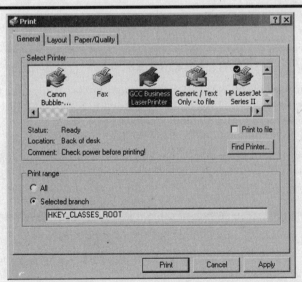

FIGURE 21.4: RegEdit's Print dialog box printing the hive HKEY_CLASSES_ROOT

2. Select options as appropriate, and then click Print.

The results of printing a Registry report are almost identical to exporting, with the exception that a printed report lacks the initial header line that's found in an exported Registry file.

TIP

Is a printed Registry report very readable? Generally not. The RegEdit print facility is basic and simply wraps lines at 80 characters. Any line more than 80 characters wraps and is difficult to read. A better solution is to export the Registry to a file, load the file into a word processor, format it so that it is readable, and print it from the word processor.

Creating, Deleting, and Renaming Entries

RegEdit allows you to quickly create, delete, or rename an entry. Entries can consist of keys, subkeys, or value entries.

Creating a New Key   To create a new key, follow these steps:

1. Select the hive or key in which the new key is to be created.

2. Chose Edit ➤ New ➤ Key.

WHY CAN'T I CREATE A KEY HERE?

Not all hives allow you to create keys directly under the hive itself. For example, you can't create a key under HKEY_LOCAL_MACHINE, but you can create a key under HKEY_CURRENT_USER.

Why? Because the HKEY_LOCAL_MACHINE hive is not "saved" when Windows 2000 shuts down. Rather it is re-created each time Windows boots—therefore, any key or subkey created would be lost at the next boot-up time.

3. RegEdit creates the new subkey, giving it a default name of New Key #*n*; *n* is a number beginning with 1. You can and should edit the new subkey's name at this time. Give the subkey a meaningful name or the name that is expected for this subkey, and then press Enter.

Once the new subkey is created, you can populate it with additional subkeys and value entries.

NOTE

A hive, key, or subkey can contain both value entries and other subkeys at the same time.

Creating a Value Entry   To create a new value entry, follow these steps:

1. Select the hive or key in which the new value entry is to be created.

2. Choose Edit ➤ New, and then select String Value, Binary Value, or DWORD Value, depending on the type of data that this value entry will have. You should select the data type for your key.

3. RegEdit creates the new value entry, giving it a default name of New Value #*n*; *n* is a number beginning with 1. You can and should edit the new value entry's name at this time. Give it a meaningful name or the name that is expected for it, and then press Enter.

TIP

At any point, you may rename a key or value entry by right-clicking the item to be renamed and selecting Rename from the shortcut menu.

4. To enter data in the new entry, double-click the entry to open the Edit dialog box.

You can now enter data in the new value entry as necessary.

NOTE

You don't necessarily need to enter a data value for a key. A key is valid without any data, though no-data defaults vary depending on the type of data the key contains: String values have a zero-length string as their default. Binary values have a zero-length binary value (which is different from having a value of zero). DWORD values have a value of zero.

Figure 21.5 shows RegEdit with a new subkey containing another subkey, a string value, a binary value, and a DWORD value, exactly as created by RegEdit. Note that I've named the initial subkey `Test Key`.

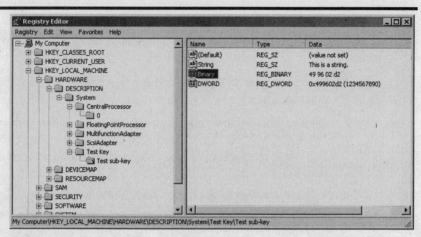

FIGURE 21.5: RegEdit after creating the subkey called Test Key and a further subkey called Test sub-key

In this example, each value entry was given a name to match the type of data stored in it. You can edit each entry at any time. To rename an entry, select it, and choose Edit ➢ Rename, which highlights the entry and encloses it in a box. Type a new name, and then click outside the box. To change the value entry's contents, select the entry, and choose Edit ➢ Modify. You can also double-click the value entry or right-click the item and choose Modify to change the value.

Copying Key Names

Is this as simple as it seems? A long, convoluted name without having to type it? Yes, it is!

To copy a key's name to the Clipboard, select the key name, and choose Edit ➢ Copy Key Name, or right-click the key and choose Copy Key Name from the shortcut menu. The information is copied to the Clipboard in text format, and you can then paste it into other applications or documents as needed. For example, when I copied the new key created for Figure 21.5, the following text was placed on the Clipboard:

```
HKEY_LOCAL_MACHINE\Hardware\Description\System\Test Key\Test
sub-key
```

This means it is not necessary to manually type long Registry keys into other applications and documents and then carefully proofread them.

Searching: Find and Find Next

Searching a Registry is one of the most important tasks you'll have to undertake. Before you modify, debug, or start browsing, you usually need to search for something.

Now, as I've mentioned, RegEdit's search capabilities are a bit limited. However, RegEdit does have the best search of the two Registry editors; RegEdt32 is even more limited in its searching capabilities.

TIP

RegEdit searches downward only. If what you are searching for is located above the current selection, you'll never find it. When in doubt, start at My Computer. You can then be assured that the search will include the entire Registry.

Searching allows you to look at keys, data value names, and data value contents. You can choose to search any or all of these (see Figure 21.6), and you can also limit the search to whole strings only, which applies only to searching text strings.

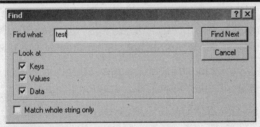

FIGURE 21.6: RegEdit searches for keys, values, and data.

NOTE

RegEdit's search program is not case sensitive, so you can enter search terms in uppercase, lowercase, or a combination. This is nice, since the case of many Registry entries is mixed.

Once the search finds the item, it stops on the word(s). If the search is unable to find the item, RegEdit displays an error dialog box. Press F3 to continue the search.

Using RegEdit from the Command Line

You can run RegEdit from the command line, using the commands described below. Not all commands are available under all operating systems, however.

WARNING

Be careful; be very careful. Running RegEdit in the command-line mode can be damaging to the Registry—it is possible to utterly destroy the Registry with a single command.

▶ To import a Registry file into RegEdit, use the command:

```
REGEDIT [/L:system] [/R:user] filename1
```

▶ To create a Registry object from a file, use the command:

```
REGEDIT [/L:system] [/R:user] /C filename2
```

▶ To export a Registry (or part of the Registry), use the command:

```
REGEDIT [/L:system] [/R:user] /E filename3 [regpath1]
```

▶ To delete part of a Registry, use the command:

```
REGEDIT [/L:system] [/R:user] /D regpath2
```

In all the above commands, the parameters are:

/L:system   Specifies the location of the system.dat file. Note that there is a colon between the /L and the parameter system.

/R:user   Specifies the location of the user.dat file. Note that there is a colon between the /R and the parameter user.

filename1   Specifies the file(s) to import into the Registry.

/C filename2   Specifies the file to create the Registry from. Note that there is a space between the /C and the parameter filename2.

/E filename3   Specifies the file to export the Registry to. Note that there is a space between the /E and the parameter filename3.

regpath1   Specifies the starting Registry key to export from (defaults to exporting the entire Registry).

/D regpath2   Specifies the Registry key to delete. Note that there is a space between the /D and the parameter regpath2.

Tips for RegEdit Users

Using RegEdit, you can export the Registry or parts of it to a text file. You can use this file as any of the following:

- A snapshot of the condition of the Registry at the time the export was made.

- A limited backup of the Registry that might have value in restoring the Registry in the event of a failure.

- A file that when compared with another export file, using FC or WinDiff, can quickly show differences between the two versions of the Registry.

- A file that can be edited with any text editor (Notepad, for example); you can then incorporate the results of the editing into a Registry using RegEdit's import facilities.

Using RegEdit, you can add simple keys, subkeys, and values (with limited data types) to any Registry. Although you can't add, edit, or create the more complex data types that Windows 2000 supports (such as data types REG_MULTI_SZ, REG_FULL_RESOURCE_DESCRIPTOR, and so on), much of your work with the Registry can be handled with simple character and numeric data types.

Installing Microsoft Remote Registry on Windows 95 and Windows 98/98 SE

Though Windows NT Workstation and Windows 2000 Professional have Microsoft Remote Registry installed already, Windows 95 and Windows 98/98 SE do not. The installation process is similar on both operating systems, though the source of the necessary drivers differs with each version.

You have to install a network service to enable Microsoft Remote Registry. This program is found in the following locations:

Windows 95   Look on the Windows 95 distribution CD, in the directory \tools\reskit\netadmin\remotreg, for the regserv program files.

Part iv

Windows 98/98 SE   Look on the Windows 98 distribution CD, in the directory \admin\nettools\remotreg, for the regserv program files. In Windows 98 SE, look in \tools\reskit\netadmin\remotreg for the regsrv program files.

In each operating system, follow these steps to install Microsoft Remote Registry:

1. Open Control Panel, and click Network to open the Network dialog box.

2. In the Configuration tab, click Add to open the Select Network Component Type dialog box.

3. Select Service from the list, and click Add to open the Select Network Service dialog box.

4. Click the Have Disk button to open the Install From Disk dialog box, provide the directory information given earlier, and click OK.

5. Select Microsoft Remote Registry.

6. Install Microsoft Remote Registry, and reboot the computer when prompted.

TIP

The Microsoft Remote Registry files are identical in Windows 95 and Windows 98/98 SE. Either will work with either version of the operating system.

RegEdt32

RegEdt32 is specifically designed for the Windows 2000/NT Registry. (RegEdit was actually designed for the Windows 95/98 Registry.) Unlike RegEdit, RegEdt32 works as an MDI program, opening each of the main hives in the Registry in a different window, which is both helpful and not so helpful. Each hive is separate, which means you don't inadvertently move from one hive to another, especially when doing searches; but at the same time, searching can be difficult because things are not always where you expect.

RegEdt32 is actually more powerful than RegEdit. Additional functionality includes the ability to manage security (noticeably missing on

Windows 95/98 machines), more control of how data is displayed, more options, and the ability to add more data types to the Registry.

Using RegEdt32

You start RegEdt32 the same way that you start RegEdit—by typing **regedt32** at a command prompt or by choosing Start ➢ Run, typing **regedt32** in the Open box, and clicking OK. You can also add a shortcut to the Desktop, as you can with any command or program, but I don't recommend doing so. RegEdt32 is a powerful tool, and you don't want access within easy reach of an uninitiated user.

By default, RegEdt32 opens the local Registry, as does RegEdit. You can also open the Registry on a remote computer as well; however, not all hives will be available on the remote Registry.

Opening and Closing Registries

As I mentioned, the local Registry is open by default when you start RegEdt32. To close it, choose Registry ➢ Close. To open it again, you can restart RegEdt32 or choose Registry ➢ Open Local. To close the currently selected Registry, which may be either the local Registry or a remote Registry, click in any window and choose Registry ➢ Close.

Remote Registries

To open a remote Registry, follow these steps:

1. Choose Registry ➢ Select Computer to open the Select Computer dialog box, as shown in Figure 21.7.

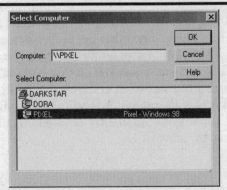

FIGURE 21.7: RegEdt32 is ready to open the Registry on the remote computer Pixel.

2. Select the computer whose Registry you want to open, and click OK, or simply double-click it.

The Registry hives that can be opened on the remote computer will be displayed, and a Warning dialog box will advise you if not all hives could be opened.

NOTE

Not all remote computers will allow you to edit or open their Registries remotely. Windows 95/98/98 SE machines must specifically authorize remote Registry editing (Windows NT systems do this automatically). See the "Installing Microsoft Remote Registry on Windows 95 and Windows 98/98 SE" section, earlier in this chapter, for information on installing Microsoft Remote Registry on these two operating systems.

WARNING

As with a local Registry, any changes you make to a remote Registry take effect immediately. There is no saving, no tossing the changes away, no just closing RegEdt32 and losing the changes. Once entered, the change takes effect, with possible disastrous results for remote users who may not even realize that their Registry was modified.

Loading and Unloading

You can use RegEdt32 to load a subkey into the current Registry, modify it, and later unload it. Why?

I described a classic example in Chapter 20. This example, configuring a modified new user profile, concerns the file NTUSER.DAT, which contains the HKEY_CURRENT_USER hive. Within this hive are settings, such as internationalization, colors, schemes, and other items. The Windows 2000 installation process creates a default user profile—nothing spectacular, a plain configuration. Whenever a new user logs on to a workstation (or a domain), this default user profile is copied to the user's profile. After that, the user can modify this default profile to suit their requirements and needs. Of course, you might want to establish some organizational defaults, such as a company scheme.

WARNING

The techniques shown next are advanced use of the Registry editor. Back up the Registry *before* doing the following.

The default user profile is saved in the following folders:

- ▶ For new Windows 2000 installations: `%sysdrive%\Documents and Settings\Default User` (this folder may have the hidden attribute set, so that it is not displayed when using either Explorer or a command session)

- ▶ For Windows NT 4, and Windows 2000 installations that are upgraded from Windows NT 4: `%systemroot%\Profiles\ Default User\`

The name of the user profile is `NTUSER.DAT`. There is an entire configuration for new users in the folder `%sysdrive%\Documents and Settings\Default User`; check out the Start Menu, Desktop, and other folders as well. You will find that you can make interesting modifications that enable new users to become proficient quickly without spending too much time customizing their computers.

First, to make this new user profile accessible to remote users (users other than those who log on locally), you must copy the `Default User` folder to the NETLOGON share. This share is typically located in `C:\ WINNT\sysvol\sysvol`.

Placing files in `Export` will cause replication to copy them locally to `Import`, along with any BDCs (Backup Domain Controllers). Note that the share might be located elsewhere. You can locate the NETLOGON share quickly by typing the following command at a command prompt:

```
net share
```

The computer's shares will be displayed.

One way to copy these files is to create a new custom profile and then copy it using the System applet's User Profiles tab.

WARNING

If you are even slightly smart, you'll make a backup copy of the `NTUSER.DAT` file *before* you make any changes in it!

Part iv

To modify the default new user profile, follow these steps:

TIP

Remember to create a new Default User directory, saving the current Default User directory as a backup.

1. Start RegEdt32. (Don't use RegEdit for this process.)

2. Click on the title bar of the HKEY_USERS On Local Machine window to make it active.

3. Choose Registry ➢ Load Hive to open the Load Hive dialog box.

4. Open the hive file in %sysdrive%\Documents and Settings\Default User. (If your system is configured, or installed, with different folder names, choose the correct name.) This hive has a filename of NTUSER.DAT.

CAN'T FIND THE LOCATION FOR NTUSER.DAT?

Remember that the NTUSER.DAT file will have the hidden attribute, so it will not normally be displayed in either a command window or in Explorer. Either tell Explorer to display hidden files or, at a command prompt, use the **dir** command with the **/ah** option to display hidden files and folders.

Worse comes to worst, open a command window (tough to do this in Explorer) and, in the root of the system drive, use the command:

```
DIR /ah /s ntuser.dat
```

This command will list all copies of the NTUSER.DAT file, allowing you to change the appropriate one. One thought though: don't change the "current user" NTUSER.DAT file—it won't work! Windows will rewrite the file when the user next logs off, causing any changes you made to disappear!

5. RegEdt32 will prompt for a new Key Name. Use the name NTUSER.

6. Change whatever keys in NTUSER need to be modified. You'll find a slew of changeable items in the new profile, including `AppEvents`, `Console`, `Control Panel`, `Environment`, `Keyboard Layout`, `Software`, and `Unicode Program Groups`. When adding new keys, do be careful to ensure that all users have at least read access to the new keys. No read access means that the key won't be accessible to the person named "user."

TIP

To set the permissions for a key, select the key, and then choose Security ➤ Permissions to open the Permissions dialog box for that key. Ensure that the Everyone group has at least read access. Resist the urge to give everyone more than read access to this key. Too much power can be a dangerous thing!

7. After making all modifications to NTUSER, choose Registry ➤ Unload Hive. Unload the hive to the file `NTUSER.DAT`. (You did back up the original file, right?)

8. Exit RegEdt32.

Once this profile is saved in the NETLOGON share location, each time a new user logs on to the network, the user will get this new profile.

Save Subtree As

To save a hive, a key, or a subkey and all descendants' contents, choose Registry ➤ Save Subtree to open the Save As dialog box. The data is saved in text format, and you can edit it with an editor such as Notepad. Information about the hive and keys is found in the saved file. Extensive data about the Registry hive, including the date the Registry file was last written to, are also saved in this file. The file is relatively easy to read, and it will be many, many times larger than the Registry, as the small example in Figure 21.8 shows.

```
Key Name:        HARDWARE\DESCRIPTION\System\ScsiAdapter
Class Name:      Adapter
Last Write Time: 7/16/99 - 6:58 PM

Key Name:        HARDWARE\DESCRIPTION\System\ScsiAdapter\0
Class Name:      Adapter
Last Write Time: 7/16/99 - 6:58 PM
Value 0
  Name:          Component Information
  Type:          REG_BINARY
  Data:
00000000   61 22 01 80 00 00 00 00 - 01 00 00 00 ff ff ff ff   a".........yyyy

Value 1
  Name:          Configuration Data
  Type:          REG_FULL_RESOURCE_DESCRIPTOR
                   Interface Type:    Internal
                   Bus Number:        0
                   Version:           0
                   Revision:          0


Key Name:        HARDWARE\DESCRIPTION\System\ScsiAdapter\0\CdRomController
Class Name:      Controller
Last Write Time: 7/16/99 - 6:58 PM

Key Name:        HARDWARE\DESCRIPTION\System\ScsiAdapter\0\CdRomController\0
Class Name:      Controller
Last Write Time: 7/16/99 - 6:58 PM
Value 0
  Name:          Component Information
  Type:          REG_BINARY
  Data:
00000000   26 00 00 00 00 00 00 00 - 01 00 00 00 ff ff ff ff   &.........yyyy

Value 1
```

FIGURE 21.8: An example of the Save Subtree As file output

NOTE

Just a suggestion: don't print these files without first determining how long they are. For me, saving a simple object generated almost 700 lines of output.

Save Key

To save a hive, a key, or a subkey and the saved object's contents, choose Registry ➤ Save Key to open the Save Key dialog box. RegEdt32 writes the data saved in a binary format; no hacking or editing is allowed here. To re-read this file later, choose Registry ➤ Restore to open the Restore Key dialog box. The file is saved with the filename and extension you specify, unlike with RegEdit, which automatically uses an extension of .reg.

NOTE

Actually, to save an object, you must have sufficient privileges to read the entire object. If you do not have these privileges, you will get an error message, "Insufficient privilege to save the key." If this becomes a problem, choose Security ➢ Permissions to open the Permissions dialog box for this key, and modify the permissions.

Information saved by Save Key contains unqualified hive and key information. For example, if you save the HKEY_LOCAL_MACHINE\ Hardware\Description\System key, the only name saved to the file will be System. The HKEY_LOCAL_MACHINE component of the object's name will *not* be saved. Again, think about how file and folder names are sometimes either fully qualified or not.

Restoring

Restoring is what Joe and Ed on the Learning Channel do to old furniture, right?

Well, maybe so, but it's also possible to restore an object in the Registry using RegEdt32. The process is straightforward, although like everything else, you must have something to restore from. As I just explained, you can save a Registry object to a file. Since the file extension is user determined, making filenames as descriptive as possible is a really good idea.

A suggestion: If you have a strong desire to play with the save and restore functionality of RegEdt32, install a practice copy of Windows 2000. Don't do this on a working version—at least not a copy of Windows 2000 that you or anyone else cares about.

NOTE

When an object is restored, the data overwrites the existing object. It becomes permanent, as everything that RegEdt32 does is immediately written to the Registry.

WARNING

More important: When an object is restored, it is written on top of the currently selected object. Be sure that the object you are restoring belongs at the current selection. Again, be sure that you name your file well so that you know exactly which object a given file represents. Imagine coming back to a saved file, perhaps weeks later, and trying to restore it without knowing which object it was saved from.

WARNING

Even *much* more important: Restoring an object may override the read-only mode option—it will write to the Registry no matter what! Care to guess how I found that out?

When an object is restored, the selected object itself is not renamed, even though the contents of the object are replaced.

Printing the Registry

In RegEdt32, choose Registry ➤ Printer Setup to open the Print Setup dialog box. Printing subkeys of the Registry with RegEdt32 results in a much nicer printout than you get with RegEdit. The printout consists of virtually the same data that is saved when you choose Registry ➤ Save Subtree. An example of what a printout looks like is shown in Figure 21.8, earlier in this chapter.

TIP

Be careful not to select too much to print. The printout capabilities of RegEdt32 can generate massive reports.

Adding Keys and Subkeys

Adding keys, subkeys, and value entries is easy enough with RegEdt32. First, be sure the Registry is not in read-only mode (see "Setting Options," later in this chapter). Next, select the location where the new subkey or key is to be located, and then use the tools on the Edit menu to add the new item.

Adding Keys and Subkeys   To create a new key, choose Edit ➤ Add Key to open the Add Key dialog box (see Figure 21.9). Specify the name and, optionally, a class.

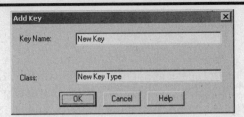

FIGURE 21.9: Adding subkeys with the Add Key dialog box

You can assign a class to a subkey. The class can be any of the following:

- ▸ REG_BINARY
- ▸ REG_SZ
- ▸ REG_EXPAND_SZ
- ▸ REG_DWORD
- ▸ REG_MULTI_SZ
- ▸ A user-supplied string describing the key's type

Since subkeys are not normally assigned a value, the class attribute is rarely used, and often it is left blank.

Adding Values and Data   To add a new value entry, with a specified data type, choose Edit ➣ Add Value to open the Add Value dialog box (see Figure 21.10). Enter a value name, and select a data type.

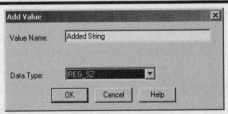

FIGURE 21.10: Adding a value with the Add Value dialog box

Unlike a key, a value *must* have a data type. Valid selections for the data type are:

- ▸ REG_BINARY
- ▸ REG_SZ

Part iv

▶ REG_EXPAND_SZ

▶ REG_DWORD

▶ REG_MULTI_SZ

You cannot add or create the specialized types, such as REG_FULL
_RESOURCE_DESCRIPTOR, using the RegEdt32 Add Value dialog box.
(I'll leave it up to you to figure out how to create a key with a nonstandard
data type, with this hint: it can be done, but it's not that easy.)

NOTE

OK, I'll tell... You use RegEdit to create a data value with a data type not supported by RegEdit or RegEdt32. Create a . reg file (export the subject key), and
edit the . reg file with any compatible text editor. Create entries in the format:
"*entry name*"=hex(n):*hh hh* ...The *entry name* option is the name for the
data value, *n* is a number corresponding to the type desired, and *hh* is one or
more pairs of hex data.

After you create a new key, one of the data value editors appropriate
for the data type selected is displayed (see Figure 21.11).

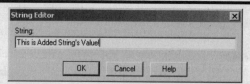

FIGURE 21.11: The RegEdt32 String Editor, just after a text string has been
entered

After you create a key, you can edit its data with a different editor. The
contents may not make much sense, though, if displayed in the wrong
format.

Each editor displays the data in its particular format, but does not
change the data type. If I were designing the Registry editor, I'd configure a
single default dialog box in which you could edit the data using all formats.

Select a key, and then from the Edit menu, select one of the following:

Binary   Edits the item in binary format.

String   Edits the item in string format.

DWORD   Edits the item in the DWORD format. It will truncate objects longer than 4 bytes.

Multi String   Edits the item using the multiline string editor.

WARNING

If you use the DWORD editor to edit an object that is more than 4 bytes, the object will be truncated to 4 bytes—permanently, irrevocably, without recourse—when you click OK.

NOTE

To change a key's data type, you must create a new key. Start by renaming the key to be changed to a temporary name. Next, create a new key with the original name, using the new data type. Finally, edit the original key, copy the key's data to the Clipboard, edit the new key, and then paste the data into the new key.

Deleting the Unwanted   Getting rid of the unwanted is easy. Select the object, either a key or a value entry, and then either choose Edit ➢ Delete or press the Delete key. RegEdt32 will prompt you to confirm that the object is to be deleted, if the Confirm On Delete option is selected (see the "Confirm on Delete" section later in this chapter).

WARNING

Once deleted, 'tis gone forever! Be careful not to delete anything that you will want later. Prior to deleting, it's appropriate to back up the Registry. It might also be a good idea to rename the object, just in case you need to restore it at a later time.

Searching

The RegEdt32 search is somewhat different from the search program in RegEdit. Unlike RegEdit, RegEdt32 can search either up or down and match case. To start a search, choose View ➢ Find Key to open the Find dialog box, as shown in Figure 21.12.

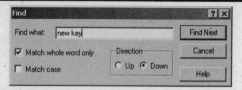

FIGURE 21.12: The RegEdt32 Find dialog box has better search criteria than the search criteria in RegEdit.

However, there is one big *gotcha*: RegEdt32 can search only on hive, key, and subkey names. RegEdt32 cannot find value names or data, which is a major limitation if you ask me. (OK, they did ask me, but I didn't say anything at the time.)

NOTE

Perhaps it's a bug, but the Match Whole Word Only check box actually forces the search tool to match the contents of the entire name, not just a single word in the name. The check box probably should actually read Match Whole Name Only.

If the search fails (which it usually does for me, since I'm always searching for data names or values, not keys), a small dialog box will tell you that the item was not found. Don't forget to search in both directions if you are in the middle of the Registry.

Security

Security is paramount in a Windows 2000 installation. The Registry, just like the NTFS file system, can be protected from unauthorized access. This can be a critical issue, because Windows 2000 supports remote Registry editing.

NOTE

It is possible to make changes in a Registry from another computer without the recipient of these changes even knowing that a change has been made (that is, until they see the results of the change).

RegEdit does not support any security modifications. If a hive is not accessible to RegEdit, you cannot view the hive or change it, depending on the level of access granted by the system. However, you can use the items on the RegEdt32 Security menu to change the security attributes for a hive and any keys if you have sufficient authority to do so.

Initially, when you choose Security ➤ Permissions, the Permissions dialog box is displayed (see Figure 21.13). You establish basic security settings in this dialog box, and you configure advanced functionality (permissions, auditing, and owner) in the Access Control Settings dialog box.

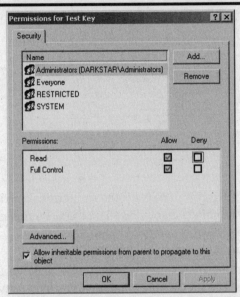

FIGURE 21.13: Setting the permissions for Test Key in RegEdt32

In the Permissions dialog box, click the Advanced button to display the Access Control Settings dialog box, which is shown in Figure 21.14. The Access Control Settings dialog box has three tabs: Permissions, Auditing, and Owner.

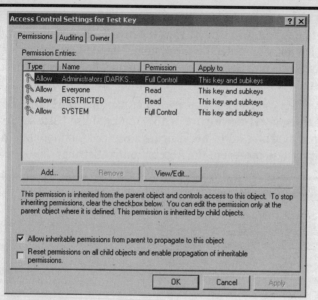

FIGURE 21.14: Specific users and administrative units can have their own permissions.

Permissions The Permissions tab displays the currently selected object and the current permissions granted to that object. The default permission for everyone is typically, but not always, Read; the Administrator accounts and the system both have Full Control.

Check the Allow Inheritable Permissions From Parent To Propagate To This Object check box if you want the current object to include its parent's permissions. Check the Reset Permissions On Child Objects And Enable Propagation Of Inheritable Permissions check box if you want to change the permissions for both the selected item and any subkeys it contains.

To set detailed permissions, click the View/Edit button to open the Permission Entry dialog box, as shown in Figure 21.15. In the Permissions section, the current permissions are organized by name. To set the type of access, select a permission name, and then click the Allow or the Deny check box. When you select Allow, you give the following accesses to the object:

Query Value The selected user can read the object.

Set Value The selected user can write to the object.

Create Subkey   The selected user can create a subkey of the object.

Enumerate Subkeys   The selected user can obtain a list of subkeys contained within the object.

Notify   Windows 2000 will notify the owner of the object when the object is modified.

Create Link   The selected user can create a link to the object from another object.

Delete   The selected user can delete the object.

Write DAC   The selected user can modify Discretionary Access Control information.

Write Owner   The selected user can modify the owner record information.

Read Control   The selected user has standard Read, Query Value, Enumerate Subkeys, and Notify permissions.

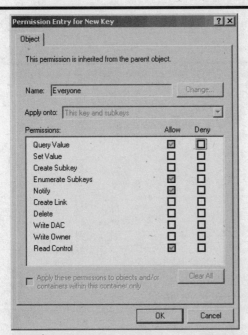

FIGURE 21.15: You can customize permissions on a user-by-user basis in the Permission Entry dialog box.

WARNING

Of course, the standard warnings apply: *Do not grant more permission than is necessary to do the job.* Understand what permissions are being granted, and consider granting permissions temporarily and removing a permission as soon as it is no longer needed.

Auditing   The word *auditing*, when mentioned with the word *government*, generally gets us weak in the knees and starts us sweating profusely. However, auditing Registry interaction can be somewhat less troublesome and very beneficial.

Auditing, like permissions, is based on users. You set up auditing in the Auditing tab of the Access Control Settings dialog box (see Figure 21.16). The Auditing Entries list is empty if auditing has not been set for the selected object. First, be sure that the Allow Inheritable Auditing Entries From Parent To Propagate To This Object check box is checked, and then click the Add button to open the Select User, Computer, Or Group dialog box, as shown in Figure 21.17. You can select both groups and individual users. Select a name in the Name list, and click OK to add that name to the list of names to be audited and open the Auditing Entry dialog box.

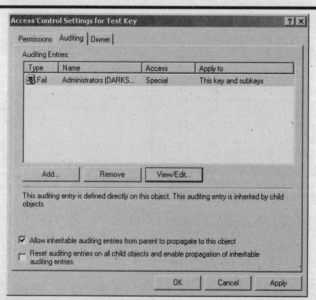

FIGURE 21.16: The Auditing tab, in which you set auditing permissions

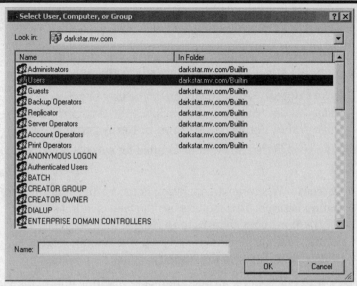

FIGURE 21.17: Add users or administrative units to be audited in this dialog box.

You can audit the following events:

Query Value   Audited whenever the user or group in the Name list reads the object.

Set Value   Audited whenever the user or group in the Name list writes to the object.

Create Subkey   Audited whenever the user or group in the Name list creates a key.

Enumerate Subkeys   Audited whenever the user or group in the Name list enumerates a list of keys contained within the object.

Notify   Audited whenever the user or group in the Name list does anything that generates a notification to the owner.

Create Link   Audited whenever the user or group in the Name list creates a link to the object from another object.

Delete   Audited whenever the user or group in the Name list deletes the object.

Write DAC   Audited whenever the user or group in the Name list modifies the Discretionary Access Control information.

Write Owner   Audited whenever the user or group in the Name list modifies the owner record information.

Read Control   Audited whenever the user or group in the Name list does anything that includes the standard Read, Query Value, Enumerate Subkeys, or Notify permissions.

You can specify that an event be audited for success, for failure, or for both:

Success   Whenever an operation is successful, auditing information is saved. This mode is useful when creating a log of information about changes to the Registry. When a problem occurs, auditing for success can help you determine what changes were made to the Registry.

Failure   Whenever an operation fails, auditing information is saved. Whenever security is an issue (any time the system is used by more than one person), auditing for failure can help point to attempts to compromise system security.

TIP

Check the Successful check box for critical objects that shouldn't be changed often. Select the Failed check box for any object that is security related.

Owner   I own things; you own things. To keep the records straight, we have titles for cars, deeds for property, and other documents that trace ownership of anything that is nontrivial. With computers, and especially with Windows 2000, ownership is important. I "own" my computer, and probably I don't want you messing with it.

When using NTFS, you can set ownership for files. In addition, objects in the Registry can have ownership. Ownership implies ultimate control: the owner can restrict access, audit, and do whatever he or she wants.

In RegEdt32, you use the Owner tab in the Access Control Settings dialog box to take "ownership" of a Registry object (see Figure 21.18).

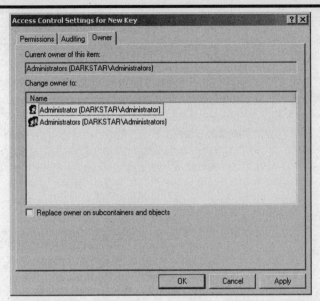

FIGURE 21.18: The Owner tab lists the current owner and allows ownership to be set to the current user.

The owner of any object can allow or disallow another user from taking ownership; however, once another user has ownership, the original owner's rights are terminated.

NOTE

Both the current owner and the system administrator can assign ownership of the object to a user or to the system administrator.

Setting Options

RegEdt32 has a number of options that you can set through the Options menu.

Font   You can change the font in which all Registry information is displayed. Most often the font you choose is a personal preference, but you might need to change fonts due to multiple language support—for example, you might be running RegEdt32 on one computer and remotely editing a Registry on another computer in which the Registry has strings that are in a different language or character set.

Part iv

Choose Options ➤ Font to open a standard Font dialog box (see Figure 21.19), in which you can select the font, style (Regular, Italic, Bold, or Bold Italic), and font size. You can also select the script (language). Choices for script include Western, Hebrew, Central European, and others.

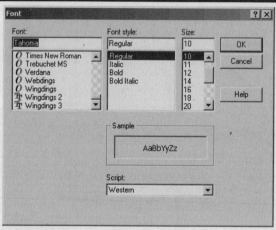

FIGURE 21.19: The font can be a personal preference, or it can support a different language or character set.

Auto Refresh   Choose Options ➤ Auto Refresh to update all the RegEdt32 Registry windows for the local Registry.

▶ If Auto Refresh is checked, Refresh All and Refresh Active on the View menu are disabled.

▶ If Auto Refresh is not checked, Refresh All and Refresh Active on the View menu are enabled.

NOTE

You cannot use Auto Refresh with a remote Registry. Even if Auto Refresh is checked, remote Registries are not updated, nor will the Refresh All and Refresh Active selections be enabled in the View menu. (With the View menu refresh options disabled, it is rather difficult to refresh the remote Registry!) When editing remote Registries, always turn off Auto Refresh.

Read Only Mode   If you want the current Registry to be un-editable, choose Options ➢ Read Only Mode. This functionality serves as a safety net, making it possible to browse the Registry without changing it. When this mode is active, Read Only Mode is checked in the Options menu.

WARNING

Unless you are specifically changing the Registry, it is best to keep Read Only Mode checked at all times. Making an inadvertent change to the Registry can be the beginning of the end of the Windows 2000 installation!

Confirm On Delete   Whenever Confirm On Delete is checked, RegEdt32 will ask the user to confirm a deletion by displaying a Warning dialog box (see Figure 21.20). The amount of time lost using Confirm On Delete is minimal compared with inadvertently deleting an object that is necessary to the well-being of Windows 2000.

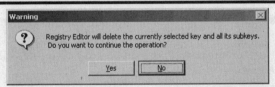

FIGURE 21.20: When you check Confirm On Delete, Windows 2000 warns you each time you delete an object in the Registry.

NOTE

Confirm On Delete is not available if Read Only Mode is checked.

Save Settings On Exit   Options, such as those previously listed, may be either temporary (for the current session) or permanent. When you choose Options ➢ Save Settings On Exit, the options you selected in the current session are saved when you exit RegEdt32.

Part iv

WARNING

Only the settings of options are saved on exit. All changes to the Registry are saved as they are made. There is no separate saving of the Registry.

Tips for RegEdt32 Users

Several tips come to mind when using RegEdt32:

- ▶ First, when saving a hive using Save Key (under the Registry menu), make absolutely sure that the filename saved to is descriptive enough to enable the successful restoration of the hive at a later time. RegEdt32 doesn't check whether a hive being restored is the same hive as the one being replaced.

- ▶ Second, as with RegEdit, be aware that printing can create reports of incredible size. Do not print the entire Registry, especially if you are over the age of 22 or so: life is just too short.

- ▶ Finally, the RegEdt32 Save Subtree As functionality allows saving a detailed text report, identical to the printed report, to a disk file. You can then load this report into a text editor or word processor and edit and print it.

BACKUP'S EMERGENCY REPAIR DISK FEATURES

The ERD (Emergency Repair Disk) that you create in Windows 2000 has slightly different contents than the ERD you created in Windows NT.

The ERD holds some of the system configuration components. The Backup program backs up Registry files to a location on the hard drive (the `repair` directory) and configuration files to a diskette. The diskette version of this information is called the ERD, and it contains files used to help Windows 2000 restore the system to a known state in the event of damage to the working copy of the Registry.

Generally, copies of the Registry contained in the `repair` folder are only usable with the Setup program's repair facility. This may seem to limit their usefulness; however, when disaster strikes, anything is better than nothing. Actually, spending half an hour running the Setup repair function is a small price to pay to recover from a damaged Registry.

There can be only one `repair` folder on a Windows 2000 system, always at `%systemroot%\repair`; however, many ERDs can exist at one time. Since an ERD's contents are (generally) matched to the Registry, it is best to simply keep one or two copies of the most recent Registry backed up.

TIP

Actually, you can copy the files in the `repair` folder to another safe location, as well, and then copy them back to the `repair` folder if necessary. Make sure that *all* files are copied or backed up and restored as a set—don't attempt to back up only some of the files in the `repair` folder. If you copy the `repair` folder files to another location, also create a copy of the ERD and save that as well.

Creating an Emergency Repair Disk

To create an ERD, follow these steps:

1. Choose Start ➤ Programs ➤ Accessories ➤ System Tools ➤ Backup to start Backup.

2. Choose Tools ➤ Create An Emergency Repair Disk to open the Emergency Repair Diskette dialog box, as shown in Figure 21.21.

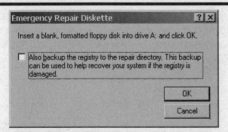

FIGURE 21.21: Backup will write backup files to the ERD diskette and, optionally, to the `repair` folder.

3. Insert a formatted diskette that contains nothing of value. If you also want to back up the Registry to the `repair` folder, click that option, and then click OK.

4. When the backup is complete, you'll see a dialog box prompting you to label the ERD and place it in safekeeping. You can then create another ERD, update the repair information on the hard disk, perform other backup tasks, or exit.

NOTE

Remember to remove the floppy diskette from the drive once Backup finishes writing the repair information to it. Attempting to boot this diskette won't cause a problem; however, it will have to be removed before the system can reboot.

THE REG.EXE REGISTRY EDITOR

The Windows 2000 Resource Kit contains a number of useful tools. Many run from a command prompt, although one has a Windows-type interface. The Resource Kit has changed substantially in Windows 2000. Gone are all the old Registry utilities, leaving only the multipurpose `reg.exe` program.

If nothing else, the Windows 2000 Resource Kit is an excellent source of both information and a whole bunch of really neat utilities and tools for the Windows 2000 user.

TIP

While I've got you in support mode, make a link on your Desktop for the URL `http://support.microsoft.com/support/search/c.asp?SPR=`. This URL links to the online TechNet search support. TechNet contains a vast amount of technical information oriented toward system administrators. I don't know what I'd do without TechNet.

WARNING

Many earlier versions of the Windows Resource Kit utilities work with both Windows NT 4 and Windows 2000. However, be cautious when using the older utilities with Windows 2000; they have not been thoroughly tested on the Windows 2000 platform!

`Reg.exe` is a tool that combines the functionality of a number of other command-line–driven Windows NT 4 Resource Kit Registry tools. It improves the interaction between the command line and the Registry and is somewhat easier (and a whole lot more consistent) to use than the other utilities. `Reg.exe` has the following functions:

- ► ADD
- ► BACKUP
- ► COPY
- ► DELETE
- ► LOAD
- ► QUERY
- ► RESTORE
- ► SAVE
- ► UNLOAD
- ► UPDATE

In the following sections, I'll cover each of the functions, showing parameters and results as examples of how to use `Reg.exe`.

The ADD Function

You use the ADD function, invoked with the command `REG ADD <options>`, to add an object (key or value entry) to the Registry. Options include the Registry object to be added with the object's value, an optional machine name (you can add objects to remote Registries), and an optional data type, as described next.

The command line for ADD is:

```
REG ADD RegistryPath=value [data type][\\Machine]
```

As with other Registry tools, the Registry path can be a ROOTKEY or a hive (with or without a value entry). The ROOTKEY can be one of the following (HKLM is assumed if none is entered):

- ► HKLM (for HKEY_LOCAL_MACHINE)
- ► HKCU (for HKEY_CURRENT_USER)
- ► HKCR (for HKEY_CLASSES_ROOT)

Part iv

- HKU (for HKEY_USERS)

- HKCC (for HKEY_CURRENT_CONFIG)

The hive will be further qualified to determine the object to be added.

The data type parameter will be one of the following (the default, if the data type is not specified, is REG_SZ):

- REG_SZ

- REG_DWORD

- REG_EXPAND_SZ

- REG_MULTI_SZ

Here's an example of executing the ADD function:

```
Windows 2000 8:56:09 C:\
REG ADD HKLM\Software\MyCo\MyApp\Version=1.00
The operation completed successfully.

Windows 2000 9:00:48 C:\
REG QUERY HKLM\Software\MyCo\MyApp\Version
REG_SZ     Version 1.00
Windows 2000 9:00:59 C:\
```

The BACKUP Function

You use the BACKUP function, invoked with the command REG BACKUP <options>, to save the Registry object specified to the file specified. Options include the Registry path to be saved, the output filename, and an optional machine name (you can save a backup on remote Registries).

The command line for BACKUP is:

```
REG BACKUP RegistryPath OutputFileName [\\Machine]
```

As with other Registry tools, the Registry path to be queried can be a ROOTKEY or a hive, with or without a value entry. The ROOTKEY can consist of one of the following (HKLM is assumed if none is entered):

- HKLM

- HKCU

- HKCR

▶ HKU

▶ HKCC

When backing up objects to a remote Registry, you can specify only HKLM and HKU.

NOTE

The REG SAVE and REG BACKUP commands are identical in functionality.

An example of executing the BACKUP function is shown below. In this example, I've saved a small key to the file C:\temp\MyCo.reg:

```
Windows 2000 9:34:19 C:\
REG BACKUP HKLM\Software\MyCo\MyNewApp c:\temp\MyCo
The operation completed successfully.


Windows 2000 9:34:21 C:\
dir c:\temp\myco.*
 Volume in drive C is (c) - Boot drive
 Volume Serial Number is CC56-5631

Directory of c:\temp

07/17/99 09:34a          8,192          MyCo
        1 File(s)      8,192 bytes
               183,407,104 bytes free

Windows 2000 9:34:27 C:\
```

The COPY Function

Use the COPY function, invoked with the command REG COPY <options>, to copy the Registry object specified to a new name. Options include the Registry path to be copied (the source) and a destination name.

The command line for COPY is:

```
REG COPY OldPath [\\Machine] Newpath [\\Machine]
```

As with other Registry tools, the Registry path to be copied (both the old path and the new path) can be a ROOTKEY or a hive. You can specify the path with or without a value entry. The ROOTKEY can consist of one of the following (HKLM is assumed if none is entered):

- ▶ HKLM

- ▶ HKCU

- ▶ HKCR

- ▶ HKU

- ▶ HKCC

You can specify only HKLM and HKU when copying objects to a remote Registry.

NOTE

Consider what happens when you copy a Registry object from one Registry to another Registry on a different machine. This command is more powerful than is apparent at first glance.

You can further qualify the hive to determine the contents of a specific key or value entry. If you don't specify a value entry, all value entries in the key are copied. Here's an example of executing the COPY function:

```
Windows 2000 9:10:52 C:\
REG QUERY HKLM\Software\MyCo\MyApp\

Listing of [Software\MyCo\MyApp\]

REG_SZ      Version 1.00

Windows 2000 9:15:18 C:\
REG COPY HKLM\Software\MyCo\MyApp\ HKLM\Software\MyCo\MyNewApp
The operation completed successfully.


Windows 2000 9:15:43 C:\
REG QUERY HKLM\Software\MyCo\MyNewApp

Listing of [Software\MyCo\MyNewApp]

REG_SZ      Version 1.00

Windows 2000 9:15:51 C:\
```

The DELETE Function

You use the DELETE function, invoked with the command REG DELETE <options>, to delete the specified Registry object. Options include the Registry path to be deleted, an optional machine name (you can query remote Registries), and an optional parameter, /F, that forces the deletion without recourse.

The command line for DELETE is:

```
REG DELETE RegistryPath [\\Machine] [/F]\
```

As with other Registry tools, the Registry path to be queried can be a ROOTKEY or a hive (with or without a value entry). The ROOTKEY can consist of one of the following (HKLM is assumed if none is entered):

- ► HKLM

- ► HKCU

- ► HKCR

- ► HKU

- ► HKCC

You can specify only HKLM and HKU when deleting objects from a remote Registry.

Using the /F option forces the deletion without any prompt or confirmation. Microsoft recommends that the /F option be used only with extreme care. I agree.

An example of executing the DELETE function is shown next. Notice that I had to respond with a y to the prompt to delete the specified object.

```
Windows 2000 9:05:30 C:\
REG QUERY HKLM\Software\MyCo\MyApp\Version
REG_SZ      Version 2.00


Windows 2000 9:09:30 C:\
REG DELETE HKLM\Software\MyCo\MyApp\Version
Permanently delete Registry value Version (Y/N)? y
The operation completed successfully.


Windows 2000 9:09:40 C:\
REG QUERY HKLM\Software\MyCo\MyApp\Version
The system was unable to find the specified Registry key.

Windows 2000 9:09:43 C:\
```

The LOAD Function

You use the LOAD function, invoked with the command REG LOAD
<options>, to load the Registry object from the file specified. The
object must have been saved using the REG SAVE or REG BACKUP
command. Options include the name of the file to load from, the
Registry path to be restored, and an optional machine name (you
can restore to remote Registries).

The command line for LOAD is:

```
REG LOAD FileName keyname [\\Machine]\
```

As with other Registry tools, the Registry path to be queried can be a
ROOTKEY or a hive, with or without a data key. The ROOTKEY can consist of one of the following (HKLM is assumed if none is entered):

- ► HKLM

- ► HKCU

You can specify only HKLM and HKCU in this command.

Objects in the key will be loaded, overwriting existing objects if there
are any. Here's an example of executing the LOAD function:

```
Windows 2000 9:47:58 C:\
 REG LOAD c:\temp\myco HKLM\TEMP\
The operation completed successfully.

Windows 2000 9:48:01 C:\
REG QUERY HKLM\TEMP /s
Listing of [TEMP\]
REG_SZ     Version 1.00
Windows 2000 9:48:35 C:\
```

The QUERY Function

You use the QUERY function, invoked with the command REG QUERY
<options>, to search the Registry for a specific value entry and display
its contents. Options include the Registry path to be queried, an optional
machine name (you can query remote Registries), and an optional parameter, /S, that forces a query of all keys.

The command line for QUERY is:

```
REG QUERY RegistryPath [\\Machine] [/S]
```

As with other Registry tools, the Registry path to be queried can be a ROOTKEY or a hive, with or without a value entry. The ROOTKEY can consist of one of the following (HKLM is assumed if none is entered):

▶ HKLM

▶ HKCU

▶ HKCR

▶ HKU

▶ HKCC

You can further qualify the hive to determine the contents of a specific key or value entry. If you don't specify a value entry, all value entries in the key are retrieved. Here's an example of executing the QUERY function:

```
Windows 2000 8:54:08 C:\
REG QUERY HKLM\Software\Microsoft\ResKit\Setup\InstallDir
REG_SZ    InstallDir    C:\NTRESKIT

Windows 2000 8:54:11 C:\
```

The RESTORE Function

You use the RESTORE function, invoked with the command REG RESTORE <options>, to restore the Registry object from the file specified. The object must have been saved using the REG SAVE or REG BACKUP command. Options include the name of the file to restore from, the Registry path to be restored, and an optional machine name (you can restore to remote Registries).

The command line for RESTORE is:

```
REG RESTORE FileName RegistryPath [\\Machine]
```

As with other Registry tools, the Registry path to be queried can be a ROOTKEY or a hive, with or without a value entry. The ROOTKEY can consist of one of the following (HKLM is assumed if none is entered):

▶ HKLM

▶ HKCU

▶ HKCR

▶ HKU

▶ HKCC

You can specify only HKLM and HKU when restoring objects to a remote Registry.

Objects in the key will be restored and overwritten by the information contained in the specified file. Here's an example of executing the RESTORE function:

```
Windows 2000 9:39:17 C:\
 REG BACKUP HKLM\Software\MyCo\MyNewApp c:\temp\MyCo
The operation completed successfully.

Windows 2000 9:40:20 C:\
 REG RESTORE c:\temp\myco HKLM\Software\MyCo\MyNewApp
Are you sure you want to replace Software\MyCo\MyNewApp (Y/N)
y
The operation completed successfully.


Windows 2000 9:40:44 C:\
```

The SAVE Function

You use the SAVE function, invoked with the command REG SAVE <options>, to save the Registry object specified to the file specified. Options include the Registry path to be saved, the output filename, and an optional machine name (you can save on remote Registries).

The command line for SAVE is:

```
REG SAVE RegistryPath OutputFileName [\\Machine]
```

As with other Registry tools, the Registry path to be queried can be a ROOTKEY or a hive (with or without a value entry). The ROOTKEY can consist of one of the following (HKLM is assumed if none is entered):

► HKLM

► HKCU

► HKCR

► HKU

► HKCC

You can specify only HKLM and HKU when saving objects to a remote Registry.

An example of executing the SAVE function is shown next. In this example, I've saved a small key to the file C:\temp\MyCo.reg:

```
Windows 2000 9:16:27 C:\
REG SAVE HKLM\Software\MyCo\MyNewApp c:\temp\MyCo.reg
The operation completed successfully.

Windows 2000 9:18:35 C:\
dir c:\temp\myco.reg
 Volume in drive C is (c) - Boot drive
 Volume Serial Number is CC56-5631

 Directory of c:\temp

07/17/99 09:18a           8,192         MyCo.reg
      1 File(s)      8,192 bytes
             183,407,104 bytes free

Windows 2000 9:19:08 C:\
```

The UNLOAD Function

You use the UNLOAD function, invoked with the command REG UNLOAD <options>, to unload (delete) the Registry object specified. The object must be a single-level key, such as HKLM\TEMP. Options include the name of the key to unload and an optional machine name (you can unload objects from remote Registries).

The command line for unload is:

```
REG UNLOAD keyname [\\Machine]
```

As with other Registry tools, the Registry path to be queried can be a ROOTKEY or a hive, with or without a value entry. The ROOTKEY can consist of one of the following (HKLM is assumed if none is entered):

► HKLM

► HKCU

You can specify only HKLM and HKCU in this command.

Objects in the key will be unloaded and will not be saved. There is no recovery in the event of a user error with this command. Here's an example of executing the UNLOAD function:

```
Windows 2000 9:47:58 C:\
REG UNLOAD HKLM\TEMP\
The operation completed successfully.

Windows 2000 9:48:01 C:\
```

```
REG QUERY HKLM\TEMP /s

The system was unable to find the specified Registry key.

Windows 2000 9:48:35 C:\
```

The UPDATE Function

You use the UPDATE function, invoked with the command REG UPDATE
<options>, to update an existing object (key or value entry) to the Reg-
istry. Options include the Registry object to be added (with the object's
value) and an optional machine name (you can update remote Registries).

The command line for UPDATE is:

```
REG UPDATE RegistryPath=value [\\Machine]
```

As with other Registry tools, the Registry path to be queried can be a
ROOTKEY or a hive, with or without a value entry. The ROOTKEY can
consist of one of the following (HKLM is assumed if none is entered):

▶ HKLM

▶ HKCU

▶ HKCR

▶ HKU

▶ HKCC

The hive will be further qualified to determine the object to be added.

Below is an example of executing the UPDATE function. First I show
the original value, then I update the object, and then I show the new
value.

```
Windows 2000 9:00:48 C:\
REG QUERY HKLM\Software\MyCo\MyApp\Version
REG_SZ     Version 1.00

Windows 2000 9:01:33 C:\
REG UPDATE HKLM\Software\MyCo\MyApp\Version=2.00
The operation completed successfully.


Windows 2000 9:03:47 C:\
REG QUERY HKLM\Software\MyCo\MyApp\Version
REG_SZ     Version 2.00

Windows 2000 9:03:53 C:\
```

HINTS AND KINKS FROM THE EXPERTS

In this section, we provide a few hints for using the two Registry editors.

How Do You Restrict Access to the Registry Editor?

In RegEdt32, follow these steps:

1. Highlight HKEY_USERS, and choose Registry ➤ Load Hive to open the Load Hive dialog box.

2. Browse to their profile directory, select NTUSER.DAT, and click Open to open yet another Load Hive dialog box.

3. In the Key Name text box, input their user ID, and click OK.

4. Navigate to \Software\Microsoft\Windows\Current-Version\Policies.

5. If no System subkey exists in Policies, add it. Then choose Edit ➤ Add Value to open the Add Value dialog box, add a value named DisableRegistryTools under the System key using type REG_DWORD, and set the value to 1.

6. Choose Registry ➤ Unload Hive.

(Courtesy of John Savill.)

Should You Use RegEdit or RegEdt32?

You can use either. RegEdit does have a few limitations; the greatest limitation is that it does not support the full RegEdt32 data types, such as REG_MULTI_SZ. If you edit this type of data with RegEdit, RegEdit will change its type.

RegEdit is based on the Windows 95 version and has features that RegEdt32 lacks, such as a good search feature. In general, RegEdit is nicer to work with. RegEdit also shows your current position in the Registry at the bottom of the window.

(Courtesy of John Savill.)

Part IV

How Do You Restrict Access to a Remote Registry?

Access to a remote Registry is controlled by the ACL (Access Control List) on the key `winreg`. To set access, follow these steps:

1. Start the Registry editor (`regedt32.exe`).

2. Move to `HKEY_LOCAL_MACHINE\System\CurrentControl-Set\Control\SecurePipeServers`.

3. Check for a key called `winreg`. If it does not exist, create it (choose Edit ➤ Add Key).

4. Select the `winreg` key.

5. Choose Security ➤ Permissions to open the Permissions For `winreg` dialog box.

6. Click the Add button to open the Select Users, Computers, Or Groups dialog box, and give the user Read access.

7. Once the key is added, click the user, and select Special Access.

8. Double-click the user, and you can select which actions the user can perform.

9. Click OK when finished.

It is possible to set up certain keys to be accessible even if the user does not have access by editing the value `HKEY_LOCAL_MACHINE\System\CurrentControlSet\Control\SecurePipeServers\winreg\All` (using RegEdt32). You can add paths to this list.

(Courtesy of John Savill.)

NOTE

For more information, see Knowledge Base article Q153183 at `http://www.microsoft.com/kb/articles/q153/1/83.htm`.

WHAT'S NEXT?

To complete our look at the Windows 2000 Registry, Chapter 22 lists some common Registry hives and keys, along with their subkeys and a description.

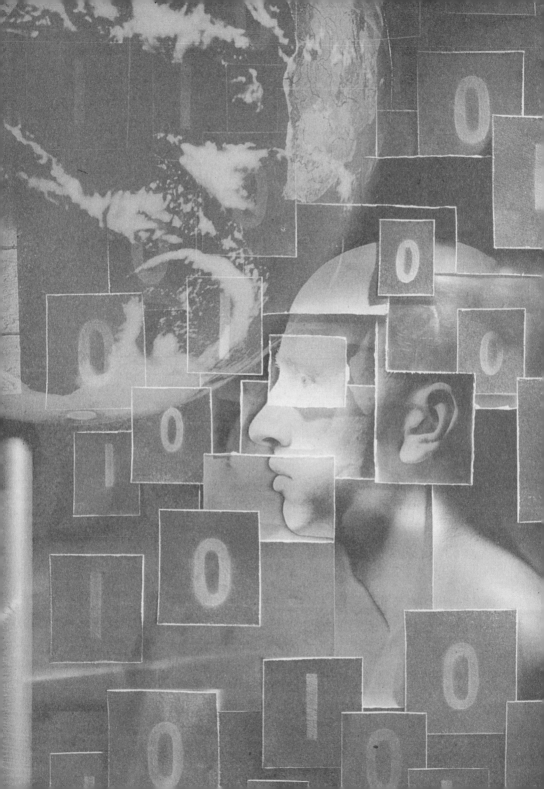

Chapter 22

COMMON HIVES AND KEYS

Virtually all Registries contain a number of common entries. These entries, mostly for basic system components, usually have either the same values or predictable values. Table 22.1 lists some common Registry hives and keys.

Adapted from *Mastering Windows 2000 Registry*,
by Peter D. Hipson
ISBN 0-7821-2615-4   725 pages $39.99

TABLE 22.1: Common Registry Hives and Keys

Subkey	Description
HKEY_LOCAL_MACHINE	
All keys	The main system description hive. This hive is critical to the execution of Windows 2000.
HKEY_LOCAL_MACHINE\Hardware\Description	
All keys	Contains information on installed hardware. This key is created at boot time, though some entries may be retained from previous executions.
System	Contains system device information, excluding NIC (Network Interface Card) and video devices.
System\CentralProcessor	Contains CPU information, such as make, model, and version.
System\FloatingPointProcessor	Contains floating-point processor data, such as make, model, and version.
System\MultifunctionAdapter\2\DiskController\0\DiskPeripheral	Contains installed disk controller information. Systems may have one, two, or three controllers in a typical configuration: primary IDE, secondary IDE, and SCSI.
System\MultifunctionAdapter\2\KeyboardController	Contains keyboard controller information at the hardware level.
System\MultifunctionAdapter\2\ParallelController	Contains printer (parallel) port information.
System\MultifunctionAdapter\2\PointerController	Contains mouse port information.
System\MultifunctionAdapter\2\SerialController	Contains information on installed serial ports.
System\MultifunctionAdapter	Contains information on device classes, other than network and disk.
System\PCMCIA PCCARDs	Contains information on installed PCMCIA (PC Card) devices.

CONTINUED ➡

TABLE 22.1 continued: Common Registry Hives and Keys

SUBKEY	DESCRIPTION
HKEY_LOCAL_MACHINE\Hardware\DeviceMap	
All keys	Contains basic device-mapping and control information.
KeyboardClass	Contains keyboard device-mapping information.
KeyboardPort	Contains keyboard port configuration information.
PARALLEL PORTS	Contains printer (parallel) port configuration information.
PointerClass	Contains mouse information.
PointerPort	Contains information on the port (mouse port, PS/2 mouse port, serial port, and so on) the mouse (pointer) connects to.
Scsi	Contains general disk interface information on IDE and SCSI devices.
Scsi\Scsi Port 0	Contains information on the first disk drive interface adapter (although labeled as SCSI, this may be an IDE device).
Scsi\Scsi Port 1	Contains information on the second disk drive interface adapter (although labeled as SCSI, this may be an IDE device).
SERIALCOMM	Contains information on serial communications device configurations.
VIDEO	Contains video configuration information.
HKEY_LOCAL_MACHINE\Hardware\ResourceMap	
All keys	Contains information on (hardware) system mapping.
Hardware Abstraction Layer\PC Compatible Eisa\Isa HAL	Describes the system configuration to Windows 2000. HALs exist for generic systems and for computers that have special hardware configurations, such as multiple processors or special bus configurations.
KeyboardPort\PointerPort	Contains general keyboard/mouse interface information.
KeyboardPort\Pointer-Port\msi8042prt	Contains mouse/keyboard interface information.
LOADED PARALLEL DRIVER RESOURCES	A description of currently loaded printer (parallel) port driver configurations.
LOADED SERIAL DRIVER RESOURCES	A description of currently loaded serial port driver configurations.

Part iv

CONTINUED ➡

TABLE 22.1 continued: Common Registry Hives and Keys

SUBKEY	DESCRIPTION
HKEY_LOCAL_MACHINE\Hardware\ResourceMap	
OtherDrivers	Contains general information on devices not otherwise classified.
OtherDrivers\<NIC>	A description of the NIC.
ScsiAdapter	Contains information about SCSI and IDE adapters.
ScsiAdapter\atapi	A description of the installed IDE (ATAPI) disk interface.
System Resources	Contains general information on system resources.
System Resources\Reserved	Contains reserved system resources information.
System Resources\Physical Memory	Contains system memory resources information.
VIDEO	Contains information on video configurations supported by the system.
VIDEO\chips	Contains information on the installed VGA adapter for the Chips & Technology VGA system.
VIDEO\VgaSave	Contains information on the originally installed VGA video system, generally a generic VGA system.
VIDEO\VgaStart	Contains information on the VGA driver used to start the system.
HKEY_LOCAL_MACHINE\SAM	
SAM	The SAM subkey. Usually protected from user browsing and modification. (Yes, the key is named SAM\SAM.) In a Windows 2000 domain using Active Directory, SAM is not used.
SAM\Domains\Account\Aliases	Contains SAM alias information.
SAM\Domains\Account\Aliases\Members	Contains member alias information.
SAM\Domains\Account\Aliases\Names	Contains domain name alias information.
SAM\Domains\Account\Groups	Contains Groups information.
SAM\Domains\Account\Groups\Names	Contains group name information.
SAM\Domains\Account\Users	Contains specific user information.

CONTINUED ➡

TABLE 22.1 continued: Common Registry Hives and Keys

SUBKEY	DESCRIPTION
HKEY_LOCAL_MACHINE\SAM\	
SAM\Domains\Account\Users\ Names	Contains username information.
SAM\Domains\Account\Users\ Names\Administrator	Contains user administrator information.
SAM\Domains\Account\Users\ Names\Guest	Contains user guest information.
SAM\Domains\Builtin\Aliases\ Members\S-1-5-21-xxxxxxxxxx- xxxxxxxxxx-xxxxxxxxxx	Contains information on built-in users: Administrator and Guest.
SAM\Domains\Builtin\Aliases\ Members\S-1-5-21-xxxxxxxxxx- xxxxxxxxxx-xxxxxxxxxx\ 000001F4	Contains information on the built-in user: Administrator.
SAM\Domains\Builtin\Aliases\ Members\S-1-5-21-xxxxxxxxxx- xxxxxxxxxx-xxxxxxxxxx\000001 F5	Contains built-in user information.
SAM\Domains\Builtin\Aliases\ Members\S-1-5-21-xxxxxxxxxx- xxxxxxxxxx-xxxxxxxxxx	Contains Domain Groups information.
SAM\Domains\Builtin\Aliases\ Members\S-1-5-21-xxxxxxxxxx- xxxxxxxxxx- xxxxxxxxxx\00000200	Contains Domain Admins group information.
SAM\Domains\Builtin\Aliases\ Members\S-1-5-21- xxxxxxxxxx-xxxxxxxxxx- xxxxxxxxxx\00000201	Contains Domain Users group information.
SAM\Domains\Builtin\Aliases\ Members	Contains member alias information for user groups.
SAM\Domains\Builtin\Aliases\ Names\Administrators	Contains member alias information for Administrators.
SAM\Domains\Builtin\Aliases\ Names\Backup Operators	Contains member alias information for Backup Operators (users who perform system backups).

Part iv

CONTINUED ➡

TABLE 22.1 continued: Common Registry Hives and Keys

Subkey	Description
HKEY_LOCAL_MACHINE\SAM	
SAM\Domains\Builtin\Aliases\ Names\Guests	Contains member alias information for Domain Guests.
SAM\Domains\Builtin\Aliases\ Names\Power Users	Contains member alias information for Power Users.
SAM\Domains\Builtin\Aliases\ Names\Replicator	Contains member alias information for Replicator accounts.
SAM\Domains\Builtin\Aliases\ Names\Users	Contains member alias information for Domain Users.
SAM\RXACT	The SAM RXACT key. Used by the Registry transaction package. A number of RXACT keys are located in the Registry. Typically these keys contain nothing.
HKEY_LOCAL_MACHINE\Security	
All keys	The protected Windows 2000 security key.
HKEY_LOCAL_MACHINE\Software	
All keys	Contains information about installed user and system software.
Classes	Contains information about extensions and the usage of file types.
Classes*	Contains information about files in general—that is, files that are not otherwise classified.
Classes\CLSID	Contains information about CLSID (class ID) assignments. Almost all applications, and those that support OLE, have a CLSID.
Classes\Interface	Contains information about OLE interface assignments. Almost all applications that support OLE have an OLE interface.
Description	Contains information about RPC objects and configurations.
Windows NT\CurrentVersion	Contains information on the currently installed version of Windows 2000.

CONTINUED ➡

TABLE 22.1 continued: Common Registry Hives and Keys

SUBKEY	DESCRIPTION
HKEY_LOCAL_MACHINE\Software	
Program Groups	Contains information on program groups as used by Program Manager.
Secure	Contains security information.
Windows 3.1 Migration Status	Contains information on migration from Windows NT 3.x to Windows NT 4/2000.
HKEY_LOCAL_MACHINE\System\ControlSet001	
All keys	The control set used to manage system resources.
HKEY_LOCAL_MACHINE\System\ControlSet002	
All keys	Backup control sets are numbered 002, 003, 004, and so on. Typically, there will only be two control sets.
HKEY_LOCAL_MACHINE\System\ControlSet003	
All keys	Backup control sets are numbered 002, 003, 004, and so on. Typically, there will only be two control sets.
HKEY_LOCAL_MACHINE\System\ControlSet004	
All keys	Backup control sets are numbered 002, 003, 004, and so on. Typically, there will only be two control sets.
HKEY_LOCAL_MACHINE\System\CurrentControlSet	
All keys	The current control set is mapped to the control set used for starting the computer.
Control\BootVerification-Program	That program used to verify that the system booted correctly.
Control\Class	Contains information about CLSIDs (OLE).

CONTINUED ➡

TABLE 22.1 continued: Common Registry Hives and Keys

Subkey	Description
HKEY_LOCAL_MACHINE\System\CurrentControlSet	
Control\ComputerName\Active-ComputerName	Holds the computer's current name.
Control\ComputerName\ComputerName	Holds the computer's name.
Control\CrashControl	Determines events when/if the system fails.
Control\FileSystem	A description of the system file system (FAT or NTFS).
HKEY_LOCAL_MACHINE\System\Disk	
All keys	A description of the system disk.
HKEY_LOCAL_MACHINE\System\Select	
All keys	A description of the control set used.
HKEY_LOCAL_MACHINE\System\Setup	
All keys	A description of the system setup state.
HKEY_LOCAL_MACHINE\System	
All keys	A description of the system.
HKEY_USERS	
All keys	Contains general user information.
HKEY_USERS\.DEFAULT	
All keys	The default user active when no other user is logged on. All information in .DEFAULT would also be found for specific users.
AppEvents\EventLabels	Event labels are used to notify users (with sound) when events happen.

CONTINUED ➡

TABLE 22.1 continued: Common Registry Hives and Keys

SUBKEY	DESCRIPTION
HKEY_USERS\.DEFAULT\	
AppEvents\Schemes	Schemes are used to apply which sounds are used for events.
AppEvents	Contains application events, such as Startup, Document Open, and so on.
Console	The system's command prompt for window(s) configuration.
Control Panel	The System Control Panel used to configure Windows 2000.
Control Panel\Accessibility	The Control Panel's Accessibility applet.
Control Panel\Appearance	The Control Panel's Appearance applet.
Control Panel\Colors	The Control Panel's Colors applet.
Control Panel\Current	The Control Panel's Current applet.
Control Panel\Custom Colors	The Control Panel's Custom Colors applet.
Control Panel\Desktop	The Control Panel's Desktop applet.
Control Panel\International	The Control Panel's International applet.
Control Panel\IOProcs	The Control Panel's IOProcs applet.
Control Panel\Keyboard	The Control Panel's Keyboard applet.
Control Panel\MMCPL	The Control Panel's MMCPL applet.
Control Panel\Mouse	The Control Panel's Mouse applet.
Control Panel\Patterns	The Control Panel's Patterns applet.
Control Panel\Screen Saver .3DFlyingObj	The Control Panel's Screen Saver.3DFlyingObj saved configuration.
Control Panel\Screen Saver .3Dpipes	The Control Panel's Screen Saver.3DPipes saved configuration.
Control Panel\Screen Saver .Bezier	The Control Panel's Screen Saver.Bezier saved configuration.
Control Panel\Screen Saver.Marquee	The Control Panel's Screen Saver.Marquee saved configuration.

Part iv

CONTINUED ➡

TABLE 22.1 continued: Common Registry Hives and Keys

Subkey	Description
HKEY_USERS\.DEFAULT	
Control Panel\Screen Saver.Mystify	The Control Panel's Screen Saver.Mystify saved configuration.
Control Panel\Screen Saver.Stars	The Control Panel's Screen Saver.Stars saved configuration.
Control Panel\Sound	The Control Panel's Sound applet.
Environment	Contains definitions of environment variables, used with both Windows and command prompts.
Keyboard Layout	The keyboard layouts for NLS (National Language Support).
Software\Microsoft\Windows Help	Contains configurations for the Windows Help system.
Software\Microsoft\Windows NT\CurrentVersion	Contains the Windows current software configurations.
Software\Microsoft\Windows NT\CurrentVersion\Devices	Contains configurations of software drivers for hardware.
Software\Microsoft\Windows NT	Contains Windows configuration items.
Software\Microsoft\Windows\CurrentVersion	Contains Windows configuration items.
Software\Microsoft\Windows	Contains general information about Windows.
Software\Microsoft	Contains information about Microsoft components and software.
Software	Contains software configurations (as compared to hardware configurations).
UNICODE Program Groups	Unused on most systems.
HKEY_USERS\<SID>	
All keys	Contains information for specific users as identified by <SID>.
AppEvents\EventLabels\.Default	Contains information regarding application event labels, as in .DEFAULT.

CONTINUED ➡

TABLE 22.1 continued: Common Registry Hives and Keys

SUBKEY	DESCRIPTION
HKEY_USERS\<SID>_Classes\	
<None>	New to Windows 2000, this key contains no usable information.

WHAT'S NEXT?

As you may remember from Part I of this book, Windows 2000 is actually a family of operating systems. In Part I, we looked at Windows 2000 Professional, the operating system that can run on a stand-alone computer, on a small network, or on a large corporate network. In Part V, we'll take a look at Windows 2000 Server, the successor to Windows NT Server 4, that can run on anything from a small home network to a network of several hundred users. In Chapter 23, we'll begin with installing Windows 2000 Server.

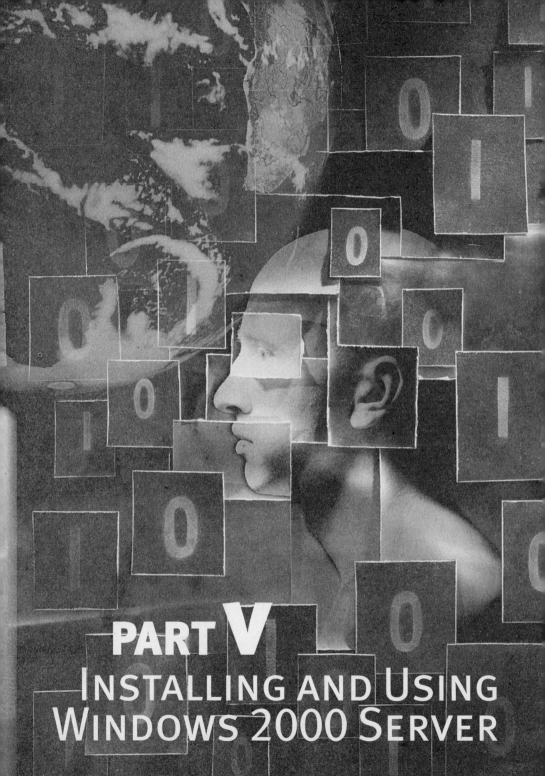

PART V
INSTALLING AND USING
WINDOWS 2000 SERVER

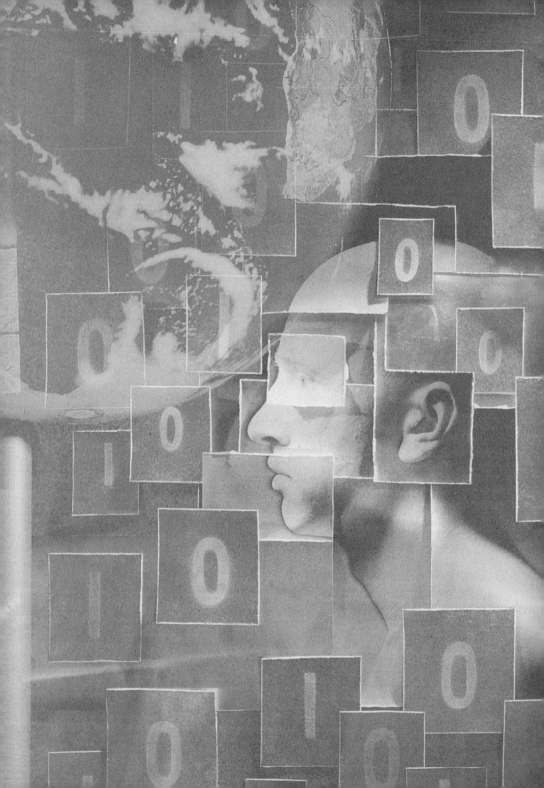

Chapter 23

INSTALLING WINDOWS 2000 SERVER

Ever since the early days of Windows 3.1, the Windows line of operating systems has become increasingly complex and cumbersome, while the installation procedures themselves have become easier and more intuitive. Windows 2000 continues in this tradition. Plug and Play becomes a functioning reality, making hardware configuration much easier and more foolproof. Domain controllers and member servers all come from the same installation seed. Unattended installs are more capable, including a remote installation option. In short, installing Windows 2000 is *usually* a straightforward affair. Anyone with a half-decent collection of hardware components and the "click Next to continue" capabilities of a 7 iron can probably install Windows 2000 Server and get it to boot up on the first try, almost every time.

Adapted from *Mastering Windows 2000 Server, Second Edition*, by Mark Minasi, Christa Anderson, Brian M. Smith, and Doug Toombs

ISBN 0-7821-2774-6   1593 pages $49.99

The hard part comes when you want not only a stable, reliable installation, but also a *repeatable process*. This repeatable process will allow one-stop shopping for all your installation needs and give you that clean and efficient install every time. However, to produce those perfect results time and time again, the planning and preparation phase of the install becomes even more important. Failure to properly plan an install will most certainly result in a reinstall.

In this chapter, I'll cover key fundamental planning steps, help you prepare your system for Windows 2000, run through an install, and, finally, troubleshoot the mess we got ourselves into.

PLANNING AND PREPARATION

First of all, what is all this hubbub about planning? Well, anyone who has done a significant number of NT installs has had to format and start over at least once. Usually this is due to a lack of planning. In my case, it is usually that I partitioned wrong, built a member server when it should have been a domain controller, or fell prey to some other simple lack of foresight. Windows 2000 does do us a favor in a few areas. For starters, with Windows NT, you had to decide early in the installation process whether you wanted a member server or a domain controller. Once you made your choice, you were stuck with it. With Windows 2000, this isn't an issue. Every initial install begins with a server. That's it, plain and simple. Once you are up and running with a stable server, you can promote it to a domain controller.

NOTE

Actually, the domain controller as we have been used to it has changed significantly. The Active Directory becomes the driving force with a whole new set of concerns that could completely throw off the balance of an install. With Windows 2000, we can just throw this factor out and deal with it later.

Next comes Plug and Play. Yes, NT 4 gave you some quasi plug-and-play functionality, but it was spotty at best and only applied to *ISA* (Industry Standard Architecture) Plug and Play, which is fairly unusual, rather than the more common PCI-based (Peripheral Component Interconnect–based) PnP boards. Windows 2000 takes another step in that direction. Plug and Play is *supposed* to make your life easier in the hardware preparation department. Sometimes, however, even the most up-to-date Plug-and-Play–based system will trip over its drivers, and hybrid PnP/legacy systems can be a bit of trouble to install.

For good or ill, however, you probably won't run into too many systems with a combination of Plug and Play and non-PnP boards. You'll find that the demands of Windows 2000 on hardware are so great that you'll probably be installing Windows 2000 only on relatively new hardware—which is likely to be entirely Plug and Play. Windows 2000 also has a Remote Installation Services option, which can serve as a central, ghost-like source for distributing Windows 2000 across your network.

These enhancements, improvements, and new features increase the possibility of a smooth installation process but still define why it's best to plan ahead of time. Planning doesn't just save you from making mistakes. It can make your installation a lot more than just installing Windows 2000. With proper planning, you can utilize the features and enhancements of Windows 2000 to save time for each install and build an entire installation process for use throughout your enterprise.

System Requirements

Once again, Microsoft has upped the ante on system requirements. No longer can we get by with a 486 Intel *processor*. A Pentium is in order, running at 166MHz or faster, although the truth of the matter is that you really should have at least a Pentium II–class processor: a Celeron, a Xeon, or a Pentium II or III. The so-called front-side bus on the processor should be a minimum of 100MHz, which means that your system should be a 350MHz or faster system. The one exception: the 366MHz processor is *not* a 100MHz front-side bus; it's only a 66MHz and so should be avoided.

However, while processing dictates how fast your computer will do the job, *memory* decides *if* your computer can do the job. Whereas NT 4 lets you get by with 16MB of RAM, Windows 2000 Server will not let you install with anything less than 64MB on an Intel box. When deciding how much memory you will need, try to consider what your server will be doing. Simple file and print sharing is not as resource intensive on a server as running applications such as Exchange, SQL Server, Web services, and so on. Any time you put the server side of a client/server application on your system, your server is performing processing that would have otherwise been done by the workstation. This directly influences your memory and processor requirements.

For example, a system that is merely serving a few print queues and shared directories can get by with the bare minimums. On the other hand, tack on Web hosting, mail servicing, and user logon validation for several thousand users, and you may need memory well up into the triple digits and a processor that could fry eggs. I'd put a *minimum* of 128MB of RAM on a Windows 2000 server (96MB for a Windows 2000 Professional workstation).

More memory means more places for the memory hardware to fail, however, and that's why you need ECC (Error Correcting Code) memory. You may recall something called *parity*, a set of circuits attached to memory systems of PCs in the '80s whose job was to monitor the memory and detect data loss in a PC's RAM. Such data loss could be caused by a bad memory chip (which you can ward off by testing your RAM with a good RAM tester program such as CheckIt or QAPlus before deploying the server), but random events also cause data loss; static electricity, power surges, and (believe it or not) infrequent extremely low-level radioactivity from the memory chips *themselves* can damage memory data. (Don't worry, you won't get cancer or mutations from your memory chips. Many, many everyday things in our world are mildly radioactive: the bricks cladding your house and indeed most kinds of ceramic produce an extremely small amount of radioactivity. Memory chips produce a radioactive particle once in a great while, and when they do, that particle may happen to cross paths with a location in memory—and when *that* happens, the memory may be flipped from a 0 to a 1 or vice versa!)

In any case, parity was kind of frustrating in that it could detect that *something* was wrong, but it didn't know *what* was wrong. PCs with parity memory were usually designed to simply shut down the PC when a memory error was detected using the parity method (which the error message would usually incorrectly call "a parity error" rather than a "memory error"—after all, if parity detected the memory error, parity was working fine!), and shutting down an entire system just because parity discovered one damaged bit is a trifle extreme.

In contrast, most of today's Pentium II–based systems (which, again, include the Xeon and Celeron) can go a step further and implement ECC. ECC is cool because it not only *detects* memory errors, it *corrects* them automatically. So when that stray alpha particle or (more likely) power glitch scrambles a bit, ECC finds that problem and fixes it without ever bothering you.

Now you may be wondering, "How much would such a wonderful feature cost?" Well, back in the old days, I worked on minicomputer systems with ECC that cost thousands of dollars. But most Pentium II–based systems can do it for about $20 per 128MB of RAM. Here's the trick: most PC memories these days are implemented as Synchronous Dynamic Random Access Memory, or SDRAM, packages. SDRAMs come in a 64-bit version or a 72-bit version. When I last priced 128MB SDRAMs, the difference in price between a 64-bit and 72-bit SDRAM was $20 on a $200 SDRAM, a fairly cheap "insurance policy" in my opinion.

You may have to go into your system's setup BIOS in order to turn on the ECC feature. Not all systems activate ECC by default.

Hard disk space requirements for Windows 2000 Server have been upped to 850MB plus an additional 100MB for each 64MB of system RAM. Of course, this will depend on your optionally installed components and future intentions for the server. I recommend 1GB as the bare minimum and as much as 2GB for servers that have numerous server components installed.

A *bootable CD-ROM drive*, although not required, is always highly recommended. A time always comes when your server crashes and you need a reinstall fast. Rather than scrambling for boot disks to get you connected to your installation source on the network, you simply pop the CD in and off you go.

All your hardware requirements can be further summed up by referencing the *Hardware Compatibility List (HCL)*. Every piece of hardware in your system should be on the list. Anything not on the list could generate problems from application failures to system crashes and probably won't even install at all. Why? Most likely, if your hardware is not on the list, you will have a hard time locating a driver. Should you happen to have an OEM (Original Equipment Manufacturer) driver that came with the hardware, you are risking system instability because Microsoft hasn't tested or guaranteed it to work.

Why do you care? Because if you get on the phone to Microsoft and give them the requisite $200 in order to get them to help you with a problem, and *then* you tell them that you've got hardware that's not on the HCL, the Microsoft support person gets to say, "Golly, I'm sorry, your stuff isn't on the HCL, that's the problem," and hang up. Result: a free 200 bucks for Bill and no solution for you. If you trust the manufacturer of the hardware who provided the driver to have fully tested it with all aspects of Windows 2000, fine. Be cautious, though. The best recommendation is

Part V

that if you are buying new hardware, consult the list first. You can find the HCL on your Windows 2000 CD or on the Web at `www.microsoft.com/ hwtest/hcl/`.

Preparing the Hardware

Once you have your hardware, it is highly advisable that you get it working and compatible first. Throughout the process, Setup will examine, activate, reexamine, configure, poke, and prod at every piece of hardware in your system that it can find. This is where the Plug-and-Play intricacies come in. If everything in your system is true Plug and Play, this process should go off without a hitch. Mix in a few older devices that don't fit this bill, and you could get some serious problems, including complete setup failure.

In this section, we'll do whatever we can to avoid these problems before we even launch Setup.

Preparing the BIOS

Most machines have highly configurable BIOSs, which can really play an important role in how Windows 2000 operates. For the pre-Setup phase, you can look for obvious settings that may interfere with your installation. Your boot device order may need customizing to allow you to boot to the CD. This, I find, is one of the most convenient ways to do an install. But then again, if you weren't expecting the CD to be bootable, you could inadvertently keep rebooting into the initial install phase from the CD over and over again, thinking you were getting the hard drive. Nothing major, but it has happened to the best of us.

The most important parts of the BIOS you'll prepare are Plug-and-Play configuration and interrupt reservations. Because most systems capable of running Windows 2000 are fairly up-to-date by default, this step gets a little bit easier. The problem comes when you try to add older, non–Plug-and-Play components into your Plug-and-Play system. For example, you may have a non–Plug-and-Play device that is an old ISA network adapter, hard-coded for interrupt 10. When your Plug-and-Play devices come online, one may prefer to initialize on interrupt 10, not knowing that your ISA card will soon request the same. As soon as the driver initializes the ISA card...conflict.

The best thing to do is to configure interrupt 10 under your Plug-and-Play BIOS settings to be reserved for a non–Plug-and-Play card. This tells any Plug-and-Play device to leave that interrupt alone. But now we have the problem of determining *what* those interrupts are *before* we start the install. Your non–Plug-and-Play device may have a configuration disk that programs it for specific settings. There may be jumpers on the hardware. Most troublesome, there may be no obvious clue as to what these jumpers are set for. In this case, a DOS-level hardware analyzer may be required to identify those resources being used.

Once you have identified and recorded all required hardware information, return to your BIOS configuration. You may have a Plug-and-Play configuration screen that lets you define whether certain interrupts are available for general use—including being allocated by Plug-and-Play boards—or if they should be reserved for ISA boards. Since non–Plug-and-Play boards are generally not BIOS aware, they will continue to use the IRQ that has been reserved, but when your Plug-and-Play boards initialize, they will be denied the resource usage as defined by the BIOS.

In most cases, the procedure of reserving resources through the BIOS will allow all hardware to work in harmony. If not, you may find it necessary to remove all nonessential, non–Plug-and-Play devices from your system before you begin. Then, once you have a successful install, add your hardware.

Partitioning

In my opinion, planning the partitioning scheme seems to be one of the most overlooked portions of the installation process. Although Windows 2000 gives you some more advanced features for managing your partitions after the install, what you decide on prior to the install will most likely stick with you throughout the life of your server.

Knowing what type of server you are building plays a tremendously big part in the planning process. For example, think about a simple member server that serves out several shared directories and a few print queues. You may find it more convenient in the long run to keep your data on one partition and the system on another. Keeping that in mind, you may want to size your system partition based on your minimum requirements, 400MB, plus some breathing room, let's say a few hundred MB, plus some extra room to grow as your business needs grow. Planning this extra room is a delicate balance between how much you anticipate adding to the server side for running applications and how much additional data space your users may require. With storage space as cheap as it is today, I wouldn't create a system partition any less than 1 gigabyte.

If you are intending to use the Remote Installation Services, be sure to set aside a *big* partition solely for its use. RIS cannot store system images on either the boot partition (the partition that the system boots from, usually C) *or* the system partition (the one containing \WINNT).

With the introduction of dynamic volume attachments, you will find your partitions more easily expandable in the future. This will help eliminate the problem of having too small a system partition. Simply mount a new partition to any directory on your NTFS 5 partition, and you're back in business.

File Systems

Choosing file systems for your partitions is usually a bit more straightforward. You have your standard choices of FAT, FAT32, and NTFS. NTFS offers obvious advantages over FAT and FAT32, which will play an extremely large part in your file system decisions. However, at times the FAT formats are required. Mostly, this comes into play when you are keeping a machine in a dual-boot format with DOS, Windows 3.*x*, Windows 95, or Windows 98/98 SE and want those operating systems to be able to access data on those partitions. There may also be times when you want your system partition in one of the FAT formats. Corrupt or missing files on the system partition can be difficult and time-consuming to repair if you are dealing with NTFS. FAT, on the other hand, allows you to boot with a simple boot disk and either replace whatever files happen to be damaged or back up essential data files before rebuilding.

WARNING

You used to have a safe feeling when you made your system partition NTFS — that no one could simply sit down at the console, pop in a DOS boot disk, reboot your server, and have full access to your data. NTFS was not readable from a DOS boot disk, and the NTFS file system itself was just too big to fit on a single disk. Well, those safe feelings can now be tucked into the same category as the feelings you get when sitting in your car at a stoplight in downtown Washington, D.C., with your wallet lying casually on the passenger seat and your windows rolled down. Anyone can download the necessary drivers to boot up a simple DOS disk with NTFS access. My point here: NTFS is more secure than FAT, but NTFS only provides the same level of protection as locking your car door and rolling up the windows. If someone wants your data and has access to your server, they can get it. Physically securing the server is the only way to truly protect your data.

That said, I've always been partial to creating a C drive formatted as FAT that's 2GB in size. I then put the system installation files (\i386) on there and the system as well. That way, I can easily work on the system by just booting from a DOS floppy. But wait, doesn't Windows 2000 have a built-in "safe boot" mode that works even with an NTFS C drive? Sure, but the system still can't get you to a C: prompt unless a lot of the system is functioning right, which kind of defeats the purpose of providing an "emergency" command prompt. I'm more comfortable knowing that I can get to my boot and system drive—C—with just DOS in the event of a disaster. I then format the rest of the drives as NTFS and put applications and data on those drives.

When choosing NTFS for Windows 2000, there are still considerations. Windows 2000 has new features added to NTFS that are not available in NT 4, pre–Service Pack 4. Those features unique to NTFS 5 are:

▸ Encryption

▸ Dynamic volume extensions

▸ Disk quota capabilities

▸ Distributed link tracking

▸ Volume mount points

▸ Indexing

These new file system features make NTFS 5 volumes unavailable locally to NT 4, pre–Service Pack 4. If you were confident enough to upgrade NT 4 servers to Service Pack 4 or later, you will be in the clear.

NOTE

Keep in mind that all these file system incompatibilities I have been talking about are only relevant in cases of dual-boot systems. For example, boot into Windows 98, and you won't see your NTFS partitions. However, once data is shared out to the network, any Windows 2000–capable client will have access to the share.

Knowing what type of file systems you will want for your finished product is essential prior to installation, but just in case there is any question, go with the lowest common denominator, which is FAT. You can always convert up to NTFS later, but you can't convert NTFS back to FAT.

Server Name

This seems like a no-brainer, but it's a good idea to plan your naming convention. There are two ways that most people make living with server names difficult. The first is underestimating the importance of server names. The second is overdoing it when it comes to a standard convention.

By underestimating naming conventions, you end up with server names such as GEORGE, ELROY, JUDY, and ASTRO on your network. This is fine for a small office local area network (LAN) that will never grow too far beyond your ability to remember these names. When you start getting more than those few servers, it gets difficult to remember who is what.

Sometimes people overdo standard conventions by defining so many formats, items, and indexes into the name that it becomes just as confusing. Some of the things people put in a name are the server's geographical location, building location, room number, role, and an index. For example, a server in Annapolis residing in the Commerce Center building that is an Exchange server might be named ANNCCBEXC01. This information is fine, but keep it to useful information that resembles the important features in your network. Do your network or users really care what building the server is in? What about the city? What if you add another Exchange server in the courthouse? That would be named ANNCRTEXC01. Perhaps a better method here would be to put the EXC first. Simplicity is key. You may want to define your network into systems, and that's it. If you had two Exchange systems, one for the Commerce Department and one for the Treasury Department, you may want COM-MAIL01 and TREMAIL01. This may allow a better grouping of servers.

The bottom line here is to really think about it. Get the customers and the people who will manage the network involved. Get a consensus on what is important and what is not important. Although you can easily change the names of the servers later, you can't easily change the hundreds or thousands of users' workstations that connect to them.

WARNING

And never name the machine and the user the same! Several errors crop up when you're logged on to a machine named X using a user account that's also named X.

Network Connection and Options

Not knowing your network configuration ahead of time isn't usually going to be a show stopper. Knowing it can save you time, though.

Protocols

You will most likely be using either TCP/IP (Transmission Control Protocol/Internet Protocol) or NetBEUI (NetBIOS Extended User Interface). Find this out ahead of time. By default, Windows 2000 installs only TCP/IP. Some configuration concerns are associated with TCP/IP that will make a tremendous difference in your ability to connect to the network later. If you use TCP/IP, do you have a DHCP (Dynamic Host Configuration Protocol) server on the network? If you don't have a DHCP server, you will need static information. The most critical elements are your IP address, subnet mask, and some sort of name resolution, whether WINS (Windows Internet Naming Service), DNS (Domain Name System), or a HOSTS or LMHOSTS file. Without those components, you will not get anywhere with TCP/IP. If the servers you need to contact are on another subnet, you will need to define your default gateway.

If you are using NetBEUI on your network, you don't have the same concerns with configuring the protocol. NetBEUI is a simple, straightforward protocol designed for small LANs and has extremely low configuration requirements. It does, however, have another concern. NetBEUI does not route. This means that your routers between subnets of your network will not pass the NetBEUI protocol. You are as good as stranded. If you use bridging between subnets, you're back in business. Find out how your network is configured before you try to rely on NetBEUI.

TIP

Resistance is futile. Just use TCP/IP.

Domain Membership

Almost every server will be a member of a domain rather than a workgroup. Windows 2000 makes this decision easier. In NT 3.*x* and 4.*x*, you had the choice of making your server a member of a workgroup, a member of a domain, a primary domain controller, or a backup domain controller. This was a critical decision during the install. You could switch a server from a workgroup to domain and back very easily, but you could not change roles between a member server and domain controller. You also could not change the domain you controlled. Once you had a domain controller in one domain, you couldn't then make it a controller of another domain. You don't need to make that decision to install Windows 2000. You'll only have the choice of joining a workgroup or a domain.

If you're joining a domain, you will need to have a computer account created in the domain. A computer account is almost identical to a user account, and like a user account, it resides in the accounts database held with the domain controllers. If the server is a member of a domain, it can assign rights and permissions to users belonging to its member domain or any of its trusted domains. This is important to your users. They should log on once to the network and never have to be asked for a password again. If the server resides in a workgroup, the ability to give rights to domain users is out of the question, causing multiple login points.

Whether you're a member of a workgroup or a domain, you can promote the server to a domain controller later by running the Active Directory Installation. This feature sounds like a nice, simple advantage, but it has a bigger impact than is obvious. In an NT 4 environment, you have to define a standard installation for member servers and one for domain controllers. Let's say you want to automate the installs for NT servers across the network. Defining which domain you want a server to control can get tricky. Do you build a different installation setup for each domain? Do you force someone to sit at the console during the installation to answer this question? With Windows 2000, you can build one installation for all servers by putting them in a workgroup and change the membership later.

Networking Components

These are the additional services to be installed, such as Internet Information Server and DNS Server. This is where I like to say things like "Ooh...Quality of Service Admission Control Protocol...sounds neat, gimme that." That's exactly what we shouldn't say. Don't overdo it here. Every option selected installs another service or utility that will consume more resources on your server.

Also be aware of the effect certain services may have on the rest of your network. Some services will require clients to be connected explicitly to a given server. On the other hand, some, like DHCP Server, act on a broadcast level and can affect clients just by being present. In addition, most services, just by being present, have an adverse effect on available system resources. Hard disk space is consumed for additional files, memory is taken up by loading more programs, and processor cycles are consumed by running excessive services that really don't have anything to do with what your server is intended to do. Unless you will specifically be using the service on this particular server, don't install these additional components.

Server Licensing

Licensing options remain the same in Windows 2000. You are given per-seat or per-server licensing modes:

▶ Per-seat licensing requires that every client on the network that accesses your server has its own license. This is the easiest method of adding up your licensing because you only account for how many clients you have; you don't need to worry about either concurrent connections from those clients into a single server or to how many servers each client holds a connection.

▶ Per-server licensing differs in that each client-to-server connection requires a license. If a client connects to 25 different servers, that client will take up 1 license on each server, totaling 25 licenses. You may know this as a "concurrent use license." It's simpler because it's easy to track—once that 26th person tries to attach, he's just denied the connection—but it's usually more expensive because you've then got to buy a bunch of licenses for *each* server.

Microsoft licensing has always been complex; here's a quick bit of advice about which way to go.

Per-seat is usually the cheapest licensing method if you have more than one server. Under per-seat licensing, you buy a Client Access License, or CAL, for every *computer* that will attach to your enterprise's servers. Again, that's *computer*, not person. So if Joe Manager reads his Exchange mail from the computer on his desktop sometimes, reads it on the road with his laptop sometimes, and once in a while comes in through the firewall from home, you need to buy *three licenses for Joe Manager*. Surprised? Most people are. On the one hand, it means that if three people share a computer, those folks only need one CAL. On the other hand, nowadays everyone's got one *or more* computers, so CALs start to add up. By the way, CALs list for about $40, although you can buy them in bulk more cheaply, and large organizations usually have some kind of an unlimited-client deal. But you don't want to run afoul of the software watchdogs, so if you go with per-seat licensing, be darn sure that you've got every computer covered! (And, sadly, that may mean that you've got to disallow employees from checking their e-mail or using other corporate resources from their home, unless they're using a company-issued laptop.)

Per-server licensing is simpler. You tell a server that you've purchased some number of CALs. The server's Licensing Service (a built-in part of Windows 2000) then keeps track of how many people are connected to the server at any moment. If you've got X licenses and the X+1st person tries to attach to the server, that person is denied access.

This sounds simple, but the problem is that you've got to buy a CAL for each connection for each server. For example, suppose you've got 4 servers, 25 employees, and 40 workstation PCs—there are more PCs than employees because of laptops and "general access" PCs. Suppose your goal is that all 25 employees can access any and all servers at any time.

Under per-server licensing, you'd have to buy 25 CALs for *each* server, or 100 CALs total.

Under per-seat licensing, you'd license each of the machines—all 40 of them—with a CAL. That one CAL would enable someone sitting at a machine to access any and all of the servers, no matter how many domains your system contains. Thus, in this case, 40 CALs would do the trick. In general, you'll find that per-seat is the cheaper way to go, but again, be careful about remembering to license all the laptops and (possibly) home PCs..

Most likely, especially in larger environments, the licensing has already been worked out ahead of time. Before starting your first install, make sure that your licensing is best suited not just for your network, but also for the way your clients use the network.

Installation Type

Finally, you need to decide whether you will be upgrading an existing operating system or performing a clean install. In most cases, this decision is a no-brainer; however, with each type also comes some unique advantages and disadvantages, which will affect your decision.

For the decision phase, let's start with a machine that is currently an NT 4 server that you want to upgrade to Windows 2000. Before you jump straight into an upgrade, you should think about how a Windows 2000 clean install will compare. Maybe your partitioning scheme currently has your system partition maxed out. Perhaps your NT 4 installation has left you with some residual problem that has just never gone away. Even if you're reinstalling the same operating system, there are performance benefits to running a clean install every so often anyway. The Registry has a unique ability to grow, and grow, and grow, without ever cleaning itself up.

If you have ever run a disk defragmenting utility, you also know how fragmented a well-used system can become. When it comes to fragmentation, one of the heaviest hit files happens to be the system pagefile, which takes enough of a toll on system resources as it is. All this clutter and excessive work being placed on your system just so it can manage itself consumes excessive amounts of otherwise free cycles left to serve your users. Backing up your data and system information, and even wiping your partitions, could yield a cleaner, more efficient, and even more stable server following the install.

This, however, is where too many people go overboard. When doing a clean install, many people want to revisit server options, service configurations, and even naming conventions. Although this is the best time for the system administrator to reinvent the wheel, it puts an unnecessary burden on your users. The more integrated your systems become, the more effect one slight configuration change will have on another. You must take careful note of all services, configurations, shares, and other settings that are defined within your system. A full system backup and a rollback plan are invaluable. If you are rebuilding an NT 4 primary domain controller, you will want to promote a backup to primary before you do anything. This will ensure that all of your account and security information is safe on another system. Finally, be ready to test every function of the server from the client's point of view when you are done. This will give you the necessary lead time to resolve any problems before your users discover them.

If you've decided on a clean install, there isn't much more you need to do. If you're running an upgrade, there are still a few considerations. The last thing you want to do is upgrade a cluttered system and carry over any issues that belong to the clutter. Many people sit in front of the server so much that they install their mail client, office suite, and other programs and utilities that are not related to what the server is supposed to be doing. These should all be uninstalled before running an upgrade. Look at your services on the server. Any third-party services, such as anti-virus, Web publishing, disk defragmenting, or other types of software, should also be removed before beginning an upgrade. By doing so, there is much less to get in the way of your install.

Which way is the best? That depends on your needs and those of your users, but let me finish this section with a bit of advice that you'll probably find unpleasant. When you look at the time involved in rebuilding user accounts, shares, services, permissions, and who-knows-what else, you'd think that upgrades are the way to go. But in my experience upgrading from NT 3.1 to 3.5 (I lost my printer shares), 3.5 to 3.51 (some domain controllers simply refused to work), and 3.51 to 4 (a number of miscellaneous problems), I must admit that I'd be *very* wary of simply upgrading a machine, particularly a domain controller, to Windows 2000. If there's any way at all to do a clean install of Windows 2000 on your former NT 4 servers, I strongly recommend it. I should stress that this isn't a fear based on any actual NT-4-to-Windows-2000 problems that I've experienced, just general experience with upgrades.

SETTING UP AND INSTALLING

Now that we have analyzed the life out of planning for an install, we should be ready to go. The actual installation is broken into three stages. The first is the preinstallation Setup Wizard. This process defines those options that configure *how* to do the install. The second stage is the text-based setup, which simply defines where to install. Finally, the graphical-based setup stage, also called a Setup Wizard, customizes everything from installed protocols and services to computer name and domain membership to the system time and date. After this final stage is complete, your server should be ready for final cleanup.

Preinstallation: Phase 1

The first thing you need to do is, of course, connect to your install source. Preferably, you would connect directly to your CD or a network copy of the CD. However, certain circumstances may make this impossible, such as, for example, a system with no operating system, no CD drive, and no DOS-based network drivers to connect you to your install source. In these cases, you'll need the dreaded boot disks. Once you have connected to your source, you need to be in the directory that corresponds to your processor—i386 for Intels. With boot disks, you simply boot the system to the first disk.

WINDOWS 2000 SETUP BOOT DISKS

Boot disks are no longer created using the WINNT command-line parameters. Disk images are stored on your Windows 2000 CD's bootdisk directory with a simple batch file and utility that allows you to create them. Another change is that boot disks no longer come in sets of three; instead, they come in sets of four. (As we all know, bigger software is always better, right?) Here's how you create the disks:

1. Prepare four blank 1.44MB floppy disks.

2. Change to your CD's bootdisk directory.

3. Execute **makeboot.exe:**.

4. Follow all prompts to create the four disks.

From MS-DOS, Windows 3.1, or Windows for Workgroups 3.11, you will need to start your setup in the DOS-based mode found with WINNT.EXE.

From a Windows 95/98/98 SE system or from earlier versions of NT, you'll launch the installation from the WINNT32.EXE. This GUI version of the setup executable gives you that user-friendly, yes-or-no click method of initiating the install. For this example, I'm using the drive letter F as the CD source on an Intel-based system. To follow along, choose Start ➢ Run, and enter the following:

```
F:\i386\WINNT32.EXE
```

If you have a system that can be upgraded to Windows 2000 Server, you will immediately reach the prompt to decide whether to run a clean install or an upgrade. If you do not have an upgrade-capable machine, you will be informed that an upgrade is not available, and the upgrade option will be grayed out.

NOTE

Only Windows NT servers can be upgraded to Windows 2000 Server. Windows 95/98/ 98 SE and Windows NT workstations can be upgraded to Windows 2000 Professional.

Following the licensing agreement, you may continue to the Special Options screen. You use this screen to define language options, advanced options, and accessibility options:

Language options   Give the choice of installing multiple languages by holding the Control key down while selecting or deselecting languages with the left mouse button. You can also select your default language, which Setup uses to define all default date, time, currency, number, character set, and keyboard layouts.

Advanced options   Customize the way the installation actually happens (see Figure 23.1):

Location Of Windows 2000 Files   Refers to the place from which you will be installing Windows 2000. I'm installing from an Intel system from F:\i386. This entry is filled in based on where you launch the install. However, if you would like to redirect Setup to another location, enter that location here.

Windows Installation Folder   Indicates the folder in which Windows 2000 will be installed. This defaults to \WINNT, but you can change it to another folder if you want. If you are dual-booting with other installations of NT or Windows 2000, you may need to specify a unique folder name. Do not include the drive letter designation.

Copy All Setup Files   Creates a complete setup source on one of your local hard drives under the folder \$win _nt$.~ls. In this folder, you will find the i386 source we are so familiar with.

NOTE

Most systems won't need the Copy All Setup Files option selected. Windows 2000 will do a pretty good job of loading the right drivers to reconnect you to your source after the reboot. However, if you fail to find your source for the text-based setup, this option will get you back on track.

I Want To Choose The Installation Partition During Setup   Allows you to specify the partition on which you will be installing Windows 2000. If you select this option, you will get a prompt following the reboot to choose your partition.

Accessibility options Include the Narrator and Magnifier. By selecting these options now, the tools will be available during the next installation phase.

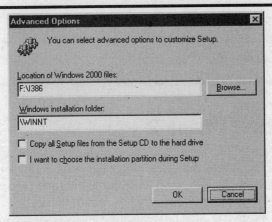

FIGURE 23.1: Advanced Options

At this point, the installation files will be copied to your hard disk, the system will be prepared for the text-based portion of Setup, and you will be prompted for a reboot.

ANATOMY OF A MACHINE READY FOR SETUP PHASE 2

Ever wonder what makes a system continue along its setup path after a reboot? Or have you ever started into the second phase of the setup, had all sorts of problems, and wanted to start from scratch? It will help to know exactly what causes the second phase to start upon reboot so you can easily remove it later. The following components will be present on your system after you complete the preinstallation phase:

▶ On the boot partition, a folder named win_nt.~bt has been created.

▶ All critical Windows 2000 boot files, including enough drivers to access the network or CD source, have been copied to the win_nt.~bt folder.

CONTINUED ➡

> ▶ In the win_nt.~bt folder, a file named winnt.sif contains the information you provided from the first phase of the setup.
>
> ▶ The Windows 2000 boot files have been copied to the boot partition if not already present. The system is now Windows 2000 bootable.
>
> ▶ The boot.ini is configured to default to the win_nt .~bt\bootsect.dat after 5 seconds.

Text-Based Setup: Phase 2

The text-based portion of Windows 2000 Setup is similar to previous versions of Windows NT, only less cluttered. We get our welcome screen, make a few selections on where we want to do our install, and then we sit back and watch the Setup program copy a whole bunch of files. It's a really simple click-Next-to-continue process, but some gotchas are hiding in the deeps.

As soon as your machine boots into the text-based portion of Setup, you may notice a prompt at the bottom of the screen that tells you to press F6 if you need to install additional SCSI or RAID (Redundant Array of Inexpensive Disks) drivers. If you don't want these additional drivers, just wait a few seconds, and the prompt will go away. In the real world, you don't use that F6 selection a whole lot anyway, so it is more convenient to just wait a few seconds rather than to keep having to say, "No, I don't want additional drivers." It's kind of like the press-F1-tab-F10 or some other machine-specific command to enter the BIOS setup. How would you like to have to press Escape to bypass the BIOS setup utility every single time you reboot your machine? To make a long story short, this F6 prompt comes up quickly. If your system has a SCSI or RAID controller that you know isn't going to initialize without an OEM-provided driver, you'll need to pay attention and hit F6.

The install starts off with a Welcome To Setup screen. You have the choice to set up Windows 2000, repair an existing Windows 2000 installation, or quit. The press-F3-to-quit option will live with you throughout this phase of the setup. If at any time during this phase you decide that you want to abort your setup attempt, this will be your escape route. Upon this exit, your system will be rebooted, but be aware that your boot.ini file has not been changed. Subsequent reboots will still by default cause your machine to restart the setup after 5 seconds at the boot menu. To get rid of this permanently, edit your boot.ini to reflect the default equal to your other operating system boot path of choice. My machine looked like the following:

```
[Boot Loader]
Timeout=5
Default=C:\$WIN_NT$.~BT\BOOTSECT.DAT
[Operating Systems]
multi(0)disk(0)rdisk(0)partition(2)\WINNT="Microsoft Windows
2000 Server"/fastdetect
C:\="Microsoft Windows 98"
C:\$WIN_NT$.~BT\BOOTSECT.DAT="Microsoft Windows 2000 Server
Setup"
```

To restore my machine to its original boot preferences, I changed the Default line back to my Windows 2000 Server boot selection and deleted the entire Windows 2000 Server Setup option. Consequently, my boot.ini looked like this:

```
[Boot Loader]
Timeout=5
Default=multi(0)disk(0)rdisk(0)partition(2)\WINNT
[Operating Systems]
multi(0)disk(0)rdisk(0)partition(2)\WINNT="Microsoft Windows
2000 Server"/fastdetect
C:\="Microsoft Windows 98"
```

To continue along with the setup, press Enter, and you'll arrive at the Disk Partitioning And Installation Location Selection screen. Be careful here. There are two things to do. The most obvious is selecting the partition in which you want Windows 2000 installed. Highlight the partition where you would like Windows 2000 installed, and press Enter.

Let's take this a step further. Beneath this screen is a handy disk-partitioning utility. From here, you can completely redo your partitioning scheme. You can delete existing partitions, create new partitions out of unpartitioned space, and format partitions in either the NTFS or FAT format file systems.

Before we begin partitioning our drives, let's go back to the planning session we had earlier. Let's say that our ideal goal is to have a 1GB Windows 98 C partition (on which we will leave our current operating system), a 2GB system partition on drive D, and a 4GB data partition on drive E. Just to give us all the necessary scenarios to describe how the setup phase partitions drives, we'll assume we have a current partition scheme of a 1GB C with Windows 98, a 1GB D, a 2GB E, and a 3GB F partition. To go from a 1-1-2-3 gigabyte partition scheme to a 1-2-4 giga-byte partition scheme, we are forced to delete almost all partitions, since we cannot reorder partitions. In other words, we cannot massage our existing second partition of 1GB into a 2GB partition without giving it more room first.

Let's start by deleting the 1GB D partition. Use the arrows to highlight the D partition, and press D to delete. A confirmation screen will appear, asking you to now press either L to continue the partition deletion or Escape to abort.

WARNING

Always take this opportunity to second-guess yourself. Once you press L to confirm the deletion of the partition, your partition and everything that was on it are gone. Ask yourself what data was on the D drive. Make sure you can afford to lose it all. Do you have a backup of the data? If the D drive contains a previous NT or Windows 2000 installation, do you have a backup of the security and accounts databases? If you are rebuilding a domain controller, have you promoted someone else to PDC (Primary Domain Controller)? Do you have a recent Emergency Repair Disk available? If you are 100 percent confident that you don't need anything on the partition, press L.

When you come back to the main Disk Partitioning screen, you'll see that the second partition of 1GB is now marked as unpartitioned space. Of course, it does no good to repartition this space now because the most you'll get is 1GB again. That would defeat the purpose of the exercise. You need 2GB. So move on down the list to what was the 2GB E partition and delete it in the same fashion. When you return to the main screen again, after confirming the deletion of the 2GB partition, you'll find that the adjacent, unpartitioned spaces have turned into a single block of unpartitioned space equaling 3GB. Just to keep it simple, we now have our 1GB C, a 3GB unpartitioned space from our combined, deleted 1GB and 2GB partitions, and a remaining 3GB partition.

At this point, we'll go ahead and create our new 2GB D partition. Highlight the 3GB free space, and press C for create. You'll move into a new screen where you're shown the total available space within which you can create a partition and are asked how large a partition you want to make. By default, the maximum available space is filled in...3GB. We want to drop that down to 2GB. Press Enter and presto! We have a 2GB new (unformatted) partition, followed by our remaining 1GB that we left out and the 3GB data partition.

After we delete our 3GB partition, it will melt into the adjacent 1GB partition, forming a 4GB unpartitioned space. We can create the new 4GB space and we're set...with partitioning anyway.

Now we still have to format our partition before we can use it. To format a partition, highlight the space listed as New (Unformatted), and press Enter to select the partition as your Windows 2000 installation directory. Really, you're not selecting a partition to format; you're just selecting a partition in which to install Windows 2000. If Setup finds that your chosen installation partition is not formatted, you'll get an additional screen to do just that. You are shown options to format FAT or NTFS. Once again, go back to your planning phase of the setup. You should already know what format you want. Once the format is complete, continue with the installation.

TIP

If you want to simply partition and format drives without doing an installation, you can always choose to go backward after the format and select another partition to format or install to, or you can simply exit the installation program.

Setup will now examine your disks. This examination is not an intensive look into the reliability of your disk. It merely runs a CHKDSK-like utility to verify a clean file and directory structure. After the examination, Setup will copy all Windows 2000 files to your chosen install location. Finally, the system will ready itself for the graphical setup phase and reboot.

CHANGES IN THE WINDOWS 2000 TEXT-BASED SETUP

You may notice some things missing from this phase of Windows 2000 Setup compared with the setup for previous versions of Windows NT. You no longer get the options to define the following:

▶ Basic PC type

▶ Video system

▶ Keyboard

▶ Country layout for keyboard (defined in phase 1)

▶ Mouse

CONTINUED ➡

Perhaps these deletions from the text-based setup can be attributed to the better hardware detection found with Plug and Play. With these changes, or reductions, to the text-based setup, you will find this stage much quicker and easier than it was in NT.

Graphical-Based Setup: Phase 3

As soon as you boot into the graphical-based setup phase of the install, Windows 2000 will run a Plug-and-Play detection phase to configure all your hardware. (This will take a while—it's often the most lengthy part of Setup—so now's a good time to go grab a Pepsi, check the voicemail, or run 5 miles.) Surprisingly enough, Windows 2000 did a better job on my particular system than Windows 98 ever did. How could that be? It's simple, really. The Plug-and-Play detection phase tries to attach the correct driver to each device in your system, so a driver must be present for each device. If no driver is available, you'll get an "unknown device" message or a generic device driver will be installed.

Since Windows 2000 has a more recent compilation of drivers, you can expect that some newer hardware will show up for Windows 2000 that otherwise wouldn't in Windows 98. More than anything, this should stress the importance of the Hardware Compatibility List (HCL). Once again, it doesn't hurt to double-check the HCL. Go to www.microsoft .com/hwtest/hcl/, and check for any recent updates or additions to the list. Some devices that were once thought unsupported may be found. If your device isn't on the HCL, it won't have a driver immediately available. You will be able to install a device driver later, however, if one becomes available.

TIP

If you have a device that isn't supported on the HCL or doesn't have a prepackaged device driver on the CD, you can use the /copysource or /copydir switch to copy an additional directory to be used during the setup. This can be used to make your device drivers available for detection. You'll find details in "Performing Unattended Installs" later in this chapter.

Once the Plug-and-Play detection phase is finished, the first dialog box we come to is the Regional Configuration screen. This stop defines settings such as number, currency, time, date, and keyboard locale formats.

Next is the Name And Organization dialog box. The name and organization listed here show who the product is registered to; it isn't used for anything related to the computer name or any other means of defining the server on the network.

The next dialog box configures your licensing options, which are the same as previous versions of NT. There is per-seat licensing and per-server licensing. Enter this information in accordance with how you purchased Windows 2000.

Next comes the computer name and administrator password definition. The computer name has already been thought out. The administrator password, especially for a clean install, is extremely important. For a clean install, this is going to be your only way to log on. Don't forget this. And please don't leave it blank unless this is just a machine you're playing around with. The default Administrator account is both powerful and dangerous because, by default, it can't be locked out. Someone can potentially crack your system by running a program that tries to log on with the default Administrator account by trying every word in the dictionary or every combination of numbers, letters, and characters. Make their work harder by putting a long and complex—numbers, letters, and characters—password on your default Administrator account.

The Components Selection dialog box defines the additional server components that are bundled with Windows 2000, including:

- ▶ Certificate Services
- ▶ Internet Information Services
- ▶ Management and Monitoring Tools
- ▶ Connection Manager Component
- ▶ Directory Services Tools
- ▶ Network Monitor Tools
- ▶ SNMP
- ▶ Message Queuing Services
- ▶ MS Indexing Services

- ▶ MS Script Debugger
- ▶ Networking Services
- ▶ COM Internet Services Proxy
- ▶ Domain Name System
- ▶ Dynamic Host Configuration Protocol
- ▶ Internet Authentication Services
- ▶ QOS Admission Control Service
- ▶ Simple TCP/IP Services
- ▶ Site Server LDAP Services
- ▶ Windows Internet Name Service
- ▶ Other Network File and Print Services
- ▶ File Services for Macintosh
- ▶ Print Services for Macintosh
- ▶ Print Services for Unix
- ▶ Remote Installation Services
- ▶ Remote Storage
- ▶ Terminal Services
- ▶ Terminal Server Licensing

Individually select each component that will be used on your server, and click Details to view subcomponents (see Figure 23.2). A white box with a check mark means the entire component, including all subcomponents, will be installed. A white box with no check mark means that none of the components or subcomponents will be installed. A gray check box with a check mark means that only some of the subcomponents of the main component will be installed.

If a modem was detected, a modem configuration screen will be next. This is where you define your calling options—in particular, your area code and what number to dial to get an outside line. These options are included in the setup so that you (hopefully) won't have to configure each dial-up session in the future to dial a 1 for long distance, a 9 for an outside line, and so on. This little part was not included in the setup phase of Windows NT.

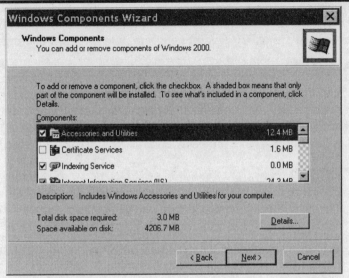

FIGURE 23.2: Windows components

The standard date, time, and time zone configuration gives you a last chance to set your system clock. Setting the correct time zone is important, especially in networks that span multiple time zones. Many utilities automatically take into account the time zone and adjust the displayed time accordingly. A server configured with the wrong time zone, even if the time is correct, would display the wrong time.

WARNING

Windows NT and Windows 2000 services have become extremely sensitive to time synchronization. Certain services rely on expiration dates, which could be greatly affected if one server has an incorrect time or date setting. Users can even be denied access to network resources if the time is off by a certain amount. Under Windows 2000, you need not synchronize time on all servers any more because that's done automatically. But that means that the Primary Domain Controller—the first domain controller you install—must have accurate time, as every other system looks to that machine for the proper time. Windows 2000 Server now has a built-in Time Service that can be used to synchronize the time. Alternatively, spend about 100 bucks, and get a desktop clock from Arcron Zeit that gets its time from radio signals from the U.S. atomic clock in Colorado and then connects to a server with an RS-232 port to deliver the correct time to your server whenever you want; I'd just schedule the server to read the time from the clock twice a day. They're available from many sources, but I got mine at www.thegoodies.com.

The network settings give you two choices: typical and custom. The typical settings assume that you will want the Client for Microsoft Networks, TCP/IP using DHCP addressing, and File and Print Sharing.

By choosing custom settings, you can add, remove, or customize protocols, clients, and services. If you want to assign static IP information, highlight TCP/IP, and click Configure. By clicking the Add button, you will be given a choice of Client, Protocol, or Service. This is also reminiscent of a Windows 95/98/98 SE machine. You can add more clients, such as Client for Novell Networks, more protocols, such as NetBEUI, or more services.

NOTE

The terminology for network settings has changed in Windows 2000. For NT-based systems, the Server service is responsible for passing information out to the network, and the Workstation service is responsible for accessing other servers and your local system. Windows 2000 has adopted the Windows 95/98/98 SE terminology. Instead of having a Workstation service per se, you have a Client service. Client service means the same thing as Workstation service, but Client service more explicitly defines the Workstation service as a client, which corresponds to Client for Microsoft and Client for Novell. The Server service is now broken into two standard services: File Sharing for Microsoft Networks and Print Sharing for Microsoft Networks.

At the WORKGROUP/DOMAIN selection screen, you can join either a workgroup or a domain by selecting the appropriate radio button and typing the workgroup or domain name in the corresponding box. If you join a domain, you must have an account created for your machine name. You can do this two ways.

The first way is to click the Create Computer Account button. After clicking OK to join the domain, you will be asked to enter an administrative account name and password. This account must be one with either Administrator or Account Operator rights. If you're using an account from the domain you are joining, enter the account name and password. If you're using an account from a trusted domain of the one you are joining, type the full domain and account name in the *DOMAIN\USERNAME* format. This will inform the validating domain controller of the location of your account. The account creation will be initiated from the server you are installing.

The second method is to not select Create Computer Account and create one ahead of time. You may want to employ this method if the person running the install doesn't have the appropriate rights and doesn't want to hunt down an administrator when this step comes up. In this scenario, go to Server Manager for the domain on which you want to add the server, and select Computer/Add To Domain, or go to Active Directory Users And Computers, and select New/Computer. Select NT Workstation Or Server, and type the name of the computer. During the installation of the server, leave the Create Computer Account option unselected, enter the correct domain name, and you should be set.

Because of security concerns, though, the computer account you create will change its password immediately upon a successful joining of the domain. This means that if you for some reason redo a clean install of a machine that already has a computer account, you can't have your new install assume that account. You must either delete and re-create the account with the same name or build the new server with a different name.

COMPUTER ACCOUNTS

Computer accounts are just like user accounts except they are "hidden" accounts. They do not appear in the User Manager window with your users. If you have enabled auditing of successful account management on the domain, you will see an Account Manager security event #624 logged on the PDC. A 624 event is a "create user account" event. Let's say we create a computer account for a new server named CADDY in the LAB domain. Under the details of the security event, the account name that was created will show as CADDY$. This CADDY$ account will be used for all communication between the server and the domain, such as validating user passwords. Once the new server and the PDC "shake hands," the server will initiate a password change for the CADDY$ account. Every 7 days thereafter, the server will again initiate a password change. The same procedure of account and password maintenance is used between domains for trust relationships.

So why is changing a password such a big deal? Well, the server is going to assign permissions to its resources based on domain user accounts. The server isn't going to blindly trust that anyone who claims to be from the LAB domain is a valid user; it wants to make certain that she is in fact a LAB user from the real LAB domain. By having this unique account with a highly secured password, the server can do just that. If the server asks the LAB domain to validate a user but the LAB domain doesn't recognize the correct CADDY$ account and password, authentication fails. This makes it nearly impossible to transport a server out of its domain and gain access to its data.

We're just about done with the install. The Setup Wizard finishes copying the files, configures the system, and performs a final cleanup. The boot.ini will now be changed to reflect the new Windows 2000 install as the default boot option. There is, however, one more step that can optionally be done here. If you need to run another program, perhaps a setup program for some utility or application, you can tell Setup to run it automatically, using the WINNT32.EXE command-line parameter /cmd:command. (Of course, using this command-line parameter means that you needed to add that /cmd option when you *started* running Setup, so if you've been doing Setup while following along, this advice is a bit late.) This could be used to run a batch file or utility to perform such tasks as transferring user data, installing programs, or other means of further automating your installs. (This is covered in more detail later in this chapter in the section on unattended installs.) The system will now reboot into a full-fledged Windows 2000 operating system.

POST-INSTALLATION PROCEDURES

After the installation is complete, you still need to perform a few more steps to finalize the server and prep it for production:

- ▶ On the first reboot, the Server Configuration Wizard will pop up automatically. It will identify the last few steps that must be completed to configure your server based on the additional network components you installed. It will also ask you some questions about your existing network to help you determine if you want to install an Active Directory.

NOTE
See Part II for more information about Active Directory.

- ▶ Check your device manager for undetected or nonfunctioning hardware components. If you removed any hardware prior to the install due to conflicts, add them back in now. Before we are truly done with the install, every piece of hardware should work properly.

- ▶ You'll want to finalize your disk partitions. In many clean install scenarios, you may have unpartitioned space left on your hard drive.

▶ For most new installations using TCP/IP, a DHCP address will be in effect. This may not be a standard practice for production servers. If necessary, acquire and configure the appropriate static TCP/IP information.

▶ In many larger network environments, certain services, utilities, tools, or other programs are loaded on all servers. For example, some sites may utilize enterprise management tools that require the use of an agent that runs on the server to collect and pass information up to a management console. Most likely, some sort of backup software will need to be installed also. Find out what additional software is needed, and install it now.

TIP

You always want to completely configure a server and install all its additional components before it goes into production. By production, we mean the point at which the first user connects to the server. Since many additional services, configurations, and software components will require a reboot, you'll want this out of the way up front to avoid further disruptions of your users' work.

▶ Run through the Control Panel applets to set all server configurations the way they should be for the long haul. Especially noteworthy are the System Control Panel settings for the pagefile and maximum Registry size.

▶ At this point, you may get the urge to walk away. Well, hold on just a minute. Too many times, people make some last-minute changes, like the Control Panel settings, and leave it at that. Even though you were never told to reboot the system—your changes were instantly accepted—there may be some unexpected side effects the next time you reboot. Just in case, give it another reboot now, before your users begin counting on the server being available.

▶ If the system is a dual-boot machine, which is usually not the case on a server, boot into all operating systems to make sure the system integrity is intact and that all data is available from all required operating systems.

▶ Once the system itself is complete, create an Emergency Repair Disk. And as an extra safeguard, you may also want to run a full backup.

▶ Finally, a step we rarely perform is documenting the server. Ask yourself if anyone else could take care of the server should you decide to take a week off for a golf vacation. If there are any special things you have to do, such as restart a service every day, it should be documented. This is a step you *must* take before you can consider your operating system "installed."

At this point, you should have a production-ready server and a method for creating this same server time and time again. It seems like, in addition to actually installing Windows 2000 Server, a lot of extra work is required, but it is well worth the trouble.

PERFORMING UNATTENDED INSTALLS

Got 50 servers to install? Getting a little tired of shoving CD-ROMs into drives and baby-sitting the setup process, answering the same dumb questions over and over again? Then you need to learn about unattended installs!

An unattended install is simply a method of providing the answers for the setup questions before they are asked in order to automate the installation process. There is no other difference in the install itself. But why do we need to automate? Usually, automation is most beneficial in large networks where Windows 2000 machines will frequently be built. By automating these installs, numerous hours can be spared that would otherwise be spent sitting at the console. Another benefit of unattended installs is that they can be run by non–Windows 2000 experts and produce the same wonderful results every time. This could help in those environments where the only on-site server operator is not an experienced administrator. Rather than spend hours walking them through an install to your specifications, you can merely give them a single command line and be done with it.

You can reduce the time spent at the console in two ways. First, you can use the command-line parameters attached to the WINNT.EXE or WINNT32.EXE. These parameters define how the first preinstallation phase will copy files and prepare your system for setup. The second way is to create an *answer file* that Setup uses to answer questions about server components and options in the graphical-based setup phase.

Command-Line Automation

The command-line parameters tell the Setup program where your source installation files are, where you want to install Windows 2000 Server, and where your answer file is located and provides other information needed to prepare for the setup. You can also use a command-line parameter to copy an additional folder to your setup source so that those files will be available during the installation. This is handy when you have OEM drivers for the hardware you want to install during the setup rather than waiting until afterward.

Before you start using command-line parameters, it is important to *really* understand them. They can have a profound impact on the installation process, so let's go over them:

/checkupgradeonly   Whenever Windows 2000 Setup begins, it checks to see if an upgrade is possible. Setup will not attempt to actually run the install.

/cmd:command   This option will launch the given command line before the setup process has completed, which will allow you to perform some additional customization or launch other programs.

/cmdcons   If you have a failed installation on your system, this option will add a Recovery Console item to your boot.ini operating system selection menu.

/copydir:folder   When you're doing automated installs for a large number of machines, this may be one of the most useful options in your arsenal. How many times have you been stopped in the middle of an installation because your network card drivers are, well, on the network? You resort to copying files to a floppy, spend 10 minutes trying to find one, format it, copy files, and hike them back to your server. What a bother. The copydir option can really help you out here. It will copy the specified folder to your installation directory during setup—while you're still connected to your network.

/copysource:folder   Similar to the copydir option, the copysource option copies a specified folder to your installation directory. The major difference between the two is that the copysource folder is deleted after setup is complete.

/debug[level][:filename]   You can tell Setup to log debugging information to a given file based on the following criteria. Level 0 logs severe errors only, 1 adds regular errors, 2 includes warnings, 3 adds all informational messages, and 4 incorporates detailed information about the setup for complete debugging purposes.

/m:folder   This option can be dangerous. When the setup process begins to copy files, the /m option tells it to look in the specified folder first. If that folder contains files to be used in setup, those files be will used. If the files are not present, they will be retrieved from the regular installation source. This can be helpful if a hotfix or alternative version of a file that you choose to utilize for every install (rather than the default version on the CD) is available. Instead of running your install and then running an update or replacing files, you can use /m and perform these tasks in one swift step.

/makelocalsource   Have you ever had problems reconnecting to your installation source after you've rebooted and started the setup? This could be due to things like Setup not recognizing your CD-ROM or network card. This option tells Setup to copy the entire source to your hard drive so that you can guarantee it will be available later.

/noreboot   There may be times when you want to launch the first stage of Setup, get your machine ready for the installation, but not reboot quite yet. This option will bypass the screen at the end of the first Setup Wizard and return you to your existing operating system without a reboot. When you do reboot, though, Setup will continue.

/s:sourcepath   This seems like a redundant switch. You've already found your source path if you've gotten as far as launching the setup. Setup even knows where it's coming from. This parameter does help identify where your source is—the i386 directory—but it also does something better. You can specify multiple source paths and have Setup copy files from each simultaneously. This can really save you time if you have a slow CD and a slow network. Be careful, though; if the first source path identified is not available, Setup will fail.

/syspart:drive   Another powerful option when you're considering mass deployments is the syspart parameter. This will
start your setup to the specified drive and mark that drive as
active. Once Setup is complete, you can physically take that
hard drive out of the system, place it in a new system, and boot
right into Setup. You must use the /tempdrive parameter with
syspart.

/tempdrive:drive   Setup will use the specified tempdrive to
place temporary setup files. If you have space concerns with
drives or merely a preference on where you want temporary files
to go, use this parameter.

/unattend   The unattend option will do an automated, no-
input-required upgrade of your previous operating system. All
configurations and settings of the old operating system will be
used for the upgrade.

/unattend[num]:answer_file   This launches one of the most
powerful features of unattended installations—the answer file.
The answer file is a text file containing any or all answers to be
used throughout the entire setup process. We'll talk about
building the answer file in the next section. If your current
operating system is Windows 2000, you can also specify a time
delay for the reboot, determined by [num].

/udf:id[,udf_file]   One of the problems with automated
installations is that you can't fully automate an install unless
you provide a name for the server, and all servers—all machines
for that matter—on your network *must* have a unique name.
This requires that you either enter the name during the setup
or use an answer file on all machines, giving them the same
name. Neither of those are viable options. The /udf parameter
allows you to specify unique information about each installation based on the file specified in the UDF file—uniqueness
database file. Here's how it works. The UDF file contains a listing of names and a section matching each name with computer-
specific information. Usually the computer-specific information
will be just the computer name, but anything you put in this

file will override the same entry in the answer file. Take a look at a sample UDF file named `unattend.udf`:

```
;SetupMgrTag
[UniqueIds]
     BS01=UserData
     BS02=UserData
     BS03=UserData
     BS04=UserData
     BS05=UserData
[BS01:UserData]
     ComputerName=BS01
[BS02:UserData]
     ComputerName=BS02
[BS03:UserData]
     ComputerName=BS03
[BS04:UserData]
     ComputerName=BS04
[BS05:UserData]
     ComputerName=BS05
```

I have five specified, unique computers defined—BS01 through BS05. If I'm sitting down to install a Windows 2000 machine for BS03, I would send the /udf:BS03,unattend.udf parameter. The Setup program will look in the UDF file and have any entries under the BS03 section override those in the standard answer file. So if the ComputerName entry in the answer file is BSxx, Setup will substitute BS03 in its place for my installation.

Those are all the possible command-line parameters that you can feed the WINNT32 program. To better see how they work, let's try a few samples of running WINNT32 from the CD located in F.

We are installing to a server that is very specific about using OEM drivers for the network card. If we start the setup and reboot, the default drivers with Windows 2000 won't get us back online. We'll use the /copysource option to copy down our drivers from the network folder of `z:\nic\oem`. Just to be on the safe side, we also want to use a /makelocalsource option so we have all files available for use. We'll launch the following command:

```
F:\i386\WINNT32 /copysource:z:\nic\oem /makelocalsource
```

During the first phase of Setup, the entire `z:\nic\oem` folder will be copied to the hard drive to be used during the installation. Once completed, the folder will be removed to free up our space again. We will also get a complete copy of the i386 folder copied to our local installation source. Between the two, we should have no problems with the installation not being able to find files.

Now, we want to launch a setup using an answer file named C:\w2k\ setup\unattend.txt and a uniqueness database file named c:\ w2k\setup\unattend.udf. To keep parity with the earlier scenario, we'll install this machine with the BS03 ID. In this case, we run this command:

```
F:\i386\WINNT32 /unattend:c:\w2k\setup\unattend.txt
/udf:BS03,c:\w2k\setup\unattend.udf
```

Answer Files

I've talked about how to launch Setup using answer files; now let's look into them to see what they are and how to create them. For starters, an answer file is like a typical INI file, around since the early days of Windows. Sections of the file are broken into groups; they're identified by their headers and surrounded by square brackets, like *[HEADER1]*. Within each section are different settings and the corresponding values to be used during the setup, formatted as *ITEM=VALUE*. Here is an answer file that I created, designed to provide every single answer for the setup:

```
;SetupMgrTag
[Unattended]
    UnattendMode=ProvideDefault
    OemPreinstall=Yes
[GuiUnattended]
    AdminPassword=Caddy^Green
    TimeZone=35
[UserData]
    FullName=BS
    OrgName=BSI
    ComputerName=BS01
[Display]
    BitsPerPel=16
    Xresolution=800
    YResolution=600
    Vrefresh=72
[LicenseFilePrintData]
    AutoMode=PerServer
    AutoUsers=5
[TapiLocation]
    CountryCode=1
```

```
        Dialing=Tone
        AreaCode=410
[RegionalSettings]
        LanguageGroup=1
        Language=00000409
[MassStorageDrivers]
[OEMBootFiles]
[OEM_Ads]
[SetupMgr]
        DistFolder=c:\nt5dist
        DistShare=nt5dist
[GuiRunOnce]
        Command0=\\setupserver\winnt\welcome.bat
[Identification]
        JoinDomain=BS
        CreateComputerAccountInDomain=Yes
        DomainAdmin=bs\brian
        DomainAdminPassword=lemmein
[Networking]
        InstallDefaultComponents=No
[NetAdapters]
        Adapter1=params.Adapter1
[params.Adapter1]
        INFID=*
[NetClients]
        MS_MSClient=params.MS_MSClient
[params.MS_MSClient]
        RPCSupportForBanyan=No
[NetServices]
        MS_SERVER=params.MS_SERVER
[params.MS_SERVER]
[NetProtocols]
        MS_TCPIP=params.MS_TCPIP
        MS_NetBEUI=params.MS_NetBEUI
[params.MS_TCPIP]
        DNS=Yes
        UseDomainNameDevolution=No
        EnableLMHosts=Yes
        AdapterSections=params.MS_TCPIP.Adapter1
[params.MS_TCPIP.Adapter1]
        SpecificTo=Adapter1
        DHCP=Yes
        WINS=No
        NetBIOSOptions=0
[params.MS_NetBEUI]
```

The first section is [Unattended]. The Unattended mode defines how you want the answers in the answer file fed to the Setup program. Here, I've chosen "provide defaults," which will fill in the answers I've selected but allow the person running the setup to override my answers with his own.

NOTE

See the next section, "The Setup Manager Wizard," for complete information on all unattended mode options.

The [GuiUnattended] section contains answers for some basic questions asked during the graphical-based setup. Look at the AdminPassword setting. This password is going to be used as the local machine's Administrator account password. It is not encrypted. If you are going to be using an answer file to build servers, you may want to make sure that your answer file itself is secured.

[UserData] contains user-specific or installation-specific information, such as name and organization entries and computer name. Remember, any of these values are overridden with the use of the UDF.

[GuiRunOnce] contains the various command lines you want to execute once Setup is complete and the new server boots up. I've chosen to have the server run a welcome batch file from a single location on the network. In this batch file on the network, I'll put in some customization routines to finalize my production-ready server. The RunOnce commands—and I'm sorry to put it this way—run once. After the commands in RunOnce execute, they will never be called again.

The [Identification] section tells Setup where to have this new server report, whether to a workgroup or domain. In my example, I've elected to put the server in the BS domain. As mentioned earlier, each Windows 2000 machine in a domain needs a computer account. I'm going to have Setup create this account for me on-the-fly by setting the CreateComputer-AccountInDomain entry to YES. The next step in creating a computer account is, of course, having permission to create the account. You must be an Account Operator or Administrator on the domain to do this honor. The DomainAdmin specifies the account I'm going to be using, and DomainAdminPassword, the corresponding password.

WARNING

Again, and I hate to harp, but this password is *not* encrypted. This one, however, is a little more dangerous than the local Administrator password. You can change the local Administrator password after the install, and the change affects only the one machine. The DomainAdmin account and password have administrative rights to the entire domain. If this account and password are jeopardized, the entire domain is jeopardized.

TIP

Notice my entry for DomainAdmin—bs\brian. The bs\ portion tells the target domain that the brian account is coming from the bs domain. Granted, since I'm joining the bs domain, the validating server will assume that I'm coming from the bs domain. However, if I wanted to use an account from a trusted domain, I could use a fully specified domainname/username to avoid confusion.

The [Networking] section allows you to use either default components or custom components. Default components include File and Print Sharing (your basic server service or ability to share files on the network), Client for Microsoft Networks (your basic workstation service or ability to connect to other resources on the network), and a dynamically assigned TCP/IP address for your TCP/IP protocol. In my installation, I chose not to use the default settings.

The next set of sections works a little differently. You'll see that one section has a value that points to yet another section—for example, the [NetClients] MS_MSClient= params.MS_MSClient. This is telling Setup to, first of all, install the MS_MSClient (this is Client for Microsoft Networks, by the way). Next, it tells Setup that the parameters to be used for MS_MSClient are found in the params.MS_MSClient section. Look a little farther down in the answer file and, lo and behold, a [params.MS_MSClient] section.

As you can see, the answer file contains a lot of information. It's actually quite easy to create an answer file, but using the right sections, items, and answers can be difficult.

The Setup Manager Wizard

The easiest way to create answer files and launch automating installs is to use the Windows 2000 Setup Manager Wizard, which is found in the Windows 2000 Resource Kit Deployment Tools. This Wizard walks you through all the questions you will need answered during a setup and builds your answer file for you.

Building the Answer File

Upon launching the Setup Manager Wizard, you will be asked whether you want to:

- ▶ Build a new answer file
- ▶ Build an answer file based on your current computer's configuration
- ▶ Modify an existing answer file

The easiest way to duplicate an install is to build the absolutely perfect Windows 2000 system and run the Setup Manager from that machine using the option to duplicate the current configuration. No muss, no fuss. Select that option and out comes an answer file that will provide all the options you have already installed. Using the New Answer File option, you can specify any options for the setup that you want, but you can also leave some unanswered for the user to input. This lets you create completely unattended installations or just partially unattended installations.

In the Installation Product screen, your options are Windows 2000 Server, Windows 2000 Professional, Remote Installation Services, or a Sysprep Install. Select the type of operating system installation you want to automate, and the Wizard immediately begins walking you through all relevant setup options to build an answer file.

As shown in Figure 23.3, the User Interaction Level screen defines how Setup is to proceed in regards to the level of input required from the user.

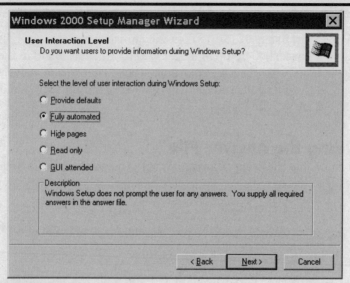

FIGURE 23.3: The Setup Manager User Interaction Level screen

You have the following options:

Provide Defaults You fill in the default answers, and the user has to accept only those defaults or make changes where deemed necessary.

Fully Automated You fill in all answers, and the user just sits back and watches. This option is, of course, the most automated and will be extremely useful when building multiple servers that have the exact same load. There won't, however, be too many cases in which this will be 100-percent effective for servers. The most you could expect is to build baseline servers with the automation and configure your additional software and components later. Most likely, you'll primarily use this option for building Windows 2000 Professional desktops.

Hide Pages The user will only get a chance to interact with Setup where you did not provide information. All pages where you did provide information are skipped. This could be a useful alternative to those scenarios in which a fully automated install just doesn't quite make sense. You'll still need someone to provide some data, but you can automate entries that will be standard.

Part V

Read Only   This option is similar to the Hide Pages option with the exception that the install will still show all pages but will not allow the user to change the defaults that you provide.

GUI Attended   This option will automate only the second phase, or the text-based portion, of the setup. The third graphical phase of Setup will be like a normal install, asking the user to manually enter all information. This option could be handy when you merely want to save yourself some time at the console. You should have fairly standard partitioning schemes for this option to work consistently, but you have added flexibility when it comes to customizing server hardware and components during the install.

Once you've selected the type of install, the next series of questions will be almost identical to the questions you encounter during the actual setup process. For each question covered during the normal, manual installation, there will be a similar question in the Setup Manager Wizard. In addition, you will get the chance to define SCSI devices that were typically done via the F6 command during Setup, as well as the option to define an additional Hardware Abstraction Layer—HAL—if your particular server requires one to recognize the system. You'll see many questions that have an option to not specify an answer at all. This will allow the user to fill in the appropriate information.

WARNING

Be careful when automating Setup options. If you consider the planning phases of a setup important, double that importance for automated installs. You will have to live with the choices you make for an automated install not only once, but for as many times as you use the answer file. Really think things through here.

WARNING

Remember the security risks when creating the answer file. You'll be asked to specify the Administrator password for each machine that uses the answer file. This is helpful for skipping the need to enter that information, but as discussed earlier, the output answer file does not encrypt this password even though the Wizard displays only asterisks in the password box as you type.

Building a Distribution Folder

Now that your answer file is complete, the Setup Manager Wizard needs to know how you plan to use it. You can use the file in conjunction with the installation source on the Windows 2000 Server CD, or you can build a *distribution folder*.

A distribution folder is a single source that contains the installation source files, the unattended answer files, batch files to kick off the setup with answer files, OEM drivers, and other custom files that you choose to include. This could be most helpful in large networks where you want to be able to create your unattended installation with the least amount of future maintenance. How? Well, instead of installing from a CD (where the path would be F:\i386), getting your OEM drivers from Z:\OEM (in which case Z is mapped to \\SETUPSERVER\WINNT), and using an answer file from a floppy disk, you can have one location to remember, one source, one batch file, and, most important, only one set of data to maintain. If connecting to a single source for installations is a concern due to network issues such as a slow wide area network (WAN) connection, a CD source may still be your best bet. We're going to walk through the creation of a distribution folder, but remember to focus on the advantages of a distribution folder—a single source.

The first thing you need to do is come up with a name for your distribution folder and a location, as shown in Figure 23.4. I've chosen to place the folder in my c:\w2k\dist folder and to share it as w2kdist.

You can also select an existing distribution folder to modify. This will allow you to change your answer files in the folder, incorporate new OEM drivers, and so on.

Two dialog boxes will present opportunities for you to incorporate additional mass storage drivers or Hardware Abstraction Layers.

Mass storage drivers are used in the event your hardware requires an OEM driver that otherwise has no support from the default Windows 2000 installation source. To install additional drivers, in the Additional Mass Storage Drivers screen, click the Browse button, and browse through your computer's drives and network connections to point to the driver's file location. You can repeat this process to add as many additional drivers as you like.

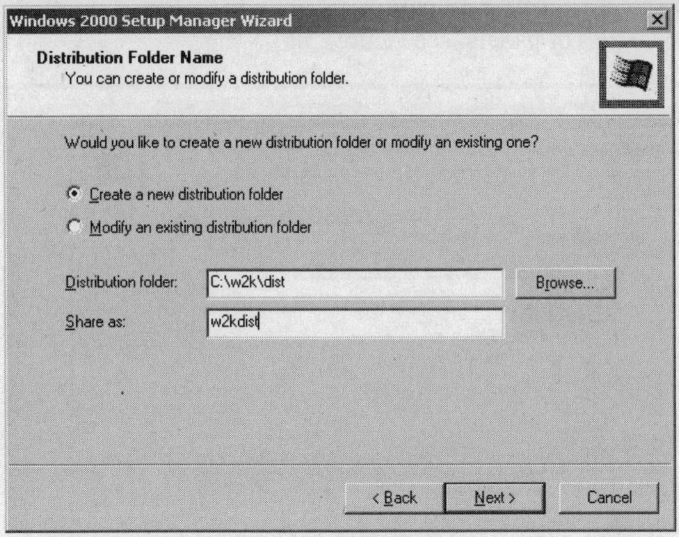

FIGURE 23.4: Modifying a distribution folder

The Command To Run option will launch the specified commands at the end of the setup but before the system has rebooted and logged back on.

To add a command, in the Additional Commands screen, type it in the Command To Run box, and click Add. Repeat this process to get as many commands into the Command List as you like. To remove a command, select it in the Command List box, and click Remove. The types of commands you might want to consider here could be simple copy statements to customize your server. For example, you might want to copy a shortcut to your Administrative Tools folder to your Desktop. You can also use the Move Up and Move Down buttons to change the order of the commands.

OEM branding is a nice way to customize what your screen will look like while the GUI portion of Setup is running. To look right, the background must be 640 by 480 with 16 colors. The logo will be placed in the upper-right corner of the screen during setup.

For both entries, in the OEM Branding screen either enter the path to your bitmap, or click the Browse button to search for it. Once you find the files, they will be copied to your distribution folder. So even though you selected a file that is local to your machine, it won't tell all installations to look for the files in that exact folder. Instead, the files will be referenced from the distribution folder share.

Here comes a really neat part of distribution folders—the selection of additional files or folders (see Figure 23.5).

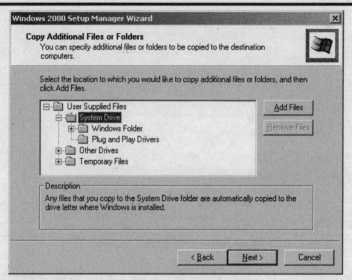

FIGURE 23.5: Copying additional files or folders

You can add as many files or folders as you like into several locations, and they will be added to your distribution folder. These folders are defined as follows:

System Drive   The System Drive folder is our installation location for Windows 2000. Click the plus sign next to the System Drive folder to display additional folders named Windows Folder and Plug And Play Drivers. Click the plus sign under Windows Folder to display the SYSTEM32 folder. Anything you put into these folders will be copied down to the installing computer's corresponding location and will stay there after the install.

Other Drives   You can also add files or folders to specific drives. Expand your Other Drives folder to display a list of hard drives to copy files to. Again, these files and folders will stay after the setup is complete.

Temporary Files   There could be times when you just want files, like maybe the Command To Run batch file routines, to be available for the setup but gone afterward. Add those here.

Keep in mind, though, once Setup is done, these files or folders will be deleted.

So let's figure out what our goal is, where we need to put the file or folder to accomplish it, and, of course, how to get it there. Let's say we have a new Plug-and-Play device—an ATI video card—that won't have the latest and greatest drivers available on the Windows 2000 CD. In this case, the Plug And Play Drivers folder under the System Drive selection is our target. Expand System Drive, and then select the Plug And Play Drivers folder. Click Add Files, and then browse for the folder that contains the drivers. Mine is a folder named ATI (see Figure 23.6). Once you select the folder, you'll see it under the Plug And Play Drivers folder.

If you want to install a set of batch files and commands that you use on your servers to the D partition, you'd add those to the Other Drives/D folder. Repeat this process as many times as necessary to put all files and folders into your distribution folder.

We're almost done. Now you need to select a name and location for the answer file in the Answer File Name screen. Make sure you put it in a location where it is readily accessible to those using it, such as the distribution folder. This falls into that category of remembering why we're using distribution folders. If I'm building my distribution folder on c:\w2k\dist, I don't want to put my answer file in c:\.

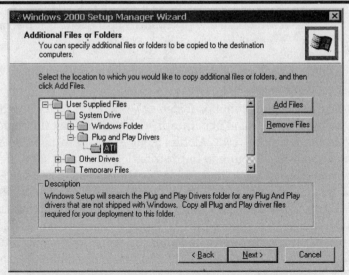

FIGURE 23.6: The Plug And Play Drivers folder expanded

WARNING

Now here is a *big* problem. I'll call it an inadvertent feature of the Setup Manager distribution folder creation process. I have chosen to place my answer file in the C:\w2k\dist folder. Guess what else happens in this folder? The installation source files, or the CD's i386 folder, gets copied in here next. In that folder on the CD is a sample unattend.txt file. My unattend.txt file is going to be overwritten as soon as the CD source file copy takes place. You should name your answer file something else, such as myanswerfile.txt, to prevent it from being overwritten.

Next, in the Location Of Setup Files screen choose the location from which you want to copy the files to build your installation source. You can use the CD or some other source. If you've already customized your installation source on a network share with updated driver files, you might want to use that source.

After the files are copied from your specified source, you are given confirmation that the Setup Manager Wizard has completed successfully and are told where the answer file, sample batch file, and, if applicable, the uniqueness database file has been created.

TIP

It might be a good idea to take a look at these files now, just to make sure they have been created the way you thought they would. This is where I found out that my unattend.txt file was overwritten with the default file that came on the CD.

For a better look at your distribution folder, open Explorer. Figure 23.7 shows my distribution folder.

At the root of the distribution folder, c:\w2k\dist, you'll see the icon of a folder with a hand underneath, which means that this folder is shared to the network already. All files required for the installation are mirrored from the CD source to the distribution folder root. This includes all files under the c:\W2k\dist folder and the folders COMPDATA, LANG, SYSTEM32, UNIPROC, WIN9XMIG, WIN9XUPG, and WIN-NTUPG. You can also see an OEM folder. This contains all those additional files and folders that I added to the setup. In the root of OEM are copies of my specified command lines and my OEM branding bitmaps. Look back at Figure 23.5, earlier in this chapter, to correlate where those files and folders were actually placed. The folders below OEM are $$, which corresponds to Windows Folder and has the SYSTEM32 subfolder, and $1, which is my System Drive folder with a Drivers subfolder beneath it, containing my specified Plug-and-Play drivers (my ATI file was placed here). Finally, I have a C and D subfolder, where anything placed under Other Drives goes.

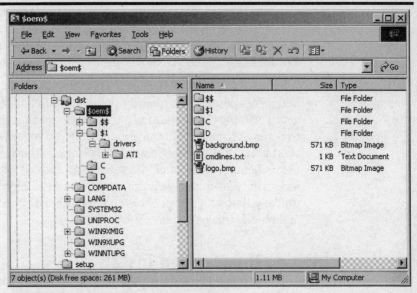

FIGURE 23.7: My distribution folder in Explorer

Setup Wizard Output Components

Whether you used a distribution folder or not, the Setup Manager Wizard creates two or three files:

Unattend.txt   This file is the actual answer file. It contains all your answers from the Setup Wizard in an INI file format.

Unattend.udf   The UDF is the uniqueness database file. This file will be created only if you specified multiple computer names to be used with the unattended installation. When launching the unattended install, you will need to use unattend.bat.

Unattend.bat   This batch file includes a sample command line required to launch the unattended install that you have just created. Several environment variables are set within the batch file:

► AnswerFile is set to the location where you saved Unattend.txt.

► UdfFile is set to the location of your uniqueness database file.

► ComputerName is fed to Unattend.bat by a parameter that you must specify. This parameter must match one of the computer names that you specified during the Setup Wizard because the install will try to match this parameter to one contained in the UDF file.

► SetupFiles points to the distribution folder's UNC (Universal Naming Convention) name. This parameter is fed to Setup as the source file location. Before you try to use Unattend.bat, you might want to look at how this variable is being set. Although the share name created with a distribution folder defaults to nt5dist, it is highly unlikely that your server is also named nt5dist. Check and modify this path if necessary.

Launching an Unattended Install

All you need to do now is actually use your answer file. To launch the unattended install, simply connect to your distribution folder, or go to the location of the files we created and launch Unattend.bat with a parameter containing your appropriate server name. If, instead of defining multiple computer names to be used with your answer file, you left the entry blank, selected uniquely generated names, or specified only a single name, the UdfFile and ComputerName variables will be left out of the install. In these cases, simply launching Unattend.bat will work just fine.

Alternatively, you could launch the setup and answer file manually, using the command-line parameter /unattend:filename. So, for example, if you had a CD in drive F and an unattended installation script named unattend.txt in C, you could start the unattended install with the following command:

```
F:\i386\winnt[32] /s:f:\i386 /unattend:c:\unattend.txt
```

USING SYSDIFF

The SYSDIFF utility is an install automation of another sort. Typical automation generally deals with walking through an installation *process*. I say "process" because the typical installation of an application such as, let's say, Microsoft Project, not only copies its files to a specific application folder on your hard drive, but to your Windows folder, probably to the System or the System32 folder, and makes all sorts of Registry changes. This prevents you from simply copying the source files to your machine and launching the program. If the installation doesn't perform all these little tasks, the program doesn't work, leaving you with two options: run the install manually or feed the installation program the answers automatically. Sometimes, this can be inconvenient.

This is where SYSDIFF comes in. SYSDIFF is really simple. SYSDIFF allows you to take a snapshot of your computer. This snapshot is a picture of everything on your system—every file, every Registry setting, everything. Next, you install whatever program you want, make whatever changes you want, and take another snapshot. SYSDIFF then calculates the difference between the two snapshots. It records everything from files copied, changed, and replaced to Registry changes. This difference file can now be used on other systems to make the same changes.

Creating the SYSDIFF Package

Before you create the package, you need a baseline system. The more complicated your pre-snapshot system is, the harder it will to be to get a difference file that can be accurately used on multiple target machines. If you plan to use SYSDIFF for repetitive clean installs, start the same way you would typically start.

The first step is the preinstall snapshot. To take this snapshot, run SYSDIFF /snap snap_file. Snap_file is the filename of the snapshot file that you will be creating. Next, install your application and run SYSDIFF /diff snap_file diff_file. This will compare your current system with your snap_file and produce your difference file. A key point to remember here is that you cannot run a difference file unless your snapshot file was created on the same installation of Windows 2000. In other words, you can't take your first snapshot on a machine, reinstall Windows 2000, install your applications, and then take your difference snapshot.

Applying the Difference File

Once your difference file is ready, you can either apply it to new target machines or build an installation source in your distribution folder that was created using the Setup Manager Wizard.

To apply the difference file to a target machine, run SYSDIFF /apply diff_file. A major caveat here is that the system root directory must be the same on the target machine as it was on the source machine. This includes the drive letter and folder name. I hate to harp on it, but refer to "Planning and Preparation" earlier in this chapter. I can't stress strongly enough that even the smallest details will come back to haunt you if you don't plan properly.

Now we'll do a walk-through of a SYSDIFF package creation and application to a new machine. We'll assume that I have a typical Windows 2000 Server installation for my network. The first thing I need is my before snapshot. I'll run the following command:

```
SYSDIFF /snap c:\snapshot.1
```

Now I have a picture of my server. The next step is to install the new program, utility, service, or whatever. I run the application setup program, let it do its own thing, and reboot the server if necessary. To conclude the difference file creation process, I need to let SYSDIFF find out everything on my server that has changed since I took my first snapshot. So I run the following command:

```
SYSDIFF /diff c:\snapshot.1 c:\diff.1
```

I've taken my c:\snapshot.1 file, used the /diff option to calculate the difference, and sent the resulting differences to the C:\diff.1 file. That's it—I now have a difference file that will effectively reproduce the installation process that I went through between the two SYSDIFF commands. All I have to do now on any new server installations where I would have otherwise wanted to run the application setup is to merely apply the difference file I created. What I'll do is copy the difference file to \\SETUPSERVER\WINNT\diff.1. Now I know it will be available to any new Windows 2000 installation. From my new server, I'll run the following command:

```
SYSDIFF /apply \\SETUPSERVER\WINNT\diff.1
```

All changes that were recorded into the difference file will be applied to my new server. Just to be on the safe side, I'm going to do a reboot to make sure all new Registry entries are read, DLLs are loaded, and my obsessive-compulsive attitude toward server reboots is satisfied. Once the server is rebooted, it should look like I ran the setup as I normally would.

TROUBLESHOOTING AN INSTALLATION

Windows 2000 produces a relatively smooth installation. Plug and Play helps in many ways by eliminating the need to know and preconfigure all your hardware prior to launching an install. You will have problems in a few instances though.

I discussed failed hardware components earlier. If your system locks up during the hardware detection and configuration phase, you have something that does not play nicely in the sandbox. Sometimes it will be obvious which component is the culprit. Sometimes it won't. Start with the obvious troubleshooting methods—the debug setup parameter discussed in "Command-Line Automation" earlier in this chapter. This will definitely help identify where the install goes wrong. The next step is to either resolve or work around the problem.

If hardware conflicts are causing problems with your install, you have a couple of options. First, you could configure the hardware and BIOS, as discussed earlier in "Preparing the Hardware," to get along with the other hardware. Maybe the troublesome hardware is a sound card that refuses to accept the detection phase. Rather than spend x amount of time trying to get it to work, pull it out of the system. Get your Windows 2000 system running first, and then add the component.

Let's say you completely blow an install at some point. You want to start over from scratch, but you don't want to format your partition and lose potential data. Before starting over, you'll want to clean up three things on your hard drive related to the install:

- ▶ The win_nt.~ls folder if you copied all files to the system

- ▶ The win_nt.~bt folder

- ▶ A line in your `boot.ini` pointing to `$win_nt$.~bt\ bootsect.dat`

Removing these entries will make your system completely forget that an install was ever happening, allowing you to start over at square one. Be careful when modifying the `boot.ini` file. If you're reverting to an old operating system, make sure your `boot.ini` default is put back to the way it was. Leaving an entry pointing simply to C:\ will let your DOS or Windows 95/98/98 SE operating system's files boot the system. Here's a sample `boot.ini` file for a dual-boot Windows 2000 and Windows 98 machine:

```
[boot loader]
timeout=30
default=C:\
[operating systems]
multi(0)disk(0)rdisk(0)partition(2)\WINNT="Microsoft Windows
2000 Server"
C:\="Microsoft Windows 98"
```

The [boot loader] section defines how your boot menu will act. This example shows a time-out of 30 seconds, at which point the default operating system on C:\ will be booted. Once the boot process continues to the C:\, it will require the standard boot files of that operating system. In Windows 98, that is the `MSDOS.SYS` and `IO.SYS`. The [operating systems] section defines the selection menu and specifies where the operating system corresponding to each choice resides. Here, Windows 98 resides in C:\, and Windows 2000 resides on `multi(0)disk(0)rdisk(0)partition(2)\WINNT`. This translates into the \WINNT folder of the disk and partition defined by the address of `multi(0)disk(0)rdisk(0)partition(2)`.

NOTE

If you want to get rid of the Windows 2000 boot menu altogether and return to your single boot up into Windows 95/98/98 SE, you must delete `boot.ini`, NTDETECT, and NTLDR from your boot partition. After they are gone, you will need to re-SYS your boot partition to make it fully DOS- or Windows-bootable again. The best way to make sure this will work is to first boot into your DOS or Windows 95/98/98 SE operating system, format a bootable floppy, and copy `SYS.COM` to the floppy. Delete the Windows 2000 boot files listed above, reboot your system to the floppy, and run a SYS C: command.

The Recovery Console

Windows 2000 has a nifty new Recovery Console that can go miles farther than the old methods of fixing broken installations. Take this scenario—one that I've dealt with numerous times. An important system file gets corrupted, umm...deleted. You know how it goes, "Let's see, NTFS.SYS, I

Part v

never use NTFS.SYS, let's just delete it to make more space." The next time you reboot, the system won't come up. Go figure. Now you need to copy a new NTFS.SYS to your hard disk. You make a bootable floppy, put NTFS.SYS on it, reboot to the floppy, and find out that your system partition is NTFS. We all know that you can't boot to a DOS floppy and access an NTFS partition. Enter the Recovery Console.

What is the Recovery Console? It is a scaled-down cross between a DOS command-line environment, certain Windows 2000 Setup functions, and partition-correcting utilities, all with the capability to access NTFS partitions.

The first thing you need to do is get into the Recovery Console. You can do this in two ways. First, you can launch the WINNT32 Setup program with the /cmdcons parameter. A brief setup routine and file-copying session will take place to create your console. Once that is completed, your boot.ini will reflect a new operating system selection, Microsoft Windows 2000 Command Console. Simply boot your machine, and then select that menu item. Of course, this method only works if one had the foresight to install the console before the system broke down. If you haven't created it ahead of time, don't worry, you can get there from the normal setup routine.

Launch Setup as you normally would—from the CD, the boot floppies, whatever you prefer. At the Welcome To Setup screen, select the repair option. From there, you will get the option to repair your installation using either the emergency repair process or the Recovery Console, and off you go.

Once you enter the console, you get a selection of all Windows 2000 installations on the system. Enter the number of the installation you want to work on, and press Enter.

NOTE

When entering the console from Setup, you go straight into the console. When entering the console from your boot menu, you'll need to press F6 at the "Press F6..." prompt to install SCSI drivers. This will let you access your SCSI hard drives or CD-ROMs that require a driver.

The next step is validation. One of the major differences between the FAT and NTFS file systems is security. Even though you can see the NTFS partitions now, you still need access to the file system. The console will ask you to enter the Administrator password. After you enter the password, you are dropped at a command prompt in the SystemRoot folder of the installation you chose. Simple!

Well now what? You're at this command prompt. What do you do with a command-prompt-only version of Windows 2000? Start off with a HELP command, which shows you a list of all available commands. You can do things like copy files, change directories, format drives, and other typical DOS-like file operations. To resolve the current problem, you would just copy your NTFS.SYS file from your floppy to your Windows 2000 installation folder, and you should be back in business. In addition, some other commands can help you get back into Windows 2000:

DISKPART   This command launches a disk partitioning utility almost identical to the utility we used during the text-based phase of Setup.

FIXBOOT   This command makes a new boot sector on your drive of choice and makes that partition your new boot partition. If you happened to destroy your boot sector information and can't boot at all, this may be your best bet.

FIXMBR   The FIXMBR command repairs the master boot record on the selected drive.

DISABLE   If you are having problems with a device that is not letting Windows 2000 boot completely—let's say you accidentally changed a device's startup parameter or installed a new service that keeps killing your system—the DISABLE command lets you prevent that service or device from starting.

ENABLE   This is just the opposite of DISABLE. Let's say you disabled an important boot device; reenabling it may be the easiest solution.

LISTSVC   Both the DISABLE and ENABLE commands require that you tell them *which* service or device to alter. This command displays a list of all devices and services.

SYSTEMROOT   This command gives you a quick return path to your SystemRoot folder without having to fight those long pesky CD commands. It also helps you when you forget which drive and folder your chosen Windows 2000 installation resides in.

LOGON   The LOGON command takes you back to your first prompt of the Recovery Console so you can choose another installation to repair.

HELP In case you can't remember the command, this is a nice little reminder.

Now that you know what the Recovery Console does, let's run through a couple of examples. I'll take the first example from our earlier scenario, a known missing or corrupt NTFS.SYS file. Once I've logged in to the Recovery Console for my Windows 2000 installation and copied a fresh NTFS.SYS to my A drive, I need to copy it to my SystemRoot folder. I should already be in the SystemRoot folder, but just to be sure, I type **SYSTEMROOT**. Now, I type **COPY A:\NTFS.SYS**. Easy, huh?

Here's another problem. You've recently installed a new service named BillyBobY2KChecker. It is set to start automatically during bootup, but as soon as it does, blue screen! Into the Recovery Console you go. At the prompt, type **LISTSVC**. You should see amongst your many devices and services that the BillyBobY2KChecker service is set to automatic. Now, type **DISABLE BillyBobY2KChecker**. The next time you reboot into Windows 2000, you should get in just fine and should probably uninstall the problem software.

The Recovery Console is a handy utility that can get you out of a lot of trouble. Once you install Windows 2000, it might not be a bad idea to run WINNT32.EXE with the /cmdcons parameter. This won't actually launch Setup; it will just configure the console. You will always have the console available in your boot menu, although it won't be set as default.

INSTALLING WINDOWS 2000 ON WORKSTATIONS WITH REMOTE INSTALLATION SERVICES

Well, by now, you've probably tried shoving the CD-ROM into some computer's drive and installed Windows 2000. You may well have had some luck at it and found that after a bit of twiddling, you could make it work quite well. "Cool," you might have thought, "Installing Windows 2000 will be a snap."

But then, you probably realized that you'd have to do it for *several hundred machines*. Let's see now, doing the exact same set of twiddling several hundred times would take...well, more patience and time than many of us have. It would be nice to be able to spend a fair amount of time on just one computer, getting it just right, and then to "Xerox" that configuration onto dozens or hundreds of other computers.

And for years, many of us did just that. Back when I worked in training labs teaching Windows 3 running atop DOS 5, it was a simple matter to boot up a workstation with a floppy containing the Novell client software, format the workstation's C drive, and then XCOPY an entire drive image from a Novell shared volume onto the workstation. The whole process was completely automated once I got it started and took no more than about 20 minutes.

Later on, with the advent of bigger operating systems such as Windows 95, drive copier programs such as Ghost and Drive Image Pro came out. These drive copiers didn't care what files were on a computer; they'd just copy a physical hard disk or partitions from that hard disk to a network folder for you. You could then set up a new computer to look just like the prototypic computer by booting the new computer from floppy and then pulling down the Ghost or Ghost-like (would that be "Ghostly"?) image.

That worked fine for Windows, but not for NT. Because NT is secure, each computer on which NT is installed has long and machine-specific strings of numbers embedded in it, numbers called Security IDs, or SIDs. Cloning one machine's NT image onto thousands of machines would lead to thousands of machines with identical SIDs. While that might not *sound* terrible, it could have some very bizarre side effects.

For example, suppose you start up a new PC with a cloned copy of NT Workstation/Windows 2000 Professional on it, logging in the first time as the default administrator. The first order of business is to create a local user account for yourself. But inside NT, that account would get an SID. Because this is the first account created besides the built-in Administrator and Guest accounts, that account's SID will be the first available in the range of SIDs on this machine.

Now imagine that Janice down the hall, who has a machine containing the exact same cloned image on her system, also logs on to her new machine as its default administrator and creates herself an account. It'll have a different name than your account—but that won't matter. NT doesn't really care what your name is; it cares what your SID is. And what value SID does Janice have? Well, because it's the first created account, you guessed it—her account now has the same SID as yours.

What does that mean? Well, suppose you made your local account an Administrator account. That means that when Janice is logged on to her own machine with her own account, she can use the Windows 2000 remote control tools to do administrator-like things to your system over the network. That's not a good thing, unless you and Janice are really good buddies.

As a result, disk-cloning vendors have come up with "SID scrambler" programs. You copy the cloned image onto a new machine and then run the SID scrambler. It creates a unique set of SIDs on the newly cloned machine, and all should be well. Microsoft, however, says that the SID scramblers from the two big players, Symantec's Ghost and PowerQuest's Drive Image Pro, won't do the whole job. I honestly don't know if this is true or if it's just Microsoft...well...being Microsoft. In any case, now Microsoft's got a method for rolling out a single workstation image to dozens, hundreds, or thousands of machines while simultaneously ensuring that each machine has unique SIDs. It's a service called the Remote Installation Services, or RIS. In this section, you'll learn how to set it up and how to get those images out to all of those PCs hungering for an operating system.

RIS Overview

RIS lets you designate a server or a set of servers as *RIS servers*. A RIS server contains the files necessary to install Windows 2000 *Professional*—yes, sadly, RIS only helps you distribute the workstation software, not the server software, onto a computer from across the network. RIS can deliver an operating system to a waiting PC in one of three formats:

Simple i386-based installation   In this simplest form, RIS is just a place to store the Windows 2000 Professional installation files. How's it different from just putting i386 onto a folder on any old file server and then sharing that folder? Not very much except in one way: you can go to the PC that you intend to put Windows 2000 Professional on and boot it with just one floppy. You'll be off and running—no messing around with the DOS Client for Networks or the like. Of course, once this installation starts up, you've got to sit at the computer and answer all of Setup's questions, baby-sitting the computer while Setup runs.

Scripted i386 install This installation is like the preceding situation, with the added benefit of unattended installation. You just go out to the target PC, boot the floppy, and away it goes. These first two options are called *CD image format* images.

Complete system image with minimal setup interaction This option is really the more interesting. In this situation, you build an entire prototypical machine, complete with applications, and then use RIS to create an image of that machine on a RIS server. You then boot the target PC with a RIS-built floppy again, and RIS transfers the entire disk image, complete with operating system and applications, to the target PC. It's not entirely hands-off, however, because it needs a bit of machine-specific customization: you need to punch in a unique machine name, for example. This kind of image is called a *RIPRep image format* image.

RIS Limitations

Before getting too excited about RIS—it's nice, but the Ghost guys needn't worry about being put out of business—let's look at what it *can't* do.

RIS Delivers Only Windows 2000 Professional Images

You can't use RIS to deliver images of Server, NT 4, Windows 95/98/98 SE, Linux...only Windows 2000 Professional images. Microsoft says they're working to make it more generic, and I hope they accomplish that, but for now, it's only a Windows 2000 Professional deployment tool.

RIS Clients Must Have Particular PCI Network Cards; Laptops Need Not Apply

I'll cover this later, but you can only get a RIS system image onto a computer that knows how to ask for one, and the only way that a system knows how to ask is if you boot that system with a floppy generated by the Remote Boot Floppy Generator, a program supplied with RIS. The problem is that the resulting floppy just contains drivers for 25 PCI-based network cards. Because it only supports PCI cards, laptops—which in general use PC Card or Cardbus network cards—can't be helped by RIS. So you're back to Ghosting for the mobile users, which is kind of silly; at least in my experience, I end up reinstalling operating systems on laptops far more frequently than on desktops.

RIS Can Image Only the C Drive

When you build a prototypic computer whose image you will then propagate all over the enterprise, you'd better build a computer with just one hard disk partition C. RIS will merely copy the C drive and whatever's on it.

RIS Has a Fairly Sparse Administrative User Interface

Although RIS doesn't require a *lot* of administration, there are a few tasks that you'll do frequently, and RIS doesn't provide a good way to do them. For example, if you had a RIS server that contained many system images, but you didn't want every user to see every possible image (which is very likely—odds are that you'd have one image for the accounting folks, another for the programmers, and so on), the only way to restrict the choice of images that a user sees is through NTFS permissions rather than via some simple administrative interface.

Steps to Making RIS Work

The first time you set up a RIS server, it can seem a bit complicated if you're not ready for it, because RIS is a bit different from other Windows 2000 services. What I'm referring to is that to install most Windows 2000 network services, such as IIS or WINS, you just install them on a server, reboot the server, and you're done. Setting up RIS on a server, however, requires fiddling a bit with Active Directory.

TIP

Before you can use RIS, you must have a Windows 2000–based domain running with an Active Directory domain controller. You also need a functioning DNS server integrated with the Windows 2000 domain—that is, a DNS server that supports RFC 2052 SRV records and RFC 2136 dynamic updates.

To get a RIS server working, follow these steps:

1. Set up a Windows 2000 server, and make it a member of a Windows 2000 domain. The server must have a fairly large drive available, and that drive can't be the boot drive or the drive containing the operating system.

2. Authorize the soon-to-be-RIS server in the Active Directory as a DHCP server, even though it's *not* a DHCP server.

3. Add the Remote Installation Services service to the server, and then reboot the server.

4. Run RISetup, the Remote Installation Setup Wizard, to prepare the large drive for receiving RIS images and to put an initial image on the drive—it's just a simple copy of i386.

5. At that point the RIS server is ready. You can add new images to it with a Wizard called RIPRep.

We'll examine each of these steps in the following pages.

Getting Ready for RIS

RIS's job is to let you take a PC with an empty hard disk, attach the PC to your enterprise network, put a RIS-created floppy disk into the PC's A drive, and boot the PC. The small program on the floppy disk is just smart enough to get an IP address for the PC, locate an Active Directory domain controller, and ask the Active Directory domain controller where to find a RIS server. Once the PC finds the RIS server, it can then start the process of pulling down a particular system image so that the PC becomes useful.

Necessary Infrastructure

But Windows 2000 needs some infrastructure to make all of this work correctly. The PC gets an IP address from a DHCP server—so you'll need at least one DHCP server running in your enterprise to make RIS work. (In case you've never worked with an IP-based NT network before, DHCP's job is to automatically assign unique network addresses to each server and workstation on the network. TCP/IP *requires* that every machine have a unique IP address; if this is not the case, the network software just doesn't work.)

Once it has an IP address, the PC finds an Active Directory server by looking it up in DNS—so you'll need a DNS server. And the PC can't query an Active Directory domain controller for the location of a RIS server unless you've got an Active Directory domain controller—so you'll need an Active Directory–based domain (as opposed to a bunch of Windows 2000 servers in a domain built out of NT 4 domain controllers). Of course, if you're running an Active Directory–based domain, you've *got* to have DNS running, so the simplified list of things you'll need before RIS will work is an Active Directory–based domain and at least one DHCP server.

A Drive for SIS

Furthermore, the RIS server needs a partition to store the RIS images. For some reason, RIS will not store images on the boot partition—which is usually drive C—or the system partition, which is the drive that contains \WINNT and the other NT system files. I found this kind of frustrating the first time I went to set up RIS, because the server that I intended to put RIS on had only two drive letters and Windows 2000 installed on the D drive. Because C was the boot and D was the system, RIS wouldn't install. I reinstalled Windows 2000 on the C drive, freeing up D, and RIS worked fine. You can have other things on RIS's drive, such as files of other types; you just can't have the system files on the drive. Remember that, although RIS will make an image of whatever file system is on the original workstation, it must be placed onto an NTFS partition on the server.

Although it's not entirely clear to me why RIS is allergic to system files, there's a good reason for it to want a drive pretty much to itself. Imagine a RIS server that contained 20 system images—how much space would that need? Well, Windows 2000 Professional itself takes up about 450MB on a hard disk, so let's be generous and say that the applications added to the image only total 50MB, leading to a 500MB image; it's just easier to calculate this way. Ten half-gigabyte images totals 5 gigabytes. But now let's look more closely at those 10 images. The vast majority of the files in the images are identical: for example, each image contains a file named DRIVERS.CAB that's nearly 50MB in size, and the file is exactly the same for each of the 10 images. That's a terrible waste of space—500MB to store 10 identical copies of a 50MB file!

RIS solves that problem with a service called the Single Instance Store, or SIS. SIS runs in the background and searches a particular drive letter—for some reason, it's only built to attach itself to a single drive letter rather than system-wide—looking for duplicate files. It then frees up space by deleting the duplicate files, putting in their place a directory entry that makes it appear as if the duplicate is still in place. In actuality, however, the duplicate is no more than a sort of pointer to the complete copy of the file. Clearly a trick like this will require a bit of magic, and that magic comes from a combination of SIS and the Windows 2000 version of NTFS—that dedicated-to-RIS drive must be an NTFS volume.

It's a shame that SIS only loads as part of RIS; I could easily imagine many cases wherein recovering space from duplicate files could be beneficial, such as a server containing hundreds of users' home folders—there's likely to be *plenty* of duplication there.

Authorizing RIS in Active Directory

Microsoft figured—probably rightly—that you wouldn't want just *anybody* putting a RIS server on the network. So before you can get the RIS service working on a server, that server must be authorized in the Active Directory. For some reason, however, you don't authorize it as a RIS server; you authorize it as a DHCP server.

To do that, find a DHCP server, and log on to it with an account with administrative powers. Follow these steps:

1. Choose Start ➤ Programs ➤ Administrative Tools ➤ DHCP to open the DHCP dialog box, as shown in Figure 23.8.

2. Choose Action ➤ Manage Authorized Servers to open the Manage Authorized Servers dialog box. You'll see a list of currently authorized DHCP servers.

3. Click Authorize to open the Authorize DHCP Server dialog box. In the Name Or IP Address text box, enter the IP address of the server that you're going to make into a RIS server.

4. Click OK, and then confirm your choice.

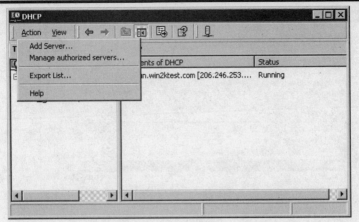

FIGURE 23.8: The DHCP dialog box and its Action menu

NOTE

If you *don't* know the IP address of the soon-to-be RIS server, go over to that server and log in to it. Choose Start ➢ Programs ➢ Command Prompt to open a command prompt window, type **ipconfig**, and press Enter. You'll see the IP address; if you have several IP addresses, select the one in the Ethernet Adapter Local Area Connection section rather than PPP Adapter.

Now that Active Directory is ready for RIS, let's get RIS ready.

Installing RIS

Next, you'll put the RIS service on the server. Follow these steps:

1. Log on to the server that you want to add RIS to using an Administrator account, and choose Start ➢ Settings ➢ Control Panel to open Control Panel.

2. Click Add/Remove Programs to open the Add/Remove Programs dialog box.

3. Click the Add/Remove Windows Components icon to start the Windows Component Wizard.

4. Click Next to display the optional server components, as shown in Figure 23.9.

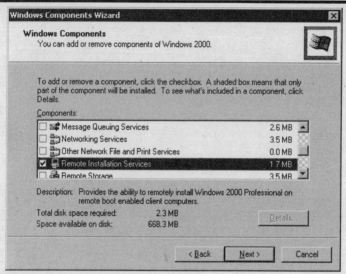

FIGURE 23.9: The Windows Components screen

5. Scroll down and check the Remote Installation Services box, and then click Next and Finish.

6. You'll be prompted to reboot, so reboot the server.

Running RISetup

When installing most Windows 2000 services, you simply choose the option in Windows Components, wait for Control Panel to pull the new service off i386, reboot the computer, and it's up and running. RIS is a bit more work than that, however, because RIS must claim its drive and set up SIS. For good measure, RIS also creates a first image. That first image is the simplest one possible—it's just a copy of the i386 directory from the Windows 2000 Professional CD-ROM.

To run RISetup, follow these steps:

1. Log on to the would-be RIS server with an administrative account and run RISetup (either from a command prompt or choose Start ➢ Run, enter **risetup** in the Open box, and press Enter).

2. Click Next, and the Wizard quickly scans your drives, looking for a likely place to keep RIS's files. In my case, it found drive

F. It wants to create a folder named RemoteInstal, as you can see in Figure 23.10.

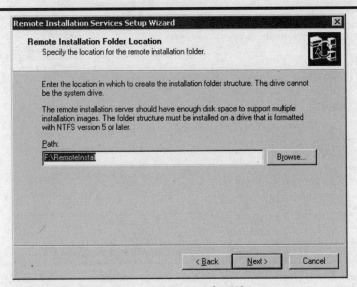

FIGURE 23.10: The suggested location for RIS images

3. Click Next to display the Initial Settings screen. The Wizard asks if you want the server to respond to requests from PCs for operating systems. Inasmuch as you don't have any useful images on the RIS server at the moment, tell the server not to respond to those requests.

4. Click Next, and the Wizard asks where to find a Windows 2000 Professional CD-ROM.

Now's a good time to pop the Windows 2000 Professional disc into your CD-ROM drive—more than likely you've *currently* got the Windows 2000 *Server* disc in there from when you installed RIS. RISetup usually isn't bright enough to know that the files are in i386, so it'll typically just suggest the drive letter of your CD-ROM. For example, if your CD-ROM drive is G, it'll suggest that the Windows 2000 Professional files are at G rather than G:\i386, so you'll probably have to help it out and tell it where to find the files. Alternatively, if you have Windows 2000 Professional's i386 folder on one of your hard disks, you can point RISetup there.

5. Click Next to display the screen you see in Figure 23.11.

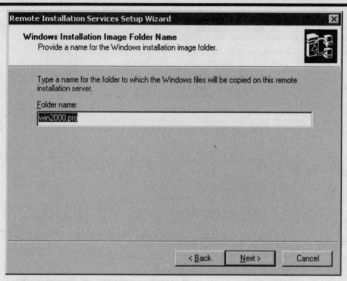

FIGURE 23.11: The folder name for the simple i386 option

Recall that a RIS server can have many images on it. Each image gets a folder within the \RemoteInstall folder. This first, simple i386 image needs a name too, and RISetup suggests just win2000.pro, which is probably fine for our needs.

6. Click Next to continue, and you'll see a screen in which you can describe the image. When you plug a new machine into the network and boot from the RIS-prepared boot floppy, you may be offered a number of choices of OS images to download. (After all, one of the things that RIS is supposed to offer is the ability to keep a bunch of images around for different uses.) This screen lets you add some descriptive text.

7. Click Next, and you'll get a summary "this-is-your-last-chance" screen.

8. Click Finish, and go away for a while. A screen similar to that in Figure 23.12 will appear.

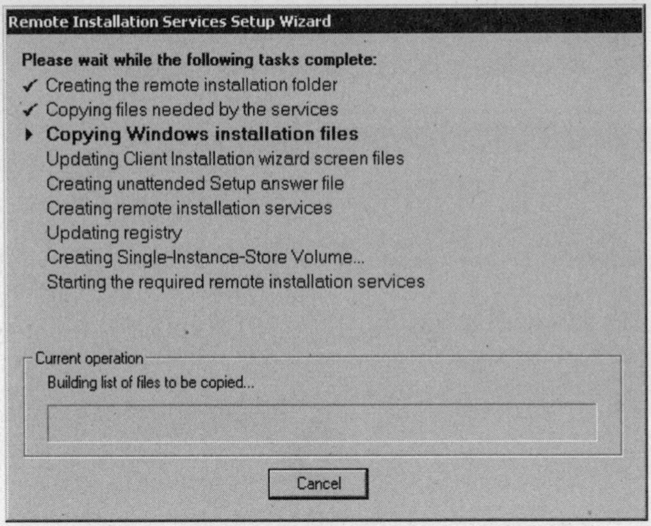

FIGURE 23.12: Progress indication screen

As you see from the screen, RISetup has got a lot to do. It copies the i386 files over to its local folder, starts SIS, and does other housekeeping. Expect it to take about 10 minutes at least.

Enabling RIS for Clients

Amazingly, after RISetup does its work, the RIS server does not reboot! But it's time to put the RIS server to work or at least to respond to requests for i386 installs. Make sure you are logged in as a domain administrator at the RIS server, and then choose Start ➢ Run, enter **DSA.MSC** in the Open box, and press Enter. If the RIS server happens to be a domain controller, it's even easier—simply choose Start ➢ Programs ➢ Administrative Tools ➢ Active Directory Users And Computers. (Notice that you've got to start the DSA in the Run dialog box because for some reason Setup *installs* the Active Directory tools on all servers, but only puts entries for those tools on the Programs menu of domain controllers.)

In the left pane of the window, you'll see an icon depicting a number of computers, intended to represent your domain. Open it (double-click or click the plus sign) to display a number of folders, including one named Computers. It's likely that your RIS server is there. Right-click the RIS computer's icon, and choose Properties from the shortcut menu to open a Properties dialog box.

My RIS server is named D (it came after A, B, and C...and yes, some days I'm just not as creative as I would like to be), and there are several tabs. Select the Remote Install tab, as shown in Figure 23.13.

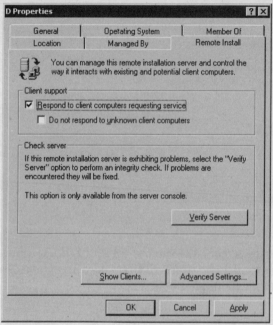

FIGURE 23.13: The Remote Install tab of the Properties dialog box for a RIS server

There's not much in the way of an administrative and management interface for RIS, just this dialog box and a few tabs in the Advanced Settings dialog box. On this tab, there's not all that much to do except to turn it on. Check Respond To Client Computers Requesting Service, click OK, and you're ready to go!

Installing Windows 2000 Professional on a Workstation from the RIS Server

It's working; let's give it a try. The RIS server is up on the network, and Active Directory knows about it. Let's suppose I have a computer that I want to put Windows 2000 Professional on (call it the target computer).

The target computer gets the attention of the RIS server through something called the Preboot eXEcution, or PXE, protocol, pronounced "pixie." (Is that acronym a reach or what?) Some computer vendors sell PCs with PXE in the BIOS. To connect a PXE-equipped PC to a RIS server, you don't even need a floppy disk; you simply plug the PC into the network and turn it on. You'll eventually get a prompt such as "boot from the network y/n?" If you let the PC boot from the network, it'll first seek out a DHCP server, then find an Active Directory server with DNS, and kick off RIS–all the code for doing that is in the PC's BIOS ROM.

Those of us less fortunate, however, are not let out of the fun. Microsoft includes a utility with RIS that will generate bootable floppy disks that replace the PXE BIOS for the PXE-deaf among us. It's called RBFG.EXE, and you'll find it on any RIS server in the \RemoteInstall\Admin\i386 directory. Run it, and you'll see a screen such as the one in Figure 23.14.

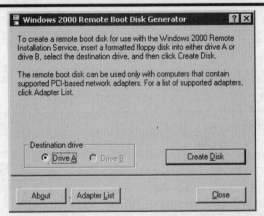

FIGURE 23.14: The Windows 2000 Remote Boot Disk Generator dialog box

Running RBFG.EXE is simple–just put a floppy into A and click the Create Disk button. A great improvement over its older cousin, the Network Client Administrator, the Remote Boot Disk Generator doesn't require that you provide it with blank floppies. That's the good news.

The *bad* news is that this will only work if your computer has PCI expansion slots and one of the 25 supported PCI network cards. Fifteen years' experience with network software has made me conservative enough that almost all my NICs are made by 3Com–not because I think 3Com makes a better card, but because I don't want to have to search for drivers–and so RBFG supports all my machines. But that might not be the case for all your systems.

Actually, let me take that back. Not all of my systems will work with an RBFG floppy—my laptops won't. Laptops don't have PCI slots in them (unless they're in some kind of docking station), so if your laptop connects to a network with a PC Card or CardBus slot (as 99.9 percent of them do), you won't be able to use RIS to get Professional on your system, sadly.

But what about the fact that new network cards appear all the time? It's not unreasonable to suggest that a year after the release of Windows 2000 you might find yourself trying to install Professional on a system with a brand-spanking-new network card that RBFG simply doesn't know how to handle. How do you introduce RBFG to a new set of drivers?

Unfortunately, you can't. Microsoft has said that they'll update RBFG.EXE regularly and perhaps distribute it over the Web, and it could be that they will—but we'll see.

In any case, if you generate a PXE boot disk, stick it into the target machine and boot the machine.

You'll see a screen with something like the following text:

```
Windows 2000 Remote Installation Boot Floppy
© Copyright 1999 Lanworks Technologies Co. a subsidiary
of 3Com Corporation
All rights reserved.
3Com 3C90XB / 3C90XC EtherLink PC
Node: 00105AE2859F
DHCP...
TFTP..............
Press F12 for network service boot
```

Press F12, and a text screen appears that says:

```
Welcome to the Client Installation wizard. This wizard
helps you quickly and easily set up a new operating sys-
tem on your computer. You can also use this wizard to
keep your computer up-to-date and to troubleshoot com-
puter hardware problems.
In the wizard, you are asked to use a valid user name,
password, and domain name to log on to the network. If
you do not have this information, contact your network
administrator before continuing.
Press Enter to continue
```

You are looking here at some client software downloaded from the RIS server called the Client Install Wizard. Look back to the first screen, and notice the TFTP with all the periods after it—that was the Trivial File Transfer Protocol transferring a simple text-based operating system to your computer.

What's kind of interesting about this is that the introductory screen, and all of the other text screens that you'll see from the Client Install Wizard, are built on a slightly modified version of HTML. You can see the "source code" for that first screen by looking on the RIS server in \RemoteInstall\OSChooser\English folder and examining the file named welcome.osc. It looks like the following:

```
<OSCML>
<META KEY=ENTER HREF="LOGIN">
<META KEY=F3 ACTION="REBOOT">
<META KEY=ESC HREF="LOGIN">
<META KEY=F1 HREF="LOGIN">
<TITLE>  Client Installation Wizard Welcome</TITLE>
<FOOTER>  [ENTER] continue </FOOTER>
<BODY left=5 right=75>
<BR>
<BR>
<BR>
Welcome to the Client Installation wizard. This wizard
helps you quickly and easily set up a new operating system
on your computer. You can also use this wizard to keep your
computer up-to-date and to troubleshoot computer hardware
problems.
<BR>
<BR>
In the wizard, you are asked to use a valid user name,
password, and domain name to log on to the network. If you
do not have this information, contact your network
administrator before continuing.
</BODY>
</OSCML>
```

If you've got any familiarity with HTML, understanding this is simple—things surrounded by angle brackets <> are *tags*, commands to the computer. They're often in pairs like right and left parentheses—<oscml> starts the "program;" </oscml> ends it. That forward slash (/) indicates that it's the end of a command—for example, <TITLE>Client Installation Wizard</TITLE> indicates that there's a command, <TITLE>

(which, as you can guess, puts a title in the screen), then there's the text that's supposed to go into the title, and then </TITLE>, which says, "That's the end of the title text." Again, they're like left and right parentheses. The <META KEY> commands tell the Wizard what to do when you press particular keys. <META KEY=ENTER HREF="LOGIN"> means, "When the user presses the Enter key, run the program login.osc." <META KEY=F3 ACTION="REBOOT"> means that if the user presses the F3 key, just reboot the system.

My intent here isn't to document the entire programming language—Microsoft hasn't completely documented it yet, to my knowledge—but to point out that you could *easily* change the generic welcome text to something customized to your particular company.

Anyway, once you press Enter, you're prompted for a username, password, and domain. The account that you log in with must have the ability to create new computer accounts. You'll next be advised that the process will delete any data on the existing hard disk:

```
The following settings will be applied to this computer
installation.
Verify these settings before continuing.
Computer account: ADMINMARK1
Global Unique ID: 00000000000000000000000105AE2859F
Server supporting this computer: D
To begin Setup, press Enter. If you are using the Remote
Installation Services boot floppy, remove the floppy diskette
from the drive and press Enter to continue.
```

Here, the RIS client software has chosen a name for the computer, ADMINMARK1, that it constructed by taking my login name—ADMINMARK was the account I used at the time—and adding a number to it. The Global Unique ID, or GUID (pronounced "gwid") is just an ID number that RIS assigned to that computer. PXE-capable machines all have a GUID built right into them, but machines using RIS boot floppies get a GUID constructed for them consisting of 20 hex zeros followed by their NIC's MAC (Media Access Control) address. Finally, the Client Install Wizard tells you the name of the RIS server from which it's getting its image. Once you press Enter to confirm, pop the floppy out of the A drive, and walk away for a half hour or so. When you return, Windows 2000 Professional will be installed completely hands-off on the machine.

RIS sets the system up like so:

- ▸ The new machine joins the RIS server's domain.

- ▸ RIS repartitions the machine's hard disk into just one large partition and formats that partition as NTFS, no matter how the drive was previously partitioned.

- ▸ The new Windows 2000 Professional system has all the settings you'd find in a typical install.

Want to change any of that? Then you'll need to create some system images.

Creating a System Image with RIPRep

Even doing a no-frills installation on a new system with RIS is rather nice. It would be nicer, however, to provide not only a vanilla operating system but perhaps a few settings and certainly an application or two—now, *that* would make the Ghost guys sweat! (But not sweat all *that* much, as you'll see. Ghost is still better than RIS. But Ghost costs money, and RIS comes free with Windows 2000.) You can do such a thing, creating what's called a *RIPRep image format* image. Here's how:

1. Set up a prototypical Windows 2000 Professional system as you'd like it. Make sure that all the code and data are on drive C—no other drives will be copied by RIS.

2. Run the Remote Installation Preparation Wizard, RIPRep, which strips the SIDs off the prototypical machine.

3. Once the image is on the RIS server, it's available to new systems for installation.

For my example, I've installed Office 2000 onto a Windows 2000 Professional workstation. To create the RIPRep image, I log on to that prototypical machine with a domain administrator account. I then open My Network Places and navigate to my RIS server, the machine named D. RIS creates a share called REMINST on every RIS server. Then I follow these steps to create the RIPrep image:

1. Open REMINST, then the Admin folder, and then the i386 folder inside that. Inside is a file named `riprep.exe`.

2. Double-click `riprep.exe`. The opening screen appears.

3. Click Next to display the screen shown in Figure 23.15.

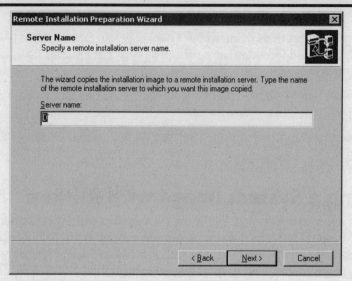

FIGURE 23.15: Choosing the destination RIS server

4. You can send the resulting image to any RIS server; I'll choose the one I've been working with, the server named D. Click Next.

5. As with the CD image that RISetup insisted upon, this new image will need a folder name. Name the folder and click Next. A screen in which you add a description appears.

6. Finally, in the next two screens, confirm that RIPRep will actually do the work.

Reconfiguring the Prototype

After transferring the system image to the RIS server, you're directed to reboot the prototype. You'll then see something odd—it looks as if the prototype is running Windows 2000 Setup all over again! In order to make the prototype's image usable to RIS, RIPRep scrubs all the user-specific settings and SIDs off the machine. Once you reboot, your system runs a kind of "mini-setup" to restore that information. Once the system reboots, you'll be prompted to do the following:

▶ Agree to the license agreement.

▶ Choose a keyboard and localization.

- ▶ Fill in a username and organization.

- ▶ Specify a computer name and password for the default Administrator account.

- ▶ Choose a time zone.

- ▶ Decide whether to do typical or custom network settings.

- ▶ Join either a workgroup or domain.

The mini-setup doesn't take nearly as long as Setup did, however, because it's not necessary to run Plug and Play.

Delivering a RIPRep Image to a Target PC

Now how do you deliver that operating-system-with-applications image to a target PC? In exactly the same way that you got the first one onto a target PC. Either press F12 when the PXE ROM tells you to, or boot from an RBFG-generated floppy.

NOTE

You do not need to build a separate RBFG-generated floppy for each system. You can build just one and carry it with you, using it to start as many different RIS image transfers as you'd like.

Now that you've got more than one image on your server, the Client Installation Wizard will offer you one more screen. After you log in, it'll list the available images and their descriptions, allowing you to choose one. Then, as before, it'll remind you that it's about to destroy any data on the hard disk, and, from there, all you need do is to pop that RBFG floppy out of the floppy drive, walk away, and come back in a half hour— the entire install is hands-off.

WARNING

Once again, don't take the "this will zap the hard disk" warning lightly. If (for example) your RIPRep image is based on a system with a 1500MB C drive formatted as FAT32, RIS will repartition and reformat the C: drive of the target PC to 1500MB and FAT32 no matter how the drive was partitioned on the target PC before. RIS will leave any remaining space unpartitioned.

Enabling Users to Start RIS Transfers

The idea, then, with RIS is this: Joe comes into your office and tells you that his computer's hosed and would you reinstall his operating systems and applications when you get a chance? You reply that you've got an even better idea and hand him an RBFG floppy. You tell him to boot it, press F12 when prompted, log in to the Client Installation Wizard, and then choose the Standard Productivity Desktop option, an image that you've built with all the company's standard desktop software—Office, the PalmPilot HotSync software, and Lotus Organizer.

Now, if Joe goes back and tries this, he'll see an error message like this:

```
The user Joe currently logged on to this computer does not
have the permissions needed to create a computer account or
modify the computer account NEWPC (NEWPC$) within the domain
apex.com.
This error may also indicate that the server D supporting
this client cannot contact the directory service to perform
the operation.
Restart this computer and try again. If the problem persists,
contact your network administrator for assistance.
```

What's going on here is that, in the process of installing the RIS image on Joe's machine, RIS must also create a *machine account*—remember, in Windows 2000 domains, machines have accounts just as people do—and not just any old user can create machine accounts. By the way, he's also got to be able to delete machine accounts, as there's probably already a machine account floating around that has the same name as the one he's about to create, as well as a few other machine permissions.

You *could* make him a member of the Account Operators group for just a day so that he could do the install, but that's an awful lot of power to give a user just so he can kick off a RIS image transfer. So instead, let's create an altogether new group called Installers, which will have the power to create and delete machine accounts but nothing else. Now, creating the Installers group will be a bit of a lengthy procedure, but you'll only have to do it once. Once you've got the Installers group defined, you can then just simply add any user to that group before giving him an RBFG floppy to reinstall his system. (And for safety's sake, you can remove him the next day, after he's got his system back up and running.)

Creating the Installers Group

You'll find that creating the Installers group is easiest if you are sitting at a domain controller. Follow these steps:

1. Log in using an account with domain administrator rights, and then start the Directory Service Administrator DSA.MSC by choosing Start ➤ Programs ➤ Administrative Tools ➤ Active Directory Users And Computers. In the left pane, you'll see an icon representing your domain with a plus sign next to it; click the plus sign to expand the domain.

2. Next, create the Installers group. Right-click the Users folder, and choose New/Group from the shortcut menu to open the Create New Object-(Group) dialog box.

3. In the Name Of New Group field, enter **Installers**. This will create a global group named Installers, which is what we want, so click OK to close the dialog box.

4. Choose View ➤ Advanced Features to open the Properties dialog box at the Security tab, which is essential to give Installers the permissions that it needs.

5. Next, we're going to give some domain-wide permissions to the Installers group, so right-click the domain's icon and choose Properties from the shortcut menu to open the *Domain Name* Properties dialog box.

6. Click the Security tab. Installers doesn't currently have any permissions, so we'll need to add a record for them. Click the Add button to open the Select Users, Computers Or Groups dialog box.

7. Click the Installers group, click Add, and then click OK to close the dialog box.

8. Back in the *Domain Name* Properties dialog box, find Installers in the Name list box, click it, and then click the Advanced button to open the Access Control Settings For *Domain Name* dialog box.

9. Again, locate Installers—this part of the operating system isn't intended for regular old users, so the UI's a bit convoluted here—to indicate the Installers record that you created.

It'll currently have some basic permission such as Read or the like. Click the View/Edit button to open the Permission Entry For *Domain Name* dialog box.

10. Scroll down in the Permissions list box to find the Create Computer Objects permission. You'll see two columns of check boxes, one labeled Allow and the other Deny. Check the Allow box, and do the same for the next permission, Delete Computer Objects. In the Apply To list box, choose This Object and All Child Objects. What you're doing here is giving Installers the right to create and destroy new objects in the folder, but *only* computer objects—machine accounts. Click OK to close the Permission Entry For *Domain Name* dialog box.

11. That permission made the folders accept the new machine objects. But once created, Installers have no control over the machine accounts themselves, so we'll add another permission record to give Installers complete control over machine accounts. From the Access Control Settings For *Domain Name* dialog box, click Add, choose Installers, and click OK to open the Permission Entry For *Domain Name* dialog box.

12. Click the Apply Onto drop-down list box, and choose Computer Objects. Check the Allow box next to the Full Control permission. Click OK to return to the Access Control Settings For *Domain Name* dialog box.

13. Scroll down in the Permission Entries list box, and you'll see a new entry for Installers, a "create/delete" permission—that's what you just created—as well as a "full control" record for "machine objects."

14. Click OK to close the Access Control Settings dialog box.

15. Click OK to close the *Domain Name* Properties dialog box.

Now that that's done, you can put Joe into the Installers group:

1. Open the Users folder, and locate the Installers group.

2. Right-click Installers, and choose Properties from the short-cut menu to open the Properties dialog box.

3. Click the Members tab.

4. Click the Add button.

5. Find Joe's account, click Joe, click OK, and then click OK again.

Finally done. Yes, that was a bit of work, and you'd kind of wonder why Microsoft didn't just build the group for us. I sure don't know.

Restricting RIS Image Choices

Once you turn Joe loose with that floppy, you just might not want him accidentally loading the wrong image. He might decide that he'd *love* to download the Programmer's Workstation image, complete with the C++ and Java compilers, interactive debuggers, and the like—none of which he has any use for. You can, as it turns out, keep him from seeing all the images on the RIS server. But you'd never guess how you do it.

The RIS server has a set of directories that exist in \RemoteInstall\ setup\English\Images\. If you've got a simple i386 installation called win2000.pro, its image is in \RemoteInstall\Setup\English\ Images\Win2000.Pro. Each RIS image, then, has a folder inside \RemoteInstall\Setup\English\Images\; remember that.

Each image contains a folder named i386, which contains yet *another* folder named Templates. *That* folder contains a file named with the extension .sif. It's an answer file that RIS uses to be able to do the installation without any user intervention. So, for example, if you have an image called Programmers, there's an SIF file in \RemoteInstall\Setup\English\Images\i386\Templates.

The way that you keep Joe out of the Programmers image is to set the NTFS permissions on the SIF file so that he's denied Read access. Once RIS sees that he's not supposed to see the file, the Programmers image won't even be offered to him.

PUTTING IT ALL TOGETHER

Before you can say that you have truly mastered installing Windows 2000, you will need to apply all the bits and pieces of the install to your network. Exactly what are you tasked with? Building a single server? Probably a manual install will suffice. Building a Windows 2000 Server rollout for a large enterprise? You might consider building an unattended install using a distribution folder. Use the option to include additional folders under the distribution folder so that all your OEM drivers are included. You may also want to include all additional server components in your distribution folder, like our network management agent. Finally, use the /cmd parameter to launch an installation batch file or even a SYSDIFF to have those last components installed. Just to cover all components, let's do a high-level walk-through of a best-case installation scenario:

- ▶ The actual installation is going to use a fully automated answer file that we've built with the Setup Manager Wizard.

- ▶ We'll specify multiple computer names and use a uniqueness database file with our answer file, or we'll have a randomly generated computer name. This way, we don't need to worry about duplicate names on the network.

- ▶ In the Setup Manager Wizard, we'll tell Setup to have the Administrator account automatically log on once the installation is done. This will help kick off the next step, without requiring us to come back to log on.

- ▶ We'll incorporate the GUIRunOnce command of \\setupserver\ winnt\welcome.bat in our answer file. That will run after Setup has completed and Windows 2000 boots up into normal operational mode for the first time.

- ▶ \\setupserver\winnt\welcome.bat will contain, amongst other things, a SYSDIFF /apply \\setupserver\winnt\diff.1 command that will apply all new applications that are not bundled with the regular Windows 2000 setup routine.

- ▶ \\setupserver\winnt\welcome.bat could also contain a SHUTDOWN command from the Resource Kit to reboot the server.

Our end result should be that we kicked off an unattended installation, came back later, and sat down at a server that was 99-percent production ready. The last 1 percent will be left to our post-installation procedures, such as assigning a static IP address, documenting our server, and performing a follow-up reboot.

Ideally, your installation itself should be considered a deliverable product—a single-point-and-click process that completely builds a server that is ready for production. True, the odds of an enterprise-wide Windows 2000 rollout being that simple are really slim. However, the amount of time you spend putting an installation package together up front will be saved for each server that uses it later on. Let's say it takes you a solid, uninterrupted 40-hour week to build this installation source, an average of 4 hours per manual install, but only 1 hour per automated install. Compare the time commitments between building an automated installation source and using automated installs with running all manual installs when dealing with only 15 server installations:

$$40 \text{ hrs} + (15 \times 1 \text{ hr}) = 55 \text{ total hrs}$$

$$15 \times 4 \text{ hrs} = 60 \text{ hrs}$$

Remember, even though an automated install may still take several hours to complete, we only need to be at the server for a very small portion of that time. Using similar estimates, the time difference in a network on which you are installing 100 servers would be 140 hours to 400 hours. As I said before, anyone can install Windows 2000. Making that installation a repeatable process that works for an entire enterprise while reducing the amount of time and cost required for such a rollout is the tricky part. Look beyond the actual installation, plan it ahead of time, and treat your installation as more than just installing Windows 2000.

WHAT'S NEXT?

As we mentioned earlier in this book, if you've used previous versions of Windows or NT, you'll find in both Windows 2000 Professional and Windows 2000 Server that some items are in new locations. In Windows 2000 Server, you'll also find that some tools have been combined into other tools. In the next chapter, we'll take a look at the Windows 2000 Server interface and describe in detail the new Microsoft Management Console.

Chapter 24

THE WINDOWS 2000 SERVER USER INTERFACE AND MMC

When I first installed Windows 2000, it looked to me a lot like Windows NT 4. So they added a couple of snazzy new icons on the Desktop—big deal. "This'll be a snap," I thought. "What's all the fuss?" But then I opened Control Panel. Don't bother looking for the Network applet, because it's not there. And it's not the only thing missing. The Services applet? Gone. The Administrative Tools group is still there, but most of our old friends, such as Server Manager and User Manager For Domains, have been eaten by this ever-present thing called the Microsoft Management Console (MMC).

Adapted from *Mastering Windows 2000 Server, Second Edition,* by Mark Minasi, Christa Anderson, Brian M. Smith, and Doug Toombs

ISBN 0-7821-2774-6   1593 pages $49.99

Where is everything? What's an old administrator to do? If you've already been fooling around with Windows 2000, you know the answers to these questions, and you can safely skip this chapter. If you are completely new to Windows 2000, this chapter will help you find those tools in their new homes. Plus we'll take a peek into the MMC framework and get you started customizing MMC tools to fit your administrative needs.

WHERE ARE THEY NOW?

When NT 4 was released, NT 3.51 administrators were comforted by the fact that most of the administrative tools were the same. We didn't have to relearn those everyday tasks. To add network services and protocols, you went to the Network applet in Control Panel; for user and group configuration, you went to User Manager and User Manager For Domains. To administer servers and shares and services remotely, we had Server Manager. So it is very disconcerting to see, upon loading Windows 2000 Server, that the three most commonly used tools seem to have disappeared. Microsoft has decided that Control Panel will now be for user options and simple configuration changes, so several items have been moved out of Control Panel and integrated into new administrative tools.

In this section, we'll take a look at some of the most glaring interface changes that an NT 4 administrator must face, and I'll show you the new procedures for those common tasks. I won't bore you with too many details; rather, I just want to get you pointed in the right direction. Specifically, I'll answer these questions:

- ▶ Where'd they put the Network applet?

- ▶ What happened to User Manager and User Manager For Domains?

- ▶ No more Server Manager?

- ▶ Where is the Disk Administrator?

- ▶ What happened to the device management tools in Control Panel (SCSI, Tape Device, and so on)? Where do I install a new device now?

- ▶ Where is the Services applet?

- ▶ What is this Network And Dial-Up Connections tool?

- ▶ Did they do away with NT Diagnostics?

This quick reference should help you weather the interface changes gracefully and have you navigating Windows 2000 Server like a pro in no time at all.

Where'd They Put the Network Applet?

Under NT 4, to configure almost any network-related information, you only had to open the Network applet in Control Panel. There you could change the machine name and workgroup name, join a domain, and add/remove adapters, protocols, and network services such as DHCP (Dynamic Host Configuration Protocol), WINS (Windows Internet Naming Service), or DNS (Domain Name System). Windows 2000 Server takes a different approach. These functions have been dispersed into several tools.

Changing a Machine Name or Workgroup/Domain

To change a machine's name or a workgroup name or to join a domain, follow these steps:

1. Open the System Properties dialog box in one of the following ways:

   ▶ Choose Start ➢ Settings ➢ Control Panel ➢ System.

   ▶ On the Desktop, right-click My Computer, and choose Properties from the shortcut menu.

2. Select the Network Identification tab, as shown in Figure 24.1. The rules that apply for joining a workgroup or domain in NT 4 also apply to Windows 2000; you must be logged on as a local administrator, and if you want to join the computer to a domain, you must also have a valid username and password to create the machine account.

NOTE

If the machine is a domain controller, you will not be able to change the identification information here.

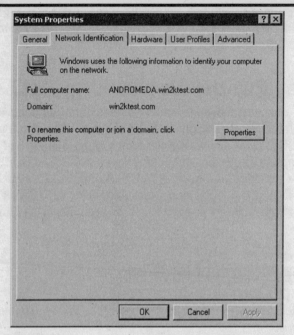

FIGURE 24.1: The Network Identification tab in the System Properties dialog box

3. Click the Properties button to open the Identification Changes dialog box. From here, you can change the machine name and workgroup or domain affiliation. Click the More button if you want to change the DNS suffix (domain name) or the NetBIOS name for the computer as well.

4. Click OK when you finish making your changes.

Adjusting Network Protocols

Under Windows 2000, you use the Network And Dial-Up Connections folder to install protocols. Follow these steps:

1. Open the Network And Dial-Up Connections folder (see Figure 24.2) in one of the following ways:

- ▶ Choose Start ➢ Setting ➢ Network And Dial-Up Connections.

- ▶ On the Desktop, right-click My Network Places, and choose Properties from the shortcut menu.

As shown in Figure 24.2, each connection displays an icon. For example, if the server has a modem and two network cards, you'll see an icon for each network adapter (they are labeled Local Area Connection by default, but you can rename them), one for each dial-up networking connection, plus the Make New Connection icon. The dial-up networking connections don't represent different modems, but rather what we used to call Address Book entries in NT 4. You can see the type of connection and status on the left in the window when you highlight the icon. It's a good idea to rename the Local Area Connection icons to something meaningful, especially if the machine has multiple networking devices.

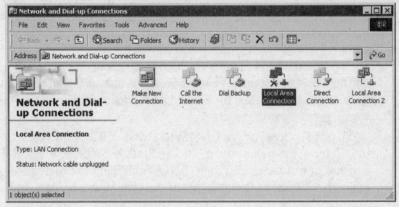

FIGURE 24.2: The Network And Dial-Up Connections folder

2. To add a protocol, right-click the Local Area Connection icon for the device that will use the protocol, and choose Properties to open the Local Area Connection Properties dialog box. Now this is beginning to look familiar.

3. Click the Configure button to display the device information, or click Install to add a client, a protocol, or a service to this device. Clicking Install opens the Select Network Component Type dialog box.

4. To add a protocol, select Protocol, and click Add to open the Select Network Protocol dialog box.

    If you add a protocol, it becomes available to every connection. Likewise, if you remove a protocol as opposed to just

unchecking the box that indicates the device driver is to use
that protocol, it is removed for all connections. Also, you
can't add or remove all of the same network components here
as you could in the Network applet in NT4, but you can add
and remove the Microsoft and NetWare redirector and server
components.

5. Click OK twice.

Adjusting and Adding/Subtracting Network Services

To load, unload, or configure Microsoft File and Print Services or the
Gateway (and Client) Services for NetWare, use the Properties dialog box
for the correct connection in the Network And Dial-Up Connections folder,
as described in the preceding section. By the way, the Workstation service
is now called the Client for Microsoft Networks, and the Server service is
called File and Printer Sharing for Microsoft Networks. Presumably this
provides consistency with Windows 95 and Windows 98/98 SE. However,
these items are still called the Server and Workstation services if you want
to stop, pause, or restart them.

You add services such as DNS, WINS, and DHCP using the
Add/Remove Programs applet. Choose Start ➣ Settings ➣ Control Panel
to open Control Panel, and then choose Add/Remove Programs ➣ Add
Or Remove Windows Components to start the Windows Components
Wizard. Select Networking Services, and then click Details to open the
Networking Services dialog box, as shown in Figure 24.3.

If you still happen to be using the Web view instead of the classic view
for your folders, there is also a helpful link (called Add Network Components) in the Network And Dial-Up Connections folder, visible on the left
side of the window. Clicking this link starts the Windows Optional Networking Components Wizard. Although Web view for folders is generally
annoying, and I'll show you how to turn it off later in the chapter, this
link is worth mentioning because it saves you a few mouse-clicks (or touch-
pad taps, as the case may be). As you see in Figure 24.4, this Wizard provides a subset of the components from the Windows Components Wizard,
namely management tools such as SNMP and Network Monitor, Other
Network File and Print Services (Print Services for Unix, Services for Macintosh), plus the full list of networking services shown in Figure 24.3.

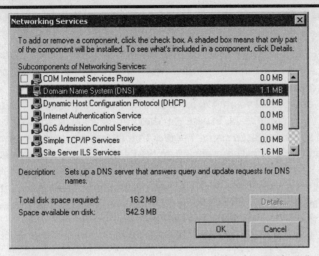

FIGURE 24.3: The Networking Services dialog box in the Windows Components Wizard

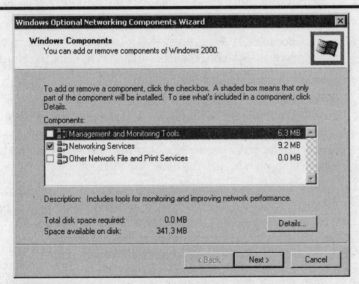

FIGURE 24.4: Optional networking components

Configuring and Installing/Removing Network Adapters

How do you add a network adapter under Windows 2000 Server? Hopefully, you won't have to. Plug and Play takes away most of your hardware woes, but once in a while you might need to add an adapter manually. For example, at one point I wanted to load the Microsoft loopback adapter on my laptop to run some tests. In case you don't already know, the loopback adapter is a software-based *virtual adapter* that allows you to load network protocols and services without having an actual network card installed. The problem is, it's not Plug-and-Play compliant, as you would deduce—how do you auto-detect a virtual adapter? The trick to remember here is that an adapter (even the Microsoft loopback adapter) is considered hardware, so you'll need to invoke the Add/Remove Hardware Wizard.

To add an adapter, follow these steps:

1. Start the Add/Remove Hardware Wizard in one of the following ways:

   ▶ Choose Start ➤ Settings ➤ Control Panel ➤ Add/ Remove Hardware.

   ▶ Choose Start ➤ Settings ➤ Control Panel ➤ System to open the System Properties dialog box, click the Hardware tab, and click the Hardware Wizard button .

2. From the Welcome screen, choose Next, and then select Add/Troubleshoot A Device in the next window, as shown in Figure 24.5. The annoying thing is that the Wizard now searches for new Plug-and-Play hardware. It would be nice to have an option to skip the detection attempt.

3. Next, the Wizard presents a list of devices installed on your system. Select Add A New Device, and click Next to open the Choose A Hardware Device screen.

4. The Wizard now asks you whether to search for new hardware (again!) or choose it from a list. Actually, if you choose to search for new hardware, Windows 2000 Server searches for hardware that is not Plug-and-Play compatible. If you choose to select your device from a list, the Wizard will display a list of device types. Scroll through the list, choose the device type you want to install, such as a network adapter, and click Next.

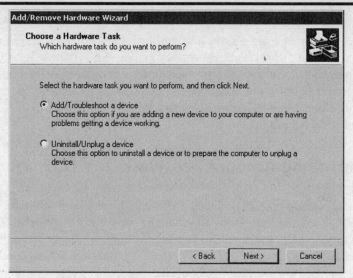

FIGURE 24.5: Choosing a hardware task

5. Select your adapter from a list of known devices, or choose Have Disk if your adapter is not on the list and you have the driver from the manufacturer. Click Next.

6. If you've selected from a list of known devices, confirm the choices you've made, and finish the Wizard. If you've chosen Have Disk, point the Wizard to the driver files (on a hard drive, floppy, or other location). From that point, the installation procedure depends on the device. You may or may not be prompted for device settings.

What Happened to User Manager and User Manager for Domains?

I'll discuss user and group management more thoroughly in Chapter 25, but for now, just remember that whereas NT 4 created both local user accounts and domain accounts with slightly different versions of the User Manager, Windows 2000 stores local user and domain accounts in very different places and with somewhat different tools. You create *local* user accounts (on stand-alone and non–domain controller systems) using the Computer Management tool, and you create *domain* accounts, or any accounts on a domain controller for that matter, with Active Directory

Users And Computers (by the way, what an awkward name for an admin tool). You can use these tools to add and modify user accounts; assign home directories, login scripts, and profiles; create and manage groups; and reset a user's password. However, you may recall that the NT 4 User Manager tools are also used to set account password and lockout policies, assign user rights, and even create trust relationships. Except for trust relationships, these functions are now administered using Group Policy or the Local Security Policy tool.

Controlling Account Password and Lockout Policies

To set account password and lockout policies for the local machine, use the Local Security Policy tool. However, if your system is part of an Active Directory domain, you'll set the domain-wide password and lockout policy using the Domain Security Policy tool. Details about setting local and group policies are included in Chapter 25, but here's a quick rundown, from the domain perspective. Log on to a domain controller as a domain administrator, and follow these steps:

1. Start the program named Domain Security Policy in the Administrative Tools group.

2. In the left pane, open Account Policies (shown in Figure 24.6). From this point on, setting account and lockout policies for the domain is similar to using the Local Security Policy tool to set policy for a stand-alone server. Expand Password Policy or Account Lockout Policy, and double-click the policy items that appear in the right pane. You'll see check boxes to turn on the policy (Define This Policy Setting) and, depending on the policy, parameters to set, such as Minimum Password Age or Account Lockout Count.

3. Once you've defined your setting, click OK, and you'll see the changed setting displayed in the right pane of the window.

4. Simply close the tool to save the change. There is no menu item to apply or save changes.

Audit policy, user rights, and some other miscellaneous security options that were previously available only by editing the Registry (or using some Resource Kit tool) are found in the Local Policies component under Security Options.

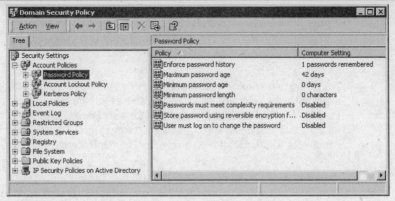

FIGURE 24.6: Setting the machine's password policy

Building Trust Relationships

In Windows 2000, you shouldn't have to create trust relationships at all; trust is implicitly built when new domains are created in an existing forest. Only when you want to set up access to resources in other preexisting forests will you need to create trust relationships. This is done using Active Directory Domains And Trusts. In Control Panel, open the Administrative Tools applet, and then select Active Directory Domains And Trusts. Right-click the icon representing your domain and choose Properties from the shortcut menu to open the Properties dialog box. Select the Trusts tab. From this point, it's just like establishing a trust relationship in NT 4. You can add a trusted domain or add domains that trust your domain.

No More Server Manager?

There is no more Server Manager tool in Windows 2000. Okay, it's still there, like the File Manager from NT 3.51 persisted in NT 4. It's not included in the Administrative Tools group any more, but you can open it by choosing Start ➢ Run and then entering **srvmgr.exe** in the Open text box. And Server Manager is still useful for administering NT machines in a domain. But the problem with the Server Manager tool is that it attempts to cover two different areas of remote administration: those functions that are machine specific, such as shares and services, and those functions that relate to domain administration, such as promoting backup domain controllers. Windows 2000 Server attempts to clear up the confusion by separating types of functions into separate components (although not necessarily into separate tools).

TIP

You'll find that Windows 2000 comes with a number of tools that Microsoft didn't put in the Programs menu. Many of those tools are implemented as MMC snap-ins (see "A Microsoft Management Console Primer" later in this chapter for more information on MMC), and a great way to locate them is to search for `*.msc` files (choose Start ➢ Search ➢ For Files Or Folders).

The functions of Server Manager that are machine related (such as shares and services) have moved to the Computer Management tool. Those related to domain management have moved to Active Directory Users And Computers and, to a lesser extent, Active Directory Sites And Services.

Shares, Services, and Alerts

To create and manage file shares on your local machine or on a remote machine, open Computer Management in the Administrative Tools group. To create a share remotely, follow these steps:

1. Select Computer Management, and choose Action ➢ Connect To Another Computer to open the Select Computer dialog box.

2. Select the remote machine from the list, and click OK.

3. In the Tree pane, expand System Tools To Shared Folders, and then open Shares, as shown in Figure 24.7.

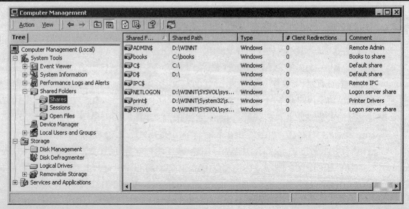

FIGURE 24.7: Viewing shared folders

4. Choose Action ➤ New File Share to start the Create Shared Folder Wizard. (You can also right-click in the pane on the right, and choose New File Share from the shortcut menu.)

    You use this new Wizard to select the directory to share by browsing; you can even create a new folder, which is a big improvement over the remote sharing in Server Manager, where you had to magically remember the full path of the directory you wanted to share.

5. Supply the necessary info such as the local path, share name, and description, and then click Next.

6. Choose one of the basic share permissions, or set custom permissions. Click Finish to create the share.

7. Right-click the new share, and choose Properties from the shortcut menu to open the Properties dialog box for that share. You can change the description or share permissions and set NTFS security on the folder. Click OK when you are done.

NOTE

The Shared Folders tool also allows you to view user sessions and open files as Server Manager did, with the option to disconnect the session or the file if necessary.

To configure alerts for particular events on specific servers, you use the Performance Logs And Alerts tool. In Computer Management, this tool is under System Tools. This tool doesn't have to be running in the foreground any more to do performance logging or generate alerts. Plus, now you can configure Windows 2000 Server to respond to alert events by creating log events, by sending a network message, or by running a command file. These are Big Improvements.

Domain Management Functions

To create a new machine account in a domain, follow these steps:

1. Open Active Directory Users And Computers.

2. Select the domain and container where you want to add the machine account. There is already a Computers container for computer accounts, but you don't really have to use it.

3. Select the Computers container (for example), and choose Action ➢ New ➢ Computer.

4. Supply the computer name in the dialog box that appears. If you are creating an account for an NT machine, be sure to check the box to allow pre–Windows 2000 computers to use the account.

5. Click OK to create the new machine account.

Promote/Demote a Domain Controller

Windows 2000 doesn't require a Primary Domain Controller (PDC) as NT 4 did. In Windows 2000 Server, Primary Domain Controllers are called *Replica Domain Controllers,* and all DCs are more or less equal, although there is a PDC emulator to accommodate certain requirements of legacy clients. So we really don't promote and demote domain controllers in the NT 4 sense. However, a stand-alone machine or a member server can become a domain controller (without reinstalling!), and a domain controller can become a stand-alone machine or a member server (also without reinstalling). You will still have to reboot the machine after running DCPROMO to complete the transformation, though.

To create a new domain controller account, follow these steps:

1. In Administrative Tools, choose Active Directory Sites.

2. Open the Sites folder, and choose the site where you want to create the new domain controller.

3. Right-click Servers, and choose New ➢ Server.

4. When prompted, supply the name of the new domain controller.

You can also create the domain controller account during the process of converting a non–domain controller into a domain controller, if you have the appropriate local and domain administrative rights. Run DCPROMO.EXE on the machine to be promoted, and a Wizard kicks in that lets you join the machine to a domain, create a new domain, or become a domain controller in an existing domain.

Control Services on a Remote Machine

To view and configure services on a remote machine as you did in Server Manager, follow these steps:

1. Open the Computer Management tool, and choose Action ➤ Connect To Another Computer.

2. Select the remote machine from a list, or just type in the machine name.

3. Once you are connected to the remote machine, expand Services And Applications to reveal the Services node.

4. Highlight Services to display a list of services on the remote machine in the right pane. You can now stop, start, and even restart services using your ever-useful right-click function, or you can use the Action menu. You can even use those cute tape recorder–like icons on the toolbar. The Properties option leads you to the equivalent of the old (NT 4) Configure button with more information and configuration options, such as a Recovery tab and a Dependencies tab.

NOTE

The Services tool in the Administrative Tools group also replaces the Services applet; see "Where Is the Services Applet?" for more details.

Where Is the Disk Administrator?

The Disk Administrator is now called Disk Management, and it can be found in the Storage component of Computer Management (see Figure 24.8).

Disk Management deserves a separate discussion, but let's just say that all the old functions are still there, more or less intact, plus the tool is now "remoteable." In other words, you can create and remove partitions on remote Windows 2000 machines, with the proper administrative credentials, of course. But if you're in a rush and need to partition and/or format a drive, open Computer Management, open the Storage folder, and then open the Disk Management folder. From there, partitioning, volume naming, and formatting are all GUI driven.

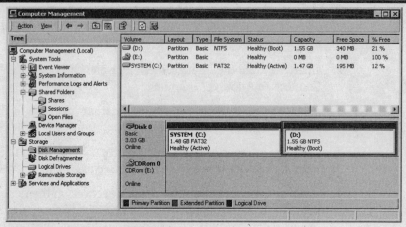

FIGURE 24.8: The Disk Management tool

What Happened to the Device Management Tools in Control Panel?

Some applets in Control Panel, such as Mouse, Display, and Sounds And Multimedia, still exist, but Windows 2000 now takes the attitude that Control Panel is for setting user-level options and not for advanced configuration. So you can still adjust your display and mouse settings, but the SCSI and Tape Device applets are gone (see Figure 24.9 for a typical view of the new Control Panel applets).

The Devices applet has been replaced by the long-awaited and much more useful Windows 2000 version of Device Manager (accessible through the Hardware tab of the System applet or the System Tools component of the Computer Management tool). Actually, Device Manager is much more useful than its Windows 95/98/98 SE predecessors because it is remoteable. That's right; now you can view devices and update drivers on your servers from the comfort and luxury of your own cubicle, assuming that you've got administrative privileges on the remote machine.

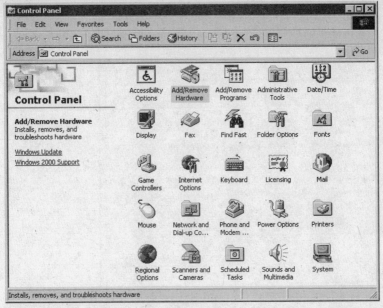

FIGURE 24.9: A typical view of Control Panel

To view existing devices and drivers on a local or a remote machine, follow these steps:

1. In Administrative Tools, open the Computer Management tool.

2. For a remote machine, highlight the root of the console (Computer Management), and choose Action ➤ Connect To Another Computer.

3. In the System Tools component, open Device Manager.

4. Right-click the machine name at the top (or any device type on the list) to scan for hardware changes. For anything that is not detected, however, open the Add/Remove Hardware applet on the local machine. This Wizard allows you to manually add and configure a device.

If you haven't noticed already, it will be a relief to learn that the System applet persists, although with a noticeable face-lift; use the Advanced tab to configure virtual memory settings and environmental variables as well as startup and recovery options (see Figure 24.10).

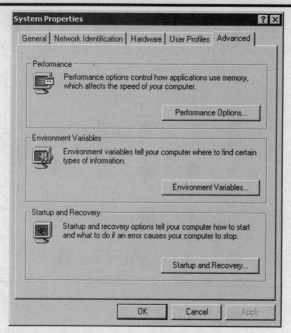

FIGURE 24.10: The System applet's Advanced tab

Where Is the Services Applet?

The functions of the Services applet are now managed and configured using the Services tool. This is accessible as a stand-alone administrative tool but also takes the form of a snap-in or an extension, where it can be used remotely in the Computer Management tool. To use the Services tool, follow these steps:

1. Choose Start ➤ Programs ➤ Administrative Tools ➤ Computer Management, or right-click My Computer, and choose Manage from the shortcut menu to open Computer Management.

2. Expand Services And Applications, and then click Services, as shown in Figure 24.11.

3. Right-click a service from the list on the right, and then choose to stop, start, pause, resume, or restart the service.

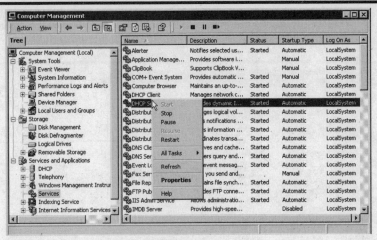

FIGURE 24.11: Services in Computer Management

Windows 2000 Server has improved on the old Services applet significantly; you can now see a brief description of the service (so you don't accidentally disable something important) and its current status, start-up value, and security context all in one view. At least, you could if the descriptions weren't as long as postdoctoral theses.

To configure a Windows 2000 Server service, follow these steps:

1. Double-click a service, or right-click it and choose Properties from the shortcut menu to open the Properties dialog box for that service.

2. Use the options on the General tab to change the description and even the display name of the service. You can change the description of a service to something meaningful, such as "Do not stop this service under any circumstances." You can also change the status or the start-up value here.

3. To change the security context (to have the service log on as a particular user) or to change the password of the user account the service uses, select the Log On tab.

The Recovery tab, shown in Figure 24.12, displays a new set of options, including what to do if the service fails. In addition to choosing the response (from Take No Action all the way to Reboot The Computer) that will occur on the first, second, and subsequent attempts, you can provide the details. You use the Dependencies tab to find out which services depend on this one and which services this one depends on, which is good to know *before* you stop the service. In NT 4 you had no way of knowing about dependencies (other than from experience or through a separate Resource Kit application) until you tried to stop the service.

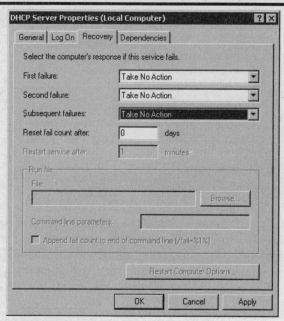

FIGURE 24.12: Options in the Recovery tab

NOTE

It's a small thing, but when you right-click a service, you'll notice that in addition to Stop, Start, Pause, and Resume, there's a new option, Restart. This is deceptively cool—you see, choosing Restart causes Windows 2000 to stop a service and then start it again in just one click, a great time-saver compared with NT 4, in which you had to first stop the service, then wait for the service to stop, and then start it again.

What Is This Network And Dial-Up Connections Tool?

The Network And Dial-Up Connections tool brings together the functions of Dial-Up Networking and NT 4's Network applet. The idea here is that a connection is a connection, whether it's a serial cable to another computer on your desk, a dial-up connection to the Internet, or a network connection using an Ethernet card that provides access to the corporate network in your office.

Each connection represented in this tool contains the necessary device and protocol-specific information for its purposes. In other words, each connection's properties and configuration information is specific to the connection type and instance. For example, a Dial-Up Connection is much like an Address Book entry in NT 4 Dial-Up Networking; it knows which device (modem), phone number, and authentication protocol to use, and network protocols and services are specified for it. A Local Area Connection entry is really not so different, containing information about the device to use (the network card type and hardware address), as well as network protocols and services to be used.

Microsoft has just simplified the Network applet options by removing the Network Identification and Services configuration options. Different types of connections are all grouped together in this tool. So you may see several different dial-up connection entries (the dial-up icon includes a telephone), just as you saw multiple Address Book entries in Dial-Up Networking under NT 4, but you'll also see different Local Area Connection icons if you have multiple network cards (the connection in the network icon appears to be a BNC T-connector). If your server contains another type of networking device, such as an X.25 card or an ISDN device, it will have an icon as well.

Where Did They Put NT Diagnostics?

WINMSD is gone. Well, the tool as we knew it is gone, replaced by a tool called System Information, which can be found in the Computer Management console under System Tools. Like many other tools we knew under NT 4, WINMSD has been replaced by a snap-in to the MMC. However, if you enter **WINMSD** in the Run dialog box, the System Information tool opens by itself in a console, as shown in Figure 24.13. So if you really want to, you can put a shortcut to WINMSD in your Administrative Tools folder and feel right at home. The System Information tool is a huge improvement over WINMSD.EXE and is an invaluable resource for system information.

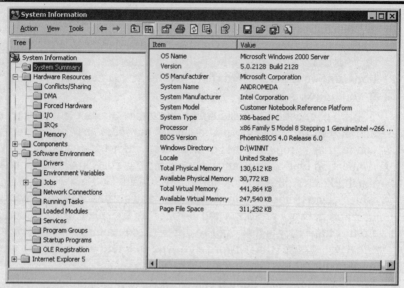

FIGURE 24.13: The System Information tool

FIXING THE WINDOWS 2000 GUI

If you're an administrator, you may find the Windows 2000 slightly new Desktop a bit annoying. Personally, I find the Web content that appears on the left side of every window to be just a waste of space. Additionally, whenever I want to go do some maintenance in the Program Files or System folders, I've got to click past patronizing user-proofing screens that essentially say, "Hey, look, buddy, you're probably too stupid to mess with these files, are you *sure* you want to see this folder?" I need to see the hidden and system files, and in general, Details view is best for maintenance operations. Additionally, I've never found the Address bar or standard buttons of much value in administrative tasks; they just rob me of screen space.

The first thing that I must do, then, when faced with a new system is to get it into "administrator-friendly" mode. To save you time, here are the steps:

1. Open My Computer.

2. Choose Tools ➤ Folder Options to open the Folder Options dialog box.

3. In the Web View section of the General tab, choose Use Windows Classic Folders.

4. Click the View tab.

5. Check the Display The Full Path In Title Bar check box.

6. Click the Show Hidden Files And Folders radio button.

7. Click the Hide File Extensions For Known File Types check box to clear it.

8. Click the Hide Protected Operating System Files (Recommended) check box to clear it, and then click Yes when you're asked to confirm your choice.

9. Click OK.

10. Back in the My Computer folder, choose View ➤ Details.

11. Right-click any blank space to the right of the menu bar, and click Standard Buttons to remove the check mark.

12. Right-click any blank space to the right of the menu bar, and click Address Bar to remove the check mark.

13. Hold down Shift, and then click the Close button in the My Computer folder—the icon in the upper-right corner that looks like an *X*. You hold down Shift so that the user interface will remember these settings.

Now that you've "saved" these settings with Shift+Close, you'll reopen My Computer and apply those settings to all folders:

1. Choose Tools ➤ Folder Options to open the Folder Options dialog box.

2. Click the View tab.

3. Click the Like Current Folder button.

4. Click Yes to confirm the message.

5. Click OK to close the Folder Options dialog box.

6. Close My Computer.

From now on, you'll be ready to get work done instead of appreciating the lovely "Web content"!

A MICROSOFT MANAGEMENT CONSOLE PRIMER

Let's face it, NT 4 admins. Our old familiar administrative tools—such as the User Manager and User Manager For Domains, Server Manager, Event Viewer, and even Disk Administrator—have been assimilated into these things called Microsoft Management Console (MMC) tools.

I've discussed the shocking absence of the Network applet and how to deal with that. I've explained how to add a protocol or service. If only that were enough. To master the Windows 2000 Server graphical changes, you must fully understand the Microsoft Management Console. In this section, I'll explain how MMC is not evil just because it has assimilated our friends, discuss key MMC terms you should know, briefly look at the Computer Management console, and finally, introduce you to creating your own MMC-based administrative tools.

What Is This MMC Thing?

In NT 4, administrators had to master multiple administration tools. A whole set of built-in tools, plus independent third-party tools, made administration sort of a mess. Although many admin tools functioned remotely, you had to install some of them separately (unless your desktop happened to be an NT server), and with third-party tools, you often had to jump through hoops to get them to work remotely, if at all. Even worse, with menus, buttons, toolbars, Wizards, tabs, HTML, Java (you get the picture), just learning how to navigate new software was a chore. Also, there was no simplified version of User Manager For Domains that could be given to account operators and no way to hide menu items in administrative tools for those without full administrator rights.

So we complained. "As administrators, we need to be able to administer our networks from the comfort and luxury of our cubicles. And we don't want to waste time exploring all the windows, Wizards, and tabs in every new tool. And we need more flexible tools," we said. Behold, Microsoft has heard our cries, and their response was the Microsoft Management Console.

MMC is a framework for management applications that provides a unified interface for Microsoft and third-party management tools. MMC doesn't replace management applications; it integrates them into one single interface. MMC contains no inherent management functions. It uses component tools called snap-ins, which do all the work. MMC provides a user interface; it doesn't change how the snap-ins function.

Why Is MMC Good and Not Evil?

MMC provides the following benefits:

- ▸ You have to learn only one interface to drive a whole mess of tools.

- ▸ Third-party (ISV—Independent Software Vendor) tools will probably use MMC snap-ins. At best, Microsoft is encouraging software vendors to do so.

- ▸ You can build your own consoles, which is practical and fun. Admins can even create shortcuts on the console to non-MMC tools such as executables, URLs, Wizards, and scripts.

- ▸ By customizing MMC consoles, admins can delegate tasks to underlings without giving them access to all functions and without confusing them with a big scary tool.

- ▸ Help in MMC is context sensitive; it displays topics for only the appropriate components. Okay, that's not really new, but it's still cool (the Action menu is also context sensitive, but nobody uses menus any more; everybody just right-clicks instead).

MMC Terms to Know

This section defines important terms you'll need to know when working with MMC.

A *console*, in MMC-speak, is one or more administrative tools in an MMC framework. The prebuilt admin tools, such as Active Directory Users And Computers, are console files. You can also create your own consoles without any programming tools—you needn't be a C or Visual Basic programmer, as I'll discuss a bit later. The saved console file is a *Microsoft saved console (MSC)* file, and it carries the .MSC extension.

NOTE

It's important to distinguish between Microsoft Management Console and console tools. MMC provides a framework to create customized console-based tools. MMC.EXE is a program that presents administrators (and others creating console tools) with a blank console. It might help to think of a new instance of MMC.EXE as providing the raw material for a tool. In that case, Microsoft Management Console provides the rules and guidelines for building the tool, and the new console you create is the finished product.

Snap-ins are what we call administrative tools that can be added to the console. For example, the DHCP admin tool is a snap-in, and so is the Disk Defragmenter. Snap-ins can be made by Microsoft or by other software vendors. (You *do* need programming skills to make these, in other words.) A snap-in can contain components called nodes, or containers, or even leaves, in some cases. Although you can load multiple snap-ins in a single console, most of the prebuilt administrative tools contain only a single snap-in (including the Computer Management tool).

An *extension* is basically a snap-in that can't live by itself on the console but depends on a stand-alone snap-in. It adds some functionality to a snap-in. Some snap-ins work both ways. For example, the Event Viewer is a stand-alone snap-in, but it's implemented as an extension to the Computer Management snap-in. The key point is that extensions are optional. You can choose not to load them. For example, Local Users And Groups is an extension to the Computer Management snap-in. If you remove the extension from the COMPMGMT.MSC file used by your support folk, or simply don't include it in a custom console that uses the snap-in, those who use the tool won't have the option to create or manage users and groups with the tool. They won't even see it.

NOTE

This will not prevent them from creating users and groups by other means, if they have the correct administrative privileges.

Admins can create new MSC files by customizing an existing MSC file or by creating one from a blank console. The MMC.EXE plus the defined snap-ins create the tool interface. Also, it's possible to open multiple tools simultaneously, but each console runs one instance of MMC. Open an MSC file, and look in Task Manager while it's running—you see only the MMC.EXE process running, not the MSC file, just as you see WINWORD.EXE running in Task Manager, but not the Word document's name.

By default, prebuilt console tools open in *User mode*. Changes cannot be made to the console design. You can't add or remove snap-ins, for example. To create or customize a console, use *Author mode*. When a user is running a tool and not configuring it, the tool should be running in one of the *User modes*. The tool will actually look different in User mode than it does in Author mode.

Figure 24.14 shows a sample console tool, with the parts of the interface labeled. This console is running in Author mode to show all the parts of the MMC interface. This is a custom console, but to open any existing tool in Author mode, invoke it from the Run dialog box with the /a switch.

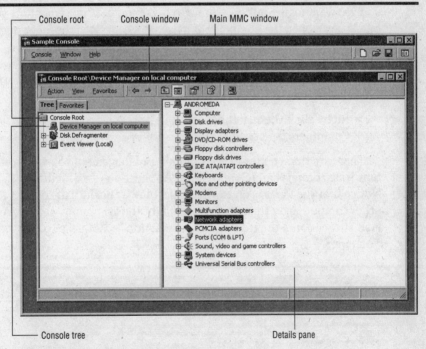

FIGURE 24.14: Anatomy of a console tool

In Figure 24.14, the Main MMC window is present because the tool is open in Author mode. In User mode, the Main MMC window, with menus and buttons, is hidden, and you only see the Console window. The Console menu in the Main window is basically a File menu, but you can also use it to add and remove snap-ins and set console options. The Action menu in the Console window is context sensitive and will reflect the options of the selected snap-in tool or component. The hierarchical list of items shown by default in the left pane is called the *console tree* (hence the "tree" label on the tab), and at the top is the *console root*. The Favorites tab displays any created links to places in the console tool. The right pane is called the *details pane*. Snap-ins appear as nodes on the console tree. The contents of the details pane depend on the item selected in the console tree.

The Computer Management Console

The Computer Management console is *the* main tool for administering a single server, local or remote. If you have only one server on your network and you want to use only one admin tool, Computer Management fits the bill. You can open the Computer Management console in the following ways:

- ▶ Select the tool from the Administrative Tools folder.

- ▶ Right-click My Computer, and choose Manage from the shortcut menu.

- ▶ Right-click the machine's icon in Active Directory Users And Computers, and choose Manage.

There are three nodes in the Computer Management console tree: System Tools, Storage, and Services And Applications (see Figure 24.15). Notice that the focus is on the local machine by default; to connect to other computers on the network, highlight the Computer Management icon at the root of the tree, and choose Action ➢ Connect To Another Computer.

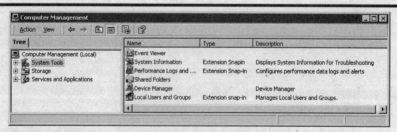

FIGURE 24.15: The Computer Management console tree

Expand the nodes in the Computer Management console tree to display the configuration tools and objects, as shown in Figure 24.16. Most of the core functions are under System Tools. Some functions even work remotely on NT 4 machines (you can view a remote machine's Event Logs, for example), but new features require the remote machine to be a Windows 2000 box.

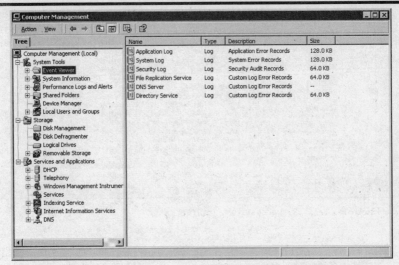

FIGURE 24.16: The expanded Computer Management console tree

In the System Tools node, you can complete the following tasks:

- ▶ View events and manage the Event Logs. Basically the Event Viewer tool turned into an MMC snap-in. Notice that some services, such as DNS and Directory Service (Active Directory software) now have their own logs.

- ▶ View system information. The export option in these consoles is great for generating reports and documenting your server configuration. System Information provides details about hardware resources, system components configuration information, and software components (see Figure 24.17).

- ▶ Set up performance logs and alerts without opening Performance Monitor.

- ▶ Manage shared folders. View, create, and manage shares; view sessions and open files; and disconnect sessions. This replaces those functions in the Control Panel's Server applet for local management and the remote shares management feature in Server Manager.

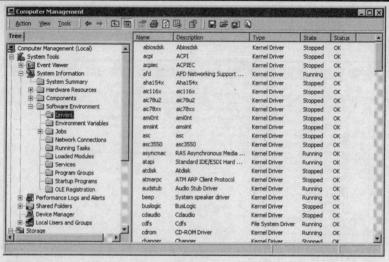

FIGURE 24.17: Viewing system information

▶ Manage devices. The long-awaited Device Manager is fully remoteable and a great place to track down information about your hardware, to update drivers, and to troubleshoot resource conflicts.

▶ Create and manage local users and groups (Chapter 25 is all about creating and managing users and groups).

The Storage node (shown back in Figure 24.16) includes options for managing removable storage (a new feature), along with the new Disk Defragmenter tool and the Disk Management tool, which is the equivalent of the Disk Administrator in NT 4. There is also a component to view logical drives, including network drive mappings, and their properties. This is useful if you want to quickly view free space or set NTFS security at the root of a partition, for example. Too bad you can't browse folders like you can in Explorer. Oh well, I guess we don't need *another* desktop shell program, do we?

The Services And Applications node (also shown in Figure 24.16) includes telephony settings, services configuration, Windows Management Instrumentation (WMI), indexing, and IIS management stuff, the last of which is also available in the Administrative Tools group by itself (the tool is called Internet Services Manager, while the extension in Computer Management is called Internet Information Services). The Services tool replaces the Services applet and the remote service management feature of Server Manager. Expect the components available in the Services And Applications node to change depending on which services are installed. For example, if the server is a DHCP server or is running DNS, these management components will appear under Services And Applications—otherwise, you won't see them.

Other MMC Tools

If you're like me, you don't want to click here and click there and basically get carpal tunnel syndrome just to open something from the Administrative Tools group. If you prefer to use the Run dialog box to invoke your tools, it's nice to know their filenames. Table 24.1 outlines some of the core MMC-based tool files to save your hand and your sanity. Keep in mind that some tools, such as DNS and DHCP, might not be present on the system if the corresponding service is not installed. Also, you need to include the program extension in the Run box. Just entering **DSA**, for example, doesn't work. You'll need to enter **DSA.MSC**.

TABLE 24.1: The Main MMC-Based Files

MSC FILE	COMMON NAME
MSINFO32.MSC*	System Information
COMPMGMT.MSC	Computer Management
DCPOL.MSC	Domain Controller Security Policy
DEVMGMT.MSC	Device Manager
DFRG.MSC	Disk Defragmenter
DFSGUI.MSC	Distributed File System
DISKMGMT.MSC	Disk Management
DOMPOL.MCS	Domain Security Policy
DOMAIN.MSC	Active Directory Domains And Trusts
DSA.MSC	Active Directory Users And Computers
DSSITE.MSC	Active Directory Sites And Services
EVENTVWR.MSC	Event Viewer
FAXSERV.MSC	Fax Service Management
FSMGMT.MSC	Shared Folders

CONTINUED ➡

TABLE 24.1 continued: The Main MMC-Based Files

MSC File	Common Name
GPEDIT.MSC	Group Policy
LUSRMGR.MSC	Local User Manager
NTMSMGR.MSC	Removable Storage Manager
PERFMON.MSC	Performance Monitor
RRASMGMT.MSC	Routing And Remote Access
SECPOL.MCS	Local Security Policy
SERVICES.MSC	Services Configuration
TAPIMGMT.MSC	Telephony
COMEXP.MSC*	Component Services
DHCPMGMT.MSC	DHCP
DNSMGMT.MSC	DNS
IIS.MSC*	Internet Information Services

Another caveat: most of these tools are found in the /winnt/system32 folder and are, therefore, in the default search path. A couple, however, are found in other folders that are not included in the default search path. The tool to manage Internet Information Services (IIS.MSC) is a good example; it's found in /winnt/system32/inetsrv. These errant tools are marked with an asterisk (*) in Table 24.1.

The quickest way to find them is to use the Search option. Once you locate them, there are a bunch of options. You can copy the tool to /winnt/system32 or just put a shortcut right on the Desktop if you don't mind the clutter. The other alternative is to change the search path to include these folders. It's a bit more of a pain; you'll need to open the System applet in Control Panel, go to the Advanced tab, and click the Environmental Variables button. Edit the system variable called Path. Oh, yes, and then reboot. Is it worth it? Many don't think so.

One strategy I like to use combines these approaches. I copy all the tools I want to a separate folder and then add *that* folder to my search path. That way I don't have to edit the path variable multiple times. I just edit it once to add my tools folder, and then I copy tools into the folder to make them quickly accessible from the Run routine. You may think this is a lot of trouble to use a couple of tools, but just wait until you install a bunch of third-party tools on your server. They all use their own installation folders. Although Microsoft is reportedly requiring new third-party admin tools to go in the /winnt/system32 folder, they've caved in on requirements before, so it's best to be prepared.

CREATING MICROSOFT MANAGEMENT CONSOLES

If the existing MMC tools don't fit your needs exactly, you can create a customized tool with your most frequently used components. Creating your own admin tool is easy using the MMC framework and snap-ins provided by Microsoft and third-party software vendors. Yes, keep in mind that your next version of a backup program or virus scanner or who knows what could be managed by a vendor-supplied MMC snap-in.

Although it's actually quite simple to create a customized MMC tool, there are so many options for customizing that I can't tell the full story here. Nevertheless, no discussion of the new Windows 2000 Server interface would be complete without an example or two of authoring administration tools.

Building a Simple Microsoft Saved Console

To configure your own custom admin tool, open a blank MMC in Author mode by typing **mmc.exe** in the Run dialog box. This will open up an untitled console (Console1) and display a generic console root, as shown in Figure 24.18. You can now open existing MSC files (just as you open DOC files in Word or XLS files in Excel) by choosing Console ➤ Open. These files will automatically open in Author mode if you open them in a blank console. If you want to open and fiddle with existing MSC files, most (but not all) of them are in the winnt/system32 folder. Just be sure to leave the original MSC files intact; you might need them again. In the example that follows, you'll be creating a tool from scratch, starting with a blank console and loading snap-ins.

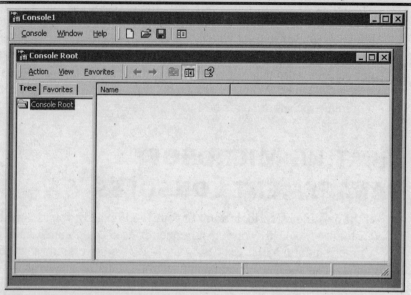

FIGURE 24.18: A generic console root

Suppose you need a tool for hardware management and troubleshooting. To create it, follow these steps:

1. Start by renaming Console Root to Hardware Tools; right-click Console Root, and choose Rename from the shortcut menu (you can actually do this step later if you prefer).

2. Now you're ready to add snap-ins. Choose Console ➢ Add/Remove Snap-In to open the Add/Remove Snap-In dialog box. As you can see in Figure 24.19, you must choose where to add the snap-in. Right now, it's only possible to add snap-ins to Console Root (now called Hardware Tools), but you can also group related tools by first adding folders to Console Root.

3. To add folders to Hardware Tools, click the Add button to open the Add Standalone Snap-In dialog box . You'll now see both dialog boxes, sort of cascaded. Items chosen from the list in the Add Standalone Snap-In dialog box will appear in the list of snap-ins in the parent dialog box. Scroll through the list until you see a folder called Folder. Click Add to place the folder in your list of snap-ins in the Add/Remove Snap-In dialog box. Click Add again, and you'll see two Folder folders. Close the Add Standalone Snap-In dialog box to return to the Add/Remove Snap-In dialog box, and then click OK to close it.

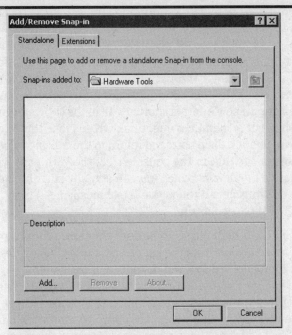

FIGURE 24.19: Choosing where to add snap-ins

> **4.** Back at the console in progress, right-click the folders to rename them. Figure 24.20 shows a Hardware Tools console with three folders, renamed to Disk Tools, Other Tools, and Web Sites.

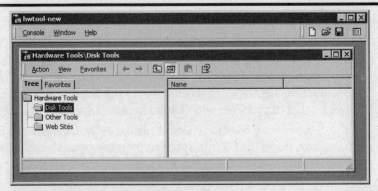

FIGURE 24.20: Customizing the console

5. The Web Sites folder will contain snap-ins that are actually hyperlinks to hardware vendor and support sites. To add links to the Web Sites folder, open the Add/Remove Snap-In dialog box again (choose Console ➤ Add/Remove Snap-In), select the Web Sites folder as the container, click Add, and then scroll through the list until you find Link To Web Address. Click the Add button, and from this point, it's just like creating a new Internet shortcut; fill in the URL, and give the shortcut a friendly name. Click OK to close the Add/ Remove Snap-In dialog box and return to the console. When you select the link in the console tree, the Web page will appear in the details pane. You can actually surf the Web from the console, although you'll technically need links to get off that particular site.

To add tools to the other folders, go through the same process, and choose the appropriate tools from the list of snap-ins available. Presumably, third-party software vendors will provide tools as snap-ins, so this list will expand and vary with the configuration and software installed. Some tools will prompt you to select a computer to manage. Others, such as the Event Viewer snap-in, also present the option to choose the machine when you start the tool from the command line. To change the focus of the tool when you kick it off, enter **tool.msc /computer=*computername*** in the Run box or at a command prompt.

While adding the stand-alone snap-ins, be sure to check out the available extensions for them. The Computer Management snap-in components are all implemented as extensions, although most also exist as independent snap-ins. You can load the Computer Management snap-in and deselect the extensions that aren't needed for your custom tool. All available extensions are added by default.

In Figure 24.21, you can see what your final tool could look like, a customized Hardware Tools console. This one consists of a Disk Tools folder (with Defragmenter and Disk Management), a folder called Other Tools that includes the Device Manager and System Information, and a Web Sites folder that can be filled with helpful hardware support–related links.

To save the custom console, choose Console ➤ Save to open the Save As dialog box, name the file and specify a path to save it in, and then click Save. Now the MSC file is ready to use.

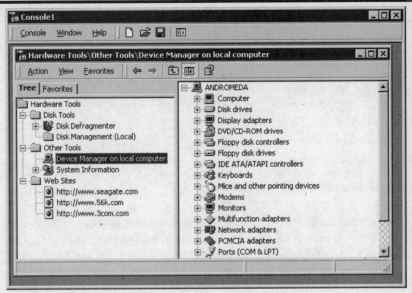

FIGURE 24.21: A custom Hardware Tools console

Designing Tools with Taskpad Views

It's possible to design simple views of an MMC tool for newbie administrators, forgoing their need to learn the different tools and navigate the console tree nodes. You might also want to present a limited set of tasks and hide others that are normally available in a regular MMC tool view. Taskpad views fill this need and allow you to create a tool that looks like the one shown in Figure 24.22. This tool presents a limited set of tasks instead of the entire console tree structure. Now novice administrators can perform delegated tasks without drilling down through the tree, expanding and collapsing, hoping to find the right tool, and then looking for the choice on the Action menu. Instead, they can just click the icon and go right to the task.

Taskpad views are HTML-based pages that can include links to console menu commands, Wizards, scripts, other executables, and even URLs. At least one snap-in is required to create a taskpad view, although you can create links to tasks that are unrelated to the snap-in, such as scripts. To include menu command and Properties dialog box tasks, however, the corresponding snap-in must be loaded beforehand.

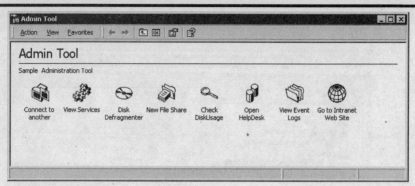

FIGURE 24.22: A simple taskpad tool

Before designing a console with taskpad views, or any type of console for that matter, put your thinking cap on, and visualize the tool you need. Which tasks will the tool include? Which snap-ins will be required? You'll need to be somewhat familiar with the available snap-ins and their functions. Will your tool include only one taskpad view with a bunch of tasks in a single window? Or do you need a tool with several tabs, each containing a set of related tasks? Figure 24.22 shows a tool with only one taskpad view; tasks are all together in one window, and the console tree is hidden from the user. Figure 24.23 illustrates a multiple taskpad tool, perhaps for a more experienced support person who needs to perform several types of tasks and doesn't want to load a different tool for each one.

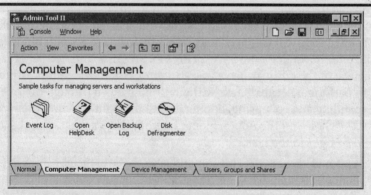

FIGURE 24.23: A multiple taskpad tool

There are a couple of possible strategies for creating taskpad views. One is to simply assemble a specific set of tasks into one or more taskpad views.

For example, when the tool is opened, you might see a single taskpad view called Routine Admin Tasks with links labeled Create New User and Create New Share. If you click the Create New User link, the dialog box or Wizard to create new users appears. In a tool like this, you might want to hide the console tree to prevent users from navigating around.

Another technique is to create taskpad views for particular items in the tree, for example, a taskpad for Users And Groups, another for Shared Folders, and a third for the Event Viewer. Again, you might choose to hide the actual console tree and normal views for this tool. In that case, you should create a main taskpad with links to the other taskpads located at different branches of the tree. So imagine a taskpad view called Main Taskpad that contains links called Open Services and Manage IIS. Click the former to display another taskpad that contains a list of services and links to stop, start, or restart a service. Click the Forward and Back buttons on the toolbar (like you do in Explorer) to return to the Main Taskpad view.

Alternately, you might choose to present these taskpad views in addition to the normal views without hiding the console tree. In this case, the taskpad will enhance the functionality of the console tool by presenting a set of simple task options (for people who don't like playing Marco Polo in admin tools) without imposing any limitations on what the user can see or access.

Whichever approach you choose, keep in mind that taskpad views are meant to simplify and facilitate the use of a console. They can even limit, to some extent, the administrative options that are presented. However, you should not consider them a foolproof way to limit admin types from performing certain tasks. Even if they can't get around the limitations of the custom console, which is by no means certain, they may have access to other tools that are not restricted. The best way to limit another admin's power is to use all the other built-in security options that are available in appropriate combinations: security group memberships, rights, group policies, and delegation of control are some of the more reliable tools for this purpose. Don't rely on a customized, locked-down console tool.

In this section, I'll show you how to create a Main Taskpad view for the Computer Management snap-in and how to create tasks. Then I'll demonstrate how to set up taskpad views for particular items in the console tree, with links from the main taskpad. Finally, I'll show you how to customize the interface to hide the console tree and present a simplified interface to the user.

Creating Taskpad Views

Once you've decided which tasks your user or admin person will perform with this tool and have identified the necessary snap-ins, you are ready to create the console. In this example, you'll create a view and a select set of tasks from the Computer Management snap-in to keep things simple. This tool will be for gathering information; we'll use the Event Logs, System Information, and Device Manager functions. Open a blank console as described earlier (enter **mmc.exe** in the Run dialog box), and load the required snap-ins. You can also use an existing custom console that contains the necessary snap-ins as long as you open it in Author mode.

To follow along with this example, load the Computer Management snap-in in your blank MMC console; it encompasses all the tasks for this tool. It's also possible to add the three snap-ins separately (Event Logs, System Information, and Device Manager), but the Computer Management snap-in has a special capability that will facilitate remote information gathering, as you'll see in a moment.

To create a taskpad view at the top of the Computer Management node, follow these steps:

1. Right-click the Computer Management node in the console tree, and choose New Taskpad View from the shortcut menu to start the New Taskpad View Wizard.

2. Click Next to continue.

3. Select the style of the taskpad view (shown in Figure 24.24). Choose whether to display the actual items that would normally appear in the details pane (such as a list of users or a list of services) and, if so, whether you want a vertical list (to accommodate lots of columns) or a horizontal list (for longer lists). In this case, we're just going to create a view of links and don't want to see the details pane information, so choose No List. If you were to choose a list type, however, you would use the List Size option box to determine how much of the window pane can be taken up by the list. I'll demonstrate a taskpad view with a list in a moment. Now, select the style you want for your task descriptions. If you needed a longer explanation to appear alongside the link, choose Text. However, we want a description that just pops up when you hover over the link, thus leaving more room for task links, so choose

InfoTip. All the tasks created later will use this style. Click
Next to continue.

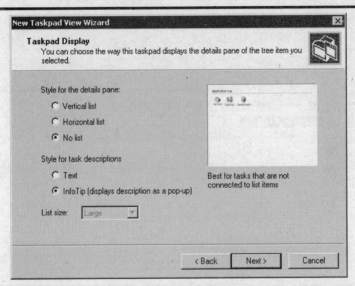

FIGURE 24.24: Configure the style of the taskpad.

4. In the next screen, you must decide whether to apply the view
   to the selected tree item only or to any other tree item of the
   same type. If you choose the latter, you can change the
   default details pane display for those items to the taskpad -
   view (although the normal view will still exist). However, let's
   choose to apply the view only to the selected tree item. This
   taskpad view will only display when the Computer Management root node is selected. Click Next.

5. Now, supply a name for your taskpad (mine is called Main
   Taskpad) and a description if you wish. The description you
   supply will appear under the title in the details pane. That's it!
   In the final screen of the Wizard, you can kick off the New Task
   Wizard and start creating tasks (uncheck the box beside Start
   New Task Wizard to avoid creating a new task for now). Click
   Finish to close the Wizard and create the new taskpad view.

Figure 24.25 shows the new taskpad before any tasks are created.
Notice the squared-off tabs that allow you to move between the taskpad
view and the normal view of the details pane. In a moment, I'll show you

how to hide the console tree on the left and remove the Normal tab to achieve the look and feel of the console shown in Figure 24.22.

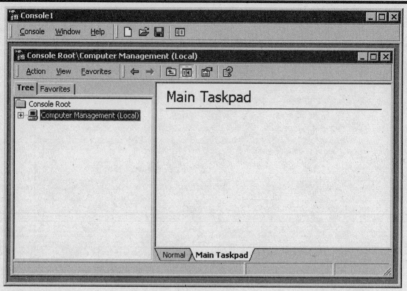

FIGURE 24.25: A console with a taskpad view

If you want to create another taskpad view, like the one in Figure 24.23, just choose Action ➢ New Taskpad View again. Or choose Delete Taskpad View to delete a selected one. If you want to make changes to a taskpad, select Action ➢ Edit Taskpad View (you may have to click the taskpad's tab first—blast those pesky context-sensitive menu commands!). In the Main Taskpad Properties dialog box, you can go back and change the style of the view and add, remove, or modify tasks.

Creating a Task

To create tasks for the new taskpad, select the Start New Task Wizard check box in the last screen of the New Taskpad Creation Wizard, or choose Action ➢ Edit Taskpad View. Select the Tasks tab, and click New to start the same Wizard. The following steps illustrate how to create a task that uses the Connect To Another Computer command (in the Computer Management snap-in):

1. In the New Task Wizard, click Next to begin creating a new task. The Wizard asks whether the task will be a menu command

Part V

(from the shortcut or Action menu in the console), a shell command, or a navigation command, which points to a link in the Favorites tab. Although shortcut menu commands are limited to the functions of a loaded snap-in, a shell command could be an executable (such as a Wizard), a shell script or other type of script, or even a URL. In any of these cases, the shell command task actually kicks off the command called, so in that sense, it's just a taskpad's version of a shortcut to something outside the tool itself. For example, you can create a shell command task and point it to the Calculator (CALC.EXE) if you want (that way, it's handy for those binary-to-decimal conversions). Click the radio button beside the desired type of task. We'll create a menu command in this example, but if you choose to create a shell command at another time, you'll need to specify the path to the command and any command-line parameters (also called arguments), the "start in" folder, and whether the command should run in a normal window, minimized, or maximized. Figure 24.26 shows the dialog box in which you create a shell command task.

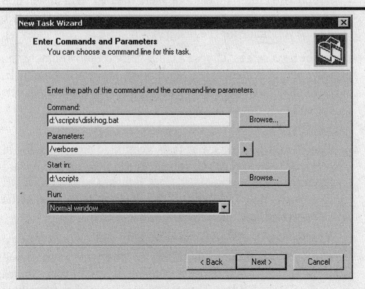

FIGURE 24.26: Creating a shell command task

NOTE

In contrast to shell command tasks, which refer to commands outside the tool, navigation command tasks are shortcuts to places within the console. For example, if you want a shortcut to the Disk Defragmenter, find it in the tool, and then add it to the tool's favorites (choose Favorites ➢ Add To Favorites). Then, when you create your task, simply choose the shortcut to Disk Defragmenter from the list of existing favorites. Once the shortcut is created, clicking the task icon whisks you down to the Disk Defragmenter tool.

2. After choosing to create a menu command, select a source for the command in the next screen, and choose a command from those available on the right. You can choose whether the source of the command will be an item in the details pane or a specific item in the console tree. In this case, we are creating the latter, a tree item task. Now you'll see the Computer Management node in the left pane, and Connect To Another Computer is among the available commands on the right. Highlight Connect To Another Computer, and click Next.

3. Give the task a name and a description. The description you supply will either appear alongside the task icon or will pop up when you hover over the icon, depending on the style choice you made for the taskpad. Click Next.

4. In the next screen, choose a task symbol. Unfortunately, the selection of symbols is rather limited. However, some tasks have recommended symbols; the Wizard may highlight one for you but will, of course, leave the final choice up to you. Click Next.

5. The Wizard confirms your task creation, displaying a list of created tasks and giving you the option to run the Wizard again to create another task. Click Finish, and then click OK to close the New Task Wizard. The new task will appear in the taskpad as a link. Just click the link to run it.

6. Just for practice, run the New Task Wizard again, creating a new menu command based on another tree item. Scroll through the Computer Management tree and locate Shares under Shared Folders. The task you're looking for is New File Share. Create a task to create a new share on the computer. Now your taskpad should look like the one shown in Figure 24.27.

Using the tasks you've created, you can now connect to remote machines and create shares on them.

Steps 1 through 5 illustrate how to create a task to connect to another computer, which is important if the tool is to function remotely. This is why the Computer Management snap-in was used instead of the individual component snap-ins. When adding individual component snap-ins such as the Event Viewer, you must specify that it always manage the local machine or a particular remote machine.

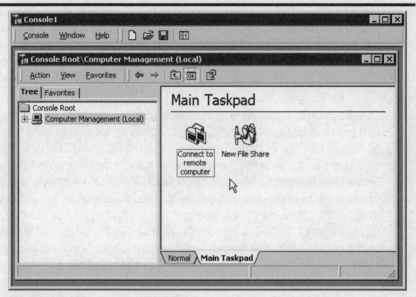

FIGURE 24.27: A taskpad with tasks

TIP

When you load a snap-in, you can choose to specify the machine to be managed when the tool is started from the command line, but this requires that you close and reopen the tool to administer a different machine; that's just too much trouble. With the Connect To Another Computer task that's built in to the Computer Management snap-in, you can easily change the focus for any task created without closing and reopening the console.

Some Notes about Taskpads and Tasks

When you were creating the taskpad in our example, you had the choice in step 4 under "Creating Taskpad Views" to apply the view to the selected tree item only or to any other tree item of the same type. When a taskpad view is applied to the selected tree item, it will only be visible when you navigate to the node in the console tree or use a link such as a Favorite to get there. When a taskpad view applies to other tree items and is set to display by default instead of the normal details pane view, the taskpad would theoretically contain mostly generic menu commands, such as Open or Properties, so that as you navigate to a certain part of the tree, you see a consistent taskpad view and set of link commands in the details pane on the right. Unfortunately, Microsoft is still working out the kinks in this area, because taskpad views created in this way don't seem to display except at the node where they are created, and the documentation is rather silent about it.

When you're choosing a menu command source, your choices are limited to menu commands available at that level if your command source is the list in the details pane. However, you can still create tree item tasks that point to any item on the tree. Menu item command tasks are not limited by the item to which the taskpad is linked. So why would you want to create tasks that are limited to the commands in the details pane at all? Well, this capability is useful if you need to apply the same tasks to different items in the list. You see, with tasks that use the command list in the details pane, you first choose the item from a horizontal list in the taskpad, for example, and then you choose the task link. The command applies to the selected item.

As an example, let's create a taskpad view for the Services node and create tasks to stop, start, and resume the selected service in the taskpad:

1. First, create the new taskpad for services configuration. Go to the Services node in the console tree (it's under `Computer Management\Services` and `Applications\Services`), and choose Action ➤ New Taskpad View to start the Wizard. Click Next to continue.

2. Select display options for the taskpad. Services will have a long list, so a vertical list is appropriate, although selecting a horizontal list will allocate more room to display the columns.

I also recommend leaving the task description style on InfoTip, as this will allow more room for task links. Click Next.

3. Choose to apply the taskpad view to the selected tree item. These commands will be specific to the Services node. Click Next.

4. Give the taskpad a name (I just called mine Services) and a description, which will appear under the name in the details pane. Click Finish to create the taskpad and start the New Task Wizard (if you left the box checked, it's selected by default).

5. To create a task, click Next in the New Task Wizard. Choose to create a menu command, and click Next.

6. This time, in the Shortcut Menu Command screen, you'll choose your command from the list in the details pane for Services. These are also the commands that are available in the shortcut menu when you select a service and right-click it. Select Restart (it doesn't really matter which service is selected on the source side at this point), and click Next.

7. Supply a name for the task and a short description. I changed the description for the Restart task because the default description, which appears when you hover your cursor over the symbol in the taskpad, was incorrectly service- and machine-specific (another small kink). Click Next.

8. Choose an icon from the list, click Next, click Finish in the confirmation screen, and you're done.

9. Repeat steps 5 through 8 as necessary to create tasks for Start, Stop, Pause, Resume, and Properties.

Now the Services taskpad should appear with the list of services displayed in a list. The tasks you've created appear alongside (or under) the details pane. To restart a service, select it from the list, and click Restart. Figure 24.28 shows the final Services taskpad with several service-related tasks, although you might not want to include the Properties task if you don't want the user of the tool to change the configuration of the services.

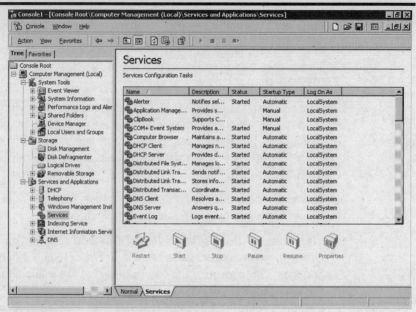

FIGURE 24.28: The Services taskpad

Customizing the Console Interface

You can give the customized tool a simplified look and feel by hiding the console tree and those navigation tabs that allow users to move between the normal view and the taskpad views.

Ya know, that reminds me, if we hide the console tree and the navigation tabs, lock the tool down, and prevent the user of the tool from navigating the console tree, they have no way of getting to the Services taskpad we created in our earlier example. They'll be stuck at the Main taskpad. So before we customize the console interface, we need a task in the Main taskpad that acts as a link to the Services taskpad. You can take care of this in two ways, and both seem to work equally well.

The first way to create a link to another taskpad is to navigate to the node while the console tree is visible in Author mode and add that location to the list of Favorites. Then, create a navigation task in the Main taskpad, and select the Services Favorite as the destination. The Favorites link must exist, however, before you can create a navigation task for it.

If you don't want to use the Favorites method, create a menu item task in the Main taskpad, and select as the source a tree item task. Navigate down the tree to Services, and select the Open command (shown in Figure 24.29). This will create a task to open the Services node where the taskpad will display by default.

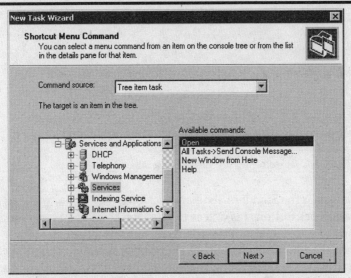

FIGURE 24.29: Creating a task to open a console taskpad view

Now, to customize the console interface, choose View ≻ Customize in the Console window. A set of view options is shown in Figure 24.30. Items are shown when the boxes are checked and hidden when they are cleared. Although clearing the Console Tree check box does hide the Tree tab in the console pane on the left, it doesn't hide the pane itself; you'll still see the Favorites tab. If that's not agreeable to you, click the Show/Hide Console Tree button on the toolbar. It actually hides the entire tree side of the Console window.

Hide the Action and View menus by clearing the Standard Menus check box. Removing the Action menu prevents the user from selecting an item from a horizontal or vertical list in a taskpad and pulling down the Action menu to see a complete set of task options, but he can still use the shortcut menu by right-clicking if you don't disable it (see the next section for instructions on disabling the shortcut menu).

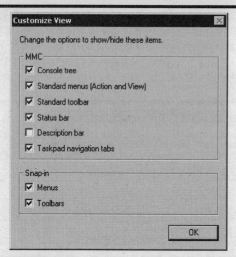

FIGURE 24.30: Customizing the view of a console

If you clear the Standard Toolbar check box, the toolbar with the Forward and Back buttons (as well as the Up One Level and Show/Hide Console buttons) disappears. You need those buttons if the tool has to navigate the tree. Consider our earlier example of a Main taskpad with a link to the Services taskpad. If the Standard toolbar is removed, you cannot return to the Main taskpad from the Services taskpad without a link in the Services taskpad. If the console tool is only running Wizards or scripts, however, removing the navigation buttons won't be a problem.

To really simplify the window, clear both the Status Bar and the Description Bar check boxes (the status bar is displayed by default, but the description bar is not). Clear the Taskpad Navigation Tabs check box to remove the Normal tab from the bottom of the details pane, and users will be able to view only the taskpads you've created.

Each snap-in can have its own menu items and toolbar buttons. To hide these for all snap-ins in the tool, clear the two check boxes in the Snap-In section of the dialog box. You can't pick and choose which toolbars and buttons to hide; you either hide them for all snap-ins or display them for all snap-ins.

Packaging the Tool for Users

When the tool is ready to be published, choose Console ➢ Options to open the Options dialog box, and change the tool's name (from Console1 to something descriptive). The new name will now appear in the title bar. You might also want to assign a different icon than the generic MMC icon. Finally, assign a default mode to the MSC file. Choose Author mode, and the file will always open with the main MMC window and main menu/ toolbar, allowing changes to be made to the tool. Otherwise, only the Console window is available. If you aren't sure what I mean by the terms *Main MMC window* and *Console window*, glance back at Figure 24.14. Use one of the three User modes to prevent changes, such as adding and removing snap-ins. The three User modes represent varying degrees of restrictions, such as whether the user can open multiple windows. LimitedAccess Single Window is the most restrictive.

There are three configuration check boxes at the bottom of the Options dialog box. To disable all shortcut menus on all taskpads in the console, click the Enable Context Menus On Taskpads In This Console check box to clear it. If you created that Services taskpad and left out a Properties task, for example, the user could still right-click a service in the list and choose Properties, unless the shortcut menus are disabled (see the preceding section for instructions on removing the Action menu, which also shows a full set of possible tasks when an item is selected). Check Do Not Save Changes To This Console to prevent users from saving any changes to the console. Users can customize views by default. To prevent this, click the Allow The User To Customize Views check box to clear it. Click OK, and then save the console as an MSC file if you haven't already.

Figure 24.31 shows our basic Admin Tool running in User mode with limited access and a single window. The console tree and taskpad navigation tabs, as well as the Action and View menus, are hidden. This tool does display the Standard toolbar, however, since it's necessary to be able to go forward and back in the tool. Too bad you can't hide some buttons and not others. The buttons to show the console tree and to go up a level are also available.

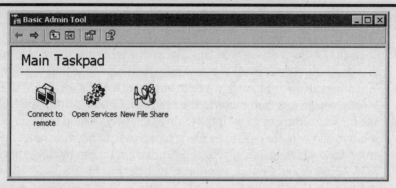

FIGURE 24.31: The final product

Distributing the Tool

When the tool is finished, distribute it as you would a normal file; e-mail it to someone, put it on the network file server in a shared folder, or use Active Directory Services to publish it. Appropriate administrative permissions for the tasks and access to the snap-ins, either on the local machine or on the network, are required to use the tool.

Unfortunately, these custom tools will only run on other Windows 2000 machines, unless Microsoft has plans to distribute a compatible version of MMC for Windows 95/98/98 SE and NT 4 clients.

Editing a Custom Console Tool

Making changes to the console is easy, even when the tool opens in User mode by default. You can open the tool in Author mode in the following ways:

▶ In the Run dialog box, enter the filename with the /a switch.

▶ Right-click the file's icon, and choose Author from the shortcut menu.

▶ In the Run dialog box, enter **mmc.exe**, and then choose Console ➢ Open.

But how can you keep others from making changes to the tool using these tricks? Chapter 25 explains how to restrict access to Author mode, and even particular snap-ins, using group policies.

What's Next?

In Windows 2000, all computers and all people on the system must have accounts. In the next chapter, we'll look at how to create and modify user and group accounts.

Chapter 25

CREATING AND MANAGING USER ACCOUNTS

By now you've learned the basics of Active Directory (AD), how to install and configure major components of Windows 2000 Server, the ins and outs of the new user interface and Microsoft Management Console (MMC), as well as the care and feeding of the Registry. Now let's tackle something at the heart of an administrator's job: creating and managing users and groups. This chapter will take you through the steps to create users and help you to understand the new group structure in Active Directory. Then I'll take on managing the users' work environments and explain Group Policy in plain, simple English.

Adapted from *Mastering Windows 2000 Server, Second Edition*, by Mark Minasi, Christa Anderson, Brian M. Smith, and Doug Toombs

ISBN 0-7821-2774-6   1593 pages $49.99

USE COMPUTER MANAGEMENT FOR LOCAL ACCOUNTS

The bulk of this chapter assumes an AD context. At this point, you know the benefits of using AD on your network. In many cases, particularly if you have NT 4 workstations or Windows 2000 systems as clients, it is desirable to create a domain, even if you have only one server, in order to take advantage of all the additional features of AD.

It is possible, however, that a small organization might want to keep life simple or even (brace yourself here) that the company's primary network operating system is not Windows 2000 or NT. For example, in a Unix or NetWare network, you may need to set up a special-purpose NT server without all that AD stuff. In that case, if your Windows 2000 machine is not a domain controller and you aren't using AD, create your user accounts using the Computer Management tool (COMPMGMT.MSC). Users and groups that you create with COMPMGMT.MSC are local accounts, which is to say they exist and are valid on that local machine only. However, COMPMGMT.MSC is a remoteable tool, so you can use it to create and manage Local Users And Groups on remote member servers in a domain or on remote stand-alone servers. To do so, choose Action ➢ Connect To Another Computer.

The Action menu (instead of the File menu) is at the top left in the Microsoft Management Console tool. (See Chapter 24 for an overview of MMC and console anatomy.)

TIP

If the machine you are working on is a domain controller, you have to use Active Directory Users And Computers (DSA.MSC) to create accounts. On a domain controller, the Local Users And Groups node is disabled in COMPMGMT.MSC, and there is an *X* in a red circle over the function to indicate that it's disabled.

Creating user accounts on a non–Active Directory server in Windows 2000 is much the same as creating local accounts on a non–domain controller in NT 4 except that you use the Computer Management tool instead of User Manager. In Computer Management, open System Tools, and then open Local Users And Groups, as shown in Figure 25.1. Notice the users and groups that are created by default when you install Windows 2000 Server. On a stand-alone server, with no particular network services such as IIS (Internet Information Server), Terminal Services, DHCP (Dynamic

Host Configuration Protocol), or DNS (Domain Name System) installed, the only built-in accounts are Administrator and Guest.

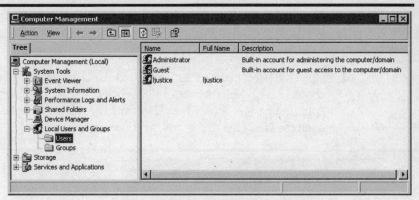

FIGURE 25.1: Computer Management Local Users And Groups

The Guest account is disabled by default as a security precaution. This account, on a stand-alone server or in an AD context, is used primarily to blow a huge hole in the security of a system by allowing unauthenticated access. That's right, unauthenticated access. No password is required for the Guest account. You can use it without any knowledge of a username or password, which is why it's disabled by default. It's a good thing that Guest is a poor account as far as powers and abilities are concerned. The Administrator account, of course, has powers and abilities well beyond those of mortal users. It cannot be deleted or disabled, even if you set stringent account lockout policies (which lock the account after a certain number of bad logon attempts). The Administrator account is not ordinarily subject to this policy and, therefore, cannot be locked out, even after a million bad logon attempts—which could be more than enough to crack a weak password.

NOTE

One common, and highly recommended, security practice is to rename both the Guest and Administrator accounts. This prevents a would-be intruder from taking advantage of the well-known usernames when attempting to log on.

The standard local groups that are built into a stand-alone server are Administrators, Backup Operators, Guests, Power Users, Replicator, and Users. Additional built-in groups are created on a domain controller system, as you'll see in a moment. These built-in groups have a predefined set of rights and permissions. To empower users with those rights and permissions, make them members of the appropriate group. For a rundown of the built-in groups and their rights, see Table 25.2 later in this chapter.

To create a new user account on a non–domain controller Windows 2000 system, follow these steps:

1. Open the Users folder under Local Users And Groups, and then choose Action ➤ New User, or right-click Users in Local Users And Groups, and choose New User from the shortcut menu to open the New User dialog box, as shown in Figure 25.2.

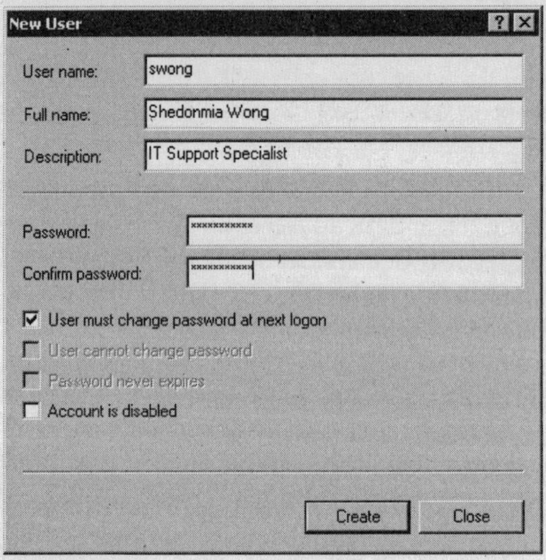

FIGURE 25.2: Creating a local user

2. Fill in the User Name, Password, and Confirm Password fields (the others are optional), and choose Create.

3. To change account properties, to assign group memberships, a login script, and a home folder, or to grant dial-in permission to the user, right-click the user account, and choose Properties from the shortcut menu.

4. To set a user's password, right-click the account, and then choose Set Password from the shortcut menu. (I'll discuss all these options and more a bit later in this chapter when we create AD accounts.)

NOTE

The local accounts you create on a stand-alone server, member server, or workstation are stored in the SAM (Security Accounts Manager) database, just as they are in NT 4. The SAM is still located in \winnt\system32\config.

That's it! If you want to set account policies such as lockout restrictions or auditing, use the Local Security Policy tool (SECPOL.MSC) or the Group Policy snap-in (GPEDIT.MSC). The process is similar to configuring Group Policy with the AD tools except that, since the machine is not a domain controller, changes will apply to the local policy for the machine. (I'll show you how to use the Group Policy snap-in to set account lockout and password policy for the domain later in the chapter.). The policies you create will be local policies, which will live in the local machine's Registry database. Not surprisingly, the scope of policy settings is more limited for local polices than for group policies in an AD environment. I'll also discuss group policies, and how they differ from local policies, later in this chapter.

USE ACTIVE DIRECTORY USERS AND COMPUTERS FOR DOMAIN ACCOUNTS

In Windows 2000, Active Directory Users And Computers (DSA.MSC) is the primary administrative tool for managing user accounts, security groups, organizational units, and policies in a single domain or in multiple domains. Because the tool is an MMC application, you can run it on any Windows 2000 machine, although it's only installed on Windows 2000 servers (and it appears only in the Start menu on domain controllers) by default. To run DSA.MSC on a Windows 2000 non–domain controller system, you can publish the application using AD and then install it on Windows 2000 Server or Professional desktops using the Add/Remove Programs applet. The Admin Pack is a prepackaged set of admin tools (found in winnt\system32\ADMINPAK.MSI) that you can publish using Group Policy, which installs the three AD tools on a machine. DSA.MSC is also useful for managing computer accounts, organizational units, resources such as printers and shared folders, and even domain controllers. In this chapter, however, I'll focus on creating and managing users and groups, including users' environments and group policies.

TIP

Computer accounts in Windows 2000 are now more like user accounts in that they can be included in groups and organizational units.

Where Do User and Group Accounts Live?

As in NT 4, local user accounts on a stand-alone server, member server, or Windows 2000 Professional workstation are stored in a Security Accounts Manager (SAM) database, usually located in C:\winnt\system32\config, but it depends on where you created your WINNT (system root) directory.

For AD, the file is called NTDS.DIT, and it's in %systemroot%\NTDS by default, but you can specify a path in the DCPROMO routine. The NTDS.DIT database stores a lot more information than the SAM does. It also stores information about servers and workstations, resources, published applications, and security policies. NTDS.DIT and the software that runs it are generally referred to together as the *directory service*, or the Active Directory. This data structure is replicated throughout the domain to all replica domain controllers for fault tolerance and load balancing. It's actually a modified Access database based on the Lightweight Directory Access Protocol (LDAP) specified in RFC 1777. Unfortunately, you can't open it in Access or otherwise view or edit it directly. You can, however, query and modify it using the Active Directory Services Interface (ADSI). As I'll discuss later, the Windows 2000 Resource Kit includes several VBScript files created for just that purpose (at least, it did as I was writing this).

Security Identifiers

User accounts, when first created, are automatically assigned a *security identifier* (SID). A SID is a unique number that identifies an account. SIDs have been used since the first release of NT; the system doesn't really know you by your name, but rather by your SID. User IDs are just there for the human interface. SIDs are never reused; when an account is deleted, its SID is deleted with it. A SID looks like this:

S-1-5-21-D1-D2-D3-RID

S-1-5 is just a standard prefix (actually, the 1 is a version number, which hasn't changed since NT 3.1, and the 5 means that the SID was assigned by NT); 21 is also an NT prefix; and D1, D2, and D3 are 32-bit numbers that are specific to a domain. Once you create a domain, D1 through D3 are set, and all SIDs in that domain henceforth have the same three values. The *RID* stands for relative identifier. The RID is the unique part of any SID. Each new account always has a unique RID number, even if the username and other information is the same as an old account. This way, the new account will not have any of the rights and permissions of the old account, and security is preserved.

Quick Tour of User and Group-Related Functions in Active Directory Users And Computers

Active Directory Users And Computers provides the network administrator with the means to perform the following tasks:

- ▶ Create, modify, and delete user accounts
- ▶ Assign logon scripts to user accounts
- ▶ Manage groups and group memberships
- ▶ Create and manage group policies

You can open Active Directory Users And Computers in the following ways:

- ▶ Choose Start ≻ Run, and enter **DSA.MSC** in the Open box.
- ▶ Choose Start ≻ Programs ≻ Administrative Tools ≻ Active Directory Users And Computers.

By default, Active Directory Users And Computers will seek out the Operations Master DC and send any change or create requests directly to that machine. If the Operations Master is offline or cannot be contacted, you can connect to another DC that will make the changes you request and synch up with the Operations Master at a later time. Just be aware that the DC honoring your request cannot guard against conflicts— namely, it cannot verify the uniqueness of a new account ID—until the Operations Master can be contacted. You will see a message to that effect if you create a user ID while the Operations Master is unavailable. In Active Directory Users And Computers, you will see the name of the contacted domain controller at the top of the console tree and your domain name right under the console root, as shown in Figure 25.3.

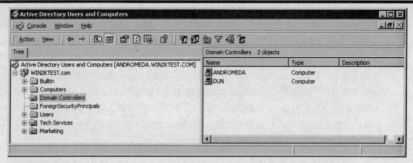

FIGURE 25.3: The Active Directory Users And Computers console

In the left pane, you see a list of containers and organizational units that were created automatically with the domain:

- ▶ Builtin

- ▶ Computers

- ▶ Domain Controllers

- ▶ ForeignSecurityPrincipals

- ▶ Users

Tech Services and Marketing are organizational units created by an administrator.

As with all the console applications, click an object in the console tree (on the left) to display its contents and information in the details pane (on the right). Notice also that the description bar for the details pane tells you how many objects are in the container. You can hide the description bar, as well as the status bar and the toolbars, if you want a more simplified view. Choose Action ➢ Customize View, and click the Description Bar check box to clear it.

The Users and Computers containers are the default locations for user, group, and computer accounts when a machine is upgraded from NT 4. They gotta go somewhere. But you don't have to put new ones there, and you can move them to organizational units (OUs) as needed. As you'll quickly discover, you can put a user account in any OU, even directly in the "domain" container. When I first created a few user and group and machine accounts, I just created them in the domain root and then moved them to OUs as they were set up.

Builtin is the container for those special built-in local groups—such as Administrators, Account Operators, Guests, and Users—that exist on every Windows 2000 Server machine, including domain controllers. More on this in a bit.

Domain Controllers (DCs) is the default OU for new Windows 2000 domain controllers. This is where the accounts are located when you first create a DC. Like the accounts in the Computers container, DC accounts can be moved to other OUs.

ForeignSecurityPrincipals is a default container for objects from external, trusted domains. In this chapter, we'll be working only with users and groups from this domain.

To create something new, select the container object where you want to locate it, and then choose Action ➢ New, or right-click the container object, and choose New from the shortcut menu. You can choose to create a shared folder, a user account, a printer, an OU, a group account, a contact, or a computer account. Any of these choices kicks off a corresponding Wizard to create the object. In each case, to fill in all the details, go back and edit the properties of the object after creating it (right-click the object, and choose Properties from the shortcut menu).

NOTE   Because they aren't really OUs, but instead mere "containers," you can't create an OU inside the Users or Computers containers, and you can only create users, computers, and groups inside the Builtin container.

Right-clicking an object displays its shortcut menu. The choices depend on the object you right-click. For example, right-click a user account, and you can disable it or reset the password; right-clicking a computer account displays options such as Move and Manage. (Manage opens COMPMGMT.MSC connected to the selected computer.)

This chapter is really not about managing machine accounts or printers or shared folders; however, contacts and OUs do relate to user and group management, so we'll take a look at those new items in a moment.

Prebuilt Accounts: Administrator and Guest

If you have just created a new domain, you'll notice that the Administrator and Guest accounts are built already. The Administrator account is, as you've guessed, an account with complete power over a machine or a domain, depending on the context. You can't delete the Administrator account, but you can rename it.

You assigned the password for the Administrator account when you installed Windows 2000 and then again when you ran DCPROMO.EXE to create a new domain. The first was a local Administrator account and password, but once you create a domain, the new Administrator account and password for the domain replace it. Don't lose that password, because you can't get it back! (Well, you can always rebuild from scratch, but it's no fun.)

A *guest* is "anyone that Windows 2000 doesn't recognize." By default, the Guest account is disabled, and it should *stay* that way. If you've ever worked with a different network, such as a Unix or NetWare network, you're probably familiar with the idea of a guest account—*but Windows 2000 works differently, so pay attention!* You can get access to most other operating systems by logging on with the username Guest and a blank password. That Guest account is usually restricted in the things it can do. That's true with Windows 2000 as well, although the Everyone group also includes guests.

Here's the part that *isn't* like other operating systems. Suppose someone tries to access a shared printer or folder on a Windows 2000 server or domain that has the Guest account enabled. She logs on to her local machine as melanie_wilson with the password happy. Even without an account on the server or domain, Melanie can still work on her local machine. Windows 95/98/98 SE machines don't care who you are, having no local accounts at all. On an NT 4 or Windows 2000 workstation, she would have to log on to an account on the local machine. However, none of these operating systems require you to log on to a server or domain in order to get access to the local workstation. Suppose that this domain or server doesn't even *have* a melanie_wilson account. Now she's working at a computer and tries to access a domain resource. Guess what? She gets in.

Even though an explicit domain login requires that you use a username of Guest, you needn't explicitly log on to a domain to use guest privileges. If your network is attached to my network and your Guest account is enabled, I can browse through your network and attach to any resources that the Guest account can access. I needn't log on as Guest; the mere fact that there *is* an enabled Guest account pretty much says to Windows 2000, "Leave the back door open, okay?" So be careful when enabling the Guest account.

Creating a New User Account

Before I discuss the ins and outs of all the user settings such as account properties, UPNs (User Principal Names), profile information, and so forth, let's just go through the steps to create a new user account with the Wizard. Then I'll go back and discuss all the settings for the newly created account.

To create a user account, follow these steps:

1. In Active Directory Users And Computers, select the Users container (or any other container/OU where you want the account to be located), and then choose Action ➤ New ➤ User to start the New Object Wizard, as shown in Figure 25.4.

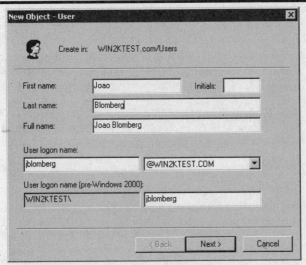

FIGURE 25.4: Creating a new user

2. Fill in the First Name, Initials, Last Name, and Full Name fields as shown in Figure 25.4 (Intitials and Last Name are optional fields). Next, fill in the user logon name (jblomberg), and choose the UPN suffix to be appended to the username at logon time. The UPN suffix is typically the DNS name of the domain, and unless you've set up alternate suffixes, you won't be able to choose any but the default domain name (win2ktest.com, in this case).

NOTE

UPN names are modeled after e-mail names, thus the @ symbol. The UPN suffix is a pointer to the domain containing the user account, so it's important when a user is logging on in a multiple-domain environment. We'll talk about UPN names in a moment. For logging on to an NT 4 or Windows 95/98 machine, there is also a downlevel logon name, which uses the old-style DOMAINNAME\username syntax from previous versions of NT.

USERNAMES IN WINDOWS 2000

Usernames in Windows 2000 must follow these rules:

▶ The name must be unique to the machine for local accounts (or unique to the domain in the case of domain accounts). However, a domain user account name may be the same as a local account name on a non–domain controller that is a member of the domain, a fact that causes much confusion because they are completely separate entities.

▶ The username cannot be the same as a group name on the local machine for a local account (or the same as a group name on the domain in the case of domain accounts).

▶ The username can be a maximum of 20 characters, upper- or lowercase or a combination.

▶ To avoid confusion with special syntax characters, usernames may not include any of the following:

" / \ [ ] : ; | = , + * ? < >

▶ The name may include spaces and periods, but may not consist entirely of spaces or periods. Avoid spaces, however, since these names would have to be enclosed in quotes for any scripting or command-line situations.

3. Once you've filled in all the username information, click Next.

4. Set a password for the user account and confirm it.

5. Set the password and account options summarized in Table 25.1, and then choose Next. None of the account options are selected by default, so it's a good idea to go ahead and select User Must Change Password At Next Logon.

TABLE 25.1: Password and Account Options for Creating a New User Account

OPTION	DESCRIPTION
User Must Change Password At Next Logon	Forces a user to change their password the next time they log on; afterward, the box will be unchecked.
User Cannot Change Password	If checked, prevents the user from changing the account's password. This is useful for shared accounts and accounts that run services such as Exchange.
Password Never Expires	If checked, the user account ignores the password expiration policy, and the password for the account never expires. This is useful for accounts that run services and accounts for which you want a permanent password (such as the Guest account).
Account Is Disabled	If checked, the account is disabled, and no one can log on to it until it is enabled (it is not, however, removed from the database). This is useful for accounts that are used as templates and for new user accounts that you create well in advance, such as new hires that will not begin work for several weeks.

6. The final screen of this Wizard simply confirms all the information you've supplied, including the container/OU where the account will live, the full name, the logon name, and the password or account options selected. Choose Finish to create your user account.

User Account Properties

Now let's go back and look at the properties of the account we just created. Right-click the user account object to open the shortcut menu. From here you can quickly copy the account, manage the user's group memberships, disable or enable the account, reset the user's password, move the account to a different container or OU, open the user's home page, or send him mail (these last two require that the home page URL and e-mail address be specified in the account information). You can also choose to delete or rename the user account from this menu.

WARNING

Each user and group account is assigned a unique identifier, called a SID, when it is created. Deleting a user or a group account deletes the unique identifier. Even if you re-create an account with the same name, the new account will not have the rights or permissions of the old account.

From the shortcut menu, choose Properties to display the Properties dialog box that the user specified. In the General tab, which is shown in Figure 25.5, you can add a description of the user account, put in the name of the office where the user works, and add telephone numbers, an e-mail address, and even Web page addresses.

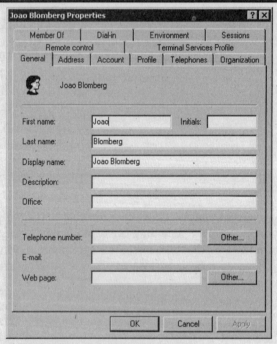

FIGURE 25.5: General user properties

The Address tab contains fields for a user's mailing address. The Telephones tab provides a place for home, pager, mobile phone, fax, and IP phone numbers, as well as a place to enter comments. You use the Organization tab, shown in Figure 25.6, to enter information about someone's actual job title and position in the pecking order of the organization.

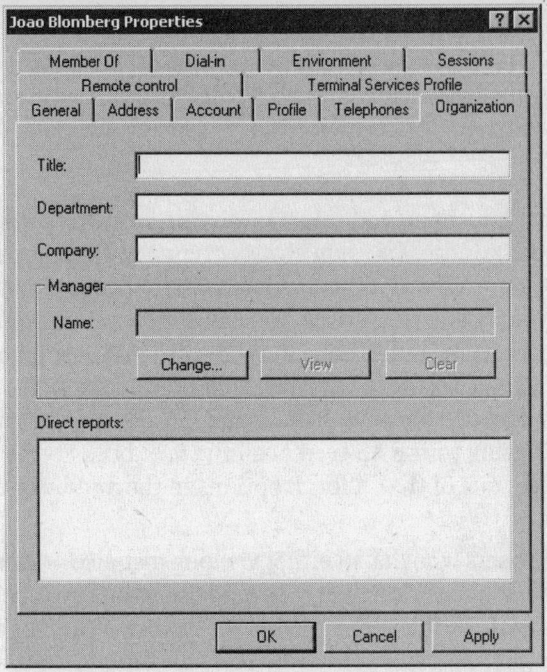

FIGURE 25.6: The Organization tab

So four of the tabs in the Properties dialog box for the user are about contact information, not what we old-time NT admins would call account properties. You know, you could enter almost all this stuff in the Exchange mailbox properties, so I know you are wondering, as I did, "What's the deal, are they integrated now? Will Exchange actually use Active Directory to create mailboxes?" At this writing, Exchange and Windows 2000 Active Directory are not actually integrated, so you still have to create Exchange mailboxes and fill out the related contact information in parallel (if you choose to do so). However, the next version of Exchange (code-named Platinum), which is in beta at this time, is supposed to integrate with Active Directory and eliminate the need for parallel user accounts and mailboxes. We shall see.

You use the Dial-In tab to grant dial-in permissions to a user account. By default, the user account you selected will probably have the Deny Access option selected at the top of the dialog box. Click Allow Access to grant dial-in permissions to this user. You also have the option to edit some user-specific settings in this dialog box.

NOTE

Before your users can actually have dial-in access, you must install the Routing and Remote Access Service (RAS). You'll find information about this in Chapter 22 of *Mastering Windows 2000 Server*, the book from which this chapter was adapted.

If you'd like to implement an additional measure of security by making sure that a user's remote access session always originates from a specific phone number, you have a few options available. First, if your modem and phone line support Caller-ID service, you can simply select the Verify Caller-ID check box and enter the phone number that this user must dial to call in. However, if you are using hardware that doesn't support Caller-ID or that service is unavailable in your area, you can achieve the same type of security by having your RAS server call the user back at a certain phone number. Select one of the Callback options in the middle of the Dial-In tab.

If you have home users who dial in either via long distance or local long distance, callback options might save you money when it comes to your remote access costs. If the telephone service in your office has a better per-minute rate than the rates your users typically have in their homes, you can save money by having your RAS server call users back at the cheaper rates.

In addition to callback options, you can specify a fixed IP address for a user. This new Windows 2000 feature can be exceptionally useful when you're setting up internal access policies based on IP addresses (firewalls, for example).

NOTE

If Terminal Services are installed on your Windows 2000 box, there will be several additional User Properties tabs to configure.

Account Settings

If you need to modify the user's login name or UPN suffix, go to the Account tab. This is also the place to specify permissible logon hours, account options, and all that stuff. By default, users are allowed to log on any day of the week at any time of the day (24/7), but you can choose the Logon Hours button to specify particular hours and days (see Figure 25.7).

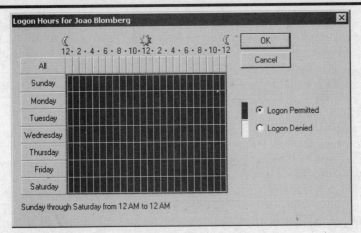

FIGURE 25.7: Setting logon hours

NOTE

By default, a user will not be logged off automatically when logon hours expire, but there is a setting to accomplish this. The setting is called Automatically Log Off Users When Logon Hours Expire, and it's found in the Group Policy snap-in, under Computer Configuration\Windows Settings\Security Settings\Local Policies\Security Options. You can also set this parameter using the Domain Security Policy tool or the Local Security Policy tool (depending on the context). In either case, look for the setting under Local Policies\Security Options.

By default, users can log on to the domain from any workstation, but logon workstations may still be specified by NetBIOS name (see Figure 25.8). However, you must still be using NetBIOS on your network in order for this to be enforced.

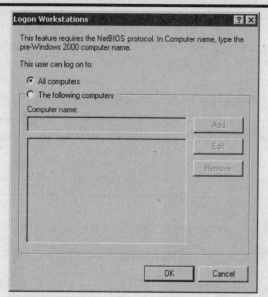

FIGURE 25.8: Permitted logon workstations

If the account is locked as a result of bad logon attempts (which you can configure using one of the Policy tools, as I'll explain later), the Account Is Locked Out box will be checked. If you want to manually unlock the account, uncheck the box. The account expiration setting is at the bottom of the Account tab. By default, an account never expires, but if you enable the option, the default interval is six weeks. Notice also that there are more account options than were offered in NT 4 (scroll down in the Account Options box to see all the options). Several of these, such as User Must Change Password At Next Logon, are familiar to NT 4 administrators and fairly self-explanatory to others. Several options are new and more obscure:

▶ The Store Password Reversible Encryption option is used for Windows 95/98/98 SE clients. That's not really new; it was just not an exposed option in NT 4.

▶ The smart card option is new, and you can use it if you opt for a public key infrastructure such as X.509.

▶ Select the Do Not Require Kerberos Preauthentication option if the account will use an implementation of the Kerberos protocol other than the one supplied with Windows 2000. Not all versions of the Kerberos protocol use this feature, but Windows 2000 does.

▸ Select the Use DES Encryption Types For This Account option if you need the Data Encryption Standard (DES). DES supports multiple levels of encryption, including MPPE (Microsoft Point to Point Encryption) Standard (40-bit), MPPE Standard (56-bit), MPPE Strong (128-bit), IPSec DES (40-bit), IPSec 56-bit DES, and IPSec Triple DES (3DES).

Notice that you cannot reset the user's password from the Account tab. To reset the user's password, close the Properties dialog box, and right-click the username in the details pane of Active Directory Users And Computers. Choose the option to reset the password to open the Reset Password dialog box. Enter and confirm a new password. If you want the user to change the password, check the User Must Change Password At Next Logon check box.

What's in a UPN Name?

I'd like to take a moment to explain how the user naming convention has changed in Windows 2000. In the Account tab in the user's Properties dialog box are two types of user logon names:

▸ The Windows 2000 name is `jblomberg@win2ktest.com`.

▸ The pre–Windows 2000 logon name is `WIN2KTEST\jblomberg`.

In NT 3 and 4, usernames followed the convention `MACHINAME\username` or the convention `DOMAINNAME\username` if the user account was in a domain (although most users weren't aware of this fact). Usernames in Windows 2000 are based on an Internet standard (RFC 822), *Standard for the Format of ARPA Internet Text Messages*, which in English means that Windows 2000 usernames follow common e-mail naming conventions. Each user account has a Universal Principal Name (UPN) consisting of a prefix, which is the username, and a suffix, which is the domain name. The prefix and suffix are joined by the @ sign. The UPN suffix indicates where to look for the user account at logon and is by default the DNS domain name. However, you'll notice that you can't just change the UPN suffix arbitrarily in a user's account record. It must be a UPN suffix specified for the domain in Active Directory Domains And Trusts. The tool allows you to specify alternate UPN suffixes for the domain. Only then can you change the UPN suffix from the default to one of the alternate UPN suffixes.

That said, the alternate UPN suffix you set up in Active Directory Domains And Trusts doesn't have to be an actual domain name. You can make it any domain name you want. For instance, during the research phase of this book, I logged on to the `win2ktest.com` domain as `mark@microsoft.com`. The idea here is to tell the machine in which domain to look for your account. For example, Joao's account may be located in the `win2kgeeks.com` domain, but he works for a company called Green Onion Resources, which consists of the `win2kgeeks.com` domain and four other domains. So his default UPN name might be `jblomberg@win2kgeeks.com`, but if Green Onion doesn't want to advertise their various Windows 2000 domains to the world, or confuse their employees, they can designate `green-onion.com` as an "alternate" UPN suffix for `win2kgeeks.com`. So Joao can log on as `jblomberg@green-onion.com` and have that on his business cards as an e-mail address.

If a person changes jobs within an organization and his user account is moved to a new domain, it's not necessary to change his e-mail address each time, and it's very inconvenient to change logon names just because you got a promotion. So UPN names allow the account to be located easily and make the account's location transparent to the user. All he has to know is "I'm jblomberg@green-onion.com." He doesn't need to be bothered with "well, your user account has to moved to the `win2kgeeks.com` domain, so you'll have to log on from now on as...oh yes, and your e-mail address is changing so tell all your friends and business contacts...."

Profile Information

The Profile tab, shown in Figure 25.9, is the place to specify a user's profile path, a logon script, and a home folder. Mostly, these options are for *downlevel clients* (a condescending new term for any pre–Windows 2000 clients) because you can specify these settings and many more with Group Policy settings. However, Group Policy only works on Windows 2000 systems, and it may be a while before companies begin to standardize on Windows 2000 Professional desktops. Until then, you'll want to use these options. I'll be discussing user profiles and login scripts in more detail in the sections to come, but the following paragraphs will give you the main ideas about these features.

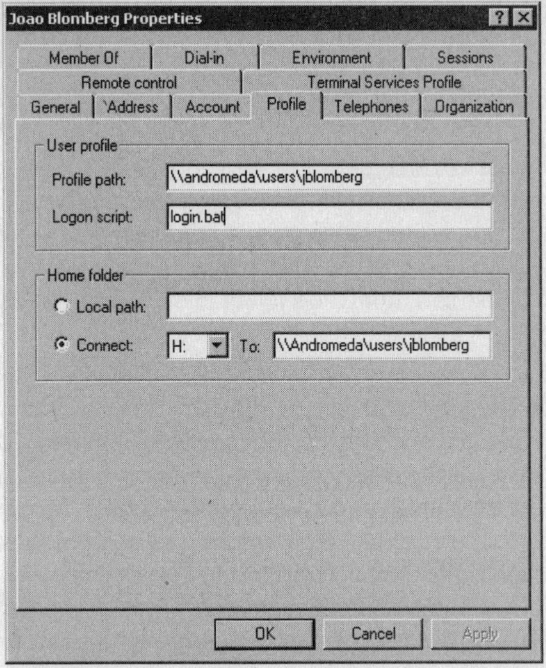

FIGURE 25.9: User profile properties

A user's Desktop settings, from Start menu content right down to a color scheme and mouse orientation, can be stored in a network location so that the user can log on from any system on the network and see the same Desktop. You can specify a shared network location for that purpose. This is also useful if you want to force a user (or group of users) to keep the same settings all the time. Such a thing is called a *roaming profile* if it's not forced on a user and if they can make changes. If the user is compelled to load that profile and can't log on without it, it's called a *mandatory profile* (or a *shared mandatory profile*, if more than one user is shackled to it). Windows 2000 group policies allow you to configure folder redirection and other Desktop settings, eliminating much of the need for NT 4–style roaming and mandatory profiles, so this feature is most useful for NT 4 clients.

A *logon* or *login script* is one that runs at logon time to configure a user's environment and to assign network resources, such as mapped drives and printers. Though the art of the login script is well known in other network operating systems, such as NetWare, login scripts in Microsoft networks have not always been emphasized. Many Microsoft networks were small in the beginning, and users could "browse" for network resources. Login scripts are, however, filling a more important role for Windows environments; networks are larger now, and administration of resources and users is becoming increasingly more complex. Windows 2000 has a default path where the login script will be stored (in the SYSVOL, which is by default in the \WINNT folder, but it's configurable). That's why you need to specify only the script's name in the dialog box. However, it is possible that the login script could be stored in a subdirectory of SYSVOL, for example in SYSVOL\Sales\saleslogin.bat. In that case, you would need to specify the relative path from the SYSVOL root, such as Sales\saleslogin.bat.

A *home folder*, also known as a *home directory*, is a folder assigned to the user for their private use. Although applications may have their own default folder for saving and opening files, the home folder is the default working folder for a user at the command prompt. It is possible to specify a local path for a user's home folder, but that's only useful if the user will be logging on locally to the machine. For users logging on from the network, you need to choose the Connect option and specify a network path following the UNC (Universal Naming Convention) *machinename**servername**directoryname*. You can also use a variable as a folder name, %username%, to indicate that the home folder name is the same as the user ID.

When you specify a home folder path for the user, Windows 2000 will create the user's home folder automatically if the network share already exists and you have permission to write to it. This saves admins a lot of time.

In any discussion about home folders, questions arise about how to limit disk space consumption. In NT 4, there was no built-in mechanism to set or enforce disk quotas. One strategy was to set up a separate partition for user folders, confining the problem to that partition (kind of like growing horseradish). The hapless admin might then run routine "diskhog" scripts and ask, beg, or publicly humiliate users into cleaning up their home folders. Others threatened to start deleting files at random if users didn't comply. But the best option was to purchase a third-party disk quota tool. Now Windows 2000 comes with a simple quota management system; you simply enable it for a volume and then set thresholds for warnings and so forth.

Group Memberships

To specify group memberships for a user account, open the Member Of tab in the Properties dialog box. As you see in Figure 25.10, by default a new user is a member of the group Domain Users. The Active Directory Folder column on the right indicates the container or OU path for the group.

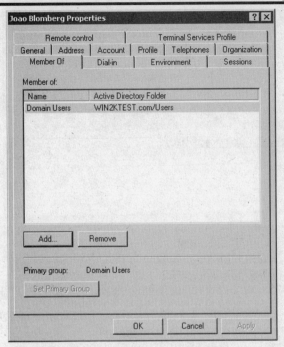

FIGURE 25.10: Setting group memberships

To add a user to another group, follow these steps:

1. Click Add to open the Select Groups dialog box, which is shown in Figure 25.11.

2. Double-click the group name, or click the Add button to add the group name to the bottom pane. If scrolling through the list is too tedious for you, just type in the group names, separated by semicolons.

3. Click Check Names to confirm that the names you typed are valid.

4. Click OK, and you're back at the Member Of tab with the new groups showing in the window.

5. Click OK again, and you're done.

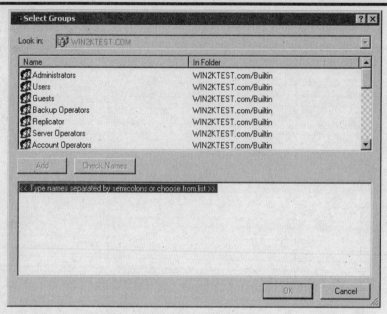

FIGURE 25.11: Selecting users and groups

To remove users from groups, select the user, and then click the Remove button in the Member Of tab. See the section "Working with Security Groups" for the skinny on group memberships.

Managing Accounts

In the previous sections, I discussed how to make changes to a single user account. Now let's talk about how to make changes to several (or many) accounts at once. While we're on the subject, I'll cover a couple of other multiple-account issues, such as how to create a bunch of users at a time.

In Active Directory Users And Computers, you can select multiple accounts in the details pane by holding down the Shift key while you work the down arrow, or you can hit the Ctrl key as you click each of the accounts, and then right-click to display the shortcut menu while those accounts are selected. As you see in Figure 25.12, you can choose to move them all to another container or OU, add them to a group, disable accounts, or enable accounts. (To remove members of a group, you'll need to go to the Properties dialog box of the group itself.) You can also send them all mail, assuming you have specified e-mail addresses for the accounts.

TIP

Remember, changes to a user's account, such as group memberships, will not take effect until the next time the user logs on.

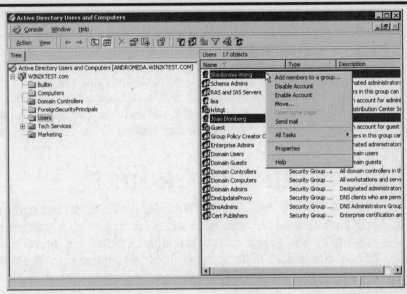

FIGURE 25.12: Selecting multiple users in Active Directory Users And Computers

You can also create an account template and copy it to create users with like settings. Properties that are copied include account settings (such as Password Never Expires), group memberships, account expiration date (if supplied), and the UPN suffix. The profile information (home directory, user profile path, and logon script) is also copied, and if you used the %username% variable to set up the template user's home folder, it will be created automatically for new users when the account is copied.

Okay, those are nice options, but where is the Select Members By Group option from our old friend the User Manager For Domains (USRMGR.EXE)? You could use that tool to select all the members of a group at once instead of scrolling through a list and selecting the users one-by-one. Come to think of it, you could manage a wider set of account properties with USRMGR.EXE, such as logon hours and home directories, and even make them all change their passwords at next logon. There doesn't seem to be a way to do these things with Active Directory Users And Computers. I actually did stumble across a Properties On Multiple Objects dialog box by selecting several accounts and pressing Alt+Enter, but it didn't work. It only set the properties of the first account selected.

So how do I make changes to several users at once, and how will I create, say, 50 or 500 users at a time?

It seems as if the answer to these questions is more complicated than it has to be, unless Microsoft is hiding something from us. You can query and modify the Active Directory using the Active Directory Services Interface (ADSI). So if you master ADSI and learn about Active Directory class objects and attributes and so forth, and if you know some VBScript or JScript, some Java or VB or C, or even some C++, you could create your 50 users at a time, presumably. Or even better, some bright, shining third-party vendor will figure it out for us and slap a user-friendly interface on it. We only have to wait for it to appear.

Understanding Groups

Assigning users to groups makes it easier to grant them both rights to perform tasks and permissions to access resources such as printers and network folders. To assist you in this endeavor, there are several built-in groups with built-in rights that you should be familiar with. You'll also want to create your own user groups and assign them certain rights and permissions. The members of the groups you create may in turn be granted the ability to administer other groups and objects, even whole organization units. To top it all off, groups in Windows 2000 can now contain computers and contacts as well as users and other groups. They can also be used as e-mail distribution lists. So it's important to understand the different types of groups that exist and how to work with them to delegate control, grant access to necessary resources, and configure rights. This is the subject of the next few sections.

Creating Groups

To create a new group in Active Directory Users And Computers, navigate to the container where you want the group to live. You can create groups at the root of the domain, in a built-in container such as Users, or in an OU. Follow these steps:

1. Highlight the container, and choose Action ➢ New ➢ Group to open the New Object – Group dialog box, as shown in Figure 25.13.

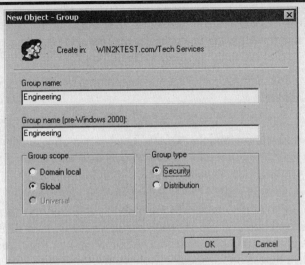

FIGURE 25.13: New group information

2. Supply the name of the group (Engineering) and the down-level name if it will be different, and then choose the group scope and group type. By default, the group scope is Global, and the type is Security. For an explanation of group types and group scope, see the following sections.

3. Click OK to create the group in the selected container.

Now let's fill in the rest of the group information and add users to the new group. Follow these steps:

1. Find and double-click the group you just created to open the Group Properties dialog box.

2. In the General tab, fill in a description if you wish and an e-mail address if a distribution list exists for the group.

3. To populate the group, select the Members tab, and click Add to open the Select Users, Contacts, Computers, Or Groups dialog box.

Windows 2000 allows users, other groups, and even computers to belong to groups, although there are rules for group nesting, as you'll read in the next few sections. Group members can also come from different OUs.

4. Highlight the users or groups and choose Add, or type the names, separated by semicolons, and then choose Check Names to verify the typed-in names (it's not necessary to check the names if you selected them from the list).

5. Click OK to finalize your additions and return to the Properties dialog box.

To view or modify the local and universal groups Engineering belongs to, for example, select the Member Of tab. The Managed By tab is for optional contact information and does not necessarily reflect any direct delegation of control.

Another way to add members to a group is to right-click the user account and choose Add Members To A Group. If you want to add several selected users to the same group at once, hold down the Ctrl key while you select users, and then right-click and choose Add Members To A Group. You'll also find a button on the toolbar in the Active Directory Users And Computers to add one or more selected objects to a group. As I mentioned earlier, there is unfortunately no option to select all the members of a group, which would allow you to manage other account properties as well.

One final how-to note: It will probably be necessary to move a group from one container to another at some point, since having groups in OUs facilitates delegation. To do this, right-click the group icon in the details pane of the Active Directory Users and Groups, and choose Move to open the Move dialog box, which is shown in Figure 25.14. Navigate to the container that will be the new home for the group, select it, and click OK.

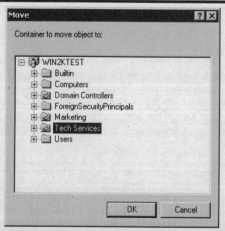

FIGURE 25.14: Moving a group to another container

Group Types: Security Groups versus Distribution Groups

When creating group accounts in Windows 2000, you can classify a group as a *security group* or as a *distribution group*. Security groups are not really new; they are equivalent to user groups as we knew them in all versions of Windows NT. They are only being called security groups now in order to distinguish them from distribution groups, which are sort of "non-security groups" and are new to Windows 2000.

Security Groups Overview

Security groups are groups used to assign rights and permissions. Like user accounts, security groups are assigned SIDs. When you view or edit an object's Access Control List (ACL), for example, the group names that appear on the list are security groups (sometimes they show up as SIDs if the friendly names are slow to resolve). These user and group SID entries on the ACL are matched up with a user's credentials to permit or deny access to the object.

There are three major types of security groups—local, global, and universal—although you might prefer to think of them as four groups: local, domain local, global, and universal.

Local groups are the kinds of groups you find on a stand-alone server, a server that is a member of a domain, or a Windows 2000 Professional workstation. Local groups are local to the machine. That is, they exist and are valid only on that workstation or on a non–domain controller server.

Domain local group is the special name for a local group that happens to be on a domain controller. Domain controllers have a common active directory that is replicated between them, so a domain local group on one replica DC will also exist on its sibling DC. As you'll see when we start getting into the details, they are different from other local groups.

Global, universal, and, of course, domain locals live on the domain controllers in the Active Directory. Global groups are still much as they were in NT 4; they are used to grant access rights and permissions across machine (and domain) boundaries.

Universal groups are new to Windows 2000 and can also serve the function of global groups, granting rights and object permissions throughout domains and between domains. They are more useful than globals or locals because they are infinitely more flexible with regard to nesting, but you can really only use them when your domain has gone "native," which requires that all NT 4 domain controllers be upgraded to Windows 2000.

Distribution Groups and Contacts

In NT 4, every group was a security group and could be used for controlling access to resources and granting rights. A distribution group is simply a non-security group. Distribution groups don't have SIDs and don't appear on ACLs. So what are they for? If you've worked with Exchange or a similar product, you are familiar with distribution lists. These are groups of recipient addresses. It's easier to send mail to ACME Managers, for example, than to individually select each manager's name from a list.

Assuming that you have entered e-mail addresses for your users, your security groups in the Active Directory are also unofficial distribution lists. Just right-click a group name in Active Directory Users And Computers to display the option to send e-mail to the group members, just as you see the option to send e-mail to a user account when you right-click it. This will kick off your default e-mail–handling program, and the system will try to send mail using the e-mail address supplied in the account information. So, if you have a group of people working in the finance department and you place all those people in a security group called Finance, you can not only assign permissions for resources to the Finance group, but you can also send e-mail to the members of the Finance security group, assuming you have filled in the e-mail information for each member.

The interesting part about these distribution groups is Windows 2000's close integration with the next version of Exchange. If you have administered Exchange and NT together, you know that it's a pain to maintain two lists, one for security and one for communication purposes. The next version of Exchange is supposed to integrate Exchange with Active Directory so you won't have to keep separate mailboxes and user accounts.

 NOTE

If you are upgrading to Windows 2000 or setting up a new Windows 2000 server on a network with Exchange, you should make sure that there are no preexisting groups with the same name as the display name of an Exchange distribution list. Rename either the distribution list display name or the NT group name to avoid conflicts.

Distribution lists are not always the same as security groups, though. For example, say your company is a communications provider and has a distribution list called Outage Alert. This distribution list is used to notify certain people in the case of a major outage that will affect service to your customers. The members of this list might include people from operations, customer relations, and even the chief executive officer. Plus, the distribution list could include external e-mail addresses of key business partners (also known as *contacts*). These people will not have a security group in common, and it's silly to have to create a separate security group just because you need a distribution list.

Since Microsoft is so determined to integrate Active Directory and Exchange, you can classify a group in the Active Directory as a distribution group, a group with no security privileges. No security identifiers are created for a distribution group, so the membership is not included in a user's credentials at logon time. You can't grant permission to use a printer to a distribution list since it doesn't appear in the ACL. The group is strictly for e-mail. Presumably, this will allow us to manage a good part of Exchange mailboxes and distribution lists without using a separate Exchange administration tool.

NOTE

You can change a security group to a distribution group and back again, but not if you're still running in Mixed mode. As with everything else that's truly useful in Windows 2000, you have to be running in Native mode.

Similarly, contacts are objects that store information about people, including e-mail, telephone, and related information. Contacts can be members of security or distribution groups, but they are not accounts, so there is no SID for a contact, and no user rights or permissions can be assigned to them.

Group Scope: Locals, Globals, and Universals

Where are they recognized and what can they contain? These are the main issues surrounding local, global, and universal groups. Since they are used to grant rights and permissions, we need to know where that group membership means something, or where it is accepted (kind of like American Express). Since we want to nest groups to simplify the granting of rights and permissions, we need to know the rules and recommendations for nesting as well.

Regular local groups are the only type of group that exists on stand-alone servers and Windows 2000 Professional systems. A stand-alone server or Professional workstation, which is not a member of a domain, is like an island nation with no knowledge of the outside world. It recognizes only its own local groups and users.

Local groups are the only ones that can be granted permission to access resources, and membership is limited to local users. When the machine joins the domain, however, that island nation becomes a member of a greater governing body, like a federation of island nations. This "member server" or "member workstation" keeps its Local Users An Groups, but will now accept non-local members from the "federation" into its local group memberships. Global groups and "federation" (domain) accounts now can be referenced on object permissions lists (ACLs) as well.

Domain local groups, living on Active Directory domain controllers, exist in a different context than the local groups on workstations, stand-alones, or member servers. These machines are, by definition, aware of their home domain and any other domains in the AD forest. Domain local groups can, therefore, contain members from any domain in the forest. They can contain users, globals from your domain or a trusted one, and universals.

Although domain local groups are more flexible in their membership, they are valid only in their home domain since they are only used on ACLs in the same domain. Other domains have their own domain local groups. If the domain local group were valid in another domain, it wouldn't be "local" any more, would it? Moreover, domain local groups don't replicate to the Global Catalog, although membership information replicates between domain controllers in the same domain. Membership of domain local groups should be relatively small and use nesting.

NOTE

The Global Catalog is a domain controller that also keeps a database of basic information on all objects in the home domain, as well as information on objects in other domains in the forest. The first DC in a domain is by default a Global Catalog server, but others can be designated. The Global Catalog facilitates logins and supplies directory information on objects in other domains.

Windows 2000 global groups are like NT 4 global groups. Global groups can contain only members from the same domain. Now in Windows 2000, you can put other global groups in them, but only in Native mode. You can't put a local group or a universal group into a global group, just user accounts and global groups from the same domain.

Global group membership is exactly the reverse of membership in domain local groups; membership in global groups is limited, but its acceptance is wide. Global groups can be used on any ACL in the forest, even in other forests if you establish an old-fashioned trust relationship. Think of global groups as containers for users and groups that need to be accepted on other machines and other domains. Global group information is also replicated between sibling domain controllers, but the Global Catalog contains only group names, not members.

Universal groups are new to Windows 2000, and you can create them on any domain controller. They can contain members from any domain in your forest and can be used on an object's ACL within the forest. Membership in universal groups is infinitely flexible, and membership is universally accepted within the forest. So why don't we just use universal groups for everything and not even worry about local or global groups any more? There are two reasons:

1. Universal groups can only be used in Native mode. Native mode is only possible after you upgrade all NT 4 domain controllers; they will not be able to handle this universal group thing.

2. If you use only universal groups, your Global Catalog will become bloated and replication issues could occur.

You see, universal group names and membership are both replicated to the other Global Catalog servers (typically, there will be one for each site); global group names appear in the Global Catalog, but its members don't. With multiple domains, the Global Catalog contains replicated information for every domain in the forest, and the size (and replication time) will increase exponentially if universal groups contain a large number of objects. Therefore, universal group membership should be fairly static. Avoid adding users directly, and only nest other groups.

On the other hand, if you have only one domain for your entire organization, your Global Catalog servers don't have to replicate information from other domains, which cuts down on replication overhead immensely. In that case, you can use universal groups exclusively. In fact, you probably want to do away with global groups completely in a single-domain setting and just use universal groups instead.

TIP

A group can contain a maximum of 5,000 members. So if you have a group of 15,000 members, you have to break it up into, say, three smaller groups and put those smaller groups into a group together.

Global and universal groups can span domains, even forests. Domains and machines in different forests do not trust one another automatically and, therefore, do not exchange group information, but this can be accomplished with old-fashioned manually created trust relationships, as you handled multiple domain matters in NT 4.

So there you have it—the skinny on local, global, and universal groups. It's really not so hard once you know and understand the rules of thumb, which are as follows:

▶ Use local groups to grant local privileges and access to local resources. Put other groups into local groups and keep membership small.

▶ Use global groups to collect users and other same-domain global groups who will need the same privileges or access to the same resources. Put these global groups into local groups that have the desired privileges and access permissions.

▶ Use universal groups any way you like once you've done away with all NT 4 domain controllers, but for replication reasons, it's best to nest global groups (as opposed to user accounts) inside universal groups.

▶ Even though you can, don't nest groups too deeply. You'll get a performance hit if you do.

Oh, yes, and I think it would be helpful to summarize the new nesting rules in Windows 2000.

Local groups (on a Windows 2000 Professional workstation or a member server) can contain the following:

▶ Domain locals, globals, universals from the home domain

▶ Globals and universals from trusted Windows 2000 domains

▶ Globals from trusted Windows NT 4 domains

Domain local groups (on a domain controller) can contain the following:

▶ User accounts from any domain in the forest

- ▸ Universals and globals from any forest domain

- ▸ Locals from the same domain only

Global groups can contain the following:

- ▸ Users from the same domain

- ▸ Other global groups from the same domain

Universal groups can contain the following:

- ▸ User accounts from any domain in the forest

- ▸ Other universal groups

- ▸ Global groups from any domain in the forest

Working with Security Groups

All right, enough talk about global, local, and universal groups. You need some examples of how this works. However, let me first emphasize how important it is to think about your group structures ahead of time. Once you've "pre-nested" your larger membership groups (such as the local and universal groups) and granted access to the local groups when you set up your resources, you'll only have to fiddle with global and universal group memberships from then on. This will save time and simplify the task of granting object permissions.

Some good basic nesting examples can be drawn from the nesting patterns that are set up automatically within a domain. One is the nesting of administrator groups. The Administrator account on a Windows 2000 machine draws its powers from membership in the local Administrators group. Take Administrator out of the Administrators group, and the account has no special powers or abilities (I don't recommend it).

The Active Directory automatically creates the Domain Admins global group, although it doesn't assign broad admin rights to the group as you might think. When a Windows 2000 machine joins a domain (or becomes a domain controller), the global group Domain Admins and the universal group Enterprise Admins are automatically placed in the membership of the local Administrators group.

Figure 25.15 shows the membership of the domain local group Administrators for the win2ktest.com domain. The net effect of this nesting is that a member of the Domain Admins or Enterprise Admins group is a local administrator on every member machine in the domain. You can override this default behavior by removing Domain Admins or Enterprise Admins from the local Administrators group on a machine, but again, I don't recommend it unless there is a special reason to do so.

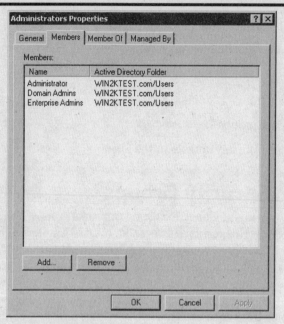

FIGURE 25.15: Members of the Administrators domain local group

You can replace the Domain Admins or Enterprise Admins group membership in the local Administrators groups with more specific Admin-type global groups, such as F&A Admins or CS Admins, but having no global or universal groups at all in the local Administrators group limits control to local Administrator accounts and unnecessarily complicates remote administration tasks.

Another example of group nesting is the membership of the local Users group. On a domain member or domain controller, Users automatically includes Domain Users. When you create a new user account in a domain, the new user is automatically assigned to the Domain Users group. It's sort of an "All Users in the Domain" group. The net effect is that a user account in a domain is automatically granted local user privileges on every domain member machine by default. The user account goes into the global group Domain Users, and the global group Domain Users goes into the local group Users, which is granted local rights and permissions on a system.

You should also know, just for the record, about a couple of other nestings. Domain Guests is automatically a member of the local group Guests on all domain member machines, and Enterprise Admins (a universal group) is a member of the local Administrators group.

Now let's look at the fictional case of Green Onion Resources (GOR), a national IT consulting and integration firm. Green Onion uses the Windows 2000 Active Directory with both Windows 2000 and NT 4 domain controllers. GOR has grouped the company's IT resources into domains by regional offices—for example, GOR South domain, GOR West domain, and GOR East domain. Finance and Accounting (F&A) people are similarly grouped into global groups by region, as are other functional units of GOR. So there are global groups called F&A South, F&A West, and F&A East.

Keeping the Finance people in different global groups in different domains allows finer control of region-specific resources and administration. But there are some central resources that must be accessible to all F&A people at GOR. Those resources are located in the Central Finance share on the Windows 2000 server called GOR_ALPHA1. Now, administrators (or their delegates) have set up a local group called F&A Central on GOR_ALPHA1 and put each global group (F&A South, F&A West, and F&A East) into the local group called F&A Central. The local group F&A Central has access to the shared resource Central Finance.

This will work and is definitely the way to go in Mixed mode. When someone is hired or leaves one of the F&A departments, admins need only to add or remove the user account from the global group to grant or deny access. This will also grant access to the region-specific resources that the global groups can already get to.

But when Green Onion Resources upgrades all existing NT 4 domain controllers, they go into Native mode, and the fun begins. Now they can maintain granularity by having global groups of functional units and regions, *and* they can also group these different F&A regional groups into a new universal group called GOR F&A. GOR enterprise admins put the three groups—F&A South, F&A West, and F&A East—into the universal group GOR F&A. They can now use the universal group to directly permit access to F&A organization-wide resources, such as the Central Finance folder, instead of using the three global groups—although it's still considered good form to put the universal group into a local group and grant access to the local group.

Why should we keep nesting global and universal groups into local groups even after Native mode? You can certainly just put a bunch of accounts into the GOR F&A universal group instead. If you have a single domain for your organization and never plan to have more, this strategy is perfectly acceptable. With multiple domains, however, remember that the Global Catalog must replicate the names and members of all universal groups throughout the forest, so grouping all 600 or so bean counter accounts from the different domains into one universal group becomes a replication (read "performance") issue.

You can also grant access to the shared resource directly to the universal group and bypass the local group nesting altogether. Current thinking holds that it's easier to set up access on the resource once and then modify it by manipulating the membership of the group that has access. This was especially true under NT 4, when managing permissions on remote shares was a bit cumbersome, but Active Directory management is likely to change all that. Granting access directly to the universal group would seem to be in keeping with that principle, though, if you plan to keep your universal group membership down and limit it to other groups.

The problem here is that domains and their global groups might come and go, especially in Windows 2000, since an entire domain can be wiped out without reinstalling the operating system. If ACL entries refer to global or universal groups that are no longer recognized as the result of a defunct domain or a broken trust relationship, ACL will report an entry as "Account Unknown," and the Forces of Darkness will increase and multiply and chaos will reign...well, maybe not. But it's messy. If you always grant access to a local group, the machine will always recognize it. You can then simply grant or deny access to a resource by manipulating the membership of that local group.

Built-In Domain Local Groups

You might have noticed in our earlier tour of Active Directory Users And Computers that all the built-in user accounts, such as Guest and Administrator, are placed by default in the Users container. There are also predefined global groups in the Users container, but some groups are listed under the Builtin container. The groups in the Builtin container are labeled Builtin Local, and the ones in the Users container are Domain Local, Global, or Universal. What's the difference?

Well, for one thing, local groups are specific to the machine, but global groups can be accepted throughout the domain or in a trusted domain.

Built-in local groups have predetermined rights and permissions for the purposes of administration. Membership in these (or any) groups grants the user all the powers and abilities granted to the group. This is a way to quickly assign well-defined administrative roles instead of having to create them from scratch.

For example, Server Operators have an inherent set of rights that allow them to create file shares and manage services. Backup Operators have the right to back up files and folders, even if they don't have permission to read or modify them. Table 25.2 lists the built-in domain local groups and their special abilities. Built-in local groups are common to all Windows 2000 systems of the same ilk (server/DC/workstation) and provide convenient container groups for granting local administrative authority.

NOTE

You can't delete these groups. You can, however, create other users and groups in the container, although they won't have any special rights unless you assign them.

TIP

In general, rights grant the ability to do something, often something admin related or otherwise restricted, and permissions grant the ability to access resources such as files and printers as well as Active Directory objects such as group policies.

TABLE 25.2: Built-In Groups and Their Rights

USER RIGHTS	MEMBERS CAN ALSO
Group: Administrators	
Log on locally	Create and manage user accounts
Access this computer from the network	Create and manage global groups
Take ownership of files	Assign user rights
Manage auditing and security log	Manage auditing and security policy
Change the system time	Lock the server console
Shut down the system	Unlock the console
Force shutdown from a remote system	Format the server's hard disk
Back up files and directories	Create common program groups

CONTINUED ➡

TABLE 25.2 continued: Built-In Groups and Their Rights

User Rights	Members Can Also
Group: Administrators	
Restore files and directories	Keep a local profile
Add and remove device drivers	Share and stop sharing directories
Increase the priority of a process	Share and stop sharing printers
Group: Server Operators	
Log on locally	Lock the server
Change the system time	Override server's lock
Shut down the system	Format the server's hard disk
Force shutdown from a remote system	Create common groups
Back up files and directories	Keep a local profile
Restore files and directories	Share and stop sharing directories
	Share and stop sharing printers
Group: Account Operators	
Log on locally	Create and manage user accounts, global groups, and local groups[1]
Shut down the system	Keep a local profile
Group: Print Operators	
Log on locally	Keep a local profile
Shut down the system	Share and stop sharing printers
Group: Backup Operators	
Log on locally	Keep a local profile
Shut down the system	
Back up files and directories	
Restore files and directories	

CONTINUED ➡

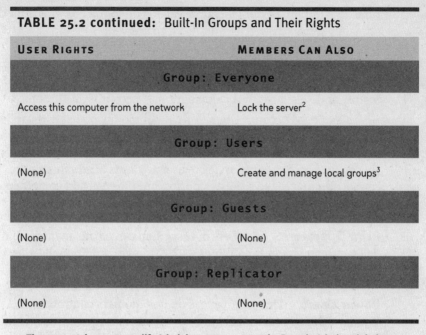

TABLE 25.2 continued: Built-In Groups and Their Rights

USER RIGHTS	MEMBERS CAN ALSO
Group: Everyone	
Access this computer from the network	Lock the server[2]
Group: Users	
(None)	Create and manage local groups[3]
Group: Guests	
(None)	(None)
Group: Replicator	
(None)	(None)

Part v

1. They cannot, however, modify Administrator accounts, the Domain Admins global group, or the local group's Administrators, Server Operators, Account Operators, Print Operators, and Backup Operators.
2. In order to actually do this, the member of the group must have the right to log on locally at the server.
3. In order to actually do this, the user must either have the right to log on locally at the server or have access to the DSA.MSC tool.

Administrators Administrators have almost every built-in right, so members are basically all-powerful with regard to administration of the system.

Backup Operators Members of Backup Operators have the right to back up and restore files whether or not they have permission to access those files otherwise.

Server Operators The Server Operators local group has all the rights needed to manage the domain's servers. Members can create, manage, and delete printer shares at servers; create, manage, and delete network shares at servers; back up and restore files on servers; format a server's fixed disk; lock and unlock servers; unlock files; and change the system time. In addition, Server Operators can log on to the network from the domain's servers as well as shut down the servers.

Account Operators   Members of the Account Operators local group are allowed to create user accounts and groups for the domain and to modify or delete most of the domain's user accounts and groups.

A member of Account Operators cannot modify or delete the following groups: Administrators, Domain Admins, Account Operators, Backup Operators, Print Operators, and Server Operators. Likewise, members of this group cannot modify or delete user accounts of administrators. They cannot administer the security policies, but they can add computers to a domain, log on at servers, and shut down servers.

Print Operators   Members of this group can create, manage, and delete printer shares for a Windows 2000 server. Additionally, they can log on at and shut down servers.

Power Users   This group exists on non–domain controllers and Windows 2000 Professional systems. Members can create user accounts and local groups and can manage the membership of Users, Power Users, and Guests as well as administer other users and groups that they have created.

Users   Users can run applications (but not install them). They also can shut down and lock the workstation. If a user has the right to log on locally to a workstation, they also have the right to create local groups and manage those groups they have created.

Guests   Guests can log on and run applications. They can also shut down the system, but otherwise their abilities are even more limited than Users. For example, they cannot keep a local profile.

Replicator   This group is strictly for directory replication. A user account is used to run the Replicator service, and it should be the only member of the group.

In the Users container, other predefined domain local groups and global groups may be created as part of the configuration of a certain service. They might serve to allow users access to certain services (such as

DHCP Users and WINS Users) or to provide a group container for administrators of the service, as in the case of DHCP Administrators and DNS Admins. These and other predefined global groups may also have special rights and/or permissions for particular things, but they don't have the broad rights and permissions of Administrators, Server Operators, or another built-in local group.

NOTE

Some predefined groups, such as Domain Computers and Domain Controllers, are designated for machine accounts, although you can add a user account to Domain Computers if it gives you a thrill.

Windows 2000 has several built-in global groups, among them Domain Admins, Domain Users, and Domain Guests. These will only appear on domain controllers. In fact, it's possible to create global groups *only* on domain controllers. Although you might use an administration tool while sitting at a non–domain controller to create the global groups, they exist only on domain controllers. Table 25.3 describes the most important built-in global groups.

TABLE 25.3: Built-In Global Groups

GROUP	WHAT IT DOES
Domain Admins	By placing a user account into this global group, you provide administrative-level abilities to that user. Members of Domain Admins can administer the home domain, the workstations of the domain, and any other trusted domains that have added this domain's Domain Admins global group to their own Administrators local group. By default, the built-in Domain Admins global group is a member of both the domain's Administrators local group and the Administrators local groups for every NT or Windows 2000 workstation in the domain. The built-in Administrator user account for the domain is automatically a member of the Domain Admins global group.
Domain Users	Members of the Domain Users global group have normal user access to, and abilities for, both the domain itself and any NT/Windows 2000 workstation in the domain. This group contains all domain user accounts and is by default a member of every local Users group on every NT/Windows 2000 workstation in the domain.
Domain Guests	This group allows guest accounts to access resources across domain boundaries if they've been permitted to do so by the domain administrators.

Special Built-In Groups

In addition to the built-in local and global groups, several special groups that are not listed in Active Directory Users And Computers (or Computer Management Users And Groups for that matter) will appear on Access Control Lists for resources and objects, including the following:

INTERACTIVE   Anyone using the computer locally.

NETWORK   All users connected over the network to a computer.

SYSTEM   The operating system.

CREATOR OWNER   The creator and/or owner of subfolders, files, and print jobs.

AUTHENTICATED USERS   Any user that has been authenticated to the system. Used as a more secure alternative to Everyone.

ANONYMOUS LOGON   A user that has logged on anonymously, such as an anonymous FTP user.

BATCH   An account that has logged on as a batch job.

SERVICE   An account that has logged on as a service.

DIALUP   Users who are accessing the system via Dial-Up Networking.

Incidentally, the INTERACTIVE and NETWORK groups together form the Everyone local group.

User Rights

User access to network resources—files, folders, devices—in Windows 2000 is controlled in two ways:

- ▶ By assigning to a user *rights* that grant or deny access to certain objects (for example, the ability to log on to a server)

- ▶ By assigning to objects *permissions* that specify who is allowed to use objects and under what conditions (for example, granting Read access for a folder to a particular user)

Consider the groups Users and Administrators. What makes administrators different from users? Well, administrators can log on right at the server; users can't. Administrators can create users and back up files; users can't. Administrators are different from users in that they have rights that users don't have. You control who gets which rights in Windows 2000 by using Group Policy. Rights generally authorize a user to perform certain system tasks. For example, the average user can't just sit down at a Windows 2000 server and log on. The ability to log on locally at a server is an example of a right, as is the ability to back up and restore day and to modify printer options on a shared printer. You can assign user rights separately to a single user, but for reasons of security organization, it is better to put the user into a group and define which rights are granted to the group.

Permissions, on the other hand, apply to specific objects such as files, folders, and printers. The ability to make changes to files in the OPERA-TIONS folder on the BIGMACHINE server is an example of a permission. Permissions regulate which users can have access to the object and in what fashion.

As a rule, user rights take precedence over object permissions. For example, let's look at a user who is a member of the built-in Backup Operators group. By virtue of membership in that group, the user has the right to back up the server. This requires the ability to see and read all folders and files on the servers, including those whose creators and owners have specifically denied Read permission to members of the Backup Operators group; thus the right to perform backups overrides the permissions set on the files and folders. But don't worry about your privacy; the Backup Operators group's rights are only valid in conjunction with a backup routine; they can't just open files on the server and read the contents, for example.

In Windows 2000, built-in groups have certain rights already assigned to them; you can also create new groups and assign a custom set of user rights to those groups. As I've said before, security management is much easier when all user rights are assigned through groups instead of to individual users.

To view or modify the local rights assignment for a user or group, open the Local Security Policy tool from the Administrative Tools group on a non–domain controller, or use the Domain Controller Security Policy tool for a domain controller. Open Local Policies\User Rights Assignment. A listing of rights and the users or groups that have been granted them will display in the details pane on the right, as shown in Figure 25.16.

To add or remove a right to a user or group, double-click the right displayed in the details pane, or right-click the selected right and choose Security. In Figure 25.17 you see the Security information for the right to change the system time. To remove a right from a group, highlight the name of the group, and choose Remove. To add a group or user to the list, click Add to open the Select Users Of Groups dialog box, and type a name or click Browse to select a name. Table 25.4 lists user rights with descriptions.

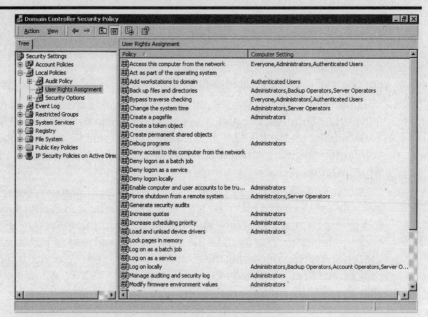

FIGURE 25.16: Local user rights policy

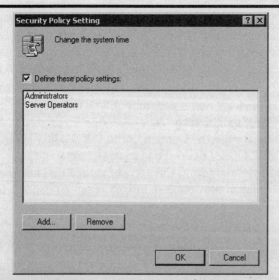

FIGURE 25.17: Local security policy setting for a user right

TABLE 25.4: Local User Rights

User Right	Description
Access this computer from the network	Connect over the network to a computer.
Act as part of the operating system	Act as a trusted part of the operating system; some subsystems have this privilege granted to them.
Add workstations to domain	Make machines domain members.
Back up files and directories	Back up files and directories. As mentioned earlier, this right supersedes file and directory permissions.
Bypass traverse checking	Traverse a directory tree even if the user has no other rights to access that directory.
Change the system time	Set the time for the internal clock of a computer.
Create a pagefile	Create a pagefile.
Create a token object	Create access tokens. Only the Local Security Authority should have this privilege.
Create permanent shared objects	Create special permanent objects.
Debug programs	Debug applications.
Deny access to this computer from the network	Opposite of the "access this computer from the network" right; specifically revokes the right to users/groups that would normally have it.
Deny logon as a batch job	Revokes the right to log on as a batch job.
Deny logon as a service	Revokes the right to log on as a service.
Deny logon locally	Revokes the right to log on locally.
Enable computer and user accounts to be trusted for delegation	Designate accounts which can be delegated.
Force shutdown from a remote system	Force a computer to shut down from a remote system.
Generate security audits	Generate audit log entries.
Increase quotas	Increase object quotas (each object has a quota assigned to it).
Increase scheduling priority	Boost the scheduling priority of a process.
Load and unload device drivers	Add or remove drivers from the system.

Part v

CONTINUED ➡

TABLE 25.4 continued: Local User Rights

User Right	Description
Lock pages in memory	Lock pages in memory to prevent them from being paged out into backing store (such as PAGEFILE.SYS).
Log on as a batch job	Log on to the system as a batch queue facility.
Log on as a service	Perform security services (the user that performs replication logs on as a service).
Log on locally	Log on locally at the server computer itself.
Manage auditing and security log	Specify what types of events and resource access are to be audited. Also allows viewing and clearing the security log.
Modify firmware environment values	Modify system environment variables (not user environment variables).
Profile single process	Use Windows 2000 profiling capabilities to observe a process.
Profile system performance	Use Windows 2000 profiling capabilities to observe the system.
Remove computer from docking station	Remove a laptop computer from its docking station.
Replace a process level token	Modify a process's access token.
Restore files and directories	Restore files and directories. This right supersedes file and directory permissions.
Shut down the system	Shut down Windows 2000.
Synchronize directory service data	Update Active Directory information.
Take ownership of files or other objects	Take ownership of files, directories, and other objects that are owned by other users.

Many rights, such as the right to debug programs and the right to profile a single process, are useful only to programmers who are writing applications to run on Windows 2000, and most are not granted to a group or user.

In general, I find that the only user right that I ever end up granting is the right to change the system time; regular users need that ability in order for their login scripts to successfully synchronize time with the time server, although members of the Power Users group already have it. Also, many third-party applications, such as backup programs and virus-scanning engines, require an Administrator-level user account that can "log on as a service."

How Do Organizational Units Fit in Here?

Organizational units (OUs) are logical containers in a domain. They can contain users, groups, computers, and other OUs, but only from their home domain. You can't put global groups or computers from another domain into your domain's OU, for example.

The usefulness of OUs is strictly for administration. Administrators can create and apply group policies to an OU, and they can delegate control of OUs as well. The idea is to have a subdivision of a domain but still share common security information and resources. Grouping users, groups, and resources into organizational units allows you to apply policies in a more granular fashion and also to decide who manages what and to what extent. So whatever anyone says about how to group your OUs, keep in mind that the tool must fit your hand; your organization may be unique, so your approach to OUs may be as well.

Rather than creating OUs for locations (that's what sites are for), departments, and so on, think about how your organization will be administered. Design your OUs with delegation in mind. Keep it simple for your own sake. Thousands of nested OUs just make more work for you. Also, OUs are unrelated to the process of locating resources on your network, so you needn't group them with a browse list in mind, either.

What's the difference between an OU and a container? An OU is a container, but not just a container like the Users container in DSA.MSC. You can delegate control of a container (you can delegate control of anything), but you can't apply Group Policy to a container.

How are OUs different from groups? A user can be a member of many groups but can only be in one OU at a time. Like groups, an OU can contain other OUs. Group names appear on ACLs, so you can grant or deny access to groups. OUs do not appear on ACLs, so you can't give everyone in the Finance OU access to a printer, for example. On the other hand, you can't assign everyone in a security group a designated set of desktop applications, but you can publish or assign the company accounting package to the entire Accounting OU.

WORKING WITH GROUP POLICIES

An administrator's work is never done. Users are constantly fiddling with their settings, it's hard to maintain "standard builds," and rolling out new applications is a big headache, in large networks or small. It's a pain to package up applications, remote management systems such as SMS are unnecessarily complex, and Admin privileges are needed to install many applications on NT or Windows 2000 machines. What a marketing opportunity!

When it comes to configuration management, a lot of buzzwords are flying around these days: system policies, Group Policy, Change and Configuration Management (CCM), and Intellimirror. What do these words mean to an everyday admin who just wants to maintain some continuity in desktop configurations?

CCM and Intellimirror are marketing monikers for a group of Windows 2000 desktop management features, including roaming profiles and folder redirection, offline folders, software distribution, and desktop configuration control (I mean management). Despite the fancy terms, many of these features (including folder redirection, software distribution, and remote desktop configuration) are easily implemented with group policies.

What kinds of things can you do with group policies? Here's a brief list:

- ▶ Publish or assign software packages to users or machines.

- ▶ Assign start-up, shutdown, logon, and logoff scripts.

- ▶ Define password, lockout, and audit policy for the domain.

- ▶ Standardize a whole bunch of other security settings for remote machines, settings that were previously only configurable by editing the Registry or using a third-party security configuration tool. Some features, such as the ability to enforce group memberships and services configuration, are completely new.

- ▶ Define and enforce settings for Internet Explorer.

- ▶ Define and enforce restrictions on users' desktops.

- ▶ Redirect certain folders in users' profiles (such as Start Menu or Desktop) to be stored in a central location.

- ▶ Configure and standardize settings for new features such as offline folders, disk quotas, and even Group Policy itself.

I'll discuss user profiles later in this chapter. Folder redirection is really a lightweight approach to user profiles ("Profiles Lite"), allowing you to use a subset of the full roaming-profile features, so I'll talk about that later in this chapter as well. The key point here is that Group Policy provides a single point of administration, allowing administrators to easily install software and apply standardized settings to multiple users and computers throughout an organization.

Before Windows 2000, a much smaller subset of these things, mostly just Desktop restriction and a few security settings, were accomplished using system policies. Group policies have improved on system policies in a couple of major ways. For one thing, system policies write permanent changes to the Registry when they are applied. This phenomenon is commonly called *tattooing*. Remove the policy, and the settings remain. You actually have to "reverse the policy" (by applying a policy with opposite settings) or change the settings manually. Group policies, on the other hand, write their information only to certain parts of the Registry, so they are able to clean up after themselves when the policy is removed. System policies are applied only once: at logon for user settings, at start-up for computer settings. Group policies are also applied this way, but they are reapplied at specific intervals. Finally, group policies do a lot more than just modify Registry settings. The bad news is that they only work on Windows 2000 Server or Professional machines, and they require Active Directory, although it is possible to apply a more limited set of "local policies" without AD.

WARNING

You can only use group policies to control Windows 2000 Server and Windows 2000 Professional machines. If your users run Windows 95/98/98 SE or Windows NT Workstation 4 on their desktops, you'll have to use the same old tools as before—Windows 95/98/98 SE profiles and system policies and Windows NT 4 profiles and group policies. Yes, you read that right—you could potentially have to worry about one set of policies for the Windows machines, another for the NT 4 machines, and a set of group policies for the Windows 2000 machines. In the same way, you might have a set of profiles for Windows 95/98/98 SE users, another for the NT 4 users, and a third set for the Windows 2000 users. If it's any consolation, you can store all these things on a Windows 2000 server—it's not like you've got to keep an old NT 4 server around to hold the NT profiles.

Group policies are stored partially in the Active Directory and partially in the SYSVOL share, so you don't have to worry about replicating them around. The File Replication Service (FRS), a grown-up version of NT 4's rather lame Directory Replication Service, automatically replicates the Active Directory and SYSVOL contents among domain controllers.

In the sections that follow, you will learn how group policies work and how to create and modify group policies. You will become familiar with the different nodes and settings in the Group Policy snap-in and look at a few examples of deploying group policies in your organization. Finally, we'll discuss some of the dos and don'ts of Group Policy.

Group Policy Concepts

First, let's discuss some important concepts, terms, and rules you need to know to master Group Policy. As I explain the functionality of Group Policy, I will mention several settings without showing you how to turn them on in the Group Policy snap-in. Just focus on the concepts for now, and later in this section, we'll take a full tour of the Group Policy snap-in. At that time, I'll point out all the settings (such as No Override and Block Inheritance) that are discussed in this section.

Administrators configure and deploy Group Policy by building *group policy objects* (*GPOs*). GPOs are containers for groups of settings (*policies*) that can be applied to users and machines throughout a network. You create policy objects using the Group Policy snap-in, usually invoked with the Group Policy tab in DSA.MSC or DSSITE.MSC. The same GPO could specify a set of applications to be installed on all users' desktops, implement a fascist policy of disk quotas and restrictions on the Explorer shell, and define domain-wide password and account lockout policies. It is possible to create one all-encompassing GPO or several GPOs, one for each type of function.

There are two major nodes in the Group Policy snap-in, User Configuration and Computer Configuration. User configuration policies apply to user-specific settings, such as application configuration or folder redirection, and computer configuration policies manage machine-specific settings such as disk quotas, auditing, and Event Log management. However, there is a good bit of overlap. It's not unusual to find the same policy available in both the User Configuration and Computer Configuration nodes. Be prepared for a certain amount of head-scratching while you search for the policy you want to activate and decide whether to use the user-based policy or the computer policy. Keep in mind that you can create a policy that uses both types of settings, or you can create separate user and computer configuration policy objects.

Contrary to their name, group policies aren't group-oriented at all. Maybe they are called group policies because a bunch of configuration management tools are *grouped* together in one snap-in (maybe "assorted policies" just didn't have the same ring to it). In any case, you cannot apply them directly to groups or users, but only to sites, domains, and OUs (which Microsoft abbreviates with the term *SDOU*). This act of assigning GPOs to a site, domain, or OU is called *linking*.

GPOs can also be linked to local policy on a particular Windows 2000 machine, as you'll see in a moment. The GPO-to-SDOU relationship may be many to one (many policies applied to one OU, for example) or one to many (one policy linked to several OUs). Once linked to a site, domain, or organizational unit, user policies are applied at login time; computer policies are applied at system start-up. Both are also periodically refreshed, with a few important exceptions.

NOTE

Group policies aren't just Registry changes. Several policies are applied with Client Side Extension (CSE) DLLs. Some examples are disk quota policy, folder redirection, and software installation. In fact, a CSE DLL processes the Registry changes, USERENV.DLL.

NOTE

When I said GPOs were stored in the AD, that wasn't exactly correct. Group policy objects are stored in two parts, a Group Policy Container (GPC), and a policy folder structure in the SYSVOL. The container part is stored in the Active Directory and contains property information, version info, status, and a list of components. The folder structure path is WINNT\SYSVOL\sysvol\ Domainname\Policies\GUID\ where *GUID* is a Global Unique Identifier for the GPO. This folder contains administrative templates (ADM files), security settings, info on available applications, and script filenames with command lines.

NOTE

Group policy objects are rooted in the Active Directory of a domain; you can't copy them to other domains, but you can link them across domain boundaries, although doing so is not recommended.

Policies Are "All or Nothing"

Each group policy object (GPO) contains many possible settings for many functions; usually you'll configure only a few of them. The others will be left "inactive," sort of like putting REM in front of a command in a script or using a semicolon at the beginning of a line in an INF file. Windows 2000 still has to read the whole policy, but it acts only on the options you've enabled. However, once you've configured a set of policies and told AD that "this GPO is linked to the win2ktest.com domain," for example, the individual settings or types of settings cannot be selectively applied. All user configuration settings will be applied to all users on Windows 2000 systems in the linked domain. All computer configuration settings will be applied to all Windows 2000 machines in the domain. Remember that neither will be applied to NT 4 or 95/98/98 SE clients.

Now, let's say you've created a GPO that deploys a set of standard desktop applications such as Word, Excel, and Outlook, and you threw in a bunch of shell restrictions to prevent users from changing their configurations. If you don't want your IT support group users to be subject to those ridiculously stringent shell restrictions (although they may need them most of all!), you can do a couple of things:

▶ You can create a separate GPO for those policies and link it to a lower-level container, such as an OU that contains all the regular users. But that OU will be the only one that gets the Office applications.

▶ You can set permissions on the GPO that prevent the policy from being applied to the IT support group (this is called filtering). However, if you use filtering to solve this problem, none of the settings in the GPO will apply to the IT support group.

Group policy application is all or nothing, so sometimes you really need separate policies for separate functions. The best way to approach this might be to create a GPO for standard software deployment and a GPO for shell restrictions. Both could be applied at the domain level, but shell restrictions can be filtered for the IT support group. The point is, it's not possible to create one monolithic policy and then specify who gets what settings, and you wouldn't want to do that anyway. At least, you wouldn't want to troubleshoot it.

Policies Are Inherited and Cumulative

Group Policy settings are cumulative and inherited from parent Active Directory containers. For example, `win2test.com` domain has several GPOs. A domain-level policy sets password restrictions, account lockout, and standard security settings. Each OU also has a policy to deploy and maintain standard desktop applications as well as folder redirection settings and desktop restrictions. Users and computers who are in both the domain and the OU receive settings both from the domain-level policy and from the OU-level policy. So some blanket policies can be applied to the entire domain, and others can be hashed out according to OUs.

Group Policy Application Order

This inheritance and accumulation is all nice and simple as long as the policies they receive from the domain are changing different settings from those specified in the OU policy. But what if they are the same? What if they both change the same setting and the domain policy says one thing while the OU policy says something else?

Policies are applied in the following order:

1. Local policy

2. Sites

3. Domains

4. OUs

5. OUs inside OUs

If the domain policy says, "You must be logged in before you can shut down the machine," and OU policy says, "Allow shutdown before logon," the OU policy is applied last and, therefore, takes precedence. If one policy says, "Lock it down," and the next one says, "Not configured," the setting remains locked down. If one policy says, "Not configured," and the next one says, "Lock it down," it's locked down as well. If one policy says, "Leave it on," and the next one says, "Turn it off," it's turned off. If one policy says, "Turn it off," and another, closer one says, "Turn it on," then a third one says, "Turn it off," guess what? It ends up turned off. However, for the preservation of your sanity, it is desirable to avoid these little disagreements between policies.

No Override and Block Inheritance

Just as filtering can counter the blanket application of policies, Block Inheritance is a special setting on a policy to prevent higher-level policies from trickling down. When it's turned on, the settings of higher policies won't be applied to lower containers. For example, if you create a GPO for a specific OU, such as Accounting, and establish all the necessary settings for the Accounting OU, and then you want to prevent the win2ktest domain GPOs from affecting the Accounting OU, turn on Block Inheritance. The only policies applied will be the Accounting OU policies.

There is also a counter to the Block Inheritance counter. (Isn't this becoming like a *Batman* episode? "Robin, they've blocked our transmission. It's time for the block-anti-block Bat-transmitter!") When No Override is turned on for a policy, settings in subsequent policies are prevented from reversing the ones in the No Override–enabled policy. For example, if domain admins have a set of highly disputed settings turned on at the domain level, and those renegade accounting admins set up their own OU with its own policies and turn on Block Inheritance, the Accounting OU effectively escapes the disputed settings...but only until the domain admins get wise and turn on No Override. Then the domain admins win, and the Accounting OU people have to live with the same restrictions as everyone else. No Override beats Block Inheritance (just like paper covers rock).

Like all secret weapons, No Override and Block Inheritance are best used sparingly. Otherwise, in a troubleshooting situation it becomes rather complicated to determine which policies are applied where. This could be detrimental to the mental health of a network administrator.

Refresh Intervals for Group Policy

Policies are reapplied every 90 minutes, with a 30-minute "randomization" to keep the domain controller from getting hit by dozens or even hundreds of computers at once. They are refreshed on DCs every 5 minutes, but there's a policy to configure all this, as you'll see in the "Group Policy Policies" section. (So, if I set a policy for the refresh interval on Blanket Vanilla Policy Policy, would that be referred to as Blanket Vanilla Policy Policy Policy?) Exceptions to the refresh interval include folder redirection and software installation. These are applied only at logon or system start-up time; otherwise, you might end up uninstalling an application while someone is trying to use it. Or a user might be working in a folder that is being redirected to a new network location. That would be bad.

Local Policies and Group Policy Objects

When you use Active Directory Users And Computers or Active Directory Sites And Services to create and link group policies, you are working with group policy *objects* to specify a collection of settings to be applied at user logon or machine boot time. The information in the GPO says things like "Change this, change that, install this, disable that." But administrators also need to be able to view the actual settings for these policies sometimes. In NT 4, you could use the System Policy Editor to view and edit those Registry entries for the local machine (instead of creating or editing a policy, you chose to open the Registry). As such, the System Policy Editor served as a more user-friendly Registry editing tool than REGEDIT.EXE or REGEDT32.EXE. Similarly, the Group Policy snap-in provides the ability to view local policy settings on a machine.

If you open the Group Policy tool provided with Windows 2000 (GPEDIT.MSC), it automatically focuses on the local machine, as shown in Figure 25.18. Administrators can use the tool as they would use the Local Security Policy tool to configure account settings (such as minimum password length and number of bad login attempts before locking the account) and set up auditing. With the exceptions of software installation and folder redirection, all the settings from Group Policy are also available for local policy configuration.

NOTE

The local group-policy-folder structure is equivalent to that of other GPOs and is found in \winnt\system32\GroupPolicy.

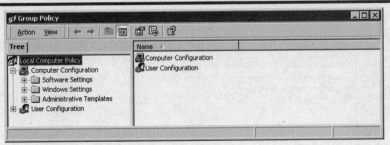

FIGURE 25.18: The Group Policy snap-in

To focus on another computer's local policy, you must have Administrator rights on that machine. You can select a computer while adding the

Group Policy snap-in to a custom management console, as shown in Figure 25.19. If you know the name of the computer, just fill it in, or click the Browse button. The snap-in can focus on a local machine or on a group policy object; the Browse button allows you to locate and find group policy objects linked to sites, domains, OUs, or computers (see Figure 25.20).

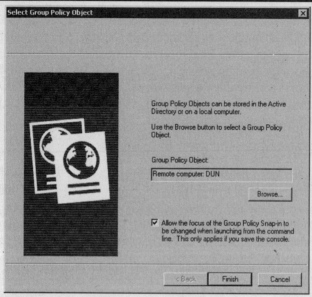

FIGURE 25.19: Adding the Group Policy snap-in

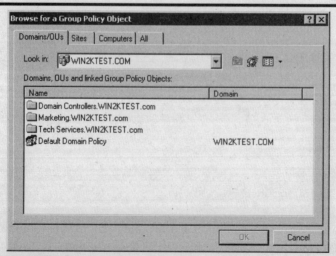

FIGURE 25.20: Selecting a group policy object

Additionally, if you select the option to allow focus to change when opening the snap-in from the command line, it's possible to select the policy object as an argument when you start the console. GPEDIT.MSC, the Group Policy console that ships with Windows 2000, has this option turned on. The syntax to open GPEDIT.MSC and look at the local policy on a remote machine is as follows:

```
GPEDIT.MSC /gpcomputer: machinename
```

So you could type, for example:

```
GPEDIT.MSC /gpcomputer: dun
```

Or you could type:

```
GPEDIT.MSC /gpcomputer: dun.win2ktest.com
```

Be sure to include a space between /gpcomputer: and the machine name.

There is one important limitation when using GPEDIT.MSC to modify policy on a remote machine. The security settings extension to the Group Policy snap-in will not work when the tool is focused on a remote machine. That's worth saying again. You cannot open GPEDIT.MSC with the switch /gpcomputer: *computername* and modify the security settings on a remote machine. Apparently, Microsoft considers this a security vulnerability. Another example of software telling us what's best for us?

NOTE

If you are using group policies, local policy is always processed before site, domain, or OU group policies.

Creating Group Policies

Now that you understand the major concepts surrounding group policies and know the difference between local policies and group policy objects, let's go through the steps of creating and editing a group policy object. In this section, I'll show you all the settings we discussed in the preceding "theory" section.

1. To open the Group Policy snap-in in DSA.MSC, right-click your domain name at the root of the console, and choose Properties from the shortcut menu.

2. Select the Group Policy tab to see what GPOs have been linked at the domain level.

If you haven't already created other policies, you'll see only the default domain policy listed. Notice the Block Policy Inheritance check box at the bottom left of the Group Policy tab. It prevents any group policy settings at a higher level from trickling down to this one. Remember the order that policies are applied: first is the site level, then the domain level, then policies for OUs.

NOTE

To view the group policy objects that are linked to a container (site, domain, or organizational unit), right-click the object in the console (DSA.MSC for domains and OUs, DSSITE.MSC for sites), and choose Properties from the shortcut menu. Then navigate to the Group Policy tab. From that point, the interface to configure policies is the same regardless of the container it's linked with.

3. To turn on No Override, highlight the policy, and choose Options to open the Default Domain Policy Options dialog box.

4. Click the No Override check box.

    When this setting is on, other policies applied down the line are prevented from defeating the settings of this one, even with Block Inheritance. Note that Block Inheritance is turned on at the link level (site, domain, or OU) and that No Override is turned on per policy.

5. Click the Disabled check box to turn off the policy so that it won't be processed or applied at this level.

    Disabling the policy doesn't disable the object itself. For example, the same policy, disabled at the domain level, could theoretically be applied at the site or OU level. If either option (No Override or Disabled) is turned on, there will be a check in the corresponding column of the Group Policy tab. You can activate both options using the shortcut menu for the policy. Simply right-click a selected policy to display the shortcut menu.

6. Back in the win2ktest.com Properties dialog box, choose New to create a new GPO. Windows 2000 will create a policy called New Group Policy Object and then allow you to rename it. If you miss that opportunity and end up with a policy

called New Group Policy Object, just highlight the policy, right-click, and choose Rename from the context menu.

7. Choose Properties to view and modify your new group policy object's properties.

   ▶ The General tab contains creation and revision information as well as options to disable the user or computer configuration portion of the policy. Depending on how you subdivide your domain into OUs, you may choose to create some policies with only computer settings and others with only user-specific settings. In that case, if the unused portion of the GPO is disabled altogether, policy application and updates are faster. If, however, your cold medicine has caused a momentary lapse of reason and there are important settings in the node you disable, those settings will be removed from the client machine. Windows 2000 will ask you to confirm that move, just to be sure.

   ▶ The Links tab gives you the opportunity to search for sites, domains, or OUs that use this GPO, if there are any. Because searching for other links takes a few moments and some resources, no linked containers will be displayed until you perform the search. Click the Find Now button to start the search.

   ▶ The Security tab displays the default permissions on the GPO. Highlight a name at the top to view the permissions in the lower section. Notice that Domain Admins and Enterprise Admins have Read and Write permissions as well as Delete and Create All Child Objects, while Authenticated Users only has Read and Apply Group Policy. Read and Write are required to change a policy, while Read and Apply are required to be a recipient of the policy.

NOTE

Don't think that Domain Admins and Enterprise Admins are not subject to a group policy's settings just because they are not granted Apply Group Policy permission by default. A user will have all the permissions of all their groups, so as members of Authenticated Users, members of Domain Admins and Enterprise Admins will also be granted Apply Group Policy permissions.

8. Back in the Group Policy tab of our `win2ktest.com` Properties dialog box, you can highlight the new GPO that you have just created and choose the Up or Down buttons to move the policy up or down in the window.

   This is an important tidbit to know: if multiple GPOs are linked to one container, as you see in Figure 25.21, they will be applied from the bottom up. Therefore, the one at the top is applied last. GPOs higher in the list have a higher priority. If settings are conflicting, the higher policy wins.

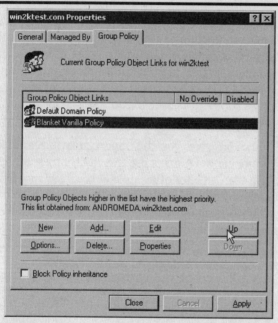

FIGURE 25.21: Increasing the priority of group policy objects

TIP

To delete a GPO or to just remove it from the list, highlight the policy, and choose Delete to open the Delete dialog box. You can delete the GPO altogether or remove it from the list while preserving the policy to be linked to another container at another time.

9. Click the Add button on the Group Policy tab to open the Add A Group Policy Object Link dialog box (see Figure 25.22), in

which you can link an existing group policy object to the desired container.

You can look for GPOs that are linked to other domains/OUs or other sites, or you can just ask for a list of all GPOs. It took me a minute to grasp this simple operation: click the container name (such as the OU for Marketing.win2ktest.com) to view the policies linked to it. Then highlight the policy, and choose OK to add it to the list back on the Group Policy tab.

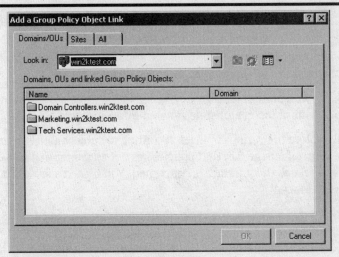

FIGURE 25.22: Adding a group policy link

Now let's view and modify our new policy. Back in the Group Policy tab, highlight the policy, and click Edit to open the Group Policy snap-in in a separate window. You'll see the policy object name at the root of the namespace, in this case Blanket Vanilla Policy [DUN.win2ktest.com] Policy. This indicates which policy is being viewed and edited. Figure 25.23 shows the policy expanded in the console tree to show the major nodes of the group policy object.

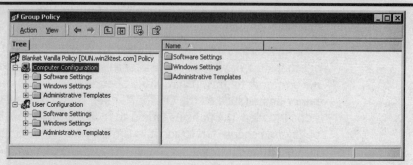

FIGURE 25.23: Group policy namespace

There are two major types of settings, as I mentioned earlier:

▶ Computer configuration settings are applied to machines at start-up and at designated refresh intervals.

▶ User configuration settings are applied to the users' working environments at logon and at designated refresh intervals.

We'll explore the various policies according to subject matter later, but prepare yourself for the fact that policies are not all configured in a uniform way as far as the interface is concerned. You'll need a few examples to see what I mean:

▶ To specify software packages under `Software Settings\ Software Installation`, open the folder, and choose Action ≻ New ≻ Package. An Open dialog box asks for the location of the package. Once it's been located and selected, you configure the package properties.

▶ To set the interval that users can wait before changing passwords, go to `Computer Configuration\Windows Settings\ Security Settings\Account Policies\Password Policy`, double-click Maximum Password Age in the details pane on the right, enable the setting by clicking the Define This Policy Setting box, and supply a time interval value.

▶ To set a policy that restricts group memberships, go to Restricted Groups under Security Settings in `Computer Configuration\ Windows Settings`, and choose Action ≻ Add Group. A dialog box asks you to enter a group or browse for it. Once the group is added to the list in the details pane on the right, double-click the group name to open a dialog box and supply the names of the users that must be or are allowed to be in the group. You can also define group memberships for the group itself.

▶ To set up folder redirection, go to `User Configuration\ Windows Settings\Folder Redirection`, and choose a folder (for example, Start Menu). The details pane on the right will be blank. Right-click on white space in the details pane (or open the Action menu), and choose Properties to open the Properties dialog box. You can now specify a location for the Start menu and configure redirection settings.

The point of this wild ride through the Group Policy snap-in interface is not to disorient you, but rather to illustrate that the Group Policy snap-in contains several nodes to accomplish various tasks, and the procedures to specify settings will vary with the node and the task. There is no one way to configure a setting, although many do follow the pattern of the second example. So, when in doubt, right-click or look in the Action menu. It's a strategy to live by.

Once you've configured your Group Policy settings, simply close the Group Policy dialog box. There is no Save or Save Changes option. Changes are written to the GPO when you choose OK or Apply on a particular setting, although the user or computer will not actually see the change until the policy is refreshed.

Filtering Group Policy

Now that you've grasped the basics of Group Policy theory and have created a policy, let's look more closely at filtering group policies for security groups. Let's go back to the Security tab in the Properties dialog box for a group policy object. Follow these steps:

1. Open `DSA.MSC` (or `DSSITE.MSC`, depending on where the link is).

2. Right-click the container linked to your GPO (in our example, the domain), and choose Properties to open the Properties dialog box.

3. Select the Group Policy tab, and highlight the policy you want to filter.

4. Click the Properties button, and select the Security tab.

Now you see the Access Control List (ACL) for the policy object. As I pointed out earlier, Domain Admins and Enterprise Admins have Read and Modify permissions, and Authenticated Users has Read and Apply Group Policy. You might create a policy to restrict desktops and then decide that you don't want to apply it to a certain group of people.

The group Authenticated Users includes everyone but guests, so by default, the policy will apply to everyone but guests—even Domain Admins and Enterprise Admins will receive the policy settings. To prevent Domain Admins and Enterprise Admins from also receiving this policy, you must check the box in the Deny column next to Apply Group Policy (see Figure 25.24).

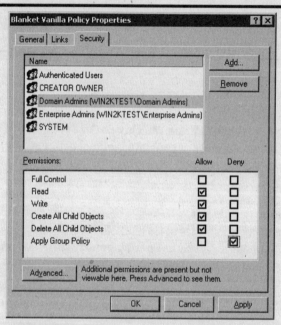

FIGURE 25.24: Denying Apply Group Policy permission

A member of both groups will only need the Deny setting for one of the two groups, but you'll need to check the Deny box for both groups if the members of Domain Admins and Enterprise Admins are not the same people. To "excuse" others from receiving the policy, put them all in a security group, and add that group to the list. It is not enough to "not check" the Allow box for Read and Apply Group Policy; the users in your special security group are also members of Authenticated Users, so you actually need to choose the Deny option for them as well. Deny takes precedence over Allow.

If you want to filter policy for a certain Windows 2000 machine (or group of machines), follow the same strategy. Add the computer accounts to a security group, add that group to the ACL for the policy object, and then deny the group Read and Apply Group Policy permissions.

There is an alternative to adding a security group to the ACL and denying it Read and Apply permissions. You could also remove Authenticated Users from the ACL altogether, preventing anyone from receiving the group policy. You would then simply add entries to the ACL for any security groups you *do* want to receive the policy. Be sure to allow them both Read and Apply Group Policy, though. Figure 25.25 shows the permissions list for Blanket Vanilla Policy in which Authenticated Users has been removed and the Engineering group has been added. This is a useful strategy if you don't want the policy to apply to all users and computers in the linked container by default.

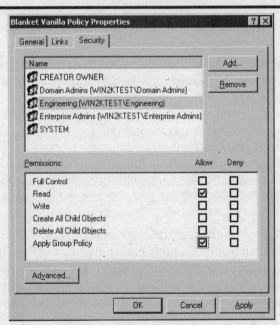

FIGURE 25.25: Group Policy ACL without Authenticated Users

By the way, there is nothing to prevent you from adding individual users to the permissions list for a group policy object. It's simply not considered good form.

NOTE

Although members of Domain Admins and Enterprise Admins by default do not have Apply permissions, administrators are also members of Authenticated Users, and Authenticated Users does have Apply permission. Because admin types are also members of Authenticated Users, policies will apply to them as well, unless they are denied the permission Apply Group Policy.

Delegating Group Policy Administration

The ability to delegate the creation and configuration of group policies to administrative personnel (or others, for that matter) is extremely useful, especially in a large organization. In this section, I'll explain how to allow persons who are not members of Domain Admins or Enterprise Admins to create and manage policies for designated sites, domains, or organizational units.

Group policy objects, by default, can be created by a member of the Administrators group for the domain or by members of the global group called Group Policy Creator Owners. However, although members of Administrators have full control of all group policy objects, members of Group Policy Creator Owners can modify only policies they have created unless they have been specifically granted permission to modify a policy. So, if you put a designated group policy administrator into the security group Group Policy Creator Owners (that's almost as awkward as Active Directory Users And Computers), they can create new policy objects and modify them.

It's one thing to create a group policy; linking that GPO to a site, domain, or organizational unit is another matter. Administrators have this power by default, but a special permission called Manage Policy Links must be granted on the ACL of the site, domain, or organizational unit before anyone else can create policy links to it. Also, there doesn't seem to be a way to create a group policy without linking it to something, at least initially. So if you want to use the Group Policy Creator Owners security group, you need to set permissions on a container object to allow them to manage policy links. You'll need to use the Delegation Of Control Wizard to accomplish this.

To allow members of Group Policy Creator Owners to create links to a particular OU, for example, follow these steps:

1. Right-click the OU in DSA.MSC, and choose Delegate Control from the shortcut menu to start the Delegation Of Control Wizard.

2. Click Next to open the screen in which you choose to add the users and groups to whom you will delegate control.

3. Click Add, and select Group Policy Creator Owners from the list.

4. Click Add again, and then click OK to return to the Users Or Groups window. The GP Creator Owners will appear in the Selected Users And Groups box.

5. Click Next, and then select Manage Group Policy Links from the predefined common tasks to delegate.

6. Click Next, and then confirm your choices in the last screen by clicking the Finish button.

Members of Group Policy Creator Owners can now create new GPOs linked to that OU. They can also modify policies that they have created, but if there are other policies on the OU, members of Group Policy Creator Owners can't edit them by default. You'll have to grant the group Read and Write permission on the policy object's ACL.

Designating a regular user or junior admin as a member of Group Policy Creator Owners and giving that person the ability to manage group policy links, even if it's just at the OU level, is a real exercise in faith and quite taxing for us control freaks (I mean "letting-go challenged" people).

If you want finer control when delegating group policy administration tasks, set up a custom MMC console. You might even limit administration to a certain GPO by loading the GP snap-in focused on that GPO. Enable only the extensions you want your delegate to use. It's further possible to configure a policy to permit the use of certain Group Policy snap-in extensions and prevent the use of others, just in case the delegate stumbles on to Author mode by accident. See the section "Group Policy Policies" later in this chapter for specifics.

TIP

See Chapter 24 for a discussion on customizing Microsoft Management consoles.

That was a lot of information, so let's review:

▶ To create a GPO, you must be a member of either the Administrators group (and this includes nesting, so membership in Domain Admins is acceptable, for example) or the Group Policy Creator Owners. If you insist on the McGyver approach, however, you at least need access to a domain controller, Read/Write permissions on SYSVOL, and Modify permission on the directory container.

▶ To edit a policy, a user must (a) have full Administrator privileges, or (b) be creator owner of the GPO, or (c) have Read and Write on the ACL of the GPO.

User and Computer Configuration Settings

Now that you've learned all about creating and linking and delegating administration of Group Policy, we'll explore some of the policy settings themselves. Since you can use various types of policies to configure a range of settings, we can't cover every single setting in the pages allotted to this chapter (otherwise it could be a book all by itself!). Rather, think of this section as an overview of the things that group policies can accomplish to make your life easier as an administrator. To follow along, open the Group Policy snap-in for a GPO by navigating to the Group Policy tab in the container's Properties dialog box, highlight an existing policy, and click the Edit button.

As you see in Figure 25.26, there are two main nodes to the Group Policy snap-in: User Configuration and Computer Configuration. Both nodes have the following subnodes: Software Settings, Windows Settings, and Administrative Templates. The difference between the two is this: policies set for User Configuration will apply to the user's settings, and those set for Computer Configuration will apply to the machine configuration.

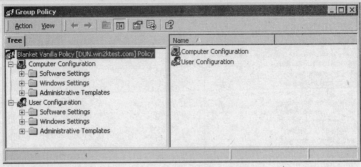

FIGURE 25.26: Group Policy nodes and subnodes

For example, if Registry settings are involved, as is the case with Administrative Templates, the changes will be written to HKEY_CURRENT_USER (HKCU) for User Configuration stuff and to HKEY_LOCAL_MACHINE (HKLM) for Computer Configuration settings. Otherwise, the differences aren't so obvious, and there is some overlap in the settings, just as HKCU contains some of the same entries as HKLM. You might want to create separate policies for machines and users, just to keep things straight, but be on the lookout for any conflicts. If a value set in the computer settings is also specified in the user policy settings, the User Configuration settings will take precedence by default.

For both User Configuration and Computer Configuration, you can use Software Settings\Software Installation to publish, assign, update, and even remove applications from a user's desktop.

Specify Scripts with Group Policy

You can specify logon and logoff scripts using Windows Settings in the User Configuration node, and you can specify scripts to run at system start-up and shutdown, using Windows Settings in the Computer Configuration node. Follow these steps:

1. Expand Windows Settings to display Scripts, and then select the script type (start-up, shutdown, logon, or logoff) in the details pane on the right. Figure 25.27 shows the scripts available in User Configuration.

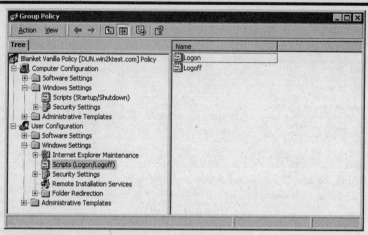

FIGURE 25.27: Group Policy start-up scripts

2. Double-click the script type (such as Logon), or highlight it and choose Actions ➤ Properties.

3. Click Add to add scripts to the list.

4. Supply a script name and parameters when prompted.

5. To edit the script name and parameters (not the script itself), choose Edit. If more than one script is specified, use the Up or Down button to indicate the order in which the scripts should run.

The scripts you create and assign should be copied to the following path in the SYSVOL directory: `\winnt\SYSVOL\SysVol\`*domainname*`\Policies\{GUID}\Machine\Scripts\Startup` or `Shutdown` (or `User\Scripts\Logon` or `Logoff`, depending on whether you are assigning scripts to the Computer Configuration or to the User Configuration node). The Global Unique Identifier (GUID) for the group policy object is a long string that looks like {FA08AF41-38AB-11D3-BD1FC9B6902FA00B}. If you want to see the scripts stored in the GPO and possibly open them for editing, click the Show Files button at the bottom of the Properties dialog box to open the folder in Explorer.

As you may know, you can also specify a login script in the Properties dialog box of the user account in DSA.MSC. Microsoft calls these *legacy logon scripts* and encourages us to assign scripts with Group Policy for Windows 2000 clients. Of course, Windows 95/98/NT clients don't use group policies, so you'll still assign their logon scripts in the account properties.

Other than that, the only real advantage to using the group policy scripts is that they run asynchronously in a hidden window. If several scripts are assigned, or if the scripts are complex, the user doesn't have to wait for them to end. Legacy logon scripts run in a window on the Desktop.

On the other hand, you might not want the scripts to run hidden (some scripts stop and supply information or wait for user input). In that case, there are several policy settings to define how group policy scripts behave. These are located in the Administrative Templates node under System\ Logon/Logoff for User Configuration and under System\Logon for Computer Configuration.

You'll find settings to specify whether to run a script synchronously or asynchronously and whether it should be visible or invisible. Legacy logon scripts can be run hidden like group policy scripts by using the setting shown in Figure 25.28. The Computer Configuration settings also include a maximum wait time for group policy scripts, which is 600 seconds by default. This changes the time-out period, which is the maximum allotted time for the script to complete.

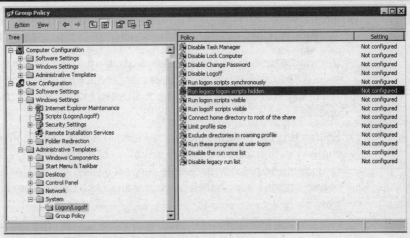

FIGURE 25.28: Policy to run legacy scripts hidden

Folder Redirection

One of the more useful things you can do with User Configuration settings in Group Policy is tell a user's Application Data, Desktop, Start

Menu, or My Documents folder to follow her around from computer to computer. These folders are important elements in a user's working environment. Application Data stores application-specific user information (Internet Explorer uses it, for example), and Desktop can contain important folders and shortcuts that need to be just one click away for the user. Start Menu contains program groups and shortcuts to programs, and My Documents is the default location for saving and retrieving files, sort of like a local home directory.

Using user profiles in NT 4 and now Windows 2000, you can preconfigure these folders' contents and assign network locations. With the System Policy Editor for 95/98 or NT, it was also possible to specify a location for these folders. But unlike the Default User profiles behavior, redirected folders live in one designated place all the time. They are not copied to each machine the user logs on to, causing "profile build-up." Instead of using the folder in the user's local profile, she will be *redirected* to the location specified in the group policy. Group policy folder redirection replaces and enhances those functions offered previously in system policies, with additional options to manage the redirected folder behavior.

There are several good reasons to use folder redirection:

▶ It's convenient for users who log on to different machines.

▶ If you specify a network location for some or all of these folders, they can be backed up regularly and protected by the IT department.

▶ If roaming profiles are still in use, setting up folder redirection speeds up synchronization of the server profile with the local profile at logon and logoff, since the redirected folders need not be updated.

▶ Redirecting the Desktop and Start Menu folders to a centralized, shared location facilitates standardization of users' working environments and helps with remote support issues, since help desk personnel will know that all machines are configured in the same way.

▶ You can mix and match. It's possible to specify a shared location for the Desktop and Start Menu folders while allowing each user to have his own My Documents and Application Data folders.

To set a network location for the Start Menu folder in Group Policy, follow these steps:

1. Go to `User Configuration\Windows Settings\Folder Redirection\Start Menu`.

Part V

2. Right-click the highlighted Start Menu folder, and choose Properties from the shortcut menu. The Properties dialog box will reveal that no policy is specified by default for Start Menu redirection.

3. Choose Basic from the drop-down box to specify a single location for the Start Menu folder, to be shared by all the users, or choose Advanced to set locations based on security group membership.

   If a single location for a shared Start Menu folder is desired, just fill in the target location with a network path or browse for it. For different locations, first choose a security group and then specify a network path. Figure 25.29 demonstrates redirecting the Start Menu folder for all members of Win2KTEST\Engineering to the Central share on the server Andromeda. In our example, all of Engineering will use the same Start Menu folder, but in either case, it's possible to set up individually redirected folders by appending %username% to the path. This creates a subfolder named after the user.

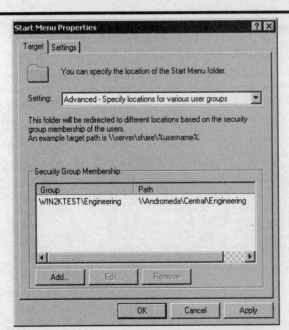

FIGURE 25.29: Policy to redirect the user's Start Menu folder

4. Click the Settings tab to configure the redirection settings.

For the sake of completeness, the redirection settings for My Documents are shown in Figure 25.30. The redirection settings for all the other folders are the same except that My Documents has the My Pictures subfolder, so there are a couple of extra items to configure.

The options you see in Figure 25.30 show default selections. The user will have exclusive access to the folder, so uncheck this box if everyone is sharing a folder. The contents of the corresponding folder will be copied to the new location by default. Even after the policy is removed, the folder will remain redirected unless you say to "un-redirect" it. One notable exception is the Start Menu folder. We can pretty much assume that a redirected Start Menu folder is a shared Start Menu folder (otherwise, why bother?), and making it private or copying over it would generally be a bad thing, so both the option to grant exclusive rights and the option to move the contents of a user's Start Menu folder to the new location are grayed out in the Settings tab.

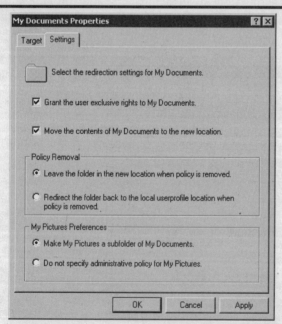

FIGURE 25.30: Policy to redirect the My Documents folder

Security Settings

Security Settings, along with Administrative Templates, makes up a large part of Group Policy. The default security settings for Windows 2000 security are purposely open to keep down administrative headaches and to ensure that users and applications work as intended. As security increases, users and applications have more restrictions, and support time goes up.

In other words, security is inversely proportionate to convenience. As you start locking down systems, something is bound to stop working. Hey, regular users can't even install applications on a Windows 2000 system by default. When you start enforcing passwords that are 8 characters or more, contain both letters and numbers, can't use any part of a user's name, and cannot be reused until 15 other passwords have been used, things get complicated for the everyday Joe. As important as security is, Microsoft judged (wisely, I believe) that functionality had to come first. For organizations that want to increase security, there are tools and guidelines. There is one problem with this approach. A big problem.

If you've ever "hardened" an NT server according to established military or other high-security guidelines, you know that you have to set particular permissions on particular folders, you must change the default permissions on certain Registry keys, and you must change or create other Registry entries as well. All in all, it takes a few hours of work on a single server, even for an efficient admin. What if you have 50 servers and 500 Professional workstations? Some things can be scripted, but others can't. Try as they might, there is no Microsoft or third-party tool that does everything automatically for all machines.

Here's where Group Policy comes to the rescue. Assuming you are going to standardize throughout the organization somewhat, you have to change those sticky Registry permissions and settings only once, using Group Policy. You have to set the NTFS permissions only once. You can even be set them up in one policy and copy them to another. Whether you need a lot of security or just a little more than the default, chances are you'll want to make at least some standardized changes, and the Security Settings node will certainly make your life easier. The bulk of Security Settings is found under `Computer Configuration\Windows Settings\ Security Settings`, although public key policies are also found in the User Configuration node in the same path. The following summarizes the major categories under Security Settings:

Account Policies   Specify password restrictions, lockout policies, and Kerberos policy.

Local Policies Configure auditing and assign user rights and miscellaneous security settings.

Event Log Centralize configuration options for the Event Log.

Restricted Groups Enforce and control group memberships for certain groups, such as the Administrators group.

System Services Standardize services configurations and protect against changes.

Registry Create security templates for Registry key permissions to control who can change which keys and to control Read access to parts of the Registry.

File System Create security templates for permissions on files and folders to ensure that files and folders have and keep the permissions you want.

Public Key Policies Manage settings for organizations using a public key infrastructure.

Importing Security Templates

A full discussion of all these security settings is certainly beyond the scope of this chapter, but you should be aware that security settings templates are available and installed with Windows 2000 Server to ease the burden of wading through and researching all the settings. It's also safer to configure settings offline and then apply them than it is to play with a live working group policy.

These templates take the form of INF files and are found in \WINNT\ Security\templates. You can choose from basic workstations or servers to secure, highly secure, and dedicated domain controller configurations. When applied directly or via Group Policy, these templates incrementally modify the default settings. You can view and modify them using the Security Templates snap-in, shown in Figure 25.31.

As you see in the figure, these settings are the same as those found in Group Policy Security Settings with the exception of Public Key Policies and IP Security Policies, which cannot be configured with templates. The values for the settings in each template are preconfigured to meet the necessary level of security. You can apply these templates or new ones that you create directly to a Windows 2000 machine's local policy by using a command-line program called SECEDIT.EXE, or you can import them into Group Policy.

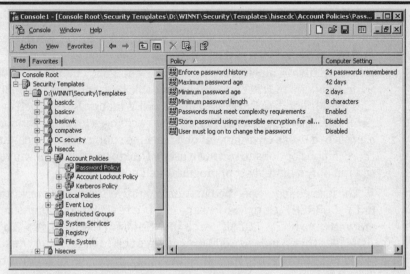

FIGURE 25.31: The Security Templates snap-in

Every fresh installation of Windows 2000 gets a standard set of local computer policies with default security settings, so it's a good idea to export your existing settings to a file by using the Group Policy snap-in focused on the local machine (GPEDIT.MSC will open that way by default) before making any drastic changes. Security settings for upgraded systems do not have their local policy changed in case the configuration has been customized. For upgraded Windows 2000 servers, Microsoft suggests we first apply the Basic configuration template and then apply an appropriate security settings template with all the settings specified explicitly.

To import a security template into Group Policy, go to Computer Configuration\Windows Settings\Security Settings, and right-click Security Settings. Choose Import Policy from the shortcut menu, and then select your policy from the list of templates. Group Policy automatically looks for the template in \WINNT\security\templates, but you can tell it to look some place else if necessary. The INF file will be imported to modify the settings in the selected group policy object.

In the spirit of this template idea, the different subcomponents of Security Settings (such as Account Policies or Local Policies) also support a copy-and-paste function, which appears in the shortcut and Action menus when the subcomponent is selected. An admin person can actually copy that part of the template information to the Clipboard and apply it to another policy.

Administrative Templates

Administrative Templates is the part of Group Policy that is most like System Policies in NT. The settings available here are based on template files (ADM files, like those used in NT and Windows 95/98 System Policies). These settings specify Registry entry changes to adjust various aspects of a user's environment or a machine configuration, including those famous options to restrict a user's Desktop to the point where they can run only a limited set of programs and nothing else.

The user changes specified in Administrative Templates are written to HKEY_CURRENT_User\Software\Policies, and computer changes are written to HKEY_LOCAL_Machine\Software\Policies. The two ADM files that Windows 2000 uses are system.adm and inetres.adm, found in \WINNT\inf. You can extend the capabilities of Administrative Templates with custom ADM files.

NOTE

When you load an Administrative Template, the ADM files are copied to \SYSVOL\Domainname\Policies\GUID\Adm.

What's the difference between User Configuration and Computer Configuration with regard to Administrative Templates? Good question. Depending on the nature of the configuration settings, some live in the user part of the Registry (HKCU), and others live in the machine part (HKLM). Other settings exist in both, which makes things really confusing. Settings for Task Scheduler, for example, are exactly the same in both places. So, other than asking yourself, Which node has the setting I want? the difference is whether the policy should apply to the machine, regardless of who logs on, or whether the policy should apply to the users and follow them from machine to machine.

What can you do with Administrative Templates settings? Among its primary functions is "keep users from changing X" or "disable or hide option Y." But mostly it's just a large collection of configuration options loosely organized together to ease our administrative burden and help us achieve the power and control of our networks and users that we crave and feel we truly deserve.

An attempt to catalog each subnode and all its policy settings would be a boring and futile exercise in the Microsoft style of documentation and is best left to those who write the Resource Kits. Besides, many of these policies should not be discussed in a vacuum and are best approached in the context of the particular application or service they configure. However, this section would be lacking if it did not include at least a few pointers on individual policies. So here are a few highly opinionated comments on some of the settings you'll find in Administrative Templates. For a few more suggestions on how to lock down a user's Desktop, see the "Systems Settings" section later in this chapter. You'll find the same options (and more) in Group Policy as you did in the System Policy Editor.

Windows Components

For every setting in Internet Explorer, there seems to be policy to disable it. Considering that much time at work is spent surfing the Web, it's a particularly cruel and clever thing to impose such control over IE settings. Unfortunately, many companies use Navigator instead of Internet Explorer.

Although you might want to implement those cool Windows Explorer restrictions to the Map Network Drive and Disconnect Network Drive options or remove particular drives in My Computer, this will only work with inexperienced users. Anyone who can access a command line can circumvent these restrictions; so be sure to check out the method (mentioned later) for restricting the programs that can run from Explorer.

A more useful setting is the one to "not track shell shortcuts during roaming." This tells Explorer to resolve shortcuts in roaming profiles to local paths instead of tracking the source and attempting to open a program or file on a remote computer (this caused me much gnashing of teeth and pulling of hair before I figured out how to stop it).

The same principle applies to the Start menu and Taskbar and Desktop options. Experienced users will not be prevented from running unblessed programs just because Run is removed from the Start menu. But the settings may be useful to guard against inexperienced users' tendency to fiddle with things randomly. Plus, there is something to be said for a simplified and consistent Start menu and Desktop throughout an organization. I personally love the options to hide "Computers Near Me" or "Entire Network" in My Network Places; with these hidden, users are not tempted to poke around on different servers to see what they can access.

Control Panel Settings

The Control Panel node includes several options to disable or remove all or part of the Add/Remove Programs applet. Disabling Add/Remove Programs will not prevent users from running setup routines in other ways.

The Display policies prevent users from changing display settings such as screen resolution, screen savers, and background wallpaper—in other words, customizing the display. Although it is desirable to prevent a user from changing the display to settings incompatible with hardware, it's not really necessary since Windows 2000 does include safeguards against that eventuality. Unless the machine is in a library or school or some place where a standardized Desktop appearance is necessary, I see no point in preventing access to these settings. Unless you work some place where everyone has to wear a blue or black suit every day, and the Desktops are subject to the same dress code, there are better ways to reassure ourselves of our superiority as network administrators.

The policies that prevent users from adding or deleting printers are useful if your users are in the habit of doing that, and then calling to say, "Why can't I print?" Also, it is helpful to specify an Active Directory path for printers to assist with searches.

System Settings

Use the Century Interpretation For Year 2000 entry to set programs to interpret two-digit date references consistently and correctly. This parameter, when enabled, defaults to 2029, so a reference to 01/06/29 is interpreted as 2029, while 01/16/30 is interpreted as 1930.

Disabling Registry editing tools prevents users from running REGEDT32 .EXE and REGEDIT.EXE, which is not a bad idea, although regular users only have Read access to the vast majority of the Registry anyway.

The famous setting Run Only Allowed Windows Applications is found in the System node under User Configuration (not Computer Configuration). If you enable the policy, you must add a list of allowed applications, or users will be able to run nothing at all. Figure 25.32 shows the policy enabled with a sample list of allowed applications. Use of this policy is often combined with the policy to hide My Network Places and Internet Explorer from the Desktop, remove Run from the Start menu, and apply other restrictions found in the Windows Explorer policies node.

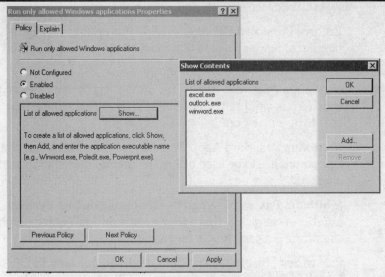

FIGURE 25.32: Policy to run only allowed applications

Using Group Policy to Set Password and Account Lockout Policy

In NT 4, any account policies set in User Manager For Domains applied to domain account and password functions, while the audited events, such as restarts, failed logon attempts, and security policy changes, were those occurring on domain controllers. Group policies are much more powerful. If you choose to create a policy at the domain level, the settings will apply to all domain member machines—servers, workstations, and domain controllers included. It is possible, however, for OU policies to override local policy settings such as auditing and user rights.

One big note about password, account lockout, and Kerberos group policies: they are applied at the domain level only. Domain controllers will receive their settings from domain-level account policies and ignore the settings in policies linked to OUs. In fact, you'll see an error in the Event Log if an OU-level policy contains these settings. So unfortunately, you still can't make administrator types change their passwords more often than everyone else does (not without a big stick, anyway). You can apply different Local Policy settings to OUs, however, so audit policy can be stricter on "high-security" OUs and more lax on others.

Password Policy includes the following options:

Enforce Password History   Enable this option and supply a number of new passwords that must be unique before a given password can be used again.

Maximum Password Age   This option sets the time period in which a password can be used before the system requires the user to pick a new one.

Minimum Password Age   The value set here is the time that a password has to be used before the user is allowed to change it again.

Minimum Password Length   This option defines the least number of characters that a user's password can contain. Eight characters is a good length for passwords.

Passwords Must Meet The Complexity Requirements Of Installed Password Filter   Password filters define requirements such as the number of characters allowed, whether letters and numbers must be used, whether any part of the username is permitted, and so forth.

Store Passwords Using Reversible Encryption   Windows 95/98 clients and Macintosh clients need to authenticate with a lower-level encryption.

User Must Log On To Change Password   This option prevents unauthenticated users from changing an account password through brute force attacks. Also prevents a user from changing his password after it's expired.

Account Lockout Policy, once enabled, prevents anyone from logging on to the account after a certain number of failed attempts:

Account Lockout Threshold   This value defines how many times the user can attempt to log on before the account will be locked out.

Reset Account Lockout Counter After   This setting defines the time in which the count of bad logon attempts will start over. For example, suppose you have a reset count of two minutes and three logon attempts. If you mistype twice, by waiting two minutes after the second attempt, you'll have three tries again.

Account Lockout Duration   This setting determines the interval that the account will be locked out. After the time period expires, the user account will no longer be locked out, and the user can try to log on again.

Using Group Policy to Manage MMC

Delegation is a great feature of Windows 2000, and the Microsoft Management Console is a big part of that. Many Windows 2000 administrators will want to create consoles to accomplish particular tasks and distribute them to the responsible parties. Group Policy offers options to control MMC so that others can't make changes to existing MMC tools or access snap-ins and extensions that are off-limits, not the least of which are the Group Policy snap-ins and extensions.

You see, in NT 4, users could either run the Server Manager tool or they couldn't. If they could run the tool, they might only be able to create machine accounts (if they were members of Account Operators) and not promote domain controllers. That didn't keep users from seeing the option in the menu or from attempting operations that were not permitted in their security context. With Windows 2000, not only can you design a tool that includes only the snap-ins and extensions that you want your admin types to use, but you can also explicitly forbid any changing of the tool (by preventing Author mode). What's more, you can completely forbid access to a particular snap-in, regardless of the tool employed by the user.

NOTE

This does not actually set a user's security level (that's what security groups and rights are for), but it can effectively limit access to certain administrative tools. Cool, eh?

The Microsoft Management Console policies are found under Administrative Templates in the User Configuration node (see Figure 25.33). The main policies shown in this figure are to restrict Author mode (which prevents the user from creating console files and from adding or removing snap-ins) and to restrict users to an explicit list of permitted snap-ins. These two policies are not exactly mutually exclusive, as you might think, nor does enabling the first eliminate the need for the second.

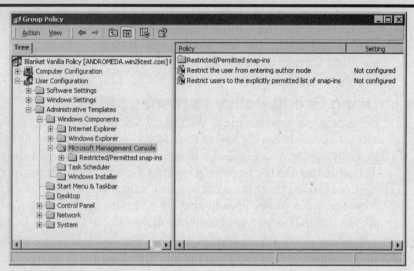

FIGURE 25.33: MMC group policies

If a user is not permitted to enter Author mode, he is unable to do the following:

▶ Run MMC.EXE from the Start menu or a command prompt; it opens, by definition, in Author mode with a blank console window.

▶ Open any console with the /a (Author mode) switch.

▶ Open any console that is configured to always open in Author mode.

All the prebuilt administrative consoles that are included in Administrative Tools are User mode tools, so they can be used when the restriction is activated. However, if you create a console and distribute it but forget to set it to open in User mode, the user will not be able to access the tool with this policy in effect.

If the policy to restrict users to only the expressly permitted list of snap-ins is enabled, users will not be able to add or remove restricted snap-ins or extensions to console files when in Author mode (they will not even appear in the list of available snap-ins). More important, if a console file already contains a restricted snap-in or extension, the restricted snap-in or extension will not appear in the console when the tool is run by a user who is subject to this policy. For example, if you don't have access to the Group Policy tab for Active Directory tools (set this policy in the Group Policy node under `Restricted/Permitted Snap-Ins`), you won't even see the tab in Active Directory Users And Computers (or AD Sites And Services) when you open the properties of the site, domain, or OU.

If you do choose to restrict users to only the expressly permitted list of snap-ins, be sure to filter the policy for exempt admin types. Also, you need to go to the `Restricted/Permitted Snap-Ins` folder and enable those that you want to be available. Otherwise, *no snap-ins will be available* to nonexempt users regardless of their power and status on the network. This could be very bad, so think carefully before you disable access to the Group Policy snap-in, or you might not be able to reverse the damage.

Even if you don't enable the policy to restrict snap-in and extension use, you can still deny access to certain snap-ins. You see, if the policy Restrict Users To The Explicitly Permitted List Of Snap-Ins is configured, enabling a certain snap-in means that it *can* be used. But if you leave the policy turned off, enabling a certain snap-in means that it *cannot* be used.

Figure 25.34 shows the snap-ins that can be permitted or restricted. There is a separate list of extension snap-ins that can be restricted/permitted (see Figure 25.35). Extensions are implemented as dependent modules of snap-ins, but sometimes they do the same things as full-blown snap-ins. For example, the Event Viewer is a snap-in and can exist by itself in a console, as it does in the Event Viewer administrative tool, but it is also implemented as an extension in the Computer Management tool. So you'll need to know whether the thing you want to restrict is a full snap-in or an extension. (See Chapter 24 for additional information on MMC consoles and snap-ins.)

There is a separate folder for the Group Policy snap-in and related extensions. These allow you to restrict or permit access to the individual parts of Group Policy so that delegated admin types can assign software to be installed, for example, without having access to the Security Settings node. *Be careful when restricting access to the GP snap-ins.* This policy should be filtered for trusted, responsible (and polite) administrators.

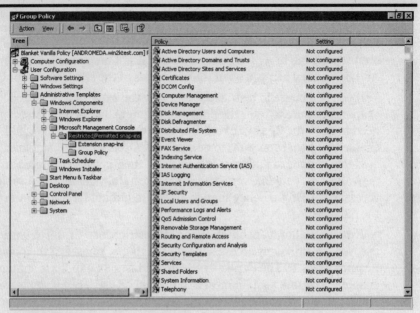

FIGURE 25.34: Permitted or restricted MMC snap-ins

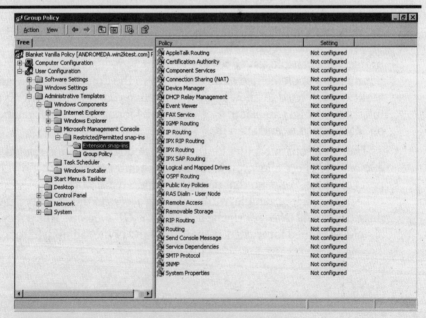

FIGURE 25.35: Permitted or restricted MMC extensions

A final note about MMC policies: If the user doesn't have all the necessary components installed on her machine, the MSC file won't work properly and may not even run. A very useful policy Download Missing COM Components directs the system to search for those missing components in the Active Directory and download them if they are found. For some reason, this policy is found in User Configuration\ Administrative Templates\System and in the corresponding path of Computer Configuration.

Managing Group Policies

In the preceding section, we touched on using Group Policy settings to restrict access to certain MMC snap-ins and extensions, including the Group Policy snap-ins. Let's finish our discussion of group policies with an exploration of the other Group Policy configuration options that are actually included as group policies ("group policy policies"). Then I'll close with a few select observations and suggestions for configuring and managing group policies in your organization.

Group Policy Policies

Policies to control Group Policy are found in Administrative Templates of both the User Configuration and Computer Configuration nodes (Administrative Templates\System\Group Policy). Figures 25.36 and 25.37 show the User Configuration and Computer Configuration options for Group Policy. The following information summarizes the most important configuration options.

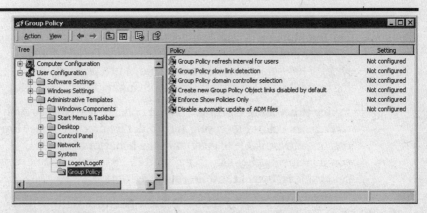

FIGURE 25.36: User configuration settings for Group Policy

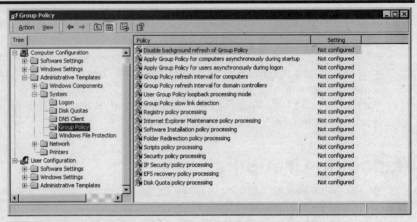

FIGURE 25.37: Computer configuration settings for Group Policy

**Group Policy Refresh Intervals For Users/Computers/
Domain Controllers**   These separate policies determine how
often GPOs are refreshed in the background while users and
computers are working. These parameters permit changes to
the default background refresh intervals and permit tweaking
the offset time.

Disable Background Refresh   If you enable this setting, policies will only be refreshed at system start-up and user login.
This might be useful for performance reasons, since having
1,500 computers refreshing policies every 90 minutes could
cause congestion on an Ethernet.

**Apply Group Policy For Users/Computers Synchronously
During Start-up**   Enable this setting to prevent users from
logging on until all group policies have been applied. Otherwise, policies apply in the background, and a user will able to
log on while policy settings are still changing.

Policy Processing Options   These policies, with names such
as Registry Policy Processing and Folder Redirection Policy Processing, are available to customize the behavior of the GPO
components. Each policy (see Figure 25.38 for an example) presents at least two of the following three options:

> **Allow Processing Across A Slow Network Connection**
> For slow connections, some policies can be turned off to

enhance performance (you can define what a "slow link" is by using the Group Policy Slow Link Detection setting). Security settings and Registry policy processing will always apply, however, and cannot be turned off.

Do Not Apply During Periodic Background Processing Specify which components will be refreshed periodically. Software installation and folder redirection policies will never be refreshed while a user is logged on, so the option is not available for them.

Process Even If The Group Policy Objects Have Not Changed   To conserve network and system resources, GPOs are, by default, not refreshed if there have been no changes. To increase security, however, and guard against a user changing a policy setting, enable the policy to ensure that all settings are reapplied at each refresh interval. Enabling this policy may cause noticeable performance degradation.

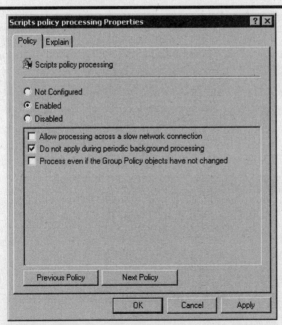

FIGURE 25.38: Script policy processing options

User Group Policy Loopback Processing Mode   By default, user policies are processed after computer configuration policies, and user policies take precedence if there are conflicts. Also by default, users receive their policy regardless of the machine they use to log on. Sometimes this is not appropriate, and policies need to be applied according to the computer's policy objects instead. For example, if I log on to a server to do administration, it's not appropriate for my office productivity applications to start installing themselves. Another example of when you would want computer policies to override user policies is if you want to apply more stringent policies for machines that are exposed to the anonymous public, such as machines in libraries, university computer labs, or kiosks in shopping malls or tourist attractions. Two modes control this behavior (see Figure 25.39):

Merge Mode   Process user policies first, then computer policies. Computer policies will therefore override conflicting user policies.

Replace Mode   Disregard user policies and processes only computer policies.

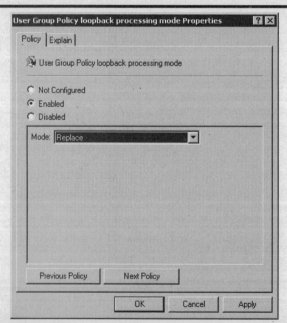

FIGURE 25.39: User Group Policy Loopback Processing Mode policy

Group Policy over Slow Links

Group Policy still works over slow links such as dial-up connections. Even better, policy is applied whether a user logs on using Dial-Up Networking or whether they log on with cached credentials and then initiate a connection. However, application of Group Policy over slow links can pose performance issues, so Windows 2000 includes policy settings to define a slow link and to define how policies are applied over a detected slow link.

The default definition of a slow link, as far as group policies are concerned, is anything less than 500 kilobits per second. The system performs a test using the Ping utility to determine the speed of the connection. If the Ping response time is less than 2,000 milliseconds, the connection is fast. You can change the definition of a slow link, however. This policy setting, called Group Policy Slow Link Detection, is available in both the User Configuration and Computer Configuration, under `Administrative Templates\ System\Group Policy` (see Figure 25.40 for the Properties dialog box of the policy). To change the default parameter, enter a number in Kbps, or enter 0 to disable slow link detection altogether. If you disable slow link detection, all policies will be applied regardless of the connection speed.

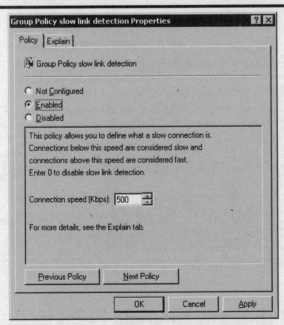

FIGURE 25.40: The Group Policy Slow Link Detection Properties dialog box

As I mentioned in the preceding section, policy processing settings for individual policy components (these have names such as Folder Redirection Policy Processing and are found in the same path as the slow link detection setting, under `Computer Configuration\Administrative Templates\System\Group Policy`) allow you to specify whether a portion of the policy object will be processed over a slow link connection. Again, this is not an option for Registry-based policies or for security settings; they will always be processed, even over slow links. The other modules will not be applied over slow links by default.

To run logon scripts over slow links, for example, open the Scripts Policy Processing policy. Enable the policy, as in Figure 25.41, and check the box beside Allow Processing Across A Slow Network Connection. Choose OK to set the policy. Repeat as necessary for the other policy processing entries.

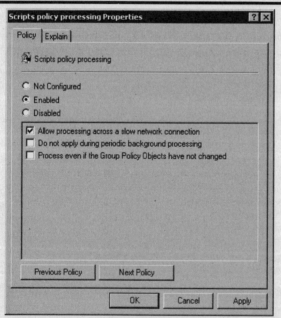

FIGURE 25.41: Policy processing options

A Few Final Thoughts on Group Policy

In the last few sections, I have discussed the concepts of group policies, including local policies. We have created a sample group policy and have seen how to turn on the various settings, such as No Override and Block Inheritance. We've looked at filtering policies for security groups and delegating policy administration to others. We have explored many of the actual policy settings, including administrative templates for desktop control, security settings, folder redirection, MMC management, even Group Policy policies. But before you close this chapter and begin to configure group policies on your network, you want to be very aware of two more big issues:

- ▶ Group policies affect network and system performance.

- ▶ Group policies are difficult to troubleshoot if something goes wrong.

The performance issue is rather simple: the more policies to apply, the longer the logon time. Each time a user logs on (or a computer is restarted), each of the GPOs associated with the user's or computer's containers (SDOUs) is read and applied. This can slow down logons considerably, and users may start calling the help desk to ask, "What's wrong with the network?" Therefore, you should keep the number of policies to a minimum.

Background refresh rate can also bog down a machine or a network. Refresh policies too often, and you'll see a hit because the machine is always busy asking for policy changes. Think about disabling the background refreshes altogether unless you're worried about users changing their settings to escape policies. If the background refresh is disabled, user policies are reapplied only at logon, and computer policies are reapplied only at start-up. The worst thing you could do for performance is have a bunch of different policies in effect and tell Group Policy to reapply at each refresh interval even if there are no changes. Another way to streamline GPO processing is to avoid assigning GPOs from different domains. Just because you can do it doesn't mean it's a good idea.

The problem with troubleshooting policies stems from an inability to view the cumulative policy settings that are actually in effect for a user or machine. This capability to display actual policy settings, currently referred to as the Resultant Set of Policy (RSOP), is necessary for managing and troubleshooting policies. Without it, you have to look at the properties of each site/domain/OU to see which policies are linked to which containers. You must then view the ACLs to see if there's any filtering and check out the disabled, Block Inheritance, and No Override options. Finally, you need to view the settings of the policies in question before you can get to the bottom of things. You'll need to take notes. Until Microsoft comes out with an RSOP tool, promised soon after the release of Windows 2000, here are a few suggestions to help minimize trouble-shooting time:

▶ Keep your policy strategy simple. Group users and computers together in OUs if possible, and apply policy at the highest level possible. Avoid having multiple GPOs with conflicting policies that apply to the same recipients. Minimize the use of No Override and Block Inheritance.

▶ Document your group policies heavily, both individual settings and framework. You may want to visually depict your policy structure and put it on the wall like your network topology diagrams. That way, when a problem arises, you can consult the documentation to see what's going on before you go fishing.

▶ Finally, test group policies before deployment! This is absolutely essential to save your help desk and ensure that applications and system services continue to run properly.

WHAT'S NEXT?

The *Windows 2000 Instant Reference,* by Jutta VanStean, is an A-to-Z listing of every command and feature in Windows 2000 Professional and Server. The last section of this book is a condensation of that reference. If you have a specific question about Windows 2000, this reference is your quickest path to an answer.

PART VI

WINDOWS 2000
INSTANT REFERENCE

WINDOWS 2000
INSTANT REFERENCE

Adapted from *Windows 2000 Instant Reference*,
by Jutta VanSteen
ISBN 0-7821-2572-7   627 pages $19.99

ACCESSIBILITY

Choose Start ➢ Programs ➢ Accessories ➢ Accessibility to access the Accessibility Wizard, Magnifier, Narrator, On-Screen Keyboard, and Utility Manager.

ACCESSIBILITY OPTIONS

Configures settings that make using the computer easier for users who have physical disabilities, such as hearing and vision impairments, as well as users who have difficulty using the keyboard and mouse.

Choose Start ➢ Settings ➢ Control Panel and double-click Accessibility Options to open the Accessibility Options dialog box. The Accessibility Options dialog box contains five tabs: Keyboard, Sound, Display, Mouse, and General. Select the appropriate check box to turn on a feature, and click the Settings button to adjust the default settings.

ACCESSIBILITY WIZARD

Wizard that helps you set up Accessibility Options to make the computer and Windows easier to use if you have difficulties with your vision, hearing, or mobility. Choose Start ➢ Programs ➢ Accessories ➢ Accessibility ➢ Accessibility Wizard to open the Welcome To The Accessibility Wizard dialog box, and then follow the on-screen instructions to establish the settings you want.

ACCESSORIES

Windows 2000 predefined program group. Windows 2000 includes many programs you can use to configure your Windows 2000 computer and perform different functions. You can find many of these programs in the Accessories program group. To access options in this group, choose Start ➢ Programs ➢ Accessories. The programs and program groups available in Accessories depend on the choices you made during the Windows 2000 installation and when you installed other programs. If you selected defaults, they will include the following:

Program groups Accessibility, Communications, Entertainment, Games, System Tools. Windows 2000 Server also includes the Microsoft Script Debugger program group, which is installed if you didn't deselect the default installation option for Internet Information Server (IIS).

Programs Address Book, Calculator, Command Prompt, Imaging, Notepad, Paint, Synchronize, Windows Explorer, and WordPad.

ACTIVE DESKTOP

Windows 2000 lets you set up your Desktop to look and function like a Web page. With Active Desktop turned on, you can display and update Web content on your Desktop. An example of this is displaying a stock ticker on your Desktop that automatically updates to show you the latest stock quotes. The fact that Web content can be automatically updated is why the Desktop is called *active*.

You can enable the Active Desktop feature in several ways:

- ► Choose Start ➤ Settings ➤ Control Panel, and then open Folder Options. On the General tab, under Active Desktop, select Enable Web Content On My Desktop.

- ► Right-click anywhere on the Desktop, and choose Active Desktop ➤ Show Web Content from the shortcut menu.

- ► Choose Start ➤ Settings ➤ Control Panel, and then open Display. Select the Web tab, and then check Show Web Content On My Active Desktop.

By default, when you enable the Active Desktop feature, your current home page displays on the Desktop. If your current home page is located on the Internet, you must be connected to the Internet for the page to display. You can change which page you want to display on your Desktop on the Web tab of Display Properties.

Once the Active Desktop is enabled, you have several other options available to configure your Active Desktop. To access these options, right-click anywhere in a blank area of the Desktop and choose Active Desktop. The following options are now available:

Show Web Content   Toggles the Active Desktop feature off and on.

Show Desktop Items   Toggles the display of Desktop icons off and on.

Lock Desktop Items   Toggles the Lock Desktop Items feature off and on. Locking Desktop items means that you cannot resize or move Active Desktop items.

Synchronize   Updates Web content.

My Current Homepage   Toggles the display of your current home page off and on.

ACTIVE DIRECTORY

Scalable directory service new in Windows 2000 Server. Active Directory lets you identify resources, called *objects*, in the network, and makes those resources accessible to users via a single logon. Examples of resources are users, users' data, groups, computers, servers, and printers. Active Directory has a component called the Directory, whose function is to store information about these resources, as well as store services that make that information available. Because all network resources are represented as objects in the Directory, Active Directory provides single-point administration.

Active Directory uses DNS (Domain Name System) for its naming system. It also supports other name formats, such as HTTP URL, UNC, RFC 822 (name @domain.extension), and LDAP URL. Active Directory supports LDAP (Lightweight Directory Access Protocol) versions 2 and 3 for accessing directory service information, and HTTP (Hypertext Transfer Protocol), which enables users of the network to display Active Directory objects as HTML pages.

Active Directory is installed on Windows 2000 domain controllers. Because in Windows 2000 all domain controllers in a domain are peers (multimaster model), each domain controller in the domain holds a copy of the Directory. When you install Active Directory on a domain controller, the Directory database and the shared system volume are created. The shared system volume is called SYSVOL, and its default location is SYSTEMROOT\SYSVOL. By default, it contains some of the domain's group policy objects as well as scripts.

ACTIVE DIRECTORY DOMAINS AND TRUSTS

Microsoft Management Console (MMC) snap-in installed on Windows 2000 domain controllers that lets you manage Active Directory domains and trusts on a Windows 2000 domain controller. To access Active Directory Domains And Trusts, choose Start ➤ Programs ➤ Administrative Tools ➤ Active Directory Domains And Trusts. The console tree displays the available domains.

Domain Properties

To access the domain's properties, select the domain object in the console tree, and choose Action ➤ Properties. You'll see the following three tabs:

General Lets you view the domain's name, the domain's pre–Windows 2000 name, the description, and the current operation mode. You can click Change Mode to change the mode from mixed to native. Once the domain is in native mode, it cannot be changed back to mixed mode.

Trusts Lets you view and edit existing trust relationships (both explicit and transitive), and add and remove explicit trust relationships between this domain and other domains. For an explicit trust relationship to be established, you must establish the applicable portion of the trust relationship in the properties of one domain and the other portion that completes the trust relationship in the properties of the other domain.

Managed By   Lets you specify the name of an Active Directory user who will manage the domain.

ACTIVE DIRECTORY USERS AND COMPUTERS

Microsoft Management Console (MMC) snap-in installed by default on Windows 2000 domain controllers that lets you create, modify, delete, and organize Active Directory user and computer accounts, groups, organizational units (OUs), contacts, printers, and shared folders in the Directory. To access Active Directory Users And Computers, choose Start ➢ Programs ➢ Administrative Tools ➢ Active Directory Users And Computers.

The Active Directory Users And Computers MMC Console Snap-In Window

Lets you manage Active Directory users, groups, computers, and other published resources through Action menu options. The options available on the Action menu depend on the item you selected in the console tree pane. Some Action menu options are also available on the toolbar.

ACTIVE DIRECTORY SITES AND SERVICES

Microsoft Management Console (MMC) snap-in installed on Windows 2000 domain controllers that lets you manage Active Directory sites and services.

Sites are created to specify the boundaries of physical sites in the network so that replication and authentication is performed, ensuring greatest efficiency. When you publish a site to Active Directory, Active Directory can then determine how to best perform replication (data is replicated both within and between sites) and which domain controller (typically within the same site) should handle service requests. This minimizes network traffic and enables you to make the best use of available bandwidth. This is particularly important in a wide area network (WAN). It is also critical because Windows 2000 uses the multimaster replication model, which enables any domain controller to service any request. Otherwise, for example, it could easily happen that a user attempts to authenticate over a dial-up connection to a domain controller located thousands of miles away.

Part VI

The Services feature is used to publish service information to Active Directory, which is then used by client applications and thus simplifies access to services. Examples are binding information (which allows Windows 2000 to automatically establish connections to services) and application configuration information. Several services are published by default.

To access Active Directory Sites and Services on a Windows 2000 domain controller, choose Start ➢ Programs ➢ Administrative Tools ➢ Active Directory Sites And Services.

ADD/REMOVE HARDWARE

Starts the Add/Remove Hardware Wizard, which helps you add, remove, and troubleshoot hardware on your system, such as network cards, modems, disk drives, and CD-ROM drives.

Choose Start ➢ Settings ➢ Control Panel ➢ Add/Remove Hardware to start the Add/Remove Hardware Wizard. This Wizard guides you through the steps to add new hardware to a Windows 2000 computer after you've physically installed it, to prepare Windows 2000 to physically remove or unplug hardware from the computer, or to troubleshoot a device that is experiencing problems. The Hardware Wizard automatically makes the necessary changes, including changes to the Registry and configuration files, and installing, loading, removing, and unloading of drivers.

Before you start the Hardware Wizard, power off your computer and install the device or plug it into the appropriate port. Turn your computer back on. If Plug and Play detects the new hardware and has the appropriate drivers for it, the hardware is added automatically, and no further action is required.

If Plug and Play does not detect your hardware, start the Add/Remove Hardware Wizard, and follow the on-screen instructions.

When you use the Add/Remove Hardware Wizard to remove hardware, Windows 2000 gives you two choices: you can completely remove hardware from the computer (physically removing the hardware and permanently removing drivers), or you can temporarily disable a device so that the physical device can stay connected to the computer but its drivers are not loaded (Windows 2000 makes the appropriate Registry changes). If you want to use the device again, you can simply enable it.

ADD/REMOVE PROGRAMS

Installs or removes programs and Windows 2000 components from your computer. Examples of programs are Microsoft Word or Microsoft FrontPage; examples of Windows 2000 components are Administrative Tools or networking options. You can also use Add/Remove Programs to install other operating systems on different partitions. Choose Start ➢ Settings ➢ Control Panel and double-click the Add/Remove Programs icon to open Add/Remove Programs. You'll see the Change Or Remove Programs screen. The left pane of the window contains three buttons for changing, removing, or adding programs and for adding or removing Windows components. The information in the right pane changes depending on which option you've selected.

ADDRESS BOOK

Lets you manage your contact information, such as postal and e-mail addresses, telephone numbers, business and personal information, and home page addresses. You can also use Address Book together with other programs, such as Internet Explorer, Outlook, and Outlook Express.

Choose Start ➢ Programs ➢ Accessories ➢ Address Book to open Address Book.

ADMINISTRATIVE TOOLS

Collection of Microsoft Management Console (MMC) tools you can use to administer every aspect of your Windows 2000 computer configuration. Which tools are available depends on whether the computer is a Windows 2000 Professional or Server computer, whether the computer is a domain controller, and which services are installed on the computer.

To access Administrative Tools, choose Start ➢ Settings ➢ Control Panel, and then double-click the Administrative Tools icon.

Commonly available options in Administrative Tools include Component Services, Computer Management, Data Sources (ODBC), Event Viewer, Local Security Policy, Performance, Services, and Telnet Server Administration. On computers configured as domain controllers with Active Directory installed, you'll also typically see Active Directory Domains And Trusts, Active Directory Sites And Services, Active Directory Users And Computers, Configure Your Server, DHCP, DNS, Licensing, and many others.

BACKUP

Lets you safeguard the data stored on your computer or on network drives to which you have access by copying the data to a data storage device, such as a tape drive or additional hard drive. Should there be a problem with your live data (such as disk failure, accidental deletion of files, or file corruption), you can restore data from a backup.

Choose Start ➤ Programs ➤ Accessories ➤ System Tools ➤ Backup to open Windows 2000 Backup.

Browse

Used to find files and directories on the computer or in the network. You'll see this button in many dialog boxes where you need to provide the name and path of a file or folder or specify an Internet or intranet address or URL. Simply click Browse to open the Browse dialog box.

Calculator

Lets you perform mathematical calculations, including standard, scientific, and statistical calculations. To open the Calculator, choose Start ➤ Programs ➤ Accessories ➤ Calculator. You can display the Calculator in either Standard view or Scientific view.

Capturing Images

Windows 2000 lets you capture screen images (full screen or active window), which you can then paste into a document. When you capture a screen image, it's saved to the Windows Clipboard, making it available for pasting at a later point in time. To capture an image and paste it into a document, follow these steps:

1. If you want to capture the entire screen, press the Print Screen key or key combination (often abbreviated as PrtSc and accessed by pressing Shift+Print Screen). If you want to capture an active window, press Alt+Print Screen.

2. Place the cursor where you want to insert the image in your document and press Ctrl+V or choose Edit ➤ Paste. Windows will paste the image into your document.

CD Player

Plays audio CDs from the CD-ROM drive installed in your computer. Choose Start ➤ Programs ➤ Accessories ➤ Entertainment ➤ CD Player to start the CD Player. You must have a sound card and speakers installed in your computer to use the CD Player.

Change Password

Lets you change the password for the currently logged-on user or another user. Press Ctrl+Alt+Delete, and then click Change Password. Either leave the User Name and Log On To information as it is (to change the currently logged-on user's password) or specify a different username and where the user logs on to (to change another user's password). Enter the old password; then enter the new password and reenter it to confirm it. Click OK to change the password.

Character Map

Lets you display and copy the available characters for each font installed on your Windows 2000 computer. This includes private characters you created with the Private Character Editor. Character Map displays Unicode, DOS, and Windows character sets.

To access Character Map, choose Start ➤ Programs ➤ Accessories ➤ System Tools ➤ Character Map. The character set for the first font in alphabetical order is displayed.

You can display character sets for other fonts by selecting a font from the Font drop-down list. Enlarge any character by simply clicking it.

When you click a character, the status bar at the bottom of the Character Map dialog box shows you the Unicode value (hexadecimal equivalent) for the character, as well as the name of the character. You may also see a keyboard equivalent displayed for the character if one is available.

Copying Characters

Character Map lets you copy characters to the Windows 2000 Clipboard and then paste them into other programs. To do this, first either click a character and then click Select, or double-click a character. Once you do, the character appears in the Characters To Copy text box. You can then click Copy to copy all selected characters to the Windows 2000 Clipboard.

Advanced View

Select Advanced View to display additional Character Map–related options. You can select the character set you want to display, group the Unicode character set by Unicode subrange, search for a specific character, or go directly to a character in the Unicode character set.

CHECKING DRIVES FOR ERRORS

You can check a floppy or hard drive for any file system and physical errors on the disk. To do so, perform these steps:

1. Right-click the drive in any Explorer window, and then select Properties.

2. Select the Tools tab.

3. In the Error-Checking section, click Check Now.

4. In the Check Disk dialog box, specify whether you want file system errors to be fixed automatically and whether you want to scan for and attempt to recover bad sectors on the disk. Click Start when you've finished.

5. Wait for all phases of the check to finish. This may take some time. When the check is done, click OK in the Checking Disk *driveletter* message box.

CLIPBOARD

The Windows Clipboard is a temporary holding place for data. When you use the Cut or Copy command in programs running on a Windows 2000 computer, any data you cut or copy is placed onto the Clipboard. You can retrieve the contents of the Clipboard by using the Paste command. To view the contents of the Clipboard, you can paste them into Notepad, for example, or you can use the ClipBook Viewer.

CLIPBOOK VIEWER

ClipBook Viewer lets you view and save the contents of the Windows 2000 Clipboard. To open ClipBook Viewer, choose Start ➤ Run, type **clipbrd**, and click OK.

The ClipBook Viewer has two windows: the Local ClipBook and the Clipboard. Maximize or resize the Clipboard to view its contents.

You can save the contents of the Clipboard either to a file or to the local ClipBook. If you do the latter, you can share ClipBook pages with other users. You can also set up permissions as well as auditing for each ClipBook page (for remote user access after you share a page) and take ownership of a page.

Close

Closes the currently open window/application. You'll find this button in the top-right corner of any open window, next to either the Restore or Maximize button.

COM+ (Component Services)

Collection of services based on the Component Object Model (COM) and Microsoft Transaction Server (MTS) extensions. COM+ provides application administration and packaging, component load balancing (CLB), improved threading and security, object pooling, transaction management, queued components, and IMDB (In-Memory Database).

Command Prompt

Used to execute command-line functions and utilities, such as MS-DOS commands and programs. Many MS-DOS commands and programs are still available in Windows 2000, although some have been removed. Check the Help system for a list of functions that still exist and those that have been removed. Examples of MS-DOS commands are del, dir, path, more, and print. An example of an MS-DOS program is Edit. Microsoft has added some new commands in Windows 2000, such as convert (to convert a FAT file system to NTFS) and start (to run a command or program in a separate window). Other examples of commands you can execute at the command prompt include the IPCONFIG command, used to view TCP/IP configuration information, and net commands, used to perform Windows 2000 networking tasks, such as net use and net print. To see a list of many of the available commands, enter **help** at the command prompt.

To access a command prompt, choose Start ➢ Programs ➢ Accessories ➢ Command Prompt. The Command Prompt window opens. You can now enter commands at the command prompt (by default, C : \).

Communications

Windows 2000 predefined program group from which you access the following communication-related program groups, programs, and functions: Fax, Hyper-Terminal, Internet Connection Wizard, NetMeeting, Network and Dial-Up Connections, and Phone Dialer. These items are described in detail throughout this book. Choose Start ➢ Programs ➢ Accessories ➢ Communications to access the Communications program group.

Part VI

CONFIGURE YOUR SERVER

Lets you configure services and options on Windows 2000 Server computers. To access Configure Your Server, choose Start ➢ Programs ➢ Administrative Tools ➢ Configure Your Server.

Configure Your Server contains links to the following server configuration options:

Home   Lets you view and return to the Configure Your Server home page. Also contains a link to new features in Windows 2000 and a link to walkthroughs on the Web. The latter takes you to Microsoft's Web site, where you can find step-by-step instructions for installing and configuring Windows 2000 Server. Back on the Configure Your Server home page, you can also select a check box to specify that you want the Configure Your Server screen to display at startup.

Register Now   Lets you register your copy of Windows 2000 Server.

Active Directory   Depending on whether Active Directory is already installed, lets you install Active Directory or access links to Active Directory Users And Computers and Active Directory help.

File Server   Lets you access links to the Create Shared Folder Wizard (to create shared folders), to Computer Management (where you can manage shared folders), and to shared folders help.

Print Server   Lets you access links to the Add Printer Wizard, to the Printers folder (for printer management), and to printing help.

Web/Media Server   Features a submenu that contains two links: Web Server and Streaming Media Server. The Web Server link lets you access the Web Server page, which has links to the Internet Services Manager (where you can perform Web and FTP server configuration) and to Internet Information Services (IIS) help. The Streaming Media Server link lets you access the Streaming Media Server page, which has links to start the Windows Component Wizard (used to set up Windows Media Services) and to Windows Media Services help. The Streaming Media Server page also contains a Next button, which you can click to start using streaming media after using the Component Wizard to set up Windows Media Services.

Networking   Lets you access links to Network and Dial-Up Connections and to the Network Identification tab of System Properties. Also has a submenu that contains four links: DHCP, DNS, Remote Access, and Routing. The DHCP link lets you access links to the DHCP Microsoft Management Console (MMC) snap-in and to DHCP help. The DNS link lets you access links to the DNS MMC console snap-in and to DNS help. The Remote Access and Routing links let you access links to the Routing And Remote Access MMC console snap-in, and to routing and remote access help.

Application Server Has a submenu with four links: Component Services, Terminal Services, Database Server, and E-Mail Server. The Component Services link lets you access the Component Services MMC console snap-in and application and programming tools help. The Terminal Services link lets you access the Component Services Wizard (also accessible through Add/ Remove Programs), which you use to install Terminal Services (an optional Windows 2000 component) and Terminal Services help. The Database Server and E-Mail Server links let you view screens explaining that Windows 2000 Server computers can be configured and used as database and e-mail servers after you install database or e-mail server applications.

Advanced Lets you view information about how you can use Windows 2000 Administration Tools to manage Windows 2000 Server computers from client computers. Also lets you access links to Windows 2000 Administration Tools help and Component and Services checklists. Also has a submenu with three links: Message Queuing, Support Tools, and Optional Components. The Message Queuing link lets you access links to the Message Queuing Installation Wizard and to Message Queuing help. The Support Tools link gives you information about how to install the Windows 2000 Resource Kit Support Tools. The Optional Components link lets you access a link to the Windows Component Wizard, which you use to install other optional Windows 2000 components.

COMPONENT SERVICES

Microsoft Management Console (MMC) snap-in administrative tool that lets you configure and manage COM and COM+ applications and components. Tasks include, for example, installing COM+ applications and managing component load balancing, application security, distributed transactions, and IMDB (In-Memory Database).

To access Component Services, choose Start ➢ Settings ➢ Control Panel, double-click Administrative Tools, and then double-click Component Services.

If you expand Component Services in the console tree, you'll see the Computers folder, and below it the My Computer object. Expand the My Computer object to see the currently installed COM+ applications in the COM+ Applications folder. Expand any COM+ application to see the Components and Roles folders, in which you can view and configure components and roles for the application.

Right-click any item in the Computers folder and below, and then choose Properties, if available, to view and configure the item. The tabs and configuration options available in the Properties dialog boxes depend on the item you've selected.

Enabling Security

To be able to use Component Services, you must first enable security on the System application and assign at least one user to the Administrator role. Microsoft recommends adding users to groups and then assigning the group to the role. Follow these steps:

1. Expand the console tree as follows: Computers, My Computer, COM+ Applications, System Application, Roles, Administrator, Users.

2. Select the Users folder, then choose Action ➤ New ➤ User.

3. Select a user or group from the list and click Add, and then click OK.

4. Reboot the computer.

Adding a Network Computer

By default, only the local computer appears under Component Services in the console tree. To be able to use Component Services on remote computers, you can add those computers to the console tree by following these steps:

1. Select Computers in the console tree.

2. Choose Action ➤ New ➤ Computer, and then enter or browse for the name of another computer in the network. Click OK.

Installing COM+ Applications

You can install additional COM+ applications on computers that have Component Services installed. Follow these steps:

1. Right-click the COM+ Applications folder of the computer where you want to install the application, and choose New ➤ Application. This starts the COM Application Install Wizard. Click Next.

2. Click Install Pre-Built Application(s).

3. Browse to and select the appropriate MSI file, then click Open.

4. In the Select Application Files screen, click Add to add additional applications, if applicable. Click Next.

5. Select an application identity. This can be either the currently logged-on user (Interactive User) or a user you specify. Click Next.

6. Click Finish. Component Services adds the application to the COM+ Applications folder.

COMPRESSING DRIVES, FOLDERS, AND FILES

You can compress NTFS-formatted drives, as well as individual folders and files on NTFS drives, to save on disk space. If you copy or add a file in a compressed drive or folder, it is automatically compressed.

To compress an NTFS drive, follow these steps:

1. Right-click a drive in an Explorer window and select Properties.

2. On the General tab, check Compress Drive To Save Disk Space, and click OK.

3. In the Confirm Attribute Change dialog box, specify whether you want only files and folders at the root of the drive to compress or subfolders and files as well. Click OK.

To compress files or folders, follow these steps:

1. Right-click the folder or file in an Explorer window and select Properties.

2. On the General tab, click Advanced to open the Advanced Attributes dialog box.

3. In the Compress Or Encrypt Attributes section, check Compress Contents To Save Disk Space, and click OK.

4. Click OK again to close the folder's Properties dialog box. If you're compressing a folder and it contains subfolders, you'll be prompted to confirm the attribute changes. Specify whether you want the changes to apply only to this folder or to any subfolders and files as well. Click OK.

COMPUTER MANAGEMENT

Microsoft Management Console (MMC) console snap-in that lets you manage various aspects of your computer. To access Computer Management, choose Start ➤ Settings ➤ Control Panel, double-click Administrative Tools, and then double-click Computer Management.

Part vi

In the console tree of Computer Management under Computer Management (Local), you'll see three categories: System Tools, Storage, and Services And Applications. Each of these items contains other items you use to manage your local computer, which is the computer you can manage by default. You can manage remote computers by selecting Computer Management (Local) in the console tree, choosing Action ➢ Connect To Another Computer, and then selecting the computer from the list and clicking OK.

With a default installation, you'll find the following items in the three categories. Other items might be available, and some items might not be available if you did not perform a default installation.

System Tools   Event Viewer, System Information, Performance Logs And Alerts, Shared Folders, Device Manager, and Local Users And Groups (not on Windows 2000 domain controllers).

Storage   Disk Management, Disk Defragmenter, Logical Drives, and Removable Storage.

Services and Applications   WMI Control (Windows Management Instrumentation), Services, and Indexing Service. On Windows 2000 domain controllers, you'll also find DHCP, Telephony, DNS, and Internet Information Services.

CONNECT TO THE INTERNET

Accessible on the Windows 2000 Desktop until you've completed the Internet Connection Wizard, which starts if you double-click the Connect To The Internet icon. The Internet Connection Wizard leads you through the process of connecting to the Internet for the first time. After you finish the Internet Connection Wizard, the Connect To The Internet icon is removed from the Windows 2000 Desktop.

CONTROL PANEL

Where you go to configure and personalize settings for many of Windows 2000's functions and features, such as Accessibility Options, Add/Remove Programs, Administrative Tools, Folder Options, Regional Options, and Scheduled Tasks. To access Control Panel, choose Start ➢ Settings ➢ Control Panel. You can also access Control Panel through My Computer and Windows Explorer.

COPY FILES AND FOLDERS

You can copy a file or folder to another location, leaving the original intact in the original location. You do this by using the Edit menu, the shortcut menu, or drag-and-drop.

Copy Files or Folders Using the Edit Menu

To copy files or folders using the Edit menu in Windows Explorer, follow these steps:

1. Select the file or folder in the right pane of the Explorer window.

2. Choose Edit ➣ Copy.

3. Browse to and select the destination folder in the Folder view of the Explorer Bar.

4. Choose Edit ➣ Paste. The file(s) or folder(s) appear in the destination folder.

Copy Files or Folders Using the Shortcut Menu

To copy a file or folder using the shortcut menu, right-click the file or folder to open the shortcut menu, and then choose Copy. Next, browse to and right-click the destination folder, and then choose Paste. Windows copies the file or folder to the destination folder.

Copy Files or Folders Using Drag-and-Drop

To copy files or folders using drag-and-drop, you must first make sure that both the source and destination folders are visible in the Folders view. Open the source folder, hold down the Ctrl key, then drag the file or folder from the source folder to the destination folder while holding down the left mouse button. When the cursor is over the destination folder (the folder is selected), let go of the mouse button, and then release the Ctrl key. Windows copies the file or folder to the destination folder.

CREATE NEW FOLDER

To be able to organize the files on your computer, you'll want to create new folders. You can do this in Windows Explorer by performing the following steps:

1. Select the folder or drive in which you want to create the new folder.

2. Choose File ➤ New ➤ Folder.

'3. A new folder with the name New Folder appears in the folder or drive you chose. Replace the name New Folder with a descriptive name of your choice, and press Enter.

CREATE SHARED FOLDER WIZARD

Windows 2000 includes the Create Shared Folder Wizard, which walks you through the process of creating shared folders. When you share a folder, it becomes visible and available to other users on the network.

To create a shared folder using the Create Shared Folder Wizard, follow these steps:

1. To start the Create Shared Folder Wizard on a Windows 2000 Server computer, choose Start ➤ Programs ➤ Administrative Tools ➤ Computer Management. On a Windows 2000 Professional computer, choose Start ➤ Settings ➤ Control Panel, and then double-click Computer Management.

2. Expand System Tools, expand Shared Folders, and then select Shares.

3. In the Action menu, choose New ➤ File Share to start the Create Shared Folder Wizard. Follow the on-screen instructions.

CREATE SHORTCUT

Shortcuts let you access programs, files, folders, printers, computers, or Internet addresses without having to go to their permanent locations.

You can create shortcuts by using the File menu, shortcut menus, and drag-and-copy.

Using the File Menu in Windows Explorer

In Windows Explorer, select an item in the right pane, and then choose File ➤ Create Shortcut. A shortcut to the item is placed into the same folder. You can now drag the shortcut to where you want it (such as another folder, the Desktop, or the Taskbar).

Using Shortcut Menus

To create a shortcut using shortcut menus, right-click an item and choose Create Shortcut. If you right-click the Desktop and choose New ➤ Shortcut, the Create

Shortcut Wizard starts, which will guide you through the process of creating a new shortcut.

Using Drag-and-Copy

To create a shortcut using drag-and-copy, in Windows Explorer select an item and drag it to where you want the shortcut to reside while pressing Ctrl+Shift. Alternatively, press the right mouse button and drag the item to where you want to place the shortcut, release the mouse button when you have reached the destination, and then choose Create Shortcut(s) Here from the resulting shortcut menu.

CTRL+ALT+DELETE

Keystroke combination that lets you access several Windows Security options through the Lock Computer, Log Off, Shut Down, Change Password, and Task Manager buttons. You can press Ctrl+Alt+Delete at any time during a Windows 2000 session to access these options. Click Cancel to return to your Windows session without using any of the available options.

DATA SOURCES (ODBC)

Lets you add, configure, and remove user, system, and file data sources and drivers so you can access data from multiple database formats, such as FoxPro, dBASE, and Access, using the same interface. To open the ODBC (Open Database Connectivity) Data Source Administrator, choose Start ➤ Settings ➤ Control Panel, double-click Administrative Tools, and then double-click Data Sources (ODBC).

ODBC Data Source Administrator has several tabs:

User DSN   Lets you add and configure data sources that will be available only to the current user on the current computer.

System DSN   Lets you add and configure data sources that will be available to all users of the computer.

File DSN   Lets you add and configure data sources that enable users to connect to a data provider.

Drivers   Displays the name, version, company, filename, and date of all ODBC drivers installed on the computer.

Tracing   Lets you configure logging of calls to ODBC drivers. Logs can be used for troubleshooting purposes. Also used to start Tracing and Visual Studio Analyzer.

Part vi

Connection Pooling   Lets you enable and configure connection pooling. If it's enabled, applications can reuse open connection handles, which increases performance.

About   Displays information about ODBC core components, including description, version, and the core component's filename and location.

DATE/TIME

Used to set the date, time, and time zone for the computer. Choose Start ➢ Settings ➢ Control Panel and double-click the Date/Time icon to open the Date/Time Properties dialog box. Alternatively, you can double-click the system clock on the right side of the Taskbar.

It's important that the date and time of the system clock are correct because this time and date information is used to specify when files on your computer are created and modified. The Date/Time Properties dialog box has two tabs: Date & Time and Time Zone.

DELETING FILES AND FOLDERS

It will at times be necessary for you to delete files or folders from your computer—for example, to free up space on your hard drive or to keep your files and folders well organized. You can do this in several ways. The first step is to select the file or folder you want to delete. Next, do one of the following:

- Choose File ➢ Delete.

- Right-click the file or folder and choose Delete from the shortcut menu.

- Press the Delete key on the keyboard.

- Drag the file or folder to the Recycle Bin icon on the Desktop (you'll have to make sure that you can see this icon on the Desktop).

Using any of the above methods and default settings, you'll have to click OK to confirm that you want to move the file or folder to the Recycle Bin. Windows then moves the file or folder to the Recycle Bin.

DESKTOP

The Desktop is what you first see when you run Windows 2000. It is meant to resemble a physical desktop on which you work and organize your papers, telephone numbers, and so forth.

By default, the Desktop contains several icons at the left of the screen (including My Documents, My Computer, My Network Places, Recycle Bin, Internet Explorer, and Connect To The Internet) and the Start button and Taskbar at the bottom of the screen. As you add new programs and make changes to your environment, new icons are added to the Desktop and Taskbar, and some may be removed. Any time you work with a program, the program's user interface appears on the Desktop so that you can use the program.

DEVICE MANAGER

Device Manager is a Windows 2000 Microsoft Management Console (MMC) snap-in. It shows you a list of all hardware installed in the computer and provides information about this hardware. Use Device Manager after you install new hardware to verify the installation. Use it also to further configure devices, check a device's status, view and update device drivers, and enable and disable devices.

To access Device Manager, choose Start ➢ Settings ➢ Control Panel, double-click System, select the Hardware tab, and click the Device Manager button.

In Device Manager, each hardware class and device is depicted by an icon and then followed by the name of the class or device. To see devices in each class, expand the class by clicking the plus sign to the left of the class icon. Unknown devices are depicted by a yellow question mark item.

As with all MMC consoles and snap-ins, Device Manager has an Action and a View menu that contain options specific to the currently active MMC console snap-in.

DHCP

Microsoft Management Console (MMC) snap-in on Windows 2000 Server computers that lets you manage the Dynamic Host Configuration Protocol (DHCP) service. DHCP eases the administrative burden of IP (Internet Protocol) address management and overall IP client configuration. Every computer in an IP network must have a unique IP address assigned to be able to communicate with other computers in the network. This IP address assignment can be done either manually or automatically (via DHCP). DHCP also enables automatic configuration of associated configuration options on DHCP-enabled client computers. Any client computer that runs a Microsoft Windows operating system can function as a DHCP client.

To be able to perform the above functions, the DHCP service in Windows 2000 Server enables the Windows 2000 Server computer to function as a DHCP server.

To access the DHCP MMC console snap-in, choose Start ➢ Programs ➢ Administrative Tools ➢ DHCP.

DHCP MMC Console Snap-In Window

By default, the Windows 2000 server on which DHCP is installed is configured to function as a DHCP server. Use the DHCP MMC console snap-in to configure the DHCP server. You can also add DHCP servers to the MMC console snap-in.

Enabling DHCP on a Windows 2000 Client

To be able to have an IP address dynamically assigned by a DHCP server to a Windows 2000 client, you must verify that DHCP is enabled at the client. To do so, follow these steps:

1. Choose Start ➤ Settings ➤ Network And Dial-Up Connections.

2. Double-click the Local Area Connection icon, and then click Properties.

3. Select Internet Protocol (TCP/IP) in the list of components used by this connection, and click Properties.

4. Check Obtain An IP Address Automatically. Click OK twice, and then click Close.

DirectX Diagnostic Tool

Lets you obtain information about Microsoft DirectX application programming interface drivers and components installed on your computer. You can also use it to check components and to disable some hardware acceleration features. You can provide the information you obtain to support personnel who are helping you troubleshoot a problem.

To access the DirectX Diagnostic Tool, choose Start ➤ Settings ➤ Control Panel, double-click Administrative Tools, double-click Computer Management, expand System Tools, select System Information, and then choose Tools ➤ Windows ➤ DirectX Diagnostic Tool.

Disk Cleanup

Finds files on your hard disk that can be deleted to free up hard disk space. Includes temporary files, unnecessary program files, no longer used Windows 2000 components, cache files, and files in the Recycle Bin. You then have the option to delete either some or all of the files, components, or programs.

Using Disk Cleanup

To free up space on your hard disk, follow these steps:

1. Choose Start ➤ Programs ➤ Accessories ➤ System Tools ➤ Disk Cleanup to start Disk Cleanup.

2. Select the drive you want to clean from the Drives drop-down list. Click OK. Wait for Disk Cleanup to scan the drive. This may take some time.

3. On the Disk Cleanup tab in the Disk Cleanup For *driveletter* dialog box, place a check mark next to the type of files you want to delete. You can also select a file type from the Files To Delete list box (without placing a check mark) and click View Files to see which files will be affected if you place a check mark next to the file type.

   Select the More Options tab to specify that you want to remove optional Windows components and programs you no longer use by clicking the appropriate Clean Up button. This will start the Windows Component Wizard or Add/Remove Programs, respectively. You can then remove any Windows components or other installed programs you no longer use.

4. When you've finished making selections, click OK.

5. Confirm that you want to delete the files by clicking Yes.

6. Wait for the utility to remove the files. This may take a while, depending on the number of files you selected for deletion.

7. Windows returns you to the Desktop when Disk Cleanup has finished.

DISK DEFRAGMENTER

A Microsoft Management Console (MMC) snap-in that lets you change the order of files and unused space on your computer's hard disk so that programs can run more efficiently, which increases overall response time.

Choose Start ➤ Programs ➤ Accessories ➤ System Tools ➤ Disk Defragmenter to start Disk Defragmenter.

Disk Defragmenter MMC Console

In the top pane of the Disk Defragmenter MMC console, you'll see the volumes available for defragmentation. Take note of the other information available regarding the volume, such as Session Status (for example, analyzing or defragmenting), File System, Capacity, Free Space, and % Free Space.

Part vi

In the lower portion of the console, you'll see a graphical representation of the data on the volume during and after analysis or defragmentation. The console also contains some of the MMC toolbar buttons, such as Action and View, as well as a status bar at the bottom of the window.

During volume analysis or defragmentation, the graphical displays Analysis Display and Defragmentation Display represent the volume's current state (during or after analysis or defragmentation). Fragmented files are indicated in red, contiguous files in blue, system files in green, and free space in white. Also, in the left portion of the status bar, you'll see the current action being performed, and to the right of this, a blue indicator bar shows you the progress of the current action.

Analyzing a Volume

To analyze a volume on your computer, perform these steps:

1. Select a volume in the list of available volumes in the upper pane of the Disk Defragmenter MMC console.

2. Click the Analyze button to start analyzing the volume. Click Pause or Stop at any time to pause or stop the drive analysis.

3. When Disk Defragmenter finishes, you'll receive a message indicating that the analysis is complete. The message also advises you whether you should defragment the volume. Click View Report to see a report about the analysis, click Defragment to defragment the volume now, or click Close to close the message and return to Disk Defragmenter.

Defragmenting a Volume

To defragment a volume on your computer, perform these steps:

1. Select a volume in the list of available volumes in the upper pane of the Disk Defragmenter MMC console.

2. Click the Defragment button to start the defragmentation. First, the volume is analyzed (or reanalyzed if it was previously analyzed), and then the defragmentation begins. This process may take quite some time to finish, depending on the size and state of the volume. Click Pause or Stop at any time to pause or stop the defragmentation process.

3. When Disk Defragmenter finishes, a message appears telling you that defragmentation is complete. You can click View Report to see a detailed report regarding the defragmentation, or you can click Close to return to Disk Defragmenter.

Viewing Reports

After you analyze or defragment a volume, a report is created that provides you with detailed information about the action. You can view this report either at the end of the operation by clicking View Report in the message that appears when the operation is finished, or you can choose Action ➤ View Report to view the report most recently created. You can also click the View Report button.

A report contains information about the volume, volume fragmentation, file fragmentation, pagefile fragmentation, directory fragmentation, and Master File Table (MFT) fragmentation. It also includes information about files that did not defragment during the defragmentation process. If you wish, you can print the report or save it to a file.

DISK MANAGEMENT

Microsoft Management Console (MMC) snap-in that lets you manage disks and volumes in a graphical environment. To access Disk Management, choose Start ➤ Settings ➤ Control Panel, double-click Administrative Tools, and then double-click Computer Management. You'll find the Disk Management snap-in under Storage.

Use Disk Management to perform operations such as changing drive letters and paths, formatting your disk, deleting partitions, creating partitions, upgrading basic disks to dynamic disks, and ejecting removable media (such as CDs). You can also create and work with simple volumes, spanned volumes, striped volumes, mirrored volumes, and RAID-5 volumes for both basic and dynamic disks.

The Disk Management Details pane by default displays a top and bottom window, with the volume list in the top window and a graphical view of your disks in the bottom window.

Basic Disks

Basic disks are hard disks that can contain primary and extended partitions, and logical drives, as well as mirrored volumes, striped volumes, spanned volumes, and RAID-5 volumes. Basic disks can be accessed by Windows 2000, as well as Windows NT 4.0, Windows 3.1, 95, and 98, and MS-DOS. Basic disks have these limits: four primary partitions per disk or three primary partitions and one extended partition. You can set up multiple volumes (logical drives) on an extended partition.

Action Menu with Basic Disks

With basic disks, you'll find many unique items on the Action menu or its All Tasks submenu. The options available depend on which item you've selected in the Details pane, and which view you've selected (Disk List or Volume List).

Refresh   Updates the disk and volume views.

Rescan Disks   Rescans all available disks.

Restore Basic Disk Configuration   Restores the disk configuration that was saved from a previous version of Windows NT.

Change Drive Letter And Path   Lets you change the drive letter and path of a volume.

Eject   Ejects the removable media from the drive.

Properties   Opens the drive's properties.

Upgrade To Dynamic Disk   Lets you upgrade a basic disk to a dynamic disk.

Open   Opens the drive in Windows Explorer without an Explorer Bar view selected.

Explore   Opens the drive in Windows Explorer with the Explorer Bar Folders view selected.

Mark Partition Active   Marks the currently selected partition as active.

Format   Lets you format the drive. You can choose a volume label, file system (NTFS or FAT32), and allocation unit size.

Delete Logical Drive   Deletes the selected logical drive.

Delete Partition   Deletes the selected partition.

Creating Partitions

To create a partition or logical drive using unallocated space, right-click unallocated space in the Graphical view and choose Create Partition, and then follow the Wizard's instructions.

View Menu with Basic Disks

The View menu contains the following unique options when working with basic disks:

Top   Contains a submenu that lets you select what to display in the top window of the Details pane. Choices include Disk List, Volume List, and Graphical View.

Bottom   Contains a submenu that lets you select what to display in the bottom window of the Details pane. Choices include Disk List, Volume List, Graphical View, and Hidden.

Settings   Lets you configure the color and pattern for each of the disk regions in the Graphical view, such as primary partition, free space, and simple volume. Also lets you configure the proportion for how disks and disk regions display in the Graphical view.

All Drive Paths   Displays all drive paths.

Dynamic Disks

Dynamic disks are hard disks that contain dynamic volumes, which you create using Disk Management. A dynamic disk can also contain dynamic mirrored, striped, spanned, and RAID-5 volumes. Dynamic disks can be accessed only by the Windows 2000 operating system. There is no limit as to how many volumes you can create on a dynamic disk. No partitions or logical drives can exist on dynamic disks. Portable computers cannot contain dynamic disks.

Upgrading a Basic Disk to a Dynamic Disk

You can upgrade basic disks to dynamic disks using Disk Management. However, once you've done that, you cannot revert the disk to a basic disk. To upgrade a basic disk to a dynamic disk, follow these steps:

1.   Choose View ➤ Top ➤ Disk List.

2.   Right-click the disk you want to upgrade in the Details pane and choose Upgrade To Dynamic Disk.

3.   Verify that the correct disk is selected, and click OK.

4.   In the Disks To Upgrade dialog box, verify that the information is correct, and click Upgrade.

5.   Read the warning message that you won't be able to boot previous versions of Windows from any volume on the disk. Click Yes to confirm the upgrade.

6.   Click Yes to verify force dismount of file systems.

7.   Click OK to reboot the computer.

After you upgrade the disk, the changes are reflected in Disk Management, showing the type as dynamic in the Details pane.

Part vi

DISK QUOTAS

Let you control how much disk space each user can use on a local or network NTFS-formatted volume. You can also use disk quotas to track disk space usage without restricting disk space.

Disk quotas are set up on the Quota tab of a volume's Properties dialog box. To access this tab, right-click a volume in an Explorer window, select Properties, and then select the Quota tab.

Quota Tab

The Quota tab lets you enable and configure disk quotas. To enable disk quotas, select the Enable Quota Management check box. If you want to use disk quotas only to track disk space usage, leave the Deny Disk Space To Users Exceeding Quota Limit check box deselected. Otherwise, select it. If this option is selected, users receive an *Insufficient Disk Space* message when they try to save a file after exceeding their disk space quota.

To specify default disk usage limits, select the radio button next to Limit Disk Space To and enter the amount of disk space in the text box. Choose a unit of measurement (KB, MB, GB, TB, PB, or EB) from the corresponding drop-down list. You can also set a warning level in the same manner next to Set Warning Level To. You can also specify that you want Windows to log an event in the event log when users exceed their quota limit and/or warning level. To do this, select the appropriate check box. You can view events with Event Viewer (to make disk quota events easier to find, you can filter the event log for Disk events). Click OK twice to implement your settings (enable disk quotas).

Windows applies the disk space and warning levels you set here to any new user the first time the user accesses the quota-enabled volume. To add quotas to existing users, you have to add a new quota entry.

Quota Entries

Quota entries give you specific disk quota information for each user. This information includes such items as the amount of disk space used, the quota limit, the warning level, and the percentage of allowed disk space used.

Quota Entries Window

To access the Quota Entries window for a quota-enabled volume, click Quota Entries on the Quota tab of the volume. The Quota Entries window consists of menus, a toolbar, the quota entry list box, and a status bar.

The quota entry list box contains information about each quota entry, including Status, Name, Logon Name, Amount Used, Quota Limit, Warning Level, and Percent Used.

Creating a New Quota Entry

You'll need to create a new quota entry for any user who existed before you enabled disk quotas for a volume.

To create a new quota entry, perform these steps:

1. Choose Quota ➢ New Quota Entry to open the Select Users dialog box.

2. From the Look In drop-down list, select the domain for which you want to display users, or select Entire Directory to display all users in the Active Directory.

3. Select one or more users in the list, and then click Add to add the users to the list of users for which a quota entry will be created. Optionally, click Check Names to verify that the names you selected are valid. Click OK.

4. In the Add New Quota Entry dialog box, you can select Do Not Limit Disk Usage or you can select Limit Disk Space To and enter the appropriate amounts and unit of measurement for disk space limits and warning levels. Click OK.

You can change the properties for any quota entry by right-clicking an entry and selecting Properties. The resulting Quota Settings dialog box contains a General tab that tells you the amount of the quota used (percent) and the quota remaining. In addition, the tab lets you change the quota disk space limit and warning level for the entry, as well as disable disk usage limits.

DISK SPACE

You can see how much disk space a file or folder uses. To do so, in any Explorer window, select a folder in the Folders Explorer Bar or a file in the right pane. The amount of space the file or folder uses appears in the status bar at the bottom of the window (the status bar must be turned on).

You can also choose File ➢ Properties, or right-click a file or folder and choose Properties from the shortcut menu. You'll find the size on the General tab. For folders, you'll also see how many files and folders are contained in the folder.

DISPLAY

Used to configure the look of your Desktop, including backgrounds, screen savers, appearance of program windows, Web options, Desktop icons, visual effects, number of colors, and resolution.

Choose Start ➤ Settings ➤ Control Panel, and double-click the Display icon. The Display Properties dialog box has six tabs, on which you can make configuration changes: Background, Screen Saver, Appearance, Web, Effects, and Settings. Click Apply any time you want changes applied to your Desktop without closing the Display Properties dialog box.

DISTRIBUTED FILE SYSTEM

Microsoft Management Console (MMC) snap-in available on Windows 2000 servers (member servers or domain controllers) that enables you to make files located on different servers (distributed) appear to users as if they are in one location. Distributed File System (Dfs) thus eliminates the need for users to try to find related files that are located on different servers. With Dfs, there is no need for drive mappings, and users are not affected if you move the physical location of a shared folder. If you use Dfs for Web servers, HTML links will still function even if you move the location of Web server resources.

To access Dfs, choose Start ➤ Programs ➤ Administrative Tools ➤ Distributed File System.

Dfs Types

You can implement Dfs using one of two types:

Stand-Alone Distributed File System   Not stored in Active Directory. Does not support automatic replication.

Domain-Based Distributed File System   Stored in Active Directory. Supports automatic replication.

Creating a Domain-Based Distributed File System

To create a domain-based Dfs, follow these steps:

1. Right-click Distributed File System in the console tree pane and choose New Dfs Root to start the New Dfs Root Wizard. Click Next.

2. Select Create A Domain Dfs Root, and click Next.

3. Select the domain you want to host this Dfs root. Click Next.

4. Type or browse for the server you want to host this Dfs root. Click Next.

5. Select to use an existing share and choose one from the drop-down list, or select to create a new share and enter the necessary share information. Click Next.

6. Type a name for the Dfs root in the Name text box. Type a comment in the Comment text box if you wish. Click Next.

7. Verify the information. If you need to make changes, use the Back button. Click Finish to create the Dfs root.

8. Reboot the computer. (If you don't, Dfs won't work.)

9. Run Distributed File System again.

10. Right-click the Dfs root in the console tree and choose New Dfs Link.

11. In the Create A New Dfs Link dialog box, type a name for the link in the Link Name text box; then type the path to or browse to the folder you want opened when a user opens the Dfs link.

12. If desired, type a comment in the Comment text box and change how long clients keep the Dfs link referral in cache.

13. Click OK to create the Dfs link.

14. To verify the creation and accessibility of the distributed file system you created, open Windows Explorer (you can do this at a client computer if you wish) and navigate My Network Places to the server where you created the distributed file system. The Dfs root appears as a network share below the server. Navigate to the Dfs link you created, which appears as a folder below the Dfs root. Verify that the contents of the folder are the same as those of the folder you specified in the Create A New Dfs Link dialog box to open when the Dfs link is opened.

DNS

Domain Name System (DNS) service and also Administrative Tools menu option that takes you to the DNS Microsoft Management Console (MMC) snap-in installed by default on Windows 2000 domain controllers with Active Directory installed. The DNS MMC console snap-in lets you manage Windows 2000 DNS servers.

DNS is a system for assigning user-friendly names (DNS names) to computers in a TCP/IP network (such as the Internet) using a domain hierarchy. This makes it easier for people to locate computers (hosts) and services in the network; for example, it's easier to remember `microsoft.com` than it is to remember the IP address `207.46.130.149`. However, hosts use each other's IP addresses to communicate. DNS names are registered with their corresponding IP addresses in DNS databases, and then the data in DNS databases is used to resolve DNS names to IP addresses when hosts request services from each other. An entry in a DNS database is called a resource record. Resource records can be one of several types, among them:

Host   Also called an A record; maps a DNS domain name to an IPv4 address

Alias   Maps an alias to an existing DNS domain name

IPv6 hosts   Maps a DNS domain name to an IPv6 address

A DNS implementation requires a DNS domain name space, resource records, a DNS server, and DNS clients.

DNS Domain Name Space

The DNS domain name space is organized to represent a conceptual tree of named domains, consisting of branch and leaf levels. At the branch level, several names represent groups of resources; at the leaf level, a single name denotes a single resource.

Each level in the domain name space has an associated name that corresponds to its function. Levels are separated by periods.

Domain Root   This is an unnamed level and is denoted by two empty quotation marks (""). In a DNS domain name, the domain root is denoted by a trailing period at the end of the DNS name, such as "`publishing.sybex.com.`". When a DNS name is used this way, it indicates an exact location in the tree hierarchy and is called a fully qualified domain name (FQDN). Contains top-level domains.

Top-Level Domain   Consists of two or three letters and denotes a country, region, or organization type. Organization type examples are `.com` and `.org`; country/region examples are `.ca` (Canada) and `.de` (Germany). Contains second-level domains.

Second-Level Domain   Name that an individual or organization registers to use on the Internet, such as `sybex.com`. Can contain either subdomains or host names.

Subdomain   Added to an organization's second-level domain name to further organize an organization's structure, such as `publishing.sybex.com` (a fictitious example used throughout this reference). Contains host names.

Host Name   Identifies a single resource in the domain, such as a computer or other device. An example might be `workstation-5 .publishing.sybex.com`.

Zones

Zones are databases of one or more DNS domain names and store name information for the domain names they include. For example, a zone could contain `sybex.com` and `publishing.sybex.com`, or you could have a separate zone for each. At the time the `sybex.com` domain is created at a server, a single zone is created for the `sybex` name space. When you add subdomains, you can either add them to the existing zone or create a new zone for them (called delegation).

Two types of zones exist:

Forward Lookup Zones   Assumes that IP addresses are required as the response to queries.

Reverse Lookup Zones   Assumes that DNS domain names are required as the response to queries.

Zone Transfers

To provide fault tolerance, you must make zones available from more than one DNS server. You accomplish this through zone transfers, which ensure that zone data is replicated and synchronized between multiple DNS servers. When a second server is configured to host a zone that exists on another server, a full zone transfer (transferring all data) is made. After that, in Windows 2000 Server incremental zone transfers occur as changes are made to the zone.

DNS MMC Console Snap-in

Use the DNS MMC console snap-in to view and configure DNS services. In the DNS console snap-in window, you can view and configure the DNS server and zones.

Action Menu

The Action and shortcut menus contain options to perform such functions as starting, stopping, pausing, resuming, and restarting the DNS service; configuring the DNS server; creating new zones; creating new resource records; adding a new domain to a zone; configuring item properties; and accessing Help. The options available depend on which item you've selected in the console tree or Details pane.

Part vi

DNS Client Configuration

In order for Windows clients to be able to use DNS services, they must know the IP address of one or more DNS servers in the network. You can have the client obtain DNS server addresses automatically (via DHCP), or you can specify an IP address for the preferred DNS server, as well as for an alternate DNS server and additional DNS servers. Follow these steps:

1. Choose Start ➤ Settings ➤ Network And Dial-Up Connections.

2. Double-click the Local Area Connection icon, and then click Properties.

3. Select Internet Protocol (TCP/IP) in the list of components used by this connection, and click Properties.

4. To use DHCP to obtain DNS server addresses, select Obtain DNS Server Address Automatically. Otherwise, select Use The Following DNS Server Addresses and enter the IP address of the preferred DNS server. To provide fault tolerance, enter the IP address of an alternate DNS server, if available.

5. Optional: To specify additional DNS server IP addresses, click Advanced, select the DNS tab, click Add, enter a DNS server's IP address, and click Add. Repeat this step until you've added all DNS server IP addresses, and then click OK.

6. Click OK, click OK again, and click Close.

DOCUMENTS

Provides access to a list of shortcuts Windows 2000 maintains to the 15 most recently accessed documents so that you can quickly access them again if you need to. Choose Start ➤ Documents to access the list. Click any item in the list to open the document in the appropriate application, saving you time and effort.

To clear the list of documents, choose Start ➤ Settings ➤ Taskbar & Start Menu, and then click Clear on the Advanced tab.

DRAG-AND-DROP

You can use drag-and-drop to copy, move, and delete files and folders in many application programs and on the Desktop. To do so, place the mouse pointer over an item, press and hold the left mouse button, and drag the item to its destination by moving the mouse. A destination might be a folder, a drive, the Desktop, and so forth. Place the pointer over the destination and release the left mouse button.

DR. WATSON

Error-debugging program that automatically diagnoses and logs Windows 2000 program errors. Support personnel can then use this information to troubleshoot the problem. Dr. Watson starts automatically when a Windows 2000 program error occurs.

To access and configure Dr. Watson, and to view application errors, choose Start ➤ Settings ➤ Control Panel, double-click Administrative Tools, double-click Computer Management, expand Systems Tools, select System Information, and then choose Tools ➤ Windows ➤ Dr Watson.

ENTERTAINMENT

Windows 2000 default program group that provides access to the following entertainment programs: CD Player, Sound Recorder, Volume Control, and Windows Media Player. You access the Entertainment program group by choosing Start ➤ Programs ➤ Accessories ➤ Entertainment.

EVENT VIEWER

Displays information about events that are logged by Windows 2000 and other installed applications. Used to monitor and troubleshoot Windows 2000 hardware and software. Also lets you manage the logged information.

To access Event Viewer, choose Start ➤ Settings ➤ Control Panel, double-click Administrative Tools, and then double-click Event Viewer.

Event Viewer Logs

By default, Event Viewer in Windows 2000 contains three logs—the Application, Security, and System logs. Each log displays different types of events. Additional logs may appear, depending on your configuration and on whether the computer is running Windows 2000 Professional or Windows 2000 Server.

Application Log

The Application log displays events generated by such applications as installation programs and database programs. The application developer programs the events to be logged into the application.

Security Log

The Security log displays such events as successful and failed login attempts, as well as events related to working with files and folders, such as creating, opening, and deleting files and folders. Security auditing is not enabled by default, and events are logged only after audit policies are set up. You must use Group Policy on a domain or Local Security Policy on a local computer to enable it. If your computer is part of a domain, Group Policy settings on the domain take precedence over Local Security Policy settings.

System Log

The System log displays events that are logged by Windows 2000 components. Examples are when drivers fail to load, a hard disk is renamed, or user disk quota data is rebuilt.

Event Types

The Event Viewer Details pane displays the following event types:

Information   Describes a successful event, such as loading a service successfully.

Warning   Describes an event that is not problematic right now but that may indicate a problem in the future, such as the browser not being able to obtain a list of servers from the browser master on a domain controller.

Error   Describes a serious problem, such as a service that fails to load.

Success Audit   Describes a successful, audited event, such as a successful system logon.

Failure Audit   Describes an unsuccessful, audited event, such as an unsuccessful system logon.

Event Log Properties

You can customize event log properties for each log. Select the log in the console tree and choose Action ➢ Properties. The Properties dialog box has two tabs: General and Filter.

General   Here you can change the log's display name and the maximum log size, configure log wrapping (when the maximum log size is reached), clear the log, and restore default settings. You can also view information about the log file, such as its current size and creation date, and when it was last modified and accessed.

Filter   Lets you filter the log by certain criteria. You can specify the types of events you want to view, the source and category of events you want to view, and the user, computer, or event ID for which you want to view events. You can also specify a time frame for viewing events. Click Restore Defaults to return to the default settings.

Event Information

When you select an event log in the console tree, the Details pane displays all events currently in the log. You can see some preliminary information about each event under the column headings. The column headings give you information about the event, such as its type; the date and time the event occurred; the source and category of the event; an event ID, if applicable; and the name of the user and computer on which the event occurred.

Viewing Detailed Information

To view additional, more detailed information about an event, right-click the event and choose Properties, or double-click it. In addition to the information available in the Details pane, you'll see a detailed description of the event and, if available, record data on the Event Detail tab. To see details for the next or previous event, click the up or down arrow button, respectively. You can also click the copy button (depicted by two sheets of paper) to copy the details of the event to the Windows Clipboard.

Ordering Events

By default, events in the Details pane display chronologically with the newest event first. You can reverse this order by choosing View ➤ Oldest First.

Finding Events

If you're looking for a specific event, it might be difficult to find the event in the log. You can search for a specific event by choosing View ➤ Find and then specifying information about the event you want to find (such as type, source, category, and user) in the Find In dialog box. Click Find Next to start your search.

Viewing Logs on a Remote Computer

By default, Event Viewer displays the event log files for the local computer. You can also access log files on remote computers. Select Event Viewer (Local) and choose the option Connect To Another Computer from the Action menu to connect to and view log files on a remote computer.

EXPLORER

Program used to work with files and folders on your computer and in the network in Windows 2000. The program's full name is Windows Explorer. It displays and lets you navigate the hierarchical structure of drives, folders, and files on your computer and of any mapped network drives. Using Explorer, you can accomplish such tasks as creating, copying, moving, renaming, and deleting files

Part VI

and folders. You can also run programs, search for files, view the properties of files, and many other file- and folder-related functions.

To open Explorer, choose Start ➤ Programs ➤ Accessories ➤ Windows Explorer. When you open Explorer in this manner, it opens to the My Documents folder (a Desktop folder). Alternatively, you can right-click Start and choose Explore. This will open Explorer to the Start Menu folder.

FAX

Configures Microsoft Fax properties, such as user information, cover pages, and fax monitoring. Choose Start ➤ Settings ➤ Control Panel and double-click the Fax icon to open the Fax Properties dialog box. It contains four tabs: User Information, Cover Pages, Status Monitor, and Advanced Options.

Microsoft Fax is part of Windows 2000 and is used to send faxes via a fax modem, also called a fax device. If one is installed, you can create a document you want to fax and then send it, as if you were printing a document. Choose File ➤ Print in any Windows application program (such as Microsoft Word) and select the fax device to which you want to send the document. Click Print and follow the instructions in the Send Fax Wizard.

FILE SIGNATURE VERIFICATION UTILITY

To maintain system integrity and detect changes to system files, system files are digitally signed. The File Signature Verification utility lets you check for critical system files that should be digitally signed but aren't.

To start the utility, choose Start ➤ Settings ➤ Control Panel, double-click Administrative Tools, double-click Computer Management, expand System Tools, and select System Information. Then choose Tools ➤ Windows ➤ File Signature Verification Utility.

To perform file signature verification, follow these steps:

1. In the File Signature Verification dialog box, click the Advanced button to configure verification options on the two tabs of the Advanced File Signature Verification Settings dialog box. On the Search tab, you can specify that you want to be notified of unsigned files, or you can specify that you want the utility to search for files of other file types that aren't digitally signed. On the Logging tab, you can specify that you want to save results to a log file, set logging options, and assign a filename for the log file. Click OK when you've finished setting advanced options.

   After you've created a log, you can return to the Logging tab in the Advanced File Signature Verification Settings dialog box at any time and click View to view the log file in Notepad.

2. Click Start to begin the file signature verification process. Wait for the process to finish. You'll see a progress bar while the utility is scanning files.

3. If all files have been digitally signed, you'll be prompted by the SigVerif message box advising you that all files have been scanned and digitally signed. Click OK and skip to step 6. If one or more files have not been digitally signed, continue with step 4.

4. The Signature Verification Results dialog box opens and lists all system files (or other files, if you selected the option for searching other files) that are not digitally signed. Information about each file includes name, folder, modified date, file type, and version. The status bar tells you how many files were found, how many were signed, how many were not signed, and how many were not scanned.

5. Click Close to dismiss the Signature Verification Results dialog box.

6. Click Close again to close the utility.

FOLDERS

Folders are part of the Windows 2000 file system structure. You use folders to organize files on your computer. In addition to files, folders can contain subfolders.

To view a folder, open a Windows Explorer window and use Explorer's navigation tools to find the folder. To view and access folder contents, double-click the folder.

FOLDER OPTIONS

Controls the appearance and use of files and folders, activates the Active Desktop, configures file associations, and enables offline use of network files. Any settings you make are reflected in how folders are displayed and used in Windows Explorer (this includes My Documents, My Network Places, My Computer and Control Panel). Choose Start ➤ Settings ➤ Control Panel and double-click the Folder Options icon to open the Folder Options dialog box, which contains four tabs—General, View, File Types, and Offline Files.

FONTS

Folder used to view and manage fonts (type styles) used by Windows 2000 and applications. To open the Fonts folder in an Explorer window, choose Start ➤

Settings ➤ Control Panel and double-click Fonts. You'll see a list of all currently installed fonts.

Font types supported by Windows 2000 include TrueType fonts, Open Type fonts (an extension of TrueType), Type 1 fonts (by Adobe Systems, Inc.), Vector fonts, and Raster fonts. The font type is indicated by the look of the font icon in the Fonts folder. For example, Open Type fonts show an *O* in the font icon; True-Type fonts show two *T*s in the icon.

You can add new fonts to your computer at any time by following these steps:

1. Choose File ➤ Install New Font.

2. Browse for the directory and folder where the new fonts are located.

3. Select one, several, or all fonts in the List Of Fonts list box. Click OK. Windows installs the fonts and returns you to the Fonts folder.

FORMAT

Lets you format floppy disks for first-time use, or completely erase the floppy disk's contents. Also lets you format fixed disks, such as your hard drive. Formatting is required in order for Windows to be able to save information to and read information from any disk device, including floppy disks.

FTP

Abbreviation for File Transfer Protocol, which is a part of the TCP/IP protocol suite used for Internet and other network communications. It is also a utility that is included with Windows 2000 that lets you transfer one or more files to or from a remote host (a computer on an IP network). It supports many file types, including American Standard Code for Information Interchange (ASCII), binary, and Extended Binary-Coded Decimal Interchange Code (EBCDIC). You can also use FTP to display directory lists and file lists.

In Windows 2000, FTP is a text-based program that you run from a Windows 2000 command prompt. To run it, follow these steps:

1. Choose Start ➤ Run.

2. Enter **ftp** and click OK. A command prompt window opens to an FTP prompt (ftp>).

You can type **?** or **help** at the ftp> prompt to display all available FTP commands. You can also type **help** followed by the name of a command to see an explanation of what the command does.

Many of the commands are used for troubleshooting purposes and to navigate the local or remote directory structure, but the following are what you need to know to use FTP for file transfer purposes:

open Opens a connection to the remote computer. You can then enter the IP address of the computer to which you want to connect to establish the connection. You can use *anonymous* as the username and your e-mail address as the password.

ascii Establishes the file transfer type as ASCII.

binary Establishes the file transfer type as binary.

put Transfers a file you specify from your computer to the remote host.

get Transfers a file you specify from the remote host to your computer.

quit Closes the connection to the remote host and ends the FTP session. You can also use the bye command for the same purpose. You'll be returned to the Windows 2000 Desktop.

Game Controllers

Installs, removes, and configures game controllers, such as game pads, joysticks, and flight yokes. Choose Start ➢ Settings ➢ Control Panel and double-click the Game Controllers icon to open the Game Controllers dialog box. It has two tabs: General and Advanced.

Games

Program group in Windows 2000 Professional that contains four games: Freecell, Minesweeper, Pinball, and, on computers running Windows 2000 Professional, Solitaire. To access the Games program group, choose Start ➢ Programs ➢ Accessories ➢ Games. (Some users claim that Solitaire helps people new to computers to learn how to control the mouse—you'll have to decide for yourself on that one.) Pinball can be played with more than one player. If you want help learning how to play any of these games, choose Help from the menu.

Group Policy

Microsoft Management Console (MMC) snap-in and Windows 2000 Server component that lets you control the Desktop environment of users in your network, including the programs users can access, the programs that are displayed on users' Desktops, the options that appear on users' Start menus, and the script files that run at certain times. Group policies consist of settings that can be applied to all users in a site, domain, or organizational unit (OU). Group policies are useful because they:

- ▸ Reduce the amount of administration needed to configure user environments.

- ▸ Enable you to control and automate application and file access.

- ▸ Reduce the number of problems that result from users making changes to their environments.

- ▸ Make the user's environment easier to work in.

Group policies are usually set for an entire site or domain by group policy administrators and are a good way to enforce company policies, such as limiting the use of applications to certain users. A group policy administrator should belong to the default Group Policy Creator Owners security group, which provides the necessary rights to modify group policies in a domain; Administrator is a member of this group by default.

Group Policy Types

Several types of group policies exist that apply settings for specific purposes:

Security   Lets you restrict user access to files and folders and specify the number of incorrect password entries before Windows locks out the user account. Also lets you specify user rights—for example, who can log on to a Windows 2000 Server computer.

Application Deployment   Lets you define application access for users. Applications can then be distributed to users in one of two ways: application assignment or application publication. With application assignment, applications and application upgrades are automatically installed on a user's computer, or a permanent connection to an application is automatically established. With application publication, an application is published to the Active Directory, making it available for installation by users using Add/Remove Programs in Control Panel.

File Deployment   Lets you specify files that Windows copies automatically to certain folders on a user's computer, such as My Documents.

Software   Lets you specify settings that will be applied to user profiles. Examples include Start menu and Desktop settings.

Scripts   Lets you specify scripts or batch files that should run automatically on users' computers at certain times—for example, when the user logs in or when the system starts. Using scripts enables task automation, such as automatically mapping network drives.

Group Policy Inheritance

Group policies are inherited in the following order: site, domain, OU. Group policies defined for a container object closer to the user override those defined for a container object farther away from the user. For example, for a user that belongs to a specific OU, a group policy applied to that OU overrides a group policy applied to the site in which the user exists.

Group Policy Objects and Templates

Group policy objects (GPOs) contain group policy configuration settings that can be applied to a site, domain, domain controller, or OU. A default GPO called Default Domain Policy is automatically created for each domain, and a default GPO called Default Domain Controllers Policy is automatically created for each domain controller.

GPOs use two different locations to store group policy configuration settings. These locations are group policy containers (GPCs) and group policy templates (GPTs). GPCs are stored in Active Directory and contain GPO properties, such as version and GPO status information. GPCs also contain subcontainers that contain user and computer group policy information. A GPT is a folder structure that is created in the system volume (sysvol) folder of a domain controller when a GPO is created. It contains all settings for all policies created in the group policy object.

Working with GPOs

You can perform many functions related to GPOs by using the Group Policy tab of site domain objects, the Domain Controllers OU, and other OU objects. Functions include creating new GPOs, adding links to existing GPOs, applying options, deleting GPOs or links to GPOs, viewing and editing GPO properties, and editing GPOs. To access the Group Policy tab, follow these steps:

1. Choose Start ➢ Programs ➢ Administrative Tools. If you want to work with GPOs applied to a domain, domain controller, or OU, choose Active Directory Users And Computers. If you want to work with GPOs applied to a site, choose Active Directory Sites And Services.

2. Right-click the appropriate object or folder (domain, the Domain Controllers OU, other OU, or site), and choose Properties.

3. Select the Group Policy tab.

In addition to offering each of the functions related to the available buttons (which will be described in more detail below), the Group Policy tab lets you specify whether you want to block policy inheritance from linked GPOs defined at higher levels than the current object. Simply select the Block Policy Inheritance check box.

Creating a New GPO

You can create new GPOs to allow further customization of your client environment. To create a new GPO, follow these steps:

1. On the Group Policy tab, click New.

2. Type a name to replace the default name New Group Policy Object, and press Enter. This creates the new GPO and automatically adds it to the list of GPOs linked to this object (site, domain, domain controller, or OU).

Adding a Link to Another GPO

You can apply one or more GPOs to a site, domain, or OU, and more than one site, domain, or OU can use the same GPO. Use the Group Policy tab to add a link to GPOs defined for a different site, domain, domain controller, or OU. Follow these steps:

1. On the Group Policy tab, click Add to open the Add A Group Policy Object Link dialog box.

2. Select the Domains/OUs, Sites, or All tab to view the currently existing GPOs. Navigate to a GPO if necessary.

3. Select the GPO to which you want to add the link, and click OK. A link to the GPO will appear in the list of GPO links.

Deleting a GPO or GPO Link

You can use the Group Policy tab to delete GPOs or GPO links. Follow these steps:

1. Select a GPO in the list of linked GPOs, and click Delete.

2. To delete only the link to the GPO, select Remove The Link From The List. To delete the link to the GPO and the GPO itself, select Remove The Link And Delete The Group Policy Object Permanently.

GPO Link Options

You can set two GPO link options: No Override and Disabled. A GPO link that has the No Override option set will not have its settings overridden by settings in other GPO objects. A GPO link that has the Disabled option set is not applied to the container.

To change GPO link options, follow these steps:

1. On the Group Policy tab, click Options to open the Link Options dialog box.

2. Select the check box next to the option(s) you want to set, and click OK. A check mark appears in the appropriate column for the affected GPO in the list of linked GPOs.

GPO Properties

You can view GPO properties on the Group Policy tab. Select the appropriate GPO in the list, and then click Properties. You'll see three tabs:

General   Displays general information about the GPO, such as creation date and revision. You can also disable or enable the user or computer settings of the GPO.

Links   Lets you view all sites, domains, or OUs that are linked to the GPO. To display locations, select a domain from the list, and click Find Now.

Security   Displays the permissions assigned to users and groups for the GPO. You can also add users and groups to the list and modify permissions. Click Advanced to access more detailed permission information and to further configure permissions, auditing, and ownership.

Group Policy Editor

To allow you to customize settings in policies contained in a GPO, Windows 2000 provides you with the Group Policy Editor, an MMC console snap-in. To access the Group Policy Editor, on the Group Policy tab select a group policy, and then click Edit.

The Group Policy Editor has two nodes: Computer Configuration and User Configuration. Policies defined under Computer Configuration apply to computers in the network and take effect when the client operating system is initialized. Policies defined under User Configuration apply to users in the network and take effect when the user logs on to a computer in the network.

Each node has three extensions (folders)—Software Settings, Windows Settings, and Administrative Templates—which in turn can contain additional extensions and policies.

Navigate the extension structure and then use the Action menu to perform actions related to policy setting, such as changing the properties of and configuring a policy. The items available on the Action menu will vary depending on which item you have selected in the console tree or Details pane.

The Windows Settings Extension

If you expand the Windows Settings extension for the Default Domain Controllers Policy or the Default Domain Policy, you'll find a node called Security Settings. The Security Settings node is where the default Domain Controller Security Policy and default Domain Security Policy, respectively, are defined and configured. The Security Settings node, in turn, has one or more levels of subnodes that contain individual policies, such as password, user rights, and event-log-related policies. Here you can also configure settings for Registry security, system service security, file security, and restricted groups.

HELP

The Windows 2000 Help system. Includes extensive explanations and step-by-step instructions for Windows 2000. You can access the information contained in the system by browsing its contents, querying the index, searching by keyword, or bookmarking and checking favorite areas of Help. The Help system pages are written in HTML, and as a result, if you're connected to the Internet, you can also follow links that point to Web pages on the Internet.

HYPERTERMINAL

Used to connect to Internet Telnet servers, online services, Bulletin Board Systems (BBS), TCP/IP hosts, and other computers via a modem or null-modem cable connection. You can use the connection to browse file systems and upload and download files.

Creating a New HyperTerminal Connection

To create a new HyperTerminal connection, choose Start ➤ Programs ➤ Accessories ➤ Communications ➤ HyperTerminal. Follow these steps:

1. In the Connection Description dialog box, enter a name for the connection in the Name text box, and choose an icon from the list of icons. Click OK.

2. In the Connect To dialog box, specify whether you want to use a modem, COM port, or TCP/IP to make the connection. Depending on your choice, you may have to enter phone number information (for modem connections) or the host address and port number (for TCP/IP connections). No additional information is required for COM port connections. Click OK.

3. If you chose a TCP/IP connection, HyperTerminal tries to establish the connection. If you chose a COM port connection, select your port settings and click OK to try to establish a connection. If

you chose a modem connection, click Dial to try to establish the connection. Click Cancel to go directly to the HyperTerminal window without trying to establish a connection.

4. To be able to use the connection later, you need to save it as a session file. In the HyperTerminal window, choose File ➢ Save. Windows saves the session (connection) in the HyperTerminal folder using the name you assigned to the connection.

Opening an Existing Connection

To open an existing connection, follow these steps:

1. Choose File ➢ Open to open the HyperTerminal folder.

2. Double-click the connection you want to open.

IMAGING

Lets you view and change graphical image files. Examples of this are digitized text documents (such as scanned documents or faxes received on a computer), photographs, or line drawings. You may want to send images in e-mails, use them in a newsletter or other document that calls for images, print them, or make annotations. Imaging lets you work on existing files, or you can send images directly into Imaging using a scanner or digital camera. Imaging lets you work with TIFF, BMP, JPG, and GIF files, and PCX/DCX, XIF, and WIFF documents.

Choose Start ➢ Programs ➢ Accessories ➢ Imaging to open Imaging.

INDEXING DRIVES, FOLDERS, AND FILES

You can enable Indexing Service to index the contents of an NTFS-formatted drive, as well as individual folders and files, so that accessing files when you use Search, for example, is faster. Before you can index any drive, folder, or file, Indexing Service must be running on the computer. Once it's started, you can include disks, folders, and files for indexing.

To index a disk, perform the following steps:

1. Right-click the drive in any Explorer window, and select Properties.

2. On the General tab, check Allow Indexing Service To Index This Disk For Fast File Searching. Click OK.

To index a file or folder, follow these steps:

1. Right-click the file or folder in any Explorer window, and select Properties.

2. On the General tab, click Advanced to open the Advanced Attributes dialog box.

3. Check the For Fast Searching, Allow Indexing Service To Index This Folder (File) option. Click OK, and then click OK again to close the folder's or file's Properties dialog box.

INDEXING SERVICE

Microsoft Management Console (MMC) snap-in that lets you index (extract information from documents and organize it in a catalog) documents on the computer for faster access. This works only with NTFS-formatted drives. Indexing Service can index different types of documents, such as HTML, Text, Microsoft Office 95 and higher, Internet mail and news, and other documents for which a filter is available. The indexed information is stored in catalogs. Indexing documents makes searches, such as those with Search or a Web browser, faster. You can also perform queries on any catalogs that have been created by using the Indexing Service Query Form.

To access Indexing Service, choose Start ➢ Settings ➢ Control Panel, double-click Administrative Tools, and then double-click Computer Management. You'll find Indexing Service under Services And Applications.

INTERNET CONNECTION WIZARD

Guides you through the process of setting up either a dial-up or LAN connection to the Internet and setting up Internet e-mail. Once you have created a connection, you can use it to connect to the Internet, where you can browse Web sites, download files, and send and receive e-mail (if you've configured e-mail account information). You can access the Internet Connection Wizard in several ways:

▶ Choose Start ➢ Programs ➢ Accessories ➢ Communications and select Internet Connection Wizard from the menu.

▶ Double-click the Connect To The Internet icon on the Desktop.

▶ Choose Start ➢ Settings ➢ Control Panel, double-click Internet Options, select the Connections tab, and click Setup.

▶ Double-click the Internet Explorer icon on your Desktop. If an Internet connection has not yet been set up, the Internet Connection Wizard starts automatically. If a connection has already been set up, Internet Explorer opens (you might be asked to connect or work offline; choose to work offline). You can then choose Tools ➤ Internet Options, select the Connections tab, and click Setup.

When the Internet Connection Wizard starts, the Welcome screen gives you three options:

▶ You can sign up for a new Internet account, meaning that you don't have an Internet Service Provider (ISP) yet. If you choose this option, you can select from a list of ISPs, or you can supply the necessary information for the ISP you want to use.

▶ You can transfer an existing Internet account.

▶ You can manually set up your Internet connection, or you can connect through a LAN.

INTERNET EXPLORER

Lets you view and download information and Web pages on the Internet or a corporate intranet. To access information on the Internet, you must have a connection established to the Internet—for example, via a modem connection and an Internet account at an Internet Service Provider (ISP), or via your corporate local area network (LAN).

To access Internet Explorer, use one of the following methods:

▶ Double-click the Internet Explorer icon on the Desktop.

▶ Choose Start ➤ Programs ➤ Internet Explorer.

▶ Open any Web file from within Windows Explorer.

▶ Enter a Web URL in the Run dialog box.

▶ Enter a Web URL in the Address bar in any Windows Explorer window, and click Go.

▶ Open an Internet network place from within My Network Places.

▶ Select Internet Explorer in the Folders view (the Explorer Bar of any Windows Explorer window).

▶ Click a link to an Internet address in an Outlook Express e-mail.

▶ Choose View ➤ Go To ➤ Home Page in any Explorer window.

Internet Explorer Window

When you open Internet Explorer, you see the Internet Explorer window. It's very similar to a standard Windows Explorer window. It contains menus, toolbars, the main viewing area, and a status bar. Many of these items are the same as in a Windows Explorer window; however, some of the toolbar buttons that appear by default, as well as several menu items, are different.

To view Internet or intranet documents in Internet Explorer, you enter the page's address in the Address bar on the Address toolbar, such as `http://www.sybex.com`, and press Enter or click Go on the toolbar. The page then loads and appears in the viewing area.

INTERNET OPTIONS

Lets you configure Internet settings and display options for your Windows 2000 computer. Among other things, Internet Options lets you:

- ▶ Configure your home page.
- ▶ Manage temporary files.
- ▶ Configure Web content colors, fonts, and languages.
- ▶ Set up security.
- ▶ Specify which applications to use for e-mail and Internet newsgroups.

Choose Start ➢ Settings ➢ Control Panel, and then double-click Internet Options to open the Internet Properties dialog box. This dialog box has six tabs: General, Security, Content, Connections, Programs, and Advanced.

INTERNET SERVICES MANAGER

Microsoft Management Console (MMC) snap-in installed by default on Windows 2000 Server that lets you manage Internet Information Services (IIS) version 5.0. Internet Information Services lets you create and manage Internet and intranet Web and File Transfer Protocol (FTP) sites. Web and FTP sites enable you to share information and files with users connected to the Internet or intranet by publishing information to the site and then having users access pages and files using a browser (or, in the case of FTP, a browser or FTP utilities). Publishing information to a Web site involves creating Web pages and copying them to a directory that is part of the Web site. Publishing files to an FTP site involves copying the files you want to share to a directory that is part of the FTP site.

Internet Information Services MMC Console Snap-in Window

To access Internet Services Manager, choose Start ➢ Programs ➢ Administrative Tools ➢ Internet Services Manager. By default, during the Windows 2000

Server installation, a default Web site is installed and appears in the Internet Information Services MMC console snap-in window. Additionally, an Administration Web site and default SMTP (Simple Mail Transfer Protocol) Virtual Server are installed.

Action Menu

Use the Action menu (or shortcut menus) to create, configure, and manage Web and FTP sites, as well as SMTP Virtual Services. Web and FTP site configuration is very complex, and the options available on the Action or shortcut menus will vary greatly depending on which item you've selected in the console tree or Details pane. Some options are also available via buttons on the toolbar.

IPCONFIG

Command that lets you view TCP/IP configuration information for each network card in your computer. Accessible from the command prompt, without the use of switches it displays basic configuration information, such as IP address, subnet mask, and default gateway IP address.

To access IPCONFIG, choose Start ➢ Programs ➢ Accessories ➢ Command Prompt, and then type **IPCONFIG** at the command prompt.

You can use switches with IPCONFIG. Examples include:

/all   Displays additional, detailed IP configuration information, such as host name; whether IP Routing, WINS Proxy, and DHCP are enabled; physical address; and IP addresses of DNS servers

/release adapter name   Releases the currently assigned IP address

/renew adapter name   Renews the DHCP lease for the currently assigned IP address

/?   Displays IPCONFIG help (syntax and switches)

Additional switches are available. Enter **IPCONFIG /?** at the console prompt to see all switches and their explanations.

KEYBOARD

Lets you configure your keyboard's settings, such as character repeat settings, cursor blink rate, input locales, and hardware-related settings.

Choose Start ➢ Settings ➢ Control Panel, and double-click Keyboard to open the Keyboard Properties dialog box, which contains three tabs: Speed, Input Locales, and Hardware.

Part vi

LICENSING

Lets you manage client access licenses to one or more Windows 2000 Server computers. Two licensing items exist in Windows 2000 Server—one accessible through Administrative Tools and one accessible through Control Panel. Licensing accessible through Administrative Tools lets you manage licenses for an enterprise; licensing accessible through Control Panel lets you manage licenses for a single Windows 2000 Server computer. To manage licensing for the enterprise, choose Start ➢ Programs ➢ Administrative Tools ➢ Licensing. To manage licensing for a single Windows 2000 Server computer, choose Start ➢ Settings ➢ Control Panel, and then double-click Licensing.

LOCAL SECURITY POLICY

Lets you view and configure account, local, public key, and Internet Protocol (IP) security policies for the local computer.

To access Local Security Policy, choose Start ➢ Settings ➢ Control Panel, double-click Administrative Tools, and double-click Local Security Policy.

Configuring Security Policies

To configure a specific security policy, navigate the console tree until individual policies appear in the Details pane. The Details pane displays each policy's name, local setting, and effective setting. To configure the policy's local setting, right-click a policy and select Security, or double-click a policy. If the computer is part of a domain and domain-level policy settings are configured, local policy settings are overridden by domain-level policy settings.

Account Policies Node

Lets you configure settings for password, account lockout, and Kerberos policies. Kerberos is an Internet standard security protocol that is used for user or system identity authentication. Policy examples for password policies include Maximum Password Age, Minimum Password Age, and Minimum Password Length. Policy examples for account lockout policies include Reset Account Lockout Counter After and Account Lockout Duration. Policy examples for Kerberos policies include Enforce User Logon Restrictions and Maximum Tolerance For Computer Clock Synchronization.

Local Policies Node

Lets you configure settings for audit policies, user rights assignments, and security options. Policy examples for audit policies include Audit Account Logon Events and Audit Directory Service Access. Policy examples for user rights assignments include Add Workstations To Domain and Manage Auditing And Security Log. Policy examples for security options include Allow System To Be Shut Down Without Having To Log On and Digitally Sign Client Communication (Always).

Public Key Policies Node

Enables you to:

- ▶ Have computers submit certificate request to a CA (Certification Authority) automatically, and then automatically install the certificate.

- ▶ Add encrypted data recovery agents and change policy settings for encrypted data recovery.

- ▶ Establish trust in a common, external root certification authority.

- ▶ Create and distribute a signed list of root certification authority certificates, also called a certificate trust list.

IP Security Policies on Local Machine

Lets you configure Windows Internet Protocol security (IPSec) to thwart network attacks (internal, private network, and Internet or extranet) by encrypting data that traverses between computers in the network. Several policies are predefined for use on computers that are part of a domain. They include Server (Request Security), Secure Server (Require Security), and Client (Respond Only).

Each policy has certain rules that apply to any computer to which the policy is assigned. You can change these rules by double-clicking a policy and making changes, or by right-clicking the policy and selecting Properties from the shortcut menu.

Assigning an IP Security Policy To assign an IP security policy to a computer, right-click the policy and select Assign. To remove the assignment, right-click the policy and select Un-Assign.

Creating a New IP Security Policy You can create new IP security policies. To do so, right-click IP Security Policies On Local Machine, and select Create IP Security Policy. Follow the steps in the IP Security Policy Wizard.

Managing IP Filter Lists and Actions You can create new IP filter lists and actions. To do so, right-click IP Security Policies On Local Machine, and select Manage IP Filter Lists And Filter Actions. In the dialog box that opens, select the Manage IP Filter Lists tab, click Add, click Add again, and then follow the Wizard's instructions to create a new IP filter list. Or select the Manage Filter Actions tab, click Add, and then follow the Wizard to create a new filter action.

Part vi

If you don't want to use the Wizards, deselect the check box Use Add Wizard in the appropriate dialog box.

Local Users And Groups

Microsoft Management Console (MMC) snap-in that lets you create and configure user and group accounts on the local computer. Local user and group accounts let you control access to resources on the local computer by assigning rights and permissions as necessary. Any user who has a local user account set up can log on to the computer using his or her username and password. Groups allow you to assign access to resources to multiple people at the same time rather than to each individual user. To do this, you create a group and add users and groups to the group. You then assign rights and permissions to a resource to the group. All users and groups added to the group then have the same rights and permissions the group has.

To access Local Users And Groups, choose Start ➢ Settings ➢ Control Panel, double-click Administrative Tools, and then double-click Computer Management. You'll find Local Users And Groups under System Tools. Local Users And Groups contains two subfolders: Users and Groups.

Lock Computer

Lets you secure the computer by locking it. Press Ctrl+Alt+Delete, and then click Lock Computer to lock the computer. To unlock the computer, press Ctrl+Alt+Delete, and then enter the name and password of the user you're logged on as or the administrator name and password to unlock the account. No other user will be able to unlock the computer.

Logical Drives

A Windows Management Instrumentation (WMI) utility that lets you manage drives (both mapped and local) either on a local or remote computer.

To access Logical Drives, choose Start ➢ Settings ➢ Control Panel, double-click Administrative Tools, and double-click Computer Management. You'll find Logical Drives under Storage.

To work with logical drives, right-click a drive in the list and choose Properties from the shortcut menu. You can then perform actions such as changing the drive label and assigning security (on NTFS-formatted drives). You can also view the drive type, the file system with which the drive is formatted, the amount of space used, the amount of free space, and the total capacity of the drive.

LOG OFF

Lets you log the current user off a Windows 2000 computer. Each user in Windows 2000 has his or her own user profile that contains such items as Desktop preferences, password, synchronization options, and accessibility options. When a user logs on, this profile is used to ensure that the environment is restored to the way the user previously configured it. Logging off enables you to log off as the current user and then log back on as another user without having to shut down the computer.

You can log off in one of two ways:

▶ Choose Start ➤ Shutdown, select Log Off *username* from the drop-down list, and click OK.

▶ Press Ctrl+Alt+Delete, and click Log Off. Click Yes to confirm that you want to log off.

LOG ON

Lets you log on to a Windows 2000 computer. Each user in Windows 2000 has his or her own user profile (either a local profile, or, if you're connected to a network and roaming profiles are configured, a roaming profile) that contains such items as Desktop preferences, password, synchronization options, and accessibility options. When a user logs on to Windows 2000, this profile is used to ensure that the environment is restored to the way the user previously configured it. This means that several users can use the same computer at different times while retaining individual Desktop and other settings.

When you start Windows 2000 or after logging off as the current user, press Ctrl+Alt+Delete, and you're prompted to log on as a specific user, either to the local computer, or, if you're connected to a network, to the applicable workgroup or domain. Enter your username, password, and the computer, workgroup, or domain you want to log on to in the respective fields in the Log On To Windows dialog box. If you're connecting from a remote computer via a modem connection, check Log On Using Dial-Up Connection. Click OK to log on.

MAGNIFIER

Used to enlarge certain areas of the screen so that they are easier to view for users with vision problems. Choose Start ➤ Programs ➤ Accessories ➤ Accessibility ➤ Magnifier. Read the message about the limitations of Magnifier. If you don't want this message to appear the next time you start Magnifier, select the Do Not Show This Message Again option. Click OK to open the Magnifier window and the Magnifier dialog box. The Magnifier window appears at the top of the screen by default.

To use the Magnifier, move the mouse pointer anywhere in the Desktop, and the Magnifier window displays that area, enlarged.

To turn off the Magnifier, click Exit in the Magnifier dialog box or right-click Magnifier in the Taskbar and select Close.

Make Available Offline

Makes network or shared files or folders available for use when you're not connected to the network.

To make a file or folder available offline, right-click the item in Windows Explorer and choose Make Available Offline. The first time you do this, you have to follow the Offline Files Wizard as outlined here:

1. In the Welcome dialog box, click Next.

2. If you don't want files to synchronize automatically when you log on and off the computer, uncheck the option Automatically Synchronize The Offline Files When I Log On And Log Off My Computer. Click Next.

3. If you don't want a message to display that reminds you that you're working offline when you're working offline, uncheck Enable Reminders, otherwise leave the option checked. If you want to have a shortcut to the Offline Files folder on your Desktop, check the option Create A Shortcut To The Offline Files Folder On My Desktop. Click Finish. The file or folder is synchronized to the Offline Files folder, and you're returned to Windows Explorer.

When you subsequently choose to make files or folders available offline by right-clicking the item and choosing Make Available Offline, the item is automatically synchronized to the Offline Files folder.

Files that are made available offline are marked with a smaller icon in the bottom-left portion of the icon so that you can easily identify files that have been made available offline. This smaller icon contains two opposite-facing arrows.

Once you go offline, you'll be able to access the files or folders that you've made available offline as if you were still connected to the network. When offline, you'll see a computer icon in the status area of the Taskbar. Click this icon to see your current offline file's status. If you have reminders set up, a pop-up message periodically tells you that you're working offline. Use the Folder Options in the Control Panel to further configure Reminders.

To work on a file offline, use Windows Explorer or My Network Places to browse to the file. Open it and make any changes you need. Alternately, access files in the Offline Files folder.

The next time you connect to the network, synchronization occurs automatically (unless you've changed default settings in Synchronization or in the Offline Files Wizard). If you need to synchronize manually, go to the Offline Files folder using the shortcut on the Desktop (created through Folder Options or the Offline Files Wizard). If necessary, change the view to Details. For files that have been modified, the Synchronization column displays Local Copy Data Has Been Modified. To synchronize all files, choose Tools ➢ Synchronize, and then click Synchronize. To synchronize an individual file, select the file and choose File ➢ Synchronize, or right-click the file and choose Synchronize.

Offline Files Folder

Offline files are also accessible through the Offline Files folder. You can create a shortcut to this folder by selecting Place Shortcut To Offline Files Folder On The Desktop on the Offline Files tab in Control Panel's Folder Options or by making the appropriate selection in the Offline Files Wizard. Double-click the shortcut to open the Offline Files folder, which displays all files marked to be available offline. You'll also see information regarding the synchronization status, availability, and the access rights you have to each file. You can also delete items in this folder. If you do, only the offline version of the file is deleted, not the network version.

MAP NETWORK DRIVE

If you're connected to a network, you can assign a drive letter to a share on the network (either on another workstation or a server). This is called mapping a drive. Assigning a drive letter lets you easily access specific shares from within Explorer windows or applications—for example, those shares that you need to access frequently.

Mapping a Network Drive

To map a network drive, perform these steps:

1. Open an Explorer window (by opening Windows Explorer, My Network Places, or My Computer).

2. Choose Tools ➢ Map Network Drive to open the Map Network Drive dialog box. Select the drive letter you want to assign from the Drive drop-down list, and enter the UNC path to the folder in the Folder text box. You can also browse to the folder by clicking Browse.

3. If you want this drive mapping to be permanent, select Reconnect At Logon. Otherwise, the drive mapping will be in effect for this Windows 2000 session only. You can also connect as a different user by clicking the link Connect Using A Different User Name and entering the username and password, or you can connect to a Web folder or FTP site by clicking that link and following the prompts in the Add Network Place Wizard.

4. Click Finish to map the drive. The mapped drive is added to My Computer, and you can see it in any Explorer window or in the Open, Save, and Save As dialog boxes when working with applications.

Disconnecting a Mapped Network Drive

After you map a drive, you can disconnect it to free up the drive letter, for example, or if you no longer need the mapping. Follow these steps:

1. In any Explorer window, choose Tools ➢ Disconnect Network Drive to open the Disconnect Network Drive dialog box.

2. Select the mapped network drive you want to disconnect, and click OK.

MAXIMIZE AND MINIMIZE

Lets you change the size of any Windows 2000 application program window.

When you click the Maximize button, the application window changes to full screen size. The Maximize button then changes to the Restore button (represented by two overlapping windows). Click this button to restore the window to its original size.

When you click the Minimize button, Windows minimizes the application window and places it on the Taskbar. To bring the application window back to its original size, click the application's icon on the Taskbar.

MICROSOFT MANAGEMENT CONSOLE (MMC)

Used to create, save, and open administrative tools, which are called MMC consoles. MMC consoles can contain tools, containers, folders, Web pages, and other administrative items, such as snap-ins, snap-in extensions, tasks, Wizards, and documentation. You use MMC consoles to administer all aspects of your computer, domain, and Active Directory.

Many MMC consoles and snap-ins already exist in Windows 2000, including Component Services, Computer Management, Event Viewer, Performance, Active Directory Users And Computers, and Services, to name just a few. You can also create new consoles using MMC.

To start MMC, choose Start ➤ Run, and enter **mmc** to open MMC. Here you can create new and open existing consoles.

MMC Window

The MMC window consists of a menu, a toolbar, and a main area, called the workspace, in which you can display existing MMC consoles or create new ones.

MMC Menus

MMC has three menus—Console, Window, and Help—that you can use to work with MMC consoles.

Console Menu   The Console menu lets you work with MMC consoles and contains the following options:

New   Lets you create a new MMC console.

Open   Lets you open an existing MMC console.

Save   Lets you save an MMC console you've created or changed.

Save As   Lets you save an MMC console using a different name than the current name.

Add/Remove Snap-In   Lets you add snap-ins to (or remove them from) the currently open console.

Options   Lets you change the name of the current console, change the console's icon, choose a console mode (console modes determine the type of access for the console), and configure additional console settings.

Exit   Closes MMC.

The Console menu also contains a list of the most recently accessed consoles for quick access.

Window Menu   The Window menu lets you control MMC console windows. It contains these options:

New Window   Opens another console in a new window.

Cascade   Cascades open console windows.

Part vi

Tile Horizontally   Displays console windows horizontally next to each other.

Arrange Icons   Arranges icons.

At the bottom of the Window menu, a list of all currently open console windows appears. The currently active console window has a check mark next to it. Select a console window from the list to make it the active window and bring it to the front.

Help Menu   The Help menu contains the following options:

Help Topics   Opens MMC-related help topics in the Windows 2000 Help system.

Microsoft On The Web   Contains a submenu that contains links to several Microsoft Web sites where you can obtain snap-ins, product news, and answers to frequently asked questions, as well as send feedback to Microsoft. Also contains a link to Microsoft's home page.

About Microsoft Management Console   Displays information about MMC, such as version number and licensing information.

MMC Toolbar

The standard MMC toolbar contains buttons to the most commonly used items also available from the MMC menus. They include Create A New Console, Open An Existing Console, Save The Current Console, and New Window.

MMC Consoles

MMC consoles are used to administer some aspect of your computer or network. They do not perform functions themselves, but rather host the tools that do.

MMC consoles have two panes. The left pane is called the console tree, where snap-ins, extension snap-ins, and other console items appear. The right pane, called the Details pane, contains functions for and information about any item you select in the console tree.

Although all MMC consoles have some menus and toolbar buttons in common, individual menu options and additional buttons may be available depending on the item you've selected in the console tree.

The Details pane in an MMC console can also display taskpad views. You can create taskpad views and add commonly used actions (tasks) to them to make using the console easier, especially for users who are not very familiar with MMC console functions and how to find actions. A taskpad view contains the items normally displayed in the Details pane along with icons for the tasks you added to the taskpad view.

MMC Console Modes

MMC consoles can be saved and then used in one of four modes:

Author Mode   Users of the console can perform all MMC functionality, including adding and removing snap-ins and extension snap-ins,
and creating new windows, taskpad views, and tasks. Users can also
see the entire console tree.

User Mode—Full Access   Users of the console can create new windows and see the entire console tree. They cannot add or remove
snap-ins, taskpad views, and tasks or otherwise change the properties
of the console.

User Mode—Limited Access, Multiple Window   Users of the console can see only the portion of the console tree that was visible when
the author of the console saved it. They can open new windows but
cannot close existing windows.

User Mode—Limited Access, Single Window   Users of the console
can see only the portion of the console tree that was visible when the
author of the console saved it. They cannot create new windows.

To open a console in Author mode that was saved in one of the user modes,
use one of the following methods (you must be a member of the Administrators
group):

▶ Choose Start ➤ Run, then enter **mmc** *pathname* /**a**, where *pathname*
represents the complete path to the console file. .

▶ Right-click the console file in a Browse dialog box, and choose Author
from the shortcut menu.

MMC Console Menus

MMC console menus include the Action, View, and Favorites menus. The Action
and View menus are available in all MMC consoles; the Favorites menu is available only in some consoles.

Action Menu   The Action menu contains options related to actions you can
perform for items that appear in the right pane.

The options available in the Action menu will vary greatly depending on the
console snap-in or extension snap-in you have selected. Some options, however,
are often available on a console's Action menu. They include:

New Window From Here   Not available if the console is opened
with User Mode—Limited Access, Single Window. Opens another window of the same console.

Part vi

New Taskpad View   Only available for consoles that are opened in Author mode. Lets you create a new taskpad view.

Edit Taskpad View   Only available for consoles that are opened in Author mode and after taskpad views have been created. Lets you edit the selected taskpad view.

Delete Taskpad View   Only available for consoles that are opened in Author mode and after taskpad views have been created. Lets you remove the selected taskpad view.

All Tasks   Brings up a submenu that contains tasks that can be performed on the selected object.

Export List   Lets you export the current list of items in the view pane to a text file.

Refresh   Refreshes the contents of the object currently selected in the console tree.

Properties   Displays properties of the object currently selected in either pane, including version, location, operating system, folder properties (in case of a folder), and any other applicable properties.

Help   Opens the Help system to the topic related to the selected item.

Connect To Another Computer   Lets you access the same type of information currently displayed for the local computer for a remote computer. For example, if you're currently viewing event logs in Event Viewer (Local), you can connect to another computer and display that computer's event logs. To connect to another computer, follow these steps:

1. Select Item (Local) in the console tree.

2. Choose Action ➢ Connect To Another Computer.

3. Select Another Computer, and enter the name of the computer in the field or browse for it. Click OK.

View Menu   The View menu contains options pertaining to how items are displayed in MMC consoles. The options available depend on the item you have selected in the console tree pane; however, you'll often see these choices:

Choose Columns   Lets you specify which columns to display in the Details pane.

Customize   Lets you specify which MMC options and snap-in options to display, such as MMC and/or Snap-In menus and toolbars.

Additionally, you'll often see the menu options Large Icons, Small Icons, List, and Details, which you would use to configure how the Details pane displays items.

Favorites Menu   The Favorites menu, which is not available in all console views, lets you add items from the console tree to your MMC favorites. This allows you to quickly access them via the Favorites menu or the Favorites tab in the console tree pane. Adding and organizing favorites in MMC functions the same way as it does in Internet or Windows Explorer. The options on the Favorites menu also are the same: Add To Favorites and Organize Favorites.

MMC Console Standard Toolbar

The buttons available on the standard MMC console toolbar depend on the item you have selected in the console tree. All or some of the following buttons are commonly available:

Back   Goes back to the previously selected item in the console tree.

Forward   Returns to the item in the console tree that was selected before you clicked the Back button.

Up One Level   Moves up one level in the console tree.

Show/Hide Console Tree   Toggles the display of the console tree on and off.

Export List   Exports the contents of the display pane to a text file.

Help   Opens the Windows 2000 Help system to the related topic.

Refresh   Updates the currently selected item.

Properties   Displays properties for the currently selected item.

Creating a New MMC Console

You can use MMC to create new MMC consoles. Follow these steps:

1. Choose Console ➢ New or click Create A New Console on the toolbar to open a new MMC console window in MMC.

2. Choose Console ➢ Add/Remove Snap-In to open the Add/Remove Snap-In dialog box.

3. On the Standalone tab, click Add, select a snap-in in the list, and click Add. If a Wizard starts, follow the prompts.

4. Select any additional snap-ins you want, and click Add. When you've finished, click Close. To add a snap-in below another snap-in, select the snap-in from the Snap-Ins Added To drop-down list

in the Add/Remove Snap-In dialog box, and click Add. If you want to remove a snap-in you've added, select it in the list, and click Remove.

5. To configure which extension snap-ins to enable (if any are available), select a snap-in in the list, and select the Extensions tab.

6. If extension snap-ins are available, uncheck Add All Extensions, and then select and deselect extension snap-ins to specify which extensions you want to enable. Click OK to return to the Add/Remove Snap-In dialog box.

7. Click OK to return to the console window.

8. Choose Console ➤ Options to open the Options dialog box.

9. On the Console tab, and enter a name for the console. If you want to change the console's icon, click Change Icon.

10. In the Console Mode drop-down list, select the console mode you want to use for this console.

11. If you selected one of the three user modes, specify whether you want to enable context (shortcut) menus on taskpads, save changes that are made to the console, or allow the user to customize views. Click OK to save your changes.

12. Choose Console ➤ Save As, enter a name for the console, browse to the folder where you want to save the console, and click Save. Console files are saved as files with an .msc extension and by default are saved in the logged-on user's Administrative Tools folder. If you use this default, you'll be able to access newly created MMC consoles by choosing Start ➤ Settings ➤ Control Panel, double-clicking Administrative Tools, and double-clicking the new console.

MICROSOFT SCRIPT DEBUGGER

Installed by default on Windows 2000 Server computers. Lets you debug (troubleshoot) and test both client and server scripts written with ActiveX-enabled scripting languages—for example, Jscript and VBScript. Additionally, you can use Microsoft Script Debugger to debug ActiveX components, Java applets, and JavaBeans. Client scripts, which are found in HTML pages, are executed when an HTML page loads or when the user clicks a button that executes a script. Server scripts are embedded in Active Server Page (ASP) files; Internet Information Service (IIS) executes server scripts when an ASP page is requested, prior to sending page content to the browser.

Use Microsoft Script Debugger to view source code, view and configure the values of properties and variables as well as script flow, and specify the pace at which a script executes.

To access the Microsoft Script Debugger, choose Start ➤ Programs ➤ Accessories ➤ Microsoft Script Debugger ➤ Microsoft Script Debugger.

MOUSE

Lets you control the settings of your mouse, such as mouse button and pointer usage, pointer speed, and hardware configuration settings.

Choose Start ➤ Settings ➤ Control Panel, and then double-click Mouse to open the Mouse Properties dialog box, which contains four tabs: Buttons, Pointers, Motion, and Hardware.

MOVE FILES AND FOLDERS

Windows 2000 lets you move files and folders in a variety of ways. You can use the Edit menu in Windows Explorer windows, drag and drop, or use the shortcut menu that appears when you right-click a file or folder. When you move a file or folder, Windows removes it from the original location and places it in the new location.

Using the Edit Menu

To move files or folders using the Edit menu, follow these steps:

1. In any Explorer window, select a file or folder you want to move.

2. Choose Edit ➤ Cut.

3. Select the destination folder.

4. Choose Edit ➤ Paste.

Using the Shortcut Menu

You can right-click files and folders to bring up the shortcut menu, which lets you perform various functions, including cutting and pasting. To move files or folders using the shortcut menu, follow these steps:

1. In any Explorer window, right-click a file or folder you want to move, and select Cut.

2. Right-click the destination folder, and select Paste.

Using Drag-and-Drop

To move files or folders using drag-and-drop, you must first make sure that both the source and destination folders are visible in the Folders view. Open the source folder, and then drag the file or folder from the source folder to the destination folder while holding down the left mouse button. When the cursor is over the destination folder (the folder is selected), release the mouse button. Windows will move the file or folder to the destination folder. If you want to use this procedure to move a file or folder, the source and destination folders must reside on the same drive. If the destination folder is on a different drive, Windows will copy the file or folder, not move it.

To move a file or folder to a different drive using drag-and-drop, you must use the right mouse button to drag the item. When you release the right mouse button, a shortcut menu appears, and you can choose to move or copy the item, or create a shortcut.

MY COMPUTER

Lets you view and navigate the contents of your computer, such as drives, folders, and files. By default, Windows places a shortcut to the My Computer folder on the Desktop. To open My Computer, double-click the My Computer shortcut, or right-click it and select Open.

The My Computer folder is part of the Windows hierarchical structure and as such opens in an Explorer window. By default, an Explorer Bar view is not selected, so you'll see the name My Computer in the left portion of the window and the top-level contents of your computer in the right portion of the window (using large icons). These contents include physical drives, mapped network drives (logical drives), and the Control Panel folder. You can change views in this window the same way you can in any Explorer window.

To see the contents of a drive, network share, or folder in My Computer, double-click the item. The right pane changes to display the contents of the item you double-clicked, and the left pane displays information about the item. Alternatively, you can choose an item from the Address drop-down list.

You can use the My Computer Desktop shortcut to quickly access System properties. To do so, right-click the My Computer icon on the Desktop, and choose Properties. This opens the System Properties dialog box. To quickly open Computer Management, right-click My Computer, and choose Manage.

MY DOCUMENTS

Folder that, by default, Windows 2000 uses to store documents that you save in such applications as WordPad and Paint. Lets you organize and quickly access your documents. A shortcut to My Documents appears on the Desktop by default. Each user of the computer has a unique My Documents folder. To change the location of the My Documents folder, right-click the My Documents shortcut on the Desktop, and choose Properties. Then, on the Target tab, enter a new path in the Target text box, and then click OK. Alternatively, you can click Move, and then browse to the new target folder.

To open My Documents, double-click the My Documents shortcut on the Desktop, or navigate to it using the Address bar in any Explorer window. By default the My Documents folder contains the folder My Pictures, which stores documents created with Paint. Additional folders might be created automatically in the My Documents folder as you work with Windows 2000. One example is the Fax folder, which is created when you create and then save personal fax cover pages using default save options.

MY NETWORK PLACES

Lets you view and navigate network resources, such as network shares and other computers. By default, a shortcut to the My Network Places folder appears on the Desktop. To open My Network Places, double-click the shortcut, or right-click it and select Open.

The My Network Places folder is part of the Windows 2000 hierarchical structure and as such opens in an Explorer window (without an Explorer Bar view selected). You'll see the My Network Places name in the left pane (and several related links) and the top-level contents in the right pane. Top-level contents include the Entire Network icon. Double-click this icon to navigate the network hierarchy, including domains, and computers belonging to the domains, all the way down to the file level.

In the My Network Places folder, you'll also see the Add Network Place icon, which you can double-click to add shortcuts to network, Web, and FTP servers using the Add Network Place Wizard.

Navigating My Network Places

My Network Places lets you navigate network resources using the Entire Network icon.

If you double-click Entire Network, you'll see links that let you search for printers, computers, people, and files and folders, and a link that lets you view the contents of the entire network. This can include Microsoft Windows networks, Novell NetWare networks, and the Active Directory (if it has been installed). Double-click the item you want to navigate to access down-level information, such as domains, computers and shares, and Active Directory components, including group, user, and computer accounts and domain controllers.

Add Network Place

Lets you add shortcuts to network shares and servers, Web folders, and FTP sites using the Add Network Place Wizard. To open the Wizard, double-click Add Network Place. Then perform these steps:

1. In the text box, type the location of the network place you want to add (use UNC paths for network servers). You can use the Browse button if you wish. Click Next.

2. Enter the necessary information, and click OK until you reach the Completing The Add Network Place Wizard screen. The type of information you'll have to provide depends on the type of network place you specified (network server, Web page, or FTP server).

3. Enter a name for the network place, and click Finish. The new network place is added to the My Network Places folder.

MY PICTURES

Folder under the My Documents folder that is used as the default folder for storing image files. For example, if you're creating an image with a program such as Paint, the default location for storing the file is My Pictures. Using the My Pictures folder to store image files means that you can easily find your image files later in this centralized location.

NARRATOR

Aids users with vision impairments by "narrating" (reading aloud) on-screen text, menus, buttons, and dialog boxes. A sound card and speakers or some other output device must be installed. Choose Start ➤ Programs ➤ Accessories ➤ Accessibility ➤ Narrator to open Narrator. You'll have to click OK to acknowledge a message dialog box explaining that Narrator has limited functionality. You can specify that you don't want Windows to display this dialog box the next time you start Narrator.

Four choices are available in the Narrator dialog box:

▶ Announce Events On Screen

▶ Read Typed Characters

▶ Move Mouse Pointer To The Active Item

▶ Start Narrator Minimized

Place a check mark in the check box next to the option you want to activate.

Three buttons are available:

Help   Opens the Windows Help system to the Narrator entry.

Voice   Lets you change voice settings, including speed, volume, and pitch, for each installed voice.

Exit   Closes Narrator.

NET

Net commands enable you to perform networking-related functions from the command prompt. Examples of this command include net print (to display print jobs and shared queues) or net group (to display all groups in the security database). To see a complete list of net commands available, at the command prompt enter **net help** or **net /?**. To see information about the net help syntax, enter **net help syntax**. To see what services you can start using the net command, enter **net help services**. To view more detailed help information about a specific net command, enter **net help** *command name*—for example, **net help group**.

If the command you're executing will prompt you to enter either yes or no at certain times, you can use the /yes and /no switches at the end of the command to automatically answer yes or no to those prompts.

NETMEETING

Lets you communicate with other people over the Internet using voice and video. This feature enables you to see images of and talk to people during meetings you conduct over the Internet. NetMeeting also enables you to engage in real-time chats, work together in shared applications, send files, and create drawings together on a shared Whiteboard.

The first time you run NetMeeting, a Wizard will guide you through the process of configuring NetMeeting and tuning your audio settings. Subsequently, you will be brought directly to Microsoft NetMeeting. To be able to configure NetMeeting correctly, you'll have to have your speakers or headphones, your microphone, and a video camera installed in the computer.

NETWORK AND DIAL-UP CONNECTIONS

Opens the Network And Dial-Up Connections folder, where you can view and configure existing and create new network and dial-up connections on the computer. You use network and dial-up connections to establish communications (connections) between computers, such as between two computers, between a computer and a local area or wide area network, or between a computer and host

Part vi

on the Internet. Once a connection is established, you can access and use resources on the computer, network, or Internet. Examples of this are using files located on the computer or network to which you are connected, and printing to printers connected to the computer or network to which you are connected. If the connection is to the Internet, you may choose to view Web sites and download files. Connections can be either local or remote. Dial-up connections you create with the Network Connection Wizard or Internet Connection Wizard appear in this folder.

You can configure security for network and dial-up connections by using such features as callback, data encryption, authentication, and Windows 2000 login and domain security.

Network And Dial-Up Connections Folder

To open the Network And Dial-Up Connections folder, where you can view, configure, and create network and dial-up connections, choose Start ➤ Settings ➤ Network And Dial-Up Connections.

When you open the Network And Dial-up Connections folder, you'll see an icon for each connection currently configured on the computer, as well as the Make New Connection icon used to create a new connection. If you select a connection in the folder, on the left side of the window you'll see some information about the connection. This information can include the name of the connection, the connection type, the current status of the connection, and the name of the device used for the connection.

You can tell by the look of each icon whether a connection is currently active. With active connections, the screen areas of the two connected computers in the icon are blue. With inactive connections, the two connected computers are grayed out.

Network and Dial-Up Connection Types

Windows 2000 supports five types of network and dial-up connections: Dial-Up, Local Area, Virtual Private Network (VPN), Direct, and Incoming. Each connection type has a different icon and default name associated with it that appears when you create a connection in the Network And Dial-Up Connections folder.

Dial-Up Connection A connection to the remote computer is established via standard telephone lines using a modem, via ISDN lines using ISDN cards, or via an X.25 network. Typically used for connections to the Internet or to connect remote users to the corporate network.

Local Area Connection A connection to another computer in a network, typically over Ethernet, Token Ring, cable modem, Fiber Distributed Data Interface (FDDI), Digital Subscriber Line (DSL), T1, Frame Relay, and others. Typically used to connect computers in a corporate local area network (LAN).

Virtual Private Connection   A dedicated, secure connection between two LANs over Point-to-Point Tunneling Protocol (PPTP) or Layer-2 Tunneling Protocol (L2TP). Lets you establish a secure connection between a remote computer and a computer on a corporate network over the Internet.

Direct Connection   A direct serial, parallel, or infrared connection between two computing devices. Typically lets you connect desktop computers with handheld computing devices.

Incoming Connections   A connection that allows other computers to connect to this computer via dial-up, VPN, or direct connection. The computer then acts as a dial-in server. You can configure both Windows 2000 Professional and Windows 2000 Server for incoming connections; however, you must use the Routing And Remote Access management console (accessible through Administrative Tools) to configure incoming connections for a Windows 2000 Server that belongs to or controls a domain. Windows 2000 Professional supports up to three incoming sessions, but only one of each type (dial-up, VPN, or direct). Windows 2000 Server supports up to 256 incoming dial-up connections.

Local Area Connection

If you have a network card installed in a computer and you install Windows 2000 on the computer, a local area connection is created automatically. The icon for this connection appears in the Network And Dial-Up Connections folder. When you connect the computer to the network, this connection automatically activates without further action required by the user. If you install additional adapters, a local area connection is created for each adapter and an icon for each connection appears in the Network And Dial-Up Connections folder.

If the connection to the network is broken (for example, if you disconnect the patch cable from the hub or network card, or if a cable connecting the computer to the network is faulty), the icon grays out, indicating that this connection is no longer connected. When the connection to the network is reestablished (for example, you plug the patch cable back in), the local area connection automatically reconnects.

As with all other connections, you can manually disconnect a local area connection by right-clicking the appropriate icon and choosing Disconnect. If you do this, the local area connection no longer connects automatically. This can be useful if you're using a laptop and don't want the adapter to try to establish a connection when you're traveling (and not connecting to the network via a local area connection). When you're back in the office and want to use the connection again, just right-click the connection's icon and choose Connect, or double-click the connection icon.

Local Area Connection Properties   To configure local area connection properties, such as installed network clients and protocols, right-click the Local Area Connection icon, and choose Properties. The Properties dialog box has one tab:

General   At the top of the tab, you'll see the network adapter used for the connection. Click Configure to access the network adapter's properties. The General tab also displays the clients, services, and protocols that are used by the connection. To configure a component, select it in the list, and click Properties.

For example, to configure your IP address, select Internet Protocol (TCP/IP), and click Properties. You can then enter your IP address, subnet mask, default gateway address, and DNS server addresses. Or you can choose to obtain your IP and DNS server addresses automatically from a DHCP server. For advanced IP, DNS, and WINS settings, click Advanced.

On the General tab, you can also click Install to install new clients, services, and protocols, or select a client, service, or protocol and click Uninstall to remove it from the system.

Select the Show Icon In Taskbar When Connected option if you want to have a visual reminder in the Taskbar after you establish a connection to the local area network.

Make New Connection

Starts the process of creating a new network or dial-up connection. Double-click the Make New Connection icon to start the Network Connection Wizard, which will guide you through the process of creating a new network or dial-up connection. First, you'll be presented with the Welcome screen. Click Next to display the Network Connection Type dialog box, where you can choose the type of connection you want to create.

The following choices are available:

Dial-Up To Private Network   Lets you create a dial-up connection to a computer on a corporate network that is set up as a dial-in server. Once the connection is established, you can access resources on the network as if you were locally attached to the network. The creation process of this type of connection is very similar to that of a dial-up connection to the Internet. During the creation of the connection, you'll have to provide the telephone number you want Windows to use to establish the connection with the dial-in server. You also have to provide an account and password on the dial-in computer or in the domain to be able to log in to the computer or domain.

Dial-Up To The Internet   Lets you create a dial-up connection to an Internet Service Provider (ISP). You must have administrative privileges to create this type of connection. If you choose this option, the Internet Connection Wizard starts and guides you through the process of setting up the connection. You'll need to know the phone number to dial your ISP and the account name and password you established with the ISP. Or, you can create a connection to the Internet through your network's proxy server. In that case, you may need to know the name and port of your company's proxy server.

Connect To A Private Network Through The Internet   Lets you create a secure, dedicated connection between your computer and a computer on a corporate network over the Internet. During setup of the VPN connection, you'll have to provide the host name or IP address of the computer to which you want to connect. If you're logged on with administrative privileges, you'll also be able to specify that you want to make the connection available to all users (instead of just yourself).

Before you can successfully connect via a VPN connection, you must have created a dial-up connection to the Internet on the computer and you must be connected to the Internet. You can choose to have the dial-up connection dialed automatically when you double-click the VPN connection, or you can choose not to have this done (in that case, you'll have to separately establish a connection to the Internet before you can connect via the VPN connection).

Accept Incoming Connections   Lets you configure a Windows 2000 computer to act as a dial-in server. The computer must be running Windows 2000 Professional, or if it's a stand-alone computer, it can be running Windows 2000 Server. If you don't have administrative privileges, this option is grayed out. If you choose this option after you've already configured the computer for incoming connections, you're effectively changing the properties of the current configuration.

Connect Directly To Another Computer   Lets you create a connection between two computers using a serial or parallel cable, or an infrared connection. You'll have to specify whether the computer is the host (the computer that will be accessed) or the guest (the computer that will access the host computer), and choose the device you want to use for the connection (serial, parallel, or infrared port). Depending on whether the computer is the host or the guest, you'll have to specify the users that are allowed to access the computer (host) or specify if you're creating the connection for yourself or all users of the computer (guest).

Part vi

Accepting Incoming Connections   To configure an eligible Windows 2000 computer to accept incoming connections and thus become a dial-in server, do the following:

1.   Double-click Make New Connection in the Network And Dial-Up Connections folder to start the Network Connection Wizard. Click Next.

2.   Select Accept Incoming Connections. Click Next.

3.   Select the device or devices you want to use to accept incoming connections (such as a modem or serial or parallel cable). If necessary, you can change the properties of any device by selecting it and clicking Properties. Properties depend on the device. They can include such items as port speed and flow control, whether the call should be operator assisted, whether the call should be disconnected after a certain amount of idle time, and hardware settings for the device. Click OK when you've finished changing a device's properties. Then click Next to continue.

4.   Select whether you want to allow VPN connections. Click Next.

5.   In the Allowed Users dialog box, specify the users that are allowed to connect to the computer. All users that currently have an account on the computer are displayed in the Users Allowed To Connect list. Place a check mark next to any user you want to allow to use this incoming connection.

    You can also add new users in this dialog box. Click Add, and specify a logon name, full name, and password for the user. Then click OK. The user is automatically added to the local SAM (Security Accounts Manager) database and appears in the Users Allowed To Connect list with a check mark in the user's check box. To change the full name, password, or callback properties of any user in the list, select a user, and click Properties. On the General tab, you can change the full name and password.

    On the Callback tab, you can configure the following callback options for incoming connections:

    Do Not Allow Callback   Callback cannot be used for this user.

    Allow The Caller To Set The Callback Number   The user can specify the number at which he or she wants the server to call him or her back. This option can reduce the cost to the user.

    Always Use The Following Callback Number   Allows the administrator to specify a telephone number that should always be used when the server makes a callback call to the user. This option can reduce the cost to the user and provides additional network security.

Click OK when you have configured a user's general and callback properties. You can also delete users from the Users Allowed To Connect list by selecting a user and clicking Delete. When you've finished, click Next.

6. In the Networking Components dialog box, select and configure the networking components, such as protocols, file and printer sharing services, and client services you want to have enabled for incoming connections. All currently installed services appear in the Networking Components list. If a check box for a service is grayed out, it means that the service cannot be disabled. Protocols (such as TCP/IP, IPX/SPS, NetBEUI, and AppleTalk) can be further configured for incoming connections. Select the protocol, and click Properties.

For example, you can configure the following settings for incoming TCP/IP connections:

▶ Allow incoming callers to access the LAN to which the computer is attached.

▶ Assign IP addresses automatically using a DHCP server.

▶ Specify a range of TCP/IP addresses that should be used for incoming connections.

▶ Allow the incoming caller to specify his or her own IP address.

Click OK when you're done making changes.

You can click Install to install additional networking components, and you can select a component and click Uninstall to remove that component from the computer. Do the latter only if you're absolutely sure this is what you want to do. Click Next to continue.

7. You cannot change the default name for incoming connections. Click Finish to create the incoming connection. Windows returns you to the Network And Dial-Up Connections folder and displays the Incoming Connections icon in the folder.

Changing Your Incoming Connections Configuration   If you need to make changes to your Incoming Connections configuration, right-click the Incoming Connections icon, and choose Properties. Use the General, Users, and Networking tabs to make configuration changes. These settings are almost identical to the settings you were able to configure when you created the connection, with some exceptions.

Part vi

For instance, on the General tab you have one additional option. You can specify whether you want Windows to display an icon on the Taskbar when users are connected to the computer. On the Users tab, you have two additional options. You can choose to require users to secure their passwords and data, and you can choose to allow directly connected devices (for example, palmtop computers) to connect without a password. If you require users to secure their passwords and data, they must select Require Secured Password and Require Data Encryption on the Security tab of the connection they are using to connect to this computer.

Connection Properties

Every connection has properties you can use to further configure the connection. To access the properties of any connection, right-click the connection, and choose Properties. The Properties dialog box has five tabs: General, Options, Security, Networking, and Sharing. (This applies to all connections but the Incoming Connections connection, which we described earlier, and the Local Area Connection, which has only one tab.)

General This is the only tab that differs significantly for each of the connection types.

Dial-Up Connections On the General tab for dial-up connections, you'll see which device will be used to make the connection. You can click Configure to configure device settings, such as connection speed and hardware features. The configuration options available will depend on the device you're using. On the General tab, you can also change the phone number the device is dialing. If you click Alternates, you can add numbers for Windows to use if the first number doesn't work, and choose to move to the top of the list the number to which the device successfully connects. Back on the General tab, you can specify to use a country/region code as well as dialing rules. Finally, you can specify whether an icon should appear in the Taskbar when a connection is established.

Local Area Connections The General tab for local area connections is very similar to the Networking tab for the other connection types. You can view and configure the device you are using to make the connection (the network adapter installed in the computer), and view and configure the networking components the connection uses (such as clients, services, and protocols). You can also install and uninstall networking components, and choose whether you want the Taskbar to display an icon when the connection is active.

Virtual Private Connections (VPN)   The General tab for the Virtual Private Connection Properties dialog box lets you specify the host name or IP address of the destination server to which you want to connect. You can specify that you want Windows to automatically dial your dial-up connection to the Internet before trying to establish the VPN connection. The dial-up connection must be established before you can establish the VPN connection. Finally, you can choose whether to display an icon in the Taskbar when this connection is active.

Direct Connections   On the General tab for direct connections, you can specify and configure the device (such as parallel or null modem) used to make the connection. The configuration options available depend on the selected device. You can also choose whether to show an icon in the Taskbar when the connection is active.

Options   Lets you configure dialing and redialing options. You can specify whether you want Windows to:

- Show information on the connection's progress while the connection is being established.

- Prompt for authentication information such as name and password, certificate, and so on before establishing the connection.

- Include the Windows logon domain information.

- Prompt for the phone number to be used for the connection (available for dial-up connections).

You can also specify how many times you want the device to redial if a connection cannot be established (the default is three times), how much time should elapse between each redial attempt (the default is one minute), and how long the connection can be idle before it disconnects (the default is never). Finally, you can specify that you want Windows to redial the connection if the line is dropped. This will work only if you have started the Remote Access Auto Connection Manager under Services in Component Services or Computer Management.

From the Options tab of dial-up connections, you can also specify X.25 logon settings by clicking the X.25 button.

Security   Lets you set up the level of security used when making a connection. You can choose to allow unsecured passwords (for dial-up and direct connections), require secured passwords, or use a smart card. If secured passwords are required, you can choose to use the user's Windows logon name, password, and domain during authentication and whether data encryption should be required. If data encryption is required, and the dial-in server to which you connect doesn't use data encryption, the connection will be disconnected. If you specify that you want Windows to use a smart card for authentication, you can also choose to require data encryption.

Alternatively, you can select Advanced (Custom Settings) and click Settings to configure advanced security settings, including making encryption optional, not allowing encryption, or requiring encryption, as well as specifying the security protocols that can be used for the connection.

Finally, on the Security tab of dial-up connections, you can also choose to display a terminal window after connecting. The remote terminal server prompts you for logon information in the terminal window, and you'll be authenticated after providing the necessary information (such as logon name and password). To automate this process, you can create a script with the necessary information, and then specify to use the script for the connection.

Networking   Lets you specify the type of dial-up server you're connecting to. For dial-up and direct connections, your choices are PPP: Windows 95/98/NT4/2000, Internet, or SLIP: UNIX Connection. PPP is by far the most common connection type for dial-up connections. For VPN connections, your choices are Automatic (which means Windows will attempt to connect via PPTP first, then via L2TP), Point-To-Point Tunneling Protocol (PPTP), or Layer-2 Tunneling Protocol (L2TP).

You can also specify the installed networking components the connection will use (by placing a check mark in the box next to the appropriate component). Additionally, on the Networking tab of dial-up connections, you can install new networking components, uninstall existing networking components, and change the properties of some of the existing networking components.

Sharing   Lets you enable or disable the ability of other computers on the network to use this connection to access external resources. If you enable this option, you can also enable or disable on-demand dialing, which means that when another computer tries to access external resources, this connection is dialed automatically.

Click Settings to configure the network applications you want to enable for any computer that shares this connection, and to specify and configure the services that will be provided to the remote network.

Connection Status

In order to see connection information about any active connection, right-click the connection, and choose Status from the menu. This opens the Status dialog box, which always has a General tab and can also have a Details tab.

General   Provides information about the connection, such as the status (for example, Connected) and the duration and speed of the connection. It also gives you activity information, such as the number of bytes sent and received, the compression ratio, and any errors that occurred during the connection.

You can also access the connection's properties (by clicking the Properties button) and disconnect the connection (by clicking Disconnect, or, if available, disable it by clicking Disable).

Details   Provides additional information and depends on the type of connection. It is not available for all connection types. It can include items such as the server type, compression level, and server and client IP addresses.

Connecting and Disconnecting a Connection

To establish a connection, select the connection and double-click the connection's icon, or right-click the connection's icon and choose Connect.

To disconnect a connection, either right-click the connection's icon and choose Disconnect, or open the connection's Status dialog box and click Disconnect on the General tab.

Finally, if you chose to display an icon in the Taskbar when the connection is active, you can also right-click the Taskbar icon and choose Disconnect.

Advanced Menu

The Network And Dial-Up Connections folder menu bar contains an additional menu, Advanced, that lets you enable or configure advanced connection options. The menu contains five options: Operator-Assisted Dialing, Dial-Up Preferences, Network Identification, Advanced Settings, and Optional Networking Components.

Operator-Assisted Dialing

If you desire, you can configure dial-up connections to allow you to either dial the number of the connection yourself through a telephone handset or have an operator dial the number for you. To enable Operator-Assisted Dialing, in the Network And Dial-Up Connections folder choose Advanced ➤ Operator-Assisted Dialing (this places a check mark next to the option, indicating that it is activated). Now, after you double-click the connection, you can either dial the number yourself through a telephone handset or have an operator dial the

Part VI

number for you. When you finish dialing, click Dial in the connection's Connect dialog box. Don't hang up the handset until the modem takes control of the telephone line (you may hear a click in the line, and the line becomes silent). To turn off Operator-Assisted Dialing, choose Advanced ➤ Operator-Assisted Dialing again to remove the check mark from the menu option.

Dial-Up Preferences

Choose Advanced ➤ Dial-Up Preferences to open the Dial-Up Preferences dialog box, where you can set preferred settings that will apply to all of your dial-up connections. The Dial-Up Preferences dialog box has two tabs: Autodial and Callback.

Autodial Lets you configure Autodial options. Autodial learns which connections you used to access remote resources, and when you try to access resources on a remote network a second time without being connected, Autodial automatically dials the connection. Options you can configure on this tab include the location(s) for which you want to enable Autodial, whether you want to be prompted before Autodial automatically dials the connection, and whether you want to disable Autodial for the current session.

Callback Lets you configure callback options for outgoing connections if you're dialing into a server that will request callback. You can specify to not use callback, to decide whether to use callback when you're dialing the connection, and to always have the server call you back at the phone number(s) you specify for your device(s) in the provided list box. Callback is not supported for VPN connections.

Network Identification, Advanced Settings, and Optional Networking Components

The Network Identification menu option takes you to the Network Identification tab of System Properties. Here you can change the computer's name, as well as the domain or workgroup the computer belongs to. From here you can also run the Network Identification Wizard to connect the computer to a network.

The Advanced Settings menu option lets you configure advanced network adapter options, such as connections and their bindings (if applicable), NetBIOS network route LANA numbers (applicable only if NetBIOS is used), and the order in which the computer accesses network resources and information (through what are called Providers).

The Optional Networking Components menu option lets you install additional Windows networking components that are not yet installed on the computer (when you select this menu option, the Windows Optional Networking Components Wizard starts and guides you through the process of adding components).

NOTEPAD

Program used to view, create, and edit small text files, such as configuration text files, readme files, or the contents of the Windows Clipboard.

Choose Start ➤ Programs ➤ Accessories ➤ Notepad to open Notepad. The Notepad window consists of a menu bar and a text area.

The Notepad menus contain standard options, as well as some unique options.

NTFS

File system for Windows 2000 computers. NTFS, which is an abbreviation for New Technology File System, has many advantages over older file systems, such as FAT and FAT32. Windows 2000 Server computers that act as domain controllers require NTFS. You can format a disk partition with the NTFS file system during the Windows 2000 operating system installation, or you can convert an older file system (FAT or FAT32) to NTFS either during the Windows 2000 operating system installation or later on using `convert.exe`.

Features that are available only if you're using NTFS include, among others:

- ▶ Active Directory
- ▶ File encryption
- ▶ Permissions set on files
- ▶ Remote Storage
- ▶ Disk Quotas

ON-SCREEN KEYBOARD

Displays a keyboard on the screen that you control with the mouse or switch input device. This feature is designed to aid users who have difficulty using a keyboard. Choose Start ➤ Programs ➤ Accessories ➤ Accessibility ➤ On-Screen Keyboard to bring up the On-Screen Keyboard. Alternatively, you can use the Windows Logo key+U shortcut. You'll have to click OK to acknowledge a message dialog box explaining that the On-Screen Keyboard has limited functionality. You can specify that you don't want Windows to display this dialog box the next time you start the On-Screen Keyboard.

Part vi

OUTLOOK EXPRESS

Program you can use to send and receive Internet e-mail and to post messages to newsgroups. Choose Start ➢ Programs ➢ Outlook Express to start Outlook Express. Alternatively, you can start Outlook Express by clicking the Launch Outlook Express button on the Quick Launch toolbar.

PAINT

Lets you create black-and-white or color drawings, which you can save as bitmap (.bmp) files. Drawings created in Paint can be pasted into other documents, printed, or used as Windows 2000 backgrounds. Choose Start ➢ Programs ➢ Accessories ➢ Paint to open Paint.

The Paint window consists of a menu bar at the top of the window, a toolbox at the left side of the window, and a drawing area to the right of the toolbar. It also contains a color box at the bottom of the toolbox and drawing area, and a status bar at the bottom of the window.

PERFORMANCE

Microsoft Management Console (MMC) console that displays system performance data as graphs and lets you configure alerts and data logs.

To open Performance, choose Start ➢ Settings ➢ Control Panel, double-click Administrative Tools, and then double-click Performance.

Performance contains two MMC console snap-ins: System Monitor and Performance Logs And Alerts.

System Monitor

The System Monitor snap-in displays system performance in one of three views: chart, histogram, or report. You can view many different performance counters for several different performance objects. Performance objects include such items as Browser, Cache, Indexing Service, Memory, Network Interface, and Processor, to name but a few. Available performance counters depend on the performance object you have selected.

Viewing Performance Information

To be able to view performance information, select System Monitor in the console tree, and then add one or more counters for a performance object to the list of monitored objects. Follow these steps:

1. Right-click anywhere in the Details pane and choose Add Counters, or click the Add button (+) on the toolbar.

2. Check Select Counters From Computer, and select the computer from the drop-down list.

3. Select a performance object from the drop-down list.

4. Check All Counters to display all counters available for the performance object, or check Select Counters From List, and choose the counter or counters you want to display.

5. Click Add. If you selected All Counters, System Monitor adds all counters to the Details pane. If you checked Select Counters From List, System Monitor adds the counter or counters you selected to the Details pane. To add other counters, select one or more additional counters in the list, and click Add. Continue in this fashion until you've added all the counters you wish to view. If you're not sure which counter to add, select a counter, and click Explain for a description of the counter.

6. Check All Instances, or check Select Instances From List, and make your selection in the list.

7. Click Close.

Each counter has an assigned color so that you can distinguish it in the graph. You'll see color assignments in the legend (the list of counters) below the graph. There, you'll also see the counter scale, counter name, instance, parent, object, and computer.

To see counter values for a specific counter, select a counter in the legend, and then view the values for that counter (last, average, minimum, maximum, and duration) in the value bar directly below the graph.

Highlighting Counters

If you have many counters selected, it might be difficult to see each counter in the graph. You can click the Highlight button on the toolbar and then click a counter in the list to bring that counter to the front in the graph and change the counter's color to white.

Deleting Counters

To remove a counter from the legend, select the counter and click the Delete button on the toolbar. To remove all counters and start over, click the New Counter Set button on the toolbar.

Changing Views

To change the view from chart to histogram, click the View Histogram button. To change the view to report, click the View Report button on the toolbar.

Clearing the Display

To clear the display for the current counters, click the Clear Display button on the toolbar.

Stopping the Display

To stop the counters temporarily, click the Freeze Display button on the toolbar. To continue the counters, click the Freeze Display button again.

After you have stopped counters, you can update the data to the most current data (snapshot) by clicking the Update Data button. This button becomes unavailable when you click the Freeze Display button again to continue displaying counter data continuously.

Displaying Data from a Log File

To display data from a log file instead of the current activity, click the View Log File Data button on the toolbar and open the log file you want to view.

Changing System Monitor Properties

Right-click anywhere in System Monitor in the Details pane, and choose Properties to customize System Monitor. Use the General, Source, Data, Graph, Colors, and Fonts tabs to choose items such as which elements to display and which counters to view (and the colors for each counter). Among other items, you can also change the view, update interval, source (current activity or log file), graph properties, and System Monitor colors and fonts.

Performance Logs And Alerts

MMC console snap-in that lets you configure performance-related logs and alerts. Two log types exist: counter logs and trace logs. Started logs (and alerts) have a green icon; stopped logs have a red icon. Right-click a log and choose Start or Stop from the shortcut menu to start or stop logging, or select the log or alert and choose Action ➤ Start or Action ➤ Stop. To delete a log or alert, select it in the Details pane, and then click Delete on the toolbar.

Counter Logs

Counter logs record information obtained from System Monitor counters you specify. To create a counter log, follow these steps:

1. Select Counter Logs in the console tree.

2. Right-click anywhere in the Details pane, and choose New Log Settings.

3. Enter a name for the log, and click OK.

4. On the General tab, click Add to add counters to the log. The process is the same as adding counters in System Monitor.

5. On the Log Files tab, configure options for the log file, such as location, name, type, and size.

6. On the Schedule tab, specify when you want the log to be started and stopped.

7. Click OK.

To view the data in the log, use System Monitor.

Trace Logs

Trace logs record data when an activity occurs, such as a process creation/ deletion, disk I/O operation, or page fault. These logs are different from counter logs, which record all activity data during a specified interval.

To create a new trace log, follow these steps:

1. Select Trace Logs in the console tree.

2. Right-click anywhere in the Details pane, and choose New Log Settings.

3. Enter a name for the log, and click OK.

4. On the General tab, specify events that are logged by the system provider, or add non-system providers to the list. Providers might include the Windows 2000 Kernel Trace Provider (system provider), Active Directory: Kerberos, Active Directory: NetLogon, Active Directory: SAM, Local Security Authority (LSA), and others. Click Provider Status to see a list of providers.

5. On the Log Files tab, set up log file settings, such as location, name, type, and size. On the Schedules tab, create a schedule for starting and stopping the log. The Advanced tab lets you configure buffer settings.

6. Click OK to create the log.

To view the data in the log file, use System Monitor.

Alerts

You can use alerts to send messages, run programs, or start a log when a counter value equals, exceeds, or is less than the value specified in the alert setting.

To create a new alert, follow these steps:

1. Select Trace Logs in the console tree.

2. Right-click anywhere in the Details pane, and choose New Alert Settings.

3. Enter a name for the alert, and click OK.

4. On the General tab, add a comment for the alert, and then click Add to add a counter using the same method you do when adding counters to the legend in System Monitor. Next, specify when you want System Monitor to trigger the alert and how frequently it should sample data.

5. On the Action tab, select the action you want to take place when an alert is triggered, such as logging an entry in the application event log, sending a message to a user you specify, starting a performance log, or running a program.

6. On the Schedule tab, choose when you want to start and stop alert scans. You can also specify whether to start a new scan when one scan is done.

Creating New Logs and Alerts from Saved Files

You can save logs and alerts as HTML files and then use them to create other logs and alerts. Right-click the log or alert, choose Save Settings As, enter a name, and click Save. To use the saved file to create a new log or alert, right-click anywhere in a blank area of the Details pane, and choose New Log Settings From or New Alert Settings From. Then select the applicable HTML file, and click Open.

PERMISSIONS

Permissions specify what kind of access is granted to users or groups for objects or object properties. The permissions you can assign depend on the object type. Some permissions are common to all object types. They include the following:

- ▶ Read

- ▶ Modify

- ▶ Change Owner

- ▶ Delete

Additional examples of permissions are Full Control, Read & Execute, Write, and so forth.

Explicit and Inherited Permissions

Permissions can be assigned either directly to an object (this is called an explicit permission) or inherited from a parent object (this is called an inherited permission). Explicit permissions are those permissions Windows assigns when an object is first created and those that are manually assigned, by an administrator, for example. By default, any permissions assigned to a container object are automatically inherited by objects that are created in that container. For example, if you create a folder called Data and then create subfolders and files in that folder, the subfolders and files inherit the permissions assigned to the Data folder. This means that the Data folder's permissions are explicit and permissions of subfolders and files in the Data folder are inherited.

PERSONALIZED MENUS

Feature that displays only the most frequently and most recently accessed menu items on Start menu menus. Enables faster access of favorite programs and menu items. You can turn off this feature by deselecting the option Use Personalized Menus on the General tab of the Taskbar & Start Menu Properties dialog box. To access this tab, choose Start ➢ Settings ➢ Taskbar & Start Menu.

PHONE AND MODEM OPTIONS

Lets you configure modem properties and telephone dialing rules. Modem properties determine the modem's configuration, and dialing rules are used to specify how you want Windows to dial phone numbers from each defined location. Choose Start ➢ Settings ➢ Control Panel, and then double-click the Phone And Modem Options icon to open the Phone & Modem Options dialog box. This dialog box has three tabs: Dialing Rules, Modems, and Advanced.

PHONE DIALER

Lets you make voice or video calls, or participate in video conference calls from your computer. You can connect by using a telephone connected to your computer, using a modem, over a network, through a telephone switch that's connected to your LAN, or via an Internet address. You'll also have to have a microphone and speakers connected to your computer, and you'll need to know the telephone number, DNS address, or IP address of the person you're calling. If you want others to see a video image of yourself, you'll need a camera attached to the computer. If

Part vi

you don't have a camera, you can still see video images of other people who do have a camera attached to their computer.

To open Phone Dialer, choose Start ➢ Programs ➢ Accessories ➢ Communications ➢ Phone Dialer.

PING

Lets you send packets to a host's IP address on a network (local area network, wide area network, Internet, intranet) to see if the host responds. Ping is often used to troubleshoot IP connectivity problems.

To use Ping, choose Start ➢ Programs ➢ Accessories ➢ Command Prompt. At the command prompt, enter **ping *host IP address***.

POWER OPTIONS

Controls the settings designed to reduce the amount of power your computer consumes. Conserving energy is becoming ever more important, both from an environmental and a cost-savings perspective. Power options can help you conserve valuable resources, such as electricity coming from standard wall outlets used to power desktop machines, as well as power from laptop batteries. The latter option extends the time you can effectively use your laptop while running on battery power. The power options you'll be able to control depend on your hardware and your hardware's configuration.

Choose Start ➢ Settings ➢ Control Panel, and double-click Power Options to open the Power Options Properties dialog box. The tabs available depend on your hardware's support for power management. Common tabs include Power Schemes, Advanced, Hibernate, and UPS. If your computer supports Advanced Power Management, you'll also see a tab called APM, where you can enable or disable Advanced Power Management. Advanced Power Management helps you reduce your computer's overall power consumption and provides battery status information if the computer is running on battery power.

PRINTERS

Used to manage all aspects of printing. From here you can perform such tasks as adding, removing, and sharing printers; assigning permissions; setting the default printer; changing printer properties; setting printer defaults; viewing and managing job queues; pausing printing; canceling printing; and setting up print server properties.

Printing in Windows 2000 is handled through the Printers folder. You can access the folder by choosing Start ➢ Settings ➢ Printers. Alternatively, you can access the Printers folder through My Computer, Windows Explorer, or Control Panel.

The majority of printer configuration is done through the printer Properties dialog box. You can also perform some printing-related actions or access configuration pages through the File menu or by right-clicking any printer icon.

PRIVATE CHARACTER EDITOR

Lets you create and add new characters to the Unicode character set. You can link characters to a specific font or all fonts. To start Private Character Editor, choose Start ➤ Run, type **eudcedit**, and click OK.

The first thing you have to do is select a Unicode code for the new character. Select the square in the Select Code dialog box that corresponds to the code you want to assign to the character. Your choice will appear in the Code area below the grid. Click OK to open the Private Character Editor window.

The Private Character Editor window consists of a toolbar, a guidebar, an Edit window, and menu options. The toolbar has several drawing tools, including Pencil, Brush, Straight Line, Hollow Rectangle, Filled Rectangle, Hollow Ellipse, Filled Ellipse, Rectangular Selection, Freeform Selection, and Eraser. Click a button to use the corresponding tool to create a new (private) character in the Edit window.

The guidebar displays such items as the character set, code, linked font, and file. The menus contain additional options you can use to create new characters.

RECYCLE BIN

A folder that holds files and folders you deleted from your hard disk until they are permanently removed from the computer's hard disk. Use the Recycle Bin to restore files that have been deleted but not yet removed from the Recycle Bin.

If deleted files are in the Recycle Bin, the icon will show paper sticking out of the top of the wastebasket. If it is empty (meaning that files have been deleted permanently), no paper shows.

You can put files into the Recycle Bin by deleting them through a shortcut menu, using the Delete key, or dragging and dropping them onto the Recycle Bin.

REGIONAL OPTIONS

Depending on where you are located geographically, you will use a specific way to display numbers with decimal fractions, large numbers, currencies, dates, and times. You will also use one of two systems of measurement, and your language and language characters will be different. Regional Options enables you to specify your geographic region; how you want Windows programs to display dates, times, numbers, and so forth; and whether Windows programs should use the metric or U.S. system of measurement. Regional Options also enables you to install and use multiple languages and keyboard layouts on the same system. Some programs can take advantage of this and may offer additional functions, such as spell-checkers and fonts for different languages. This enables you to read or type documents using characters used in other language groups (such as Cyrillic or Greek).

Choose Start ➤ Settings ➤ Control Panel, and then double-click the Regional Options icon to display the Regional Options dialog box. It contains six tabs: General, Numbers, Currency, Time, Date, and Input Locales.

REGISTRY

Database that holds all information about your system, such as defaults and properties for folders, files, users, preferences, applications, protocols, devices, and any other resources.

When you install new applications or hardware, or when you make any changes to your system using Control Panel, information about the installation or changes is saved in the Registry. You can make changes manually to the Registry using the Registry Editor. To run the Registry Editor, choose Start ➤ Run, type **regedit**, and click OK.

REMOVABLE STORAGE

Microsoft Management Console (MMC) snap-in that lets you manage hardware libraries. Hardware libraries consist of hardware devices (such as jukeboxes and changers) that can read removable media (for example, tapes and optical discs), and the removable media itself. Use Removable Storage Management to track, label, and catalog your removable media, and to control hardware libraries' physical aspects, such as door, slots, and drives. You can also use Removable Storage Management to clean hardware library drives. Removable Storage Management complements your backup software, which you would use to manage the physical data contained on your removable media. To access Removable Storage, choose Start ➤ Settings ➤ Control Panel, double-click Administrative Tools, and double-click Computer Management. You'll find Removable Storage under Storage. It has four subnodes: Media Pools, Physical Locations, Work Queue, and Operator Requests.

RESTORE

Button at the top-right corner of windows that lets you return a window to its original size after you have maximized it using the Maximize button.

ROUTING AND REMOTE ACCESS

Microsoft Management Console (MMC) snap-in that lets you configure and manage Routing And Remote Access services on a Windows 2000 Server computer. Installed by default on Windows 2000 Server computers, but not enabled or configured.

Supported routing services include Virtual Private Network (VPN), Network Address Translation (NAT), and multiprotocol local area network (LAN) to wide area network (WAN) and LAN-to-LAN routing. Routing services enable Windows 2000 Server computers to act as software routers, allowing the computer to forward packets to other computers in the network.

Supported remote access services include VPN and dial-up services, enabling remote users to access the network as if they were locally attached to the network.

To access the Routing And Remote Access MMC console snap-in where you can enable and configure Routing And Remote Access services, choose Start ➤ Programs ➤ Administrative Tools ➤ Routing And Remote Access.

Routing And Remote Access MMC Console Snap-in Window

Although installed by default on Windows 2000 Server computers, Routing And Remote Access is not enabled or configured by default. In the console tree, you'll see the Server Status node, which provides information about the current routing and remote access status, such as stopped, started, and paused. The Server (local) node (the node's name is your server's name) by default gives you information about how to start the process of setting up and configuring Routing And Remote Access.

Enabling Routing And Remote Access

To enable Routing And Remote Access, follow these steps:

1. Select the server object in the console tree, and then choose Action ➤ Configure And Enable Routing And Remote Access to start the Routing And Remote Access Configuration Wizard.

2. Select one of the Common Configurations. Choices include Internet Connection Server, Remote Access Server, Virtual Private Network

(VPN) Server, Network Router, and Manually Configured Server. Click Next.

3. Follow the Wizard's prompts. Selections and options will vary greatly depending on the configuration choice you make in step 2.

4. When prompted, click Finish to complete the Wizard.

5. Click Yes to start Routing And Remote Access immediately. To leave it stopped for now, click No (you can start the service using the Routing And Remote Access MMC console snap-in).

Action Menu

Use the Action menu to further configure Routing And Remote Access services and access Routing And Remote Access help. Routing And Remote Access involves complex configuration; accordingly, the available options on the Action (and shortcut) menus will depend on the item you have selected in the console tree or Details pane.

RUN

Used to open programs, folders, documents, and Internet resources. Most frequently used to run installation programs. Follow these steps:

1. Choose Start ➢ Run to open the Run dialog box.

2. In the Open text box, enter the name of the resource you want to open. Include the full path. If you've used Run before, the path to the most recently opened resource will appear in the Open text box. You can also choose a resource by clicking the drop-down arrow and selecting a resource from the list. If you don't know the exact path to the resource, click Browse, and browse for and select it. Click Open to return to the Run menu.

3. Click OK to open the resource.

RUN AS

Used to run a program or Microsoft Management Console (MMC) tool as a user other than the one currently logged on (for example, as an administrative user). Follow these steps to access the Run As Other User dialog box:

1. In Windows Explorer, select a program you want to run as another user.

2. Hold down the Shift key, and right-click.

3. From the shortcut menu, select Run As.

4. In the Run As Other User dialog box, make sure that the Run The Program As The Following User option is selected, and enter the name, password, and domain for the user that you want to run the program.

5. Click OK.

A related dialog box is Install Program As Other User. If you run an installation program such as `install.exe` or `setup.exe` as a user who does not have administrative privileges, the Install Program As Other User dialog box appears, and you're asked if you want to install the program as an administrative user because some programs won't install correctly if you don't. Enter information the same way you did in the Run As Other User dialog box. You can also specify to always run installation programs as the current user by selecting the corresponding check box.

SAFE MODE

Windows 2000 lets you start up the computer in Safe mode to troubleshoot Windows system problems—for example, if Windows won't start after an application installation. To access the Safe mode startup options on the Windows 2000 Advanced options menu, follow these steps:

1. Choose Start ➣ Shutdown, select Restart from the drop-down list, and click OK.

2. When the Please Select Operating System To Start screen appears, press F8.

3. Choose one of the nine options. Use the up and down arrow keys to highlight your choice, and press Enter to select it. NumLock must be off in order for the arrow keys to work.

SCANNERS AND CAMERAS

Lets you configure scanners and cameras that are installed on the Windows 2000 computer.

Choose Start ➣ Settings ➣ Control Panel, and double-click Scanners And Cameras to open the Scanners And Cameras Properties dialog box, which has one tab:

Devices   Use this tab to view, add, remove, troubleshoot, and configure the properties of scanners and cameras. Any installed scanners or cameras appear in the list of installed scanners or cameras. You can add new scanners or cameras by clicking Add and following the Wizard's instructions. You'll have to provide the manufacturer and model of your hardware, and specify the communications port you want to use for the device.

To remove a scanner or camera, select it in the list, and click Remove. If you're experiencing problems with a scanner or camera, select it in the list, and click Troubleshoot to start the Windows 2000 Troubleshooter for cameras and scanners.

If you want to view or modify the properties of a scanner or camera, select it in the list, and click Properties. The available properties will vary depending on your hardware, but may include such items as port settings used for the device and color management.

Scheduled Tasks

Windows 2000 lets you schedule tasks to run at a certain time, date, and interval. Tasks include items such as programs, scripts, and documents. Scheduled Tasks, located in Control Panel, lets you open the Scheduled Tasks folder, where you can create new scheduled tasks as well as view and configure already scheduled tasks.

Choose Start ➢ Settings ➢ Control Panel, and double-click the Scheduled Tasks icon to open the Scheduled Tasks folder. By default, no tasks are scheduled, and the folder contains only the Add Scheduled Task icon.

Add Scheduled Task

Starts the Scheduled Task Wizard, which guides you through the process of creating scheduled tasks. To create a scheduled task, follow these steps:

1. In the Scheduled Tasks folder, double-click Add Scheduled Task. The Scheduled Task Wizard starts. Click Next.

2. In the list of programs, select a program you want Windows 2000 to run, or click Browse to browse to a program located elsewhere on the computer or network. Click Next.

3. Enter a name for the scheduled task. It can be, but does not have to be, the same name as the program.

4. Decide how often you want to run this task. You can choose to perform the task daily, weekly, monthly, only once, every time the computer starts, or every time you log on to the computer. Select the appropriate radio button, and click Next.

5. The options available in next dialog box will depend on your choice in step 4. If you chose to run the task when you start the computer

or when you log on to the computer, skip to step 6. If you chose any of the other options, you will be able to specify such items as the time to start the scheduled task and on which days, weeks, or months you want the task to run. When you finish, click Next.

6. Enter your username and password. Click Next.

7. Select the check box if you want to open the Properties dialog box for the scheduled task after the Wizard creates the task. Click Finish to complete the Wizard.

Scheduled Tasks Folder

The Scheduled Tasks folder contains all of your scheduled tasks and the Add Scheduled Task icon to run the Scheduled Task Wizard.

You can identify a scheduled task by the small clock icon located in the bottom-left corner of its icon. If you select a scheduled task icon, you'll see information about the task in the left portion of the Scheduled Tasks folder. Information includes the name of the task, the schedule for the task, its next run time, its last run time, the results of the last run, and the task's creator.

Run and End Task

When you right-click any task, two options specific to scheduled tasks are available: Run and End Task. Choose Run to run the scheduled task immediately. Choose End Task to stop a scheduled task that is currently running. When a scheduled task is running, you will see status information in the left portion of the Scheduled Tasks folder.

SEARCH

Use this Windows 2000 feature to search for files, folders, Internet resources, printers, and people. Choose Start ➤ Search, and select one of the options from the submenu. Alternatively, click the Search button in Windows Explorer or Internet Explorer. You'll be able to choose any of the search options in the Search pane at the left of the window. If you ever close the Search pane, you can reopen it by clicking the Search button.

SEND FAX WIZARD

Walks you through the steps of sending a fax via a fax printer installed on the computer. In any Windows application, create a document, and then choose File ➤ Print. Select the fax printer you want to use, and click Print. This starts the Send Fax Wizard. Follow the on-screen instructions to finish sending your fax.

Part VI

SEND TO

Lets you send a file or folder directly to a destination, such as a floppy drive, the Desktop (as a shortcut), a mail recipient, and the My Documents folder.

To send an item to a destination using Send To, perform these steps:

1. In any Explorer window, right-click a file or folder to open the shortcut menu.

2. Select Send To, and select the destination.

SERVER EXTENSIONS ADMINISTRATOR

Microsoft Management Console (MMC) snap-in installed on Windows 2000 Server computers that lets you administer FrontPage server extensions for non–Internet Information Services (IIS) and IIS 3 virtual servers. For IIS 4 or later (Windows 2000 includes IIS 5), FrontPage server extensions are already integrated, and you would use the Internet Information Service MMC snap-in (accessible through the Internet Services Manager menu option in the Administrative Tools program group) to administer them.

To access the Server Extensions Administrator, choose Start ➤ Programs ➤ Administrative Tools ➤ Server Extensions Administrator.

SERVICES

Microsoft Management Console (MMC) console snap-in that lets you start and stop services that are installed or running on your Windows 2000 computer. Some examples of services are Fax Service, Indexing Service, Event Log, Plug and Play, and Utility Manager.

To access Services, choose Start ➤ Settings ➤ Control Panel, double-click Administrative Tools, and double-click Services.

In the Details pane of the Services MMC console snap-in, you can see information about all services installed on your computer, including name, description, status, startup type, and the account the service uses to log on.

Working with Services

Services lets you start, stop, pause, resume, and restart services installed on your Windows 2000 computer. To do so, right-click a service, and choose the appropriate action from the shortcut menu, or select a service, click Action, and select the action you want to perform. Alternatively, use the Start Service, Stop Service, Pause Service, and Resume Service buttons on the toolbar.

Service Properties

You can view and configure properties for any service installed on your computer. Right-click a service and choose Properties from the shortcut menu. The Service Properties dialog box has four tabs:

General   Lets you view and configure general items, such as the display name, description, startup type, status of the service (started, stopped, or paused), and start parameters. You can also click the appropriate button to start, stop, pause, or resume the service. Also lets you enter parameters to apply when the service is started.

Log On   Lets you specify an account the service should use to log on. This can be either the Local System account or a user account you specify. You can also choose to provide a user interface that anyone logged on to the computer can use to interact with the service. Finally, you can enable or disable the service for specific hardware profiles you have set up on your computer by selecting a profile in the list and clicking Enable or Disable, respectively.

Recovery   Lets you specify an action Windows 2000 should take if the service fails. You can specify different actions for the first, second, and subsequent failures. The default action varies from service to service. Available options include Take No Action, Run A File, Restart The Service, and Reboot The Computer. If you select Run A File, you must specify in the Run File area of the dialog box the file you want Windows to run. If you select Restart The Service, specify the number of minutes that should elapse before the service restarts. If you select Reboot The Computer, click Restart Computer Options to specify the number of minutes that should elapse before the computer reboots and whether you want a custom message sent to network users before the computer reboots. On the Recovery tab, you can also specify the number of days that should pass before Windows resets the fail count.

Dependencies   Lets you view any services that depend on the currently selected service and any services on which the currently selected service depends. This information can help with troubleshooting service-related problems.

SETTINGS

The Settings option on the Start menu gives you access to many Windows 2000 configuration tools, such as Control Panel, Network And Dial-up Connections, Printers, and Taskbar & Start Menu. Choose Start ➢ Settings, and make your choice from the submenu.

SHARED FOLDERS

Microsoft Management Console (MMC) console snap-in that lets you view and manage shares on the computer you're using, remote connections to that computer, and files in use by remote users.

To access Shared Folders, choose Start ➢ Settings ➢ Control Panel, double-click Administrative Tools, double-click Computer Management, and select Shared Folders under System Tools in the console tree.

SHARING

Lets you share resources on your computer (such as folders, disks, and printers) with users of a network. When you share a folder or disk, you can specify the users who should have access to the resource as well as the permissions they will have to the folder or disk. Sharing settings are configured on the Sharing tab of the resource's Properties dialog box. Users can see and access resources you've shared in any Explorer window by navigating to your computer using My Network Places.

Sharing a Folder or Disk

To share a folder or disk with users of the network, perform the following steps:

1. In any Explorer window, right-click the folder or disk you want to share, and select Sharing.

2. On the Sharing tab of the folder's or disk's Properties dialog box, select Share This Folder, and enter a name for the share. If you want, you can also enter a comment in the Comment text box.

3. Specify whether you want the maximum number of users to be able to connect to the shared folder or disk, or specify a certain number of users who can connect to the folder or disk simultaneously.

4. To change the default permissions (Everyone, Full Control, Change, and Read permissions), click Permissions. In the resulting dialog box, click Add to add users or groups to the list of users with whom you want to share the folder or disk. To remove users or groups, select a group or user in the list, and click Remove. To change the permissions, select a group or user in the list, and select the appropriate Allow or Deny option in the Permissions list box. When you've finished, click OK.

5. To configure offline access, click Caching on the Sharing tab. You can enable or disable caching of files in the folder by selecting or

deselecting the Allow Caching Of Files In This Shared Folder option. If you select it, you can then choose a setting for caching from the drop-down list. Choices include Manual Caching For Documents, Automatic Caching For Documents, and Automatic Caching For Programs. Detailed explanations are given below the drop-down list as you make a selection from the list. Click OK when you've made your choices.

6. If applicable, you can also click New Share to open the New Share dialog box, where you can create a new shared folder. Click OK to finish creating the new share. The New Share button is available only when you are sharing a network folder, not when you're sharing a local folder.

7. Back on the Sharing tab, click OK to save the sharing settings for the folder or disk.

In the Explorer window, a hand icon appears at the bottom of the folder or disk, indicating that the resource is shared.

SHUT DOWN

Shuts down the system. Choose Start ➢ Shutdown.

The drop-down list box in the Shut Down Windows dialog box contains three options by default:

Log Off *current user* **(where** *current user* **is the user you're currently logged on as)**   Ends the session by logging off the current user. You'll be presented with the Welcome To Windows window so that you can log on as another user.

Shut Down   Ends the current session and shuts down Windows. You can then turn off the computer.

Restart   Ends the current session, shuts down Windows, performs a warm boot, and starts Windows again. You'll be presented with the Welcome To Windows window so that you can log on again.

SOUND RECORDER

Lets you record, edit, play, and mix sounds from audio input devices installed in your computer. Examples of audio input devices are a microphone (using a sound card) and a CD-ROM player.

Choose Start ➢ Programs ➢ Accessories ➢ Entertainment ➢ Sound Recorder to open the Sound Recorder dialog box.

SOUNDS AND MULTIMEDIA

Lets you assign specific sounds to Windows 2000 system events, such as receiving e-mail or exiting Windows, and for sound and multimedia device configuration.

Choose Start ➢ Settings ➢ Control Panel, and double-click Sounds And Multimedia to open the Sounds And Multimedia Properties dialog box.

START

Used to gain access to system Shut Down options, Windows 2000 Help, files and other resources, configuration options, recently opened documents, programs, and Windows Updates.

By default the Start button is located in the bottom-left corner of the Taskbar. Clicking this button activates the Start menu. Right-clicking this button brings up a menu from which you can open the current user's Start Menu folder (click Open), open Windows Explorer (click Explore), and search for files, folders, computers, printers, and people (click Search). If you're logged in as a user with administrative privileges (such as Administrator), you'll have two more options: Open All Users and Explore All Users. These two options open the C:\Documents and Settings\All Users\Start Menu folders in Windows Explorer with the Folders Explorer Bar pane either not displayed or displayed.

START MENU

The Start menu is used to gain access to system Shut Down options, files and folders, Windows 2000 Help, configuration options, recently opened documents, programs, and Windows Updates. To access the Start Menu, click the Start button. The following options are part of the default Start menu:

Shut Down   Brings up the Shut Down Windows dialog box, from which you can choose to shut down the computer, restart the computer, or log off the current user.

Run   Brings up the Run dialog box. From here, you can run programs and open folders, documents, or Internet resources.

Help   Brings up the Windows 2000 Help system. Here you can find answers to all of your Windows 2000–related questions by browsing the contents, querying the index, searching by keyword, or adding and then checking back on your favorite topics.

Search   Brings up a submenu with options for searching for files or folders on the local computer and on the network, for resources on the Internet (by opening Internet Explorer and activating the IE

Search feature), for printers, and for people (in your company or on the Internet).

Settings   Brings up a submenu with options for opening Control Panel to customize and configure your Desktop and computer, accessing existing and creating new network and dial-up connections, accessing existing and creating new local and network printers, and customizing the Start menu and Taskbar.

Documents   Brings up a submenu with an option for opening the My Documents folder. Also displays a list of shortcuts to the 15 most recently accessed files. Click a file to open it.

Programs   Brings up a submenu that gives you access to program groups and programs located on your computer.

Windows Update   Connects you to www.windowsupdate .microsoft.com so that your computer can automatically be updated with new features, device drivers, and so forth.

You can add programs to the Start menu by dragging and dropping a program's icon on the Start button.

SYSTEM

Controls system properties, including network identification configuration, hardware device configuration (including hardware profile configuration), user profile configuration, and advanced properties, including performance, environment variable, and system startup and recovery configuration.

Choose Start ➤ Settings ➤ Control Panel, and double-click System to open the System Properties dialog box, which contains five tabs: General, Network Identification, Hardware, User Profiles, and Advanced.

General

The General tab provides information about your system, such as the version of the operating system you are running, to whom the operating system is registered, and information about the physical computer.

Network Identification

Use this tab to view and configure the full name of your computer and the workgroup or domain to which it belongs. Each computer in a network must have a unique name by which you and other users can identify it. If the computer is a member of a domain and you've specified a DNS domain name for the computer, then the DNS domain name becomes part of the full name.

The Network Identification tab has two buttons used for configuration of network identification: Network ID and Properties.

NOTE

If the computer is a Windows 2000 domain controller, the network identification information cannot be changed. The Properties button is grayed out, and the Network ID button does not exist.

Network ID   Starts the Network Identification Wizard. Use the Wizard to connect your computer to a different network than the one to which you're currently connected (such as connecting to a workgroup or domain to which you're not currently connected).

Properties   Opens the Identification Changes dialog box. Here you can change the name of the computer, as well as change the domain or workgroup to which the computer belongs. Click OK after you make your changes. If you're joining a domain, you'll be prompted to supply the username and password for a user who has the proper permissions to enable the computer to join the domain. By default, this is any member of the group Domain Admins. You can also specify the DNS domain name for the computer by clicking More and entering the DNS domain name for the computer. Select the Change DNS Domain Name When Domain Membership Changes option if you want to automatically adjust the DNS domain name when changing domain membership. Click OK to save your changes.

Network Identification Wizard

To change your current workgroup or domain membership, follow these steps:

1. On the System Properties dialog box's Network Identification tab, click Network ID to start the Network Identification Wizard.

2. On the Welcome screen, click Next.

3. Choose This Computer Is Part Of A Business Network, And I Use It To Connect To Other Computers At Work. Click Next.

4. Specify whether your company uses a network with a domain or without a domain, and click Next.

5. If you specified that your company uses a network without a domain, specify the name of the workgroup to which your computer should belong, click Next, and skip to step 11. If you specified that your company uses a network with a domain, read the Network Information screen and make sure that you have all the necessary information before you proceed. This information includes your

username, password, the domain for your user account, and possibly your computer name and the domain for your computer (this may not necessarily be the same domain as the domain in which your user account resides). Click Next.

6. Enter your Windows 2000 username and password and the domain in which the user account exists. Click Next.

7. If a computer account already exists, the Wizard will ask whether you would like to use the account. Click Yes (if you'd like to use the account) or No (if you don't want to use it). If a computer account does not already exist, or if you clicked No, enter your computer name and the domain for the computer. Click Next.

8. Enter the name, password, and domain of an administrative user who has the necessary rights to allow the computer to join the domain. Click OK.

9. You can add a user who has an account in a domain on the network (either yourself or another user) to the local computer to give that user access to the resources on the computer as well as to shared resources on the network. Enter the name and domain information for the user. Alternatively, you can choose not to add a user at this time. Click Next.

10. If you chose not to add a user, skip to step 11. If you chose to add a user, select the level of access the user should have. Standard means that the user will be added to the Power Users group, and Restricted means that the user will be added to the Users group. Select Other if you want to specify a group. Click Next.

11. Click Finish to complete the Network Identification Wizard.

12. Click OK to acknowledge that you must restart the computer so that your changes can take effect.

13. Click OK to close the System Properties dialog box.

14. Click Yes to restart the computer.

Hardware

Use this tab to configure your computer's hardware. This tab gives you access to the Add/Remove Hardware Wizard, Device Manager, and Hardware Profiles.

Part vi

Hardware Wizard

Click the Hardware Wizard button to start the Add/Remove Hardware Wizard. This Wizard guides you through the steps for:

- Adding new hardware to a Windows 2000 computer after you've physically installed it

- Preparing Windows 2000 to physically remove or unplug hardware from the computer

- Troubleshooting a device that is experiencing problems

The Hardware Wizard automatically makes the necessary changes, such as modifying the Registry and configuration files, and installing, loading, removing, and unloading drivers.

Device Manager

Lists all hardware installed in the computer. Also enables you to configure the properties of hardware devices, check the status of installed devices, view and update device drivers, and disable and uninstall devices.

The Device Manager area of the Hardware tab contains an additional button, Driver Signing. To maintain file integrity, files can be digitally signed. The integrity of digitally signed files can be verified before they are installed on a computer. For example, all Windows 2000 files are digitally signed and verified during installation.

Click the Driver Signing button to open the Driver Signing Options dialog box, where you can specify how you want to handle digital file signing. You can choose to ignore digital signatures and install all files, regardless of whether they're digitally signed (the default); to display a warning message if an unsigned file is about to be installed; or to not allow the installation of files that are not digitally signed. You can also make your choice the system default by clicking the Apply Settings As System Default check box. Click OK to save any changes you've made and return to the Hardware tab.

Hardware Profiles

Hardware profiles specify which drivers you want Windows to load at system startup. You may need different drivers loaded if your hardware changes, such as might be the case if you have a laptop that you place into a docking station when you're back at the office. When the laptop is undocked, you use a modem for dial-up access to the network and a physically attached printer. When it's docked, you use a network adapter to connect to the network, but you don't need the modem or the physically attached printer. To handle these different hardware configuration needs, Windows 2000 allows you to set up multiple hardware profiles. At system startup, you can then choose which profile to use.

To configure hardware profiles, click the Hardware Profiles button, which brings up the Hardware Profiles dialog box. By default, one profile, called Profile 1, is created when you install Windows 2000. It contains the settings for your current hardware. You'll see it in the Available Hardware Profiles list.

Four options are available in the Hardware Properties dialog box: Properties, Copy, Rename, and Delete.

You can copy profiles to create new profiles by selecting a profile, clicking Copy, entering a name for the copy of the profile, and clicking OK. Once you have more than one profile, use the up and down arrows to rearrange each profile's position in the list. The profile at the top of the list is the default profile.

You can rename a profile by selecting it, clicking Rename, entering a new name for the profile, and clicking OK. You can delete a profile by selecting it, clicking Delete, and confirming your choice.

Enabling and Disabling Devices   To enable or disable a device for the current profile, use Device Manager. Right-click a device, and choose Disable or Enable, depending on the current state of the device.

Profile Properties   To view and configure the properties of a profile, select the profile in the list, and click Properties. In the Properties dialog box, you can see items such as a docking station's Dock ID (provided by the hardware manufacturer) and the serial number.

You can specify that the profile is used for a portable computer by clicking the This Is A Portable Computer check box. If Windows 2000 can determine whether the portable computer is currently docked, the appropriate selection will be made automatically, and you won't be able to change it. If Windows 2000 cannot determine whether the computer is docked or undocked, the selection will read The Docking State Is Unknown, and you can manually select whether the computer is docked or undocked for this profile.

To make the profile available at system startup, select the Always Include This Profile As An Option When Windows Starts check box.

Hardware Profiles Selection   In the Hardware Profiles Selection area of the Hardware Profiles dialog box, you can choose whether you want Windows to wait at startup until you've made a hardware profile selection, or you can specify that Windows use the first profile in the list after a certain amount of time has elapsed without a choice being made. The range is 0 to 500 seconds.

User Profiles

User profiles specify the settings for a user's Desktop environment when the user logs on to the Windows 2000 computer. Settings include such items as display settings (for example, wallpapers and color schemes), printer connections, mouse settings, Start menu items, and network connections. Three types of user profiles exist: local, roaming, and mandatory (a type of roaming user profile).

The User Profiles tab lets you view, copy, and change the type of user profiles.

Advanced

Use this tab to configure advanced system settings related to the computer's performance, environment variables, and startup and recovery.

Performance

Performance Options enables you to configure the computer's virtual memory paging file size, specify the maximum size of the computer's Registry, and optimize performance for applications running either in the foreground or background.

Click the Performance Options button to open the Performance Options dialog box.

Application Response   Under Application Response, click the appropriate radio button to optimize performance for either Applications (running in the foreground) or Background Services (running in the background). If you choose the former, foreground applications receive more processor resources than background applications. If you choose the latter, all applications receive equal amounts of processor resources. The default is Applications on a Windows 2000 Professional computer and Background Services on a Windows 2000 Server computer.

Virtual Memory   A paging file (swap file) lets you hold data on disk that does not fit into physical memory. The combination of the paging file and physical memory is called virtual memory. As data is needed, it is moved out of the swap file into memory (data is moved from memory to disk to accommodate the data that needs to be moved to memory). Each physical disk can hold a separate swap file.

You can view the current size of the paging file in the Virtual Memory area of the Performance Options dialog box. To change the size of a swap file, click Change, select the appropriate drive in the Drive list, and change the values for initial size and maximum size. Click Set to make the change. You can also view information regarding the total paging file size for all drives, such as minimum size, recommended size, and current size.

If you set the initial and maximum size values to zero, you're effectively deleting the paging file.

Finally, on the Virtual Memory tab, you can see the current Windows 2000 Registry size and specify its maximum size in MB.

Environment Variables

An environment variable is a symbolic name associated with a value (string) that Windows 2000 and programs written to run under Windows 2000 can use to be able to behave in a certain way under certain conditions. Variable values are strings that hold environment information. This information might include items such as paths for saving certain file types (such as Temp files), paths to certain files (such as application files needed by an application to run), the number of processors, and the processor architecture.

Click the Environment Variables button to open the Environment Variables dialog box. Here you can view variables and their values that are already defined for both the current user and the system (these include user- or administrator-created variables as well as application-created variables).

The current user can also create, edit, and delete user-specific variables. Only members of the Administrators group can create new system variables and edit or delete existing system variables.

Startup and Recovery

Lets you specify the operating system the computer should use when it starts, and specify what to do if the computer suddenly stops running.

Click the Startup And Recovery button to open the Setup And Recovery dialog box.

Under System Startup, you can choose the default operating system if you have more than one operating system installed on the computer. You can also specify how long to display the list of operating systems before starting the default operating system if no selection is made.

Under Recovery, specify actions to perform if the computer suddenly stops. Items include writing an event to the system log, sending an administrative alert, and automatically rebooting the computer.

You can also specify whether to write debugging information to a file (this process is called a dump) and how much information you want to record. Under Write Debugging Information, you can select from None (Do Not Write Debugging Information), Small Memory Dump (64KB), or Kernel Memory Dump. You can specify a path for the dump file and choose whether to overwrite the file if it already exists.

SYNCHRONIZE

Brings up the Items To Synchronize dialog box, which you use to synchronize offline files with online files and configure synchronization settings. Choose Start ➤ Programs ➤ Accessories ➤ Synchronize to open the Items To Synchronize dialog box.

Items that appear in the Items To Synchronize dialog box are any files or Web pages you've made available offline. If you don't want to synchronize a particular item, deselect its check box.

The Items To Synchronize dialog box contains four buttons:

Properties   Displays properties for the selected item. For offline files, it opens the Offline Files folder, where you can work with and access the properties of any files it contains. For offline Web pages, it opens the Properties dialog box for the selected page.

Synchronize   Synchronizes the selected items.

Setup   Opens the Synchronization Settings dialog box. The Logon/Logoff tab lets you specify the items you want to synchronize automatically when you log on or off the computer. The On Idle tab lets you specify the items you want to synchronize when the computer is idle. The Scheduled tab lets you set up a schedule for synchronizing items (using the Scheduled Synchronization Wizard).

Close   Closes the Items To Synchronize dialog box.

SYSTEM INFORMATION

Microsoft Management Console (MMC) console snap-in that collects and displays information about your Windows 2000 computer. To access System Information, choose Start ➢ Settings ➢ Control Panel, double-click Administrative Tools, double-click Computer Management, and then expand and select System Information under System Tools in the console tree.

System Information includes a system summary, along with many different items that are grouped into four categories: Hardware Resources, Components, Software Environment, and Internet Explorer 5. You can see details about your configuration or provide the information collected by System Information to service technicians who are troubleshooting your computer.

SYSTEM TOOLS

Predefined Windows 2000 program group that contains several utilities you can use to perform system maintenance and configure your system. Utilities include Backup, Character Map, Disk Cleanup, Disk Defragmenter, Getting Started (Windows 2000 Professional only), Scheduled Tasks, and System Information.

TASKBAR

Primarily used to switch between applications and launch applications. Appears at the bottom of the screen by default. On the left end of the Taskbar is the Start button, which brings up the Start menu. Next to it is the Quick Launch toolbar.

Buttons next to the Quick Launch toolbar represent open programs. On the right end of the Taskbar is the system clock. This area of the Taskbar is referred to as the status area and can contain other items as well. For example, if you're using a laptop, you'll see an icon that indicates your battery levels. In addition, the status area displays icons that indicate you're printing a document, that you've received e-mail, and that antivirus software is running, among other useful information.

TASKBAR & START MENU

Used to customize the Taskbar and Start menu. Choose Start ➢ Settings ➢ Taskbar & Start Menu to display the Taskbar And Start Menu Properties dialog box. It has two tabs: General and Advanced.

General Tab

Use this tab to customize the look and placement of the Taskbar. You can select or deselect the following options:

Always On Top   Means that the Taskbar will be displayed on top of other windows so that you can always see it. Enabled by default.

Auto Hide   If you select this option, the Taskbar is displayed as a thin line. Move the pointer over this line to display the Taskbar.

Show Small Icons In Start Menu   If you select this option, a smaller Start menu with smaller icons and without the Windows 2000 side bar displays. The Windows side bar is the blue bar on the left of the Start menu that displays the Windows operating system name, such as Windows 2000 Professional.

Show Clock   If selected, this option displays the clock on the right side of the Taskbar. Enabled by default.

Show Personalized Menus   If you select this option, menus off the Start menu will become personalized, meaning that only recently accessed menu items appear in the menus. You can view and access all other menu items by moving the mouse pointer over the double downward pointing arrows at the bottom of a menu.

Part vi

Advanced Tab

Use this tab to customize the Start menu. Under Customize Start Menu, the following buttons are available:

Add   When you click this button, the Create Shortcut Wizard helps you through the process of adding a shortcut to the Start menu. Follow these steps:

1.   Click Add to start the Create Shortcut Wizard.

2.   Type the path for or browse to the location of the item for which you want to create a shortcut. You can specify programs, files, folders, computers, and Internet addresses. Click Next.

3.   Choose the Start Menu folder in which you want to place the shortcut or create a new folder. Click Next.

4.   Enter a name for the shortcut.

5.   Click Finish.

Remove   Lets you remove shortcuts from the Start menu. Click Remove, select the shortcut, and click Remove. Click Close when you've finished.

Advanced   Lets you add submenus to the Start menu or the Programs menu. To get started, click Advanced. This opens the Start Menu folder in a Windows Explorer window. Next, choose File ➢ New ➢ Folder, and name the folder. To add a submenu to the Programs submenu, double-click the Programs folder, then choose File ➢ New ➢ Folder and name the folder. To add shortcuts to the new submenu, you can use the Add button on the Advanced tab, or you can add items to the submenu folder you created in Windows Explorer.

Re-sort   Sorts the items on the Programs menu so that they appear in their default order.

Clear   Removes the list of recently accessed resources (files, programs, Web sites) in the Documents Start menu option.

Under Start Menu Settings on the Advanced tab, you can further customize which Start menu options are displayed and how they are displayed. Select the check box that corresponds to a setting you want to activate.

To activate Start Menu Settings changes without closing the Taskbar And Start Menu Properties dialog box, click Apply.

When you've finished customizing the Taskbar and Start menu, click OK.

TASK MANAGER

Lets you view the status of and control programs and processes that are running on the Windows 2000 computer. You can also view performance indicators for processes. Using Task Manager, you can see which programs (tasks) are running, end them if they're no longer responding, see which processes are running, and view system resource information about these processes as well as overall system usage information.

To access Task Manager, press Ctrl+Alt+Delete, and click Task Manager.

Task Manager Window

The Task Manager window consists of menus at the top of the window, three tabs (Applications, Processes, and Performance) that take up the main Task Manager window, and a status bar at the bottom.

Task Manager Menus

Task Manager has several menus: File, Options, View, Windows, and Help. The options available on the View menu change depending on the Task Manager tab you have selected.

File Menu

The File menu contains these options:

New Task (Run...)   Opens the Create New Task dialog box. Here you can enter the path to a new task and run it (click OK).

Exit Task Manager   Ends Task Manager.

Options Menu

The Options menu contains these options:

Always On Top   If this option is selected, Task Manager always runs on top of other programs.

Minimize On Use   If this option is selected, Task Manager is minimized when you switch to another running program.

Hide When Minimized   If this option is selected, Task Manager is hidden when you minimize it and won't appear in the Taskbar.

Show 16-Bit Tabs   Displays 16-bit Windows tasks. Look for these tasks under the associated ntvdm.exe file. Available only with the Processes tab selected.

View Menu

The View menu contains these options:

Refresh Now   Refreshes the Task Manager screen immediately.

Update Speed   Contains a submenu where you can specify how often the Task Manager screen is refreshed automatically. Choices are High (twice per second), Normal (every two seconds), Low (every four seconds), and Paused (no automatic refresh).

Large Icons   Displays tasks as large icons. Available only with the Applications tab selected.

Small Icons   Displays tasks as small icons. Available only with the Applications tab selected.

Details   Displays tasks with details, such as the task's status. This is the default setting. Available only with the Applications tab selected.

Select Columns   Lets you select columns you want to display on the Processes tab. Available only with the Processes tab selected.

CPU History   Lets you specify whether each CPU has its own graph. Available only with the Performance tab selected.

Show Kernel Times   Displays kernel time in the CPU Usage and CPU Usage History graphs. Available only with the Performance tab selected.

Windows Menu

The Windows menu lets you specify how to display the windows of running tasks on the Desktop. It is available only with the Applications tab selected. You can choose from Tile Horizontally or Vertically, Minimize, Maximize, Cascade, or Bring To Front. Bring To Front brings the window to the front but does not switch to it.

Help Menu

The Help menu lets you access Task Manager–specific help topics and information about Task Manager, such as the version number and licensing information.

Task Manager Tabs

Task Manager contains the Application, Processes, and Performance tabs, which you can use to view and control tasks and processes as well as view performance information.

Applications   Displays all applications (tasks) that are currently running. You can terminate a task (by selecting it and clicking End Task), you can switch to a task (by selecting it and clicking Switch To), and you can create a new task (by clicking New Task).

Processes   Displays the processes currently running on the Windows 2000 computer. Information includes the process name, process identifier (PID), CPU usage, CPU time, memory usage, and many other items. Specify columns you want to display by choosing View ≻ Columns. To terminate a process, select it in the list, and click End Process.

You can also assign priorities to processes. Right-click a process, select Set Priority, and select a priority from the list. Choices include Realtime, High, AboveNormal, Normal, BelowNormal, and Low.

Performance   Displays system performance information. CPU usage, CPU usage history, memory usage, and memory usage history are displayed as graphs. Total handles, threads, and processes; total, available, and system cache memory; and other system information about commit charge and kernel memory are displayed as text.

Status Bar

The status bar at the bottom of the Task Manager window displays information about the number of processes that are currently running, the current CPU usage, and the current memory usage.

TELEPHONY

Microsoft Management Console (MMC) snap-in installed on Windows 2000 Server computers that lets you work with telephony service providers on your computer. Telephony services enable the integration of computer application programs and telephony devices. This enables you to use Windows programs to perform such functions as connecting to telephones, sending faxes, and joining a conference. Telephony services are installed but not enabled by default.

During the performance of these functions, three software components are involved: application programs, the Telephony Application Programming Interface (TAPI), and TAPI service providers. Application programs use TAPI functionality to allow you to make phone calls and send and receive faxes, for example. Examples of application programs include Phone Dialer, NetMeeting, and HyperTerminal. TAPI enables application programs to perform telephony functions. An example of a telephony function is dialing. TAPI service providers translate commands for telephony protocols or devices. This means that if a program wants to perform a function, such as dialing a phone number, TAPI identifies the appropriate TAPI service provider that provides support for the device, and the service provider in turn sends the correct commands to the device.

Several TAPI service providers are installed on Windows 2000. Examples include the TAPI Kernel-Mode Service Provider and the Unimodem 5 Service Provider.

TELNET CLIENT

Command-line utility that enables you to connect to a remote Telnet server using the Telnet protocol (part of TCP/IP). Once connected, you can perform character-based functions at the remote computer as if you were directly at the computer.

To start the Telnet Client, perform these steps:

1. Choose Start ➢ Programs ➢ Accessories ➢ Command Prompt.

2. At the command prompt, enter **telnet *hostname***. (The host name can be either the remote computer's TCP/IP address or host name). The client connects, and you'll see a message saying, "Welcome to Microsoft Telnet Server."

To see a list of many of the commands you can execute at the remote command prompt, type **help** at the command prompt.

To quit the Telnet Client, perform these steps:

1. At the command prompt, enter **telnet**.

2. At the Microsoft Telnet> prompt, enter **quit**.

TELNET SERVER ADMINISTRATION

Lets you administer the Telnet Server service. For example, you use Telnet Server Administration to start and stop the Telnet Server service. The Telnet Server service enables remote computers to connect to the Telnet server via the Telnet protocol (part of TCP/IP). The version of Telnet Server included with Windows 2000 supports two simultaneous connections.

To access Telnet Server Administration, choose Start ➢ Settings ➢ Control Panel, double-click Administrative Tools, and double-click Telnet Server Administration. This opens the Telnet Server Administration command-prompt dialog box.

At the prompt, type the number that corresponds to the function you want to perform, such as 4 to start the Telnet Server service, or 1 to list current users. Available functions include:

0) Quit This Application

1) List The Current Users

2) Terminate A User Session

3) Display/Change Registry Settings

4) Start The Service

5) Stop The Service

You must use function 4 to start the Telnet Server service before Telnet clients can connect to the Telnet Server. Function 3 enables you display/change Registry settings that relate to Telnet Server.

UPDATE WIZARD UNINSTALL

Lets you uninstall patches, drivers, and system files that were installed using Windows Update, and restore the patch, drive, or system file to the previously installed version. You can also perform this function online on the Windows Update Web site; however, this utility is useful if you don't have a connection to the Internet when you need to restore older versions of installed files.

To access the Update Wizard Uninstall tool, choose Start ➤ Settings ➤ Control Panel, double-click Administrative Tools, double-click Computer Management, expand System Tools, and select System Information. Then choose Tools ➤ Windows ➤ Update Wizard Uninstall.

If no updates are installed, you'll receive a message informing you that no packages are available for uninstall, and the process terminates. If updates are installed, follow the Wizard's prompts to uninstall options.

USER PROFILES

User profiles are a combination of folders and data that specify the settings for a user's Desktop environment when the user logs on to the Windows 2000 computer. This way, the user's Windows 2000 environment always looks the same when he or she logs on to the computer. Settings include items such as display settings (for example, wallpapers and color schemes), printer connections, mouse settings, Start menu items, network connections, and Desktop shortcuts. Three types of user profiles exist: local, roaming, and mandatory (a type of roaming user profile).

Local User Profiles

A local user profile, created the first time a user logs on to a Windows 2000 computer, is stored on the local computer. The local user profile is available only on the computer on which it resides. Thus, any changes you make to the user profile

Part VI

are available only on that computer. If you go to another computer and want to have your Desktop environment look the same as on your original computer, you'll have to specify all of the settings for your local user profile on that computer.

By default, the local user profile directory (user_name) and its subdirectories are created off the C:\Documents and Settings directory. The full path is thus C:\Documents and Settings\user_name.

Roaming User Profiles

A roaming user profile is stored on a server. The first time you log on to the domain after the ability to use a roaming user profile has been set up for you, the local user profile is uploaded to the server. After that, the roaming user profile is downloaded from the server to any Windows 2000 computer in the domain onto which you log on. Thus, you don't have to specify your settings again and again as you move from computer to computer. If you make changes to the Desktop environment, when you log off, those changes are copied to the roaming user profile stored on the server. The complete roaming profile is copied to a computer only once; after that, only changes made to the profile are downloaded.

Creating Roaming User Profiles

To create a roaming user profile for a user, perform the following steps:

1. On a Windows 2000 server, create a shared folder with the shared folder permission Full Control assigned to the Everyone group (the default). This folder will hold roaming user profiles. The path's format should be \\server_name\ shared_folder_name.

2. Choose Start ➤ Programs ➤ Administrative Tools ➤ Active Directory Users And Computers, expand the domain, select Users, double-click the user, and select the Profile tab.

3. In the Profile path text box, enter the path to the roaming user profile using the \\server-name\shared_folder_name\user_name format. Click OK.

4. Log on to the domain as the user for whom you're creating the roaming profile to create the user's roaming user profile directory on the server and copy the local user profile to the server.

Mandatory User Profiles

A mandatory user profile is a roaming user profile whose settings cannot be changed by the user. Only network administrators have the ability to change mandatory user profiles. This way, network administrators can control the settings and options available for individuals, a group of users, or all users, creating a standardized Desktop environment, which helps ease administration.

Changing a Roaming User Profile to a Mandatory User Profile

To change a roaming user profile to a mandatory user profile, you must rename the hidden file `ntuser.dat` to `ntuser.man`. You'll find this file in the `\\..\user_name` directory for either local or roaming user profiles.

User Profiles Tab

To view, copy, or change the type of user profiles stored on the local computer, choose Start ➢ Settings ➢ Control Panel, double-click System, and select the User Profiles tab.

You can see all currently configured user profiles stored on the local computer in the list under Profiles stored on this computer. Three options are available:

Delete   To delete a user profile, select the profile, and click Delete.

Change Type   To change the user profile type from local to roaming and vice versa, select a profile, and click Change Type. This opens the Change Type dialog box. A roaming user profile must exist for the user in order for you to change the profile type (otherwise, the Roaming Profile option is grayed out). Select Roaming Profile to change the user profile from local to roaming.

Copy To   Assume you want to copy user A's profile to user B. Select user A's profile in the list of profiles stored on this computer, and click Copy To. Enter the path to user B's roaming profile directory in the Copy Profile To text box (`\\server_name\shared_profile_directory _name\user_name`). Next, click Change under Permitted To Use, click Show Users, select user B, and then click OK.

USERS AND PASSWORDS

Lets you manage local user accounts and passwords on Windows 2000 Professional computers. If the computer is part of a domain, Users And Passwords also lets you add domain users to a group on this computer to enable them to access this computer using their domain user account password. In addition, Users And Passwords lets you configure boot-up security and certificates, and access Local Users And Groups for more advanced user account management functions.

To access Users And Passwords, choose Start ➢ Settings ➢ Control Panel, and double-click Users And Passwords.

Users And Passwords contains two tabs: Users and Advanced.

Part vi

Users Tab

The Users tab lists user accounts that have access to this computer. These accounts can be local or network user accounts. The Users tab has the following buttons:

Add   If the computer is not part of a domain, lets you create a new user. If the computer is part of a domain, lets you add a domain user account to the list of users that can use the local computer.

Remove   Removes the selected user from the computer's user list. If you remove a local user in this fashion, the local user account is deleted. If you remove a domain user, the user is only removed from the list of users who can use the local computer; the user's domain user account is not affected.

Properties   For local users, displays the selected user's properties on two tabs: General and Group Membership. You can use these tabs to both view and change the name, full name, description, and group membership properties. For domain users, displays and lets you change only group membership information.

Set Password   Lets you change the password for the selected local user. You cannot change passwords for domain users.

Advanced Tab

The Advanced tab lets you perform or access additional user management functions.

The Certificate Management area of the tab has two buttons:

New Certificate   Lets you obtain a new certificate using the Certificate Manager Import Wizard.

Certificates   Lets you view, import, export, and remove certificates. For more information about certificates, see the Content Tab subheading under the main heading Internet Options.

The Advanced User Management area of the Advanced tab contains one button:

Advanced   Opens Local Users And Groups (Microsoft Management Console), where you can create users and groups, change users' group membership, and perform other advanced user account management functions.

In the Secure Boot Settings area of the Advanced tab, you can specify whether users must press Ctrl+Alt+Delete to be able to access the Windows 2000 logon screen. Microsoft recommends requiring users to press Ctrl+Alt+Delete to preserve password security and prevent damage that might occur from Trojan horse programs.

Adding a User

If your computer is not part of a domain, you can use Users And Passwords to create a new user on the local machine.

To do so, follow these steps:

1. On the Users tab of Users And Passwords, click the Add button.

2. In the Add New User dialog box, enter the user's name in the User Name text box. This name should be unique. Common naming conventions include [First_Letter_of_ First_Name][Lastname] and [First_Name][First_Letter_of_ Last_Name].

3. You can optionally enter the user's full name in the Full Name text box, and a description in the Description text box; however, the latter two are not required.

4. Click Next, enter a password in the Password text box, and then enter the password again in the Confirm Password text box. Click Next to continue.

5. Select one of the three user type options:

   Standard User   This is the default selection. This type of user is automatically added to the Power Users group. The user can install applications and change computer settings, but cannot read other users' files.

   Restricted User   This type of user is automatically added to the Users group. The user can use the computer and save files, but cannot install applications or change the computer's settings.

   Other   Lets you choose from several different groups to which to add the user. Groups include Administrators, Backup Operators, Guests, Power Users, Replicator, and Users. Each group has specific permissions and rights assigned. For more information on these groups, consult the Windows 2000 Help system.

6. Click Finish. The user is now added to the list of users for the computer.

If your computer is part of a domain, you can give domain users the ability to access the local computer by adding them to the list of users for this computer and adding them to a local group. They will use their domain user account password to access the computer.

Part vi

To add a domain user to the local computer's user list, follow these steps:

1. On the Users tab of Users And Passwords, click Add to open the Add New User Wizard.

2. Enter the username of a user in the domain and enter the domain, or use the Browse button to browse to a user in the domain or entire directory. Click Next when you've entered the information.

3. Select the level of access you want to give the user. Standard User adds the user to the Power Users group, Restricted User adds the user to the Users group, and Other lets you specify the group to which you want to add the user, such as Administrators. Click Finish.

After you add a domain user, the user is added to the list of users for this computer. The icon is a head with a globe, indicating that the user is a domain user, rather than a local user. You'll also see that the Set Password button is not available because you can't change passwords for domain users through Users And Passwords.

UTILITY MANAGER

Program used to manage the Windows 2000 Magnifier, Narrator, and On-Screen Keyboard Accessibility options. Choose Start ➤ Programs ➤ Accessories ➤ Accessibility ➤ Utility Manager to start the Utility Manager.

In the Utility Manager list box, all of the Accessibility utilities currently installed in Utility Manager are listed. Narrator and Magnifier are installed automatically. The On-Screen Keyboard can be added by a user with administrative privileges through the On-Screen Keyboard's File menu. In the list box, you can see the utilities' name and status. The status column entry will be Running, Not Running, or Not Responding. The Narrator utility is set up by default to run automatically when you open Utility Manager. If you wish, you can sort the list by name or status by clicking the respective column header.

To start a utility, select it in the list, and click Start. To stop a utility, select it in the list, and click Stop. To start a utility automatically when Windows starts or when Utility Manager starts, select the utility, and place a check mark in the appropriate check box. To run Accessibility options in secure mode, check the option Run In Secure Mode. This setting applies to all utilities added to the Utility Manager.

VOLUME CONTROL

Lets you control the balance of sound coming from your speakers, as well as control the volume and bass and treble settings of sounds you record and play back through any audio device or multimedia application.

Choose Start ➢ Programs ➢ Accessories ➢ Entertainment ➢ Volume Control to open the Volume Control dialog box.

In the Volume Control dialog box, a separate volume control slider, balance slider, and Mute check box are available for each available audio device, and you can change settings independently.

Use the sliders under Volume Control to affect all devices, and click the Mute All check box to mute all devices.

WEB SHARING

Tab that lets you share folders on a Web site in the network. Requires that Internet Information Services (IIS) has been installed and that a Web site has been created. A default Web Site is created automatically when IIS is installed. To access Web Sharing, right-click a folder or disk in Windows Explorer on a Windows 2000 Server computer, choose Properties, and select the Web Sharing tab. Here you can select the appropriate Web site from the Share On drop-down list and indicate whether you want to share the folder or disk.

To share the folder or disk, click Share This Folder, which opens the Edit Alias dialog box. Here you need to specify the name for the alias to be used on the Web site, and configure access permissions—Read, Write, Script Source Access, and Directory Browsing— and application permissions—None, Scripts, and Execute (Includes Scripts). Click OK to share the folder or disk.

After you create the alias, it appears in the Aliases list box on the Web Sharing tab. To create an additional alias for the folder or disk, click Add and complete the information in the Edit Alias dialog box.

To edit an alias, select it in the list, and click Edit Properties; to remove an alias, select it in the list, and click Remove.

WHAT'S THIS

Lets you access context-sensitive help. What's This is usually available in dialog boxes. To access What's This, right-click an item in a dialog box. If available, the What's This selection pops up. Click it to read help information about the item.

In some dialog boxes, you can also access the What's This information by selecting the question mark icon in the top-right corner of the dialog box and then placing the cursor (which now has a question mark attached to it) over an item and clicking it.

WINDOWS COMPONENTS

By default, many Windows components are installed on Windows 2000 Professional and Server computers. However, many other components are also available to suit your environment's specific needs. Also, the components available and installed by default are not identical for Windows 2000 Server and Professional.

Examples of Windows components installed by default include WordPad, Calculator, HyperTerminal, Phone Dialer, Media Player, Volume Control, Indexing Service, Internet Information Services (IIS), DNS, DHCP, Microsoft Script Debugger, and so on. Additional Windows components that are available include Certificate Services, Message Queuing Services, Remote Storage, Terminal Services, QoS Admission Control Services, WINS, and so on.

To add Windows components not installed by default, use Add/Remove Programs (found in Control Panel). For information about each of the available components, use the Windows 2000 Help system.

WINDOWS MEDIA PLAYER

Lets you play audio, video, and mixed-media files in a variety of different formats. For example, you can view video clips of a movie, listen to radio broadcasts (over the Internet), or enjoy a music video. Supports both streaming and non-streaming media files. When you play a streaming media file, playback begins before the entire file is downloaded. Streaming files are received and played using a continuous process of downloading portions of the file, storing those portions in memory, and then playing them back while more of the file is downloaded and stored in memory. This allows users to receive live media content, such as newscasts or live concerts.

Supported media file formats include audio files, such as Wave (.wav) and Sound (.snd) files, MIDI files (.mid, .midi, and .rmi), MP3 files (.mp3 and .m3u), Microsoft streaming media files (.asf and .asx), MPEG files (such as .m1v, .mp2, and .mpa), Quick Time files (.mov and .qt), and Video files (.avi).

To access Windows Media Player, choose Start ➤ Programs ➤ Accessories ➤ Entertainment ➤ Windows Media Player.

WINDOWS REPORT TOOL

Lets you create a problem report, including a description of the problem and a snapshot of system settings and system and program files. When troubleshooting a problem, you can give this information to technical support personnel.

To access the Windows Report Tool, choose Start ➤ Settings ➤ Control Panel, double-click Administrative Tools, double-click Computer Management, expand System Tools, and select System Information. Then choose Tools ➤ Windows ➤ Windows Report Tool.

Creating and Submitting a Report

To create and submit a Windows report, follow these steps:

1. Start Computer Management from Control Panel, select System Information, and start the Windows Report Tool by choosing Tools ➤ Windows ➤ Windows Report Tool.

2. Choose Options ➤ User Information and enter information about yourself. Select the option Include User Information In Submitted Report if you want this information included in the report. Make any necessary choices regarding your network proxy settings. Click OK.

3. In the Problem Description, Expected Results, and Steps To Reproduce The Problem fields respectively, enter descriptive information about the problem, what happens when the problem occurs, and steps for reproducing the problem.

4. If you want to include or exclude specific files from the report, click the Change System File Selections link, and make your selections in the list box. To add files, click Add. To select all files, click Select All. When you've finished, click OK.

5. Click Next and enter a filename for the report. Then click Save to save the report to a file that you can later send to a support technician via e-mail. The Report Tool collects system information and creates the report information file. This process can take some time.

6. When the file is created, you're returned to the Windows Report Tool, where you can create a new report or close the tool. To close the tool, click Cancel, or choose File ➤ Exit.

WINDOWS UPDATE

Connects you to Microsoft's Windows Update home page. Here you can download Windows product updates and obtain additional support information on

Part vi

how to use the Windows Update site. Click the appropriate links to find the information you're looking for, such as critical updates, recommended updates, top picks, device drivers, additional Windows features, and help on using the site.

WMI CONTROL

Microsoft Management Console (MMC) console snap-in that lets you manage settings and configuration for Windows Management Instrumentation (WMI), which is designed to let you manage your enterprise over the Internet or an intranet.

To access WMI Control, choose Start ➤ Settings ➤ Control Panel, double-click Administrative Tools, and double-click Computer Management. You'll find the WMI Control snap-in under Services And Applications.

WMI CONTROL PROPERTIES

To work with WMI Control properties, select WMI Control in the console tree and choose Action ➤ Properties. This opens the WMI Control Properties dialog box, which contains five tabs:

General   Lets you view general information about the computer to which you are currently connected (such as processor, operating system, operating system version, WMI version, and WMI location). Also lets you connect to the WMI Control service as a different user by clicking Change, deselecting Log On As Current User, specifying a username and password of a different user, and clicking OK.

Logging   Lets you specify the logging level and size and location of log files.

Backup/Restore   Lets you back up the WMI repository to a file, if a change to the repository has occurred since the last time a backup was performed. Also lets you restore from a backup and specify the automatic backup interval. To manually back up or restore the WMI repository, click the Back Up Now or Restore Now buttons, respectively, and follow the prompts.

Security   Lets you configure permissions for any name space (directory) in the WMI directory structure.

Advanced   Lets you specify advanced settings, such as the name space WMI Scripting should use by default.

WORDPAD

Basic word-processing program included with Windows 2000. Lets you create, edit, and view files using several different formats, including Word for Windows 6.0, Rich Text Format (RTF), text documents (ASCII), and Unicode text documents.

Choose Start ➢ Programs ➢ Accessories ➢ WordPad to open WordPad. The WordPad window consists of a menu bar, toolbar, Format bar, ruler, text area, and status bar.

Part vi

INDEX

Note to Reader: In this index, **boldfaced** page numbers refer to primary discussions of the topic; *italics* page numbers refer to figures.

SYMBOLS & NUMBERS

* (asterisk) wildcard character, 71

? (question mark) wildcard character, 71

A

Access Control List (ACL), 251
   and access to remote Registry, 572
   for policy objects, 792
accessibility, **86–92**, 826
   in Internet Explorer, 420
Accessibility Options dialog box, **87–88**, *88*, 826
Accessibility Wizard, **89–90**, *90*, 826
Accessories (Windows 2000), 39, 189, **826**
   Accessibility, 88–92
      Magnifier, 879–880
   Address Book, **201–205**, *202*, 831
      adding contact, 203
      adding group, 203–204
      importing and exporting, 206
      locating people, 204
      map creation, 205, *205*
      opening, **202**
      printing, 204
   Calculator, **206–209**, *207*, 832
      scientific calculator, 208–209
      standard calculator, 208

CD Player, **190–192**, *191*, 832
   volume adjustment, **193–194**
Command Prompt, 129
Communications
   NetMeeting, 179
   Phone Dialer, 363
Entertainment, 859
   Volume Control, 945
Fax, **225–228**, 862
games, **198–201**, 865
   FreeCell, 199, *200*
   Minesweeper, 200, *200*
   Pinball, 201, *201*
   Solitaire, 199, *199*
Imaging, **220–225**, *221*, 871
   Annotation toolbar, 224
   Imaging toolbar, 223
   Standard toolbar, 221–222
Notepad, **210–213**, *211*, 905
Paint, *217*, **217–220**, 906
   tools, 218–219
Sound Recorder, *194*, **194–195**, 923
Synchronize, 931–932
System Tools ➣ Scheduled Tasks, 136
Volume Control dialog box, *193*, **193–194**, 945
Windows Explorer, 60

Windows Media Player, **195–198**, *196*, 946

WordPad, **213–217**, *214*, 949

  document creation, **216**

  Format bar, 215

  sending document as e-mail attachment, **216–217**

  toolbar buttons, 214

account lockout, group policies for, 810–811

Account Operators group, 766, 768

accounts. *See also* user accounts

  Administrator, 32, 729, **735–736**

  group, **732**

  Guest, 729, **735–736**

acknowledgment packet in DHCP client configuration, 283

ACL (Access Control List), 251

  and access to remote Registry, 572

  for policy objects, 792

Active Desktop, 12, 36, 827

  enabling Web content, 99

  set up, **85–86**

Active Directory Domains And Trusts, 683, 828–829

Active Directory Installation Wizard, *333*, **333–338**, *335*

  items created, **336–337**

Active Directory Services, 231, 827–828

  authorizing Remote Installation Services in, **652–653**

  backups, 464

  database structure, 326

  Directory Service module, **254–256**

  and DNS, *298*, 298–299

enterprise management, **234–245**

  industry standard, **236**

  user acceptance, **238–245**

  vendor acceptance, **237–238**

Exchange and, 741

goals, **234–235**

hierarchical structure, *248*

  forests, 322, *322*

  single-tree environment, *321*, 321–322

installing, **329–338**

  preparing for, **331–332**

  verification, **337–338**

integrating DNS with, **288–289**

internal architecture, **256**, *256*

partitioning database, **299–301**

for Remote Installation Services, 651

security subsystem, **252–253**

server types, **323–324**

servers in, 272

single master functions, **325–327**

single namespace, **245–250**

sites and services, 829–830

in Windows 2000 Server architecture, **250–256**, *251*

Active Directory Services Interface (ADSI), 752

Active Directory Sites And Services, 684

Active Directory Users And Computers, 684, 728, **731–752**, 829

  console, *734*

  to create machine accounts, 685

  group creation, 752–754, *753*

  opening, *733*

selecting multiple accounts, 750, *751*

user and group-related functions, **733–735**

Add A Group Policy Object Link dialog box, 788–789, *789*

ADD function (Reg.exe), **561–562**

Add Printer Wizard, 143–144, *144*

for network printer, 146

Add Profile Association dialog box, 160

Add/Remove Hardware Wizard, *681*, 830, 928

for virtual adapter, 680

Add/Remove Programs applet, 130, *131*, 830–831

for installing DHCP services, 270, *270*

policies to disable or remove, 808

Add/Remove Snap-in dialog box, 706, *707*

Address Book, **201–205**, *202*, 831

adding contact, 203

adding group, 203–204

automatic additions to, 379

importing and exporting, 206

locating people, 204

map creation, 205, *205*

opening, **202**

printing, 204

Address Resolution Display and Control (ARP), **427**

Address Resolution Protocol (ARP), 262

ADM files, 806

administration model, **316–318**, *317*

Administrative templates, **806–807**

Administrative tools, 831. *See also* Microsoft Management Console

filenames, 703–705

administrative users, and Active Directory Services, **240–245**

Administrator account, 32, 729, **735–736**

Administrators account, 729–730

Administrators group, 765–766, 767

ADSI (Active Directory Services Interface), 752

Advanced Attributes dialog box, 113–114, *114*

Advanced Power Management (APM), 98

Agents layer, in Directory Service module, 254

alerts, 908–910

alias for Registry components, 444–445

alt newsgroup, 393

Always on Top option for Taskbar, 933

anonymous FTP archives, 427, 428

Anonymous Logon group, 770

answer files for unattended install, 620, **625–628**

building, **629–631**

name for, 636

APM (Advanced Power Management), 98

AppEvent.Evt file, 459

AppEvents subkey (Registry), 513

Apple QuickTime, 198

applets, 42

Application Response, 930

applications. *See also* Accessories (Windows 2000)

adding and removing, **130–133**

deployment group policy, 866

old, on Windows 2000, **122–123**

policies to restrict, 808, *809*

printing documents from, **149–151**

remote execution, 432

running

automatically when starting Windows 2000, **126**

from command prompt, **129**

from documents, **125–126**

from Explorer, **123**, *124*

minimized, **127–128**

with Run command, **45–46**, **128**

scheduling tasks, **135–138**

from Search, **124–125**, *125*

from Start menu, **122**

setting for opening document, 40–41

viewing status of running, **935–937**

and Windows 2000 Professional, 14

archive file attribute, 111

Arcron Zeit, clock, 615

area codes

dialing rules and, 356

for TAPI locations, 357, 358–359

ARP (Address Resolution Display and Control), **427**

ARP (Address Resolution Protocol), 262

asterisk (*) wildcard character, 71

AT commands, 351

for modem initialization, 353

attachment to e-mail

creating, **388–389**

saving in Outlook Express, 378–379

WordPad document as, **216–217**

attrib command (Recovery Console), 485

attributes of files, 111

audio CDs, **190–192**, 832

auditing

DHCP, **278–280**

Registry, 552–554

Authenticated Users group, 770

Author mode for consoles, 699, 724

Auto Hide for Taskbar, 933

Auto Refresh in RegEdt32, 556

Autoexec.nt file, 459, 470

automation. *See also* unattended installs

SYSDIFF utility for, **639–641**

time savings, 671

B

background

for Desktop, 95, **96**

for e-mail messages, 385

background color, for e-mail messages, **386**

background refresh, 821

for group policies, 816

backup domain controller, 330

BACKUP function (Reg.exe), **562–563**

Backup Operators account, 729–730

Backup Operators group, 766, 767

backups, **464–472**, 831–832

   to create Emergency Repair Disk, 465

   before installing Windows 2000 Professional, **20–21**

   of Registry, **457–461**, 523

      for NTFS, **467**

      RegEdit for, **470–472**

      restoring from, **473–479**

      to tape or other media, **464–465**

   using copy or xcopy, **465–469**

bad logon attempts, locked account from, 744

basic disks, 849–850

   upgrading to dynamic disk, 851

batch command (Recovery Console), 485

Batch group, 770

binary files, FTP to download, 428

BIOS, preparing for Windows 2000 install, **594–595**

Block Inheritance, in group policy objects, **782**, 786

bookmarks in Internet Explorer, 417

boot disks, for Windows 2000 Setup, 605

boot files, backups, 464

Boot Manager, 467, 477, 482

   HKEY_LOCAL_MACHINE hive rebuilt by, 501

boot menu, customizing, **468**

boot sector, 448

   inspection, 477

boot-up, Registry use at, 447–450

bootable CD-ROM drive, 593

bootable disk, creating, 466

boot.ini file, 448–449, 468

   modifying, 641–642

   Recovery Console and, 482

BootP protocol, 269

broadcast packets, 283

Browse, 832

built-in groups

   domain local, **764–769**

   global, 769–770

   rights, 771

Builtin container, 735

business unit model, **315**, *316*

C

Calculator, **206–209**, *207*, 832

   scientific calculator, 208–209

   standard calculator, 208

call waiting, disabling, 358

calling card, for telephone calls, **360–363**

Camelot, Digiphone, 437

cameras, configuring, **917–918**

canceling printing, 153

canonical name, for organizational units, 320

Caps Lock key

   and password errors, 37

   sound when pressed, 87

CD

   add-on components, 31

   bootable, 466

   starting installation from, 23

cd command (FTP), 428

CD Player, **190–192**, *191*, 832
   volume adjustment, **193–194**
CD-ROM drive, bootable, 593
CentralProcessor subkey (Registry), 503
certificates
   digital, 423
   managing, 942
Certified for Windows 2000 logo, 123
Character Map, 833
chat, 437
Chat application in NetMeeting, 181,
   182, *183*
chdir command (Recovery Console), 485
child domains, 284
chkdsk command (Recovery Console),
   485
classes of IP addresses, **265–266**
Classes subkey (Registry), 507
clean install, vs. upgrade, 602–604
clearing Clipboard, **174**
Client Access License, 601
Client for Microsoft Networks, 678
Client Install Wizard, 661
client/server networks, user account for,
   32
Client service, 616
Client Side Extension (CSE) DLLs, 779
clients
   DNS configuration, 858
   downlevel, 746
   enabling RIS for, **657–658**
Clients subkey (Registry), 507
Clipboard, **166–171**, 834
   clearing, **174**

copying, cutting and pasting,
   167–169
for screen captures, **170–171**
ClipBook Viewer, 166, **171–174**, *172*,
   834
   copying from, **173**
   pasting item into, **172–173**
   sharing pages, **173–174**
   starting, **172**
clock
   displaying on Taskbar, 933
   setting system during Windows
      2000 install, 615
closing
   registries, 537
   windows, 835
cls command (Recovery Console), 485
clustering, DHCP and, **281–282**
cmdcons directory, 482–483
CMPMGMT.MSC, 728
Collage, 170
color
   of fonts for e-mail messages, 386
   in Internet Explorer, 419
   maximum number displayed, 100
   of screen components, 98
color-blindness, 87
color profile, 160
COM+ (Component Services), 835
   Class Registration database, back-
      ups, 464
   installing applications, 838
COM ports for modem, 350
command prompt, 835

for Internet utilities, 427

for Recovery Console, 644

for RegEdit, **534–535**

for Resource Kit utilities, 522

running applications from, **129**

comm.drv, 345

communications in Windows 2000, **343**, 835. *See also* Internet; Outlook Express

    dialing rules, **356–363**

    modem installation, **345–348**

    modem properties, **348–363**

    Network And Dial-Up Connections, 893–904

    Phone Dialer, **363–367**, *364*

    placing call, **368–369**

comp newsgroup, 393

Component Services, 837–839

Components Selection dialog box, 613–614

compound documents, 175

compression, 839

    of attached files, 389

    for modem communications, 355

    in NTFS, **113–115**

        for folders, 116

    utilities to unzip, 436

computer account, 600, **617**

Computer Configuration, 778

Computer Management console, 681, 684, **700–703**, 839–840

    Connect To Another Computer, 717

    to create share, *684*, **684–685**

    creating taskpad view, 711–712

nodes, 700, *700*

opening, 700

Services and Applications, 702–703

    DHCP (Dynamic Host Configuration Protocol), 845–846

    DNS (Domain Name System), 857

    Internet Service Manager, 702, 874–875

Services tool, **690–692**, *691*

Storage, 702

    Disk Defragmenter, 847–849

    Disk Management, 687, *688*, 849–851, 849–851

    Removable Storage, 914

System Tools, 701–702

    Device Manager, 118, 688–689, 845

    Devices applet, 688

    Event Viewer, 859–860

    Local Users and Groups, **728–731**, *729*, 878

    Performance logs and alerts, 908–910

    System Information tool, 693, *694*

concurrent use license, 601

Config.nt file, 459, 470

Configuration Management, 776

configuring resources, Active Directory Services and, 241

Confirm on Delete, in RegEdt32, 557

Connect dialog box, *413*

Connect to the Internet, 54, 840

connection, 693
    for HyperTerminal, 870–871
    to remote registries, **528–529**
console root, 700
Console subkey (Registry), 513
console tree, 700
    hiding, 721
consoles, 697. *See also* Microsoft
  Management Console
    anatomy, *699*
    vs. taskpads, 711
contacts, 757
    Address Book to track, **201–205**
Contacts pane, in Outlook Express, 375
containers
    creating, **307**
    vs. organizational units, 775
    viewing group policy objects linked
      to, 786
Content Advisor, 422–424
Control Panel, 42, *43*, 83–84, 840
    Accessibility Options, **87–88**
    Add/Remove Programs applet, 130,
      131
    changes after install, 619
    changes for Windows 2000, 673,
      674, 688, *689*
    classic Windows view, *77*
    Date/Time, **103**
    Display, **95–101**
    Folder Options, 75. *See also* Folder
      Options dialog box
    Fonts, 162
    Keyboard, **92–93**, 875
    Mouse, **93–94**

    opening, **84**
    Phone And Modem Options, 343
    Printers, 143
    Regional Options, **102**
    Scanners and Cameras, **917–918**
    Scheduled Tasks, **918–919**
    Sounds and Multimedia, **924**
    System, **925–931**
      User Profiles, 941
    Users and Passwords, 32, **941–944**
    Web view, *76*, *85*
Control Panel subkey (Registry), 513
Control sets in Registry System key,
  508–509
conversation, 396
copy command (Recovery Console), 485
COPY function (Reg.exe), **563–564**
copying
    characters, 833
    from ClipBook Viewer, **173**
    files and folders, **68–69**, 841
    floppy disks, **80–81**
    for Registry backups, **465–469**
      vs. xcopy, **469**
copying and pasting, **167–169**
cost center model, **313**, *314*
counter logs, 909
Create Folder dialog box (Outlook
  Express), *378*, 378
Create Link event, auditing, 553
Create Shared Folder Wizard, 685, 842
Create Shortcut dialog box, *55*, *69*
Create Shortcut Wizard, 934
Create Subkey event, auditing, 553

Creator Owner group, 770

Ctrl+Alt+Delete, 843

CU-SeeMe, 438

cursor blink rate, 93

Customize View dialog box, 722

CuteFTP, 436

cutting and pasting, **167–169**

D

DARPA (Department of Defense Advanced Research Projects Agency), 260

Data Encryption Standard (DES), 745

Data Sources (ODBC), 843–844

data types for Registry keys, **497–500**

data value editors, 546–547

database for audio CD information, 191

Database layer in Directory Service module, 255

date format, 102

Date/Time Properties dialog box, **103**, *103*, 844

dates

computer setting for, 103

searching for files by, 72

two-digit references, 808

DCPROMO.EXE, 333, 686

Default Domain Policy Options dialog box, 786

Default file, 459

default gateway, 267

default preferences for modem, 354

default printer, 144

default user, 445

default user profile, 516

default value in Registry keys, 494

Default.sav file, 459

DEF$$$$$.DEL file, 459

delegation, and organizational unit design, 775

Delegation Of Control Wizard, 794–795

delete command (Recovery Console), 485

Delete event, auditing, 553

DELETE function (Reg.exe), **565**

Deleted Items in Outlook Express, 374

deleting

applications, **132–133**

e-mail messages, **380–381**

encryption and, 115

files and folders, **70**, 844

group policy objects, 788

identities in Outlook Express, 393

partitions, 27, 610

printers, 145

Registry objects, 547

shortcuts from Start menu, 934

users from groups, 750

Department of Defense Advanced Research Projects Agency (DARPA), 260

dependencies of server services, 691–692

DES (Data Encryption Standard), 745

description bar, clearing from Taskpad view, 722

Description key (Registry), **502–503**

Desktop, 36, *37*, 844–845. *See also* Start menu

"administrator-friendly" mode, **694–695**

background for, 95, **96**

creating folder from, 62

file creation from, 64

icons, **50–54**

    Connect to the Internet, 54

    Internet Explorer, 54

    My Computer, **52**

    My Documents, **50–51**

    My Network Places, **53**

    Recycle Bin, **53–54**

printing documents from, **148–149**

right-clicking, 109

saving configurations, 118

shortcuts, creating, **55–56**

starting Explorer from, 60

Taskbar, **48–50**

    hiding and displaying, **49–50**

    QuickLaunch toolbar, **48–49**

for Windows 2000 Professional, *5*

for Windows 2000 Server, 7

Windows 95/98 vs. Windows 2000 Professional, 12

details pane in console, 700

device drivers, 612

Device Manager, 118, 688–689, 845, **928**

DeviceMap key (Registry), **503–504**

Devices applet, 688

DHCP (Dynamic Host Configuration Protocol), **267–283**, 619, 845–846

    Active Directory Services and, 243

    adding, 678

    auditing, **278–280**

    client configuration process, **282–283**

    and clustering, **281–282**

    installing service, **269–271**

    scope creation, **273–278**

    server authorization, **272–273**

        for RIS, **652–653**

    server configuration, **272**

    server for Remote Installation Services, 650

dial-in permissions for user account, 741–742

Dial-Up Connection

    configuring, **409**

    Group Policy over, **819–820**

dialing in to ISP, **412–414**

dialing rules, **356–363**

Dialup group, 770

Digiphone (Camelot), 437

digital certificates, 423

dir command (FTP), 428

dir command (Recovery Console), 485

directory servers, **183**

    for NetMeeting, 179

    for Phone Dialer, **365**

directory service, 732

Directory Service Administrator, 667

Directory Service module, 251

Directory System Agent (DSA) layer, in Directory Service module, 255

DirectX Diagnostic tool, 846

disable command (Recovery Console), 486

DISABLE command (Recovery Console), 644

disconnect command (FTP), 429

discover packet in DHCP client configuration, 282

Disk Administrator, 687

Disk Cleanup, 846–847

Disk Defragmenter, 13, 847–849

disk drives. *See also* partitions

    checking for errors, 834

    compression, 839

    logical, 878

    mapping network, 881–882

    for Remote Installation Services, 651

Disk Management, 687, *688*, 849–851

disk quotas, 748, 852–853

disk space, 853

    limiting user consumption, 748

    operating system requirements for, 6

    for Windows 2000 Professional, 19, 593

DISK subkey (Registry), 509

DISKPART command (Recovery Console), 486, 644

Display policies, 808

Display Properties dialog box, **95**, *96*, 854

    Appearance tab, 98, *98*

    Effects tab, 99, *100*

    Screen Saver tab, *97*, 97–98

    Settings tab, **100–102**, *101*

    Web tab, 99, *99*

distinguished names, 246, *247*, **249–250**

distributed database for DNS, 286

distributed file system, 854–855

distribution folder, **632–637**

    checking, 636–637, *637*

distribution groups, **756–757**

distribution of custom consoles, **723**

division model, **315**, *316*

DNS (Domain Name System), **284–292**, 406, 855–858

    Active Directory Services and, 243–244

    adding, 678

    domains, **285–286**, **297–299**

    installing and configuring on ADS domain controller, **289–292**

    integrating with Active Directory, **288–289**

    planning naming, **286–287**

    server for Remote Installation Services, 651

    testing, **331**

DnsEvent.Evt file, 459

documentation of server setup, 620

documents

    compound, 175

    in Notepad

        creating, **210–213**, *211*

        opening and saving, **213**

    opening from My Documents folder, *51*

    printing, **147–152**

    running applications from, **125–126**

    sending as e-mail attachment, **216–217**

    setting application to open, 40–41

    in WordPad, creating, **216**

Documents (Start menu), **40–41**, 858

   clearing, 41–42

domain accounts

   Active Directory Users And
     Computers to manage, **731–752**

   creating, 681–682

Domain Admins global group, 761–762,
   769

domain-based distributed file system,
   854–855

domain controllers, 330

   vs. ADS server, 332

   and DHCP, 272

   installation decisions and, 590

   promoting or demoting, **686**

Domain Controllers organization unit,
   735

Domain Guests group, 763, 769

domain local groups, 755, 758

Domain Name System (DNS). *See* DNS
   (Domain Name System)

domain naming master, 326

domain root, 856

Domain Security Policy tool, 682, *683*

domain user accounts, 32

   adding to local computer user list,
     944

Domain Users group, 762, 769

DomainAdmin account, password for,
   627–628

domains

   in Active Directory Service,
     828–829

   as administrative boundaries,
     304–308

benefits, 232

creating machine account in,
   685–687

DNS, 284, **285–286**

DNS and NT, **297–299**

membership, 599–600

name changes, **675–676**

Organizational Unit (OU) model,
   308–327

reasons for new, **307–308**

registering with Internet Society,
   286

trusts between, **301–304**

what it is, **296–304**

.dos file extension, 428

dot notation, 405

dotted decimal, 263

DoubleSpace, and Windows 2000
   Professional upgrade, 24

downlevel clients, 746

downloading files, FTP (File Transfer
   Protocol) for, 427–429

Dr. Watson, 859

Drafts in Outlook Express, 374

drag and drop, 858

   to copy files and folders, 841

   to move files and folders, 890

   to print documents, *148*, **148–149**

drawing. *See* Paint

drive copier programs, 646

Drive Image Pro (PowerQuest), 647

drives, indexing, 871–872

DriveSpace, and Windows 2000
   Professional upgrade, 24

DSA (Directory System Agent) layer, in Directory Service module, 255

DSA.MSC, 728

dual-boot configuration
file system for, **30–31**
and installation repair, 478
partitions for, 27
setup, **28–30**
testing, 619

dynamic disks, 850
upgrading basic disks to, 851

Dynamic Host Configuration Protocol (DHCP), 619. *See* DHCP (Dynamic Host Configuration Protocol)

dynamic updates, DNS and, 288, **291–292**

E

e-mail. *See also* Outlook Express
attachments
creating, **388–389**
saving in Outlook Express, 378–379
WordPad document as, **216–217**
sending to group members, 756
WordPad document as attachment, **216–217**

ECC (Error Correcting Code) memory, 592–593

Edit menu, ➢ Paste Special, 176, 177

Edit menu (RegEdit), 525

editing
embedded objects, 176
linked objects, 178

ejecting audio CDs, 192

embedding objects, **175–176**

Emergency Repair Disk (ERD), 457, **558–560**
contents, **470**
creating, 465, **559–560**
before dual-boot setup, 28
vs. repair directory, 489
restoring Registry from, **476–479**

.EML file extension, 377

emptying Recycle Bin, 54

ENABLE command (Recovery Console), 486, 644

encryption in NTFS, **113–115**

end users, and Active Directory Services, **238–240**

Enterprise Admins group, 761–762

enterprise management, **236–245**
industry standard, **236**
user acceptance, **238–245**
vendor acceptance, **237–238**

Entertainment, 859

Enumerate Subkeys event, auditing, 553

Environment subkey (Registry), 513

environment variables, 119, **458**, **931**
Registry keys for, 498
for search path, 704
System applet to set, 689, *690*

ERD (Emergency Repair Disk). *See* Emergency Repair Disk (ERD)

error-correction scheme, for modem, 354

errors, checking drives for, 834

ESE (Extensible Storage Engine), 254, 255–256

EUDC subkey (Registry), 513

Event logs, 701

Event Viewer, 859–860

Everyone group, 736, 767

Exchange, planned integration with Active Directory, 741, 756

exit command (Recovery Console), 486

expand command (Recovery Console), 486

expiration of user account, 744

Explorer, 47, *47*, **60–62**, *61*, 861–862

    to create files, 64

    to create shortcut, 842

    creating folder in, 63

    to delete files, 70

    Make Available Offline, 880–881

    to open files, 62

    resolution of shortcuts, 807

    right-clicking objects to open, 110

    running applications from, **123**, *124*

    saving Outlook Express messages in folders, 377

    viewing file extensions in, 66

Export Registry File dialog box, *472*, *526*

exporting

    Address Book, **206**

    Registry hives and keys, **526–528**

Extensible Storage Engine (ESE), 254, 255–256

extensions for snap-ins, 698, 708

external modem, installing, 346

F

FAT16 file system, 11, **26**

FAT32 file system, 11, **26**, 464

    for dual-boot configuration, 29, **30–31**

    partition for, 597

    Registry backup for, **466**

Favorites

    in Help, 13, 45

    in Internet Explorer, 417

Favorites menu (RegEdit), 525

Fax, **225–228**, 862

Fax Service Management dialog box, *227*, 227

faxes, **225–228**

    receiving, **227–228**

    sending, **226**

    wizard to send, **919**

File and Printer Sharing for Microsoft Networks, 678

file extensions, 66

File Manager (Windows 3.1), 10

File menu (Task Manager), 935

file Properties dialog box, **111–112**, *112*

    on NTFS file system, *113*

File Rep.evt file, 460

File Replication Service (FRS), 777

File Signature Verification Utility, 862–863

file structure, *306*, 306

file system

    choices, **25–27**

        disk partitions, **26–27**

        FAT16 file system, **26**

FAT32 file system, **26**

NTFS (New Technology File System), **25–26**

when preparing for Windows 2000 install, **596–597**

for dual-boot configuration, 29, 30

Windows 95/98 vs. Windows 2000 Professional, 11

File Transfer dialog box (NetMeeting), 186

File Transfer Protocol (FTP), **427–429**

file types, **66**

for Media Player, 198

filenames, Windows 3.1 vs. 2000 Professional, 10

files. *See also* compression; Explorer

copying and moving, **68–69**, 841

creating, **64–65**

deleting, **70**, 844

deployment group policy, 866

in distribution folder, 634–635

indexing, 871–872

location option during Windows 2000 install, 606

moving, 889–890

names for, **63**

changing, **69–70**

NetMeeting to transfer, **186**

opening, **62**

printing documents to, **151–152**

removing unnecessary, 846–847

retrieving from Recycle Bin, 54

right-clicking, 109

searching for, **70–72**

sharing, **66–67**

synchronization, **73–74**, 931–932

filtering group policies, **791–794**

FilterKeys, 87

Find command. *See also* Search (Start menu)

in RegEdit, 533

Finger, **429**

FIXBOOT command (Recovery Console), 486, 644

FIXMBR command (Recovery Console), 486, 644

FloatingPointProcessor subkey (Registry), 503

floppy disks. *See also* Emergency Repair Disk (ERD)

copying, **80–81**

formatting, **79–80**

for printer install, 144

RBFG-generated, 659, 665

for Setup boot, 22, 23

folder bars, 13

Folder Options dialog box, **74–78**, 863

File Types tab, *78*, 78

General tab, *75*, 85–86, *86*, 695

Offline Files tab, 78, *79*

View tab, 69, 77, 695

folder Properties dialog box, **115–117**

General tab, *116*

folders, 863

compression, 839

copying and moving, **68–69**, 841

copying to installation directory during install, 621

creating, **62–63**, 841–842

deleting, **70**, 844

displaying in Explorer, 61

indexing, 871–872

links, 12, 13

moving, 889–890

names for, **63**

    changing, **69–70**

opening, **62**

opening in separate windows, 76

redirection, 777, **799–802**

right-clicking, 109

searching for, **70–72**

sharing, **66–67**, 842, **922–923**

fonts, **161–163**

    changing display size, 101

    in Internet Explorer, 420

    in RegEdt32, 555–556

Fonts folder, *162*, 863–864

footers in Notepad, 212

ForeignSecurityPrincipals container, 735

FORMAT command (DOS), 466, 864

format command (Recovery Console), 486

formatting

    floppy disks, **79–80**

    partitions, 611

    text in WordPad, 215, *215*

forwarding e-mail messages, **380–381**

FQDN (fully qualified domain name), 292

fragmentation, 603

FreeCell, 199, *200*

FRS (File Replication Service), 777

FTP (File Transfer Protocol), 262, **427–429**, 864–865

FTP client, 436

FullShot99, 170

fully qualified domain name (FQDN), 292

G

Game Controllers, 865

games, **198–201**, 865

    FreeCell, 199, *200*

    Minesweeper, 200, *200*

    Pinball, *201*, 201

    Solitaire, 199, *199*

Gateway Services for NetWare, 678

geographic model, **310**, *311*

get command (FTP), 429

Ghost (Symantec), 647, 663

Global Catalog Server, 244–245, **323**, 758

    Active Directory Installation Wizard and, 336

global groups, 755, 759, 760

    vs. local groups, 764

global unique ID (GUID), 662

    for group policy objects, 798

graphics. *See also* Paint

    adding to e-mail messages, **385**

    screen captures, **170–171**, *171*, 832

group accounts, location, **732**

group policies, **776–822**, 865–870

    concepts, **778–782**

    configuration possibilities, **796–815**

    Control Panel settings, **808**

to control Windows components, **807**

creating, **785–791**

delegating administration, **794–796**

on dial-up connections, **819–820**

editor, 869

filtering, **791–794**

folder redirection, **799–802**

inheritance, 867

to manage Microsoft Management Console, **811–815**, *812*

managing, **815–822**

    Group Policy policies, **815–818**

objects and templates, 867–869

for password and account lockout, **809–811**

security settings, **803–804**

setting network location for Start Menu folder, 800–802

to specify scripts, **797–799**, *798*

System settings, **808**

types, 866

Group Policy Creator Owners group, 794

group policy objects, 778

    "all or nothing", **780**

application order, **781**

Block Inheritance, **782**, 786

deleting, 788

increasing priority, *788*

inheritance and cumulation, **781**

local policies and, **783–785**

No Override, 782, **786**

properties dialog boxes, 787

    Security tab, 791–792, *792*

refresh intervals, **782**

viewing those linked to container, 786

Group Policy Slow Link Detection, 819

    properties dialog box, *819*

Group Policy snap-in (GPEDIT.MSC), 783

    Administrative templates, **806–807**

Automatically Log Off Users When Logon Hours Expire, 743

importing security template into, 805

for remote machine policies, 785

groups

    adding members to, 668–669

adding users to, 753–754

creating, **752–754**, *753*

distribution, 756–757

Installers to create machine accounts, 666, **667–669**

maximum number of members, 760

nesting, 760–761

vs. organizational units, 775

scope, **757–761**

security, **755–756**, **761–770**

user membership in, **748–750**

Guest account, 729, **735–736**

Guests account, 729–730

Guests group, 767, 768

GUID (global unique ID), 662

    for group policy objects, 798

H

HAL (Hardware Abstraction Layer), 12, 449

hard disks. *See* disk drives

hardware

compatibility for Windows 2000 Professional, **19–20**

preparing for Windows 2000 install, **594**

Registry hive for, 495, **501–504**

requirements

Windows 2000 platform, 6

and Windows 2000 Professional installation, **19**

for Windows 2000 Server, **591–594**

robustness, 456

system information about, 118

Hardware Abstraction Layer (HAL), 12, 449

Hardware Compatibility List (HCL), 19, 593, 612

hardware profiles, 118, **928–929**

hardware vendors, and Windows 2000, 8

Hardware Wizard, 118

HCL (Hardware Compatibility List), 19, 593, 612

Hcl.txt file, 19

headers in Notepad, 212

help, 870

in command prompt, 129

Favorites in, 13

for Internet utilities, 426

for Resource Kit utilities, 522

for Task Manager, 936

HELP command (Recovery Console), 486, 645

Help (Start menu), **44–45**

hibernation, 98

hidden file attribute, 111

hiding Taskbar, **49–50**

hierarchical naming, *297*

High Color, 100

history, of Internet hyperlinks, 419

hives in Registry, 443, **444–445**, 451, 492, **493**, 494

importing and exporting, **526–528**

printing, 529–530

repairing, 478

HKEY_CLASSES_ROOT, 135, **494**

HKEY_CURRENT_CONFIG, 135, **496**, **515**

HKEY_CURRENT_USER, 135, 444, 445, **494–495**, 797

\Software\Policies, 806

HKEY_DYN_DATA, 444, 497

HKEY_LOCAL_MACHINE, 135, 449, **495–496**, 797

\Hardware, **501–504**

\DESCRIPTION, **502–503**, 576

\DeviceMap, **503–504**, 577

\ResourceMap, **504**, 577–578

\SAM, 496, **505**, 578–580

\Security, **505–506**, 580

\Software, **506–508**, 580–581

\Software\Policies, 806

\System, **508–510**, 581–582

HKEY_USERS, 135, 444, **496**, **510–514**

\.DEFAULT, 582–584

\<SID>, 584

\<SID_Classes>, 585

home folder for users, 748

home page, 416

   setting, 419

horizontal line, in Outlook Express messages, 384

host, 403

Host A Meeting dialog box (NetMeeting), 184, *184*

host address, 263

host name, 857

HTML documents. *See also* Web sites

   for Client Install Wizard, 661–662

   e-mail messages as, **383–386**

   Notepad for creating, 210

   for Taskpad views, 709

   viewing source code, 417

hybrid model, *318*, **318–319**

hyperlinks

   in e-mail messages, **386**

   in Internet Explorer, 418

HyperTerminal, 870–871

I

ICMP (Internet control Message Protocol), 261

icons

   for linked objects, 177, *178*

   for shortcuts, 56

   in Start menu, 933

icons on Desktop, **50–54**

   changing, 99, *100*

   Connect to the Internet, 54

   Internet Explorer, 54

   My Computer, **52**

   My Documents, **50–51**

   My Network Places, **53**

   Recycle Bin, **53–54**

   right-clicking, **51**

identities in Outlook Express, **391–393**

Identities subkey (Registry), 513

idle modem connection, 414

   disconnecting, 354

images. *See* graphics; Paint

Imaging, **220–225**, *221*, 871

   Annotation toolbar, 224

   Imaging toolbar, 223

   Standard toolbar, 221–222

Import Registry File dialog box, 479

importing

   Address Book, **206**

   Registry hives and keys, **526–528**

Inbox in Outlook Express, 374

Indexing Service, 31, **72**, 114, 871–872

INF files, 804

infrastructure master, 327

.ini files, 442

initialization string for modem, 353, 415

Insert Attachment dialog box, *388*

installing

   Active Directory Services, **329–338**

   applications, **131–132**

   fonts, 163

   local printers, **143–145**

   modem, **345–348**

   network printers, **145–146**

   Recovery Console, **480–481**

Remote Installation Services, **653–654**

Remote Registry, **535–536**

installing Windows 2000 Professional. *See also* Remote Installation Services

add-on components, **31**

backups before, **20–21**

file system choices, **25–27**

hardware compatibility, **19–20**

hardware requirements, **19**

network information collection, **20**

preparing for, 18

from RIS server, **658–663**

Setup, **22–25**

for dual-boot configuration, **28–30**

for new installation, **22–24**

partition changes by, 27

for upgrade, **24–25**

upgrade vs. new install, **21–22**

user account creation, **32–33**

Intellimirror, 776

Interactive group, 770

Internet addresses. *See* IP addresses

Internet Architecture Board, 260

Internet connection types, **402–407**

creating new connection, **410–411**

Dial-Up Connection configuration, **409**

manual connection setup, **411–412**

modem troubleshooting, **414–415**

as remote terminal, **406–407**

using modem, **407–415**

Internet Connection Wizard, 54, 409, *410*, 840, 872–873

for manual connection setup, 411

for new dial-up connection, 410–411

and Outlook Express, 372

Internet control Message Protocol (ICMP), 261

Internet Explorer, **415–417**, 873–874

opening, 416

options, **418–425**

Advanced tab, **425**, *426*

Connections tab, **424**, *424*

Content tab, **422–424**, *423*

General tab, **419–420**, *420*

Programs tab, **425**, *425*

Security tab, **420–422**, *421*

policies to disable features, 807

searches, 435

Internet Explorer icon (Desktop), 54

Internet Information Services Web server, 31

Internet Locator Service, 365

Internet Options dialog box, 418, 874

Internet Properties dialog box, 418

Advanced tab, **425**, *426*

Connections tab, *424*, **424**

Content tab, **422–424**, *423*

General tab, **419–420**, *420*

Programs tab, *425*, **425**

Security tab, *421*

Internet Protocol (IP), 262

Internet Protocol (TCP/IP) Properties dialog box, *269*

Internet Relay Chat (IRC), 437

Internet security zone, 421

Internet Service Manager, 874–875

Internet Service Provider (ISP), 402
   dialing in to, **412–414**
   information from, **408**
Internet Society, 260
   domain registration with, 286
Internet software, searches for,
  434–438
Internet utilities, **426–434**
   ARP (Address Resolution Display
    and Control), **427**
   Finger, **429**
   FTP (File Transfer Protocol),
    427–429
   Netstat, **431**
   Ping (Packet Internet Groper), **430**
   RCP (Remote File Copy), **431**
   REXEC (Remote Program
    Execution), **432**
   ROUTE, **433**
   RSH (Remote Shell/Script), **432**
   Telnet, **432**
   TFTP (Trivial File Transfer
    Protocol), **434**
   tracert, **433–434**, *434*
interrupts, Plug and Play vs. non-Plug
  and Play, 595
IP addresses, 263, *264*, **265–266**,
  405–406
   determining current, 182
   new version, 406
   for Remote Installation Services,
    650–651
   subnetting, **266–267**
IP Configuration dialog box, 182
IP (Internet Protocol), 262
IPCONFIG, 182, 262, 875

IPhone (VocalTec), 437, *437*
IRC (Internet Relay Chat), 437
ISP (Internet Service Provider), 402
   dialing in to, **412–414**
   information from, **408**
Items to Synchronize dialog box, *73*,
  931–932

J

JET database engine, 255

K

Kerberos protocol, 744
   group policies, 809
Kerberos.dll, 253
kernel in boot process, 449
keyboard
   accessibility options, 87
   customizing, **92–93**
   menu key, 108
   on-screen, **91**, *92*, 905
   to open Start menu, 122
   Windows logo key for shortcuts,
    56–57
Keyboard Layout subkey (Registry), 514
Keyboard Properties dialog box, 875
   Hardware tab, 92
   Speed tab, *93*, 93
KeyboardClass subkey (Registry), 503
KeyboardPort subkey (Registry), 504
keys in Registry hive, 443, 451, 494. *See
  also* HKEY~EL
   adding with RegEdt32, 544
   copying names, **532–533**

creating, 530
empty, 493
importing and exporting, **526–528**
printing, 529–530
saving, **542–543**

L

landscape printing, 151
language, 102
     in Internet Explorer, 420
     keyboard setup for different, 93
     as Setup option, 606
laptop computers, RBFG.EXE and, 660
Last Known Good boot process, 510
LDAP (Lightweight Directory Access
     Protocol), 732
left-handed mouse, 94
legacy logon scripts, 798, 799
licensing, **601–602**, 876
Lightweight Directory Access Protocol
     (LDAP), 365, 732
Line In, in Volume Control, 194
linking, 779
linking objects, 175, **177–178**
LISTSVC command (Recovery Console),
     486, 644
LOAD function (Reg.exe), **566**
Local Area Connection Properties dialog
     box, 677
local area network, for Internet connec-
     tion, *404*, 404
local groups, 755, 758, 760
     built-in domain, **764–769**
     global groups vs., 764

standard for stand-alone server,
     729–730
local intranet security zone, 421
local policies, group policy objects and,
     783–785
local printers, 142
     installing, **143–145**
Local Security Authority (LSA), 251
     components, *253*
     functions, 252–253
Local Security Policy tool, 682, 731,
     876–878
local user accounts, 32
     creating, 681
     rights, 773–774
local user profiles, **939–940**
local user rights policy, *772*
local users and groups, 878
locked account, group policies for,
     810–811
locking computer, 878
.log file extension, 460
log files
     of debugging information from
          Setup, 622
     for DHCP auditing, 279–280
     for modem, 352
     performance, 908–910
Log Off, 46, 879
logging on, 33, **36–37**, 879
     Active Directory Services and, 239
     locked account from bad attempts,
          744
logical drives, 878

logoff script, group policies to specify, **797–799**

logon command (Recovery Console), 486

LOGON command (Recovery Console), 644

logon hours, for user account, *743*

logon script, 747–748

    group policies to specify, **797–799**

loopback adapter, 680

ls command (FTP), 428

LSA (Local Security Authority), 251

    components, *253*

    functions, 252–253

Lsasrv.dll, 253

M

machine account

    creating in domain, **685–687**

    group permissions for, 667–668

    for Remote Installation Services, 666

machines, name changes, **675–676**

Macintosh AIFF Resource files, 198

Magnifier, **90**, *91*, 879–880

    Utility Manager to stop and start, 92, 944

Make Available Offline, 880–881

makeboot.exe, 605

Manage Policy Links permission, 794

Management and Monitoring Tools, 31

mandatory profile, 747, **940–941**

map command (Recovery Console), 487

Map Network Drive, 881–882

mapping to network resources, Active Directory Services and, 239

maps, including in Address Book, **205**

mass storage drivers, for unattended install distribution folder, 632

Master Boot Record (MBR), 448

math, Calculator for, **206–209**

maximizing window, 882

MBR (Master Boot Record), 448

measurement system, 102

Media Player (Windows), **195–198**, **946**

member servers, and DHCP, 272

memory, 456. *See* RAM

menu item command tasks, in Taskpad views, 718

menus, personalized, 40, 911

Message Queuing Services, 31

MFT (Master File Table), 26

microprocessor

    operating system requirements for, 6

    for Windows 2000 Professional, 19, 591

Microsoft File and Print Services, 678

Microsoft Internet Directory service, 183

Microsoft Internet Referral Service, 411

Microsoft Management Console, **696–705**, 829, 882–888. *See also* Computer Management console; Taskpad views

    Administrative tools, 831

    benefits, **697**

    Component Services, 837–839

    console creation, **705–724**, 887–888

        building simple, **705–708**, *706*

console interface customization, **720-722**

distribution, **724**

editing custom console tool, **724**

packaging for users, **723**

Taskpad views, **709-722**

consoles, 884-887

group policies to manage, **811-815**, *812*

Group Policy, 865-870

opening blank, 705, *706*

other tools, **703-705**

Performance, 906-910

Routing and Remote Access, **915-916**

Server Extensions Administrator, **920**

System Information tool, 693, *694*, **932**

Telephony, **937-938**

terminology, **697-700**

what it is, **696-697**

window, 883-884

WMI Control, **948**

Microsoft Script Debugger, 888-889

Microsoft subkey (Registry), 507

MIDI (Musical Instrument Digital Interface), 194, 198

Minesweeper, 200, *200*

minimized applications, running, **127-128**

minimizing window, 882

misc newsgroup, 393

mixed mode, for ADS server, **332**

mixed model, *318*, **318-319**

mkdir command (Recovery Console), 487

MMC.EXE, 698

modem

fax capabilities, **225-228**

installing, **345-348**

for Internet connection, **407-415**

troubleshooting, **414-415**

properties, **348-363**

Properties dialog box

Advanced tab, **352-356**, *353*

Diagnostics tab, *351*, **351-352**

General tab, *349*, **349-350**

troubleshooting, **414-415**

more command (Recovery Console), 487

MountedDevices subkey (Registry), 509

mouse pointer

appearance settings, 94, *95*

controlling with numeric keypad, 87

Mouse Properties dialog box, 93-94, 889

Buttons tab, *94*, 94

Pointers tab, 94

MouseKeys, 87

moving

e-mail between folders, 376

files and folders, **68-69**, 889-890

groups, 754, *754*

Moving Pictures Experts Group (MPEG), 198

MPEG (Moving Pictures Experts Group), 198

MS-DOS, in dual-boot configuration, 29

.MSC file extension, 697

Msvl_0.dll, 253

MultiFunctionAdapter subkey (Registry), 503

multihomed computer, 433

multimedia, Media Player (Windows) for, **195–198**, **946**

multiple master environments, 325

multitasking, Windows 3.1 vs. 2000 Professional, 10

Musical Instrument Digital Interface (MIDI), 194, 198

My Computer, 890

   properties dialog box, **117–119**

     Network Identification tab, 675, *676*

My Computer folder, *52*

My Computer icon (Desktop), **52**

My Documents, 890–891

My Documents icon (Desktop), **50–51**

My Network Places, 13, *53*, 891–892

My Network Places icon (Desktop), **53**

My Pictures Folder, 13, 50, 892

N

name resolution, **247–249**, *248*

   DNS (Domain Name System) for, **284–292**

names

   for containers, 309

   for files and folders, **63**

     changing, **69–70**

   for machines, workgroup/domain, changing, **675–676**

   for organizational units, **319–320**

   for server, **598**

   for shortcuts, 56

names context, 256

namespace, **245–250**

   for DNS, 284, 856–857

Narrator, **88–89**, *89*, 892–893

   Utility Manager to stop and start, 92, 944

native mode, for ADS server, **332**

navigation command tasks, 716

nesting

   administrator groups, 761

   groups, 760–761

     example, 763–764

Net, 893

NetBEUI (NetBIOS Extended User Interface), 599

Netlogon.dll, 253

Netlogon.dnb file, 460

Netlogon.dns file, 338, 460

NetMeeting, 166, **178–186**, *180*, 893

   Chat application, 181, **182**, *183*

   configuring, 179–180

   Directory Servers, 179, **183**

   file transfer, **186**

   hosting meeting, **184**

   making call, **181**

   sharing applications, **185**

   starting, **179–180**

   video, **184**

Netscape Navigator, 416

Netstat, **431**

network adapters, configuring and installing or removing, **680–681**

network address, 263

Network And Dial-Up Connections, 42, *268*, *412*, 412–414, *677*, **693**, 893–904

  to install protocols, **676–678**

Network applet, 674

  features previously part of, **675–681**

Network group, 770

Network Identification Wizard, 118, **926–927**

Network Neighborhood, 13. *See also* My Network Places

network printers, 142

  installing, **145–146**

Network subkey (Registry), 514

network traffic, domains to control, 308

Networking Services, 31

  dialog box, 678, *679*

networks

  adding computer, 838

  adjusting and adding/subtracting services, **678**

  development, **232–234**

  and floppy disk drives, 81

  mapping disk drives, 881–882

  and Windows 2000 Professional, **14–15**

    information collection for install, **20**

New Identity dialog box, *392*

New Mail Rule dialog box, 389, *389*

New Object Wizard, 737

New Scope Wizard, *274*, 274–276

New Task Wizard, 715, *715*

New Taskpad View Wizard, 712

New Technology File System (NTFS), 11, **25–26**

New Zone Wizard, 289, *290*

news newsgroup, 393

newsgroups, 393

  account setup, **394**

  connecting to, **395**

newsreader, Outlook Express as, **393–397**

No Override in group policy objects, 782, 786

nodes in clusters, 281

nodes in snap-ins, 698

non-Plug-and-Play devices, 594

non-transitive trusts, 303–304

Notepad, *65*, **210–213**, *211*, 905

  creating files in, 64–65, **211–212**

  for Registry editing, 479

Notify event, auditing, 553

Novell NetWare 5, hardware requirements, 6

NSLOOKUP, 262, 331, 338

NTDETECT.COM, 449

Ntdsa.dll, 253

NTDS.DIT file, 732

NTDS.Evt file, 460

NTFS (New Technology File System), 11, **25–26**, 464, 905

  compression and encryption, **113–115**

  for dual-boot configuration, **30–31**

  Registry backup for, **467**

  security, 596

  unique features, 597

NTLDR, 448

NTUSER.DAT file, 516, 540

Num Lock key, sound when pressed, 87

numbering system, 102

    for scientific calculation, 209

O

object-based model, **311–313**, *312*

objects, 827

    in compound documents, 175

    in Registry, 444

octets in IP address, 263

ODBC subkey (Registry), 507

OEM Branding screen, 633

offer packet, in DHCP client configuration, 282

OLE (Object Linking and Embedding), **174–178**

    Registry hive for, 494

On-Screen Keyboard, **91**, *92*, 905

    Utility Manager to stop and start, 944

one-way trusts, 301, *302*

OpenType fonts, 161

operation master, 325

Operations Master domain controller, 733

Options dialog box (Console), 723

Options dialog box (NetMeeting), Video tab, *185*

Options dialog box (Outlook Express), **397–398**

    General tab, *375*, *398*

    Signatures tab, *387*

Options menu (Task Manager), 935

Organizational Unit (OU) model

    aspects of planning, **319–321**

        delegating administration, **320–321**

        names, **319–320**

        ownership, **320**

    qualities of good, **309–319**

        administration model, **316–318**, *317*

        cost center model, **313**, *314*

        division or business unit model, **315**, *316*

        geographic model, **310**, *311*

        hybrid or mixed model, *318*, **318–319**

        object-based model, **311–313**, *312*

        project-based model, *314*, **314–315**

Organizational Unit (OU) object class, 304, **305–307**

    container creation, **307**

organizational units, **775**

    for accounts, 734

    Active Directory Installation Wizard and, 337

OS/2 for dual-boot configuration, 29

Outbox in Outlook Express, 374

outline fonts, 161

Outlook Express, 11, 39, **372–393**, *373*, 906

    creating and sending messages, **381–382**

        adding pictures, **385**

        attaching files, **388–389**

        background color or sound, **386**

with HTML, **383–386**

hyperlinks, **386**

signatures, **387–388**

customizing, **397–398**

folders list, **374**

identities, **391–393**

message rules, **389–391**

New Message window, *381*, 381–382

as newsreader, **393–397**

    account setup, **394**

    connecting to newsgroups, **395**

    finding newsgroups, **396**

    posting, **397**

    reading newsgroup, **396**

    subscriptions, **396**

preview pane, *374*

printing, **376**

reading and processing messages, **376–381**

    deleting messages, **380–381**

    forwarding messages, **380**

    marking messages, **376**

    moving messages, **376**

    replies, **379–380**

    saving messages, **377–379**

retrieving mail, **375–376**

stationery, **384–385**

ownership, 554–555

of organizational units, **320**

P

packaging, custom consoles for users, **723**

Packet Internet Groper (Ping), 262, **430**

Page Setup dialog box (Notepad), *212*

paged pool size, 442

paging file, 930

Paint, *217*, **217–220**, 906

    to save screen capture, 170

    tools, 218–219

paper clip icon, in Outlook Express, 378

paper trays, 159

PARALLEL PORTS subkey (Registry), 503

parent domain, 284

parity, 355, 456, 592

PartitionMagic, 27

partitions, **26–27**

    of ADS database, 299, *300*

    creating, 850

    deleting, 27, 610

    formatting, 611

    RIS and, 665

    selecting for Windows 2000 install, 606, 609–610

    when preparing for Windows 2000 install, **595–596**

password

    for Administrator account, 613, 631, 736

    changing for user, 833

    for DomainAdmin account, 627–628

    group policies for, **809–811**

for Internet connection, 413

for local machine, 682

for log-on, 36–37

for Outlook Express identity, 392

restrictions, 803

for user account, 739, 942

password protection, Windows 95/98 vs. Windows 2000 Professional, 11

Paste Special dialog box, *176*

pasting, **167–169**

into ClipBook Viewer, **172–173**

path, for Administrative tools, 704

pausing

CD Player, 192

printing, 153

PDC emulator master, 326

peer-to-peer networks, user account for, 32

per-seat licensing, 601–602

per-server licensing, 601–602

performance

group policies and, 817, 821

System Properties settings for, **930–931**

Task Manager information about, 937

Performance console, 906–910

logs and alerts, 685, 908–910

System Monitor, 906–908

permissions, 770, 910–911

for ClipBook pages, 174

for groups, 667–668

for printers, 160

for Registry keys, 541, 549–551

personalized menus, 40, 911, 933

Phone And Modem Options applet, 343, *346*, 911

to change modem properties, 348

Dialing Rules tab, 356

Phone Dialer, 344, **363–367**, *364*, 911–912

directories, **365**

placing call, **368–369**

speed dial list programming, **365–367**, *367*

starting, **363–365**

Pinball, *201*, 201

Ping (Packet Internet Groper), 262, 331, **430**, 912

to test connection speed, 819

PK_UNZIP, 436

PKZIP, for Registry backups, 469

Place A Call dialog box (NetMeeting), 181, *181*

planning Windows 2000 Server install, **590–604**

BIOS preparation, **594–595**

file system, **596–597**

hardware preparation, **594**

network connections, **599–604**

partitioning, **595–596**

server name, **598**

system requirements, **591–594**

Plug and Play, 590–591

detection during Windows 2000 install, 612

in Windows 2000 Professional, 12

PnPManager subkey (Registry), 504

point of presence for Internet, 405

PointerClass subkey (Registry), 503

PointerPort subkey (Registry), 504

points, 161

policies, Active Directory Services and, 241, 245

portrait printing, 151

ports

    for modem, 350

    for printers, 156

posting to newsgroups, **397**

POSTs (Power-on self-tests), 448

Power Management, 13

Power Options Properties dialog box, 97–98, 912

Power Users account, 729–730

Power Users group, 768

PowerQuest corporation, 27

    Drive Image Pro, 647

Preboot eXEcution (PXE) protocol, 658–659

Preview pane, in Outlook Express, 373, *374*

primary domain controller, 330

    for non-Windows 2000 clients, 326

    time setting on, 615

Print dialog box, *150*

Print Operators group, 766, 768

print server, 142

print spooler, 147

printer drivers, 145

    Active Directory Services and, 241

    for network printer, 156

printer window, 152–153, *153*

printers, 912–913

    adding, **142–146**

        installing local, **143–145**

        installing network, **145–146**

    policies to prevent user changes, 808

    properties dialog boxes, **154–160**

        Advanced tab, **157–158**, *158*

        Color Management tab, **160**, *161*

        Device Settings tab, 159, *159*

        General tab, *154*, **155**

        Ports tab, **156**, *157*

        Security tab, 160, *160*

        Services tab, **158**, *159*

        Sharing tab, *147*, **155–156**, *156*

    right-clicking, 109

Printers dialog box, 42

Printers folder, *143*

Printers subkey (Registry), 514

printing, **147–152**. *See also* fonts

    Address Book, **204**

    from applications, **149–151**

    from Desktop, **148–149**

    faxes, 228

    to file, **151–152**

    managing process, **152–153**

    in Outlook Express, **376**

    Registry, **529–530**, 544

    separator page when, 158

    test page, **145**

    Web pages, 417

Printing Preferences dialog box, 155

priority of print jobs, 157

Private Character Editor, 913

problem report, Windows Report tool for, **947**

processor

    operating system requirements for, 6

    for Windows 2000 Professional, 19, 591

Program Groups subkey (Registry), 507

Program Manager (Windows 3.1), 10

programs. *See also* applications

Programs (Start menu), **39–40**. *See also* Start menu ➤ Programs

project-based model, *314*, **314–315**

properties dialog boxes, **110–111**

    for Address Book, *203*

    for Command Prompt window, 129

    for files, **111–112**, *112*

        on NTFS file system, *113*

    for My Computer, **117–119**

    Sharing tab, 66, *67*

protocols

    adjusting, **676–678**

    ARP (Address Resolution Protocol), 262

    BootP protocol, 269

    DHCP (Dynamic Host Configuration Protocol), **267–283**, 845–846

        Active Directory Services and, 243

        auditing, **278–280**

        client configuration process, **282–283**

        and clustering, **281–282**

        installing service, **269–271**

        scope creation, **273–278**

        server authorization, **272–273**

        server configuration, **272**

    FTP (File Transfer Protocol), 262, **427–429**, 864–865

    ICMP (Internet control Message Protocol), 261

    IP (Internet Protocol), 262

    LDAP (Lightweight Directory Access Protocol), 365, 732

    PXE (Preboot eXEcution) protocol, 658–659

    SMTP (Simple Mail Transfer Protocol), 262

    SNMP (Simple Network Management Protocol), 261

    TCP (Transmission Control Protocol), 261

    TFTP (Trivial File Transfer Protocol), **434**, 661

    UDP (User Datagram Protocol), 261, 434

    in Windows 2000 Professional planning, **599**

prototype, reconfiguring after transferring system image, **664–665**

PXE (Preboot eXEcution) protocol, 658–659

Q

quad address, 405

QUERY function (Reg.exe), **566–567**

Query Value event, auditing, 553

question mark (?) wildcard character, for searches, 71

QuickLaunch toolbar, **48–49**

Outlook Express icon, 372

quit command (FTP), 429

R

radioactivity, 592

RAM

operating system requirements for, 6

parity, 355, 456, 592

system information about, 118

for Windows 2000 Professional, 19, 591–592

RBFG.EXE, 659

RCP (Remote File Copy), **431**

RDisk utility, 463

Read Control event, auditing, 554

read-only file attribute, 111

read only mode, in RegEdt32, 557

Ready to Send/Clear to Send flow control, 355

rec newsgroup, 394

recording sounds, **194–195**

Recovery Console, **480–487**, **642–645**

commands and options, **485–487**

components, **482–483**

installing, **480–481**

launching, 643

starting from Installation CD-ROM, **484**

using, **483–484**

Recreational Software Advisory Council (RSAC), 422

Recycle Bin, 913

dragging files to, 70

Recycle Bin icon (Desktop), **53–54**

Red Hat Linux 6.1, hardware requirements, 6

redirected folders, **799–802**

refresh intervals

for group policies, 816

for group policy objects, **782**

.reg file, loading, **479–480**

REG program, 488

REG_BINARY objects, 497

size limit, 442

REG_DWORD data type, 499

REG_EXPAND_SZ data type, 498

REG_FULL_RESOURCE_DESCRIPTOR data type, 500

Regional Options dialog box, **102**, *102*, 913–914

Registry, **133–135**, **441–442**, 914. *See also* HKEY_~EL

backups, 452, 465

multiple copies, **462–463**

and restore, **457–461**

checking on changes in, 518

contents of exported file, 527

Control Panel and, 84

location, **458–461**

organization, **443–446**

data values, **445–446**, **497–500**

hives, 492, **493**, 494. *see also* hives in Registry

hives and aliases, **444–445**

rebooting after change, 488

restoring from backup, **473–479**
    after copying, **475–476**
    error messages, 479
    from other media, **474–475**
    from tape, **473–474**
restoring from Emergency Repair
    Disk, **476–479**
size, 526
size limit, 442
system policies and, 777
terminology, **450–452**
warnings, 134
Windows 2000 use, **447–450**
Registry editors
    disabling, 808
    installing Remote Registry,
        535–536
    RegEdit, *134*, 134, **523–536**, *524*
        changing entries, **530–532**
        from command prompt,
            534–535
        connecting and disconnecting
            from remote Registries,
            528–529
        copying key names, **532–533**
        to export Registry sections, 518
        importing and exporting hives
            and keys, **526–528**
        printing Registry, **529–530**
        vs. RegEdt32, 571
        for Registry backups,
            470–472, *471*
        searches, **533**
        tips for using, **535**
    RegEdt32, 522, **536–558**

adding keys and subkeys,
    544–547
loading and unloading,
    538–541
opening and closing Registries,
    537
options, **555–557**
printing, **544**
vs. RegEdit, 571
remote registries, 537–538
restoring, **543–544**
saving key or hive, **542–543**
saving subtree, **541–542**
searches, **547–548**
security, **548–555**
starting, 537
tips for using, **558**
Reg.exe, **560–570**
RegistryREG, 522
restricting access, 571
REG_MULTI_SZ, 445
REG_MULTI_SZ data type, 499
REG_NONE data type, 500
REG_SZ data types, 497–498
REG_UNKNOWN data type, 500
relative ID master, 326
relative identifier (RID), 733
relative names, 250
remote access
    with Devices Manager, 688–689
    restricting phone numbers for, 742
Remote Boot Floppy Generator, 648
Remote File Copy (RCP), **431**
Remote Installation Services, **645–669**

authorizing in Active Directory, **652–653**

creating Installers group, **667–669**

creating system image with RIPRep, **663–664**

enabling for clients, **657–658**

enabling users to start transfers, **666**

installing, **653–654**

installing Windows 2000 Professional on workstation from server, **658–663**

limitations, **648–649**

overview, **647–648**

partition for, 596

preparation, **650–652**

reconfiguring prototype, **664–665**

restricting image choices, **669**

running RISetup, **654–657**

Progress indication screen, *657*

steps to making it work, **649–650**

remote machine, controlling services on, 687

remote member servers, managing Local Users And Groups on, 728

Remote Program Execution (REXEC), **432**

remote registries

connecting to and disconnecting from, **528–529**

opening, 524

restricting access, **572**

Remote Registry, installing, **535–536**

Remote Shell/Script (RSH), **432**

remote terminal, Internet connection as, **406–407**

remote users, profile accessible to, 516–517, 539

RemoteAccess subkey (Registry), 514

removable storage, 914

rename command (Recovery Console), 487

repair directory, 476, 559

Emergency Repair Disk vs., 489

repeat delay for keyboard, 93

repeat rate for keyboard, 92, 93

Replica Domain Controllers, 686

Replicator account, 729–730

Replicator group, 767, 768

request packet, in DHCP client configuration, 282

Requests for Comments (RFCs), 260–261

822, *Standard for the Format of ARPA Internet Text Messages*, 745

resolution of screen display, 100–101

ResourceMap key (Registry), **504**

Restart, 46

RESTORE function (Reg.exe), **567–568**

restoring

Registry, **473–479**

after copying, **475–476**

from Emergency Repair Disk (ERD), **476–479**

error messages, 479

from other media, **474–475**

from tape, **473–474**

using Setup, **476–479**

Registry objects, **543–544**

System State from backup, 474–475

windows, 915

restricted sites security zone, 421

Resultant Set of Policy (RSOP), 821

retrieving e-mail from Outlook Express, **375–376**

reverse lookup zone, 289, *291*

REXEC (Remote Program Execution), **432**

RFCs (Requests for Comments), 260–261

    822, *Standard for the Format of ARPA Internet Text Messages*, 745

Rich Text in Outlook Express, 383

RID (relative identifier), 733

right-clicking, 41, **108–110**. *See also* shortcut menus

    to copy or move files, 68

    Desktop icons, **51**

    to print documents, 149

    Start menu, **46–48**

    Windows 95/98 vs. Windows 2000 Professional, 11

right-handed mouse, 94

rights. *See* user rights

RIPRep, **663–664**

    delivering image to target PC, **665**

RIPRep image format image, 648, 663

RIS servers, 647

    Properties dialog box, Remote Install tab, *658*

RISetup, running, **654–657**

rmdir command (Recovery Console), 487

roaming user profile, 118, 495, 747, **940**

root domain, 284, *296*, 296

rootDSA object, 256

ROUTE, **433**

routers, and broadcast packets, 283

Routing and Remote Access, **915–916**

RSAC (Recreational Software Advisory Council), 422

RSH (Remote Shell/Script), **432**

RSOP (Resultant Set of Policy), 821

Rules Editor in Outlook Express, **389–391**

Run As Other User dialog box, **916–917**

Run dialog box, *128*

Run (Start menu), **45–46**, *128*, **916**

running applications

    automatically when starting Windows 2000, **126**

    from command prompt, **129**

    from document, **125–126**

    from Explorer, **123**, *124*

    minimized, **127–128**

    from Search, **124–125**, *125*

    from Start menu, **122**

S

Safe mode, **917**

SAM (Security Accounts Manager), 330, 459, 460

    local accounts stored in database, 731

    Registry hive for, 496, **505**

Samsrv.dll, 253

.sav file extension, 460

SAVE function (Reg.exe), **568–569**

saving

    attachment to e-mail in Outlook Express, 378–379

files in Notepad, 213

keys in Registry hive, **542–543**

messages in Outlook Express, **377–379**

Registry subtree, **541–542**

scanner

configuring, **917–918**

and Imaging application, 221

Schannel.dll, 253

Scheduled Tasks, **135–138**, **918–919**

schema master, 326

sci newsgroup, 394

scientific calculator, 208–209

scope creation, for DHCP, **273–278**

screen captures, 832

with Clipboard, **170–171**, *171*

screen display

color of components, 98

Magnifier to enlarge portion, 90

resolution, 100–101

settings, **95**

screen saver, **97**

Script Debugger (Microsoft), 31, 888–889

Scripted i386 install, 648

scripts

for FTP, 429

group policies, 866

group policies to specify, **797–799**, *798*

remote execution, 432

Scroll Lock key, sound when pressed, 87

Scsi subkey (Registry), 503

ScsiAdapter subkey (Registry), 503–504

SDRAM (Synchronous Dynamic Random Access Memory), 593

Search Results dialog box, *71*

search services, 435

Search (Start menu), 12, 13, **44**, **919**

for files and folders, **70–72**

running applications from, **124–125**, *125*

searches

for Internet software, **434–438**

for newsgroups, **396**

of Registry, **533**

in RegEdt32, **547–548**

SecDC.inf file, 459

SECEDIT.EXE, 805

SecEvent.evt file, 460

second-level domain, 856

SecSetup.inf file, 459

Secur32.dll, 253

Secure subkey (Registry), 507

security. *See also* password

for answer files, 627

computer accounts and, 617

DHCP servers and, 272

and floppy disk drives, 81

in group policies, **803–804**

importing templates, **804–806**, *805*

in Internet Explorer, **420–422**

Recovery Console and, 482

for Registry, **548–555**

for Registry backups, 463

Registry hive for, 496

renaming Guest and Administrator accounts for, 729

rights assignment to groups, 771

in server Component Services, 838

Windows 95/98 vs. Windows 2000 Professional, 11

Security file, 459, 460

security group policy, 866

security groups, **755–756**, **761–770**

security identifiers (SIDs), 511–512, 732, 740

Select subkey (Registry), 509

Send Fax Wizard, **919**

Send To, **920**

sending fax, **226**

Sent Items in Outlook Express, 374

separator page when printing, 158

SERIALCOMM subkey (Registry), 503

server, 5

changing role of, 330

configuring, 836–837

for DHCP

authorizing, **272–273**

configuring, **272**

documentation of setup, 620

licensing, **601–602**

name for, **598**

properties dialog box

Dependencies tab, 691–692

Recovery tab, 691, *692*

RIS, 647

types for ADS, **323–324**

Global Catalog Server, **323**

Server Extensions Administrator, **920**

Server Manager, 683–684

Server Operators group, 766, 767–768

Server service, 616, 678

Service group, 770

service packs, and restoring Windows 2000, 461

services, **920–921**

Services tool, **690–692**, **690–692**, *691*

set command (Recovery Console), 487

Set Value event, auditing, 553

Settings (Start menu), **42**, 42, **921**. *See also* Control Panel

Setup, **22–25**

for new installation, **22–24**

partition changes by, 27

to restore Registry, **476–479**

for upgrade, **24–25**

Setup and Recovery dialog box, 931

Setup Manager User Interaction Level screen, *630*

Setup Manager Wizard

building answer file, **629–631**

building distribution folder, **632–637**

launching unattended install, **638**

output components, **637–638**

Setup subkey (Registry), 509

Setup.log file, 459, 470

shared folders, creating, 842

Shared Folders snap-in, **922**

shared mandatory profile, 747

sharing, **922–923**

ClipBook Viewer pages, **172–173**

encryption and, 115

files and folders, **66–67**

printers, 144, **146–147**, 155–156

sharing information

with NetMeeting, **178–186**

using Clipboard, **166–171**

    copying, cutting and pasting, **167–169**

using OLE, **174–178**

shell account, 403

shell command tasks, 715, 716

shortcut menus, 842

    of files and folders, 889–890

        Send To, 68–69

        Sharing, 66

    for My Computer, Make Available Offline, 73

    for My Network Places, Make Available Offline, 73

    Properties, 111

    right-clicking to open, 41

    Send To, **920**

    for Start button

        Explore, 47, *47*

        Explore All Users, 48

        Open, 47

        Open All Users, 48

        Search, 48

    for user account object, 739

    Windows 3.1 vs. 2000 Professional, 10

shortcuts

    creating, **55–56**, 842–843

    for printers, 145

        dragging files to, 148

Shut Down (Start menu), **46, 923**

SID scrambler, 647

SIDs (security identifiers), 445, 511–512, 732, 740

    and multiple installs, 646–647

.sif file extension, 669

signatures in e-mail messages, **387–388**

Simple i386-based installation, 647

Simple Mail Transfer Protocol (SMTP), 262

Simple Network Management Protocol (SNMP), 261

Single Instance Store (SIS), 652

single master functions, **325–327**

sites in Active Directory Service, 336, 829–830

smart card, 744

SMTP (Simple Mail Transfer Protocol), 262

snap-ins, 698

    loading, 717

    policies to forbid access, 811, 812–813, *814*

snapshot of system, 639

sneakernet, 79, 342

SNMP (Simple Network Management Protocol), 261

soc newsgroup, 394

SOF$$$$$.DEL file, 460

software. *See also* applications

    group policies, 866

    Registry hive for, 496

Software file, 459, 460

Software key (Registry), **506–508**

Software subkey (Registry), 514, 515

Software.sav file, 460

Solitaire, 199, *199*

sound

    in e-mail messages, **386**

    testing in NetMeeting, 180

Sound Recorder, *194*, **194–195**, **923**

SoundSentry, 87

Space Cadet 3D Pinball, 201

speaker volume for modem, 350

speed

    of modem, 350

    of mouse pointer, 94

Speed Dial list in Phone Dialer, **365–367**, *367*

SRV resource records, 288, 337

srvmgr.exe, 684

stand-alone servers

    and DHCP, 272

    standard local groups for, 729–730

standard calculator, 208

Standard for the Format of ARPA Internet Text Messages (RFC 822), 745

Standard toolbar, clearing from Taskpad view, 722

Start menu, **37–48**, *38*, **924–925**

    deleting shortcuts from, 934

    ➢ Documents, **40–41**, 125–126, 858

    ➢ Help, **44–45**

    personalizing, **103–104**

    ➢ Programs, **39–40**, 122. *See also* Accessories (Windows 2000)

        ➢ Administrative Tools ➢ Active Directory Users And Computers, 667

        ➢ Administrative Tools ➢ Configure Your Server, 836–837

    right-clicking, **46–48**, 109

    ➢ Run, **45–46**, **128**, **916**

    running applications from, **122**

    ➢ Search, **44**, **919**

        ➢ For Files and Folders, 124

        to run applications, **124–125**, *125*

    ➢ Settings, **42**, **921**

        ➢ Control Panel, 840

    ➢ Shut Down, **46**, **923**

    Windows 95/98 vs. Windows 2000 Professional, 12

    ➢ Windows Update, **38**, *39*, 131, **947–948**

Start menu folder, redirected, 802

Start Menu Properties dialog box, Target tab, *801*

start-up environment, 477

Startup folder, 39, 126, *127*

static addresses, 276

stationery, in Outlook Express, **384–385**

statistical calculation, 209

status bar

    clearing from Taskpad view, 722

    of Task Manager, 937

StickyKeys, 87

storage

    of Registry backups, 463

        safe location, 470

subdomain, 856

subject line, for e-mail messages, 382

subkeys. *See also* keys in Registry hive

subnet mask, 267

subnetting for IP addresses, **264–267**

subscriptions to newsgroups, **396**

swap file, 930

Symantec, Ghost, 647, 663

synchronization, 931–932

Synchronization Manager, **73–74**

Synchronization Settings dialog box, *74*

SYSDIFF utility, **639–640**

SYS$$$$$.evt file, 460

System applet, 689–690

   Advanced tab, *690*

system clock, setting during Windows 2000 install, 615

System file, 459, 460

system files, verification, 477

System group, 770

system image, creating with RIPRep, **663–664**

system information

   Registry hive for, 496

   viewing, *702*

System Information tool, 693, *694*, **932**

System Internals, 464

System key (Registry), **508–510**

System Monitor, 906–908

system policies, 777

System Policy Editor, 783

"System Process - Licensing Violation" message, 479

System Properties dialog box, **117–119**, **925–931**

   Advanced tab, **930–931**

   General tab, *118*, 925

   Hardware tab, **927–929**

   Network Identification tab, **925–927**

   User Profiles tab, 941

System State

   backup, 464–465, 488–489

   restoring from backup, 474–475

System subkey (Registry), 502–503, 514, 515

System Tools, **932**

system variables, 119

SYSTEM.ALT file, 460

System.ini, 442

SYSTEMROOT command (Recovery Console), 487, 644

%systemroot% environment variable, 458

System.sav file, 460

SysVol, 465

T

talk newsgroup, 394

tape backups, 465

   restoring Registry from, **473–474**

TAPI (Telephony Application Program Interface), **343–344**

   locations, 356–358

Task Manager, **935–937**

Task Scheduler, **135–138**, *136*

   adding new task, **137**

   Advanced menu, **138**

   modifying existing task, **137–138**

Taskbar, *48*, **48–50**, **933**

   hiding and displaying, **49–50**

   QuickLaunch toolbar, **48–49**

   right-clicking, 109, *110*

Taskbar and Start Menu Properties dialog box, *43*, 126, **933–934**

Advanced tab, 103–104, *104*

General tab, 40, 50

opening, 42

Taskpad views, *710*, *720*

creating, 711, **712–714**

links from console to, 720

notes about taskpads and tasks, **718–719**

task creation, **714–717**

tasks, scheduling, **918–919**

tattooing, 777

TCP/IP, 403

basics, **260–267**

addressing, **263–264**

history, **260–261**

IP subnetting, **264–267**

protocols, **261–262**

DHCP (Dynamic Host Configuration Protocol), **267–283**

how it works, **271–283**

installing service, **269–271**

DNS (Domain Name System), **284–292**

TCP (Transmission Control Protocol), 261

TechNet, 560

telephone calls over Internet connection, 437

telephone company credit cards, **360–363**

Telephony, **937–938**

Telephony Application Program Interface (TAPI), **343–344**

Telnet, 262, **432**

Telnet Client, **938**

Telnet Server Administration, **938–939**

templates

importing security, **804–806**, *805*

for user accounts, 751

temporary files

drive for Setup, 623

for Internet, managing, 419

terminal emulation software, 403

test page, printing, **145**

testing DNS (Domain Name System), **331**

TFTP (Trivial File Transfer Protocol), **434**, 661

threaded newsreader, 396

time

computer setting for, 103

synchronization, 615

time format, 102

ToggleKeys, 87

toolbar, clearing from Taskpad view, 722

toolbars, for folders, 13

top-level domain, 856

trace logs, 909

TRACERT, 262, **433–434**, *434*

transitive trusts, 304

Transmission Control Protocol (TCP), 261

Trivial File Transfer Protocol (TFTP), **434**, 661

troubleshooting

group policies and, 821–822

Internet connection

Ping for, 430

trace route command, 433, *434*

modem for Internet connection,
414–415

printing test page, **145**

Windows 2000 Server install,
641–645

True Color, 100

TrueType fonts, 161

trusted sites security zone, 421

trusts, 296

in Active Directory Service,
828–829

building relationships, **683**

between domains, **301–304**

in networks, 233

in Windows 2000 Server, **303–304**

two-way trusts, 301–302, *302*

.txt files, 210

type command (Recovery Console), 487

U

UDF file (uniqueness database file),
623–624

UDP (User Datagram Protocol), 261, 434

Unattend.bat, 637, 638

unattended installs, **620–638**

answer files, **625–628**

command line automation,
621–625

launching, **638**

Setup Manager Wizard, **629–638**

Unattend.txt, 637

Unattend.udf, 637

unauthenticated access, Guest account
for, 729

UNC (Uniform Naming Convention),
245–246

Unicode character set

adding characters to, 913

for Windows 2000 Registry, 472

UNICODE Program Groups subkey
(Registry), 514

Uniform Naming Convention (UNC),
245–246

Uniform Resource Locator (URL), 416

Unimodem, 345

uninstalling programs, and Registry, 443

Uninterruptible power supply (UPS), 98

universal groups, 755–756, 759, 760

universal modem driver, 345

Unix, 407

media file formats, 198

UNLOAD function (Reg.exe), **569–570**

unlocking user accounts, 744

unnamed value in Registry keys, 494

unzip program, 436

UPDATE function (Reg.exe), **570**

Update Wizard Uninstall, **939**

upgrade

clean install vs., 602–604

to Windows 2000 Professional,
24–25

vs. new install, **21–22**

UPN (Universal Principal Name), 745

suffix, 737, 738

UPS (Uninterruptible power supply), 98

URL (Uniform Resource Locator), 416

adding to custom console, 708

U.S. atomic clock, 615

Usenet, 393

user accounts
 changes to, 751
 creating, **32–33**, 730–731, **737–739**, 943
 location, **732**
 logon hours for, *743*
 managing, **750–752**, **941–944**
 properties dialog boxes, **739–750**
  Account tab, **743–746**
  Address tab, 740
  Dial-In tab, 741–742
  General tab, 740, *740*
  Member Of tab, **748–750**, *749*
  Organization tab, 740, *741*
  Profile tab, **746–748**, *747*
  Telephones tab, 740
 templates for, 751
user callback, 742
user configuration policies, 778
User Datagram Protocol (UDP), 261, 434
user environment, Registry entry to control, 806
User Group Policy Loopback Processing mode, 818, *818*
user logon names, **745–746**
User Manager, 674, **681–683**
User Manager for Domains, 674, **681–683**
User mode, 251
 for consoles, 699, 723
user principal names, 250
user profiles, 118, **516–517**, **929–930**, **939–941**
 default, 539
  modifying, 540
 HKEY_USERS hive for, 513

user rights, **770–775**
 for local users, 773–774
Userdiff file, 460
usernames in Windows 2000, 738
 for log-on, 36
users
 and Active Directory Services, **237–245**, 829
 adding to groups, 753–754
 Desktop settings, 747
 end users vs. administrators, 235
 group memberships, **748–750**
 home folder for, 748
 interaction with Setup Manager, 629–631
 packaging custom consoles for, **723**
 Registry hive for information, 494–495, **510–514**
 running programs as other, **916–917**
 starting RIS transfers by, **666**
Users account, 729–730
Users and Passwords, **941–944**
 dialog box, 32–33, *33*
Users group, 767, 768
USRMGR.EXE, 751
Utility Manager, **92**, **944**

V

value entry in Registry keys, 443, 494
 creating, 531–532, 545–547
vendors, and Active Directory Services, **237–238**
VGA (Video Graphics Adapter), 100

video
  Media Player (Windows) for,
    195–198
  in NetMeeting, **184**
video conferencing, with Phone Dialer,
  363
Video Graphics Adapter (VGA), 100
VIDEO subkey (Registry), 504
videoconferencing, 438
VidPhone, 438
View menu (RegEdit), 525
View menu (Task Manager), 936
views for folders, 13
virtual adapter, loopback adapter as,
  680
virtual memory, 689, 930
  managing, 118
viruses, NTFS and, 26
VocalTec, IPhone, 437, *437*
voice conferencing, with Phone Dialer,
  363
voice recordings, 194, 195
Volatile Environment subkey (Registry),
  514
Volume Control dialog box, 49, *49*, *193*,
  193–194, **945**
volume control for modem, 350
volume, defragmenting, 848

W

.wav files, 194
Web browser. *See also* Internet Explorer
Web content on Desktop. *See also*
  Active Desktop
    removing, 695–696

Web pages. *See* HTML documents
Web sharing, **945**
Web sites
  adding to custom console, 708
  on application compatibility, 14
  on application compliance, 123
  for audio CD information, 191
  for domain registration, 286
  on hardware compatibility, 8
  for Hardware Compatibility List, 20,
    593
  Microsoft on accessibility, 87
  for newsgroups, 393
Web view, enabling, 75
What's This, **945–946**
wildcard characters, for searches, 71
windiff.exe, 518
windows
  capture of, 170
  maximizing and minimizing, 882
  opening folders in separate, 76
  restoring, 915
Windows 2000 Advanced Server, **8**
Windows 2000 Data Center, **9**
Windows 2000 platform
  Advanced Server, **8**
  comparison, **9–14**
    with Windows 3.1, **9–11**
    with Windows 95/98, **11–12**
    with Windows NT Workstation,
      12–14
  Data Center, **9**
  hardware requirements, 6

installing on workstations,
645–669

usernames in, 738

Windows 2000 Professional, **4–5**, *5. See
also* installing Windows 2000
Professional

adding and removing components,
133

components, **946**

hardware requirements, 6

Installer service, 130

Internet utilities, **426–434**

ARP (Address Resolution
Display and Control), **427**

Finger, **429**

FTP (File Transfer Protocol),
427–429

Netstat, **431**

Ping (Packet Internet Groper),
430

RCP (Remote File Copy), **431**

REXEC (Remote Program
Execution), **432**

ROUTE, **433**

RSH (Remote Shell/Script),
432

Telnet, **432**

TFTP (Trivial File Transfer
Protocol), **434**

tracert, **433–434**, *434*

multiple boot configurations, 467

policies to control components, **807**

restoring from backup, **461–462**

running applications automatically
when starting, **126**

Windows 2000 Resource Kit, 522

Reg.exe, **560–570**

ADD function, **561–562**

BACKUP function, **562–563**

COPY function, **563–564**

DELETE function, **565**

LOAD function, **566**

QUERY function, **566–567**

RESTORE function, **567–568**

SAVE function, **568–569**

UNLOAD function, **569–570**

UPDATE function, **570**

Windows 2000 Server, **5–7**

Active Directory Services in architecture, **250–256**, *251*

configuring, 836–837

Desktop, 7

restarting services, 692

service configuration, 691

trusts in, **303–304**

Windows 2000 Server install

F3 to abort, 608

planning and preparation,
590–604

BIOS preparation, **594–595**

file system, **596–597**

hardware preparation, **594**

network connections,
599–604

partitioning, **595–596**

server name, **598**

system requirements, **591–594**

post-installation procedures,
618–620

preparation for phase 2 reboot,
607–608

setup

graphical-based setup, **612–618**

preinstallation, **604–607**

text-based setup, **608–611**

text-based setup changes from NT, **611–612**

troubleshooting, **641–645**

unattended, **620–638**

answer files, **625–628**

command line automation, **621–625**

Setup Manager Wizard, **629–638**

walk-through of best-case scenario, 670

Windows 3.1, *10*

applications on Windows 2000, **122–123**

vs. Windows 2000 Professional, **9–11**

Windows 3.1 Migration Status subkey (Registry), 508

Windows 95/98

applications on Windows 2000, **122–123**

in dual-boot configuration, 29

upgrade from, 24–25

vs. Windows 2000 Professional, **11–12**

Windows 98, hardware requirements, 6

Windows Components Wizard, 31, *271*, 271

for Remote Installation Services, 653, *654*

Windows Explorer, 10

Windows logo key, for shortcuts, 56–57

Windows Management Instrumentation (WMI), **948**

Windows Media Player, **195–198**, *196*, **946**

Windows menu (Task Manager), 936

Windows NT Server

hardware requirements, 6

Windows 2000 Server as successor, 6

Windows NT Workstation

hardware requirements, 6

upgrade from, 24–25

vs. Windows 2000 Professional, **12–14**

Windows 2000 Professional as successor, 4

Windows Optional Networking Components Wizard, 678, *679*

Windows Report tool, **947**

Windows Update (Start menu), 13, **38**, *39*, 131, **947–948**

Win.ini, 442

winipcfg, 182

WINMSD, 693

WINNT32.exe, 605

command-line parameters, 620, **621–625**

WINNT.EXE, 605

command-line parameters, 620, **621–625**

WINS, adding, 678

Winsock applications, 435

Winsock FTP, 436, *436*

winsock.dll, 345

WinZIP, 389

Wizards, 274

WMI (Windows Management Instrumentation), **948**

Word, temporary files, and encryption, 115

WordPad, **213–217**, *214*, **949**

    document creation, **216**

    Format bar, 215

    printing documents from, 150

    sending document as e-mail attachment, **216–217**

    toolbar buttons, 214, *214*

workgroup, name changes, **675–676**

workstation, 5. *See also* Remote Installation Services

    installing Windows 2000 Professional from server, **658–663**

Workstation service, 616, 678

Write DAC event, auditing, 554

Write Owner event, auditing, 554

X

xcopy for Registry backups, **465–469**

    vs. copy, **469**

XON/XOFF flow control, 355

Z

zone file, 285

zone transfers, 857

zones, 857

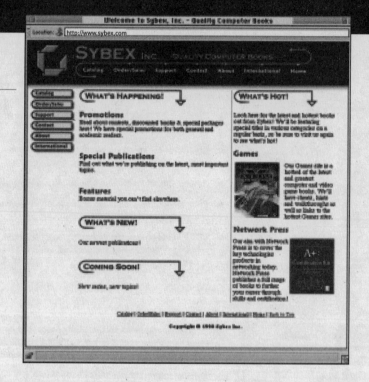

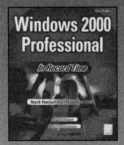

ABOUT THE CONTRIBUTORS

S ome of the best—and best-selling—Sybex authors have contributed chapters from their current books to *Windows 2000 Complete*.

Pat Coleman writes about the Internet, Windows and Windows applications. She is the co-author of *Windows 2000 Professional: In Record Time, Mastering Intranets* and *Mastering Internet Explorer 4*, all from Sybex. Pat is also an extremely accomplished editor.

Peter Dyson is a writer and software engineer with more than 20 years experience in software development and technical support. His more than two dozen books include *Windows 2000 Professional: In Record Time, Windows 98 Instant Reference, The Dictionary of Networking* and *UNIX Complete*, all from Sybex.

Peter D. Hipson is an author, consultant, and teacher. Peter's most recent book with Sybex is *Mastering Windows 2000 Registry*. When not writing computer books, he can often be found teaching computer science at the local college, where he says he "ruins the lives of hundreds of unsuspecting college students every year." An avid Microsoft beta tester, he finds time to test and use virtually every product Microsoft produces.

Robert King is a Microsoft Certified Trainer (MCT), Microsoft Certified Systems Engineer (MCSE), a Master Certified Novell Instructor (MCNI) and Master Certified Novell Engineer (MCNE). King has more than ten years of experience in designing and maintaining networks, and is the owner of King Technologies, a network consulting company. He is the author of *Mastering Active Directory* and two other upcoming MCSE Study Guides, all with Sybex.

Mark Minasi, MCSE, is recognized as one of the world's best teachers of Windows NT/2000. He teaches NT/2000 classes in 15 countries and is a much sought-after speaker at Windows NT conferences, regularly keynoting and speaking at the *NT Wizards* and *NT Professionals* conferences. He also writes three popular columns in *Windows 2000 Magazine*, as well as a column for Japan's *Nikkei* NT Magazine. His firm, MR&D, has taught tens of thousands of people to design and run NT networks. His Sybex books include *Mastering Windows 2000 Server, Mastering Windows NT Server, Mastering TCP/IP for NT Server, Troubleshooting Windows*, and *The Complete PC Upgrade & Maintenance Guide*, which has sold a million copies and been translated into twelve languages.

Jutta VanStean is a freelance technical writer with more than 10 years of experience administering networks and writing books on network operating systems. She is the editor of ZD Journal's Inside NetWare, wrote *Windows 2000 Instant Reference* (Sybex) and has served as technical editor for a number of books include the *Network+ Study Guide* (Sybex).

Windows 2000 Taskbar and Window Components

Address Toolbar —   — Menu Bar   — Standard Buttons Toolbar

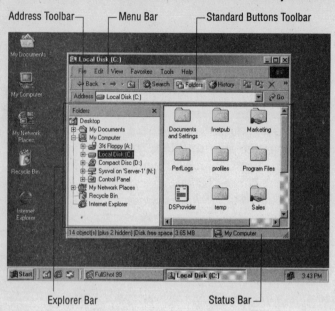

Explorer Bar   Status Bar —

Windows 2000 Desktop Components

— Control Button   Scroll Bars

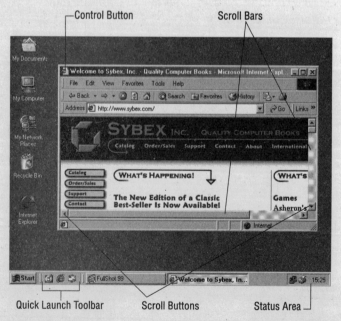

Quick Launch Toolbar   Scroll Buttons   Status Area —